DATE DUE

FEB 23			
OCT 2 0			
GAYLORD			PRINTED IN U.S.A.

MODERN BRITISH FICTION

MODERN BRITISH FICTION

EDITED BY MARK SCHORER
University of California
Berkeley

A Galaxy Book

NEW YORK
OXFORD UNIVERSITY PRESS
1961

For
E. M. Forster

Preface

The essays in this collection, taken as a whole, attempt to accomplish two purposes. The first is to define twentieth-century British fiction in general, to show how it is different from fiction that came earlier. If Thomas Hardy seems to be the last of the nineteenth-century novelists rather than the first of the twentieth, he still serves as a bridge to the present, and, more than that, as a reference backwards against which such a more modern spirit as Joseph Conrad can be measured. The second purpose is to evaluate, through their major works, the major novelists. Occasionally, in the body of the book, these novelists are treated in general terms, but most of the essays are on individual works and concern themselves with analyses of techniques, explications of themes, investigations of structures, commentaries on aesthetic and moral preoccupations. The variety of approaches should in itself suggest something of the variety of the fictional achievement.

I am indebted to my wife and Miss Ann Goolsby for assistance in the preparation of this book.

Berkeley, California   Mark Schorer
January 1961

Contents

MODERN BRITISH FICTION

VIRGINIA WOOLF

---◆◆◆---

Modern Fiction

In MAKING any survey, even the freest and loosest, of modern fiction it is difficult not to take it for granted that the modern practice of the art is somehow an improvement upon the old. With their simple tools and primitive materials, it might be said, Fielding did well and Jane Austen even better, but compare their opportunities with ours! Their masterpieces certainly have a strange air of simplicity. And yet the analogy between literature and the process, to choose an example, of making motor cars scarcely holds good beyond the first glance. It is doubtful whether in the course of the centuries, though we have learnt much about making machines, we have learnt anything about making literature. We do not come to write better; all that we can be said to do is to keep moving, now a little in this direction, now in that, but what a circular tendency should the whole course of the track be viewed from a sufficiently lofty pinnacle. It need scarcely be said that we make no claim to stand, even momentarily, upon that vantage ground. On the flat, in the crowd, half blind with dust, we look back with envy to those happier warriors, whose battle is won and whose achievements wear so serene an air of accomplishment that we can scarcely refrain from whispering that the fight was not so fierce for them as for us. It is for the historian of literature to decide; for him to say if we are now beginning or ending or standing in the middle of a great period of prose fiction, for down in the plain little is visible. We only know that certain gratitudes and hostilities inspire us; that certain paths seem to lead to fertile land, others to the dust and the desert; and of this perhaps it may be worth while to attempt some account.

Our quarrel, then, is not with the classics, and if we speak of quarreling with Mr. Wells, Mr. Bennett, and Mr. Galsworthy it is partly that by the mere fact of their existence in the flesh their work has a living, breathing, every-day imperfection which bids us take what liberties with it we choose. But it is also true that, while we thank them for a thousand gifts, we reserve our unconditional gratitude for Mr. Hardy, for Mr. Conrad, and in a much lesser degree for the Mr. Hudson, of *The Purple Land, Green Mansions,* and *Far Away and Long Ago.* Mr. Wells, Mr. Bennett, and Mr. Galsworthy have excited so many hopes and disappointed them so persistently that our gratitude largely takes the form of thanking them for having shown us what they might have done but have not done; what we certainly could not do, but as certainly, perhaps, do not wish to do. No single phrase will sum up the charge or grievance which we have to bring against a mass of work so large in its volume and embodying so many qualities, both admirable and the reverse. If we tried to formulate our meaning in one word we should say that these three writers are materialists. It is because they are concerned not with the spirit but with the body that they have disappointed us, and left us with the feeling that the sooner English fiction turns its back upon them, as politely as may be, and marches, if only into the desert, the better for its soul. Naturally, no single word reaches the centre of three separate targets. In the case of Mr. Wells it falls notably wide of the mark. And yet even with him it indicates to our thinking the fatal alloy in his genius, the great clod of clay that has got itself mixed up with the purity of his inspiration. But Mr. Bennett is perhaps the worst culprit of the three, inasmuch as he is by far the best workman. He can make a book so well constructed and solid in its craftsmanship that it is difficult for the most exacting of critics to see through what chink or crevice decay can creep in. There is not so much as a draught between the frames of the windows, or a crack in the boards. And yet— if life should refuse to live there? That is a risk which the creator of *The Old Wives' Tale,* George Cannon, Edwin Clayhanger, and hosts of other figures, may well claim to have surmounted. His characters live abundantly, even unexpectedly, but it remains to ask how do they live, and what do they live for? More and more they seem to us, deserting even the well-built villa in the Five Towns, to spend their time in some softly padded first-class railway carriage, pressing bells and buttons innumerable; and the destiny to which they travel so luxuriously becomes more and more unquestionably an eternity of bliss spent in the very best hotel in Brighton. It can scarcely be said of Mr. Wells that he is a materialist in the sense that he takes too much delight in the solidity of his fabric. His mind is too generous in its sympathies to allow him to spend much time in making things shipshape and substantial. He is a materialist from sheer goodness of heart, taking upon his shoulders the work that ought to have been discharged by Government officials, and in the plethora of his ideas and facts scarcely having leisure to realise, or forgetting to think important, the crudity and coarseness of his human beings. Yet what more damaging criticism can there be both of his earth and of his Heaven than that they are to be inhabited here and hereafter by his Joans and his Peters? Does not the inferiority of their natures tarnish whatever institutions and ideals may be provided for them by the generosity of their creator? Nor, profoundly though we respect the integrity and humanity of Mr. Galsworthy, shall we find what we seek in his pages.

If we fasten, then, one label on all these books, on which is one word materialists, we mean by it that they write of unimportant things; that they spend immense skill and immense industry making the trivial and the transitory appear the true and the enduring.

We have to admit that we are exacting, and, further, that we find it difficult to justify our discontent by explaining what it is that we exact. We frame our question differently at different times. But it reappears most persistently as we drop the finished novel on the crest of a sigh—Is it worth while? What is the point of it all? Can it be that owing to one of those little deviations which the human spirit seems to make from time to time Mr. Bennett has come down with his magnificent apparatus for catching life just an inch or two on the wrong side? Life escapes; and perhaps without life nothing else is worth while. It is a confession of vagueness to have to make use of such a figure as this, but we scarcely better the matter by speaking, as critics are prone to do, of reality. Admitting the vagueness which afflicts all criticism of novels, let us hazard the opinion that for us at this moment the form of fiction most in vogue more often misses than secures the thing we seek. Whether we call it life or spirit, truth or reality, this, the essential thing, has moved off, or on, and refuses to be contained any longer in such ill-fitting vestments as we provide. Nevertheless, we go on perseveringly, conscientiously, constructing our two and thirty chapters after a design which more and more ceases to resemble the vision in our minds. So much of the enormous labour of proving the solidity, the likeness to life, of the story is not merely labour thrown away but labour misplaced to the extent of obscuring and blotting out the light of the conception. The writer seems constrained, not by his own free will but by some powerful and unscrupulous tyrant who has him in thrall to provide a plot, to provide comedy, tragedy, love, interest, and an air of probability embalming the whole so impeccable that if all his figures were to come to life they would find themselves dressed down to the last button of their coats in the fashion of the hour. The tyrant is obeyed; the novel is done to a turn. But sometimes, more and more often as time goes by, we suspect a momentary doubt, a spasm of rebellion, as the pages fill themselves in the customary way. Is life like this? Must novels be like this?

Look within and life, it seems, is very far from being "like this." Examine for a moment an ordinary mind on an ordinary day. The mind receives a myriad impressions—trivial, fantastic, evanescent, or en- graved with the sharpness of steel. From all sides they come, an in- cessant shower of innumerable atoms; and as they fall, as they shape themselves into the life of Monday or Tuesday, the accent falls differ- ently from of old; the moment of importance came not here but there; so that if a writer were a free man and not a slave, if he could write what he chose, not what he must, if he could base his work upon his own feeling and not upon convention, there would be no plot, no comedy, no tragedy, no love interest or catastrophe in the accepted style, and perhaps not a single button sewn on as the Bond Street tailors would have it. Life is not a series of gig lamps symmetrically arranged; but a luminous halo, a semi-transparent envelope surround- ing us from the beginning of consciousness to the end. Is it not the task of the novelist to convey this varying, this unknown and uncir- cumscribed spirit, whatever aberration or complexity it may display, with as little mixture of the alien and external as possible? We are not pleading merely for courage and sincerity; we are suggesting that the proper stuff of fiction is a little other than custom would have us believe it.

It is, at any rate, in some such fashion as this that we seek to define the quality which distinguishes the work of several young writers, among whom Mr. James Joyce is the most notable, from that of their predecessors. They attempt to come closer to life, and to preserve more sincerely and exactly what interests and moves them, even if to do so they must discard most of the conventions which are commonly observed by the novelist. Let us record the atoms as they fall upon the mind in the order in which they fall, let us trace the pattern, however disconnected and incoherent in appearance, which each sight or incident scores upon the consciousness. Let us not take it for granted that life exists more fully in what is commonly thought big than in what is commonly thought small. Any one who has read *The Portrait of the Artist as a Young Man* or, what promises to be a far more interesting work, *Ulysses*,[1] now appearing in the *Little Review*, will have hazarded some theory of this nature as to Mr. Joyce's intention. On our part, with such a fragment before us, it is hazarded rather than affirmed; but whatever the intention of the whole there can be no question but that it is of the utmost sincerity and that the result, difficult or unpleasant as we may judge it, is undeniably important. In contrast with those whom we have called materialists Mr. Joyce is spiritual; he is concerned at all costs to reveal the flickerings of that innermost flame which flashes its messages through the brain, and in order to preserve it he disregards with complete courage whatever seems to him adventitious, whether it be probability, or coherence or any other of these signposts which for generations have served to support the imagination of a reader when called upon to imagine what he can neither touch nor see. The scene in the cemetery, for instance, with its brilliancy, its sordidity, its incoherence, its sudden lightning flashes of significance, does undoubtedly come so close to the quick of the mind that, on a first reading at any rate, it is difficult not to acclaim a masterpiece. If we want life itself here, surely we have it. Indeed, we find ourselves fumbling rather awkwardly if we try to say what else we wish, and for what reason a work of such originality yet fails to compare, for we must take high examples, with *Youth* or *The Mayor of Casterbridge*. It fails because of the comparative poverty of the writer's mind, we might say simply and have done with it. But it is possible to press a little further and wonder whether we may not refer our sense of being in a bright yet narrow room, confined and shut in, rather than enlarged and set free, to some limitation imposed by the method as well as by the mind. Is it the method that inhibits the creative power? Is it due to the method that we feel neither jovial nor magnanimous, but centred in a self which, in spite of its tremor of susceptibility, never embraces or creates what is outside itself and beyond? Does the emphasis laid, perhaps didactically, upon indecency, contribute to the effect of something angular and isolated? Or is it merely that in any effort of such originality it is much easier, for contemporaries especially, to feel what it lacks than to name what it gives? In any case it is a mistake to stand outside examining "methods." Any method is right, every method is right, that expresses what we wish to express, if we are writers; that brings us closer to the novelist's intention if we are readers. This method has the merit of bringing us closer to what we were prepared to call life itself; did not the reading of *Ulysses* suggest how much of life is excluded or ignored, and did it not come with a shock to open *Tristram Shandy* or even *Pendennis* and be by them convinced that there are not only other aspects of life, but more important ones into the bargain.

However this may be, the problem before the novelist at present, as we suppose it to have been in the past, is to contrive means of being free to set down what he chooses. He has to have the courage to say that what interests him is no longer "this" but "that": out of "that" alone must he construct his work. For the moderns "that," the point of interest, lies very likely in the dark places of psychology. At once, therefore, the accent falls a little differently; the emphasis is upon something hitherto ignored; at once a different outline of form becomes necessary, difficult for us to grasp, incomprehensible to our predecessors. No one but a modern, perhaps no one but a Russian, would have felt the interest of the situation which Tchekov has made into the short story which he calls "Gusev." Some Russian soldiers lie ill on board a ship which is taking them back to Russia. We are given a few scraps of their talk and some of their thoughts; then one of them dies and is carried away; the talk goes on among the others for a time, until Gusev himself dies, and looking "like a carrot or a radish" is thrown overboard. The emphasis is laid upon such unexpected places that at first it seems as if there were no emphasis at all; and then, as the eyes accustom themselves to twilight and discern the shapes of things in a room we see how complete the story is, how profound, and how truly in obedience to his vision Tchekov has chosen this, that, and the other, and placed them together to compose something new. But it is impossible to say "this is comic," or "that is tragic," nor are we certain, since short stories, we have been taught, should be brief and conclusive, whether this, which is vague and inconclusive, should be called a short story at all.

The most elementary remarks upon modern English fiction can hardly avoid some mention of the Russian influence, and if the Russians are mentioned one runs the risk of feeling that to write of any fiction save theirs is waste of time. If we want understanding of the soul and heart where else shall we find it of comparable profundity? If we are sick of our own materialism the least considerable of their novelists has by right of birth a natural reverence for the human spirit. "Learn to make yourself akin to people. . . . But let this sympathy be not with the mind—for it is easy with the mind—but with the heart, with love towards them." In every great Russian writer we seem to discern the features of a saint, if sympathy for the sufferings of others, love towards them, endeavour to reach some goal worthy of the most exacting demands of the spirit constitute saintliness. It is the saint in them which confounds us with a feeling of our own irreligious triviality, and turns so many of our famous novels to tinsel and trickery. The conclusions of the Russian mind, thus comprehensive and compassionate, are inevitably, perhaps, of the utmost sadness. More accurately indeed we might speak of the inconclusiveness of the Russian mind. It is the sense that there is no answer, that if honestly examined life presents question after question which must be left to sound on and on after the story is over in hopeless interrogation that fills us with a deep, and finally it may be with a resentful, despair. They are right perhaps; unquestionably they see further than we do and without our gross impediments of vision. But perhaps we see something that escapes them, or why should this voice of protest mix itself with our gloom? The voice of protest is the voice of another and an ancient civilisation which seems to have bred in us the instinct to enjoy and fight rather than to suffer and understand. English fiction from Sterne to Meredith bears witness to our natural delight in humour and comedy, in the beauty of earth, in the activities of the intellect, and in the splendour of the body. But any deductions that we may draw from the comparison of two fictions so immeasurably far apart are futile save indeed as they flood us with a view of the infinite possibilities of the art and remind us that there is no limit to the horizon, and that nothing—no "method," no experiment, even of the wildest—is forbidden, but only falsity and pretence. "The proper stuff of fiction" does not exist; everything is the proper stuff of fiction, every feeling, every thought; every quality of brain and spirit is drawn upon; no perception comes amiss. And if we can imagine the art of fiction come alive and standing in our midst, she would undoubtedly bid us break her and bully her, as well as honour and love her, for so her youth is renewed and her sovereignty assured.

NOTE

1. Written April 1919.

2

FREDERICK R. KARL

---◆---

The Mayor of Casterbridge:
A New Fiction Defined

FROM George Eliot to Thomas Hardy, and particularly from *Adam Bede* (1859), with its artisan protagonist, to *The Mayor of Casterbridge* (1886), with its field-worker "hero," is a distance far greater than the passage of twenty-seven years would indicate. Although Hardy's roots, like George Eliot's, were solidly within a nineteenth-century intellectual framework—a pre-Freudian world of Darwin, Spencer, and Huxley—nevertheless, his characters and plots move in a sphere unknown to his contemporaries, an area that no other Victorian, excepting Dickens in some of his minor characters, had attempted to define.

The century that began with Jane Austen's well-balanced heroines of strong will, who literally "will" themselves into normal behavior, rushes toward its end with the willful self-destructiveness of Hardy's heroines and heroes who "will" themselves not into normality but into an obsession with guilt and penance. From the suave, unquestioned inner-direction of Darcy and Mr. Knightley, who live within an intensely realistic world of everyday fact, we pass to a completely different kind of inner-direction in Henchard, whose compulsive life is played out in a fabulous puppet show rather than in a real world. In *The Mayor of Casterbridge*, as in several of his other major novels,

---

Reprinted from *Modern Fiction Studies* (VI, 3) with the permission of the Purdue Research Foundation and the author.

Hardy evidently aimed at a different kind of realism from that exhibited in George Eliot, Dickens, Jane Austen, and Thackeray. When
he wrote in 1886 that his "art is to intensify the expression of things
. . . so that the heart and inner meaning is made vividly visible," [1]
he foreshadowed Conrad's oft-repeated and justly famous definition
of realism, that "by the power of the written word to make you hear,
to make you feel—it is, before all, to make you *see*." This kind of
realism entails, among other things, a new type of protagonist and
a new way of developing scenes: one finds, for example, characters and
scenes that relate to the narrative on both a non-realistic and realistic
basis, in the same way that some of the seemingly non-functional
passages work in Conrad's major novels and in Lawrence's *The Rainbow* and *Women in Love*. To define Hardy's realism, particularly that
of *The Mayor of Casterbridge*, is to reveal a major turning point in
the development of the English novel: the novel is no longer solely
an important social document but has become as well a significant
psychological history.

Hardy once wrote that "Coleridge says, aim at *illusion* in audience
or readers—*i.e.*, the mental state when dreaming, intermediate between complete *delusion* (which the French mistakenly aim at) and a
clear perception of falsity." [2] In this "suspension of disbelief," Hardy
found a way of both raising the implausible to a philosophic system
and demonstrating that art is a "disproportioning" of reality. As
aware as George Eliot that the realism of the naturalist is not art,
Hardy used chance as a way of infusing "imaginative realism" into his
narratives, for chance not only suggested something supernatural, but
it also fitted the terms of his own beliefs.

In *The Mayor of Casterbridge*, as well as in *The Return of the
Native*, *Jude the Obscure*, and *Tess of the D'Urbervilles*, chance becomes a universal symbol of Hardy's personal philosophy; what he
calls chance is everything over which man has no control. Although
man's will is not nullified by chance, neither can will itself overcome
chance; the latter is, in its functioning, the will of the universe, what
Hardy, in his long narrative poem, *The Dynasts*, later called the
Immanent Will. This force operates in the world without conscious
design; even though it is not a controlling force, in that it does not
direct man, it frequently seems to evoke more malignity than benevolence. Hardy claimed, notwithstanding, that chance is not a sinister
intelligence, that it can work either for good or evil. With Michael
Henchard, it seems more apparently sinister because he lacks proportion and balance, is himself sinister in the original sense of the word.

That Henchard—also, Jude, Clym Yeobright, Tess, and Eustacia Vye
—happens to be constituted *this* way is, however, of no consequence to
the principle of chance. Each may have been completely different,
Hardy suggests but, except for Tess, each would still have become
a victim because he is obsessed by some inexplicable force that
wastes his energies. As D. H. Lawrence, with some disappointment,
noted, Hardy "used" chance as a way of punishing his social deviates, while at the same time claiming that chance itself is an indifferent force:

Nevertheless, this philosophy of chance, while certainly neither
original nor consistent, did allow Hardy to move from the realistic-
romantic nineteenth-century mold into his unique expression of changing values. In *The Mayor of Casterbridge*, the unreality of a chance-
filled world is at once indicated in the fable-like beginning, with its
simple evocation of distance and timelessness. Hardy writes:

> One evening of late summer, before the present century had reached its
> thirtieth year, a young man and woman, the latter carrying a child, were
> approaching the large village of Weydon-Priors, in Upper Wessex, on
> foot. They were plainly but not ill clad, though the thick hoar of dust
> which had accumulated on their shoes and garments from an obviously
> long journey lent a disadvantageous shabbiness to their appearance
> just now.[3]

The straightforward style, almost matter-of-fact in its artlessness, conveys both the immediate setting and the potential doom awaiting the
couple. They walk along the road together, yet alone, and their isolation here foreshadows their inability to connect personally, even
though later they do remarry. The fact is, Henchard must always
be alone and isolated ("his taciturnity was unbroken, and the woman
[Susan] enjoyed no society whatever from his presence" [p. 2]). She
and he walk to the fair grounds unknown and unknowing, only to
be separated even further by his perverse act of selling her and the
child. Later, the still isolated Henchard enters Casterbridge, painfully builds up a business alone, tries unsuccessfully to win a friend
in Farfrae, unsuccessfully woos Lucetta, then remarries Susan, who is
dutiful but unloving, tries unsuccessfully to win Elizabeth-Jane as
his daughter, and gradually loses each in turn, leaving Casterbridge
as alone, stripped, and alienated as when he entered.

Henchard's rashness of temperament and lack of moderation, leading to bursts of anti-social behavior while he is drunk, do not by
themselves adequately explain his character. In his bull-like force

(Hardy emphasizes his physical strength in the fight with Farfrae), in his inability to love (he offers marriage, but never love), in his need to humiliate himself (among other things, his marriage with Susan lowers him in public opinion), in his anti-heroic tendencies (he rises in stature paradoxically as he demeans himself)—in all of these Henchard is more an inexplicable force than a frail human. Like Conrad's Jim, he seems personally to make the terms of his own victimizing, and yet he is unable to help himself—the kind of forces that are to destroy him are, as Freud indicated, too deep in the unconscious to manifest themselves in easily recognizable form. Henchard's quest in life is to pursue a course of action that will satisfy both his destructive drives and the overt desires of his social life. He is, Hardy suggests, a man obsessed by a singular passion, and, therefore, a man doomed in a world that rewards flexibility.

By moving at the extremes of behavior which he himself cannot understand, Henchard recalls in part, among Hardy's contemporaries, Dickens' Steerforth (*David Copperfield*) and Bradley Headstone (*Our Mutual Friend*) and foreruns Conrad's Lord Jim, Gide's Lafcadio, and Camus' Meursault, each of whom is obsessed by demons that remain unrecognizable, although all perceive that there is something within they must control. When control, nevertheless, becomes impossible, they commit actions which directly or indirectly injure others while also laying the groundwork for their own destruction. Only Dickens among other major nineteenth-century English novelists was aware of the self-destructive demons nourished within an otherwise respectable and controlled individual, although he, like Hardy after him, was unable to account for them.

Hardy's other immediate predecessors and contemporaries, Thackeray, George Eliot, and Meredith, were so far committed to a "normal" world that they avoided all extremes of social behavior; but Hardy, like Dickens in his later novels, attempted to create a society in which the extremist, what Dostoevsky considered the criminal and later French novelists the rebel, clashed with the social norm. Hardy differed from Dickens, however, by concerning himself *primarily* with what happened to the radical who is the potential criminal and rebel: Henchard, Jude, Clym, Eustacia, and all those who are destroyed by their intransigence and/or their obsession with a single mode of behavior. Moreover, since they are unable to help themselves, Hardy's world seems excessively cruel, even antagonistic to individual needs, a world in which chance becomes a malevolent rather than an indifferent force. Yet the savagery of Hardy's world—in which con tinued cruelty, pain, and suffering become the norm for his heroes and heroines—is merely a reflection of man's insignificance when he attempts to exert more force than he has or tries to function without self-understanding. Hardy's protagonist usually means well and is, as Henchard, basically decent. But his obsessions are clearly uncontrollable—like Gide's Lafcadio and Conrad's Jim, he must defy the restrictions placed upon him, and in his defiance there lies the stuff of his self-destruction.

Henchard's fixed behavior further strengthens the fable or fairy tale atmosphere that surrounds the narrative, with its seeming simplification of character development, and also becomes the substance of Hardy's anti-realism. The Fair scene itself, with its readers of Fate, its games of chance, its auctions of animals, its waxworks and peep shows and conning medical men, with its hag-like furmity woman, who, like a Fate from *Macbeth*, stirs her large pot, is a timeless symbol of man's irrational quest for pleasure in a grim world of expedience. Moreover, at a Fair, anything goes; normal behavior is no longer adhered to, and eccentricity can itself become the norm. In Freudian terms, the id can here triumph over (or force out) the censorship of the superego, and man's ego, his ultimate behavior, is deflected into cruel acts both to his loved ones and to himself. Thus, the relatively simple act of auctioning horses at the Fair becomes an unambiguous foreshadowing of Henchard's sale of Susan, and the swallow circling through the tent trying to escape is an obvious reference to Henchard's desire to escape a marriage that he claims has bound him in penury. The Fair, then, assumes its traditional significance: a place where people are liberated from personal cares and freed from their daily burdens. Like the quickly curving swallow, Henchard is to fly from the tent alone.

Escape itself becomes, ironically, a form of isolation that Henchard can never avoid; and the sordid business at the Fair becomes the terms both of his freedom and his thralldom. When he sells Susan, that act is the only one in which *he* throws off another human being; the rest of the novel finds him "being sold" and thrown off. Hardy remarks: "Henchard's wife was dissevered from him by death; his friend and helper Farfrae by estrangement; Elizabeth-Jane by ignorance" (p. 146). Moreover, Lucetta leaves him for marriage with Farfrae; the sailor Newsom returns to claim Elizabeth-Jane; the town itself casts him out as Mayor. Further, one part of Henchard is dissociated from the other, so that his personality is split, manifest on the surface as the sober part and the drunken part, but of course the division goes far deeper. Hardy evidently lacked the psychological equipment to analyze the double role that grips Henchard, although his artistic suggestion of the type is psychologically true. Conrad, in *Lord Jim*, likewise lacked the analytical knowledge, but he was able to create a "true" type: in Jim, the split occurs between his romantic ideals and his realistic situations, and his tragedy is his inability to reconcile the two. Henchard's tragedy, similarly, is his inability to reconcile drunkenness (romance) and soberness (realism). The self-destructive Henchard cannot perceive that the latter preserves while the former destroys.

Henchard's isolation from himself is given nearly exact definition in Hardy's use of several overlapping scenes that both indicate his alienation and emphasize the element of fable. Man is split and isolated, first, by his juxtaposition to surroundings that dwarf his stature and diminish his spirit. In Chapter 19, for example, Henchard gazes at the cliffs outside Casterbridge and his eyes alight on a square mass of buildings cut into the sky. Hardy describes the bulky monument as a pedestal missing its statue, the missing element significantly being a corpse; for the buildings were once the county jail, their base forming the gallows where crowds would gather to watch executions. This passage occurs soon after Henchard has read Susan's letter telling him that Elizabeth-Jane is not his daughter, Henchard having recently tried to convince the girl that she is his. Then, after Henchard learns the facts, Newsom's daughter comes to him and says that she does accept him as her father. We recognize that the missing corpse is the doomed Henchard, caught between uncontrollable forces, one part trying to gain love and life, the other, unable to effect an attachment, caught by death.

This powerful scene in which the split Henchard foresees his own doom recurs in a different context when, after the cruel mummery, the despondent and suicidal outcast thinks of drowning in the river as a solution to his misery. The sight, however, of his straw effigy floating in the water—the same effigy that had horrified Lucetta and caused her fit—suggests his own death, acts out, as it were, a substitute death, and dissuades him. "Not a man somewhat resembling him, but one in all respects his counterpart, his actual double, was floating as if dead in Ten Hatches Hole" (p. 360). The supernatural aspect of the sight impresses Henchard, and, ironically, the effigy, which in another way has helped destroy him, here saves his life. "That performance of theirs killed her [Lucetta], but kept me alive" (p. 361).

"Supernatural" aspects of the fable further appear when man is enclosed in a historical setting that indicates his fate. The Roman amphitheatre at Casterbridge serves the purpose of a meeting-ground and at the same time frames the puny dimensions of puppet-like man against a mighty historical past. Henchard, who has been heroic amidst the townspeople, is now diminished by the immensity of the amphitheatre where he meets Susan; and their immediate problems, when viewed against the melancholy background, seem petty indeed.

This kind of scene recurs in various forms; it appears, as we saw, when Henchard gazes at the Franciscan priory with its gallows and missing corpse; it re-appears with intended irony near the end of the novel in the form of the pre-historic fort, Mai-Dun, where Henchard hides, telescope in hand, to spy on Farfrae and Elizabeth-Jane. The fort is described as "of huge dimensions and many ramparts, within or upon whose enclosures a human being, as seen from the road, was but an insignificant speck" (p. 375). Here, Henchard, already in decline because of his personal losses, squanders even his physical dimensions, dwarfed as he is by the fort and made to seem still smaller by the meanness of his objective—to scan the Roman *Via* for the two lovers. Then the ampitheatre itself recurs as a meeting-place for Henchard and Lucetta, the successor to Susan; within the huge enclosure, her pathetic figure revives in his soul "the memory of another ill-used woman who had stood there . . . [so that] he was unmanned" (p. 301). As they meet, the sun rests on the hill "like a drop of blood on an eyelid," a half-closed eyelid which sees reality only absently, masked as the latter is by personal ambition and willful revenge. His strength drained, the once heroic Henchard finds his feeling for the woman turning from revenge to pity and disdain amidst the hugeness of their overwhelming enclosure.

Not only is man insignificant in relation to natural surroundings, Hardy suggests, but also in his contacts with uncontrollable human forces. The reappearance of the furmity woman, that Fate who reveals the iniquity of Henchard's past, indicates how limited his career can be once he has offended the order of his universe. Further, his reliance on the weather-prophet, a person deep within superstition, exemplifies Henchard's growing insecurity and also puts him at the mercies of a human interpretation of the uncertain elements. That Henchard should rely on a fabulous prophet, who, mysteriously, seems to be expecting him, demonstrates his recurring fears now that Farfrae opposes him. The "hero" can no longer rely on his own devices and by taking counsel from a false prophet wills a destiny that will destroy him. The furmity woman and the weather-prophet "destroy" Henchard on the fable level as much as Farfrae, Lucetta, Elizabeth-Jane, Susan, and the town itself nullify him on the realistic level. Split by the two forces, Henchard is indeed trapped.

II

Hardy had the poetic ability, as Lawrence did after him, to suggest the whole in every part, to bring into each scene a miniature of the entire work. This is particularly evident in *The Mayor of Caster-bridge* where the structure is tight, the plot limited to essentials, and the main characters few. One recognizes the novel's stylization in the anti-realism of implausible events, in the somewhat evident symbolic patterns, and in the poetic evocation of characters and events. As Albert Guerard has pointed out, at the poetic and imaginative level, Hardy is capable of tragedy, although when he thinks philosophically he seems commonplace and his limitations become obvious. His finest scenes, consequently, are those in which 'pure thought' does not dominate, scenes which remain close to a fable tradition and can be suggested poetically rather than realistically.

Unlike George Eliot and Thackeray, whose obvious forte was real-ism, Hardy, like Conrad and Lawrence, was more at home when he could avoid a head-on realistic scene and, instead, evoke the conflict obliquely. He could, so to speak, be true to human feeling but not to human truth. Lacking the philosophical orderliness of George Eliot and Thackeray's uniformity of viewpoint, as well as the sheer vivacity of Dickens and Meredith, Hardy retreated to the oddities of life which determine man's frail existence. Thus, as we suggested above, his reliance on cosmic irony and the chance occurrences of implausible events bolstered his way of working; for a dependence on chance enabled him to touch his subject, as it were, from the side and gave substance to his oblique attacks upon complacency, deviation, and immoderation. Chance, in effect, was his weapon to strike through surface reality to areas where the poetry of man offers resistance to the drab starkness of a malevolent universe.

We can see, then, that certain short but powerful scenes fulfill Hardy's genius, although they may well seem peripheral or incidental to the unsympathetic reader. In Chapter 29, for example, Lucetta and Elizabeth-Jane encounter a rambling bull, whose uncertainty seems to be theirs as well as Henchard's. The bull proves to be dangerous, an old cranky one, and uncontrollable except by an experienced hand. It begins to pursue the two women, the air from its nostrils blowing fear over them, until Henchard runs up, seizes the stick attached to the nose-ring, and subdues the frustrated animal. How ironical the scene becomes! for Henchard is recognizably the bull, or at least suggestive of the bull first in its brazen fierceness and then in its flinching half-paralysis once a stronger force masters it. Henchard himself is literally imprisoned in a nose-ring of events, and the two women whom he saves are, ironically, the Furies who will not give him rest.

This kind of intense scene, otherwise ordinary, joins with several others of the same type to comment indirectly upon the main characters and to create an atmosphere of lost opportunities and muddled human relationships. Earlier, upon recognizing that Lucetta and Farfrae are lovers, Henchard is offered an apple by the nervous Lucetta, which he rejects just as she has rejected his proposal: both offers are based on deceit and both are to bring unhappiness. Then, late in the novel, the dead body of the goldfinch in Henchard's gift to the Farfraes is a sentimentalized but effective symbol of the isolated Henchard, his life snuffed-out, forgotten, and alone in the darkness. The selling-scene itself, which runs like a leitmotif through the novel—for it becomes the basis both of Henchard's potential salvation and his real destruction—contains the grotesqueness and expediency that are essential to a world that pays only lip service to the amenities of life. Similarly, the grotesqueness recurs in Henchard's fight with Farfrae; the declining mayor realizes that he cannot kill his rival, for at the moment of triumph he is struck by the sadness of his inhuman act in the past, and to think of killing Farfrae is to relive his former shame at the Fair.

This scene itself is duplicated by one shortly after. As Farfrae is defeated by Henchard at the height of his good fortune (as, conversely, the Scotsman had triumphed over the Mayor), so too Lucetta, at her peak of assurance, is trapped by the satirical mummery, which causes her death. Everyone closely associated with Henchard's past is tainted by his misfortune. Only Farfrae and Elizabeth-Jane can escape because they are outside Henchard's range and remain flexible: they can move *with* chance and defy the Fates, although Farfrae escapes death or serious injury only because Henchard is guilt-ridden. The tragedy of Lucetta, on the other hand, is the tragedy of any Hardy woman who seeks a clear path to happiness without the perceptive awareness of potential evil, and who tries to defy the precepts of a malevolent universe that demands obedience to its strict terms of behavior.

Henchard himself, confused by the pressures of the outside world, declines rapidly once he foregoes his twenty-year penance and returns to drink, his position in the town having been exploded by the return of the furmity woman. He honors the breaking of his oath, appropriately, with the recitation of verses from the 109th Psalm, to the effect that a wicked man shall lose his family, his riches, even all semblance of dignity; and, his name despised, he will be swiftly destroyed. Hardy evidently conceived of Henchard as an enduring Job, an inarticulate sufferer of destiny's wager, but one without the possibility of salvation through faith. Henchard, like Job, is caught amidst forces he cannot understand, caught among forces, however, created by the terms of his own character rather than those strictly imposed upon him. Therefore, Henchard's tragedy is potentially greater than Job's (he is closer to the Greeks than he is to the Hebrews), for his only salvation would be to transcend himself, an impossibility for one who is condemned to be destroyed.

All of Henchard's acts reveal a fatalism, as if he must drive himself until he falls. Thus, his seeming impetuousness in ignoring all advice is more than mere rashness or ill temper. It is the chief constituent of an innate need to debase himself, to act out a role that will ultimately diminish him. Nowhere more than in the scene when the obsessed ex-Mayor kneels to welcome the Royal Personage passing through Casterbridge is his growing insignificance stressed. Fortified by drink and carrying a small Union Jack, Henchard, wearing a brilliant rosette over his weatherbeaten journeyman garments, tries to regain some of his former glory without disguising his present misery. Advancing to the Personage, Henchard waves the flag and attempts to shake his hand, until, seized by Farfrae, he is removed forcibly. From the large-sized individual who struggled against powers he could not understand, Henchard here dwindles into the court fool, whose pathetic figure, however, causes not comedy but vexation and annoyance. Reduced from his former self and diminished by the blows of chance, Henchard allows his former employee to sweep him aside as a foolish meddler.

Nevertheless, Hardy's Henchard, although dwarfed by his natural surroundings, isolated by his townsmen, and made absurd by his grotesque acts, is still of heroic stature, evidently a nineteenth-century counterpart of an Aeschylean or Euripidean protagonist. Hardy had early recognized that Aristotle's definition of classical tragedy needed to be transformed or amended to suit present-day realities and wrote his own definition shortly after completing *The Mayor of Caster-bridge:* "Tragedy. It may be put there in brief: a tragedy exhibits a state of things in the life of an individual which unavoidably causes some natural aim or desire of his to end in catastrophe when carried out." [4] Within these terms, Henchard, as well as Clym, Jude, and several others of low birth, is a tragic hero, frustrated and hindered by the very things he hopes to attain and blinded by the obsessive nature of his quest. Clearly, Henchard's flaw is, as we suggested, more than a rash temper; his whole character, Hardy is careful to indicate in his definition, is his fate.

His character, like Lear's, is of heroic proportions, although so molded that the vast energies are dissipated in foolish acts of pride and vanity. As an outcast, Henchard gains identification with a whole host of alienated figures, Oedipus, the Ancient Mariner, Lear himself, but, most of all, the Cain of the Bible, whom Hardy made the prototype of all outcasts. Once fallen from his eminence, Henchard, now no different from the "naked" man who had entered Casterbridge nearly a quarter of a century before, leaves the town: "'I—Cain—go alone as I deserve—an outcast and a vagabond. But my punishment is *not* greater than I can bear'" (p. 379). Henchard's ordeal—all part of the universe's unconscious design—is a peculiarly nineteenth-century one even though Hardy carefully drew attention to its Greek and Biblical counterparts. True, Henchard is caught within the workings of a destiny he cannot understand, but he has committed a crime against the universe, the unnatural act of ridding himself of a family burden, and this while frenzied (drunk). Further, while his free will can work successfully within a certain sphere—only by sheer energy and drive has he become mayor, for Henchard is a man of small ability—it nevertheless is restricted to a line of action in which the whole person is not engaged. Still further, while the novel is subtitled "A Story of a Man of Character," indicating that the emphasis is to be on man and on character, the definitive acts in the novel clearly derive from an area outside Henchard's control. A split individual, a mysterious universe, a misdirected will—all these elements help define a new type of nineteenth-century man.

If, once again, we compare Henchard with Adam Bede, we can distinguish sharply between two kinds of lower class protagonists and show further how Hardy was moving from the traditional matter of the novel. Adam is in the line of somewhat prosaic young men whose aims are restricted to what they can possibly attain. Imperfect in certain ways, these characters do not set goals that are outside their reach, and they display relative equanimity and moderation in their quests. Adam himself is by no means perfect, but his imperfections are of a kind that will provide only disappointment, not nullification. Moreover, the terms of his desires are themselves small and always bounded by the explicable. There is little in the world that Adam could not understand, George Eliot leads us to believe, provided he was mature and intelligent enough to extend himself. What is true of Adam is also true of Dickens' protagonists, Thackeray's middle-class gentlemen, Jane Austen's genteel provincials, and Meredith's romantic heroes: the world holds few secrets from those who would banish ego and vanity in favor of common sense. Henchard's world is obviously quite different. While a simple frettish woman disappoints Adam, a whole series of re-appearing women seem to doom Henchard, and each time he fails it is almost always over a woman or related to one. Moreover, while imperfections of character are merely a sign of immaturity in Adam, they *constitute* the character of Henchard. While Adam has to go through an emotional ordeal in order to purge himself of his temper and to gain an insight into real love, the ordeal of Henchard is not a matter of development but of life and death, the ordeal of the tragic hero set back by phenomena outside his control. In addition, while Adam has to understand only visible things, Henchard must master invisible forces and obviously he cannot succeed, for he himself engenders several of the forces which help destroy him. Furthermore, Adam is the lower-class "hero" who is *like* everyone else despite low birth, while Henchard is *unlike* anyone else—he is marked, like Cain, almost from the beginning, and marked he goes through the novel, a grotesque figure of wasted energies and misdirected will. Adam was not intended to be, and cannot be, a tragic hero, while Henchard could not be the center of a conventional love story or the protagonist in a dramatic narrative lacking tragedy.

George Eliot was interested in presenting the detailed grandeur of passions that Wordsworth considered "incorporated with the beautiful and permanent forms of nature." Hardy, also, was interested in the "permanent forms of nature," though not as something necessarily ennobling; rather, as a background for human tragedy and as a silent force supposedly indifferent both to man and to its own powers. Nature, like society, gives Henchard something to be isolated from, helping to define the terms of his alienation, while in George Eliot it brings about attachment and purification. This distinction is important, for Hardy turned the Victorian lower-class "hero" into an unreasonable, guilt-stricken, and alienated figure who is denied even the saving powers of nature.

The seeming simplicity of Henchard's actions should not obscure Hardy's not so simple conception of his character. The grotesqueness and obsessiveness of Henchard's position—in several ways he is not unlike a muscular version of Kafka's K.—become more meaningful when we see that his tragedy, like K.'s, is played out against a relatively calm and imperturable background. The townspeople themselves are under no pall of tragedy; even Farfrae is untouched by the deeper aspects of Henchard's position, as is Elizabeth-Jane, whose insubstantiality precludes her suffering too much. Susan, likewise, is too simple and flexible to suffer little more than shame at her position, and her early removal from Henchard would seem more a source of happiness than misery. Perhaps Lucetta suffers for a short time on a scale comparable to that of Henchard, but she, like Elizabeth-Jane and Susan, is not solid enough to transform suffering into tragic feeling. Only Henchard is tragic, only Henchard really suffers, and this emphasis helps convey his monumental anguish. His profile dominates Casterbridge, and even in decline he has size and scope.

Although Henchard is diminished by juxtaposition with the amphitheatre, as well as with the Roman road and the Chapel on the Cliff, he nevertheless gains identity from their massive impressiveness at the same time he is dwarfed by their grandeur. One is reminded here of that great scene in *Tess of the D'Urbervilles* (1891) in which Tess lies immolated on the stone slab of Stonehenge, the pretty dairy girl identified with a vast history of martyrs and victims. So too, Henchard gains in massiveness and substance through identification with his surroundings. Like many other Hardy heroes, together with several from Wordsworth through Lawrence, Henchard cannot be separated from the earth, which denotes both defeat and life to him. The spirit of place remains close to him: he works in the earth before coming to Casterbridge and dies close to the earth after leaving. He places his trust in the earth, and when it, like everything else, fails him, he willingly forsakes life.

III

The outline of *The Mayor of Casterbridge,* as befitting a tragedy, is quite simple, despite the several new incidents occurring in each chapter. Hardy himself was afraid that the demands of weekly publication, with the need to force an incident into each installment, would strain the credulity of the reader of the novel as a whole; but while the play of intercrossing incidents—especially those concerning the returned sailor Newsom—does seem overworked at times, the main profile is clear. Perhaps the very simplicity of the novel caused Henry James to call the author, "the good little T ———— H ————," a remark that caused Hardy considerable discomfort.

The important elements, however, do stand out boldly, so boldly that Joseph Warren Beach thought the spareness was closer to a motion picture scenario than to a novel. Yet fullness of development could not have been Hardy's intention, certainly not the fullness of *Tess of the D'Urbervilles* or *The Return of the Native,* both of which are longer novels with fewer single incidents. What Hardy evidently intended was a Greek tragedy appropriate for his own time. Certainly the formal patterns of the novel (although these elements are not necessarily its virtues) attempt the simple line of Greek tragedy, with the evident rise and fall of incident leading to the hero's recognition of his situation. Even the moral alienation of Henchard, which places him close to a twentieth-century "hero," finds its source in the isolation of Aeschylus' and Euripides' protagonists. Consider, also, the leitmotif of the furmity woman, together with the recurrence of themes of isolation, the reappearance of key people, the use of the weather prophet, the prevalence of classical architecture, the starkness of the landscape, the morbidity of Henchard's "sickness," the victimizing of the hero by women, the use of folk customs like the skimmity ride, the presence of the townspeople as a chorus, the aura of fatalism cast over the main character because of events lying outside his control, the inability of the main character to find happiness as long as there is a taint on his conscience— all these are a throwback to the chief elements of Greek tragedy now reproduced and brought to bear upon the novel, elements, moreover, that have become the common staple of the novel after Hardy.

Henchard is an Oedipus who instead of marrying his mother after twenty years remarries Susan after a similar lapse of time; in another way, he is an Orestes whose revenge is against himself, not his mother, for having killed a part of his own being. Henchard can never be free from himself, just as he can never be free from society. Often, the conflict in a Hardy protagonist is between social convention, which restricts, and the individual need to be free, which can never be fulfilled in the terms the individual expects. This conflict can take several forms, although rarely does Hardy shape it solely along the simple line of duty versus passion. Frequently, he complicates the terms of the inner conflict by showing that duty itself can be and often is degrading, while passion can as frequently lead to fear and insecurity as it does to personal happiness. Doubtless, Hardy changed the terms of the traditional conflict (especially strong in the Victorian novel) because they would, under certain conditions, lead to qualified happiness and heroization, both of which he felt falsified a tragic sense of life. As several critics have remarked, the criticism of Hardy during his novel-writing days was directed more toward his pessimism than toward his so-called sexual themes. Perhaps Hardy's readers would have more readily accepted Lucetta's happiness (after sufficient penance) than the cruel death that she must suffer. D. H. Lawrence, for instance, was outraged that Hardy killed off his "living" characters and let the prosaic ones escape, and Lawrence, here, was not far from the general public's dismay at Hardy's lack of optimism. Hardy himself wrote in 1886: "These venerable philosophers seem to start wrong; they cannot get away from a prepossession that the world must somehow have been made to be a comfortable place for man." [5] Hardy suggests his own prepossession in the last line of *The Mayor:* "that happiness was but the occasional episode in a general drama of pain."

The frequent criticism is that Hardy as a counter to mid-Victorian optimism (or what passed for it) would not allow anyone to be happy who could feel deeply or think widely. There is some truth to this stricture, for Hardy had been strongly influenced by Darwin's work during his maturing years prior to his first published novel in 1871. The battle between man and nature, manifest in the mysterious and even malevolent power that determines the process of natural selection, becomes translated into a cosmic pessimism in which man is countered at every turn by antagonistic forces. Because man can never be sure of himself—like the Greek hero, he can be struck down at the peak of his success—Hardy's novels seem cruel. Henchard undergoes rebuffs that appear in excess of what his original crime demands, and his punishment appears more than what a basically decent man deserves. That Hardy will not give him the chance to recover after penance, a kind of resurrection traditional in the nineteenth-century novel, is evident in his relationship with Elizabeth-Jane. During his decline, Henchard has hopes of living closer to the girl: "In truth, a great change had come over him with regard to her, and he was developing the dream of a future lit by her filial presence, as though that way alone could happiness lie" (p. 352). This passage is measured against a later one in which the girl, now married, rebuffs his attempt at reconciliation: " 'Oh how can I love, or do anything more for, a man who has served us like this [deceived her about her real father]' " (p. 396). Thus, one of Henchard's few real acts of demonstrable affection is rejected out of hand, and rejected, moreover, by a girl now secure with a husband and a father. The cruelty here is unbearable for the reason that Henchard has been discarded by one who is solidly part of society, while, previously, his rejections had at least been at the hands of people equally insecure. Now, Elizabeth-Jane, respectable, cared-for, loved, confident, and youthful, strikes at Henchard's last vestige of dignity: he indeed becomes the dead goldfinch forgotten in the dark cage.

The cruelty of the main lines of the novel does help prevent a potentially sentimental tale from getting mawkish. Hardy, like Conrad, Lawrence, Joyce, and Virginia Woolf after him, was clearly reacting to Victorian sentimentality, although he did not evade it on several occasions when he was sure his audience desired tears. However, by imposing the starkness of Greek classical tragedy on an 1820's rural English setting, and intermixing that with a Darwinian cosmos, Hardy tried to avoid an excess of direct feeling. Nevertheless, he failed to recognize that Greek tragedy is not necessarily bleak and pessimistic but merely the working out of man's conflicts with himself or with his state and gods. He did recognize, though, that to approximate such tragedy he would have to manipulate much artificially in order to make his philosophy—one necessarily alien to the surrounding culture—work out consistently. The Greek tragedian could write with his entire culture behind him, while Hardy was generally isolated from the practices of his literary contemporaries and certainly from the beliefs of a dominant part of his audience. Therefore, we sense the strain, the need to impose consistency even at the expense of art.

The cruelty of Hardy's pursuit of Henchard is mitigated, if only partially, by the latter's stubborn resistance to forces that would soon have defeated a man of lesser stature. The mere array of circumstances aligned against Henchard—in this sense comparable to Job's ordeal—makes his struggle seem epical. Henchard's standing up to the onslaughts of chance incidents, each of which might demolish him, exemplifies his power of defiant endurance. When he declares scornfully, " 'But my punishment is *not* greater than I can bear,' " he seems, in his Promethean strength, to become as large as the forces which are attempting to nullify him. The fact that Henchard *is* tragic—that despite several excessive circumstances, Hardy is still able to convey a tragic sense—gives him a power beyond that of a mere mortal, who would appear pathetic, not Promethean. When Henchard has been defeated, one has witnessed the conflict of a powerful will with an implacable force, and his dying wishes give him the unearthly power of a maddened Lear, whose defiant cry of " 'Ere they shall make us weep! We'll see 'em starved first.'" should be the epitaph for Casterbridge's former mayor. Hardy wrote significantly in his diary just two days after finishing *The Mayor* his own epitaph on Henchard's struggle: "The business of the poet and novelist is to show the sorriness underlying the grandest things, and the grandeur underlying the sorriest things."

Henchard, we should remember, is a decent man whose early sins are not indicative of a cruel or ill-intentioned character, rather the mistakes of a man carried away by a frenzy he finds impossible to control. In his dealings in Casterbridge, he is particularly fair and honest. He willingly destroys himself by admitting the furmity woman's accusation in court, and his action in remarrying Susan is an attempt to do what is right even though no love is involved. Although Henchard is a primitive in his inarticulateness, he recognizes the need for a softer side at the same time he is unable to summon these feelings. He agrees, out of duty, to take care of Susan, Elizabeth-Jane, Farfrae, and Lucetta, feeling intimately only about Farfrae, who returns mere decency for the Mayor's compulsive need for companionship. Henchard, however, so dominates all relationships that he disallows any opposition; lacking love, which itself forces flexibility, he loses all hold upon humanity, including his own. His inability to love is equated to his self-destructive tendencies, and it is difficult to distinguish where each begins or ends. Consequently, Henchard often seems harsher than his character warrants simply because he smashes certain moral bonds by acting from duty rather than love. Moreover, Hardy appears to nullify him exactly as he, in turn, nullifies others by refusing them the deeper feelings that he himself is unable to summon. The disparity between Henchard's abortive attempts to be decent and the ill results of his efforts is the extent to which Hardy's philosophy precluded uncontested happiness.

The quality of one's happiness is determined by his flexibility and aims; if he can, like Farfrae and Elizabeth-Jane, remain outside any dominating obsession and live more by common sense than force of will, he will not be destroyed or even seriously injured. Hardy indicates that if one is an idealist—that is, one who tries to impose his will upon an antagonistic or indifferent world—then his exertions create a Promethean conflict leading to his destruction; if, however, one is a realist and does not attempt to change himself or the world, his chances of destruction are minimized. This pattern is not of course always true for Hardy's characters—Tess is an evident exception—but it does define the major figures of *The Mayor*.

Nevertheless, even to suggest that the other characters in the novel have individual lives is to see how far Henchard overshadows them and how much of *The Mayor* is his novel alone. To a much larger extent than either George Eliot, Thackeray, Meredith, or the later Dickens, Hardy used a single character to dominate his narratives. Even Becky Sharp fails to predominate in *Vanity Fair* to the degree that Henchard controls Hardy's novel, and we must return to *Wuthering Heights* to find a comparable figure, that of the all-powerful Heathcliff. We recognize that for Hardy the domination of the central character, even though he be an anti-hero, was another carry-over from Greek tragedy, the nature of whose protagonist determined the nature of the drama. If the novel is, as Hardy believed, an outgrowth of events from a particular character who shapes them (except those things which chance controls), then the novel must be directed in its details by this single force. Thus, the events that help nullify Henchard are those that develop from his own character: he literally makes the world that first envelops and then squeezes him to death. The title, we note again, is "A Story of a Man of Character."

Hardy's use of the town, similar to George Eliot's presentation of Middlemarch as a comment upon the main characters, creates a chorus that is as malevolent in its gossip as it is a form of social commentary. Hardy took the Greek chorus as both a representation of public opinion and a force for warning the protagonist of excesses, and remolded it into an interfering group of townspeople who directly influence the protagonist's fortunes. Accordingly, the town is both public opinion and participant in the drama: its opinion is more than mere warning, it can force its way. George Eliot and Hardy realized that the town's opinion in a democratic age would entail more than mere commentary; with class mobility less restricted, the individual's business was no longer his sole concern: the individual now belonged to everyone. In *Middlemarch*, town gossip cuts through Bulstrode's hypocrisy and ruins his reputation, while in *The Mayor* the skimmity ride destroys Lucetta's hopes for happiness. In each, the town becomes a force for reliving the past, whose unwelcome recurrence is the basis for gossip and hearsay.

Both George Eliot and Hardy showed a sharp awareness of social structure, recognizing that the mighty (Bulstrode) and the outsider (Lucetta and Henchard) can each be destroyed by a demonstration of majority opinion, whether it be justified or not. Further, both use country customs, implicit in the chorus, as a way of trapping the urbanized characters, and by so doing remove the country from mere picturesqueness and take the romance from the pastoral. This is not to claim that George Eliot and Hardy forsake the picturesque quality of rural life—one need think only of the Poysons in *Adam Bede* or of the dairy workers in *Tess*—but it is to suggest that in their later work they discount the pictorial quality in favor of a more individualized comment. The farmer and his wife are no longer merely decorative; they now have sentiments that must be heeded and values that can upset those whom they oppose. Thus, the chorus of townspeople and farmers has come full turn; in a democratic age, it loses its aloofness and sense of cosmic justice. Now, it too is involved, and no one can escape its approval, condemnation, or interference in his personal life. The chorus, as Kafka's K. was to learn, can impose its will regardless of the individual's rights, more often than not sending the alienated protagonist into exile. Hardy's Henchard, then, is in some ways the English prototype of the twentieth-century's isolated hero, the dominating figure in a world suddenly inexplicable by human reason.

Hardy is important, therefore, not only intrinsically but also historically. If we compare him again with Jane Austen, Thackeray, Dickens, Meredith, and George Eliot and then with the nearest pivotal English novelist after him, Joseph Conrad, we can see how he has changed the nineteenth-century novel, although change in itself is of course no criterion of quality. Granted, obviously, that his major predecessors and contemporaries had each brought individual genius to the novel, it is nevertheless in Hardy that we find the first sustained attempt to examine new aspects of late Victorian reality and to probe into areas barely suggested before. In Hardy, almost for the first time, we have an author who is counter to the central tendencies of his age, what we can claim for Dickens and Meredith only marginally. Hardy recognized that idealism is a component of egoism, and that the true idealistic hero is not one who conquers or triumphs as Christ did, but one who can destroy himself in muddle and noncomprehension. Hardy was primarily interested in the stranger whose attempts to get inside society are self-destructive. Already, we recognize a world that is somewhat subversive and anti-social; Greek tragedy now serves modern sensibilities, and its external determinism is now internalized and seen as of man's own making. The stranger is indeed Promethean in his quest for a particular kind of truth, but the mere fact that he is a stranger is sufficient to doom him. In his perception of the great grotesque depths lying beneath conventional morality, Hardy, in *The Mayor of Casterbridge* and his other major novels, wrote a parable for our times. The lesson is that life itself destroys even when man is basically good.

NOTES

1. Florence Hardy, *The Early Life of Thomas Hardy, 1840–1891* (New York, 1928), pp. 231–232.

2. Florence Hardy, p. 197.

3. *The Mayor of Casterbridge* (New York, 1922), p. 1. All further references will be to this Harper's Modern Classics Edition and will appear in the text of my paper.

4. Florence Hardy, p. 230.

5. Florence Hardy, p. 234.

3

DOROTHY VAN GHENT

On Tess of the D'Urbervilles

It was Hardy who said of Meredith that "he would not, or could not
—at any rate did not—when aiming to represent the 'Comic Spirit,' let
himself discover the tragedy that always underlies comedy if you only
scratch deeply enough." Hardy's statement does not really suggest that
comedy is somehow tragedy *manqué*, that writers of comedy would
write tragedies if they only "scratched deeply enough." What he says
is what Socrates said to Aristophanes and Agathon at the end of the
Symposium—that the genius of tragedy is the same as that of comedy.
It is what Cervantes knew, whose great comic hero, Quixote, walks
in the same shades with Orestes and Oedipus, Hamlet and Lear. It
is what Molière knew. Even Jane Austen knew it. The precariousness
of moral consciousness in its brute instinctual and physical circumstances, its fragility as an instrument for the regeneration of the
will: this generic disproportion in the human condition comedy develops by grotesque enlargement of the imbalance between human
motive and the effect of action. The special point to our purpose is,
however, another: neither tragic figure nor comic figure is merely
phenomenal and spectacular if it truly serves the function common
to both genres—the catharsis; acting as scapegoats for the absurdity
of the human dilemma, they are humanity's thoughtful or intuitive

From *The English Novel: Form and Function* by Dorothy Van Ghent, Holt,
Rinehart and Winston, Inc., 1953; the quotations are reprinted from *Tess
of the D'Urbervilles* by Thomas Hardy, Macmillan and Co. Ltd., 1891 by
permission of the publishers and the Trustees of the Hardy Estate.

comment on itself. We return, thus, deviously by way of the kinship of tragedy and comedy, to the matter of "internal relations." The human condition, whether in the "drawing-room of civilized men and women" or on a wild heath in ancient Britain, shows, if scratched deeply enough, the binding ironies that bind the spectacular destiny of the hero with the unspectacular common destiny; and it is in the internal relations of the art form, the aesthetic structure, that these bonds have symbolic representation. The aesthetic failure of *The Egoist* is thus a diagnostic mark of a crucial failure of vision, a weakness and withdrawal of vision before the common dilemma and the common destiny.

To turn to one of Hardy's great tragic novels is to put "internal relations" in the novel to peculiar test, for there is perhaps no other novelist, of a stature equal to Hardy's, who so stubbornly and flagrantly foisted upon the novel elements resistant to aesthetic cohesion. We shall want to speak of these elements first, simply to clear away and free ourselves from the temptation to appraise Hardy by his "philosophy"—that is, the temptation to mistake bits of philosophic adhesive tape, rather dampened and rumpled by time, for the deeply animated vision of experience which our novel, *Tess*, holds. We can quickly summon examples, for they crop out obviously enough. Before one has got beyond twenty pages one finds this paragraph on the ignominy and helplessness of the human estate:

> All these young souls were passengers in the Durbeyfield ship—entirely dependent on the judgment of the two Durbeyfield adults for their pleasures, their necessities, their health, even their existence. If the heads of the Durbeyfield household chose to sail into difficulty, disaster, starvation, disease, degradation, death, thither were these half-dozen little captives under hatches compelled to sail with them—six helpless creatures, who had never been asked if they wished for life on any terms, much less if they wished for it on such hard conditions as were involved in being of the shiftless house of Durbeyfield. Some people would like to know whence the poet whose philosophy is in these days deemed as profound and trustworthy as his song is sweet and pure, gets his authority for speaking of "Nature's holy plan."

Whenever, in this book, Hardy finds either a butt or a sanction in a poet, one can expect the inevitable intrusion of a form of discourse that infers proofs and opinions and competition in "truth" that belongs to an intellectual battlefield alien from the novel's imaginative concretions. On the eve of the Durbeyfield family's forced deracination and migration, we are told that

to Tess, as to some few millions of others, there was ghastly satire in
the poet's lines:

> *Not in utter nakedness*
> *But trailing clouds of glory do we come.*

To her and her like, birth itself was an ordeal of degrading personal
compulsion, whose gratuitousness nothing in the result seemed to
justify, and at best could only palliate.

Aside from the fact that no circumstances have been suggested in
which Tess could have had time or opportunity or the requisite development of critical aptitudes to brood so formidably on Wordsworth's lines, who are those "few millions" who are the "like" of Tess?
as, who are the "some people" in the previous quotation? and in what
way do these statistical generalizations add to the already sufficient
meaning to Tess's situation? At the end of the book, with the "Aeschylean phrase" on the sport of the gods, we feel again that intrusion
of a commentary which belongs to another order of discourse. The
gibbet is enough. The vision is deep and clear and can only be marred
by any exploitation of it as a datum in support of abstraction. We
could even do without the note of "ameliorism" in the joined hands
of Clare and Tess's younger sister at the end: the philosophy of an
evolutionary hope has nothing essential to do with Tess's fate and
her common meaning; she is too humanly adequate for evolutionary
ethics to comment upon, and furthermore we do not believe that
young girls make ameliorated lives out of witness of a sister's hanging.

What philosophical vision honestly inheres in a novel inheres as the
signifying form of a certain concrete body of experience; it is what the
experience "means" because it is what, structurally, the experience *is*.
When it can be loosened away from the novel to compete in the general field of abstract truth—as frequently in Hardy—it has the weakness
of any abstraction that statistics and history and science may be allowed
to criticize; whether true or false for one generation or another, or for
one reader or another, or even for one personal mood or another, its
status as truth is relative to conditions of evidence and belief existing
outside the novel and existing there quite irrelevant to whatever
body of particularized life the novel itself might contain. But as a
structural principle active within the particulars of the novel, local
and inherent there through a maximum of organic dependencies,
the philosophical vision has the unassailable truth of living form.

We wish to press this difference a bit further by considering—deliberately in a few minor instances, for in the minor notation is the

furthest reach of form—the internality and essentiality of Hardy's vision, just as we have previously considered instances of its externalization and devitalization. Significantly, his "ideas" remain the same in either case. They are abruptly articulated in incident, early in the book, with the death of Prince, appearing here with almost ideographical simplicity.

> The morning mail-cart, with its two noiseless wheels, speeding along these lanes like an arrow, as it always did, had driven into [Tess's] slow and unlighted equipage. The pointed shaft of the cart had entered the breast of the unhappy Prince like a sword, and from the wound his life's blood was spouting in a stream, and falling with a hiss into the road.
>
> In her despair Tess sprang forward and put her hand upon the hole, with the only result that she became splashed from face to skirt with the crimson drops . . .

The mail cart leaves, and she remains alone on the road with the ruin.

> The atmosphere turned pale; the birds shook themselves in the hedges, arose, and twittered; the lane showed all its white features, and Tess showed hers, still whiter. The huge pool of blood in front of her was already assuming the iridescence of coagulation; and when the sun rose, a million prismatic hues were reflected in it. Prince lay alongside still and stark, his eyes half open, the hole in his chest looking scarcely large enough to have let out all that had animated him.

With this accident are concatenated in fatal union Tess's going to "claim kin" of the D'Urbervilles and all the other links in her tragedy down to the murder of Alec. The symbolism of the detail is naïve and forthright to the point of temerity: the accident occurs in darkness and Tess has fallen asleep—just as the whole system of mischances and cross-purposes in the novel is a function of psychic and cosmic blindness; she "put her hand upon the hole"—and the gesture is as absurdly ineffectual as all her effort will be; the only result is that she becomes splashed with blood—as she will be at the end; the shaft pierces Prince's breast "like a sword"—Alec is stabbed in the heart with a knife; with the arousal and twittering of the birds we are aware of the oblivious manifold of nature stretching infinite and detached beyond the isolated human figure; the iridescence of the coagulating blood is, in its incongruity with the dark human trouble, a note of the same indifferent cosmic chemistry that has brought about the accident; and the smallness of the hole in Prince's chest, that looked "scarcely large enough to have let out all that had animated him," is the minor remark of that irony by which Tess's great cruel trial appears as a vanishing incidental in the blind waste of time and space and biological repetition. Nevertheless, there is nothing in this event that has not the natural "grain" of concrete fact; and what it signifies —of the complicity of doom with the most random occurrence, of the cross-purposing of purpose in a multiple world, of cosmic indifference and of moral desolation—is a local truth of a particular experience and irrefutable as the experience itself.

In the second chapter of *Tess* the gathering for the May-day "club-walking" is described, a debased "local Cerealia" that has lost its ancient motive as fertility rite and that subsists as a social habit among the village young people. Here Clare sees Tess for the first time, in white dress, with peeled willow wand and bunch of white flowers. But it is too late for him to stop, the clock has struck, he must be on his way to join his companions. Later, when he wants to marry Tess, he will tell his parents of the "pure and virtuous" bride he has chosen, when her robe is no longer the white robe of the May-walking but the chameleon robe of Queen Guinevere,

> *That never would become that wife*
> *That had once done amiss.*

In the scene of the May-walking, the lovers are "star-crossed" not by obscure celestial intent but by ordinary multiplicity of purposes and suitabilities; but in the submerged and debased fertility ritual—ironically doubled here with the symbolism of the white dress (a symbolism which Clare himself will later debase by his prudish perversity)—is shadowed a more savage doom brought about by a more violent potency, that of sexual instinct, by which Tess will be victimized. Owing its form entirely to the vision that shapes the whole of Tess's tragedy, the minor incident of the May-walking has the assurance of particularized reality and the truth of the naturally given.

Nothing could be more brutally factual than the description of the swede field at Flintcomb-Ash, nor convey more ·economically and transparently Hardy's vision of human abandonment in the dissevering earth.

The upper half of each turnip had been eaten off by the live-stock, and it was the business of the two women to grub out the lower or earthy half of the root with a hooked fork called a hacker, that this might be eaten also. Every leaf of the vegetable having previously been consumed, the whole field was in color a desolate drab; it was a complexion without features, as if a face, from chin to brow, should be only an expanse of skin. The sky wore, in another color, the same likeness; a white vacuity of expression with the lineaments gone.

The visitation of the winter birds has the same grain of local reality, and yet all the signifying and representative disaster of Tess's situation—its loneliness, its bleak triviality, its irrelevance in the dumb digestion of earth—is focused in the mirroring eyes of the birds.

> . . . strange birds from behind the North Pole began to arrive silently . . . gaunt spectral creatures with tragical eyes—eyes which had witnessed scenes of cataclysmal horror in inaccessible polar regions, of a magnitude such as no human being had ever conceived, in curdling temperatures that no man could endure; which had beheld the crash of icebergs and the slide of snow-hills by the shooting light of the Aurora; been half blinded by the whirl of colossal storms and terraqueous distortions; and retained the expression of feature that such scenes had engendered. These nameless birds came quite near to Tess and Marian, but of all they had seen which humanity would never see they brought no account. The traveller's ambition to tell was not theirs, and, with dumb impassivity, they dismissed experiences which they did not value for the immediate incidents of this upland—the trivial movements of the two girls in disturbing the clods with their fragile hackers so as to uncover something or other that these visitants relished as food.

There is the same sensitive honesty to the detail and expression of fact, the same inherence of vision in the particulars of experience, in the description of the weeds where Tess hears Clare thrumming his harp.

> The outskirt of the garden in which Tess found herself had been left uncultivated for some years, and was now damp and rank with juicy grass which sent up mists of pollen; and tall blooming weeds, emitting offensive smells—weeds whose red and yellow and purple hues formed a polychrome as dazzling as that of cultivated flowers. She went stealthily as a cat through this profusion of growth, gathering cuckoospittle on her skirts, brushing off snails that were climbing the appletree stems, staining her hands with thistle-milk and slug-slime, and rubbing off upon her naked arms sticky blights that, though snow-white on the tree-trunks, made blood-red stains on her skin; thus she drew quite near to Clare, though still unobserved of him.

The weeds, circumstantial as they are, have an astonishingly cunning and bold metaphorical function. They grow at Talbothays, in that healing procreative idyl of milk and mist and passive biology, and they too are bountiful with life, but they stain and slime and blight; and it is in this part of Paradise (an "outskirt of the garden"—there are even apple trees here) that the minister's son is hidden, who, in his conceited impotence, will violate Tess more nastily than her sensual seducer: who but Hardy would have dared to give him the name Angel, and a harp too? It is Hardy's incorruptible feeling for the actual that allows his symbolism its amazingly blunt privileges and that at the same time subdues it to and absorbs it into the concrete circumstance of experience, real as touch.

The dilemma of Tess is the dilemma of morally individualizing consciousness in its earthy mixture. The subject is mythological, for it places the human protagonist in dramatic relationship with the nonhuman and orients his destiny among preternatural powers. The most primitive antagonist of consciousness is, on the simplest premise, the earth itself. It acts so in *Tess*, clogging action and defying conscious motive; or, in the long dream of Talbothays, conspiring with its ancient sensuality to provoke instinct; or, on the farm at Flintcomb-Ash, demoralizing consciousness by its mere geological flintiness. But the earth is "natural," while, dramatically visualized as antagonist, it transcends the natural. The integrity of the myth thus depends, paradoxically, upon naturalism; and it is because of that intimate dependence between the natural and the mythological, a dependence that is organic to the subject, that Hardy's vision is able to impregnate so deeply and shape so unobtrusively the naturalistic particulars of the story.

In *Tess,* of all his novels, the earth is most actual as a dramatic factor—that is, as a factor of causation; and by this we refer simply to the long stretches of earth that have to be trudged in order that a person may get from one place to another, the slowness of the business, the irreducible reality of it (for one has only one's feet), its grimness of soul-wearying fatigue and shelterlessness and doubtful issue at the other end of the journey where nobody may be at home. One thinks, in immediate comparison, of Egdon Heath in *The Return of the Native.* Except for one instance—when Mrs. Yeobright has a far walk to Clym's cottage, and Clym, unforewarned, fails to meet her, and she turns away—the heath in *The Return* exists peripherally and gratuitously in relation to the action, on the one hand as the place where the action happens to happen (an action has to happen somewhere), and on the other, as a metaphor—a metaphorical reflection of the loneliness of human motive, of the inertia of conscious life, of the mystery of the enfolding darkness; but it is not a dramatically causative agent and its particular quality is not *dramatically* necessary. In *The Mayor of Casterbridge*, the Roman ruins round about the town of Casterbridge are a rather more complicated metaphor, for they are works of man that have fallen into earth; they speak mutely of the anonymity of human effort in historical as well as in geological time; their presence suggests also the classic pattern of the Mayor's tragedy, the ancient repetitiveness of self-destruction; and they provide thus a kind of guarantee or confirming signature of the heroism of the doomed human enterprise. But the Mayor could have had his tragedy in a town with no Roman ruins about it at all; they are, even more than Egdon Heath, gratuitous, and their gratuitousness leads Hardy into some pedantry of documentation to support their metaphorical standing in the story. In *Tess* the earth is *primarily not a metaphor but a real thing* that one has to move on in order to get anywhere or do anything, and it constantly acts in its own motivating, causational substantiality by being there in the way of human purposes to encounter, to harass them, detour them, seduce them, defeat them.

In the accident of Prince's death, the road itself is, in a manner of speaking, responsible, merely by being the same road that the mail cart travels. The seduction of Tess is as closely related, causally, to the distance between Trantridge and Chaseborough as it is to Tess's naïveté and to Alec's egoism; the physical distance itself causes Tess's fatigue and provides Alec's opportunity. The insidiously demoralizing effect of Tess's desolate journeys on foot as she seeks dairy work and field work here and there after the collapse of her marriage, brutal months that are foreshortened to the plodding trip over the chalk uplands to Flintcomb-Ash, is, again, as directly as anything, an effect of the irreducible *thereness* of the territory she has to cover. There are other fatal elements in her ineffectual trip from the farm to Emminister to see Clare's parents, but fatal above all is the distance she must walk to see people who can have no foreknowledge of her coming and who are not at home when she gets there. Finally, with the uprooting and migration of the Durbeyfield family on Old Lady Day, the simple fatality of the earth as earth, in its measurelessness and anonymousness, with people having to move over it with no place to go, is decisive in the final event of Tess's tragedy—her return to Alec, for Alec provides at least a place to go.

The dramatic motivation provided by natural earth is central to every aspect of the book. It controls the style: page by page *Tess* has a wrought density of texture that is fairly unique in Hardy; symbolic depth is communicated by the physical surface of things with unhampered transparency while the homeliest conviction of fact is preserved ("The upper half of each turnip had been eaten off by the live-stock"); and one is aware of style not as a specifically verbal quality but as a quality of observation and intuition that are here—very often—wonderfully identical with each other, a quality of lucidity. Again, it is because of the *actual* motivational impact of the earth that Hardy is able to use setting and atmosphere for a symbolism that, considered in itself, is so astonishingly blunt and rudimentary. The green vale of Blackmoor, fertile, small, enclosed by hills, lying under a blue haze—the vale of birth, the cradle of innocence. The wide misty setting of Talbothays dairy, "oozing fatness and warm ferments," where the "rush of juices could almost be heard below the hiss of fertilization" —the sensual dream, the lost Paradise. The starved uplands of Flintcomb-Ash, with their ironic mimicry of the organs of generation, "myriads of loose white flints in bulbous, cusped, and phallic shapes," and the dun consuming ruin of the swede field—the mockery of impotence, the exile. Finally, that immensely courageous use of setting, Stonehenge and the stone of sacrifice. Obvious as these symbolisms are, their deep stress is maintained by Hardy's naturalistic premise. The earth exists here as Final Cause, and its omnipresence affords constantly to Hardy the textures that excited his eye and care, but affords them wholly charged with dramatic, causational necessity; and the symbolic values of setting are constituted, in large part, by the responses required of the characters themselves in their relationship with the earth.

Generally, the narrative system of the book—that is, the system of episodes—is a series of accidents and coincidences (although it is important to note that the really great crises are psychologically motivated: Alec's seduction of Tess, Clare's rejection of her, and the murder). It is accident that Clare does not meet Tess at the Maywalking, when she was "pure" and when he might have begun to court her; coincidence that the mail cart rams Tess's wagon and kills Prince; coincidence that Tess and Clare meet at Talbothays, *after* her "trouble" rather than before; accident that the letter slips under the rug; coincidence that Clare's parents are not at home when she comes to the vicarage; and so on. Superficially it would seem that this type of event, the accidental and coincidental, is the very least credible of fictional devices, particularly when there is an accumulation of them; and we have all read or heard criticism of Hardy for his excessive reliance upon coincidence in the management of his narratives; if his invention of probabilities and inevitabilities of action does not seem simply poverty-stricken, he appears to be too much the puppeteer working wires or strings to make events conform to his "pessimistic" and "fatalistic" ideas. It is not enough to say that there is a certain justification for his large use of the accidental in the fact that "life is like that"—chance, mishap, accident, events that affect our lives while they remain far beyond our control, are a very large part of experience; but art differs from life precisely by making order out of this disorder, by finding causation in it. In the accidentalism of Hardy's universe we can recognize the profound truth of the darkness in which life is cast, darkness both within the soul and without, only insofar as his accidentalism *is not itself accidental* nor yet an ideology-obsessed puppeteer's manipulation of character and event; which is to say, only insofar as the universe he creates has aesthetic integrity, the flesh and bones and organic development of a concrete world. This is not true always of even the best of Hardy's novels; but it is so generally true of the construction of *Tess*—a novel in which the accidental is perhaps more preponderant than in any other Hardy—that we do not care to finick about incidental lapses. The naturalistic premise of the book—the condition of earth in which life is placed—is the most obvious, fundamental, and inexorable of facts; but because it is the physically "given," into which and beyond which there can be no penetration, it exists as mystery; it is thus, even as the basis of all natural manifestation, itself of the quality of the supernatural. On the earth, so conceived, coincidence and accident constitute order, the prime terrestrial order, for they too are "the given," impenetrable by human *ratio*, accountable only as mystery. By constructing the *Tess*-universe on the solid ground (one might say even literally on the "ground") of the earth as Final Cause, mysterious cause of causes, Hardy does not allow us to forget that what is most concrete in experience is also what is most inscrutable, that an overturned clod in a field or the posture of herons standing in a water mead or the shadows of cows thrown against a wall by evening sunlight are as essentially fathomless as the procreative yearning, and this in turn as fathomless as the sheerest accident in event. The accidentalism and coincidentalism in the narrative pattern of the book stand, thus, in perfectly orderly correlation with the grounding mystery of the physically concrete and the natural.

But Hardy has, with very great cunning, reinforced the *necessity* of this particular kind of narrative pattern by giving to it the background of the folk instinctivism, folk fatalism, and folk magic. If the narrative is conducted largely by coincidence, the broad folk background rationalizes coincidence by constant recognition of the mysteriously "given" as what "was to be"—the folk's humble presumption of order in a rule of mishap. The folk are the earth's pseudopodia, another fauna; and because they are so deeply rooted in the elemental life of the earth—like a sensitive animal extension of the earth itself—they share the authority of the natural. (Whether Hardy's "folk," in all the attributes he gives them, ever existed historically or not is scarcely pertinent; they exist here.) Their philosophy and their skills in living, even their gestures of tragic violence, are instinctive adaptations to "the given"; and because they are indestructible, their attitudes toward events authoritatively urge a similar fatalism upon the reader, impelling him to an imaginative acceptance of the doom-wrought series of accidents in the foreground of the action.

We have said that the dilemma of Tess is the dilemma of moral consciousness in its intractable earthy mixture; schematically simplified, the signifying form of the *Tess*-universe is the tragic heroism and tragic ineffectuality of such consciousness in an antagonistic earth where events shape themselves by accident rather than by moral design; and the *mythological* dimension of this form lies precisely in the earth's antagonism—for what is persistently antagonistic appears to have its own intentions, in this case mysterious, supernatural, for it is only thus that the earth can seem to have "intentions." The folk are the bridge between mere earth and moral individuality; of the earth as they are, separable conscious ego does not arise among them to weaken animal instinct and confuse response—it is the sports, the deracinated ones, like Tess and Clare and Alec, who are morally individualized and who are therefore able to suffer isolation, alienation, and abandonment, or to make others so suffer; the folk, while they remain folk, cannot be individually isolated, alienated, or lost, for they are amoral and their existence is colonial rather than personal. (There is no finer note of this matter—fine in factual and symbolic precision, and in its very inconspicuousness—than the paragraph describing the loaded wagons of the migrating families:

> The day being the sixth of April, the Durbeyfield wagon met many other wagons with families on the summit of the load, which was built on a well-nigh unvarying principle, as peculiar, probably, to the rural laborer as the hexagon to the bee. The groundwork of the arrangement was the position of the family dresser, which, with its shining handles, and finger marks, and domestic evidences thick upon it, stood im-

portantly in front, over the tails of the shaft-horses, in its erect and natural position, like some Ark of the Covenant which must not be carried slightingly.

Even in the event of mass uprooting, the folk character that is preserved is that of the tenacious, the colonial, the instinctive, for which Hardy finds the simile of the hexagon of the bee, converting it then, with Miltonic boldness, to its humanly tribal significance with the simile of the Ark of the Covenant.) Their fatalism is communal and ritual, an instinctive adaptation as accommodating to bad as to good weather, to misfortune as to luck, to birth as to death, a subjective economy by which emotion is subdued to the falling out of event and the destructiveness of resistance is avoided. In their fatalism lies their survival wisdom, as against the death direction of all moral deliberation. There is this wisdom in the cheerful compassion of the field-women for Tess in her time of trouble: the trouble "was to be." It is in Joan Durbeyfield's Elizabethan ditties of lullaby:

> I saw her lie do-own in yon-der green gro—ve;
> Come, love, and I'll tell you where.

—the kind of ditty by which women of the folk induce maturity in the child by lulling him to sleep with visions of seduction, adultery, and despair. It is in the folk code of secrecy—as in Dairyman Crick's story of the widow who married Jack Dollop, or in Joan's letter of advice to her daughter, summoning the witness of ladies the highest in the land who had had their "trouble" too but who had not told. Tess's tragedy turns on a secret revealed, that is, on the substitution in Tess of an individualizing morality for the folk instinct of concealment and anonymity.

While their fatalism is a passive adaptation to the earthy doom, the folk magic is an active luxury: the human being, having a mind, however incongruous with his animal condition, has to do something with it—and if the butter will not come and someone is in love in the house, the coexistence of the two facts offers a mental exercise in causation (though this is not really the "rights o't," about the butter, as Dairyman Crick himself observes; magical lore is not so dainty); yet the magic is no less a survival wisdom than the fatalism, inasmuch as it does offer mental exercise in causation, for man cannot live without a sense of cause. The magic is a knowledgeable mode of dealing with the un-knowledgeable, and it is adaptive to the dooms of existence where moral reason is not adaptive, for moral reason seeks congruence between human intention and effect and is therefore always inapropos (in Hardy's universe, tragically inapropos), whereas magic seeks only likenesses, correspondence, analogies, and these are everywhere. Moral reason is in complete incommunication with the "given," for it cannot accept the "given" as such, cannot accept accident, cannot accept the obscure activities of instinct, cannot accept doom; but magic can not only accept but rationalize all these, for the correspondences that determine its strategies are themselves "given"—like is like, and that is the end of the matter. As the folk fatalism imbues the foreground accidents with the suggestion of necessity, the folk magic imbues them with the suggestion of the supernaturally motivated; and motivation of whatever kind makes an event seem "necessary," suitable, fitting. The intricate interknitting of all these motifs gives to Hardy's actually magical view of the universe and of human destiny a backing of concrete life, as his evocation of the earth as Cause gives to his vision the grounding of the naturalistic.

The folk magic is, after all, in its strategy of analogy, only a specialization and formalization of the novelist's use of the symbolism of natural detail, a symbolism of which we are constantly aware from beginning to end. Magical interpretation and prediction of events consist in seeing one event or thing as a "mimicry" of another—a present happening, for instance, as a mimicry of some future happening; that is, magic makes a system out of analogies, the correlative forms of things. Poets and novelists do likewise with their symbols. Burns's lines: "And my fause luver staw my rose, / But ah! he left the thorn wi' me," use this kind of mimicry, common to poetry and magic. When a thorn of Alec's roses pricks Tess's chin, the occurrence is read as an omen—and omens properly belong to the field of magic; but the difference between this symbol which is an omen, and the very similar symbol in Burns's lines, which acts only reminiscently, is a difference merely of timing—the one "mimics" a seduction which occurs later, the other "mimics" a seduction and its consequences which have already occurred. And there is very little difference, functionally, between Hardy's use of this popular symbol as an *omen* and his symbolic use of natural particulars—the chattering of the birds at dawn after the death of Prince and the iridescence of the coagulated blood, the swollen udders of the cows at Talbothays and the heavy fertilizing mists of the last summer mornings and evenings, the ravaged turnip field on Flintcomb-Ash and the visitation of the polar birds. All of these natural details are either predictive or interpretive or both, and prediction and interpretation of events through analogies are the profession of magic.

When a piece of blood-stained butcher paper flies up in the road as Tess enters the gate of the vicarage at Emminster, the occurrence is natural while it is ominous; it is realistically observed, as part of the "given," while it inculcates the magical point of view. Novelistic symbolism *is* magical strategy. In *Tess*, which is through and through symbolic, magic is not only an adaptive specialization of the "folk," but it also determines the reader's response to the most naturalistic detail. Thus, though the story is grounded deeply in a naturalistic premise, Hardy's use of one of the commonest tools of novelists—symbolism—enforces a magical view of life.

Logically accommodated by this view of life is the presentation of supernatural characters. Alec D'Urberville does not appear in his full otherworldly character until late in the book, in the episode of the planting fires, where we see him with pitchfork among flames—and even then the local realism of the planting fires is such as almost to absorb the ghostliness of the apparition. The usual form of his appearance is as a stage villain, complete with curled mustache, checked suit, and cane; and actually it seems a bit easier for the reader to accept him as the Evil Spirit itself, even with a pitchfork, than in his secular accouterments of the villain of melodrama. But Hardy's logic faces its conclusions with superb boldness, as it does in giving Angel Clare his name and his harp and making him a minister's son; if Alec is the Evil One, there will be something queer about his ordinary tastes, and the queerness is shown in his stagy clothes (actually, this melodramatic stereotype is just as valid for a certain period of manners and dress as our own stereotype of the gunman leaning against a lamppost and striking a match against his thumbnail). Alec is the smart aleck of the Book of Job, the one who goes to and fro in the earth and walks up and down in it, the perfectly deracinated one, with his flash and new money and faked name and aggressive ego. If he becomes a religious convert even temporarily it is because he is not really so very much different from Angel (the smart aleck of the Book of Job was also an angel), for extreme implies extreme, and both Angel and Alec are foundered in egoism, the one in idealistic egoism, the other in sensual egoism, and Angel himself is diabolic enough in his prudery. When Alec plays his last frivolous trick on Tess, lying down on one of the slabs in the D'Urberville vaults and springing up at her like an animated corpse, his neuroticism finally wears, not the stagy traditional externals of the Evil Spirit, but the deeply convincing character of insanity—of that human evil which is identifiable with madness. Both Angel and Alec are metaphors of extremes of human behavior, when the human has been cut off from community and has been individualized by intellectual education or by material wealth and traditionless independence.

Between the stridencies of Angel's egoism and Alec's egoism is Tess —with her Sixth Standard training and some anachronistic D'Urberville current in her blood that makes for spiritual exacerbation just as it makes her cheeks paler, "the teeth more regular, the red lips thinner than is usual in a country-bred girl": incapacitated for life by her moral idealism, capacious of life through her sensualism. When, after Alec's evilly absurd trick, she bends down to whisper at the opening of the vaults, "Why am I on the wrong side of this door?" her words construct all the hopelessness of her cultural impasse. But her stabbing of Alec is her heroic return through the "door" into the folk fold, the fold of nature and instinct, the anonymous community. If both Alec and Angel are spiritually impotent in their separate ways, Tess is finally creative by the only measure of creativeness that this particular novelistic universe holds, the measure of the instinctive and the natural. Her gesture is the traditional gesture of the revenge of instinct, by which she joins an innumerable company of folk heroines who stabbed and were hanged—the spectacular but still anonymous and common gesture of common circumstances and common responses, which we, as habitual readers of newspaper crime headlines, find, unthinkingly, so shocking to our delicate notions of what is "natural." That she goes, in her wandering at the end, to Stonehenge, is an inevitable symbolic going—as all going and doing are symbolic—for it is here that the earthiness of her state is best recognized, by the monoliths of Stonehenge, and that the human dignity of her last gesture has the most austere recognition, by the ritual sacrifices that have been made on these stones.

4

ARTHUR MIZENER

————◆◆————

Jude the Obscure as a Tragedy

> . . . *who cannot see*
> *What Earth's ingrained conditions are.*
> —*"Seventy-four and Twenty."*

I suppose no one will question Hardy's right to the title of "the first great tragedian in novel form," taking *tragedy* in its looser sense. Yet there seems to be a general feeling that somehow his novels are not successful, are not, for all their deep sense of the horror of ordinary life, really tragic. "There is," as Mr. E. M. Forster says, "some vital problem that has not been answered, or even posed, in the misfortunes of Jude the Obscure." The cause of that feeling is, I think, an attitude which is probably more the product of his age than of Hardy's own understanding. In a sense the courage of Hardy's profoundest conviction failed him, precisely as Tennyson's did, under the pressure of the reasoning of his age.

Hardy, to be sure, refused to identify what he called "the ideal life" with the conventional views of his times, and this refusal saved him from the superior fatuousness of people like Tennyson and Browning at their worst. He could, indeed, be devastating about these conventional views: "How could smug Christian optimism worthy of a dissenting grocer find a place inside a man [Browning] who was so vast a seer and feeler when on neutral ground?"[1] Yet at bottom Hardy's attitude suffered from the same kind of fault as Browning's. Browning

Reprinted from *Southern Review* (VI, 1) with the permission of the author and the Louisiana State University Press.

tried to convince himself that because God was in his heaven all must be right with the world. Hardy's objection to this view of things was that it believed in heaven at all; for Hardy, using Browning's logic in reverse, tried to convince himself that because all was obviously not right with the world, there could be no heaven. The only source of hope left him, therefore, was the belief that the world would, by a process of moral evolution, become a kind of heaven in time.[2] This kind of hope was the only kind Hardy could discover, once he had denied any independent reality to the dream of perfection, and without some hope not only tragedy but life itself is impossible.

The trouble with this view, for tragedy, is that its possessor is incapable of facing squarely the paradox of evil. Browning felt that, having accepted the proposition that God is the all-great and the all-loving too, he had committed himself to a denial of evil; life was therefore an exhilarating battle in which one proved his worth for heaven—

> Only they see not God, I know,
> Nor all that chivalry of his,
> The soldier-saints who, row on row,
>
> Burn upward each to his point of bliss—
> Since, the end of life being manifest,
> He had burned his way thro' the world to this.[3]

Hardy, feeling profoundly the ingrained evil of human and animal life, thought that feeling committed him to a denial of heaven. Thus both Browning and Hardy found it impossible to deny, for the sake of a smaller consistency, one of the realities which must be recognized and accepted for the larger consistency of tragedy. Both found it impossible to believe in "the goodness of God" and "the horrors of human and animal life"; neither, in Keats's phrase, was "capable of being in uncertainties, mysteries, doubts, without any irritable reaching after fact and reason." They felt called upon either to explain the real life as a logical corollary of the ideal life, or to explain the ideal life as a logical corollary of the real. They were thus incapable of representing in the same fiction the meaning and splendor of both lives and of using each to illuminate the limitations of the other.

But this inability to escape the smaller consistency was the central weakness of late nineteenth-century literature as a whole: "there is the assumption that Truth is indifferent or hostile to the desires of men; that these desires were formerly nurtured on legend, myth, all kinds of insufficient experiment; that, Truth being known at last in the form of experimental science, it is intellectually impossible to maintain illusion any longer, at the same time that it is morally impossible to assimilate Truth." [4] It is in this sense that Hardy's attitude is more the product of his age than of his own understanding. It is probably more remarkable, under the circumstances, that he came as close as he did to escaping from the trap his age unconsciously set for itself than that he was, in the end, caught.

The code Hardy evolved as a description of the ideal life is a secularized version of the Sermon on the Mount, a thoroughly fumigated New Testament morality. The real subject of *Jude* is the evolution of this code in Jude's mind ("a species of Dick Whittington, whose spirit was touched to finer issues than a mere material gain" [89]). In so far as this code is a statement of the potentialities of humanity, it is the possibility of their realization somewhere, somehow, which gives Jude's death meaning. In so far as it is not a statement of the potentialities of humanity Jude is mad and his death meaningless: this alternative was obviously no part of Hardy's intention. But Hardy had no place outside of the actual world of time where he could visualize these potentialities as being realized; he saw no possibility that the nothing of death itself, when the long sickness of health and living begins to mend, would bring all things. So he ended by implying the realization of these human potentialities in this world; ended, that is, by denying his most profound conviction, that earth's conditions are ingrained. And if it is difficult to believe that life is evil and God good, it is even more difficult to believe that the evil of life is ingrained and that it will nevertheless presently come unstuck.

That Hardy produced such powerful novels, in spite of his inability to conceive an ideal life with an existence either very strong or outside of time and in spite of the formal limitations which this attitude inevitably imposed on him, is a tribute to his profound rectitude. The power of Hardy's novels is the power of Hardy's character; the consistency and purity of the feeling throughout both the novels and the poems proves that his vision of evil is, quite simply, what he saw. Such feeling cannot be faked. This power makes itself felt in spite of Hardy's fumbling inability to think his way through to an understanding of his personal impressions or to a form which would organize them in terms of their meaning.

II

About his idea in *Jude* Hardy was quite explicit: *Jude* was "to show the contrast between the ideal life a man wished to lead, and the

squalid real life he was fated to lead. . . . [This] idea was meant to
run all through the novel." It was to be a tragedy "of the WORTHY
encompassed by the INEVITABLE." [5] Such an idea requires for its successful representation a form which is consciously an artifice, a verisimilar and plausible narrative which the novelist values, not for its
own sake, but as the perfect vehicle for his idea. He must keep his
narrative alive at every turn with his idea, for he cannot, once committed to it, afford the luxury of a meaningless appeal to his reader's
delight in recognition and suspense. The characters of such a novel,
as Aristotle said of the characters in the tragedy of his day, are there
for the sake of the action, and the action or fable is there, ultimately,
for the sake of the idea—*is* the idea.

Yet Hardy, with such an essentially tragic idea never freed himself
wholly from the naturalistic assumption that narrative must be significant historically rather than fabulously.[6] In the case of *Jude* this
assumption forced him to identify himself as author with his hero
instead of with the action as a whole. Jude is not a character in a
larger composition, the dramatization of one of several presented points
of view which go together to make up the author's attitude, because
Hardy's attitude was not complex and inclusive but simple and exclusive. He therefore sought to contrast the ideal life with the real life,
not of man but of *a* man. That is to say, he wrote a naturalistic novel,
a history of his hero, in which the hero is the author, for Jude is obviously autobiographical in the general sense.[7] The essential meaning
of his fiction for Hardy is its narrative or "historical" meaning, and
Jude's understanding of that history is Hardy's. All that the narrative
which is a perfect artifice ever proves according to Hardy is the historical existence of a "consummate artist"; all that it even tempts us
to believe in is the historical reality of the events it presents. Hardy
never really faced the possibility that a great work of art aims at a
kind of truth superior (but not necessarily contradictory) to a scientific and historical verisimilitude.[8] For Hardy, therefore, the true
narrative was one which conformed to a historical conception of the
truth from which the fabulous was very carefully excluded; and the
truest of these was, in the general sense, autobiographical, since
only the man who had lived through experiences generally like those
described in the narrative could represent with historical accuracy
not only the external events but the thoughts and opinions of participant in these events.

Yet because Hardy had an idea he was not content simply to tell a
story. If that idea was not finely enough conceived to drive him to dis-

card the naturalistic form, it was strong enough to make him stretch that form to the breaking point by the use of devices which have no place in his kind of novel. There is, for example, nothing to be said against the use of a certain amount of coincidence in the novel which is consistently an artifice, but it only weakens a novel which depends for its acceptance on the reader's conviction of the distinguishably historical truth of its hero's career. In the same way Hardy's carefully devised contrasts fail of their full purpose because he is writing a novel at whose center there is no final contrast.[9] These contrasts are not, therefore, means for enriching a central contrast between a vision of the ideal life and a vision of the real life; they are but means for contrasting a single view of things, which is true, with all other views of things, which are false. And this is the contrast of melodrama rather than of tragedy. In the same way, too, Hardy's use of symbolic incident, for all its immense immediate effectiveness, remains a kind of desperate contrivance in a novel which is not itself a symbol but "a true historie." These incidents do not, that is, have in them implications of contrasted views of experience; they are merely poetic projections of the hero's view of things. The result of all this is a novel which is formally neither fish, flesh, nor good red herring, a novel whose tremendous verisimilar life is constantly being sapped by a series of irrelevant devices and yet remains, as a systematic artifice, "a paradise of loose ends."

III

The nearest Hardy came to escaping from the strangling limitations of his attitude and the naturalistic form to which it committed him was in his pastoral idealization of the life of his Wessex peasants. He might, by completing this idealization, have produced profound romantic comedy; for he could see so clearly that "it is the on-going—*i.e.*, the 'becoming'—of the world that produces its sadness. If the world stood still at a felicitous moment there would be no sadness in it. The sun and the moon standing still on Ajalon was not a catastrophe for Israel, but a type of Paradise" (*The Early Life*, p. 265). It is his feeling that the world had come perceptibly closer to standing still at a felicitous moment for his Wessex peasants in the old days which tempted him to see their life as a type of Paradise.

Yet he did not know how to subdue the rational fact of the matter. The on-going of the world worked among the Wessex people too, if more slowly; and even if it did not, only the illusion of nostalgia could make one who knew that earth's conditions are ingrained suppose there had even been a felicitous moment in the past. The life of these peasants can be, for Hardy, only a charming anachronism; and their comments, though Hardy uses them chorically in his novels, are really irrelevant to any meaning which is possible for him. When Mrs. Edlin comments on Sue's marriage—"In my time we took it more careless, and I don't know that we was any the worse for it!" (438)—or when she is to be heard "honestly saying the Lord's Prayer in a loud voice, as the Rubric directed" (333), she is only an example of how much simpler and easier life was before man had progressed in the hands of inescapable time to his present high state of nervous and emotional organization. She cannot be, as Hardy's use of her sometimes seems to imply she is, an image from a timeless and ideal pastoral world, an Arden to which his hero will escape from the squalid real world of Duke Frederick's court. For much as Hardy longed, however unconsciously, to make out of the world of his Wessex peasants an ideal pastoral world, the weary weight of its unintelligible actuality so burdened him that he was never able to see it as a type of Paradise, to make it a part of his means for "holding in a single thought reality and justice." It was indeed Hardy's tragedy as a writer that he never found any such means. Mrs. Edlin and the rest of his peasants remain meaningful only at the level of history; they are samples of the simpler and easier way of life in the past, preserved for Hardy's day by an eddy in time.

The moments of happiness which come in most of Hardy's novels just before the catastrophes are particular instances of his inability to make the country life a type of Paradise. Grace and Giles in Sherton Abbey while they still believe the divorce possible, Tess and Angel between the murder of Alec and the arrest at Stonehenge, Jude and Sue at the Wessex Agricultural Show, these felicitous moments are always moments when the protagonists believe they have won their way back to the Garden of Eden, to purity of heart and to a kindly country world which will be a satisfactory home for the pure in heart. Only a rather staggering amount of coincidence in the narrative or naïveté in the characters can provide moments of such delusion in the real world as Hardy knew it; and because Hardy was committed to a naturalistic form he not only had to produce these moments by coincidence and naïveté, but to demonstrate that, except as faint foreshadowings of a reformed humanity, they were fool's paradises. Thus Hardy's time-bound universe and the naturalistic form which it forced on him as a novelist prevented his imagining or presenting an artificial world which contained both reality and justice.

Committed as he was to the truth of abstract reason rather than the truth of imagination, Hardy therefore had no choice but to conceive his ideal life as a felicitous moment some place in the future of the real life, since this ideal life was the only kind which could be reached by strict reason from his premise. Hardy's faith in this kindly country world to which humanity would win in the course of history is seldom explicit in the novels, since to make it explicit is to make explicit also the contradiction between this faith and Hardy's overwhelming conviction that Earth's conditions are ingrained. That faith is, however, of necessity everywhere implicit in his presentation of the events of human and natural life; it is his only source for the light which reveals the horror of these events.[10]

In that Hardy's novels rest, in this indirect fashion, on a belief in the world's progress toward a felicitous future, their meaning is the meaning of sentimental pastoral. They are what *As You Like It* would be without Jaques to remind us and the senior Duke that "the penalty of Adam" was not merely "the season's difference" but the knowledge of good and evil, without Touchstone to show us that weariness of the legs is as significant in its way as weariness of the spirit in its, and his love of Jane Smile as real as Silvious's love of Phebe or Orlando's of Rosalind. For however much Hardy failed to recognize it, his whole view of things was based on the assumption that the world of *The Woodlanders* without Fitzpiers and Mrs. Charmond and an educated Grace would be an ideal world, a world of

> Men surfeited of laying heavy hands
> Upon the innocent,
> The mild, the fragile, the obscure content
> Among the myriads of thy family.
> Those, too, who love the true, the excellent,
> And make their daily moves a melody.
> [*The Dynasts*, Fore Scene]

The success of such poems as "In Time of 'The Breaking of Nations' " depends on the implication that the life of the man harrowing clods and the maid and her wight is not only eternal—a world that stands still; but felicitous—a world which knows only the sweet adversity of "the season's difference" and not the adversity of evil. Such a pastoral vision of a still point of the turning world was the source of Hardy's sense of the squalid evil of real life. But because he refused to use the life of his Wessex peasants, or any other life, to body forth his forms of things unknown, he was unable to turn those forms to shapes at all.

But if Hardy's combination of half-despairing, scientific humanitarianism, and the naturalistic form which he thought it committed him to, was incapable of pastoral, it was even more incapable of tragedy. Hardy's feeling that the evil of this world was incurable is tragic. But because he was unable to place the source of the idealism by which he measured the world and found it wanting outside of time and therefore, *faute de mieux*, came to believe "in the gradual ennoblement of man," his attitude is such as to preclude a formal structure which pits the idealist against the practical man in equal combat. There is no basic, unresolvable tragic tension between the real and the ideal in his attitude, and there is as a consequence no tragic tension in the formal structure it invokes as its representation. The objection to Hardy's form for tragedy is, therefore, not a matter of his occasional awkwardness or carelessness; it is radical.[11]

The assumption which justifies the naturalistic novel is that there can be only one kind of reality, and this is Hardy's assumption. But if there is only one kind of reality there can be also only one kind of truth, and that truth, in *Jude* is the melioristic view of the world that is the only belief Hardy can find.[12] As author Hardy is therefore unable to represent justly in *Jude* those kinds of men according to whose ideas the world must be run if earth's conditions are ingrained. In his fictional world such people can be shown only in the light of the single true view of things which Hardy and Jude share. It is as if Shakespeare had first made Hamlet altogether incapable of believing the evil of the world incurable and had then shown us Claudius only as Hamlet saw him. Hardy's Claudiuses are not mighty opposites; they are inexplicable villains. At best he can give them credit for being better adjusted to the world as it is at the moment. And for the same reason the only irony he can direct against his hero is the irony to be derived from a demonstration of his temporary maladjustment in a world which, if it is not meaningless, will presently realize that hero's ideal. There is thus neither permanent justification in Hardy for the Arabellas nor permanent irony for the Judes. *Jude* cannot display the very real if limited truth of Claudius's

> For what we know must be, and is as common
> As any the most vulgar thing to sense,
> Why should we in our peevish opposition
> Take it to heart? Fie! 'tis a fault to heaven,
> A fault against the dead, a fault to nature,
> To reason most absurd . . .

nor the very real if terrible absurdity of Hamlet's "Go to, I'll no more on't; it hath made me mad. I say, we will have no moe marriage: . . ."

But if the actions of the Arabellas are seen only as Jude saw them, they must remain for the reader what they were for Jude, the consequences of an inexplicable and brutal stupidity rather than of a different kind of wisdom to Jude's. Thus Hardy's attitude and the form it invoked excluded from his representation, despite the fact that no one knew them better than he did, the point of view of those men and women for whom "the defence and salvation of the body by daily bread is still a study, a religion, and a desire." It excluded, too, an understanding of how a woman like Sue might, not in weakness but in strength, deny the validity of Jude's humanitarian idealism. It is one thing, that is, for Jude to preach to Sue the horror of her final surrender to Phillotson and conventional conduct or for Hamlet to preach to his mother the horror of surrender to Claudius and a "normal" life. It is quite another for Hardy, who does, or Shakespeare, who does not, to commit himself completely as author to this sermon.

At the same time, however, that Hardy presents the almost universal opposition to Jude as inexplicably cruel, he is forced to present people and animals—of which there are a great many in Hardy—in such a way as to support Jude's view of them. In other words, Hardy presents the same kinds of objects at once unjustly and sentimentally. And this is the manifestation in the "verbal correlative" of Hardy's attitude of the contradiction inherent in that attitude. Because he can see only a single reality, that of the time-bound actual world, the life of that reality has to be at once incurably evil and potentially good.

IV

Jude the Obscure is, then, the history of a worthy man's education. Part One, for example, is primarily an account of Jude's youth up to the moment he departs for Christminster in search of learning. From the very beginning, however, Jude and the world through which he moves are presented as they appear to the eyes of one who has accepted the view of things which will be the end-product of Jude's education. In so far as Jude understands this view of things, he is not dramatized; he is the author. In so far as, in his innocence, he ignores the necessities and their implications which this view sees, he is dramatized, objectified by Hardy's irony. Hardy's narrative is, then, secondarily, a demonstration of the consequences of Jude's innocent ignorance of "Nature's logic"—in Part One in the matter of sex. Nature takes its revenge by entangling Jude irretrievably with Arabella. Hardy gives this demonstration a complex poetic elaboration, and it is easy to suppose as a consequence that his narrative is fundamentally symbolic, the pitting of two different views of experience—Jude's and Arabella's—against each other in a neutral arena. That it is not is evident from the fact that Hardy as the narrator takes advantage of every opportunity to support Jude's attitude. Furthermore, this part cannot, as symbolic narrative, be fitted into any pattern which runs through the book as a whole, for the only pattern *Jude* has is the pattern of history.

Nevertheless the poetic elaboration of this episode is interesting as an example, characteristic of the procedure of the book as a whole, of how Hardy's idea, striving to establish a form which will make sense of it, is constantly breaking through the limits of the naturalistic form. The meeting of Arabella and Jude, for example, is brought about by Arabella's hitting Jude with a pig's pizzle. No better image for what drew Arabella and Jude together could be found, and, a symbol of their meeting, the pig's pizzle hangs on the bridge rail between them throughout their first meeting. Thereafter, Arabella scarcely appears in this part unaccompanied by pigs. In the same way Jude's dream of an education which will take him through Christminster to a career as a philanthropic bishop is associated with a vision of Christminster as seen from the roof of the old Brown House against the blaze of the setting sun, like the heavenly Jerusalem, as the child Jude says solemnly to the tiler. It is also associated with the New Testament. The New Testament, in its strictly moral aspect, is the textbook of Hardy's humanitarian morality, and in so far as Jude values its morality he is demonstrating his instinctively humanitarian feelings. But Jude's Testament represents for him also religion and, in that it is a Greek text, learning; and in valuing it on these counts he is demonstrating his illusions.

During the wooing of Arabella by Jude there are sporadic recrudescences of these symbols. For example, Hardy is constantly bringing the two lovers back to the rise on which the old Brown House stands, from which Jude had once seen his vision of the heavenly Jerusalem and where, under the influence of an impulse rather awkwardly explained on the narrative level, he had also once knelt and prayed to Apollo and Diana, the god and goddess of learning and chastity (33). Under the influence of Arabella, Jude "passed the spot where he had knelt to Diana and Phoebus without remembering that there were any such people in the mythology, or that the sun was anything

else than a useful lamp for illuminating Arabella's face" (46). Hardy
carefully notes, too, that a picture of Samson and Delilah hangs on
the wall of the tavern where the two lovers stop for tea but instead,
partly at Arabella's suggestion, drink beer (48, 79, 451). The linkage
of Arabella and liquor (she had been a barmaid) is valuable to
Hardy not only as a piece of naturalism but because it makes Arabella an incarnation of what Jude later calls "my two Arch Enemies
. . . my weakness for women and my impulse to strong liquor"
(420).

Yet these symbols, effective as they are, are sporadic and unsystem-
atized. Hardy never deserts his naturalistic narrative and commits his
meaning to them completely, and so the reader never feels to the full
in him what Henry James once so beautifully called the renewal "in the
modern alchemist [of] something like the old dream of the secret of
life." Hardy never thought of himself as a modern alchemist but only
as a historian. This fact is plain enough in the climactic scene of this
part, the pig-killing scene, for here the pig is not primarily a symbol
but an object at the naturalistic level. Arabella takes toward it, as such,
an attitude perfectly consistent with the attitude she has maintained
throughout. Her concern is for the salableness of the meat, and even
her urging that Jude kill the pig quickly when it cries out is determined by her conventional fear lest the cry reveal to the neighbors
that the Fawleys have sunk to killing their own pig. "Poor folks
must live," she says when Jude protests against the inhumanity of
slowly bleeding the pig to death (72). And though Hardy's description of the incident precludes any sympathy for Arabella, this statement is profoundly true within the limits of the world Arabella is
aware of.

In direct contrast to Arabella's practical view of this killing, Hardy
sets Jude's idealistic view of it: "The white snow, stained with the
blood of his fellow-mortal, wore an illogical look to him as a lover
of justice, not to say a Christian; . . . " (73). There is irony here, of
course, but it is directed solely to the point that Hardy "could not
see how the matter was to be mended" (73), not at all to the point
that in one very real sense—the sense that Arabella understood—it
could and ought never to be mended.[13] This is so because Hardy
is in fact and, as a consequence, by the form he has chosen committed to Jude's view of this incident. That commitment is clear in
every word Hardy himself writes about the pig; for example: "The
dying animal's cry assumed its third and final tone, the shriek of
agony; his glazing eyes rivetting themselves on Arabella with the

eloquently keen reproach of a creature recognizing at last the treachery of those who had seemed his only friends" (71).

The consequence of the author's putting the full weight of his authority in this way behind one of the conflicting views of the events is to take the ground out from under the other. The events are presented only as Jude saw them, so that Arabella's view of them seems to the reader simply inexplicably hard-hearted, however commonplace. Hardy can see that Arabella's attitude, in its complete ignorance of Jude's, is grimly funny: "'Od damn it all!' she cried, 'that ever I should say it! You've over-stuck un! And I telling you all the time—'" (71). But he cannot see that it is in any sense justified. The result of this commitment of the author is that the scene as a whole becomes sentimental; and it is difficult to resist the temptation to read it as "a burlesque of the murder of Duncan" with the pig substituted for the king ("Well—you must do the sticking—there's no help for it. I'll show you how. Or I'll do it myself—I think I could." [70]).

This pig-killing scene is of course meant to connect in the reader's mind with the earlier episode where Farmer Troutham whips Jude for allowing the rooks to eat his corn. For Jude the rooks "took upon them more and more the aspect of gentle friends and pensioners. . . . A magic thread of fellow-feeling united his own life with theirs. Puny and sorry as those lives were, they much resembled his own" (10).[14] Here again Hardy presents these birds and Jude only as Jude sees them. For all his knowledge of "the defence and salvation of the body" he signally fails to do justice to Farmer Troutham's view of them, just as he fails to do justice to Arabella's view of Jude and the pig, because he cannot present two kinds of truth in a naturalistic novel. Hamlet, to say nothing of Shakespeare, could understand and yet defy augury both for himself and the sparrow, since he knew well in the end from experience what was well enough known to him from his reading from the start, that there is a "special providence" in these matters, so that "the readiness is all." Hardy, like Jude and Jaques, could only weep, knowing no providence at all. Shakespeare could therefore write "The Phoenix and the Turtle," Hardy only "Compassion: An Ode in Celebration of the Centenary of the Royal Society for the Prevention of Cruelty to Animals."

Part Two (at Christminster) brings Hardy's spiritual Whittington to his London where he is taught that his desire for learning had been only "a social unrest which had no foundation in the nobler instincts; which was purely an artificial product of civilization" (151). At the very beginning he catches a glimpse of the truth: "For a moment there fell on Jude a true illumination; that here in the stone-yard was a centre of effort as worthy as that dignified by the name of scholarly study within the noblest of the colleges" (96).[15] Apart from his narrative function, Phillotson is used in this part to foreshadow Jude's discovery of this truth and to reveal what happens to a weaker person at such a disappointment (116–17). Arabella's temporary conversion after Cartlett's death has the same kind of formal relation to Sue's conversion, with the additional irony that Sue's conversion involves a return to active sexual life which she hates, Arabella's a loss of it which she cannot endure (373). Jude's discovery of the fraudulence of learning leaves him only his Christianity; that he will discover this too is "as dead as a fern-leaf in a lump of coal" Hardy tells us directly (96–7). That it has been replaced by a German-Gothic fake he suggests by his references to the tearing down of the "hump-backed, wood-turreted, and quaintly hipped" Marygreen church and to the "tall new building of German-Gothic design" erected in its place (6, 146).

Meanwhile Jude meets his cousin Sue, whom Hardy always keeps before the reader as Jude first saw her in the picture at Marygreen, "in a broad hat, with radiating folds under the brim like the rays of a halo" (88), not only because she remains always for Jude a saint but because, by a terribly irony, she literally becomes one at the end of the book. Sue has twice Jude's quickness of wit and half his strength of character.[16] She therefore saw from the beginning that there was nothing in the universe except "Nature's law"; but because of her lack of real profundity, she thought also that it was "Nature's . . . raison d'être, that we should be joyful in what instincts she afforded us . . ." (403). When she discovered that nature had no raison d'être and that paganism was as false as Christianity had seemed to her, she did not have the strength to face it and went back to conventional wifehood and conventional Christianity. All this, even the impermanence of Sue's paganism (the figures of Venus and Apollo are plaster and come off on her gloves and jacket), is implicit in the episode of the images in Chapter II and in the recollections of Sue's childhood in Chapter VI. By a fine piece of irony—since Sue is, while her strength lasts, a saint of Hardy's humanitarian faith—Hardy has Jude focus not only his physical but his religious feelings on Sue. Gradually he learns from her and experience the omnipotence of Nature's law. But meanwhile Jude sees this imperfect saint of humanitarianism as an Anglican saint. Of the irony of this illusion Hardy makes much (e.g., 123), and in incident after incident, until Jude

unlearns his Christianity, he reëmphasizes the irony of this love between the pagan and delicately sexed Sue and the Christian and
passionate Jude.

In Part Three Jude, having realized that learning is vain and that
only his "altruistic feeling" had any "foundation in the nobler instincts,"
goes to Melchester, partly because it is "a spot where worldly learning
and intellectual smartness had no establishment" (152), partly because Sue is there. There follows a series of episodes which represent
the conflict between Sue's daring humanitarian faith and her weak
conventional conduct, on the one hand, and Jude's "Tractarian" faith
and courageously honest conduct, on the other. In the end, of course,
Hardy arranges events so as to demonstrate the omnipotence of "the
artificial system of things, under which the normal sex-impulses are
turned into devilish domestic gins and springes to noose and hold
back those who want to progress" (257), and Sue marries Phillotson.
In Part Four Jude's education is almost lost sight of in the welter of
narrative detail. Occasionally its progress is marked for the reader,
as when Jude replies to Sue's question whether she ought to continue to live with Phillotson: "Speaking as an order-loving man—
which I hope I am, though I fear I am not—I should say yes. Speaking
from experience and unbiassed nature, I should say no" (248).
Though Sue and Jude determine to sacrifice their love to right conduct, their coming together on the occasion of their aunt's death at
Marygreen finally forces Jude to recognize the evil of the church's
marriage system and Sue to realize that she must leave Phillotson for
Jude. Sue tries at first to avoid marriage and an active sexual life, but
Arabella's return, ironically, forces her to yield to Jude in order to
hold him.[17]

There follows in Part Five a period when "the twain were happy—
between their times of sadness . . ." (341). Hardy shows them as
devoted lovers at the Great Wessex Agricultural Show, where they
are carefully contrasted with the conventional married couple Arabella
and Cartlett (Chapter V). But the pressure of the conventional world
on them as unmarried lovers forces them down and down until Jude,
"still haunted by his dream" (395), brings Sue and the children to a
"depressing purlieu" of Christminster. Here Jude makes a speech, from
the cross, as it were, to the Roman soldiers of Christminster in which
he states the result of his education: "I perceive there is something
wrong somewhere in our social formulas: what it is can only be discovered by men or women with greater insight than mine—if, indeed,
they ever discover it—at least, in our time" (388).

It is here at Christminster that Hardy makes the most extreme use of his one completely symbolic character, Father Time.[18] All through Part Five he has been used to strike the ominous note which reminds us that Sue and Jude's moderate happiness is a snare and a delusion. Now, under the influence of his perfectly arbitrary melancholy and the misinterpretation of something Sue says, he kills all the children, including himself. Father Time is Jude and Arabella's son brought up by Jude and Sue, in order that Hardy may say (400):

> On that little shape had converged all the inauspiciousness and shadow which had darkened the first union of Jude, and all the accidents, mistakes, fears, errors of the last. He was their nodal point, their focus, their expression in a single term. For the rashness of those parents he had groaned, for their ill-assortment he had quaked, and for the misfortunes of these he had died.

The effect of this incident on Jude and Sue is to place each of them in the position from which the other had started at the beginning of the book (409):

> One thing troubled him more than any other, that Sue and himself had mentally travelled in opposite directions since the tragedy: events which had enlarged his own views of life, laws, customs, and dogmas, had not operated in the same manner on Sue's. She was no longer the same as in the independent days, when her intellect played like lambent lightning over conventions and formalities which he had at that time respected, though he did not now.

Sue returns to Christianity and Phillotson as a consequence of this change; and Jude, partly because of a kind of stunned indifference (he takes to drink), and partly because of Arabella's predatory sexuality, returns to his first wife. It is perfectly apparent that in Hardy's opinion Sue has done an unforgivably inhuman thing to save a perfectly imaginary soul.[19]

But Hardy is at least willing to suggest a conflict in Sue between her affection for Jude and her religious belief, even if he is capable of seeing only one right in that conflict. Thus, when Jude departs from their last meeting, to which he had gone knowing that he was committing suicide, "in a last instinct of human affection, even now unsubdued by her fetters, she sprang up as if to go and succor him. But she knelt down again, and stopped her ears with her hands till all possible sound of him had passed away" (466). On his way home

Jude feels "the chilly fog from the meadows of Cardinal as if death-claws were grabbing me through and through" (469); Hardy catches the whole complex of "stern reality" in this symbolic statement by Jude. College, church, social convention, the very things which Jude had at the beginning believed in as the representatives of his ideal, have killed him, either by betraying him directly or by teaching Sue to betray him.

When Hardy comes to Jude's actual death, he also presents Arabella with a choice, the choice of staying with the dying Jude or going to the Remembrance games. The representation of her here is perhaps the best brief illustration in the book of the melodramatic effect which resulted from Hardy's exclusive attitude toward his material. There is not the slightest sign of conflict in Arabella over her choice; she goes without question to the games, flirts with the quack physician Vilbert, and is upset only by the thought that "if Jude were discovered to have died alone an inquest might be deemed necessary" (485). As in the pig-killing scene, Arabella is shown as feeling only brute passion and fear of convention; she is the parody villainess of melodrama, not the mighty opposite of tragedy. Thus the immediate pathos of Jude's death in part derives from Arabella's villainous neglect of him; like the cheers of the Remembrance day crowd which are counterpointed against Jude's dying quotation from *Job*, however, this neglect illustrates only the complete indifference of society to Jude's dream of an ideal life. The rest of the pathos derives from Jude's uncertainty as to why he had been born at all. But the meaning of his death, in so far as it has one, derives from such conviction as Hardy can muster that Jude's life has not been in vain, but the unfortunate life of a man who had tried to live the ideal life several generations before the world was reformed enough to allow him to. Jude's death is not, therefore, in our ordinary understanding of the word, tragic; since it is the result of a conflict between the ideal life a man wished to lead and the only temporarily squalid real life which he was forced to lead.

Jude the Obscure is then, not a tragedy, not a carefully devised representation of life the purpose of which is to contrast, at every turn, the permanently squalid real life of man, with the ideal life (or, if you will, man's dream of an ideal life). It is the history of how an obscure but worthy man, living a life which Hardy conceived to be representative, learned gradually "that the social moulds civilization fits us into have no more relation to our actual shapes than the conventional shapes of the constellations have to the real star-patterns" (242), learned what the true morality of "unbiassed nature" is. In the process of learning this optimistic morality he discovered also that neither nature nor society even recognized it, to say nothing of living by it. In so far as Hardy gave him hope at the end that in time they would, he denied what he otherwise saw so clearly, that earth's conditions are ingrained; in so far as he did not give Jude this hope he denied the possibility of the only ideal life he could conceive and made his hero's life and death essentially meaningless.

The instructive comparison to *Jude* is of course *Hamlet*. For Shakespeare too saw most profoundly the horror of life's ingrained conditions. But because he could also understand and represent the attitude of those who sought to adjust themselves to life's conditions, he saw that the only hope he could give his hero was for that consummation he so devoutly wished, and death is the only felicity Hamlet ever deems possible. Hamlet's death is not death in a universe in which there is no place without bad dreams; neither is it a death justified by a hope that some day the world's ingrained conditions will come unstuck. Jude's death is a little bit of both.

Hardy says in the preface to *Jude* that it "is simply an endeavor to give shape and coherence to a series of seemings, or personal impressions, the question of their consistency or their discordance . . . being regarded as not of the first moment." In that the feeling of the presented life in *Jude* has a powerful coherence this is a justified defense of it. But it is precisely because Hardy never really posed for himself the question of how the meaning of his impressions could be coherent without being consistent that *Jude*, for all the power of its presented life, is not a tragedy.

NOTES

1. Hardy to Sir Edmund Gosse, 3 March 1899. This letter is reproduced in T. J. Wise, *A Browning Library*, opposite p. 118. Cp., *Jude*, p. 410. For convenience's sake I have made all page references to the Modern Library edition of *Jude*.

2. When Dr. A. B. Grosart, having found "abundant evidence that the facts and mysteries of nature and human nature have come urgently before Mr. Hardy's penetrative brain," wrote in that wonderful Victorian way to ask Hardy for his views on the problem of reconciling the absolute goodness of God with "the horrors of human and animal life, particularly parasitic," Hardy characteristically replied: "Perhaps Dr. Grosart might be helped to a provisional view of the universe by the recently published Life of Darwin,

and the works of Herbert Spencer and other agnostics." F. E. Hardy, *The Early Life of Thomas Hardy*, p. 269.

3. "The Statue and the Bust." This was Hardy's favorite Browning poem, presumably because its doctrine that "he who endureth to the end shall be saved" was Hardy's, though he could not, I think, have said, as Browning—perhaps too surely—can, what he meant by *saved*. (*The Early Life*, pp. 252, 261; *Jude*, p. 281.) It should be said for Browning that he was capable, in such poems as "A Toccata of Galuppi's," of doing full justice to the splendor of human life as an autonomous existence.

4. Allen Tate, *Reactionary Essays on Poetry and Ideas*, p. 96.

5. F. E. Hardy, *The Later Years of Thomas Hardy*, pp. 41 and 14.

6. Let me repeat that I think this is not simply a case of Hardy's making an unfortunate choice. In any age when history and fable seem mutually exclusive there is no fortunate choice.

7. Hardy frequently and quite rightly denied that *Jude* was autobiographical in the specific sense (see *The Later Years*, pp. 44, 196), for the events of Jude's life are not in any specific sense the events of Hardy's. But Hardy certainly thought of Jude's experiences as representative of the same kind of experiences he had had and therefore believed it would be scientifically accurate to make the history of his own mind the history of Jude's. "April 28 [1888]. A short story of a young man—'who could not go to Oxford'— His struggles and ultimate failure. Suicide. There is something [in this] the world ought to be shown, and I am the man to show it to them—though I was not altogether hindered going, at least to Cambridge, and could have gone up easily at five-and-twenty." (Hardy's journal, quoted in *The Early Life*, pp. 272–73). What is crucial here is the evidence that Hardy identified himself with Jude so far as thoughts and feelings go, that Jude's attitude toward the events of the narrative is, with minor qualifications to be noted presently, Hardy's.

8. "But in these Bible lives and adventures there is the spherical completeness of perfect art. And our first, and second, feeling that they must be true because they are so impressive, becomes, as a third feeling, modified to, 'Are they so very true, after all?' Is not the fact of their being so convincing an argument, not for their actuality, but for the actuality of a consummate artist who was no more content with what Nature offered than Sophocles and Pheidias were content?" *The Early Life*, p. 223.

9. "Of course the book is all contrasts—or was meant to be in its original conception. . . . e.g., Sue and her heathen gods set against Jude's reading the Greek testament; Christminster academical, Christminster in the slums; Jude the saint, Jude the sinner; Sue the Pagan, Sue the saint; marriage, no marriage, &c., &c." *The Later Years*, p. 42.

10. "It may be added here that the war destroyed all Hardy's belief in the gradual ennoblement of man, a belief he had held for many years. . . . He said he would probably not have ended *The Dynasts* as he did end it if he could have foreseen what was going to happen within a few years." (*The Later Years*, p. 165.) See also Hardy's remarks on the Golden Rule, *Early Life*, p. 294.

11. Hardy, like so many naturalistic novelists, seems to have had considerable faith in the efficacy of carelessness: "The whole secret of a living style and the difference between it and a dead style, lies in not having too much

style—being—in fact, a little careless, or rather seeming to, here and there."
(*The Early Life*, p. 138.) " 'Why!' he said, 'I have never in my life taken
more than three, or perhaps four, drafts for a poem. I am afraid of it losing its freshness.' " (Robert Graves, *Good-bye to All That*, p. 362.) The
result is, as Maugham once wrote, that "he gave you the impression of writing with the stub of a blunt pencil." (*Cakes and Ale*, p. 134.)

12. ". . . the time was not ripe for us! Our ideas were fifty years too
soon to be any good to us" (478). "Christminster is . . . any old-fashioned
University about the date of the story, 1860–70, before there were such
chances for poor men as there are now." (*The Later Years*, p. 249.)

13. It is interesting here to compare the way Shakespeare handles Jaques's
moralizing of the wounded deer. To begin with, Shakespeare makes precise
and explicit what is only vaguely implicit in Hardy's fiction because Hardy
is too much concerned with the actual level, that is the fact that this grief
for an animal is really the image of a grief for the neglect of the exceptional
man in an indifferent world—"Sweep on you fat and greasy citizens." In
the second place, Shakespeare does not present Jaques "weeping and com-
menting/Upon the sobbing deer"; we hear of it from another lord who,
though not without sympathy for the deer ("and indeed, my lord,/The
wretched animal heaved forth such groans. . . ."), conveys quite clearly
the absurdity of Jaques's grief in the practical world. Shakespeare is as sure
of the justice of this anonymous lord's view of the matter as he is of the
different justice of Jaques's view of it. It is as if Hardy had given Arabella
as eloquent a statement of her view of the pig-killing as he gives Jude of his.

14. Birds also occasionally achieve the status of symbols in Hardy—"All
are caged birds; the only difference lies in the size of the cage." (*The Early
Life*, p. 224.) Thus the pair of pigeons which Jude and Sue are forced to
sell to the poulterer and which Sue later surreptitiously releases (363) are
an image of Jude and Sue caged and sold by society for reasons quite
independent of their own feelings and worth. For other uses of this bird
symbol, see *Jude*, pp. 316, 318, 398, 436; *The Mayor of Casterbridge*,
Chap. XLIV–XLV; *The Dynasts*, Pt. 2, p. 214. Hardy would not, of course,
have used these birds at all if he had not thought their dilemma terrible
in its own right. In other words, their primary meaning is still their naturalistic meaning. The same thing is true of the trapped rabbit (252).

15. This passage is an example of what Henry James called "the platitude
of statement." Hardy indulged in it constantly, both in the prose and the
poems, without, apparently, any sense that it was destructive of the life
of his representation. Like his description of the objects of his narrative
from Jude's point of view, it is an outgrowth of his inability to see how
necessary it was for him not to commit himself as author to one view of
things.

16. Hardy seems to have felt that this kind of spiritual weakness was an
inherent characteristic of the more delicate sex (165, 263). It was a common
enough Victorian idea—

> Woman is the lesser man, and all thy passions, match'd with mine,
> Are as moonlight unto sunlight, and as water unto wine—

but it is a little difficult to see how Hardy reconciled this conviction with
Tess. The resemblance between "Locksley Hall" and *Jude*, however, even

down to the parallel uses of Arabella and Tennyson's "savage woman," is astonishing. The only difference between them is that Tennyson, like Browning, found it a little easier to view conventional life optimistically— at least officially he did, for there is much to be said for the argument that Tennyson was at bottom pure mystic and that "The Mystic" rather than "Locksley Hall" represents his deepest feelings about the secular and material faith of his day.

17. On the marriage question, from Sue's point of view: ". . . she fears it would be breaking faith with Jude to withhold herself at pleasure, or altogether, after it; though while uncontracted she feels at liberty to yield herself as seldom as she chooses. This has tended to keep his passions as hot at the end as at the beginning, and helps to break his heart. He has never really possessed her as freely as he desired. (*The Later Years*, p. 42.) Hardy confessed that the delicacy of public sentiment in the period prevented his dwelling on this point as he wished to, made it impossible for him to show clearly, for example, that Jude's spending the night with Arabella when they met unexpectedly at Melchester (216) was a demonstration of how powerfully sheer physical desire was fighting against suppression in him.

18. Father Time as an excellent illustration of the kind of sensational sentimentality which results from trying to represent the essence of life's squalor in a naturalistic narrative: "The doctor says [says Jude] there are such boys springing up amongst us—boys of a sort unknown in the last generation—the outcome of new views of life. . . . He says it is the beginning of the coming universal wish not to live" (400).

19. "Do not do an immoral thing for moral reasons! You have been my social salvation. Stay with me for humanity's sake! You know what a weak fellow I am. My two Arch Enemies you know—my weakness for women and my impulse to strong liquor. Don't abandon me to them, Sue, to save your own soul . . ." (420).

5

MORTON DAUWEN ZABEL

Chance and Recognition

Conrad's title pages always taxed his scruples as severely as any part of his manuscripts, not always to his own satisfaction or to ours in the titles he arrived at, but with notable success in the epigraphs he placed below them. These he used consistently. Mrs. Conrad has said that they were always chosen with extreme care, Conrad taking pains that these "quotations had always a close and direct relation to the contents of the book itself" and that they should express "the mood in which the work was written." Sometimes it is the mood, whether of memory, pathos, irony, or tragic conviction, that is emphasized. More often the epigraph hints of the motive or attitude that directed Conrad's shaping of his material and the conception of experience it dramatizes.

The quotation he fixed below the title of *Lord Jim* is a clue not only to the narrative method which, in his long recitatives, monologues, and self-inquisitions, Conrad made his special instrument for the achieving of realism and form, but to the psychological compulsion under which his characters, caught in the moral or circumstantial prisons of their lives, are forced to speak, and by which Conrad himself, if we trace his nature in his tales and personal writings, was compelled toward his special kind of art and revelation. "It is certain my conviction

From *Craft and Character in Modern Fiction* by Morton Dauwen Zabel; Copyright © 1957 by Morton Dauwen Zabel; reprinted by permission of The Viking Press, Inc.

gains infinitely, the moment another soul will believe in it": Novalis's aphorism is a key to the necessity that is a source both of Conrad's imaginative method and of his appeal to psychological realists.

Sometimes the complex of fate requires solution by something more violent than an ordeal of personal exoneration. Shakespeare's "So foul a sky clears not without a storm" at the head of *Nostromo* suggests a prevailing symbol. When the novel is of a more exotic or melodramatic tendency, it sustains a sense of the marvelous or miraculous, of a thrilled response to the incredible turns and hazards of fate, of "marvels and mysteries acting upon our emotions and intelligence in ways so inexplicable that it would almost justify the conception of life as an enchanted state"—so reflecting the romantic tendency in Conrad's temperament that involved him in the fortunes of his career and that took a lifetime of discipline to bring to terms with the critical force of his moral intelligence. A French nursery rhyme sets the tone for *A Set of Six:* "Les petites marionnettes / Font, font, font, / Trois petits tours / Et puis s'en vont." A phrase from Boethius—". . . for this miracle or this wonder troubleth me right gretly"—stands at the head of the autobiographical *Mirror of the Sea. Victory* begins under the spell of three lines from Milton's "Comus":

> Calling shapes and beckoning shadows dire
> And airy tongues that syllable men's names
> On sands and shores and desert wildernesses.

But there is another series of these quotations that indicates even more clearly the idea that possessed Conrad in his reading of experience. It was an idea that doubtless originated in a profoundly significant root-experience of his own temperament and history. He was to employ it as the incentive of his greatest tales. It is suggested repeatedly in his epigraphs from his first book to his last. The quotation on *Almayer's Folly* in 1895 is from Amiel: "Qui de nous n'a eu sa terre promise, son jour d'extase, et sa fin en exil?" Baudelaire's "D'autres fois, calme plat, grand miroirs / De mon désespoir" serves as heading to *The Shadow Line* in 1917. An aphorism from La Bruyère acts as a clue to *The Arrow of Gold* in 1918: "Celui qui n'a connu que des hommes polis et raisonnables, ou ne connaît pas l'homme, ou ne le connaît qu'à demi." The motto for *The Rescue* in 1920 is from Chaucer's "Frankeleyn's Tale":

> "Alas!" quod she, "that ever this sholde happe!
> For wende I never, by possibilitee,
> That swich a monstre or merveille mighte be!"

Most specific of all, the quotation below the title of *Chance*, in 1913, is from Sir Thomas Browne: "Those that hold that all things are governed by Fortune had not erred, had they not persisted there."

The meaning and consistency of these passages is clear. They permit us to summarize briefly, if too simply, the basic theme of Conrad's fiction. His work dramatizes a hostility of forces that exists both in the conditions of practical life and in the moral constitution of man himself. Men who show any fundamental vitality of nature, will, or imagination are not initially men of caution, tact, or prudence, "polis et raisonnables," and they are certainly unlikely to remain so. They are possessed by an enthusiasm that makes them approach life as an adventure. They attack the struggle with all the impulsive force of their illusion, their pride, their idealism, their desire for fame and power, their confidence that Chance is a friend and Fortune a guide who will lead them to a promised goal of happiness or success, wealth or authority. Chance, under this aspect of youthful illusion, is the ideal of expectation and generosity. She is the goddess of the ignorance we prize as sincerity before we learn that sincerity is a virtue which, like James's cipher in arithmetic, depends for its value on the number to which it is attached. She takes the color of her benevolence from youth's impetuosity and ardor, before those qualities have revealed their full cost in experience and disillusionment. It sometimes happens that the illusion we impose on our lives at their outset is not enthusiastic but cynical or pessimistic. The cost then proves all the greater. The hero of "Youth," *The Arrow of Gold* and *The Shadow-Line* is at times supplanted by a man like Heyst in *Victory* or Razumov in *Under Western Eyes*, whose untested misanthropy is as fatally romantic a presumption on the conditions of the responsible life or the obligations of character as an untested optimism. ("Woe to the man whose heart has not learned while young to hope, to love—and to put its trust in life!") An equal enemy lies in wait for both. That enemy—"our common enemy"—leaps from unknown coverts: sometimes from the hiding-places that fate or accident has prepared, but more often and seriously, like the beast in the jungle, from the unfathomed depths of our secret natures, our ignorance, our subconscious or unconscious selves.

When the moment comes the victim is forced to commit himself to it. It is the signal of his destiny, and there is no escape for the one who meets it unprepared. The terms of life are reversed by it. It is the stroke by which fate compels recognition—of one's self, of reality, of illusion, error, mistaken expectation, and defeat. At that moment,

if a man can measure up to it, his conscious moral existence begins,
an existence for which previous intellectual or theoretical anticipation
can never fully prepare. "We begin to live when we have conceived
life as tragedy." Chance is no longer beneficent. She is a setter of traps
and snares. Her opportunities have become the measure of risk and
peril, and her favorites are no longer adventurers or idealists but
those who can say, in another sentence of Yeats's that is an explicit
phrasing of Conrad's idea: "When I think of life as a struggle with
the Daemon who would ever set us to the hardest work among those
not impossible, I understand why there is a deep enmity between
a man and his destiny, and why a man loves nothing but his destiny."

The crisis in almost every one of Conrad's novels—many of which
form a prolonged and exhaustive analysis or sublimation of crisis—
arrives when, by a stroke of accident, or by an act of decision or error
rising from the secret necessities of temperament, a man finds himself
abruptly committed to his destiny. It is a commitment to which all
men of morally significant quality are bound. It is the test and opportunity of fundamental selfhood, and there is no escape from it. Its
necessity is variously stated in Conrad's books—most memorably
perhaps in "Typhoon":

> The sea . . . had never put itself out to startle the silent man, who
> seldom looked up, and wandered innocently over the waters with the
> only visible purpose of getting food, raiment, and house-room for three
> people ashore. Dirty weather he had known, of course. He had been
> made wet, uncomfortable, tired in the usual way, felt at the time and
> presently forgotten. So that upon the whole he had been justified in
> reporting fine weather at home. But he had never been given a glimpse
> of immeasurable strength and of immoderate wrath, the wrath that
> passes exhausted but never appeased—the wrath and fury of the pas-
> sionate sea. He knew it existed, as we know that crime and abomina-
> tions exist; he had heard of it as a peaceable citizen in a town hears
> of battles, famines, and floods, and yet knows nothing of what these
> things mean—though, indeed, he may have been mixed up in a street
> row, have gone without his dinner once, or been soaked to the skin in
> a shower. Captain MacWhirr had sailed over the surface of the oceans
> as some men go skimming over the years of existence to sink gently
> into a placid grave, ignorant of life to the last, without ever having
> been made to see all it may contain of perfidy, of violence, and of
> terror. There are on sea and land such men thus fortunate—or thus
> disdained by destiny or by the sea.

The full implications of this final sentence extend beyond Conrad's
tales and even his life; they give us his judgment on a world lapsed

into the anarchy that results from a morality of casuistry and opportunism. It was not only in political and commercial society that he saw that violence at work, with the ramifying evil he depicted in *The Secret Agent* and *Under Western Eyes*—novels whose wholly European or English settings give little occasion for an occluding exoticism, and so bring out the full force of Conrad's critical powers. He saw it in the crisis of civilization which he witnessed in Europe, and he saw it there in terms of a question whose import he felt with personal intensity and even with guilt—the question of the fate of Poland. A few of his essays suggest his long scrutiny of this problem, but explicitly he rarely, if ever, elucidated it. It remains involved in the complex of his tales, which is what makes it memorable and dynamic. To grasp the larger significance of Conrad's vision of the violence in his age requires a special attention to what the tales contain and convey.

Conrad's temperament, like that of his characteristic heroes, was rooted in an impulse, an impetuosity, that involves the poet, as much as the man of action, in a presumption on the laws of moral responsibility. He was initially, by his emotional disposition—and perhaps inevitably, by the dramatic circumstances of his Polish youth and revolutionary heritage—an idealist whose passions were early set at a pitch of heroic resolution, committed to a struggle that called on the fullest indomitability of will and spirit. The stoic sentiment of contemporary romantics—"Nothing ever happens to the brave"— could never be the principle of such a tradition. The fiery hopes of Polish nationalism and the cause of Poland's freedom had already exacted the fullest share of bravery, suffering, and ignominy from Conrad's people, and from his own family. Yet even here the illusion of Providence was not missing. Conrad's father was a nationalist of Shelleyan tendencies, translator of Vigny's *Chatterton* and Hugo's *Hernani* and *La Légende des Siècles*. In his note to *A Personal Record* Conrad protested that his father should not be called revolutionist since "no epithet could be more inapplicable to a man with such a strong sense of responsibility in the region of ideas and action and so indifferent to the promptings of personal ambition," and that he was "simply a patriot in the sense of a man who, believing in the spirituality of a national existence, could not bear to see that spirit enslaved." But Danilowsky, the Polish historian, describes this father as "an honorable but too ardent patriot," who was known to the Tzarist police as an "agitator," author of the seditious mandate that brought about his arrest in October 1861, his imprisonment in War-

saw, and his subsequent deportation to the Government Vologda for
a four-year exile which brought on the death of his wife and eventually his own death as well. Apollo Korzeniowski's verse is passionate
in its defiance of misfortune:

> Ready is your boat, and in the outspread sails
> Blows the wind, lighthearted,
> Some of us life may deceive,
> You will choose the right way.

> May cowards tremble at lofty waves,
> To you they bring good fortune!
> You know the hidden reefs,
> And are familiar with the tempest!

> Your eager boat, with eagle's wings,
> Will make a rapid passage,
> And, steered by reason, governed with strength,
> Will reach the shores of fame!

> But, resting from your journey,
> In the golden lands of fortune,
> Remember, O remember with a sigh
> Those who perished in the tempest!

This "Korzeniowski strain," as his wife's relatives called it, with
its devotion to Utopian ideals and revolutionary hazards—impulsive,
sarcastic, impatient—seems to have served as a warning to the members of the Bobrowski family, whose daughter he courted and who
considered him "an undesirable pretender." The Bobrowskis, who
were, like the Korzeniowskis, of the land-owning gentry and had a
brilliant record as soldiers and patriots, were of more conservative,
reformist leanings. They were agricultural, closely devoted as a
family, apparently more realistic and cautious in their view of the
nationalist cause than the young poet whom they knew as a "red"
and who, despite his sensitive character and human sympathies,
was famed for his recklessness and scurrilous impatience with tem-
porizers. The hazardous conditions of Conrad's youth (he was only
five when his father was arrested and deported), the unsettled fortunes of the family, and his knowledge of his father's courage, must
have fostered his early ambitions about his own career. When he
turned from the East of Europe which he always feared and disliked, since it represented the national enemy Russia as well as those

unfathomed conflicts that reflected his own severe doubt of himself, he looked toward the countries that promised a career of greater certainty. He looked toward France, with her marine service and political opportunities, and more particularly, in these earliest years of his travels, toward Spain of the Carlist cause, in whose service he was to take his first great chance, as a gun-runner and agitator. Conrad's celebrations of the hope and illusion of youth, of innocence, of courage and the bravery it supports in the untested nature of the immature man, of the sincerity which blesses this primitive kind of emotion—these are too evident in his work to be doubted as revivals, in his later memory, of the excitement with which he launched himself on life when he left Poland behind in 1874, at the age of seventeen, and boarded the west-bound Vienna express for Venice and Marseilles, "as a man might get into a dream."

Once Conrad had embarked on that adventure, however, a rival strain of his inheritance asserted itself. How early we cannot tell, for the documents on this part of his life, from 1873 until the middle eighties, are few. Apparently it did not appear during his first years in Marseilles, when he frequented the conservative *légitimiste* circle of the banker Delestang and his wife, or during his first two sea-voyages that ensued from this acquaintance—that in 1875 on the *Mont-Blanc* to Martinique and Le Havre, and that in 1876 on the *Saint-Antoine* to St. Pierre, Port-au-Prince, and the Gulf of Mexico. It apparently did not deter him during the romantic episode among the Spanish legitimists of Don Carlos's cause which involved him between October 1877, and February 1878, in the exploits of the gun-running tartane *Tremolino*, his love affair with the prototype of Rita de Lastaola, his duel with the American J. M. K. Blunt, and the other escapades (later to be recorded in *The Arrow of Gold*) that caused so much alarm among his relatives in Poland that his guardian uncle, Tadeusz Bobrowski, threatened to stop his allowance and compel him to come home. These experiences terminated in fiasco. Wounded in the duel, Conrad was barely on his legs when his alarmed uncle arrived in Marseilles from Kiev to find his nephew deserted by his Carlist friends, embittered by humiliation, and ready to throw up all adventurous political schemes in favor of a job on an English coaster, the *Mavis*, carrying coal and linseed-oil cargoes between Lowestoft and Constantinople.

When Conrad arrived in Lowestoft on June 18, 1878, he stepped for the first time on English soil, knowing only as much English as he had picked up on the voyage, practically without money, without acquaintances in England, and, as his biographer tells us, "alone in the world." This is the first of two decisive dates in Conrad's life. (The other was to come in 1895.) Poland, Marseilles, Carlism, and youth were behind him. Poverty and the rigorous routine of a merchant vessel descended on him and fixed his life for the next seventeen years.

What now rose in Conrad's personality was a force more familiar to us in his books than the ecstatic emotion of youth which he often celebrates but which he was able to recapture only in moments of lyrical memory and which, as a consequence, never rings as authentically as the darker emotions which now announced themselves and persisted in his nature to the end of his life. His benevolent uncle Tadeusz began to write him in response to the letters which Conrad was sending back to Poland. Conrad's shift from youth, Poland, and France to the unsparing exactions of sea-life was one great transition in his fortunes. He was to submit another, of even severer conditions, in 1895, when he threw up the sea and ventured on a career in literature. He did this not with convinced determination, for he tried repeatedly to get a new command even as late as 1900, when his first five books had been published. These breaks or changes have, as we now observe them, the appearance of having been undertaken with a kind of compulsion of inherent vocation, to test his strength and fortitude in the face of a long-delayed creative necessity; but conscious intention as yet played little part in his actions. Troubled, in the early eighties, by the growing melancholy and passionate introspection induced by long sea-watches, by solitary duties, and by the racking boredom which in later life he confessed to be the one sensation he remembered from his sailing days, he found welling up within him symptoms of the tragic inheritance of his race and family.

His life had begun in disturbance, danger, and a great ascendant hope. It had become vividly adventurous in France, Spain, and the West Indies. Now, abruptly, it became confined, ruthlessly vigilant, curtailed to the most tyrannous necessities, calculated to the hour and moment by the charts on the captain's table, the needle in the binnacle, the movements of the stars. His voyages to African coasts, the Americas, and the Malay and China seas brought contrasts of novelty and exotic discovery, but by the time Conrad took his journey to the Congo in 1890, reality had become unconditional. The continent of Africa and his voyage up its coiled, snakelike river figured as his descent into Hell. His journal of the trip still conveys the agony of that palpable damnation. He returned ravaged by the illness and mental disruption which undermined his health for the remaining thirty years of his life.

Between 1891 and 1895 his voyages were broken by intervals spent alone and homeless in London, with only his uncle remaining of his immediate family (and he was to die in 1894) and a distant cousin by marriage, the Polish-Belgian novelist Marguerite Poradowska, of Brussels, to serve as his confidante in Western Europe. When Conrad lay ill in London in 1891 he received a letter from his uncle Tadeusz which we may take as an account of his predicament written from the point of view of a privileged observer:

My dear boy:

I begin as I always do, but I ought to address you as "my dear pessimist"; for judging from your letters that description would fit you best. I cannot say that I am pleased by your state of mind, or that I am without apprehension about your future. . . . Thinking over the causes of your melancholy most carefully I cannot attribute it either to youth or to age. In the case of one who is thirty-four and has had as full a life as you have had, I am forced to attribute it to ill-health, to your wretched sufferings on the African adventure, to your illness which resulted from them, and to the fact that you have had lately plenty of time to give yourself up to the habit of reverie which I have observed to be part of your character. It is inherited; it has always been there, in spite of your active life.

I may be mistaken, but I think this tendency to pessimism was already in you as long ago as the days when you were at Marseilles, but it was then part of youth. I am sure that with your melancholy temperament you ought to avoid all meditations which lead to pessimistic conclusions. I advise you to lead a more active life than ever and to cultivate cheerful habits.

Our country, as Slowacki well says (although he himself was not free from the reproach), is the "pan" of the nations, which in plain prose means that we are a nation who consider ourselves great and misunderstood, the possessors of a greatness which others do not recognize and will never recognize. If individuals and nations would set duty before themselves as an aim, instead of grandiose ideals, the world would be a happier place. . . . Perhaps you will reply that these are the sentiments of one who has always had "a place in the sun." Not at all. I have endured many ups and downs; I have suffered in my private life, in my family life, and as a Pole; and it is thanks to these mortifications that I have arrived at a calm and modest estimate of life and its duties, and that I have taken as my motto "usque ad finem"; as my guide, the love of the duty which circumstances define.

It is not to be argued that Conrad's life explains his art in its fullest dimensions, any more than his "ideas" explain his novels, or that we can use his personal documents and letters as a substitute for that explanation. Indeed, his defensive nature made it unlikely that he should write these as such an explanation. The reproofs he expressed to several students of his career indicate that he would have endorsed Eliot's sentence which his own preface to The Nigger of the "Narcissus" to some degree anticipated: "The more perfect the artist, the more completely separate in him will be the man who suffers and the mind which creates." Conrad was a dramatic genius and an artist in character; his creations are always more than the sum of his conscious motives and critical intelligence. Any comparison of his personal writings with his novels shows that he found his full voice only when writing imaginatively. Only then does he resist the charge made against him by E. M. Forster when he said that "the secret casket of his genius contains a vapor rather than a jewel." At the same time it is impossible to neglect the value which the events of Conrad's life and the testimony of his intimate correspondence contribute toward the interpretation of his fiction. At the least, these provide us with a comment on the problem he dramatized in a language which almost perfectly coincides with the spirit of his plots and situations. We know, in addition, how strongly he protested against the purely impersonal order of art advocated by the naturalists; how he considered their novels a perpetuation of the worst vices of the old convention of arbitrary omniscience in fiction; how lifeless he found the critical objectivity of his friend Galsworthy; how he disagreed as vigorously as Yeats did with Stendhal's conception of art as "un miroir qui se promène sur la grande route." Five of his narratives were never denied as autobiographies. He said that all his characters were "at one time or the other known by me." And although it is inevitable that we can never prove the personal basis of his greater novels, we cannot read them without sensing the existence of such a basis, or observing that Conrad's repeated hints of such relevance were expanded and explored from one end of his production to the other.

The letters he wrote Mme. Poradowska between 1890 and 1900 reveal that almost every fundamental problem of his later fiction was sketched or suggested in that correspondence and applied there with remorseless intimacy not to fictitious characters but to his own plight and state of mind. They also reveal that during those critical years of his life, when he was making a harassed transition from maritime service to the profession of novelist, he was already groping for the means and courage to translate these experiences into fictional form, to objectify them dramatically, and thus to come into an intelligent realization of their meaning: to save himself, as he once expressed it, "from the madness which, after a certain point in life is reached, awaits those who refuse to master their sensations and bring into coherent form the mysteries of their lives."

Conrad's sense of the crisis of moral isolation and responsibility in which the individual meets his first full test of character is repeatedly emphasized in his tales, to a degree which has put a special stamp on his heroes. These are men marked by a number of conditions which have become much more familiar during the past half-century than they were when Conrad began to write. Even then, however, they had been established by serious novelists and dramatists. James and Ibsen, to name only two, had dramatized the plight of the man or woman on whom life closes down. By divesting him or her of the familiar supports and illusory protection of friendship, social privilege, or love; by throwing the individual violently out of an accepted relationship with family or society, this crisis suddenly makes him aware of a hostile or unknown world which must be learned anew, conquered or mastered, before survival is possible. Obviously this order of drama has a classic ancestry. It is the oldest mode of tragedy. But the social and psychological emphasis of modern times has given it a substance, a basis of practical moral conditions, not always apparent even in Shakespeare. It is this drama of alienation and spiritual recognition which appears in the characteristic novels of Mann, Gide, and Kafka, in Robinson's poems, in Joyce and Hemingway. It is carried to lengths of symbolic extension in *Death in Venice, The Trial, Nightwood,* and ultimately in *Finnegans Wake.* One of its latest appearances is in the novels of the French existentialists, who have given tragedy a new dimension in the irrationality or absurdity of the universe. But it is doubtful if any of these writers has achieved a more successful *dramatic* version of the problem than Conrad did—a more complete coincidence of the processes of psychic recognition and recovery with the dramatic necessities of the plot; and this for a reason which distinguishes Conrad's contribution to modern fictional method: his imposition of the processes of psychological experience, notably the experience of recognition, on the structure of the plot. Even in James, as later in Thomas Mann and André Gide, whose moral drama also took this direction, the ratiocinative element and structural manipulation of the action did not permit an equal immersion in the "destructive element" of psychic reality, an equal coincidence of moral sensibility with form.

The conditions that mark the plight of a Conrad character who is caught in the grip of circumstances that enforce self-discovery and its cognate, the discovery of reality or truth, are remarkably consistent in his books. The condition of moral solitude is the first of them —the isolation of Razumov in *Under Western Eyes*, of Heyst in *Victory*, of Flora de Barral in *Chance*, of Jim himself in *Lord Jim*, and of a large number of other outcasts, exiles, or estranged souls—Willems, Lingard, Mrs. Travers, Mrs. Verloc, Peyrol; even men whom age or accident has suddenly bereft of the solid ground of security or confidence—Captain Whalley, Captain MacWhirr, the young captain on his first command in *The Shadow-Line*, or Kurtz of "Heart of Darkness" in his last abandonment of soul. The isolation varies in its nature. Willems is alone because he is a banished wastrel who has made life a law to himself; Mr. George is alone because he is young and irresponsible; Lingard and Captain Whalley have accepted stoically their estrangement from the ties of normal life; Jim and Flora feel themselves excommunicated from society by disgrace and by the false confidence or idealism that has betrayed them; Razumov is isolated by an impenetrable mystery of birth and social alienation; Heyst by the disgust, induced by a fatal vein of skepticism in his nature and so tending toward a nihilism of all values, which follows a misplaced trust in his fellow men. In all these more serious cases, isolation tends to become so absolute that it can be bridged again only by some irresistible compulsion that rises out of the psychic and ethical necessities of character. Life demands justification by love or honor, as with Flora and Razumov; it exacts justice from the disillusioned, as with Mrs. Verloc; it demands, in the case of Heyst, the last and absolute testimony of honor which only suicide can give. Conrad leaves no doubt of the extreme to which he pushed this condition. Of Heyst we hear that "Not a single soul belonging to him lived anywhere on earth . . . he was alone on the bank of the stream. In his pride he determined not to enter it." And of Razumov: "He was as lonely in the world as a man swimming in the deep sea. . . . He had nothing. He had not even a moral refuge—the refuge of confidence."

But if isolation is the first condition of these lives, it is never an isolation that brings independence or liberty. Freed by choice from normal human ties and obligations, Conrad's men find themselves in the inescapable presence of conscience. "I am being crushed—and

I can't even run away," cries Razumov. The solitary may take to
debauchery and self-law like Willems: even that does not permit
him to escape. He may rise to power and fame like Kurtz: that permits escape least of all. He may believe he has formed a world of
his own like Heyst:

> Heyst was not conscious of either friends or enemies. It was the
> very essence of his life to be a solitary achievement, accomplished not
> by hermit-like withdrawal with its silence and immobility, but by a
> system of restless wandering, by the detachment of an impermanent
> dweller amongst changing scenes. In this scheme he had perceived
> the means of passing through life without suffering and almost with-
> out a care in the world—invulnerable because elusive.

But the world allows no such independence. "No decent feeling was
ever scorned by Heyst," and that fact proves his undoing and finally
his moral salvation. These men are all brought to discover what the
oldest religious systems of the world have advocated: that the more
liberty we have, the less we can use. The man who is alone in the
world can never escape, for he is always with himself. Unless he is
morally abandoned beyond the point of significance through prof-
ligacy or irresponsibility, he lives in the company of a ruthless inquisitor, a watcher who never sleeps, a perpetually vigilant judge:
with his instinct of identity, the moral imperative of his existence.
A novelist who proposes to explore the full experience of the justice
imposed on our faculties by conscience will be impelled, like Conrad,
to penetrate a world that lies below the appearances of conduct. The
explorations made by Conrad in that dimension have advanced, in
our time, to the farthest reaches of the unconscious self. If Conrad
did not reach those depths he pointed the way to them. *Lord Jim,
Chance*, and *Under Western Eyes* join the experiments of Melville,
Dostoevsky, James, and Joyce in charting the experience of the unconscious, and the means by which it is to be explored.

It is here that Conrad's work enters a dimension which is ostensibly
psychological and which, for purposes of drama and characterization,
must appear validly so. But it goes farther. It encounters the problem
of appearance and reality, of bringing into single focus the processes
of subjective intuition and the conditions of social and moral necessity
—the values of egotism and those of ethical fact. It may treat these
in terms of the relativity of appearances and sentiments as Proust
defined it, but it will also insist on relating the psychic and moral
ambiguity of human nature to the ambivalence of reality as art em-

bodies and struggles with it, and finally to the metaphysical condition of value itself. When Conrad enters that dimension fully he leaves his sentimental limitations and prejudices behind him and takes his place as one of the authentic creative imaginations of our time—one who certainly outdistances the other English novelists of his generation.

The order of art to which Conrad addressed himself, less apparently by conscious intention than by instinct and personal necessity, is one that has become paramount in the literature of the Twentieth Century. The ambiguity of truth, the conflict of appearance and reality, the rival claims of the secret and the social self—these are now integral to modern fiction in its major manifestations, whether in Proust or Mann, James or Kafka, Gide or Sartre. They arrive at something like the condition of paradigm in Pirandello's *Six Characters in Search of an Author*.

The six characters emerge from their half-created, unrealized lives and make their claim for the reality of their existence. The play they see being devised on the stage shocks and appals them by its failure to do justice to the truth of their experience. They plead that their agony be given the truth it had in life itself; that their passions and motives be understood; that reality be brought to terms not only with art but with moral insight and compassion. The actors and director who grapple with their plea can make nothing but a travesty of the tragedy they attempt to enact. Their struggle to render it justice produces, in Pirandello's hands, a metaphysical dilemma. It is not only art that is at odds with life; it is human comprehension itself. But the question insists: can life ever do justice to its own reality? Are suffering, agony, tragedy comprehensible in their own condition? Is it possible for them to achieve comprehension until consciousness, moral sympathy, or art intervene to interpret and define them? Can man, or life, be said to exist in terms of significance until these modes of definition and justice succeed in embodying them? The dilemma, driven to the extreme lengths of suspense and contradiction, ends finally in enigma and fiasco. The question remains unresolved. It collapses under the test of resolution. Conrad's problem in *Lord Jim* was this same problem. There too, in spite of driving Jim's fate to the logic of catastrophe, the question of the reality of his moral identity ends in enigma. But the problem of resolving it had become an obsession with Conrad. It taxed him continuously to the end of his life. At times he resorted to desperate measures of heroism, suicide, or moral compromise to resolve it; sometimes he fell back on the arbitrary formulas of ethical duplicity or stoicism. But it remained to the end the essential theme and animus of his drama.

It is instructive to turn again to Conrad's letters for confirmation of his sense of the crisis which induces the test of selfhood to which he subjects his heroes. When Conrad passed, around 1895, out of the perfectly controlled and adjusted mechanism of sea-life, with its accurate regimen of human relations and balances, he entered into a freedom which he soon discovered to be no liberation but a prison. For him, in those middle years of the nineties, the self was doubly trapped. He found himself alone not only with his poverty and rigorous self-discipline but with his creative conscience, now struggling to express itself.

His dramatizations of the trapped sensibility were preceded by that harrowing period in London in which he decided to face a kind of labor that meant daily and yearly solitude, with no give-and-take of human approval or disagreement, with no one to judge his principles or results but himself, and with a brutal aesthetic judgment—soon divested of the amateur excitement with which he wrote *Almayer's Folly*—ruling his waking and sleeping life. It is small wonder that Conrad, who was to make the trapped man the object of his special study, should have always remembered this period of his life, for it marked the beginning of an anxiety and a discipline that were not to end until his death. We find him recurring to the idea of the convict with an insistence, and with none of the defiance, that marks Rimbaud's salutations to that form of fate in the *Saison en Enfer*. Tormented all his life by the "stérilité des écrivains nerveux" which he shared with Baudelaire, Conrad began the grinding labor of his books. Years later, in 1909, he wrote to Norman Douglas that "there's neither inspiration nor hope in my work. It's mere hard labor for life —with this difference, that the life convict is at any rate out of harm's way—and may consider the account with his conscience closed: and this is not the case with me. I envy the serene fate and the comparative honesty of the gentlemen in gray who live in Dartmoor. I do really. I am not half as decent or half as useful." But earlier, in the nineties, he was already acknowledging that fate to his "cousin" in Brussels, Mme. Poradowska:

> I am not so happy to be working as you seem to think. There is nothing very exhilarating in doing disagreeable work. It is too much like penal servitude, with the difference that while rolling the stone of Sisyphus you lack the consolation of thinking of what pleasure you had in committing the crime. It is here that convicts have the advantage over your humble servant.

Again:

> I astonish and perhaps scandalize you by my joking about criminals, while you think me capable of accepting or even admitting the doctrine (or theory) of expiation through suffering . . . there is no expiation. Each act of life is final and inevitably produces its consequences in spite of all the weeping and gnashing of teeth and the sorrow of weak souls who suffer as fright grips them when confronted with the results of their own actions. As for myself, I shall never need to be consoled for any act of my life, and this because I am strong enough to judge my conscience rather than be its slave, as the orthodox would like to persuade us to be.

And again:

> Remember, though, that one is never entirely alone. Why are you afraid? And of what? Is it of solitude or of death? O strange fear! The only two things that make life bearable! But cast fear aside. Solitude never comes—and death must often be waited for during long years of bitterness and anger. Do you prefer that?
>
> But you are afraid of yourself; of the inseparable being forever at your side—master and slave, victim and executioner—who suffers and causes suffering. That's how it is! One must drag the ball and chain of one's selfhood to the end. It is the price one pays for the devilish and divine privilege of thought; so that in this life it is only the elect who are convicts—a glorious band which comprehends and groans but which treads the earth amidst a multitude of phantoms with maniacal gestures, with idiotic grimaces. Which would you be: idiot or convict?

The alter ego of the conscience was an inevitable corollary—as Conrad here indicates—of his conception of inescapable selfhood. The *Doppelgänger* becomes part of the drama of character and self-determination. When Jim delivers his long monologues to Marlow; when Flora bares her soul to Marlow, Mrs. Fyne, or Captain Anthony; when Razumov writes his passionate entries in his diary and disburdens his soul to the old language-teacher and finally to Nathalie Haldin herself; when Decoud or Gould ruminate their secret histories, these people are really carrying out the drama of their divided natures, objectifying under the compulsion which psychoanalysts have seized upon as therapeutic necessity their souls' dilemmas and thus trying to save themselves from madness. But the divided man—the face and its mask, the soul and its shadow—figures even more concretely than this in Conrad's dramatic method (though rumination and monologue were usually his own means of giving genuine substance to his realism). The rival character—sometimes a villain, sometimes a friend or lover, sometimes a fellow-fugitive like the "secret sharer" in the story of that name—serves the hero as a transferred embodiment of his other self.

Thus love, or the sense of honor, or the obligation of duty, or even the social instinct itself, enters the novels as a means by which the individual is lifted out of his isolation and morbid surrender. The inward-driving, center-fathoming obsession of the tale becomes reversed and takes a centrifugal direction toward external standards of value. It is finally the world which saves us—the world of human necessities and duty. It may be the world of a ship and its crew, as in *The Shadow-Line;* it may be the world of an island and a single fellow-soul, as in *Victory;* it may be that wider world of social and political relationships which Conrad seldom explored fully but which he did build in solid form in *Nostromo* and *Chance.* In one of the most perfect of Conrad's tales, "The Secret Sharer," the allegory of the alter ego is achieved within the narrowest possible limits. In one of the finest of his novels, *Under Western Eyes,* the conception is made to embody the whole complex of Russian history. "The Secret Sharer," as Miss M. C. Bradbrook has pointed out, is the microcosm of the basic concept in Conrad's fiction. Leggatt, the swimmer, has committed murder and so, by a moment's blind action, has ruined his life. He escapes, but finds refuge, naked, under cover of night on a strange ship—"a fugitive and a vagabond on the earth, with no brand of the curse on his sane forehead to stay a slaying hand." The captain hides him in his cabin, learns his guilt, and thus becomes allied to that guilt, the refugee's secret becoming an embodiment of the captain's own secret life. The hidden self of the captain is "exactly the same" as that of the fugitive, who is of necessity concealed from the world, is dressed in a sleeping suit, the garb of the unconscious life, and appears out of and again disappears into the sea, naked again, under cover of darkness. But before he disappears at last, "a free man, a proud swimmer striking out for a new destiny," the captain has come to know the secret self he lives with. His life is changed. He too must address himself to a "new destiny." A new vision of humanity has broken in upon the impersonal regimen of his days—upon the "ideal conception of one's own personality," abstract, illusory, and therefore insecure and perilous, which "every man sets up for himself secretly." The "sharing" has recreated him, stirred him to a sense of his latent moral insecurity, and so enforced in him the necessity of human community—that "unavoidable solidarity" which Conrad persistently invokes as the inescapable commitment of men: "the solidarity in mysterious origin, in toil, in joy, in uncertain fate, which binds men to each other and all mankind to the visible earth."

For Conrad, however existential he may have been by inclination, the commitment could never remain arbitrary. It is a necessity which defines man as human, his moral consciousness as imperative, and his persistence in that consciousness as the fundamental law of life. From this germinal presentation of the case Conrad's drama of the self widens until, in his most ambitious books, it comes to include the larger workings of that law in society and politics, even in the destiny of nations and of races. The growth in his thought from an idealistic conception of life to a critical one, from his temperamental romanticism to his later realism of values, is the drama of his genius in its difficult emergence, its strenuous self-discipline, and its eventual successes. That growth appears most typically in the three novels that show his dramatic method most explicitly—*Lord Jim, Under Western Eyes,* and *Chance,* but it is extended to more sheerly creative feats of dramatization in three other books—*Nostromo,* his most complex historical and political drama, a comprehensive matrix of his moral and ethical sensibility, resonant of a profoundly riddled debate of moralities and creeds of conduct; *The Secret Agent,* his highest achievement in tragic irony; and *Victory,* his most concentrated symbolic narrative.

The romantic element in his work, like the romantic impulse in his nature, was never effaced. It persisted as the basis of his popularity and of the excesses of style and treatment which appear in his evocative tendency in language, in his treatment of the sea, of woman, and of fortune as inscrutable entities, in his exotic and rhetorical effects, in his sentimental emphasis on the heroic and the miraculous in human fate and character, in the fatigued naïveté of fatalism that reasserts itself in his last three novels. But if it was not effaced, it was recognized. Conrad himself admitted an inherent romanticism as a component of his imagination and of his ordeal in moral and creative responsibility. He referred to it late in life in a passage of apology:

> The romantic feeling of reality was in me an inborn faculty. This in itself may be a curse, but when disciplined by a sense of personal responsibility and a recognition of the hard facts of existence shared with the rest of mankind becomes but a point of view from which the very shadows of life appear endowed with an internal glow. And

such romanticism is not a sin. It is none the worse for the knowledge of truth. It only tries to make the best of it, hard as it may be; and in this hardness discovers a certain aspect of beauty.

His success came when responsibility and discipline opposed the self-indulgence which a romantic impulse had encouraged in his early emotions and sensibility. When these correctives assert themselves in his pages, they produce the rigor of style and feeling which stiffens and gives structure to the natural extravagance of his emotions, his impulsiveness in sentiment, the untested enthusiasm of his responses to scene, character, and experience. Conrad's development as an artist —with due allowance made for the weakening powers of his later novels—reproduces the ordeal of self-mastery and moral exoneration which he repeatedly dramatized in the lives of his characteristic heroes. "All a man can betray is his conscience," his Razumov says in *Under Western Eyes*. The measure of Conrad's character and his artistry may be taken from the fact that neither his sense of honor nor his sense of realism permitted him to betray the conscience which it took him half his life to discover in himself, and the other half to test and dramatize in his books.

1945 [1956]

6

F. R. LEAVIS

———◆———

Minor Works and *Nostromo*

AN ANNOUNCEMENT once appeared in a quarterly, against the name
of the present writer, of an article to be entitled *Conrad, the Soul and
the Universe*. The exasperation registered in this formula explains,
perhaps, why the article was never written. For that Conrad has done
classical work is as certain as that his classical status will not rest
evenly upon his whole *œuvre*, and the necessary discriminations and
delimitations, not being altogether simple, clearly oughtn't to be
attempted in any but a securely critical frame of mind. He has, of
course, long been generally held to be among the English masters; the
exasperation records a sense that the greatness attributed to him
tended to be identified with an imputed profundity, and that this "profundity" was not what it was taken to be, but quite other, and the
reverse of a strength. The final abandonment of the article may have
been partly determined by Mr. E. M. Forster's note on Conrad that
appeared in *Abinger Harvest*:

> What is so elusive about him is that he is always promising to make
> some general philosophic statement about the universe, and then re-
> fraining with a gruff disclaimer. . . . Is there not also a central
> obscurity, something noble, heroic, beautiful, inspiring half-a-dozen
> great books, but obscure, obscure? . . . These essays do suggest that he
> is misty in the middle as well as at the edges, that the secret casket

From *The Great Tradition* by F. R. Leavis, 1948. Reprinted by permission
of George W. Stewart Publisher, Inc., and Chatto and Windus Ltd.

of his genius contains a vapour rather than a jewel; and that we needn't try to write him down philosophically, because there is, in this direction, nothing to write. No creed, in fact. Only opinions, and the right to throw them overboard when facts make them look absurd. Opinions held under the semblance of eternity, girt with the sea, crowned with stars, and therefore easily mistaken for a creed.

—This might well have gratified the exasperation, and made its expression seem unnecessary.

Mr. Forster, however, doesn't attempt discriminations or precisions (his note is a reprinted review of *Notes on Life and Letters*). And he doesn't suggest those manifestations of the characteristic he describes in which we have something simply and obviously deplorable—something that presents itself, not as elusively noble *timbre*, prompting us to analysis and consequent limiting judgments, but as, bluntly, a disconcerting weakness or vice. Consider, for instance, how *Heart of Darkness* is marred.

Heart of Darkness is, by common consent, one of Conrad's best things—an appropriate source for the epigraph of *The Hollow Men:* "Mistah Kurtz, he dead." That utterance, recalling the particularity of its immediate context, represents the strength of *Heart of Darkness:*

> He cried in a whisper at some image, at some vision—he cried out twice, a cry that was no more than a breath—
> "The horror! The horror!"
> I blew the candle out and left the cabin. The pilgrims were dining in the mess-room, and I took my place opposite the manager, who lifted his eyes to give me a questioning glance, which I successfully ignored. He leaned back, serene, with that peculiar smile of his sealing the unexpressed depth of his meanness. A continuous shower of small flies streamed upon the lamp, upon the cloth, upon our hands and faces. Suddenly the manager's boy put his insolent face in the doorway, and said in a tone of scathing contempt—
> "Mistah Kurtz—he dead."
> All the pilgrims rushed out to see. I remained, and went on with my dinner. I believe I was considered brutally callous. However, I did not eat much. There was a lamp in there—light, don't you know— and outside it was so beastly, beastly dark.

This passage, it will be recognized, owes its force to a whole wide context of particularities that gives the elements here—the pilgrims, the manager, the manager's boy, the situation—their specific values.

Borrowing a phrase from Mr. Eliot's critical writings, one might say that *Heart of Darkness* achieves its overpowering evocation of atmosphere by means of "objective correlatives." The details and circumstances of the voyage to and up the Congo are present to us as if we were making the journey ourselves and (chosen for record as they are by a controlling imaginative purpose) they carry specificities of emotion and suggestion with them. There is the gunboat dropping shells into Africa:

> There wasn't even a shed there, and she was shelling the bush. It appears the French had one of their wars going on thereabouts. Her ensign dropped limp like a rag; the muzzles of the long six-inch guns stuck out all over the low hull; the greasy, slimy swell swung her up lazily and let her down, swaying her thin masts. In the empty immensity of earth, sky and water, there she was, incomprehensible, firing into a continent. Pop, would go one of the six-inch guns; a small flame would dart and vanish, a tiny projectile would give a feeble screech— and nothing happened. Nothing could happen. There was a touch of insanity in the proceeding, a sense of lugubrious drollery in the sight; and it was not dissipated by somebody on board assuring me earnestly there was a camp of natives—he called them enemies!—hidden out of sight somewhere.
>
> We gave her her letters (I heard the men in that lonely ship were dying of fever at the rate of three a day) and went on. We called at some more places with farcical names, where the merry dance of death and trade goes on in a still and earthy atmosphere as of an overheated catacomb. . . .

There is the arrival at the Company's station:

> I came upon a boiler wallowing in the grass, then found a path leading up the hill. It turned aside for the boulders, and also for an undersized railway-truck lying there on its back with its wheels in the air. One was off. The thing looked as dead as the carcass of some animal. I came upon more pieces of decaying machinery, a stack of rusty nails. To the left a clump of trees made a shady spot, where dark things seemed to stir feebly. I blinked, the path was steep. A horn tooted to the right, and I saw black people run. A heavy, dull detonation shook the ground, a puff of smoke came out of the cliff, and that was all. No change appeared on the face of the rock. They were building a railway. The cliff was not in the way of anything; but this objectless blasting was all the work going on.
>
> A slight clanking behind me made me turn my head. Six black men advanced in a file, toiling up the path. They walked erect and slow,

balancing small baskets full of earth on their heads, and the clink kept
time with their footsteps. Black rags were wound round their loins,
and the short ends behind waggled to and fro like tails. I could see
every rib, the joints of their limbs were like knots in a rope; each had
an iron collar on his neck, and all were connected together with a chain
whose bights swung between them, rhythmically clinking. Another
report from the cliff made me think suddenly of that ship of war I had
seen firing into a continent. It was the same kind of ominous voice;
but these men could by no stretch of imagination be called enemies.
They were called criminals. . . .

There is the grove of death:

At last I got under the trees. My purpose was to stroll into the shade
for a moment; but no sooner within it than it seemed to me that I had
stepped into the gloomy circle of some Inferno. The rapids were near,
and an uninterrupted, uniform, headlong, rushing noise filled the mourn-
ful stillness of the grove, where not a breath stirred, not a leaf moved,
with a mysterious sound—as though the tearing pace of the launched
earth had suddenly become audible.

Black shapes crouched, lay, sat beneath the trees, leaning against
the trunks, clinging to the earth, half coming out, half effaced within
the dim light, in all the attitudes of pain, abandonment, and despair.
Another mine of the cliff went off, followed by a slight shudder of the
soil under my feet. The work was going on. The work! And this was the
place where some of the helpers had withdrawn to die.

They were dying slowly—it was very clear. They were not enemies,
they were not criminals, they were nothing earthly now,—nothing but
black shadows of disease and starvation, lying confusedly in the green-
ish gloom. . . . These moribund shapes were free as air and nearly as
thin. I began to distinguish the gleam of the eyes under the trees. There,
glancing down, I saw a face near my hand. The black bones reclined
at full length with one shoulder against the tree, and slowly the eyelids rose and the sunken eyes looked up at me, enormous and vacant,
a kind of blind, white flicker in the depths of the orbs, which died out
slowly.

By means of this art of vivid essential record, in terms of things
seen and incidents experienced by a main agent in the narrative, and
particular contacts and exchanges with other human agents, the
overwhelming sinister and fantastic "atmosphere" is engendered. Ordinary greed, stupidity and moral squalor are made to look like behaviour in a lunatic asylum against the vast and oppressive mystery of
the surroundings, rendered potently in terms of sensation. This mean

lunacy, which we are made to feel as at the same time normal and insane, is brought out by contrast with the fantastically secure innocence of the young harlequin-costumed Russian ("son of an archpriest . . . Government of Tambov"), the introduction to whom is by the way of that copy of Tower's (or Towson's) *Inquiry into Some Points of Seamanship*, symbol of tradition, sanity and the moral idea, found lying, an incongruous mystery, in the dark heart of Africa.

Of course, as the above quotations illustrate, the author's comment cannot be said to be wholly implicit. Nevertheless, it is not separable from the thing rendered, but seems to emerge from the vibration of this as part of the tone. At least, this is Conrad's art at its best. There are, however, places in *Heart of Darkness* where we become aware of comment as an interposition, and worse, as an intrusion, at times an exasperating one. Hadn't he, we find ourselves asking, overworked "inscrutable," "inconceivable," "unspeakable" and that kind of word already?—yet still they recur. Is anything added to the oppressive mysteriousness of the Congo by such sentences as:

> "It was the stillness of an implacable force brooding over an inscrutable intention"?

The same vocabulary, the same adjectival insistence upon inexpressible and incomprehensible mystery, is applied to the evocation of human profundities and spiritual horrors; to magnifying a thrilled sense of the unspeakable potentialities of the human soul. The actual effect is not to magnify but rather to muffle. The essential vibration emanates from the interaction of the particular incidents, actions and perceptions that are evoked with such charged concreteness. The legitimate kind of comment, that which seems the inevitable immediate resonance of the recorded event, is represented here:

> And then I made a brusque movement, and one of the remaining posts of that vanished fence leaped into the field of my glass. You remember I told you I had been struck at the distance by certain attempts at ornamentation, rather remarkable in the ruinous aspect of the place. Now I had suddenly a nearer view, and its first result was to make me throw my head back as if before a blow. Then I went carefully from post to post with my glass, and I saw my mistake. Those round knobs were not ornamental but symbolic; they were expressive and puzzling, striking and disturbing—food for thought and also for the vultures if there had been any looking down from the sky; but at all events for such ants as were industrious enough to ascend the pole. They would have been even more impressive, those heads on the stakes,

if their faces had not been turned to the house. Only one, the first I had made out, was facing my way. I was not so shocked as you may think. The start back I had given was really nothing but a movement of surprise. I had expected to see a knob of wood there, you know. I returned deliberately to the first I had seen—and there it was, black, dried, sunken, with closed eyelids,—a head that seemed to sleep at the top of that pole, and, with the shrunken dry lips showing a narrow white line of the teeth, was smiling too, smiling continuously at some endless and jocose dream of that eternal slumber.

I am not disclosing any trade secrets. In fact, the manager said afterwards that Mr. Kurtz's methods had ruined the district. I have no opinion on that point, but I want you clearly to understand that there was nothing exactly profitable in those heads being there. They only showed that Mr. Kurtz lacked restraint in the gratification of his various lusts, that there was something wanting in him—some small matter which, when the pressing need arose, could not be found under his magnificent eloquence. Whether he knew of this deficiency himself I can't say. I think the knowledge came to him at last—only at the very last, but the wilderness had found him out early, and had taken on him a terrible vengeance for the fantastic invasion. I think it had whispered to him things about himself which he did not know, things of which he had no conception till he took counsel with this great solitude—and the whisper had proved irresistibly fascinating. It echoed loudly within him because he was hollow at the core. . . . I put down the glass, and the head that had appeared near enough to be spoken to seemed at once to have leaped away from me into inaccessible distance.

—That the "admirer of Mr. Kurtz," the companion of the narrator here, should be the fantastically sane and innocent young Russian is part of the force of the passage.

By such means as it illustrates we are given a charged sense of the monstrous hothouse efflorescences fostered in Kurtz by solitude and the wilderness. It is a matter of such things as the heads on posts— a direct significant glimpse, the innocent Russian's explanations, the incidents of the progress up the river and the moral and physical incongruities registered; in short, of the charge generated in a variety of highly specific evocations. The stalking of the moribund Kurtz, a skeleton crawling through the long grass on all fours as he makes his bolt towards the fires and the tom-toms, is a triumphant climax in the suggestion of strange and horrible perversions. But Conrad isn't satisfied with these means; he feels that there is, or ought to be, some horror, some significance he has yet to bring out. So we have an adjectival and worse than supererogatory insistence on "unspeakable rites," "unspeakable secrets," "monstrous passions," "inconceivable mystery," and so on. If it were only, as it largely is in *Heart of Darkness*, a matter of an occasional phrase it would still be regrettable as tending to cheapen the tone. But the actual cheapening is little short of disastrous. Here, for instance, we have Marlow at the crisis of the episode just referred to:

I tried to break the spell—the heavy, mute spell of the wilderness—that seemed to draw him to its pitiless breast by the awakening of forgotten and brutal instincts, by the memory of gratified and monstrous passions. This alone, I was convinced, had driven him out to the edge of the forest, towards the gleam of the fires, the throb of drums, the drone of weird incantations; this alone had beguiled his unlawful soul beyond the bounds of permitted aspirations. And, don't you see, the terror of the position was not in being knocked on the head—though I had a very lively sense of that danger too—but in this, that I had to deal with a being to whom I could not appeal in the name of anything high or low . . . I've been telling you what we said—repeating the phrases we pronounced—but what's the good? They were common everyday words—the familiar vague sounds exchanged on every waking day of life. But what of that? They had behind them, to my mind, the terrific suggestiveness of words heard in dreams, of phrases spoken in nightmares. Soul! If anybody had ever struggled with a soul, I am the man. And I wasn't arguing with a lunatic either. . . . But his soul was mad. Being alone in the wilderness, it had looked within itself, and, by heavens! I tell you, it had gone mad. I had—for my sins, I suppose—to go through the ordeal of looking into it myself. No eloquence could have been so withering to one's belief in mankind as his final burst of sincerity. He struggled with himself too, I saw it—I heard it. I saw the inconceivable mystery of a soul that knew no restraint, no faith, and no fear, yet struggling blindly with itself.

—Conrad must here stand convicted of borrowing the arts of the magazine-writer (who has borrowed his, shall we say, from Kipling and Poe) in order to impose on his readers and on himself, for thrilled response, a "significance" that is merely an emotional insistence on the presence of what he can't produce. The insistence betrays the absence, the willed "intensity" the nullity. He is intent on making a virtue out of not knowing what he means. The vague and unrealizable, he asserts with a strained impressiveness, is the profoundly and tremendously significant:

I've been telling you what we said—repeating the phrases we pronounced—but what's the good? They were common everyday words—

the familiar vague sounds exchanged on every waking day of life. But what of that? They had behind them, to my mind, the terrific suggestiveness of words heard in dreams, of phrases spoken in nightmares.

—What's the good, indeed? If he cannot through the concrete presentment of incident, setting and image invest the words with the terrific something that, by themselves, they fail to convey, then no amount of adjectival and ejaculatory emphasis will do it.

I saw the inconceivable mystery of a soul, etc.

—That, of course, is an ambiguous statement. I see that there is a mystery, and it remains a mystery for me; I can't conceive what it is; and if I offer this inability to your wonder as a thrilling affair of "seeing an inconceivable mystery," I exemplify a common trait of human nature. Actually, Conrad had no need to try and inject "significance" into his narrative in this way. What he shows himself to have successfully and significantly seen is enough to make *Heart of Darkness* a disturbing presentment of the kind he aimed at. By the attempt at injection he weakens, in his account of Kurtz's death, the effect of that culminating cry:

He cried in a whisper at some image, at some vision—he cried out twice, a cry that was no more than a breath—"The horror! The horror!"

—The "horror" there has very much less force than it might have had if Conrad had strained less.

This final account of Kurtz is associated with a sardonic tone, an insistent irony that leads us on to another bad patch, the closing interview in Brussels with Kurtz's "Intended":

The room seemed to have grown darker, as if all the sad light of the cloudy evening had taken refuge on her forehead. This fair hair, this pale visage, this pure brow, seemed surrounded by an ashy halo from which the dark eyes looked out at me. Their glance was guileless, profound, confident, and trustful. She carried her sorrowful head as though she were proud of that sorrow, as though she would say, I—I alone know how to mourn for him as he deserves.

It is not part of Conrad's irony that there should be anything ironical in this presentment of the woman. The irony lies in the association of her innocent nobility, her purity of idealizing faith, with the unspeakable corruption of Kurtz; and it is developed (if that is the word)

with a thrilled insistence that recalls the melodramatic intensities of
Edgar Allan Poe:

> I felt like a chill grip on my chest. "Don't," I said in a muffled voice.
> "Forgive me. I—I—have mourned so long in silence—in silence. . . .
> You were with him—to the last? I think of his loneliness. Nobody near
> to understand him as I would have understood. Perhaps no one to
> hear. . . ."
> "To the very end," I said shakily. "I heard his very last words. . . ."
> I stopped in a fright.
> "Repeat them," she murmured in a heart-broken tone. "I want—I
> want—something—something—to live with."
> I was on the point of crying at her "Don't you hear them?" The
> dark was repeating them in a persistent whisper all around us, in a
> whisper that seemed to swell menacingly, like the first whisper of a
> rising wind. "The horror! the horror!"
> "His last words—to live with," she insisted. "Don't you understand
> I loved him—I loved him—I loved him!"
> I pulled myself together and spoke slowly.
> "The last word he pronounced was—your name."
> I heard a light sigh and then my heart stood still, stopped dead
> short by an exulting and terrible cry, by the cry of inconceivable tri-
> umph and of an unspeakable pain.
> "I knew it—I was sure!" . . . She knew. She was sure.

Conrad's "inscrutable," it is clear, associates with Woman as it does
with the wilderness, and the thrilling mystery of the Intended's innocence is of the same order as the thrilling mystery of Kurtz's corruption: the profundities are complementary. It would appear that the
cosmopolitan Pole, student of the French masters, who became a British
master-mariner, was in some respects a simple soul. If anyone should
be moved to question the propriety of this way of putting it, perhaps
the following will be found something of a justification:

> Woman and the sea revealed themselves to me together, as it were:
> two mistresses of life's values. The illimitable greatness of the one, the
> unfathomable seduction of the other, working their immemorial spells
> from generation to generation fell upon my heart at last: a common
> fortune, an unforgettable memory of the sea's formless might and of the
> sovereign charm in that woman's form wherein there seemed to beat
> the pulse of divinity rather than blood.

This comes from a bad novel, one of Conrad's worst things, *The
Arrow of Gold*. It is a sophisticated piece of work, with a sophistica-

tion that elaborates and aggravates the deplorable kind of naïvety illustrated in the quotation. Not that the author's talent doesn't appear, but the central theme—and the pervasive atmosphere—is the "unfathomable seduction" of the "enigmatic" Rita; a glamorous mystery, the evocation of which (though more prolonged and elaborated) is of the same order as the evocation of sinister significance, the "inconceivable" mystery of Kurtz, at the close of *Heart of Darkness*. If any reader of that tale had felt that the irony permitted a doubt regarding Conrad's attitude towards the Intended, the presentment of Rita should settle it.

"Woman" figures in *The Rescue*, the book that in publication preceded *The Arrow of Gold* (both came out just after the 1914 war, though *The Rescue* belongs essentially to Conrad's early period). The glamour here is a simpler affair—less sophisticated and more innocent. But if *The Rescue* lacks the positive badness of *The Arrow of Gold*, it is, on a grand scale, boring in its innocence. The seduction of Woman as represented by Mrs. Travers is less insistently and melodramatically "unfathomable" than in the later book, but cannot sustain the interest Conrad demands for it; so to say that it is, in the formal design, adequate to balancing Heroic Action as represented by Lingard—King Tom, idealized seaman-adventurer—is not to say anything very favourable about the whole. *The Rescue*, in short, is an Academy piece— "sombre, colourful, undeniably a classic" the reviewers may have said, and its Grand Style staging of the conflict between Love and Honour (a kingdom at stake) against a sumptuously rendered *décor* of tropical sea, sunset, and jungle is, in its slow and conscientious magnificence, calculated to engender more deference than thrill, and so can't even be recommended as good boy's reading—though it offers little to adults. The book, in fact, is not altogether a surprising kind of thing to have come from a sailor of pertinacious literary talent and French literary education. The reason for bringing it in just here is to enforce the point that Conrad, for all his sophistication, exhibits a certain simplicity of outlook and attitude. About his attitude towards women there is perceptible, all the way through his literary career, something of the gallant simple sailor.

The sailor in him, of course, is rightly held to be a main part of his strength. It is not for nothing that *Heart of Darkness*, a predominantly successful tale, is told by the captain of the steamboat—told from that specific and concretely realized point of view: appraisal of the success of the tale is bound up with this consideration. But the stress up till now has fallen upon Conrad's weaknesses. It is time to ask where the strength may be found in its purest form. There will, I think, be general approval of the choice of *Typhoon* as a good example. But I am not sure that there is as general a recognition of just where the strength of *Typhoon* lies. The point may be made by saying that it lies not so much in the famous description of the elemental frenzy as in the presentment of Captain MacWhirr, the chief mate Jukes and the chief engineer Solomon Rout at the opening of the tale. Of course, it is a commonplace that Conrad's distinctive genius comprises a gift for rendering the British seaman. But is it a commonplace that the gift is the specific gift of a novelist, and (though the subtler artist doesn't run to caricature and the fantastic) relates Conrad to Dickens? Consider, for instance, this:

> He was rather below the medium height, a bit round-shouldered, and so sturdy of limb that his clothes always looked a shade too tight for his arms and legs. As if unable to grasp what is due to the difference of latitudes, he wore a brown bowler hat, a complete suit of a brownish hue, and clumsy black boots. These harbour togs gave to his thick figure an air of stiff and uncouth smartness. A thin silver watch-chain looped his waistcoat, and he never left his ship for the shore without clutching in his powerful, hairy fist an elegant umbrella of the very best quality, but generally unrolled. Young Jukes, the chief mate, attending his commander to the gangway, would sometimes venture to say, with the greatest gentleness, "Allow me, sir,"—and, possessing himself of the umbrella deferentially, would elevate the ferrule, shake the folds, twirl a neat furl in a jiffy, and hand it back: going through the performance with a face of such portentous gravity, that Mr. Solomon Rout, the chief engineer, smoking his morning cigar over the skylight, would turn away his head in order to hide a smile. "Oh! aye! The blessed gamp. . . . Thank 'ee, Jukes, thank 'ee," would mutter Captain MacWhirr heartily, without looking up.

Consider the exchanges between Captain MacWhirr and Jukes over the Siamese flag, deplorably, poor Jukes feels ("Fancy having a ridiculous Noah's ark elephant in the ensign of one's ship"), substituted for the Red Ensign. Consider the accounts of the home backgrounds, of MacWhirr and the chief engineer.

It is to be noted further that these backgrounds in their contrast with the main theme of the tale afford a far more satisfactory irony (it is, in fact, supremely effective) than that, in *Heart of Darkness*, of the scenes at Brussels. At the same time it is to be noted that there is in *Typhoon* no sardonic Marlow, commenting on an action that he is made to project; whereas, though *Heart of Darkness* is given from the point of view of the captain of the steamboat, that captain *is* Marlow—Marlow, for whom Conrad has more than one kind of use, and who is both more and less than a character and always something other than just a master-mariner. For comment in *Typhoon* we have the letters home of Solomon Rout, the chief engineer, and the letter of Jukes to his chum. In short, nothing in the story is forced or injected; the significance is not adjectival, but resides in the presented particulars—the actors, the incidents and the total action: we are given the ship, her cargo and her crew of ordinary British seamen, and the impact on them of the storm.

The ordinariness is, with a novelist's art, kept present to us the whole time; the particular effect of heroic sublimity depends on that.

> And again he heard that voice, forced and ringing feeble, but with a penetrating effect of quietness in the enormous discord of noises, as if sent out from some remote spot of peace beyond the black wastes of the gale; again he heard a man's voice—the frail and indomitable sound that can be made to carry an infinity of thought, resolution and purpose, that shall be pronouncing confident words on the last day, when heavens fall, and justice is done—again he heard it, and it was crying to him, as if from very, very far—"All right."

—Conrad can permit himself this, because the voice is that of the unheroically matter-of-fact Captain MacWhirr, whose solid specific presence, along with that of particularized ordinary sailors and engineers, we are never allowed to forget:

> A lull had come, a menacing lull of the wind, the holding of a stormy breath—and he felt himself pawed all over. It was the boatswain. Jukes recognized these hands, so thick and enormous that they seemed to belong to some new species of man.
> The boatswain had arrived on the bridge, crawling on all fours against the wind, and had found the chief mate's legs with the top of his head. Immediately he crouched and began to explore Jukes' person upwards, with prudent, apologetic touches, as became an inferior.

Or take this:

> The boatswain by his side kept on yelling. "What? What is it?" Jukes cried distressfully; and the other repeated, "What would my old woman say if she saw me now?"
> In the alleyway, where a lot of water had got in and splashed in the dark, the men were still as death, till Jukes stumbled against one

of them and cursed him savagely for being in the way. Two or three voices then asked, eager and weak, "Any chance for us, sir?"

"What's the matter with you fools?" he said brutally. He felt as though he could throw himself down amongst them and never move any more. But they seemed cheered; and in the midst of obsequious warning. "Look out! Mind that manhole lid, sir," they lowered him into the bunker. The boatswain tumbled down after him, and as soon as he had picked himself up he remarked "She would say, 'Serve you right, you old fool, for going to sea.' "

The boatswain had some means, and made a point of alluding to them frequently. His wife—a fat woman—and two grown-up daughters kept a greengrocer's shop in the East-end of London.

The seamen are their ordinary selves, the routine goes forward in the engine-room, and the heroic triumphs of the *Nan-Shan* emerge as matters-of-fact out of the ordinariness:

> "Can't have . . . fighting . . . board ship,"

says Captain MacWhirr through the typhoon, and down into the 'tween-deck, into the human hurricane of fighting coolies, go Jukes and his men as a routine matter-of-fact course, to restore order and decency:

> "We have done it, sir," he gasped.
> "Thought you would," said Captain MacWhirr.
> "Did you?" murmured Jukes to himself.
> "Wind fell all at once," went on the Captain.
> Jukes burst out: "If you think it was an easy job—"
> But his captain, clinging to the rail, paid no attention.
> "According to the books the worst is not over yet."

And the qualities which, in a triumph of discipline—a triumph of the spirit—have enabled a handful of ordinary men to impose sanity on a frantic mob are seen unquestionably to be those which took Captain MacWhirr, in contempt of "Storm-strategy," into the centre of the typhoon. Without any symbolic portentousness the Captain stands there the embodiment of a tradition. The crowning triumph of the spirit, in the guise of a matter-of-fact and practical sense of decency, is the redistribution—ship devastated, men dropping with fatigue—of the gathered-up and counted dollars among the assembled Chinese.

In *The Shadow-Line,* also in common recognition one of Conrad's masterpieces (it is, I think, superior to *Heart of Darkness* and even to *Typhoon*), we have the same art. It has been acclaimed as a kind of prose *Ancient Mariner*, and it is certainly a supremely sinister and beautiful evocation of enchantment in tropic seas. But the art of the evocation is of the kind that has been described; it is not a matter of engendering "atmosphere" adjectivally, by explicitly "significant" vaguenesses, insistent unutterablenesses, or the thrilled tone of an expository commentator, but of presenting concretely a succession of particulars from the point of view of the master of the ship, who, though notably sensitive, is not a Marlow, but just a ship's master; an actor among the other actors, though burdened with responsibilities towards the crew, owners and ship. The distinctive art of a novelist, and the art upon which the success of the prose *Ancient Mariner* essentially depends, is apparent in the rendering of personality, its reactions and vibrations; the pervasive presence of the crew, delicately particularized, will turn out on analysis to account for the major part of the atmosphere. The young captain, entering the saloon for the first time and sitting in the captain's chair, finds he is looking into a mirror:

> Deep within the tarnished ormolu frame, in the hot half-light sifted through the awning, I saw my own face propped between my hands. And I stared back at myself with the perfect detachment of distance, rather with curiosity than with any other feeling, except of some sympathy for this latest representative of what for all intents and purposes was a dynasty; continuous not in blood, indeed, but in its experience, in its training, in its conception of duty, and in the blessed simplicity of its traditional point of view on life. . . .
> Suddenly I perceived that there was another man in the saloon, standing a little on one side and looking intently at me. The chief mate. His long, red moustache determined the character of his physiognomy, which struck me as pugnacious in (strange to say) a ghastly sort of way.

The disobliging and disturbing oddity of the mate turns out to be due to the sinister vagaries and unseemly end of the late captain:

> That man had been in all essentials but his age just such another man as myself. Yet the end of his life was a complete act of treason, the betrayal of a tradition which seemed to me as imperative as any guide on earth could be. It appeared that even at sea a man could become the victim of evil spirits. I felt on my face the breath of unknown powers that shape our destinies.

The sinister spell that holds the ship is characteristically felt in terms of contrast with the tradition and its spiritual values, these being embodied in the crew, a good one, who carry on staunchly against bad luck and disease. The visiting doctor himself is "good" in the same way. The story ends, it will be noted, on the unexpected parting with the faithful Ransome, the exquisitely rendered seaman with a voice that is "extremely pleasant to hear" and a weak heart:

> "But, Ransome," I said, "I hate the idea of parting with you."
> "I must go," he broke in. "I have a right!" He gasped and a look of almost savage determination passed over his face. For an instant he was another being. And I saw under the worth and the comeliness of the man the humble reality of things. Life was a boon to him—this precarious, hard life—and he was thoroughly alarmed about himself.
> "Of course I shall pay you off if you wish it."
>
> .   .   .
>
> I approached him with extended hand. His eyes, not looking at me, had a strained expression. He was like a man listening for a warning call.
> "Won't you shake hands, Ransome?" I said gently. He exclaimed, flushed up dusky red, gave my hand a hard wrench—and next moment, left alone in the cabin, I listened to him going up the companion stairs cautiously, step by step, in mortal fear of starting into sudden anger our common enemy it was his hard fate to carry consciously within his faithful breast.

These things are worth many times those descriptions of sunsets, exotic seas and the last plunge of flaming wrecks which offer themselves to the compilers of prose and anthologies.

This is at any rate to confirm the accepted notion of Conrad to this extent: that his genius was a unique and happy union of seaman and writer. If he hadn't actually been himself a British seaman by vocation he couldn't have done the Merchant Service from the inside. The cosmopolitan of French culture and French literary initiation is there in the capacity for detachment that makes the intimate knowledge uniquely conscious and articulate. We are aware of the artist by vocation, the intellectual who doubles the seaman, only when we stop to take stock of the perfection of the rendering and subtle finish of the art.

But this fine balance, this identity, isn't always sustained. In Marlow, who (as remarked above) has a variety of uses, the detachment is separated off. As a main participant in events though, by his specific rôle as such, a detached one, he gives his technical function a dramatic status in the action, and the author a freedom of presence that, as we have seen, constitutes a temptation. Elsewhere Marlow is frankly a method of projection or presentation—one that we learn to associate with Conrad's characteristic vices and weaknesses. In *Youth,* for instance, one of the best-known of the tales, though not one of the best, he goes with the cheap insistence on the glamour, and with that tone which, here and in other places, makes one recall the formula of the early reviewer and reflect that the prose laureate of the British seaman does sometimes degenerate into a "Kipling of the South Seas." (And this is the point at which to note that Conrad can write shockingly bad magazine stuff—see the solemnly dedicated collection called *Within the Tides.*)

In *Lord Jim* Marlow is the means of presenting Jim with the appropriate externality, seen always through the question, the doubt, that is the central theme of the book. Means and effect are unobjectionable; it is a different matter from the use of Marlow elsewhere to pass off a vaguely excited incomprehension as tremendous significance. But *Lord Jim* doesn't deserve the position of pre-eminence among Conrad's works often assigned it: it is hardly one of the most considerable. There is, in fact, much to be said in support of those reviewers who (Conrad tells us) "maintained that the work starting as a short story had got beyond the writer's control," so that what we have is neither a very considerable novel, in spite of its 420 pages, nor one of Conrad's best short stories. The presentment of Lord Jim in the first part of the book, the account of the inquiry and of the desertion of the *Patna,* the talk with the French lieutenant—these are good Conrad. But the romance that follows, though plausibly offered as a continued exhibition of Jim's case, has no inevitability as that; nor does it develop or enrich the central interest, which consequently, eked out to provide the substance of a novel, comes to seem decidedly thin.

The eking out is done mainly from the world of *Almayer's Folly, An Outcast of the Islands,* and *Tales of Unrest,* those excessively adjectival studies in the Malayan exotic of Conrad's earliest vein. Those things, it had better be said here, though they are innocuous, and no doubt deserved for their originality of setting some respectful notice when they came out, will not be urged by judicious admirers of Conrad among his claims to classical rank. In their stylistic eloquence, which suggests a descent from Chateaubriand, their wearying exoticism, and their "picturesque" human interest, they aren't easy to re-read.

No, *Lord Jim* is neither the best of Conrad's novels, nor among the best of his short stories. If, on the other hand, his most considerable work had had due recognition, it would be known as one of the great novels of the language. For *Nostromo* is most certainly that. And it complicates the account of Conrad's genius in that it doesn't answer to the formula arrived at above. He is not here the laureate of the Merchant Service, the British seaman happily doubled with the artist—an artist whose "outsideness" with regard to the Merchant Service is to be constated only in the essential degree of detachment involved in an adequately recording art. In *Nostromo* Conrad is openly and triumphantly the artist by *métier*, conscious of French initiation and of fellowship in craft with Flaubert. The French element so oddly apparent in his diction and idiom throughout his career (he learnt French before English) here reveals its full significance, being associated with so serious and severe a conception of the art of fiction.

The controlling conception of the novelist's art is severe, but the novel is luxuriant in its magnificence: it is Conrad's supreme triumph in the evocation of exotic life and colour. Sulaco, standing beneath snow-clad Higuerota, with its population of Indians, mixed-bloods, Hidalgos, Italians and English engineers, is brought before us in irresistible reality, along with the picturesque and murderous public drama of a South American State. This aspect of Conrad's genius in *Nostromo* has had full recognition; indeed, it could hardly be missed. What doesn't seem to be a commonplace is the way in which the whole book forms a rich and subtle but highly organized pattern. Every detail, character and incident has its significant bearing on the themes and motives of this. The magnificence referred to above addresses the senses, or the sensuous imagination; the pattern is one of moral significances.

Nostromo has a main political, or public, theme, the relation between moral idealism and "material interests." We see the Gould Concession become the rallying centre for all in Costaguana who desire peace and order—the constitutionalists, the patriotic idealists, the Robin Hood of the oppressed, the representatives of the financial power of Europe and North America. The ironical end of the book shows us a Sulaco in which order and ideals have triumphed, Progress forges ahead, and the all-powerful Concession has become the focus of hate for workers and the oppressed and a symbol of crushing materialism for idealists and defenders of the spirit. This public theme is presented in terms of a number of personal histories or, it might be said, private themes, each having a specific representative moral significance.

The Gould Concession is in the first place the personal history of its inheritor, Charles Gould—and the tragedy of his wife. He, like the other main characters, enacts a particular answer to the question that we feel working in the matter of the novel as a kind of informing and organizing principle: what do men find to live *for*—what kinds of motive force or radical attitude can give life meaning, direction, coherence? Charles Gould finds his answer in the ideal purpose he identifies with the success of the Gould Concession:

> What is wanted here is law, good faith, order, security. Anyone can declaim about these things, but I pin my faith to material interests. Only let the material interests once get a firm footing, and they are bound to impose the conditions on which alone they can continue to exist. That's how your money-making is justified here in the face of lawlessness and disorder. It is justified because the security which it demands must be shared with an oppressed people. A better justice will come afterwards. That's your ray of hope.

Charles Gould's faith is parodied by his backer, the American financier Holroyd, whose interest in furthering a "pure form of Christianity" and whose rhetorical faith in the manifest destiny of the United States cannot without irony be said to give ideal significance to his love of power. Charles himself is absorbed by the Concession that killed his father, and Emilia Gould, standing for personal relations and disinterested human sympathy, looks on in starved loneliness at the redeeming triumph that is an ironical defeat of the spirit.

Nostromo, picturesque indispensable to his patrons and popular hero, has no ideal purpose. He lives for reputation, "to be well spoken of"—for his reflection in the eyes of others, and when, tempted by the silver, he condemns himself to clandestine courses the mainspring of his life goes slack. His return to find the new lighthouse standing on the lonely rock hard by his secret, and his consequent betrayal into devious paths in love, are magnificent and characteristic triumphs of symbolism. His appropriately melodramatic death is caused by the silver and occurs during a stealthy visit to it.

Martin Decoud, intellectual and "dilettante in life," Nostromo's companion in that marvellously rendered night of the Gulf (it is one of the most vivid pieces of sensuous evocation in literature), also has no ideal purpose. The voice of sceptical intelligence, with "no faith in anything except the truth of his own sensations," he enjoys conscious advantages, and has no difficulty in summing up Nostromo:

> Decoud, incorrigible in his scepticism, reflected, not cynically but with general satisfaction, that this man was made incorruptible by his

enormous vanity, that finest form of egoism which can take on the aspect of every virtue.

He can also place Charles Gould, that "sentimental Englishman" who

cannot exist without idealizing every simple desire or achievement. He could not believe his own motives if he did not make them first a part of some fairy tale.

Decoud himself, contemptuously free from the "sentimentalism of the people that will never do anything for the sake of their passionate desire, unless it comes to them clothed in the fair robes of an ideal," is frankly moved by his passion for Antonia Avellanos, and that alone, when he initiates the step through which the mine is saved and the aims of the patriots and idealists achieved. In this respect he provides a criticism of Charles Gould's subtle infidelity to his wife. Yet, even apart from his passion, he is not quite self-sufficient. At a moment when we might have expected him to be wholly engrossed in practical considerations we find him, significantly, illustrating an essential human trait:

all the objectless and necessary sincerity of one's innermost life trying to react upon the profound sympathies of another's existence.

For

In the most sceptical heart there lurks at such moments, when the chances of existence are involved, a desire to leave a correct impression of the feelings, like a light by which the action may be seen when personality is gone, gone where no light of investigation can ever reach the truth which every death takes out of the world. Therefore, instead of looking for something to eat, or trying to snatch an hour or two of sleep, Decoud was filling the pages of a large pocket book with a letter to his sister.

Marooned on the Great Isabel (site of the subsequent lighthouse) he discovers that his self-sufficiency is indeed radically qualified:

Solitude from mere outward condition of existence becomes very swiftly a state of soul in which the affectations of irony and scepticism have no place. It takes possession of the mind, and drives forth the thought into the exile of utter unbelief. After three days of waiting for the sight of some human face, Decoud caught himself entertaining a doubt of his own individuality. It had merged into the world of

cloud and water, of natural forces and forms of nature. . . .
    . . . He had recognized no other virtue than intelligence and had
erected passions into duties. Both his intelligence and his passion
were swallowed up easily in the great unbroken solitude of waiting
without faith.

He shoots himself. The whole episode is given in painful immediacy.
    Of all the characters the one nearest to self-sufficiency is Dr.
Monygham, the disliked and distrusted, and he, for all his sardonic
scepticism about human nature, does hold to an ideal. His scepticism is based on self-contempt, for his ideal (he is, in fact, a stronger
and quite unequivocal Lord Jim) is one he has offended against; it
is an exacting ideal of conduct. He offers a major contrast with
Nostromo too, since his success in the desperate venture that saves
the situation and rehabilitates him (in his own eyes—he expects death)
depends upon his having no reputation except for "unsoundness"
and a shady past, and his being ready to be ill-spoken of and ill-
thought of. His ideal, of course, isn't merely personal—it is of the same
order as the moral idea of the Merchant Service (he is "an officer
and a gentleman"): it owes its strength to a traditional and social
sanction; and he has an outer stay in his devotion to Mrs. Gould.
    Perhaps the completest antithesis to Decoud is Giorgio Viola, the
serene old Garibaldino, also self-sufficient, or very near it—he by
reason of his libertarian idealism, the disinterestedness of which is
above all question. He represents with monumental massiveness
the heroic age of the liberal faith—of *Songs before Sunrise* and the
religion of humanity, and so provides a contrasting background for
the representatives of Progress in Costaguana politics (by the end of
Nostromo the Marxists are on the scene). He is commandingly real;
but it is part of the irony of the book that the achievements he stands
for should have produced the South America we are shown.
    Captain Mitchell represents the Merchant Service. He is sane
and stable to the point of stupidity. His inability to realize that he,
Joe Mitchell ("I am a public character, sir"), has anything to fear
from a ridiculously menacing Dago whose ruffians have stolen his
presentation pocket-chronometer actually cows the all-powerful Dago
into restoring both chronometer and freedom:

> The old sailor, with all his small weaknesses and absurdities, was
> constitutionally incapable of entertaining for any length of time a fear
> of his personal safety. It was not so much firmness of soul as the lack
> of a certain kind of imagination—the kind whose undue development

caused intense suffering to Señor Hirsch; that sort of imagination which adds the blind terror of bodily suffering and of death, envisaged as an accident to the body alone, strictly—to all the other apprehensions on which the sense of one's existence is based. Unfortunately, Captain Mitchell had not much penetration of any kind; characteristic, illuminating trifles of expression, action, or movement, escaped him completely. He was too pompously and innocently aware of his own existence to observe that of others. For instance, he could not believe that Sotillo had been really afraid of him, and this simply because it would never have entered into his head to shoot anyone except in the most pressing case of self-defence. Anybody could see he was not a murdering kind of man, he reflected quite gravely.

These traits, it will be seen, qualify him for an essential function in the presentment of the action, to which he is related in a way symbolized by his triumphant sense—a sense uninformed by any comprehension of what is going forward—of being at the centre of things, whence history is directed, as he sits, an *habitué*, in Mrs. Gould's drawing-room.

On the significance of the other characters there is no need to enlarge: Señor Avellanos, the liberal idealist, who dies of disappointment, and the sheets of whose *Fifty Years of Misrule* are "fired out as wads for trabucos loaded with handfuls of type" during the "democratic" *émeute;* the fanatical Father Corbelàn; Hirsch, the embodiment of fear, and so on. Instead, a negative point had better be made by way of stressing the distinctive nature of the impressiveness of *Nostromo.* The impressiveness is not a matter of any profundity of search into human experience, or any explorative subtlety in the analysis of human behaviour. It is a matter rather of the firm and vivid concreteness with which the representative attitudes and motives are realized, and the rich economy of the pattern that plays them off against one another. To suggest, as Edward Garnett does in his introduction to *Conrad's Prefaces,* that perhaps this or that character wouldn't really have behaved just as he does in the book is misdirected criticism. The life-like convincingness of Conrad's persons (which is complete as we read, and undisturbed by properly critical reflection) doesn't entitle us to psychologize them as lives existing outside the book. I am reminded of certain remarks of T. S. Eliot's:

A "living" character is not necessarily "true to life". It is a person whom we can see and hear, whether he be true or false to human nature as we know it. What the creator of character needs is not so much knowledge of motives as keen sensibility; the dramatist need not understand people, but he must be exceptionally aware of them.

It is an Elizabethan dramatist Eliot has in front of him; and it strikes me that there is something that recalls the strength of Elizabethan drama about the art of *Nostromo*—something Shakespearean, in fact. The keen sensibility and the exceptional awareness are apparent in the vividness with which we see and hear Conrad's persons, and there is nothing about them that, on reflection, we find untrue to human nature as we know it. But the seeing and hearing is adequate understanding: they are present to us and are plainly what they are; and to try, by way of appreciation or criticism, to go behind that is to misunderstand what the book offers us. There is plainly no room in *Nostromo* for the kind of illustrated psychology that many critics think they have a right to demand of a novelist (and of Shakespeare). Consider the number of personal centres of moral interest, and the variety of themes. Consider the number of vivid dramatic scenes and episodes. Consider the different strands that go to the totality of the action. There is the private tragedy of the Goulds; there is Nostromo's history, involving that of the Viola family; there is the story of Decoud and Antonia; there is that of Dr. Monygham and his self-rehabilitation; and all these and so much else are subsumed in the public historical drama——the study, concretely rendered, of the play of moral and material forces, political and personal motives, in the founding of the Occidental Republic.

Clearly, Conrad's study of motives, and of the relation between the material and the spiritual, doesn't depend for its impressiveness on any sustained analytic exhibition of the inner complexities of the individual psyche. The impressiveness lies in the vivid reality of the things we are made to see and hear, and the significance they get from their relations in a highly organized and vividly realized whole. It lies in such effects as that of the presence of Decoud and Nostromo in the lighter as it drifts with its load of silver and of Fear (personified by the stowaway Hirsch) through the black night of the Gulf; and that of the unexpected nocturnal encounter between Nostromo and Dr. Monygham, two sharply contrasted consciousnesses, in the vast deserted Custom House, and their discovery that the "shapeless high-shouldered shadow of somebody standing still, with lowered head" seen on the wall through a doorway, is thrown by the hanging body of the tortured Hirsch. We have it characteristically when Charles Gould, going out from his interview (consummate satiric comedy) with Pedrito Montero, would-be Duc de Morny to the new Napoleon, runs into the "constitutionalist" deputation he has refused to support ("The acceptance of accomplished facts may save yet the precious vestiges of parliamentary institutions"):

> Charles Gould on going out passed his hand over his forehead as if to disperse the mists of an oppressive dream, whose grotesque extravagance leaves behind a subtle sense of bodily danger and intellectual decay. In the passages and on the staircases of the old palace Montero's troopers lounged about insolently, smoking and making way for no one; the clanking of sabres and spurs resounded all over the building. Three silent groups of civilians in severe black waited in the main gallery, formal and helpless; a little huddled up, each keeping apart from the others, as if in the exercise of a public duty they had been overcome by a desire to shun the notice of every eye. These were the deputations waiting for their audience. The one from the Provincial Assembly, more restless and uneasy in its corporate expression, was overtopped by the big face of Don Juste Lopez, soft and white, with prominent eyelids and wreathed in impenetrable solemnity as if in a dense cloud. The President of the Provincial Assembly, coming bravely to save the last shred of parliamentary institutions (on the English model), averted his eyes from the Administrador of the San Tomé mine as a dignified rebuke of his little faith in that only saving principle.

Charles Gould's quiet unyieldingness in the face of Pedrito's threats and blandishments has already invested him for the moment with a larger measure of our sympathy than he in general commands. The brush with the deputation confirms this effect, while at the same time reinforcing dramatically that pattern of political significance which has a major part in *Nostromo*—a book that was written, we remind ourselves in some wonder, noting the topicality of its themes, analysis and illustrations, in the reign of Edward VII.

Again, we have the symbolic pregnancy of Conrad's dramatic method in such a representative touch as this (the context is the flight of aristocrats and adherents of "law and order" to the protection of the "master of the Campo"):

> The emissary of Hernandez spurred his horse close up.
> "Has not the master of the mine any message to send the master of the Campo?"
> The truth of the comparison struck Charles Gould heavily. In his determined purpose he held the mine and the indomitable bandit held

the Campo by the same precarious tenure. They were equals before the lawlessness of the land. It was impossible to disentangle one's activities from its debasing contacts.

There is—the adjective proposes itself at this point—something rhetorical, in a wholly laudatory sense, about Conrad's art in *Nostromo*. One might add, by way of insisting further on the Elizabethan in it, that it has a certain robust vigour of melodrama. The melodrama, of course, is completely controlled to the pattern of moral significance. Consider, for instance, how the climax of the public drama is given us: it is a thrilling nick-of-time *peripeteia*, but it is given in retrospect through the pompous showmanship and uncomprehending importance of Captain Mitchell ("Fussy Joe"). The triumphs of the Progress he hymns are already assured and commonplace, and already (a few pages on) Dr. Monygham is asking:

> "Do you think that now the mine would march upon the town to save their Señor Administrador? Do you think that?"

He has just pronounced:

> "There is no peace and no rest in the development of material interests. They have their law, and their justice. But it is founded on expediency, and it is inhuman; it is without rectitude, without the continuity and the force that can be found only in a moral principle."

This is only one instance of that subtle play of the order of presentment against the time-order which the reader finds himself admiring in the book as a whole—subtle, yet, once taken stock of, appreciated as inevitable. It is characteristic of Conrad's method, to take another instance, that we should have seen, in a prospective glimpse given us at the very opening of the book, the pitiable *débâcle* of the Ribierist dictatorship of "reform" before we are invited to contemplate the hopes and enthusiasms of its supporters at the inauguration.

It will probably be expected, after so much insistence on the moral pattern of *Nostromo*, that something will be said about the total significance. What, as the upshot of this exhibition of human motive and attitude, do we feel Conrad himself to endorse? What are his positives? It is easier to say what he rejects or criticizes. About the judgment on Decoud's scepticism we can have no doubt. And even Decoud concedes that the illusions "those Englishmen" live on "somehow or other help them to get a firm hold of the sub-stance." To this concession we can relate the observations of the engineer-in-chief:

> "Upon my word, doctor, things seem to be worth nothing by what they are in themselves. I begin to believe that the only solid thing about them is the spiritual value which everyone discovers in his own form of activity—"
>
> "Bah!" interrupted the doctor.

The engineer has in mind Holroyd the millionaire and his preoccu-pation with a "pure form of Christianity." But although Dr. Mony-gham, himself devoted to a moral idea, is as such clearly not disapproved by the author, he is made to seem Quixotic, and it is difficult to feel that the ironic light in which the "spiritual values" discovered by the other main characters in their forms of activity are shown is less essentially dissociating than the irony focussed upon Holroyd. In fact, though Decoud is so decisively dealt with in the action, he remains at the centre of the book, in the sense that his consciousness seems to permeate it, even to dominate it. That con-sciousness is clearly very closely related to the author's own personal *timbre*, that which becomes representable in quotation in such char-acteristic sardonic touches as:

> They had stopped near the cage. The parrot, catching the sound of a word belonging to his vocabulary, was moved to interfere. Parrots are very human.
>
> "Viva Costaguana!" he shrieked. . . .

It is not a question of a "philosophy"; Conrad cannot be said to have one. He is not one of those writers who clear up their fundamental attitudes for themselves in such a way that we may reasonably, in talking of them, use that portentous term. He does believe intensely, as a matter of concrete experience, in the kind of human achievement represented by the Merchant Service—tradition, discipline and moral ideal; but he has also a strong sense, not only of the frailty, but of the absurdity or unreality, in relation to the surrounding and underlying gulfs, of such achievement, a sense so strong that it often seems very close to Decoud's radical scepticism, which is, in the account of those last days, rendered with such sig-nificant power. In fact, Decoud may be said to have had a considerable part in the writing of *Nostromo;* or one might say that *Nostromo* was written by a Decoud who wasn't a complacent dilettante, but was positively drawn towards those capable of "investing their activities with spiritual value"—Monygham, Giorgio Viola, Señor Avellanos, Charles Gould.

At any rate, for all the rich variety of the interest and the tightness of the pattern, the reverberation of *Nostromo* has something hollow about it; with the colour and life there is a suggestion of a certain emptiness. And for explanation it is perhaps enough to point to this reflection of Mrs. Gould's:

> It had come into her mind that for life to be large and full, it must contain the care of the past and of the future in every passing moment of the present.

That kind of self-sufficient day-to-dayness of living Conrad can convey, when writing from within the Merchant Service, where clearly he has known it. We are made aware of hostile natural forces threatening his seamen with extinction, but not of metaphysical gulfs opening under life and consciousness: reality on board ship is domestic, assured and substantial. "That feeling of life-emptiness which had made me so restless for the last few months," says the young captain of *The Shadow-Line,* entering on his new command, "lost its bitter plausibility, its evil influence." For life in the Merchant Service there is no equivalent in *Nostromo*—no intimate sense conveyed of the day-by-day continuities of social living. And though we are given a confidential account of what lies behind Dr. Monygham's sardonic face, yet on the whole we see the characters from the outside, and only as they belong to the ironic pattern—figures in the futilities of a public drama, against a dwarfing background of mountain and gulf.

This kind of vision, this sense of life, corresponds, there can be no doubt, to something radical in Conrad. All his readers must have noticed how recurrent and important the theme of isolation is in his work. And they must have noticed too the close relation between the Decoud consciousness and the sympathetic hero of *Victory*, the English-speaking Swede, Axel Heyst.

ALBERT J. GUERARD

———◆———

The Journey Within

"HEART OF DARKNESS" is the most famous of these personal short
novels: a *Pilgrim's Progress* for our pessimistic and psychologizing age.
"Before the Congo I was just a mere animal." [1] The living nightmare
of 1890 seems to have affected Conrad quite as importantly as did
Gide's Congo experience thirty-six years later. The autobiographical
basis of the narrative is well known, and its introspective bias obvious;
this is Conrad's longest journey into self. But it is well to remember that "Heart of Darkness" is also other if more superficial things:
a sensitive and vivid travelogue, and a comment on "the vilest scramble
for loot that ever disfigured the history of human conscience and geographical exploration." [2] The Congo was much in the public mind in
1889, when Henry Stanley's relief expedition found Emin Pasha (who
like Kurtz did not want to be rescued), and it is interesting to note
that Conrad was in Brussels during or immediately after Stanley's
triumphant welcome there in April 1890. [3] This was just before he set
out on his own Congo journey. We do not know how much the
Georges Antoine Klein who died on board the *Roi des Belges* resembled the fictional Kurtz, but Stanley himself provided no mean
example of a man who could gloss over the extermination of savages
with pious moralisms which were very possibly "sincere."

"Heart of Darkness" thus has its important public side, as an

Reprinted by permission of the publishers from Albert J. Guerard, *Conrad
the Novelist*, Cambridge, Mass.: Harvard University Press, Copyright 1958,
by the President and Fellows of Harvard College.

angry document on absurd and brutal exploitation. Marlow is treated
to the spectacle of a French man-of-war shelling an unseen "enemy"
village in the bush, and presently he will wander into the grove at the
first company station where the starving and sick Negroes withdraw
to die. It is one of the greatest of Conrad's many moments of compassionate rendering. The compassion extends even to the cannibal
crew of the *Roi des Belges*. Deprived of the rotten hippo meat they
had brought along for food, and paid three nine-inch pieces of brass
wire a week, they appear to subsist on "lumps of some stuff like half-
cooked dough, of a dirty lavender color" which they keep wrapped
in leaves. Conrad here operates through ambiguous suggestion (are the
lumps human flesh?) but elsewhere he wants, like Gide after him, to
make his complacent European reader *see:* see, for instance, the
drunken unkempt official met on the road and three miles farther on
the body of the Negro with a bullet hole in his forehead.[4] "Heart of
Darkness" is a record of things seen and done. But also Conrad was
reacting to the humanitarian pretenses of some of the looters precisely
as the novelist today reacts to the moralisms of cold-war propaganda.
Then it was ivory that poured from the heart of darkness; now it is
uranium. Conrad shrewdly recognized—an intuition amply developed
in *Nostromo*—that deception is most sinister when it becomes self-
deception, and the propagandist takes seriously his own fictions. Kurtz
"could get himself to believe anything—anything." The benevolent
rhetoric of his seventeen-page report for the International Society for
the Suppression of Savage Customs was meant sincerely enough. But a
deeper sincerity spoke through his scrawled postscript: "Exterminate
all the brutes!" The conservative Conrad (who found Donkin fit to
be a labor leader) speaks through the journalist who says that "Kurtz's
proper sphere ought to have been politics 'on the popular side.'"

Conrad, again like many novelists today, was both drawn to
idealism and repelled by its hypocritical abuse. "The conquest of the
earth, which mostly means the taking it away from those who have a
different complexion or slightly flatter noses than ourselves, is not a
pretty thing when you look into it too much. What redeems it is the
idea only. An idea at the back of it; not a sentimental pretence but an
idea; and an unselfish belief in the idea . . ." Marlow commits himself to the yet unseen agent partly because Kurtz "had come out
equipped with moral ideas of some sort." Anything would seem preferable to the demoralized greed and total cynicism of the others, "the
flabby devil" of the Central Station. Later when he discovers what has
happened to Kurtz's moral ideas, he remains faithful to the "nightmare

of my choice." In *Under Western Eyes* Sophia Antonovna makes a distinction between those who burn and those who rot, and remarks that it is sometimes preferable to burn. The Kurtz who had made himself literally one of the devils of the land, and who in solitude had kicked himself loose of the earth, burns while the others rot. Through violent not flabby evil he exists in the moral universe even before pronouncing judgment on himself with his dying breath. A little too much has been made, I think, of the redemptive value of those two words—"The horror!" But none of the company "pilgrims" could have uttered them.

The redemptive view is Catholic, of course, though no priest was in attendance; Kurtz can repent as the gunman of *The Power and the Glory* cannot. "Heart of Darkness" (still at this public and wholly conscious level) combines a Victorian ethic and late Victorian fear of the white man's deterioration with a distinctly Catholic psychology. We are protected from ourselves by society with its laws and its watchful neighbors, Marlow observes. And we are protected by work. "You wonder I didn't go ashore for a howl and a dance? Well, no—I didn't. Fine sentiments, you say? Fine sentiments, be hanged! I had no time. I had to mess about with white-lead and strips of woolen blanket helping to put bandages on those leaky steam-pipes." But when the external restraints of society and work are removed, we must meet the challenge and temptation of savage reversion with our "own inborn strength. Principles won't do." This inborn strength appears to include restraint—the restraint that Kurtz lacked and the cannibal crew of the *Roi des Belges* surprisingly possessed. The hollow man, whose evil is the evil of *vacancy*, succumbs. And in their different degrees the pilgrims and Kurtz share this hollowness. "Perhaps there was nothing within" the manager of the Central Station. "Such a suspicion made one pause—for out there there were no external checks." And there was nothing inside the brickmaker, that papier-maché Mephistopheles, "but a little loose dirt, maybe."

As for Kurtz, the wilderness "echoed loudly within him because he was hollow at the core." Perhaps the chief contradiction of "Heart of Darkness" is that it suggests and dramatizes evil as an active energy (Kurtz and his unspeakable lusts) but defines evil as vacancy. The primitive (and here the contradiction is only verbal) is compact of passion and apathy. "I was struck by the fire of his eyes and the composed languor of his expression . . . This shadow looked satiated and calm, as though for the moment it had had its fill of all the emotions." Of the two menaces—the unspeakable desires and the apathy—apathy surely seemed the greater to Conrad. Hence we cannot quite believe the response of Marlow's heart to the beating of the tom-toms. This is, I think, the story's minor but central flaw, and the source of an unfruitful ambiguity: that it slightly overdoes the kinship with the "passionate uproar," slightly undervalues the temptation of inertia.

In any event, it is time to recognize that the story is not primarily about Kurtz or about the brutality of Belgian officials but about Marlow its narrator. To what extent it also expresses the Joseph Conrad a biographer might conceivably recover, who in 1898 still felt a debt must be paid for his Congo journey and who paid it by the writing of this story, is doubtless an insoluble question. I suspect two facts (of a possible several hundred) are important. First, that going to the Congo was the enactment of a childhood wish associated with the disapproved childhood ambition to go to sea, and that this belated enactment was itself profoundly disapproved, in 1890, by the uncle and guardian.[5] It was another gesture of a man bent on throwing his life away. But even more important may be the guilt of complicity, just such a guilt as many novelists of the Second World War have been obliged to work off. What Conrad thought of the expedition of the Katanga Company of 1890–1892 is accurately reflected in his remarks on the "Eldorado Exploring Expedition" of "Heart of Darkness": "It was reckless without hardihood, greedy without audacity, and cruel without courage . . . with no more moral purpose at the back of it than there is in burglars breaking into a safe." Yet Conrad hoped to obtain command of the expedition's ship even after he had returned from the initiatory voyage dramatized in his novel. Thus the adventurous Conrad and Conrad the moralist may have experienced collision. But the collision, again as with so many novelists of the second war, could well have been deferred and retrospective, not felt intensely at the time.

So much for the elusive Conrad of the biographers and of the "Congo Diary." Substantially and in its central emphasis "Heart of Darkness" concerns Marlow (projection to whatever great or small degree of a more irrecoverable Conrad) and his journey toward and through certain facets or potentialities of self. F. R. Leavis seems to regard him as a narrator only, providing a "specific and concretely realized point of view." [6] But Marlow reiterates often enough that he is recounting a spiritual voyage of self-discovery. He remarks casually but crucially that he did not know himself before setting out, and that he likes work for the chance it provides to "find yourself . . . what no other man can ever know." The Inner Station "was the farthest point of navigation and the culminating point of my experience." At a material and rather superficial level, the journey is through the temptation of atavism. It is a record of "remote kinship" with the "wild and passionate uproar," of a "trace of a response" to it, of a final rejection of the "fascination of the abomination." And why should there not be the trace of a response? "The mind of man is capable of anything—because everything is in it, all the past as well as all the future." Marlow's temptation is made concrete through his exposure to Kurtz, a white man and sometime idealist who had fully responded to the wilderness: a potential and fallen self. "I had turned to the wilderness really, not to Mr. Kurtz." At the climax Marlow follows Kurtz ashore, confounds the beat of the drum with the beating of his heart, goes through the ordeal of looking into Kurtz's "mad soul," and brings him back to the ship. He returns to Europe a changed and more knowing man. Ordinary people are now "intruders whose knowledge of life was to me an irritating pretence, because I felt so sure they could not possibly know the things I knew."

On this literal plane, and when the events are so abstracted from the dream-sensation conveying them, it is hard to take Marlow's plight very seriously. Will he, the busy captain and moralizing narrator, also revert to savagery, go ashore for a howl and a dance, indulge unspeakable lusts? The late Victorian reader (and possibly Conrad himself) could take this more seriously than we; could literally believe not merely in a Kurtz's deterioration through months of solitude but also in the sudden reversion to the "beast" of naturalistic fiction. Insofar as Conrad does want us to take it seriously and literally, we must admit the nominal triumph of a currently accepted but false psychology over his own truer intuitions. But the triumph is only nominal. For the personal narrative is unmistakably authentic, which means that it explores something truer, more fundamental, and distinctly less material; the night journey into the unconscious, and confrontation of an entity within the self. "I flung one shoe overboard, and became aware that that was exactly what I had been looking forward to—a talk with Kurtz." It little matters what, in terms of psychological symbolism, we call this double or say he represents: whether the Freudian id or the Jungian shadow or more vaguely the outlaw. And I am afraid it is impossible to say where Conrad's conscious understanding of his story began and ended. The important thing is that the introspective plunge and powerful dream seem true; and are therefore inevitably moving.

Certain circumstances of Marlow's voyage, looked at in these terms, take on a new importance. The true night journey can occur (except during analysis) only in sleep or in the waking dream of a profoundly intuitive mind. Marlow insists more than is necessary on the dreamlike quality of his narrative. "It seems to me I am trying to tell you a dream—making a vain attempt, because no relation of a dream can convey the dream-sensation, that commingling of absurdity, surprise, and bewilderment in a tremor of struggling revolt . . ." Even before leaving Brussels Marlow felt as though he "were about to set off for the center of the earth," not the center of a continent.[7] The intro-spective voyager leaves his familiar rational world, is "cut off from the comprehension" of his surroundings; his steamer toils "along slowly on the edge of a black and incomprehensible frenzy." As the crisis ap-proaches, the dreamer and his ship move through a silence that "seemed unnatural, like a state of trance"; then enter (a few miles below the Inner Station) a deep fog. "The approach to this Kurtz grubbing for ivory in the wretched bush was beset by as many dangers as though he had been an enchanted princess sleeping in a fabulous castle."[8] Later, Marlow's task is to try "to break the spell" of the wilderness that holds Kurtz entranced.

· The approach to the unconscious and primitive may be aided by a savage or half-savage guide, and may require the token removal of civilized trappings or aids; both conceptions are beautifully dramatized in Faulkner's "The Bear." In "Heart of Darkness" the token "relin-quishment" and the death of the half-savage guide are connected. The helmsman falling at Marlow's feet casts blood on his shoes, which he is "morbidly anxious" to change and in fact throws overboard.[9] (The rescue of Wait in *The Nigger of the "Narcissus"* shows a similar pat-tern.) Here we have presumably entered an area of unconscious crea-tion; the dream is true but the teller may have no idea why it is. So too, possibly, a psychic need as well as literary tact compelled Conrad to defer the meeting between Marlow and Kurtz for some three thou-sand words after announcing that it took place. We think we are about to meet Kurtz at last. But instead Marlow leaps ahead to his meeting with the "Intended"; comments on Kurtz's megalomania and assumption of his place among the devils of the land; reports on the seventeen-page pamphlet; relates his meeting and conversation with Kurtz's harlequin disciple—and only then tells of seeing through his binoculars the heads on the stakes surrounding Kurtz's house. This is the "evasive" Conrad in full play, deferring what we most want to know and see; perhaps compelled to defer climax in this way. The tactic is dramatically effective, though possibly carried to excess: we are told on the authority of completed knowledge certain things we would have found hard to believe had they been presented through a slow consecutive realistic discovery. But also it can be argued that it was psychologically impossible for Marlow to go at once to Kurtz's house with the others. The double must be brought on board the ship, and the first confrontation must occur there. We are reminded of Leggatt in the narrator's cabin, of the trapped Wait on the *Narcissus*. The incorporation and alliance between the two becomes material, and the identification of "selves."

Hence the shock Marlow experiences when he discovers that Kurtz's cabin is empty and his secret sharer gone; a part of himself has vanished. "What made this emotion so overpowering was—how shall I define it?—the moral shock I received, as if something altogether monstrous, intolerable to thought and odious to the soul, had been thrust upon me unexpectedly." And now he must risk the ultimate confrontation in a true solitude and must do so on shore. "I was anxious to deal with this shadow by myself alone—and to this day I don't know why I was so jealous of sharing with anyone the peculiar blackness of that experience." He follows the crawling Kurtz through the grass; comes upon him "long, pale, indistinct, like a vapor exhaled by the earth." ("I had cut him off cleverly . . .") We are told very little of what Kurtz said in the moments that follow; and little of his incoherent discourses after he is brought back to the ship. "His was an impenetrable darkness. I looked at him as you peer down at a man who is lying at the bottom of a precipice where the sun never shines" —a comment less vague and rhetorical, in terms of psychic geography, than it may seem at a first reading. And then Kurtz is dead, taken off the ship, his body buried in a "muddy hole." With the confrontation over, Marlow must still emerge from environing darkness, and does so through that other deep fog of sickness. The identification is not yet completely broken. "And it is not my own extremity I remember best— a vision of grayness without form filled with physical pain, and a careless contempt for the evanescence of all things—even of this pain itself. No! It is his extremity that I seem to have lived through." Only in the atonement of his lie to Kurtz's "Intended," back in the sepulchral city, does the experience come truly to an end. "I laid the ghost of his gifts at last with a lie . . ."

Such seems to be the content of the dream. If my summary has even a partial validity it should explain and to an extent justify some of the "adjectival and worse than supererogatory insistence" to which F. R. Leavis (who sees only the travelogue and the portrait of Kurtz) objects. I am willing to grant that the unspeakable rites and unspeakable secrets become wearisome, but the fact—at once literary and psychological—is that they must remain *unspoken*. A confrontation with such a double and facet of the unconscious cannot be reported through realistic dialogue; the conversations must remain as shadowy as the narrator's conversations with Leggatt. So too when Marlow finds it hard to define the moral shock he received on seeing the empty cabin, or when he says he doesn't know why he was jealous of sharing his experience, I think we can take him literally . . . and in a sense even be thankful for his uncertainty. The greater tautness and economy of "The Secret Sharer" comes from its larger conscious awareness of the psychological process it describes; from its more deliberate use of the double as symbol. And of the two stories I happen to prefer it. But it may be the groping, fumbling "Heart of Darkness" takes us into a deeper region of the mind. If the story is not about this deeper region, and not about Marlow himself, its length is quite indefensible. But even if one were to allow that the final section is about Kurtz (which I think simply absurd), a vivid pictorial record of his unspeakable lusts and gratifications would surely have been ludicrous. I share Mr. Leavis' admiration for the heads on the stakes. But not even Kurtz could have supported many such particulars.[10]

NOTES

1. Jean-Aubry, *Life and Letters*, I, 141, and *The Sea Dreamer*, p. 175. Reportedly said to Edward Garnett. In his *Joseph Conrad in the Congo* (London, 1926), p. 73. Jean-Aubry gives a slightly different wording: "Before the Congo I was only a simple animal."

2. *Last Essays*, p. 17. In "Heart of Darkness" Conrad makes once his usual distinction between British imperialism and the imperialism of other nations. On the map in Brussels there "was a vast amount of red—good to see at any time, because one knows that some real work is done in there." His 1899 letters to E. L. Sanderson and to Mme. Angèle Zagórska on the Boer war express his position clearly. The conspiracy to oust the Briton "is ready to be hatched in other regions. It . . . is everlastingly skulking in the Far East. A war there or anywhere but in S. Africa would have been conclusive,—would have been worth the sacrifices" (Jean-Aubry, *Life and Letters*, I, 286). "That they—the Boers—are struggling in good faith for their independence cannot be doubted; but it is also a fact that they have no idea of liberty, which can only be found under the English flag all over the world" (*ibid.*, I, 288).

3. *Life and Letters*, I, 121, 124; *The Sea Dreamer*, pp. 154–159.

4. Compare "The Congo Diary." Conrad did not use the skeleton tied to a post that he saw on Tuesday, July 29 (*ibid.*, p. 79). It might have seemed too blatant or too "literary" in a novel depending on mortuary imagery from beginning to end.

5. *Life and Letters*, I, 137; *The Sea Dreamer*, p. 171.

6. F. R. Leavis, *The Great Tradition* (London, 1948), p. 183.

7. Lilian Feder finds a number of parallels with the sixth book of the *Aeneid* in "Marlow's Descent into Hell," *Nineteenth-Century Fiction*, IX (March 1955), 280–292; Robert O. Evans finds chiefly the influence of Dante's *Inferno* in "Conrad's Underworld," *Modern Fiction Studies*, II (May 1956), 56–62. My views on literary influence differ from those of Miss Feder and Mr. Evans. But echoes and overtones may exist. We may apply to "Heart of Darkness" Thomas Mann's words on *Death in Venice:* a little work of "inexhaustible allusiveness."

8. The analogy of unspeakable Kurtz and enchanted princess may well be an intended irony. But there may be some significance in the fact that this once the double is imagined as an entranced feminine figure.

9. Like any obscure human act, this one invites several interpretations, beginning with the simple washing away of guilt. The fear of the blood may be, however, a fear of the primitive toward which Marlow is moving. To throw the shoes overboard would then mean a token rejection of the savage, not the civilized-rational. In any event it seems plausible to have blood at this stage of a true initiation story.

10. The reader irritated by the hallucinated atmosphere and subjective preoccupation of "Heart of Darkness" should turn to Robert Louis Stevenson's short novel, *The Beach of Falesá* (1892). A new trader, Wiltshire, takes a native mistress, and finds himself—thanks to a rival trader (Case)— virtually excommunicated. The situation distantly resembles that of Willems in *The Outcast of the Islands*. Later, Wiltshire goes inland to discover the source of Case's power over the natives; he has heard stories that his rival worships or traffics with devils. He finds an Æolian harp in a tree (to simulate ghostly voices) and presently the place of worship:

"Along all the top of it was a line of queer figures, idols, or scarecrows, or what not. They had carved and painted faces, ugly to view, their eyes and teeth were of shell, their hair and their bright clothes blew in the wind, and some of them worked with the tugging . . .

"Then it came in my mind that Case had let out to me the first day that he was a good forger of island curiosities, a thing by which so many traders turn an honest penny. And with that I saw the whole business, and how this display served the man a double purpose: first of all, to season his curiosities and then to frighten those that came to visit him."

Had Conrad read *The Beach of Falesá* before writing "Heart of Darkness"? The question is unimportant. The important thing is to recognize the immense distance from Case's carved faces to the skulls on Kurtz's palisade; from Case's pretended traffic with devils to Kurtz's role as one of the devils of the land; from Wiltshire's canny outwitting of a rival trader to Marlow's dark inward journey; from the inert jungle of Stevenson's South Pacific to the charged symbolic jungle of Conrad's Congo. The nighttime meeting of Case and Wiltshire is merely an exciting physical struggle. *The Beach of Falesá* is a good manly yarn totally bereft of psychological intuition.

8

IAN WATT

———◆———

Story and Idea in Conrad's
The Shadow-Line

REVIEWING Conrad's first masterpiece, *The Nigger of the "Narcissus,"* Arthur Symons, though an admirer, complained nevertheless that it had "no idea behind it"; [1] and since then this objection has been fairly common. It was most memorably expressed by E. M. Forster, who reviewed Conrad's collected essays, and found that they, at least, suggested that "the secret casket of his genius contains a vapour rather than a jewel; and that we need not try to write him down philosophically, because there is, in this particular direction, nothing to write. No creed, in fact. Only opinions . . ." [2]

"Opinions" certainly; and they are often disconcertingly typical of the main social rôles to which fate successively introduced Conrad —the Polish landowner, the French clerical *ultra*, the English quarter-deck martinet. "No creed," equally certainly; the word implies theological sanctions which had no interest for Conrad, although his rather frequent use of a tone of sacerdotal commitment may explain why Forster misses in Conrad what he would surely deplore in anyone else: the only creed to which Conrad, a child of nineteenth-century scepticism, would freely have said "Amen" was Forster's own—"I do not believe in belief." As for "writing him down philosophically," Conrad certainly did his best to discourage any such enterprise: "I don't know what my philisophy [of life] is," he once wrote sardonically

This essay in a slightly different form is reprinted from *The Critical Quarterly* (Summer 1960), with the permission of the editors and the author.

to Edward Garnett, "I wasn't even aware I had it." [3] We obviously don't find in Conrad the persistent, overtly conceptualised, and often polemic, concern with philosophical issues which characterises George Eliot or Meredith; nor are we aware of any continual pressure towards making us see the universe in a special way, as we are in reading Thomas Hardy, for example, or D. H. Lawrence. And yet we surely also sense in Conrad's narratives an intense and sustained thoughtfulness, whose larger tenor may indeed, as Forster says, sometimes seem obscure, but whose seriousness nevertheless persuades us that we are in the presence of something beyond mere "opinions."

Conrad's own statements on the kind of general meanings he attempted in his fiction do not compose a clear and systematic critical theory; what is most systematic about them, indeed, is their refusal to submit to the conceptual mode of discourse. Nevertheless their essential purport remained very consistent, from the time of their first enunciation in the Preface to The Nigger of the "Narcissus." The novelist's aim is defined there as "by the power of the written word to make you hear, to make you feel—it is, before all, to make you *see*"; and the primarily descriptive nature of Conrad's purpose is then emphasised by his insistence that the aim of art is quite different from the "clear logic of a triumphant conclusion" sought by the scientist or the philosopher. What follows, however, is less often quoted, and it shows that the impressionist rendering of the world of appearances was only a beginning; Conrad's final aim was to present the "rescued fragment" of sense-impressions with "such clearness of sincerity" that "its movement, its form, and its colour, [would] reveal the substance of its truth." "The substance of its truth" has an ominously Platonic suggestion; but the nature of the ultimate "truth" which inheres in sense experience is clarified when Conrad continues that "at last the presented vision" should "awaken in the hearts of the beholders that feeling . . . of the solidarity in mysterious origin, in toil, in joy, in hope, in uncertain fate, which binds men to each other and all mankind to the visible world."

This explanation, in turn, helps to guide our interpretation of a literary aim which Conrad asserted almost as frequently as he denied having a philosophy: "all my concern has been with the 'ideal' value of things, events and people." [4] We shall return to the problem of just what he meant by "ideal values": for the moment we can at least relate it to the notion that the reader should apparently expect to discover, in the way he is made to see the particular events and characters of the narrative, something much more general, something which stands for universal elements in man's relations to his fellows and to the natural world.

Conrad's last masterpiece, *The Shadow-Line*, is one of his most typical works. The story—about how the young narrator suddenly throws up a satisfactory job as first-mate of a steamer trading in Eastern seas, only to find himself unexpectedly thrust into his first command, which turns out to be one of unique difficulty—is characteristic. Characteristic because its subject is a sea voyage; a voyage, moreover, that is, as Conrad wrote, "exact autobiography," [5] an example, like *Heart of Darkness* and *The Nigger of the "Narcissus,"* though even more literally so, of "my personal experience . . . seen in perspective with the eye of the mind"; [6] while the nature of the personal experience, moral initiation, is one of Conrad's dominant literary themes.

In general, *The Shadow-Line* is a by no means recondite piece of writing, and its main ideas are stated with such unusual explicitness that it hardly seems to call for analysis. But actually it was the lack of understanding with which *The Shadow-Line* was received that roused Conrad to complain that "after 22 years of work, I may say that I have not been very well understood." His friend Sir Sidney Colvin, for example, hesitated to review it on the odd grounds that he had no local knowledge of its setting—the Gulf of Siam; [7] while various other critics thought that it was a ghost story,[8] or merely an illustration of the "taste for the morbid" of the *English Review*, in which it was serialised.[9] Today, other misconceptions must perhaps be removed before we can fully appreciate why it was about *The Shadow-Line* that Conrad made one of his most emphatic statements of intention: "whatever dramatic and narrative gifts I may have are always, instinctively, used with that object—to get at, to bring forth *les valeurs idéales.*" [10] This affirmation, together with the story's own inherent interest and power, and the incidental fact that some of its recent commentators are also in considerable critical disagreement about it, may justify the present attempt at a further elucidation of "the ideal values" in what Conrad "admitted" to be "in its brevity a fairly complex piece of work"; [11] an attempt which may also serve to clarify the larger problem of the connection between story and idea in Conrad's work generally.

I

The first chapter of *The Shadow-Line* is mainly concerned with a petty intrigue at the Officers' Home between two of its derelicts—

the Chief Steward and a permanently unemployed ship's officer named Hamilton—an intrigue aimed at preventing the narrator, a first mate, from receiving an urgent message from the Harbour Office about the command which awaits him. The slowness of this opening has often been criticised—most recently by Albert J. Guerard in his *Conrad the Novelist:*

> *The Shadow-Line,* while written in part in the pure unpretentious prose of "The Secret Sharer," is distinctly less perfect. It gets underway very slowly and uncertainly . . . Conrad apparently conceived of *The Shadow-Line* as dealing with the passage from ignorant and untested confidence through a major trial to the very different confidence of mature self-command. So conceived, the story ought logically to have reflected, in its first pages, a naïve and buoyant confidence . . .[12]

Actually, Conrad's deliberateness is necessary for several reasons. By the time we have observed how, on his way from the docks to the Officers' Home the narrator is indifferent alike to the glare of the sun and the pleasure of the shade, we have begun to participate in his state of mind on leaving the ship; a state of mind which has been defined retrospectively in the story's opening words:

> Only the young have such moments. I don't mean the very young. No. The very young have, properly speaking, no moments. It is the privilege of early youth to live in advance of its days in all the continuity of hope which knows no pauses and no introspection.
> One closes behind one the little gate of mere boyishness—and enters an enchanted garden. Its very shades glow with promise. Every turn of the path has its seduction. And it isn't because it is an undiscovered country. One knows well enough that all mankind had streamed that way . . .
> One goes on. And the time, too, goes on—till one perceives ahead a shadow-line warning one that the region of early youth, too, must be left behind.
> This is the period of life in which such moments of which I have spoken are likely to come. What moments? Why, the moments of boredom, of weariness, of dissatisfaction. Rash moments. I mean moments when the still young are inclined to commit rash actions . . . such as throwing up a job for no reason.

One way of refusing to see the shadow-line ahead is to rebel against all involvements: and so, as the narrator comments, he "had never . . . felt more detached from all earthly goings on." This fretful self-preoccupation—and the unconscious strategy it serves—had to be very firmly established before the reader could relish the irony of the scene where

the narrator finally tells Giles that he has discovered that Hamilton
and the Steward have kept him from receiving the message from the
Harbour Office. But he is still blind to the implications of the message,
and adds that it means "nothing" to him:

> "Nothing!" repeated Captain Giles, giving some sign of quiet,
> deliberate indignation. "Kent warned me you were a peculiar young
> fellow. You will tell me next that a command is nothing to you—and
> after all the trouble I've taken, too!"
>
> "The trouble!" I murmured, uncomprehending. What trouble? All I
> could remember was being mystified and bored by his conversation for
> a solid hour after tiffin. And he called that taking a lot of trouble.
>
> He was looking at me with a self-complacency which would have
> been odious in any other man. All at once, as if a page of a book had
> been turned over disclosing a word that made plain all that had gone
> before, I perceived that this matter had also another than an ethical
> aspect . . .
>
> . . . as soon as I had convinced myself that this stale, unprofitable
> world of my discontent contained such a thing as a command to be
> seized, I recovered my powers of locomotion . . .

When Guerard, then, complains that the narrator's "irritability"
"at last becomes irritating to the reader," [13] it is surely because he
doesn't see it as part of the novel's form and meaning that the
reader should experience for himself the irritating obtuseness of the
narrator's resistance to Captain Giles's well-meaning interference, a
resistance whose narrative climax is the comically laborious double-
take over his first command, but whose ultimate function is to exhibit
for the reader the whole complex of conflicting emotions which char-
acterise the onset of that penumbral transition from late youth to
committed adulthood which is Conrad's professed subject.

As his title indicates. Conrad disliked titles that were "too literal—
too explicit"; [14] but a shadow-line has just the right degree of suggestive mutability and indeterminacy of application to stand as a
nautical metaphor for a transit through one of what Johnson called
"the climatericks of the mind." A shadow-line is not a definite boun-
dary that one crosses consciously, whether in space, like a line of
longitude, or in time: Conrad isn't dealing with the rather obvious
temporal indicators of adulthood—political or legal, like the 21st
birthday; religious, like the first communion; or biological, like sexual
maturity. The shadow-line is inward and social; approaching it one is
only aware of some vague atmospheric change, and one may not
know its cause; yet although it is mysterious and elusive, projected
almost at random through the chance collisions of the individual

with his endlessly varying environment, it has a compelling universality. The narrator, fleeing, as he puts it, from "the menace of emptiness," is really fleeing from the shades of the prison house that lie
ahead; and he tries to alter his course because pursuing the present
one—his career as first mate—obviously involves renouncing many other
aspirations; it means acknowledging an end to the youthful dream
that one will, one day, be able to achieve everything; it means, alas,
beginning to be like everybody else.

To have contemplated a successful struggle against the common
fate may—in retrospect—seem a ridiculous form of self-confidence in
the narrator. But the "naïve and buoyant confidence" of youth is rarely
as simple as Guerard seems to assume: jejune optimism alternates
with equally intense indecision and self-doubt: the human mind
will indulge in endless "artful dodges," as Marlow put it in *Lord Jim*,
"to escape from the grim shadow of self-knowledge"; [15] and one reason
for refusing to be like everybody else is the fear that one may not
even prove to be as good.

Conrad's slowness in the first chapter enables him to present all
these perplexities concretely. And there are others, for the social
perspective of the hero's situation is as important as the psychological; *The Shadow-Line*, as Carl Benson has written, is "the communal counterpart" of "The Secret Sharer";[16] and to present this
in first-person narration, "through the medium of my own emotions"
as Conrad put it,[17] means that the larger representativeness and
thematic coherence of the hero's personal relationships must be suggested through a fairly fully described sequence of encounters in
which our understanding of the pattern of motives outstrips that of
the narrator. We can then see that the narrator's three former col-
leagues on board the ship all attempted to understand and assist
him in the light of their own characters: the misogynist second-
engineer, who gloomily suspected that sex was the great shadow-line
which the narrator was approaching; the dyspeptic first engineer,
for whom the "greensickness of youth" could be cured by two bottles
of a patent liver-medicine, which he generously offered "out of his
own pocket"; the more experienced captain, who showed greater
insight in their parting interview, and added "in a peculiar, wistful
tone, that he hoped I would find what I was so anxious to go and look
for."

On ship, then, the narrator had encountered from society—but
hardly noticed—a measure of helpfulness and sympathy; he is now
equally blind to the series of warning examples which face him in
the Officers' Home: the steward, who "had been connected with the

sea. Perhaps in the comprehensive capacity of a failure"; the com-ically supine officer from the Rajah's yacht, who was a "nice boy" before he turned to indolence and debauch; and Hamilton's corrupt ineptitude, to which—in a dangerous parallel to the narrator's own case—he himself is blinded by his sense of inner superiority to the common throng. But, as on the ship, there are also well-meaning friends; and Giles serves as a climactic reminder that the solemn rites of passage which youth must endure are comically protracted by the various attempts at help and understanding by which they are cus-tomarily attended, attempts whose purpose only the peculiar psy-chology of the protagonist at this stage of life prevents him from seeing as what they are.

II

The torpid vacillations of the first chapter, then, constitute a series of concrete enactments of the narrator's initial reactions to the ironic social and spiritual divisions which are Conrad's theme. The narrator next hurries to the harbour office, and is told to proceed that evening by steamer to Bangkok, and take over a sailing ship stranded there by the death of its captain. He meets all kinds of difficulties in getting the ship ready to sail, and even when he is clear of the harbour an unseasonable lack of wind makes it impossible for him to move out into the open sea. In these four central chapters the narrator gradually comes to realise that his new rôle as captain, which he had at first envisaged as the final, total, and, indeed, magical solution of all his life-problems, actually involves an intricate network of moral im-peratives, psychological discoveries, and social responsibilities, which had until then been too abstract, too much in the future, to be real, but which now crowd thickly upon him: the shadow line has unsus-pected depth; it can't be crossed easily, or quickly.

At first, we observe, the narrator pays as little attention to Giles's gloomy prognostications as to the later warnings of the friendly doctor at Bangkok; unreasonably but understandably he clings to the belief that once out of harbour all will be well because the sea is "pure, safe and friendly." Such security, however, is more than any-one should count on; the crew's health actually gets worse as the lack of wind makes it impossible to pass the island of Koh-Ring; and the nadir is reached at the end of the fourth chapter when the narrator discovers that the remaining five quinine bottles actually contain a worthless white powder. He informs the crew of the catas-trophe, fully expecting to be overwhelmed by their anger and reproach: actually, the "temper of their souls or the sympathy of their imagina-

tion" surprises him; and it is their stoic resignation, their refusal
to see things personally, which does most to turn him away from his
egocentric sense that all is merely a plot aimed against him personally
—a plot by which he has been "decoyed into this awful, this death-
haunted command."

Before then there had already been some signs of human inter-
dependence, and of the narrator's growing awareness of it. In contrast to the moral intransigence he had showed towards the steward
at the Officers' Home, he had listened to his sick first mate Burns's
plea "You and I are sailors," and allowed him, sick as he was, to
come back from hospital on to the ship, even though Burns, like
Hamilton, had been his rival for the command, and was now so
broken in body and mind that his mere presence on board ship was
a serious hindrance. But when the crisis comes, Mr. Burns isn't
wholly a dead loss: he steadies the narrator by telling him that it's
"very foolish, sir" to feel guilty about the quinine; and he unwittingly
seconds Giles's earlier advice about keeping to the east side of the
Gulf of Siam.

It is, however, to the clear-sighted persistence of Ransome that
the protagonist is most indebted. In the fifth chapter, after two weeks
of being virtually becalmed, Ransome points out "a broad shadow
on the horizon extinguishing the lower stars completely," and the
narrator realises that there are not enough fit men to prepare the
boat for the coming squall. Overwhelmed by the depth of his "contempt for that obscure weakness of my soul [under the] stress of
adversity," he goes below in a state of paralysed remorse and confesses in his diary: "What appals me most of all is that I shrink from
going on deck to face it . . . I always suspected I might be no
good. . . ." Gradually, however, he becomes aware that Ransome is
lingering "in the cabin as he had something to do there, but hesitated
about doing it." Hesitates long enough to make the narrator ask "You
think I ought to be on deck," to which Ransome replies "without
any particular emphasis or accent: 'I do, sir.' "

It is the final nudge into the realisation that command means
self-command. They go on deck, and the narrator finds in "the impenetrable blackness" a sense of "the closing in of a menace from all
sides."

It is in this crisis that we are closest to the Jungian analogy suggested by Guerard. The darkness of the night and the narrator's
despair certainly receive sufficient emphasis to suggest a symbolic
intent; and even to lend some support to the interpretation of *The
Shadow-Line* as essentially concerned, like "The Secret Sharer," with

an "archetypal . . . night journey" [18] which eventually causes the protagonist to subdue those aspects of his personality "which interfere with seamanship."

"The dark night of the soul" seems to be getting even more of a nuisance than the "Dark Lady of the Sonnets" used to be. The objection is not that it doesn't exist—metaphors exist once they are made—but rather that the seductive concreteness of the phrase deludes its hierophants into thinking that they have gained more than they have when the analogy has enabled them to reduce the literary work to less than it is: in the present case, to find *The Shadow-Line* inferior to "The Secret Sharer" primarily because, being much longer, it resists reduction to a single symbolic paradigm even more vigorously.

Actually, Conrad's emphasis in *The Shadow-Line* is not specifically on the forces which interfere with seamanship, but on something much more general—on "an ordeal . . . which had been maturing and tempering my character." It is true that the narrator often feels that he is a failure as captain: but this, and his consequent sense of guilt, is, as far as we can judge, a subjective—and typical—reaction to the difficulties of a first command; from the time that the doctor in Bangkok compliments him on his "very judicious arrangements," we have no reason to doubt that the narrator is right in saying that "the seaman's instinct alone survived whole in my moral dissolution."

The darkness and immobility of the night do not, of course, in themselves require symbolic explanation. The increment of suspense and pictorial vividness would be justified for its own sake; it is in keeping with Conrad's frequent use of darkness for his narrative climax; and it may well have been dark when the actual events occurred which served as basis for the story. But if one looks for larger meanings, for symbolic representations of universal elements in man's relations to his fellows and to the natural world, there are several which are clearly relevant to the main implications of the narrative. The calm before the storm, and the intensified darkness that precedes dawn, are well enough established commonplaces of human experience; and here they derive a particular significance from the fact that the calm is the climax of the long period of calm since leaving port, and that the darkness is the climax of the longer inner darkness which began when the leading edge of the shadow-line began to trouble the narrator's youthful horizon.[19]

The calm, of course, has its psychological parallel in the narrator's prolonged inward lethargy, a parallel to which Conrad draws attention in the epigraph; in Baudelaire's sonnet "La Musique" the poet's quest for "ma pâle étoile" is most deeply menaced, not by tempests

but by the "calme plat" which is the "great mirror of his despair."
More widely, the alternating rhythm of calm and storm is the equivalent in the natural order of a human perspective to which Conrad was
uniquely attentive—the duality of rest and work; of the solicitations
of inertia and the impulsions to action. In the beginning the narrator's
deepest yearnings, in his inarticulate revulsion from the "mortal
coil," [20] were for repose; later, on his way to the harbour office, he
found "something touching about a ship . . ." folding her white wings
for a rest," and then heard that Captain Ellis had attributed his delay
in coming to "funking . . . too much work."

Once at sea, the solicitations of the most extreme form of inertia,
death, increasingly pervade the consciousness of the narrator. In
the brilliant passage where he goes down to tell Burns about the
quinine, for instance, he at first mistakes his glimpse of Burns trim-
ming his beard with a pair of scissors as an attempt at suicide; while
shortly afterwards Burns's ageworn look causes him to reflect: "Envi-
able man! So near extinction." Later, when Ransome comes to report
on the darkening sky, the narrator thinks that the message must be
that "Someone's dead"; and when he finally goes up to prepare for
the squall he welcomes the utter calm and darkness of the night as
an image of death:

> When the time came the blackness would overwhelm silently the bit
> of starlight falling upon the ship, and the end of all things would come
> without a sigh, stir, or murmur of any kind, and all our hearts would
> cease to beat like run-down clocks . . . The quietness that came over
> me was like a foretaste of annihilation. It gave me a sort of comfort, as
> though my soul had become suddenly reconciled to an eternity of blind
> stillness.

It was this particular implication of the shadow-line which led
Conrad's wife to object to his title on the grounds that it suggested
the Psalmist's "valley of the shadow of death." [21] But death is only one
of the terrors which occupy the narrator's mind as he waits in the
"blackness which had swallowed up our world" for the heavens to
declare themselves; most obviously he experiences an unforgettable
reminder of man's precarious exposure to the unpredictable power
of the natural order as a whole; and the importance of this exposure
to the idea of the shadow-line was suggested in a letter which Conrad
wrote to his relative and intimate friend Marguerite Poradowska:
"One always thinks oneself important at twenty. The fact is, however, that one becomes useful only on realising the utter insignificance of the individual in the scheme of the universe." [22]

On the other hand, confronting his own "utter insignificance" in the natural order heightens the narrator's awareness of his need for the support of his fellows. This is brought home, for instance, in the scene when, after the mainsail has been hauled up close and the mainyard squared, Ransome comes to report, and then, suddenly "stepped back two paces and vanished from my sight" out of the light of the binnacle lamps. Shaken, the narrator

> moved forward too, outside the circle of light, into the darkness that stood in front of me like a wall. In one stride I penetrated it. Such must have been the darkness before creation. It had closed behind me. I knew I was invisible to the man at the helm. Neither could I see anything. He was alone, I was alone, every man was alone where he stood.

Here the vivid realization of complete human isolation in "the darkness before creation," evokes the historical dimension of the theme of human solidarity; the narrator, having been deprived, first through the loneliness of command, and then through darkness, of the support of his fellows, is brought face to face with the long tradition of civilisation since the creation, and his own utter dependence on it.

III

The historical perspective of the shadow-line has, of course, made its appearance much earlier in the narrative. For instance, as soon as the protagonist had boarded his ship, he had sat down alone in the Captain's chair, and it had occurred to him that: "A succession of men had sat in that chair"; then, reflected in the cabin mirror, he had observed his own face "rather with curiosity than with any other feeling, except of some sympathy for this latest representative of what for all intents and purposes was a dynasty; continuous, not in blood indeed, but in its experience, in its training, in its conception of duty, and in the blessed simplicity of its traditional point of view on life."

F. R. Leavis, in a Conrad centenary address largely devoted to *The Shadow-Line*, comments that this passage "very soon takes on in retrospect a profoundly ironic significance." It is true that the preceding symbol of the nautical hierarchy soon proves to have completely betrayed it, acting with a complete disregard of his ship, its crew and its owners, and even selling the vital quinine so that he could "cut adrift from everything" and pursue his own individual inclinations—sexual, in his squalid amour with the horrible female in Haiphong, and artistic, with his verse-writing and his final allegiance only to his violin. Ironical, therefore, it certainly is, that the narrator should look to this particular symbolic precursor for support. But Leavis is surely wrong in making the former captain an example of how the seaman's career had not in itself "given him fulfilment"; [23] he had failed it, not it him. In any case we should be careful before taking the irony too far, since, although it is a sign of youthful illusion to expect more from its elders than they can give, it is also a sign of maturity not to reject the inheritance of the past merely because we have discovered the imperfections of its human representatives. Dynastic, like apostolic successions, must always make a distinction between the man and the rôle; and the traditional definition of the rôle represents a value about which Conrad was the last man to be ironical, however acute and indeed obsessive his awareness of the fullness with which its actual human representatives partake of the frailty of their kind.

The late captain's lurid defections enforce the point that the tradition of the past is not handed over purged of man's selfishness and weakness; and the idea is later reinforced by the eerie presence on deck of Burns's gibbering death's head when the squall finally comes and "suddenly, the darkness turned into water." Nevertheless the mind of the narrator is sustained, and the story as a whole enacts, how the narrator finds "his place in a line of men whom he did not know, of whom he had never heard; but who were fashioned by the same influences, whose souls in relation to their humble life's work had no secrets for him."

One of F. R. Leavis's main aims in the essay is to emphasise that Conrad does not merely wish to preach the master mariner's "glamorless routine doggedly taken." Of course; but although Conrad would not have argued the equivalence of moral maturity and the acceptance of the seaman's code, he would surely have poured his wrath on anyone who proposed them as alternatives. Leavis tends to do so, in his wish to underline how Conrad stands for something more than "any mere vocational ethos"; [24] while, much more misleadingly, Guerard succumbs to the same dichotomy in an opposite direction by seeing "the conclusion" as "simply that . . . we cannot be good seamen, alone with our ships, until we have faced out, recognised, and subdued those selves which interfere with seamanship." [25] But Conrad's presentation surely denies the relevance of such oppositions: the problems of the narrator's first command are not peculiar, essentially, to seamen; an awareness of the unsuspected multiplicity of reciprocal obligations is surely one in which all mankind partakes in its measure once it leaves youth behind, although most of all when it assumes responsibility for the lives of others; as Conrad suggested in his dedication: "To Borys and all others who like himself have crossed in early youth the shadow-line of their generation."

The terms of this dedication emphasise one aspect of the generality of the story's main theme. Conrad had long planned to relate his own first voyage as captain from Bangkok to Singapore in 1888; but when he came to write the story, nearly thirty years later, what had been personal, autobiographical, and particular took on so much larger a significance that it encompassed his own eighteen-year old son's taking up the dynastic inheritance as an officer at the front in the first World War; and what was originally to have been called "First Command" became *The Shadow-Line*.

Conrad, then, is dealing with a particular version of a more general shadow-line which, under a host of different social and individual and historical circumstances, is traversed whenever youth's idealised image of the world, of itself and of its own destiny is penetrated and modified by its sense of solidarity with those who, in the past and in the present, continue man's struggle against all the powers of darkness and anarchy which pervade the natural, the historical, the social, and the personal order. And Conrad is being realistic rather than ironic— if the distinction be allowed—in presenting all the forces opposed to human solidarity so powerfully.

Burns, for example, stands for much more than the force of rivalry in advancement; his superstitious terror of the dead captain, lying in wait for the ship in latitude 8° 20′ (his place of burial), is no doubt the main reason why some critics thought that Conrad was invoking the supernatural; but in fact Burns makes a much more complex—and realistic—contribution to Conrad's theme: Burns's madness is a corruption of the legitimate power of the past over the present; his supernatural fears are a common enough caricature of a proper sense of what, in his "Author's Note," Conrad called "the intimate delicacies of our relation to the dead"; and, just as this superstitious awe is an indication of Burns's own incapacity, so it awakens uneasy echoes in the narrator's mind when he is obsessed with his own sense of powerlessness. Burns's conviction that no progress will be possible until they have passed the particular latitude where the captain was buried is itself a superstitious version of the shadow-line, the shadow-line that Burns himself is afraid to cross; while Burns's final diabolic laugh in the teeth of the squall is essentially only a melodramatic form of the hysteria in the face of impotence and terror which the narrator himself has just undergone.

The narrator, of course, needs these warning lessons: he must learn that neither the dynastic past—the dead captain—nor the present —his sick and demented first mate—live up to his ideal. But this discovery has by now been complemented by another—neither does he. Blame and regret, however, are equally futile, and in any case the reciprocities of inadequacy are not unqualified: in these depths of the narrator's self-accusation about the quinine it is the combination of Burns's pressure, the crew's understanding, and Ransome's direct intervention, which makes him shake off the sense of drifting impotence and betrayal; he determines: "Remorse must wait. I must steer"; and steering, as Conrad has earlier reminded us, is "a symbol of mankind's claim to the direction of its own fate."

So, with only himself and Ransome able to handle the anchors, the ship eventually arrives at Singapore. Conrad's thought has altered a good deal from *Lord Jim*: conceit and error and guilt are universal, but their consequences, it seems, are not irredeemable; we are all in the same boat with them, and with sickness and death, but, if we sieze our fleeting and partial opportunities, we can steer.

Here, of course, it is Ransome's "contained serenity" in the face of the most extreme physical disablement—a weak heart—which represents most fully the true dynastic inheritance. Ransome has learned to live with awareness of death, "schooled himself into a systematic control of feelings and movements"; and later, for all his devotion to duty, he asserts, "in a blue funk about [his] heart," that he "has a right," to leave the ship. Thus the narrator glimpsed at the human level what the blackness of night had suggested at the natural level—the bitterest of all the lessons of the shadow-line— the reality of death; and death, in Sir Walter Raleigh's words, is "he that puts into man all the wisdom of the world, without speaking a word." [26]

Sickness and death, then, accompany the ship's final rush into port; and in the course of this severely qualified victory both the narrator and the reader experience intense and grateful recognition of the varied efforts that have enabled the ship, after all, to survive; a sense which overwhelms the narrator when his crew is carried off to hospital, but which he has already expressed to Ransome: "I and the ship, and everyone on board of her, are very much indebted to you."

The debt, however, is soon a matter of past history, and the narrator takes on another crew to continue his voyage. There is no heroic finality; and in the narrator's last interview with Giles we can find no warrant for believing that the shadow-line is crossed once and forever; we are never, as witness the late captain, in the clear; nor are the forces of inertia ever wholly vanquished. The narrator "feels old"; he has learned Giles's lesson that there's "precious little rest in life for anybody"; he can even confess that "God only knows" whether he feels "faint-hearted" or not. Further—and most troubling of all— he still cannot be absolutely sure that he has become a full member of the dynasty. We see this in the ironic resurgence of the earlier friction between Giles and the narrator; for, after he's told Giles that he'll be "off at daylight tomorrow," and Giles has replied in his bluff, avuncular way, "You will . . . That's the way . . . You'll do," the narrator, "irritated by his tone," retorts: "What did you expect?"

IV

Whether the ideas I have attributed to *The Shadow-Line* are true or interesting, and whether (and how) Conrad made them seem so, are not directly within my present purview. That they fit into Conrad's general thought could certainly be supported by reference to his other works and to his correspondence; and one would also find evidence there for the view that Conrad is a symbolic writer only in the sense that his narratives have a larger meaning, though one which is not a matter of obscure and esoteric secrets, but only of extending and generalising the implications of his "things, events and people." That is, Conrad deals in the kind of symbolism for which I have elsewhere [27] suggested the term *homeophoric*—"carrying something similar," as opposed to *heterophoric*, "carrying something else"—as the larger import of the tale's literal meaning. To interpret the story in terms of Jung, or of the supernatural, would be *heterophoric;* it would take us *away* to *another* meaning and would slight the literal one; whereas the homeophoric interpretation would be wholly consistent with the kind of expansion of particular narrative implications suggested by Conrad in his "Author's Note": "when we begin to meditate on the meaning of our past it seems to fill all the world in its profundity and its magnitude."

Obviously many of the details in *The Shadow-Line* are there only because they were part of Conrad's memories of the past. But three decades of experience so guided the process of discovery, selection and emphasis that out of what Conrad himself called "the mere material" of the story there arose a work which is perhaps the finest

example of what Conrad meant by "bringing out *les valeurs idéales*"
—the French makes much clearer than does "ideal values" in English
that it is not, at least not directly, a question of ethical ideals, but
merely of trying to perceive and make visible the significance of a
particular individual experience: trying to "get the idea" and make
us "get it."

In that sense Conrad must be considered a philosophic writer;
and, although his frequent jests at those who tried to turn him into
a philosopher once took the form—"There is even one abandoned
creature who says I am a neo-platonist.[28] What on earth is that?"—
the analogy to Plato may serve to clarify Conrad's position. For in
the end there is something Platonic about Conrad's concern with
"ideal values"; with his insistence, for example, in the case of *The
Shadow-Line,* that the "twilight region between youth and maturity"
has certain features which are as universal as Plato's Forms. He
does not, of course, make the metaphysical assertion that these universal features are part of a unified, harmonious, and timeless system;
nor is he much concerned with the ethical preachment that we ought
to devote our lives to trying to attain them. Indeed, since the narrator
does not, after leaving the "enchanted garden," achieve "that special
intensity of existence which is the quintessence of youthful aspirations,"
we are at liberty to see the shadow-line as only the process which age
calls "settling down" but youth calls "selling out." We misread Conrad if we see his recall of vanished youthful turmoil as sharing the
vatic complacency of the initiate who has completed his analysis;
the protagonist doesn't come out on the other side of the shadow-line
into another "enchanted garden"; "experience," as he says, "means
always something disagreeable, as opposed to the charm and innocence
of illusions"; the loss of Eden brings painful exactions, not opportunities for realising dreams. So, if Conrad gives the impression, as Virginia Woolf put it, that his characters are "tested by their attitude to
august abstractions" [29] it is not because he has a "creed" but because
that is his observation of what life does: everyone in *The Shadow-Line*
is judged by the events. Conrad is not concerned to tell us that the
various general features which he discerns in the experience of the
narrator are inherently good or bad, but only that they are there;
and if we retort "So what?", shrugs agreement.

Conrad's "ideal values," then, are not intended to be ethical or
normative; and the fact that he does not bridge the gap from "is"
to "ought" is one reason why Conrad disappoints those who expect
him to have a "philosophy." Another reason is that his work falls far

short of conceptual synthesis. This is not in itself inconsistent with
the Platonic analogy: Plato thought you could not hope to describe
the Ideas, but only to guide your hearers in such a way that they
might eventually see them for themselves. But, of course, Conrad himself doesn't pretend to more than partial glimpses of any universals, and
what Marlow says of Stein's wisdom in *Lord Jim* defines only one
of the directions in Conrad's narrative: "we had approached nearer
to absolute Truth, which, like Beauty itself, floats elusive, obscure,
half-submerged, in the silent still waters of mystery." [30] Conrad's
other major narrative direction, of course, lies in the vivid presentation of empirical reality; and that is perhaps why there are, as Forster
puts it, "constant discrepancies between his nearer and his further
vision." "If," Forster remarks, Conrad "lived only in his experiences,
never lifting his eyes to what lies beyond them: or if, having seen what
lies beyond, he would subordinate his experiences to it—then in either
case he would be easier to read." [31] Conrad lets us look beyond, but
never in such a way as to subordinate actuality; and the actualities
of life, especially as he learned to see them through English eyes,
were to be respected, even if they fell short of more romantic and
ideal expectations. He was, after all, a Platonist who fell among em-
piricists; a Pole cast among Anglo-Saxons.

Conrad, then, is like many great writers, a philosopher only in the
sense that his own retrospective awareness of the continuities and
discontinuities of human experience can enlighten ours; and *The
Shadow-Line* is perhaps the most successful realisation of Conrad's
achievement in this direction. Many people, it may be hazarded,
have stumbled, first with chagrin, and later, if they are fortunate,
with re-assurance, on the discovery that most of their thoughts and
deeds are not unique, but are linked in many ways with those of the
dead and of those who are merely nearer death; that the reciprocity
is real, even though we never receive, as we never bestow, the full
measure of recognition; and that some elements of that reciprocity,
however qualified, are still, to adapt Conrad's phrase on the title
page, worthy of our mortal yet undying regard. In *The Shadow-Line*
Conrad overwhelms us with these realisations; but he also accompanies them with various melancholy ironies: for one thing, the
dynasties of experience are fragile, corruptible and intermittent; for
another, despite the Existentialist version of the shadow-line, we
do not choose our solidarities with the past and the present, but
come to them—as we come into the world—involuntarily and unconsciously: are usually, indeed, dragged into them, screaming.

NOTES

1. *Saturday Review*, LXXXV (1898), 145–6.
2. "Joseph Conrad: a Note," *Abinger Harvest* (London, 1946), p. 135.
3. *Letters from Conrad, 1895–1924*, ed. Edward Garnett (London, 1928), p. 199.
4. G. Jean-Aubry, *Joseph Conrad: Life and Letters* (London, 1927), II, 185.
5. *Life and Letters*, II, 181, 182.
6. "Author's Note," in *Collected Edition of the Works of Joseph Conrad* (J. M. Dent: London, 1950), vii.
7. *Life and Letters*, II, 185; II, 182.
8. See "Author's Note," v; *Life and Letters*, II, 195
9. *Life and Letters*, II, 181.
10. *Life and Letters*, II, 185.
11. "Author's Note," v.
12. Cambridge: Harvard University Press, 1958, p. 30.
13. *Conrad the Novelist*, p. 32.
14. *Letters from Conrad*, p. 298.
15. *Collected Edition*, p. 80.
16. "Conrad's Two Stories of Initiation," *PMLA*, LXIX (1954), 46.
17. *Life and Letters*, II, 184.
18. *Conrad the Novelist*, pp. 30–31.
19. David Bone assumes a literal shadow-line—the "darkling in the sea, the reflex of a wind in motion" which at last takes the ship out of the doldrums—the lull between trade winds. (*A Conrad Memorial Library*, ed. George T. Keating, Garden City, New York, 1929, pp. 255–260.) But it is unlikely that anything so literal is intended: the narrator, for instance, speaks of how, ever since he set sail, "all my life before that momentous day is infinitely remote, a fading memory of light-hearted youth, something on the other side of a shadow" (p. 106).
20. P. 73. This is, appropriately, but one of the many phrases from *Hamlet* in *The Shadow-Line*; e.g. "undiscovered country," p. 3; "stale, unprofitable world," p. 28; "out of joint," p. 84.
21. *Joseph Conrad and his Circle* (London, 1935), pp. 193–4. The reference is to Psalm XXIII, 4.
22. *Letters of Joseph Conrad to Marguerite Poradowska, 1890–1920*, ed. Gee and Sturm (New Haven, 1940), p. 45.
23. "Joseph Conrad," *The Sewanee Review*, LXVI (1958), p. 196, p. 197.
24. Pp. 198, 193.
25. P. 31.
26. *The History of the World*, Book V, chapter 6, section 12.
27. "Conrad Criticism and *The Nigger of the 'Narcissus',*" *Nineteenth-Century Fiction*, XII (1958), 257–283.
28. *Letters from Conrad*, p. 226.
29. "Mr. Conrad: A Conversation," *The Captain's Death Bed and Other Essays* (London, 1950), p. 76.
30. *Collected Edition*, p. 216.
31. *Abinger Harvest*, p. 137.

9

R. P. BLACKMUR

The King over the Water:
Notes on the Novels of F. M. Hueffer

It would seem now, after re-reading some seven or eight of his novels, that Ford Madox Hueffer belonged to that race of novelists whose facility for the mere act of writing is so great that their minds never quite catch up with the job under way, and whose writing seldom stops on the difficulties that make the job worth doing. If you have the ease of too much talent you cannot benefit from the hardships of genius. Twenty years ago and more, when these novels were first read, nothing of this sort could have been said by the present writer. Let us see along what lines it has become possible now.

Ford Madox Hueffer—or Ford Madox Ford; to me he remains Hueffer—wrote a great many novels, publishing the first at the age of nineteen, and between 1920 and 1928 I read as many as I could lay hands on, without ever a twinge of reaction which might lead to judgment until it was asked for in the present circumstance. The twinge will appear later, but I do not think it will reach judgment; I do not think Hueffer was the kind of writer who takes to being judged much, because he did not display the materials, or the order of materials, suitable to our means of judgment; the twinge is enough.

Meanwhile, there is the memory of reading, and how it came

Reprinted from *The Princeton University Library Chronicle* (IX, 3) with the permission of the editors and the author.

about. Joseph Conrad just then, in 1920, had come to the height
of his reputation with *The Rescue,* and in reading Conrad one found
that he had twice collaborated with Hueffer, in *Romance* and in *The
Inheritors.* These being read and indiscriminately admired, one went
on and read *The Good Soldier* out of curiosity to see what Hueffer
was like all by himself, and came out with an admiration out of all
proportion. Hueffer at the time seemed to belong to a group: he
belonged to Conrad, W. H. Hudson, Stephen Crane; but that was
only part of it, for he belonged also to Henry James, Ezra Pound,
and T. S. Eliot; he belonged to two generations and to the bridge
that over-arched them. He occupied, mysteriously but evidently, all
the interstices between all the members of both groups, and somehow contributed an atmosphere in which all of them were able to
breathe. He had something to do with the *life,* the genuineness, of the
literature written between *Lord Jim* and *The Waste Land,* between
The Dynasts and *Ulysses.* All this was actual enough at the time; *The
English Review,* dug up and read in old numbers, and *the transatlantic
review,* both of which Hueffer edited, make the history stand. Yet to
think of Hueffer in this way involved a view of him which has little
of the truth in it that goes beyond history, the kind of truth which
must somehow be our subject here. Atmospheres do not last, and
can be re-created only in the living memory. Ford Madox Hueffer
bore no real relation to Conrad and Hudson except the editorial relation; he had in his own writing, what corresponds there to the editorial, he had the relation of the chameleon-response to them. When
his work was in the felt presence of their work, the skin of his writing
changed color accordingly. What he responded with was partly the
stock baggage of English literature and partly his own sensibility. I do
not see how anybody who had not read Conrad and James could
see what Hueffer was up to by way of form and style in their separable
senses, or for that matter how anybody not knowing Conrad and
James could feel the impact of Hueffer's sensibility attempting to
articulate itself in terms of what it had absorbed of theirs. Without
that knowledge, Hueffer's novels seem stock and even hack on the
formal side and freakish or eccentric on the side of sensibility.

All this is summary description of the sensibility articulated in
The Good Soldier, and in the four novels of which Christopher Tietjens
is the central character, *Some Do Not, No More Parades, A Man
Could Stand Up,* and *Last Post.* The first was published in 1915, the
Tietjens novels in the early twenties. Aside from *Romance,* written
in collaboration with Conrad, I take it that these novels are what

we mean when we speak of Hueffer as a novelist. If they stand, we
have to put beside them at least one Utopian fantasy, *Ladies Whose
Bright Eyes* (1911) and perhaps the late Napoleonic romance, *A
Little Less than Gods* (1928); because his serious novels lie always
between fantasy and romance. *Ladies Whose Bright Eyes* is gay, light,
tender: the fantasy of a commercially-minded London publisher (himself a fantasy rather than a caricature of the type) transported in a
traumatic dream to the England of 1326; in terms of which, when he
wakes, he undergoes a kind of backwards conversion, and unearths
a corner of fourteenth-century Utopia in modern England. *A Little
Less than Gods* is the historical romance of an Englishman who finds
himself, a kind of chivalrous traitor, in the service of Napoleon between Elba and Waterloo; it is pompous, stuffy, and sloppy both
as romance and as history; but is written, so the dedicatory letter
says, in the belief that it is—or means to be—a true sight of history.
Each of these books has something to do with the glory of an arbitrary
prestige resting on values asserted but not found in the actual world:
values which when felt critically deform rather than enlighten action
in that world, so that the action ends in the destruction of the values
themselves. Like the idea of Napoleon, such values have all the greatness possible without virtue, and like the Napoleonic and the medieval
ideas, they have genuine and universal popularity. Many people—or
parts of many people—find life tolerable only because they think it is
like that; other people find literature tolerable only if it furnishes
such ideas for getting back at life. In writing light novels—more or
less unconscious pot-boilers—in the exemplification of such ideas,
Hueffer was certainly on the track of what people want in a light and
preoccupied way.

In his serious novels, *The Good Soldier* and the novels about Tietjens
listed above, what makes them serious is that these same ideas are
treated seriously, with all the fanaticism that goes with fresh conversion or the sore point of fixed prejudice. Edward Ashburnham, the
hero of *The Good Soldier,* is an extravagant princely sensualist, a
wrecker of lives in the pursuit of life; he is also a soldier and he is
seen by the narrator as a model of glory—a glory which is brought
to a climax when, because his manners make it impossible to accept
the body of a young girl brought up in his house, he cuts his throat
and drives the young girl mad. Edward is feudal and Protestant; what
modern Protestant feudalism cannot do to ruin him through his
sensuality is done for him by his wife's Roman Catholicism. Feudalism,
sensuality, Roman Catholicism, are, all three, forces which prevent

the people in this book from coping with the real world and which exacerbate their relations to it.

In the Tietjens novels Toryism replaces feudalism, as it is the modern form of it, and as Tietjens is a Tory public servant in a world of 1914, or Lloyd George, liberalism; the sensuality is given to the wife rather than to the husband; the wife, being both Roman Catholic and sensualist, is thus more exacerbated than the wife in *The Good Soldier*. Otherwise the ideas are much the same. The virtues of the deprived Tory and the deprived Catholic are seen as the living forms of damnation. The Tory becomes the object of undeserved scandal, leading to disinheritance and his father's suicide, and thus, as a result *only* of his held beliefs as to the proper relations between father, son, and brother in a Tory family, to his own ruin. For her part, the Catholic sensualist becomes a bitch *manquée*, that is to say, an unmotivated destroyer of her own goods. There is not a person of account in the four volumes who is not animated by principle so high as to be a vocation from his or her point of view; but there is not a decent, frank, or satisfying relation between any two of them till the very end; principles get in the way by determining rather than formulating or judging values in conflict. Yet these principles are shown as admirable and exemplary in Christopher Tietjens, and exemplary if not wholly admirable in his wife Sylvia. Indeed the world is shown as in conspiracy against these principles—with the war of 1914–1918 as a particularly foul part of the conspiracy. The war, in presented fact, is only a kind of international Whiggery and interested scandal-mongering—all but those aspects of it which permit Christopher Tietjens to follow the Lord and behave like a princely Yorkshire Tory gentleman. Surely, if we want an easy name for this sort of thing, it is romanticism in reverse; it is the Faustian spirit of mastery turned suicidal on contact with classical clichés; it is also to say that these serious novels are only an intensified form of whatever happens when you put together the ideas of the medieval fantasy and the Napoleonic romance.

What intensifies them is, what we began by saying, the relation they bear to the work of his two immediate masters. And this is to say that Hueffer is a minor novelist in the sense that his novels would have little existence without the direct aid and the indirect momentum of the major writers upon whom he depended. He dealt with loyalty and the conflict of loyalties like Conrad, he dealt with fine consciences and hideously brooked sensualities like James. But all the loyalty he did not find heightened by Conrad was obstinacy, and all the conscience and sensuality he did not find created by James were priggery and moral suicide. Adding this to what has already been said of the chief novels, makes a terrible simplification: it says that Hueffer supplied only the excesses of his characters' vices and virtues, and only the excesses of their situations; and it suggests that his sensibility was unmoored, or was moored only in the sense that a sensibility may be moored to lost causes known to be lost.

Known to be lost. If there is an image upon which Hueffer's sensibility can be seen to declare its own force it is in an image of devotion to lost causes known to be lost; that is what his more serious novels dramatize, that is what his characters bring to their conflicts and situations, otherwise viable, to make them irremediable—for the law is already gone that could provide a remedy. In politics and philosophy we call this the cultivation of ancestral Utopias; in literature, since we can recognize these cultivations with the pang of actuality, they make a legitimate, though necessarily always subordinate, subject matter. They are real, these causes known to be lost—as real as the King over the Water—but they depend for their reality on their relation to causes not lost, much as history depends on the present which it disturbs, not for its truth but for its validity. So it is with Hueffer's novels; the validity of his dramatizations of men and women devoted to causes known to be lost depends on our sense of these same causes in the forms in which they are still to be struggled for. To the purposes of his obsession he chose the right masters in Conrad and James. His lost English Catholic women, his lost English Tories, his lost medievalists and his strange inventions of lost Americans, depend on Conrad's sailors and James's ladies and gentlemen (since they are not men and women) of the world—in whom only the milieu, the ambience of positive sensibility, is strange or lost. The difference is that where the people in Conrad and James are beaten by the life to which they are committed and by the great society of which they believe themselves to be at heart, in Hueffer the people are beaten because they believe themselves animated by loyalties and consciences utterly alien to the life and the society in which they find themselves. Not only their fate, but also their ideals are intolerable to them. They make of their *noblesse oblige* the substance as well as the instrument of their damnation. They are ourselves beside ourselves the wrong way; and they are so because the sensibility of the novels is identical with that of the characters; there is no foil or relief, whether of aspiration or of form; only that terrible facility with the medium which goes with causes known to be lost.

That is the twinge of reaction that comes in re-reading Hueffer's novels; that as an artist as well as a man he knew his causes to be lost: which is why he had to be facile, and why he could not supply his novels with the materials for judgment. You cannot judge the King over the Water, however, you may feel a twinge at the toast proposed.

10

ROBIE MACAULEY

Parade's End

THE YEAR before he died Ford Madox Ford used to walk around the campus at Olivet College like a pensioned veteran of forgotten wars. We took him for a kind of vast, benevolent and harmless Uncle Toby, leaning on his stick in class or sitting in his dark little basement office and wheezing out his stories of Henry James as Toby might have spoken of Marlborough. His books seemed like medals achieved, perhaps, in the Crimea; and we read Auden, Kafka, Evelyn Waugh.

We were no different from the rest of the world. We knew vaguely that his Tietjens books were about the first World War and we suspected that they might be a good enough account of a soldier's disillusioning experiences—but we had read all that before. If any of us went far enough to look at the introductory letter to *A Man Could Stand Up—*, the third in the series, he would find Ford confirming it:

"This is what the late war was like: this is how modern fighting of the organized, scientific type affects the mind. If, for reasons of gain, or, as is still more likely out of dislike for collective types other than your own, you choose to permit your rulers to embark on another war, this—or something very accentuated along similar lines—is what you will have to put up with! I hope, in fact, that this series of books, for what it is worth, may make war seem undesirable."

Reprinted from Robie Macauley's "Introduction" to *Parade's End* by Ford Madox Ford, by permission of Alfred A. Knopf, Inc. Copyright 1950 by Alfred A. Knopf, Inc.

A little afterward some of us went to war ourselves and later, coming back, took Ford's novels down from the shelf to see if his easy prediction had come true. It seemed impossible that we could have been so wrong.

For some peculiar reason of his own he had hoaxed us; he was neither benevolent nor harmless and his books were by no means a simple warning as to what modern warfare is like. To read the Tietjens story for that would be like going through Henry James to improve one's manners or through Conrad to learn how to navigate a ship.

Nevertheless, this is the way the novels were taken when they were first published. They were thought to be books of "experiences" and they sold well. The reaction came when Ford's readers discovered that what he had actually given them was not another *Under Fire* or *What Price Glory?* but something complex and baffling. There was a love story with no passionate scenes; there were trenches but no battles; there was a tragedy without a denouement. Ford was quickly and easily forgotten.

We are a little older now and perhaps a little less superficial. We have been living a little longer with the great, enveloping tragedy Ford set out to describe. Perhaps in this edition we can take a second look at the Tietjens story and discover that it is less about the incident of a single war than about a whole era, more about our own world than his.

II

"The two young men—they were of the English public official class—sat in the perfectly appointed railway carriage." So begins the Tietjens story. Everything is excellent, comfortable, predictable: the leather window straps are of virgin newness, the mirrors immaculate, as if they had reflected very little, the upholstery a luxuriant scarlet and yellow design, the air smelling faintly of varnish. The train runs as smoothly as (Tietjens thinks) British gilt-edged securities. Moreover, the two young men are of the class that administers the world. "If they saw a policeman misbehave, railway porters lack civility, an insufficiency of street lamps, defects in public services or in foreign countries, they saw to it either with nonchalant Balliol voices or with letters to the *Times*, asking with regretful indignation, 'Has the British This or That come to *this?*'" Under their care are manners, the arts, diplomacy, inter-imperial trade and the personal reputations of prominent men. They do not realize that their train has got on the wrong line.

Actually it is not running from London to Rye as they think, but from the past into the future, and ahead of them on their one-way journey is a chaotic country of ripped battlefields and disordered towns. Their fellow-passengers will grow hysterical and unpredictable, station masters will put up the wrong signals, troops will come aboard and get off again, the good furnishings of the train will get worn and broken, the schedule will go to pieces. And, experiencing all this, Christopher Tietjens will learn to expect that somewhere, beyond some bridge or tunnel, the tracks themselves will finally disappear into the dry sands of the wasteland.

But to begin where Ford did we must return to take a look at the unsuspecting passenger as he sits in his comfortable seat at the start of the journey. The beginning of the Tietjens story took form in Ford's mind just after the war. He had returned to France and was spending the summer in Harold Monro's villa on the deserted Riviera, a discharged officer, a cast-off writer immersed in a sense of disaster. As he walked in the garden of the Villa des Moulins, his ideas, cloudy at first but growing more precise, began to gather around the memory of an old friend, now dead.

Arthur Marwood had been enough of a paradox in himself to suggest greater ones. He was the son of a good Yorkshire country family, a mathematician of brilliance in the government office of statistics and Ford's associate in publishing *The English Review*. His mind was "acute and scornful" Ford says. "He possessed the clear Eighteenth-century English mind which has disappeared from the earth, leaving the earth very much the poorer." However, "he was, beneath the surface, extraordinarily passionate—with the abiding passion for the sort of truth that makes for intellectual accuracy . . ." In spite of his brilliance, Marwood had no career.

It was tuberculosis, actually, that forced him into a retired and inactive life, yet Ford, going beyond that, saw a tragedy of disinheritance. His kind of intelligence and what it represented passed through the metamorphosis of the author's imagination and became Christopher Tietjens. "I seemed," Ford says, "to see him stand in some high place in France during the period of hostilities taking in not only what was visible but all the causes and all the motive powers of infinitely distant places. And I seemed to hear his infinitely scornful comment on those places. It was as if he lived again."

So Marwood furnished the outline and the intellect, but there had to be more to Tietjens than that alone. Through the course of the four books the development of his personality is one of the most elaborate and singular accomplishments of modern writing.

His character is synonymous with the character of an ordered, bounded, and harmonious past. Socially, this means the England of gentry and farms before the middle classes built it into an empire. Morally, it means a code of honor and self-respect in contrast to business honesty and puritan habits. It means that Tietjens is humane in his relationships, feudal in his outlook, Christian in his beliefs, a classicist by education, a Tory in politics. He is, in fact, "the last English Tory." Mirrored in this "clear Eighteenth-century mind," the world is an equable and logical mechanism in which God, Man, and Nature have a balanced relationship. It is not specifically an English view; it has belonged to every Western nation.

In one place in *No More Parades* Tietjens concocts a kind of fable for himself. He sees:

> The Almighty as, on a colossal scale, a great English landowner, a benevolently awful duke who never left his study and was thus invisible, but knowing all about the estate down to the last hind at the home farm and the last oak; Christ an almost too-benevolent landsteward, son of the Owner, knowing all about the estate down to the last child at the porter's lodge, apt to be got around by the more determined tenants; the Third Person of the Trinity, the spirit of the estate, the Game as it were, as distinct from the players of the game; the atmosphere of the estate, that of Winchester cathedral just after a Handel anthem has been played.

Tietjens means it as a semi-humorous comment on himself, but beyond that it is serious. Heaven is a Platonic reflection of earth, a place of feudal order and harmony and there are laws of science, morality, or theology to cover every event.

But Tietjens is out of his time in a world where the laws have lost their reality, the system has collapsed and the synthesis of knowledge and belief has lost its validity; under his feet he feels the great landslip. England (his specific example) once had a defined and integrated culture, but during the Nineteenth century it had become a kind of pseudo-civilization marked for export. Like cheap tradinggoods, imitations, her morals, manners, and religion were shipped to every part of the world. It was a process of weakening, dilution, and overextension in more than a physical sense. Earning great paper profits, she had actually been spending her capital.

Ford saw the war as simply a dramatic heightening of the inevitable processes of ruin. England's victory was only an irony, a catalytic occurrence and she emerged from it into a social and intellectual chaos. The telling thing, Ford thought, was not that the world had changed physically to any great extent, but that the lines of communication had broken down. There was no longer a recognized continuity between past and present or present and future. The traditional modes of relationship among people had disappeared and there were no new ones to take the place.

We are likely to judge history as the blind men took the elephant; it is too big for us and too misleading in its various parts. The historian may offer a splendid, documented, analytical narrative; and yet we feel the lack of a plot. The novelist of history offers us a kind of mystery-play in which the great mass of ideas and events are concentrated into a sharp and comprehensible drama. Shakespeare's historical cycle and *War and Peace* are such mystery-plays. Though I do not wish to suggest a qualitative comparison—those two works are almost the grandest of their kind—Ford's Tietjens novel at least belongs in the same category. But with a difference. Ford was trying to define dramatically a thing that was only a direction or indication in his own time and his story includes the future. Looking at England today we can see more plainly what he meant. Tolstoy left the future out or, rather, he saw it as a twin-brother to the past and the cycle of his novel goes through the sequence of revolt and disorder back to order again. Chekhov, seeing differently, implied the future and we know now that the ring of the axe on the cherry tree outside the Ranevskys' windows was a more prophetic sound than the laughter in the Behuzovs' drawing-room at the end of *War and Peace*.

Therefore, Ford took as the scheme for his allegory the life of one man, Christopher Tietjens, a member of an extinct species, which, as he says, "died out sometime in the Eighteenth century." Representing in himself the order and stability of another age, he must experience the disruptive present.

III

I have been trying to give a bare idea of the abstract concepts which govern the development of the Tietjens novel, "the game," Ford says, "as distinct from the players of the game." One of Flaubert's important insistences was that the writer deal directly and exclusively with the explicit, leaving value judgments to implication. For a novelist whose abstract meaning is readily available this is not hard. The younger Flaubert, for instance, demonstrates just the right evidence to make the case of *Madame Bovary* clear. But it is a relatively simple case. The older Flaubert, dealing with the greater and more complicated issues of *L'Education sentimentale,* produces a story whose surface is difficult, contrasting, and perplexed. Ford went along the same path; the lucidity and perfect form of *The Good Soldier* was followed ten years later by the slippery indirections of the Tietjens story. (The comparison is even more exact if we remember that Ford's early enthusiasm was for *Madame Bovary* but that in later life, he said, he read *L'Education sentimentale* fourteen times.)

There is perhaps one central question arising from the events and circumstances of the Tietjens story that seems almost unexplainable in terms of the plot alone. It is one of the chief ambiguities that must exasperate and rebuff the unwary reader and yet it seems to lie in wait for him in almost every phase of the entire story. A workable answer to it should supply a great deal.

Why is Christopher Tietjens so endlessly persecuted? Nearly everyone else in the novel, consciously or unconsciously, tries to discredit, injure, attack, or betray him. He seems to be the object of a kind of compulsive hatred, yet in himself he is honorable, amiable, apparently a danger to nobody. In various ways this enmity appears in his friends, his acquaintances, fellow-officers, superiors, but most particularly and significantly in his wife. It is the last, his relationship with Sylvia, that offers the decisive clue to the seemingly purposeless affliction that he finds on every side.

At the beginning of *Some Do Not . . .* the domestic situation of the two is outlined. Sylvia has had a child whose paternity is doubtful and more recently she has run away to the Continent with another man. Then she has changed her mind and asked Tietjens to have her back again, a proposal to which he assents by cable. Sylvia, in Germany, is shown in a scene with a Socratic Irish priest, Father Consett, who draws from her the admission that what she hates most about her husband and what she can't live with is his essential and imperturbable goodness. In the meantime Tietjens has met a young woman named Valentine Wannop at Rye and taken a long ride in the fog with her. The first part is chiefly an establishment of character and the lines are drawn between Sylvia, an arrogant, reckless, and morally chaotic woman and Christopher, the wise and enduring man.

The antagonism gets dramatic exposition in the second part of

Some Do Not . . . through a long scene which is built up by one of Ford's favorite devices, the *progression d'effet*. It is a psychological melodrama which gradually produces an intolerable pressure.

Tietjens, in the interval between the two parts, has been in the early battles of the war. A portion of his mind has been numbed by amnesia and he is wondering if this may be the first terrible sign. At the same time Sylvia is attacking his mental security in her own way. "I'll torment him," she has promised herself and she proceeds by accusation, sarcasm, lies, and open hatred. She has slandered him to his friends, whispered that he is keeping a mistress, that he has had a child by another woman; she has involved him in financial trouble. She is trying by all desperate means to reduce him to her own state of emotional anarchy—one sign of anger or weakness is all that she needs. "If," Sylvia went on with her denunciation, "you had once in your life said to me: 'You whore, you bitch . . . May you rot in hell . . .' you might have done something to bring us together."

But Tietjens grows stronger under the assault. Bit by bit his memory is returning and with it the emotional and intellectual equilibrium that belongs to him. He treats her violence with his odd courtesy, dispassion, and forgiveness.

"There is only one man from whom a woman could take '*Neither I condemn thee*' and not hate him more than she hates the fiend!" Sylvia says, and finally gives her last furious thrust: Tietjens's father, she says, was driven to commit suicide by hearing the report that Christopher had got the daughter of his oldest friend with child.

Tietjens answers. "Oh! Ah! Yes! I suspected that. I knew it really. I suppose the poor dear knows better now. Or perhaps he doesn't . . . It doesn't matter." Instead of the expected explosion there has been a deflation and Sylvia has lost again.

Later on in *No More Parades* Tietjens's relationship with Sylvia is developed in another crucial scene. It is in France during wartime and Tietjens, now in command of a base camp, is suffering from enormous nervous stresses. Sylvia has managed to get there by unofficial means and they meet at a hotel during an engagement party. She is unable to explain to herself exactly why she has come; she confronts herself with the apparently insoluble paradox that Christopher, whom she detests so much, is actually the only man in the world she can love. But once there, she gives herself up to the luxury of torturing and trying to ruin him. Though she cannot quite see what it means, her memory furnishes her with an exquisite sadistic example of her motives in the anecdote of a white purebred bulldog (looking something like Tietjens) that she had once whipped raw and left out in the weather to freeze.

Sylvia has no difficulty raising all kinds of troubles, official, domestic, and personal, around Tietjens's head. She seems to arouse the hidden or latent antagonism of everyone else towards him. ("Christopher . . . A Socialist!" gasps General Campion when Sylvia tells him an absurd lie. "By God, I *will* have him drummed out of the service . . .") It ends in a strange muddle in her hotel room and as a result Tietjens is transferred to the front lines.

The portrayal of Sylvia is as remarkable as that of Christopher. The unusual thing that Ford manages to transmit is not only Sylvia's insecurity and self-doubt, but her real terror at the idea of her husband. The intolerable fact to her is that he is sane.

And some of this terror at Tietjens is shared by everyone around. They are fragmentary people, uncertain, confused, without values. They sense that Tietjens belongs to a moral frame of reference that both makes the world intelligible and wards off its shocks. To their jumbled and neurotic lives he stands as a reproach, and they must destroy him if possible.

IV

The two middle books of the novel, *No More Parades* and *A Man Could Stand Up—* might be described as concurrent with the war rather than about it. The scene is France during the hostilities and Ford manages to show a great deal of Tietjens's life, first as an administrative officer in charge of organizing drafts of replacements and later as commander of a front-line unit. It is often vivid, always well-observed and convincing; yet the mere fact of the war has a curiously secondary importance.

Fiction about war has always been, essentially, a kind of adventure fiction. With the older novelists it was an adventure of sides or armies seen from a high hill. How will the English (or the Scotch or the French) win this battle? was the question we were supposed to hang on. Victor Hugo's Waterloo is the most elaborate example. Then came Stendhal, the innovator, and wrote the adventure story of a single man lost in the tremendous confusion. How will Fabrizio escape? he asks. It seemed to be a much more interesting question.

Tolstoy and Crane followed his line and so did nearly all of Ford's contemporaries who wrote about the first World War. To it they added their own generation's contempt for illusion and made the point that such an adventure must turn out badly. War was a savage, hideous thing and had to be shown as such. Nevertheless, it was a kind of entity in itself, an unexplained adventure that had little to do with the normal course of the world.

Ford saw the war as a concentrated specimen of the whole history of his time, a bloody dumb-show imitating the bigger drama. If there is any adventure in Ford's war it is a cerebral adventure and if there is any danger it is psychological danger. Tietjen's question: "Am I going mad?" becomes a universal one and while protagonists of other war novels see villages wrecked, Tietjens sees a civilization going to ruin.

Ford always felt somewhat embarrassed in trying to explain his own work; the great artistic immodesty of James's prefaces was something he could not understand. Consequently, his prefatory remarks to these books might have been written by a mild, slightly deprecating friend who had little idea of their subject. In a typical understatement to be found in the dedicatory letter to *No More Parades* he says that the book is about Worry:

> That immense army was . . . depressed by the idea that those who controlled it overseas would—I will not use the word "betray" since that implies volition—but "let us down." We were oppressed, ordered, counter-ordered, commanded, countermanded, harassed, strafed, denounced—and, above all, dreadfully worried. The never-ending sense of worry, in fact, far surpassed any of the "exigencies of troops actually in contact with the enemy forces," and that applied not merely to the bases, but to the whole field of military operations. Unceasing worry!

This statement hints at something, but by no means expresses it. The more valuable idea that Ford's war is seen as something like a violent intensification of all the troubles of a foundering society comes out a little more clearly in his remarks concerning his "war books" in the autobiographical volume, *It Was the Nightingale:*

> A man at this point is subject to exactly the same disasters and perplexities as his temperament prepares him for in time of peace. If he is the sort of man to have put up with the treachery of others, his interest at home will suffer from treasons; if he is the man to incur burdens of debts, debts will unaccountably mass themselves; if he is a man destined to be betrayed by women, his women will betray him exaggeratedly and without shame. For all these vicissitudes will be enlarged by the strident note that in time of war gets into both speeches and events . . . And he is indeed then *homo duplex:*

a poor fellow whose body is tied in one place but whose mind and personality brood over another distant locality.

In *No More Parades* the "disasters and perplexities" that haunt Tietjens have actually taken possession of those around him. Lt. McKechnie is the lunatic remnant of a brave officer, a classical scholar. His troubles with his wife are a wildly exaggerated version of Tietjens's relations with Sylvia and he has got to the point where he hears a kind of shelling within his brain. "The memory seemed to burst inside him like one of those enormous tin-pot crashes." For Tietjens he is like a horrible premonition.

There is the Welsh private, O Nine Morgan. His wife has gone off with a prize-fighter and when he applied for leave to go home Tietjens refused it in order to save him from being killed by the fighter. Morgan is a dispatch-runner; he is hit by a shell-burst in the street just outside the door of Tietjens's office and he falls inside to die in Tietjens's arms. "So he was better dead," Tietjens thinks. "Or perhaps not."

> Is death better than discovering that your wife is a whore and being done in by her cully? *Gwell angau na gwillth,* their own regimental badge bore the words. "Death is better than dishonor". . . No, not death, *angau* means pain. Anguish! Anguish is better than dishonor. The devil it is! . . . He was born to be a blooming casualty. Either by shellfire or by the fist of the prize-fighter.

O Nine Morgan, the semi-anonymous man, is an example or a parable. He is truly *homo duplex,* born to be a casualty wherever he might go—either from fists at home or splinters of iron abroad, both of which, in the final view, are aspects of the same thing.

The war experiences, in a way, represent Tietjens's dark night. *No More Parades* piles injustice on injustice, but one of the things that help Tietjens remain firm is the increasing realization that he is experiencing no simple personal nemesis but the total breakup. "We were fitted neither for victory nor defeat," he thinks; "we could be true neither to friend nor foe. Not even to ourselves." He sees the clearest irony in his story of a visit to the War Office in 1914 where he had seen an official preparing the one ceremony of the war for which (Tietjens thinks) England was prepared—the disbanding of troops. It would close with the band's playing *Land of Hope and Glory.* The adjutant would then say, *"There will be no more parades."* And, Tietjens adds, "Don't you see how symbolical it was? . . . For there won't. There damn well won't. No more Hope, no more Glory, no more parades for you and me any more. Not for the country . . . Not for the world, I daresay."

A Man Could Stand Up— begins with a telephone message to Valentine Wannop in England, informing her that Tietjens has come home but that he seems to have lost his mind. With this ominous suggestion about him, the novel takes a step backward in time to show the history of one day in the trenches. The major part of it takes place in Tietjens's mind, an interior monologue that mingles a thousand fragments of the past with a thousand details of the present. Tietjens is second-in-command of a thinned-out battalion awaiting a German attack. As he goes about the routine business of the day Tietjens makes an effort of memory and imagination to hold off the gathering insanity he feels all about him. He must quiet the frenzied McKechnie and deal with his colonel who, losing control, has taken to drink. He tries to keep up the morale of his men.

Most important of all, he must keep his own balance. One night Tietjens had awakened to hear a voice coming from a mine almost beneath his feet, *"Bringt dem Hauptmann eine Kerze,"* it said. "Bring a candle to the captain." Was it real? he wonders. Or is his mind becoming a tangle of fantasy like all the others'?

But Tietjens has an amulet to carry him through. It is the recurring thought of George Herbert on a hill above Bemerton parsonage composing the line, *"Sweet day so cool, so calm, so bright, the bridal of the earth and sky . . ."* It is a vision of serenity and sanity. It serves to remind Tietjens that he belongs to a consistent system of belief, that there is or has been once a regular, logical, beautiful order to nature of which he is part. As long as that idea remains, as long as he can distinguish the song of the larks from the noise of the barrage, he will be safe.

The battlefield of *A Man Could Stand Up—*, thus, is more mental than physical and only one actual shell falls on it. It comes as a climax to the scene, burying Tietjens, a lance-corporal, and a lieutenant under a pile of earth. Tietjens crawls out, uncovers the others and carries the lieutenant away under fire. Immediately he is ordered to report to General Campion who, spic and span, is visiting the trenches on a tour of inspection. He is enraged that Tietjens has not reported before, that his uniform is dirty and that he has a hand in one pocket. The general relieves him of his command and with this unexpected little irony the war is over for Tietjens.

The third part of the book begins where the first left off, bringing Tietjens and Valentine together in his empty house in London. He is not mad, but just saved from madness. At last they are ready to admit they love each other, but as the horns and bells of Armistice Night sound, the crazy spectres from the trenches drift in one by one. Now that the ordeal is over, they seem simply harmless scarecrows and Tietjens and Valentine give them something to drink to celebrate the war's end.

Before looking at the final book of the Tietjens story, I should mention the matter of style. It is quite possible that Ford knew as many of the trade-secrets of writing as did any author of his time and a real discussion of his technique would be more extensive than an introduction allows. A few important methods and intentions, however, can be noted.

The language of the Tietjens story is one of simplicity and understatement. It is neither commonplace nor rhetorical and it manages to reveal exciting events without any surface theatricality of its own.

The chief stratagems of narrative or dramatic style are somewhat more difficult to describe; they are the *progression d'effet*, the time-shift and the interior monologue. I have noted a good example of the first in the breakfast scene between Tietjens and Sylvia in *Some Do Not . . .* , in which all the nerves are slowly drawn to the snapping point.

In the Tietjens novel the time-shift and interior monologue are employed simultaneously. Ford often translates the scene of his story into the mind of one character or another and then uses all the tenses of memory as if they formed a keyboard. A scene from the far past is juxtaposed significantly with a present incident; the happening of a year ago has some bearing on yesterday. The "stream-of-consciousness" techniques (Woolf, Joyce, Proust, Richardson) bear both similarities and differences, though Ford at this time had not read the work of his contemporary experimenters.

In all, Ford cannot be called a great stylistic innovator. Rather he tried to use the best techniques of others with great care and imagination. He himself called his style "impressionistic." If a term is needed, that word seems both sufficiently general and sufficiently descriptive.

v

The Last Post is the strangely inconclusive conclusion of the Tietjens story. In form it is the most oblique of any of the books, the most extreme example of what might be called Ford's "tangential relevance." Christopher Tietjens is present physically for only one moment at the end of the book and yet he is the most central being in it. The system of the book might be thought of as a temporarily eclipsed sun with a number of visible satellite consciousnesses surrounding and defining its position. There are nine relative and interconnected interior monologues representing several people in the general vicinity of the cottage to which Christopher and Valentine and Mark and his long-time French mistress (now his wife) have gone after the war.

Each one of these monologues is a digressive collection of commentary, gloss, footnote, addenda, and paraphrase of the whole Tietjens story. The mind of Marie (Mark's wife) is described as being like a cupboard, "stuffed, packed with the most incongruous materials, tools, vessels and debris. Once you opened the door you never knew what would tumble out or be followed by what." Nearly all of the incongruous material that tumbles out of each mind, however, is pertinent somehow to the life of Tietjens.

Each one of these minds floats in the atmosphere of time, crossing and recrossing the orbits of the others, yet there must be a binding device to connect each one with the here-and-now of the book and to remind the reader of real people in a real place. Ford introduces a certain amount of present incident into the story to effect this (a woman entering the garden, Marie making cider) and each present incident is viewed from a different perspective by several different characters. The whole book is like an immense juggling act of time and point of view.

In the fantastic trench-world, Tietjens had wished for peace: "to stand up on a hill." The post-war world seems to be an image of his hope—placid and rural. But when the minds are opened we realize that nothing has actually changed and that the chaos, disorder and combat are still there. It is a non-sequitur world just as the memories of its inhabitants are non-sequitur.

Christopher's elder brother Mark becomes the Tietjens symbol. He has been paralyzed by a stroke (the Tietjenses can no longer be an effective force actually, physically), but his mind is as active and perceptive as ever (the intellectual dominance remains). He lies on a cot under a thatch roof, staring out at a landscape. He knows that he will soon die. His consciousness is thus purified of all physical dross and from him we can expect some definition, a statement removed into the realm of the absolute and final by death itself.

To the other six mental discussions of the Tietjens story, which are ambiguous, unreliable, partial views, Mark's three sequences of thought stand as a kind of framework. He appears at the beginning, middle, and end. (The actual succession follows this order: Mark; Marie-Leonie, his wife; Cramp, a farmer; an American woman, a stranger; Mark again; Marie; Sylvia Tietjens; Valentine Wannop; finally, Mark.)

In Mark's thoughts the various puzzles of the Tietjens history are solved at last. He knows now that his father's "suicide" was really an accident, that Christopher's son is truly Christopher's son. Now that the ancient tree of Groby is to be cut down and the family estate passed into the hands of a Catholic, he knows that the traditional curse will be off the Tietjenses—in effect, the dire but honorable curse of simply being what they are. Last night he had heard a rushing sound and had been "sensible of the presence of the Almighty walking upon the firmament." He is ready for death and sure of heaven.

He hears the people in the garden as voices from the past. "Damn it all could they all be ghosts drifting before the wind?" Christopher stands in front of his eyes for a moment with a chunk of the fallen Groby great tree in his hands and then Mark is dead; and the time of the Tietjenses is dead with him.

Mark's final statement is beyond emotion; the "curse" has always implied a future and it is now lifted. He presents both a summation of the Tietjenses' case and a reconciliation with its destruction. Both their strength and their failure lie in the fact that they have been true to something in a world where no one is true to anything. They are an anachronism and, as an anachronism, must disappear. It is inevitable that one theory of Truth, one systematic idea of how man may lead a "good" life, will be swallowed up in a world of Untruth, but that is according to history's law—not its equity.

VI

In his crotchety book on the English novel, Ford found much to complain of. He could see in its history no progressive intellectual maturation, no regular development of a tradition and no continuing attempt to uphold the artist's responsibility of "rendering" the life he saw. There were, however, a few writers here and there who understood that responsibility and lived up to it.

The difference between the general library of English novels and these few isolated achievements is partly a matter of method and partly of artistic integrity. Fielding, Smollett, Dickens, Thackeray—and most of the others we are inclined to call the major English novelists—failed, Ford thought, in the peculiar duty of an artist to his work. It resulted in, "mere relating of a more or less arbitrary tale so turned as to insure a complacent view of life." "Complacent" is the important word. It recalls, as a near-perfect example, the ending of *Tom Jones* when Tom, outcast and disinherited because of his honesty and courage, is welcomed back again simply because Fielding has performed the magician's trick of discovering his gentle birth. This complacency, this annihilating compromise with banality Ford thought to be a result of the English writer's continual urge to be considered "respectable" in a country where the artist had no honor and no social place.

The working toward ultimate conformity produced another commitment, which was one of method and viewpoint. The novelist presupposes a whole social scheme; within that circumference he arranges the smaller scheme of his plot and within the plot he assigns his characters various appropriate roles. When Fielding or Thackeray suddenly surprise us by showing their faces over the tops of their puppet theatres, we realize exactly what the novelist should keep us from realizing: that these are not self-directing people involved in a situation that seems to generate its own drama, but contrivances of cloth and wood assigned to their roles of good or evil.

According to Ford's view, the other kind of novel—in distinction it might be called the "intensive" novel—was produced intermittently during the eighteenth and nineteenth centuries by, first, Richardson, later Austen and Trollope, finally Conrad and James. (His own name belongs next.) In France it became a tradition; in England it remained a series of singular performances.

This kind of novelist pursues an intense inquiry into the behavior of a certain group of characters both as unique beings and as part of an interweaving, interacting system of relationship. Finally he reasons, or suggests that we reason, from the particular to the general. All society, he declares, is simply a sum total of how human beings behave towards each other and if he is fortunate enough or gifted enough to select for his study circumstances of relationship that have a widespread application, he will have achieved, into his contemporary world, the most penetrating act of inquiry possible. In this kind of novel we surprise the individual situation in the very act of turning into the general circumstance.

We can imagine Mansfield Park as the geographical center of an early nineteenth-century culture and its concerns—love, money, manners, personal virtue—being pivotal to that culture. Visibly, things changed so little during the next seven decades that these could still remain preoccupations for that great pedant of the sensibilities, Henry James.

But geological shifts had been taking place in the culture and those values, by the end of the nineteenth century, no longer represented the same importance. Conrad had to deal with an expanding world and Ford with an exploding one. In the Tietjens novel Ford had not only to consider a great multiplicity of values (all of them changing, becoming ambiguous) but the greater question of value itself. If the quiet but intricate life of Mansfield Park is the proper symbol of one period, the wartime life of the Tietjens book is a symbol of our own destructive, inchoate time.

In this way Ford expanded the dimensions of the "intensive" novel to fulfill a more complicated assignment, yet he retained the central principle of precise moral-emotional-psychological investigation. The general argument or "meaning" of his book is not, of course, unique. In different ways and under different disguises it is one of the common motives of most important twentieth-century writers; Mann, Joyce, Gide, Eliot, Proust have all shared it and projected it in their various ways.

Each one of these writers has produced his response—Ford has not. It may be that the Tietjens novel demands a greater effort of self-recognition from the world, but if this effort can be made we shall not only have added a major novel to our literature but shall have performed a major act of understanding about ourselves and our era.

VII

I have been referring to the Tietjens story as one novel divided into four different books and I think it can be comprehended in no other way. There is a misleading note in Ford's dedicatory letter to *The Last Post* which seems to indicate that he added this book as a kind of sequel to show "how things turned out." Addressing it to Isabel Paterson, he says:

> For, but for you, this book would only nebularly have existed—in space, in my brain, where you will so it be not on paper or between boards. But, that is to say, for your stern, contemptuous and almost virulent insistence on knowing "what became of Tietjens" I never should have conducted this chronicle to the stage it has now reached.

Most likely, this should be taken more as a compliment to a literary friend than as exact truth. Without *The Last Post*, the novel would have been sadly truncated and though it could never "turn out" as an ordinary novel must turn out, the recapitulation and final statement of *The Last Post* is indispensable. In his book on Conrad, Ford explains that it was necessary for him to have a whole design in mind (contrary to Conrad's procedure) before he could begin.

The entire novel was written over a period of five years, *Some Do Not . . .* appearing in 1924, *No More Parades* in 1925, *A Man Could Stand Up—* in 1926, and *The Last Post* in 1928. It was begun at St. Jean Cap Ferrat, continued during Ford's wanderings from there to Paris, from Paris to Guermantes, to Toulon, Paris again, Avignon, and was finally finished in New York on November 2nd, 1927.

Previous to this edition it has not been published in its proper form, as a unit. *Parade's End,* the present title, was Ford's own choice as a designation for the whole.

It seems the most appropriate of any. With an immense sense of tragedy, Ford saw the long and splendid procession of the Western nations coming to an end and Tietjens is the ghostly voice of the adjutant at the final disbanding. He says, "There will be no more Hope, no more Glory. Not for the nation. Not for the world, I daresay. *There will be no more parades.*"

11

RICHARD A. CASSELL

Notes on the Labyrinth of Design
in *The Good Soldier*

> If then the parts are managed so regularly, that the beauty of the
> whole be kept entire, and that the variety become not a perplexed
> and confused mass of accidents, you will find it infinitely pleasing
> to be led in a labyrinth of design, where you see some of your way
> before you, yet discern not the end until you arrive at it . . .
> John Dryden: An Essay on Dramatic Poesie

JOHN DOWELL, the narrator in Ford Madox Ford's *The Good Soldier*,
says near the end of his memoirs: "I have, I am aware, told this story
in a very rambling way so that it may be difficult for anyone to find
his path through what may be a sort of maze. I cannot help it." [1] But
there is a path, a design, for the device of the narrator is a ruse.
Dowell's rambles through conscious memory, his telling events as they
come to mind, his recalling earlier impressions, adding present ones,
repeating certain scenes and seeing them somewhat differently each
time, occasionally breaking down under the strain of recalling painful moments, intermittently posing questions he cannot answer and
then offering them to the reader to ponder, are not only artful devices
to claim the close attention of the reader's thoughts and feelings, but
also tools to mold the pattern of the novel. The discursive, associative

---

The material of this essay will appear in an expanded form in Mr. Cassell's
forthcoming book on Ford, to be published by The Johns Hopkins University Press.

patterns of memory create the *rationale* of the design, for the rambling is only apparent; the succession of events and impressions is under remarkable control, as is the language which re-creates them.

Ford claimed that he wanted to put in this novel all that he knew about writing; what results is not merely a brilliant show of technique. Dowell's manner of narration justifies the intricate shiftings in chronology and is the key to the novel's structure. The dislocations of time are controlled by the demands of the progressions of effect, which themselves create successively the contexts for the novel's central imagery. Ultimately, the narration, as it develops, shapes the meaning that can be drawn from it. Since the intricacy of the manner as much as the limitations of space prevent a thorough treatment of how Ford succeeds in squeezing everything out of this affair, I will suggest only a few representative lines of the pattern.

The plot revolves around the end of a line of good soldiers and gentlemen of honor, Edward Ashburnham, and his destruction by the women who seek to possess him. Dowell, a wealthy American, tells the story of his and his wife's acquaintanceship with the Ashburnhams in Nauheim and Paris. Dowell's ambitious wife Florence, with the full knowledge of Leonora Ashburnham, succeeds in becoming Ashburnham's mistress, and manages to hold on to him for nine years until she is frightened into suicide after discovering that he loves Nancy Rufford, the young ward of the Ashburnhams, and that Dowell has discovered a pre-marital affair of hers. Leonora, inspired by ambivalent motives, later forces Nancy to offer herself to Ashburnham, who, though he loves her, refuses her. Leonora then sends Nancy away, even after Dowell says he wants to marry the girl. On the night before Nancy leaves, Dowell learns from Ashburnham of his renounced passion for Nancy. A few weeks later, upon receiving a flippant telegram from Nancy in Brindisi, Ashburnham slits his throat with a penknife. After the funeral, Leonora exposes to the unsuspecting Dowell her husband's infidelities with Florence and other women and reveals her frantic attempts to maintain their fortune and the public view of their marriage. Dowell begins to write his memoirs immediately after the shock of these revelations. He does not finish until Leonora has married a colorless but respectable neighbor and until he has brought back the now mad Nancy from India, with whom he lives on the Ashburnham estate that he has purchased.

Exploiting all the ironies inherent in this affair, Ford molds it into a high comedy that results in a subtle, pitiless indictment of contemporary traditional ruling class manners beneath whose surface lie horror and moral chaos. To register his protest and yet to disappear as author, Ford needs a narrator who lacks strict moral preconceptions, who is, in fact, without narrow moral blinders which might prevent him from seeing or representing the view in contexts other than his own. Even as blind to facts and as gullible as he has been, Dowell becomes a disarmingly honest reporter who tells us everything so that at each stage in the story we know by both statement and implication everyone's view of the affair, including Ford's. Dowell himself is representative of a moral relativism approaching inertia that Ford saw as one destructive element of the old order of honor and integrity in public affairs. He is nevertheless capable of reporting, if not fully understanding, the horror beneath the lives of the English "good people," who suffer "broken, tumultuous, agonized, and unromantic lives, periods punctuated by screams, by imbecilities, by deaths, by agonies" (p. 238). The statement is a characteristic Dowell exaggeration of the view of life Ford ascribed to James: "a series of . . . meaningless episodes beneath the shadow of doom." [2]

The control Ford places upon the telling of his tale is that dictated by *progression d'effet*. Difficult to define precisely, it involves the employment of all narrative devices in order to gain verisimilitude and a sense of inevitability. All of the conflicts and forces released by the author must ultimately coalesce, not so much by resolutions of heretofore unrevealed actions at the climax as by the accumulation of our emotional responses and of our moral and intellectual evaluations. The focus is on the effect to be aroused cumulatively from combined effects throughout the novel. The result is a complex of information discovered, attitudes aroused, and implications drawn, the "conflicting irresolutions ending in a determination." [3]

So many conflicts and forces are released that *The Good Soldier* appears to be nothing but a series of shocks, outbursts, and breakdowns. We are literally thrown into the middle of the affair and have to face the same discontinuities, confusions, and demands upon our powers of judgment that we muddle through in everyday life. But Ford knew that a novel, if it is to make any claims to being a work of art, must discover, must clarify, the truth of the selected instances from life that it chooses to represent. In *The Good Soldier* structure is achieved by both short and long *progressions d'effet*, themselves shaped by what the narrator's dislocations in the sequence of action disclose and imply at every step of the way. Bewilderment is transformed into revelation. The novel leads us from the appearances to the realities, although the appearances also have their realities; [4]

from paralyzed silence on intimate matters to extended, frenzied talks: Florence with Leonora, Leonora with Ashburnham and Nancy, Leonora and Ashburnham with Dowell, and Dowell through his memoirs to us; from Leonora's moral certainties to her reckless abandonment of them; from Ashburnham's unrestrained passions to his regeneration through sacrifice of his love for Nancy to his traditional sense of honor: from Dowell's ignorance to his baffled knowledge and partial insights. What Ford wants to achieve is an imaginatively documented record of his age, for, as he says, "the greatest service that any novelist can render the Republic . . . is to draw an unbiased picture of the world we live in." [5]

The first chapter deftly sketches in some of the main figures and shadings in the picture that is to be drawn for us. The impression is strong but not clear.

"This is the saddest story I have ever heard," Dowell begins, and with the exact *mot juste*, for "sad" has several shades of meaning. Originally an Anglo-Saxon word meaning satisfied or sated, its current meanings range from being downcast, gloomy, melancholy, or affected with grief or sorrow, which are various intensities of the same feeling. It also refers to somber or dull colors and often playfully to something shocking or wicked. The word has ironic potentialities Ford does not let pass. In Dowell's mouth it is a sentimental understatement; in the context of the novel it is both that and an outright lie, for it is sad to see the comfortable assurances of the past slip away, but outrageous to suffer in the vacuum their disappearance has left.

One paradox follows the other. The Dowells knew the Ashburnhams "as well as it was possible to know anybody, and yet, in another sense, we knew nothing at all about them." Dowell intends "to puzzle out" the affair, but until recently he "had never sounded the depths of an English heart," for he had known only "the shallows" (p. 3). He leads us to believe Florence and Ashburnham are heart patients, though we are to discover that both ailments are deceptions and that not only the English heart but the heart of the whole matter is an impenetrable darkness. The illusion of the cohesiveness of these two couples, all "quite good people" descended from the best families, is immediately questioned by a series of paradoxical metaphors centering on decay and permanence. Dowell says he is like one who has "witnessed the sack of a city or the falling to pieces of a people" (p. 5). The collapse of his "little four-square coterie" he likens to the death of a mouse from cancer, a process which is the same as "the whole sack of Rome by the Goths" (p. 5). But they seem so secure,

like "one of those tall ships with the white sails upon a blue sea, one
of those things that seem the proudest and the safest of all the beautiful and safe things that God has permitted the mind of men to frame"
(p. 6). He likens his tranquil life before the shock of discovery to "stepping a minuet" (p. 6). Because it is a refined, genteel dance with
carefully prescribed steps, bows, and curtsies, it serves as a symbol
of the manners of public behavior that gave to Dowell, and to them all,
a sense of assurance and stability. Dowell is a man enamored of
these surfaces, who clings to the dream of their reality, for he tells us
that "the mob may sack Versailles; the Trianon may fall," society may
collapse, but the dance goes on. "You can't kill a minuet de la cour"
(p. 6). Not fully assured, he sentimentally asks, as he is to do often,
if there is not "any heaven where old beautiful dances, old beautiful
intimacies prolong themselves" (p. 6).

The question jolts him into another reality. Their life was not a
minuet but "a prison full of screaming hysterics" (p. 7). But again,
no; it was "true": the sunshine, the music, the sounds of fountains,
and the fact that they were four people with the same tastes and
desires. He tries to settle this contradiction with a rationalization
by asking that if he possessed "a goodly apple that is rotten at the
core" and did not recognize the rottenness until after nine years, did
he not still possess a goodly apple? It appears merely "a little odd"
to him that he never knew "that the physical rottenness of at least
two pillars of our four-square house never presented itself to my mind
as a menace to its security" (p. 7). He knows nothing, except perhaps
"the life of the hearth and of the smoking room."

Even the assurances these seem to offer are enigmas, and since
Dowell's impressions are not stabilized, he never allows ours to be. The
rest of the chapter slowly moves around to pose baffling questions
of personal motives and morals. How did Florence have time to
know and do so much since Dowell was her constant "sedulous,
strained nurse" (p. 8)? Is Leonora a harlot or like "every decent
woman"? Dowell assures us Ashburnham was the "excellent magis-
trate, a first-rate soldier, one of the best landlords" (p. 11). He seemed
pure, for he never in the smoking-rooms told "gross stories" or even
listened to them. He was one to trust your wife with. "And I trusted
mine—and it was madness" (p. 11).

Characteristically, Dowell turns to himself for comparison, the first
hint of his final identification with Ashburnham. He vouches for his
own clean thoughts and chastity. But if chastity of speech is the sign
of the libertine, what is he? "Am I no better than a eunuch or is the

proper man—the man with the right to existence—a raging stallion
forever neighing after his neighbour's womenkind?" (p. 12). Again,
he does not know; there are no guides to either "the morals of sex"
or to "the more subtle morality of all other personal contacts, associations, and activities [.] Or are we meant to act on impulse alone?
It is all a darkness" (p. 12). There are no intelligible limitations like
those for the minuet.

One of the consequences of the narrative method by which Dowell
juxtaposes past and present views is that a scene asks more questions
than it answers and is often misleading. According to the nature of
memoirs, much of the novel is related by a narrative summary interspersed with glimpses of scenes and snatches of dialogue. But there
are a few key scenes, which are carefully prepared for and rendered,
if not always fully developed, and the novel revolves around them.
Each scene constantly looks backward and forward, finishing a revelation already hinted at, or allowing us a new point of view, or introducing allusions to be developed later. The confusion is only apparent;
the meaning slowly unfolds.

For example, in rendering the action at the castle at M—, Ford
uses his favorite device of a scene as a framework or envelope enclos-
ing other actions, bits of information, and revelations which will clarify
and complicate our view, add ironic overtones, and comment on every
level of the novel's meaning. The scene starts casually as Dowell in
his disarming way says he will use it as an illustration of his notion
that it is difficult to get beneath the surface of the prescribed rules
and rituals of "the good people." The ostensible purpose is actually
to reveal to us that Florence is making her claim for Ashburnham,
and that it is a fact of which Leonora is aware but Dowell is ignorant,
although he senses a crisis. The whole scene is splendidly evocative
in its quickening cadences, as the foursome moves steadily up to the
room containing the copy of Luther's Protest, where Florence indirectly
declares her intentions and places one finger on Ashburnham's wrist;
and in its gradually lengthening cadences as Leonora grabs Dowell's
wrist, rushes him outside, and in the face of his innocence checks her
panic and assumes her public pose. At this point the scene is interrupted by twenty-one pages of digressions, the principal ones revealing something of Ashburnham's infidelities and reporting the earlier
scene, witnessed by Florence, of Leonora's striking Maisie Maidan,
a woman for whom Ashburnham has a passionate though not adulter-
ous attachment. We return to the lawn of the castle, where Leonora
accepts Dowell's apology for Florence's behavior as he sees it. Ash-

burnham and Florence appear, the foursome leaves for Nauheim, the scene is over.

But with its enclosed revelations it reverberates everywhere. First of all, it illuminates the brilliantly comic hotel dinner scene rendered earlier. The digression explains that Leonora and Florence had entered the dining room arm in arm because Florence had seen Leonora striking Maisie and had understood Leonora's reason for doing it, information that throws further light on Florence's sense of triumph in announcing her campaign to capture Ashburnham. Maisie's story itself serves as one of the overlapping frameworks for the castle scene. She is not introduced until early in Dowell's digression, where he tells us that Leonora had paid her way to Nauheim—the first suggestion of Leonora's pimping—and badly misleads us by saying, "We saw plenty of her for the first month of our acquaintance, then she died, quite quietly—of heart trouble" (p. 51). The remark hardly prepares us for the comic shock of Leonora's finding her upon their return from the castle with her feet sticking out of a trunk, whose lid had closed upon her, "like the jaws of a gigantic alligator" (pp. 75–76).

Dowell uses juxtapositions offered us by the digression to try to arouse our sense of pity for Ashburnham, but mostly he complicates our view of him. In the dining room scene, Ashburnham "gurgles"; in the castle he looks panic-stricken when Florence's finger touches his wrist; in neither case does he apparently say a word. We have to set this queer passiveness against Dowell's earlier suggestion that Ashburnham might be "a raging stallion" and his asserting that Ashburnham is a perfect English gentleman. And now Dowell tells us that Ashburnham is a sentimentalist whose infidelities are "inspired by the mad passion to find an ultimately satisfying woman" (p. 51). We learn that he has had to submit to Leonora's control of his estate, that he in fact does not have heart trouble, that he is truly, as Dowell had said in the dining room scene, "in a perfect devil of a fix" (p. 30); in short, that he is a victim of Leonora's "English Catholic conscience" which drove her to take over and "to fix things up" (p. 56). He is more to be pitied than blamed, even by the man he has deceived.

The scene not only sets the stage for Maisie's death and Florence's own victimizing of Ashburnham, but also foreshadows other events. Leonora's panic at the castle is placed against her striking Maisie Maidan and establishes the pattern of her angry, frustrated outbursts preparing us for her final moral breakdown when she lashes out against the "evil" of Nancy's innocence and beauty and offers her as a sacrificial victim for the preservation of her marriage. And perhaps, too, Maisie, with her innocence, in being offered by Leonora as a kind of toy for Ashburnham to play with, prepares us for Nancy, who resembles Maisie, who is equally innocent, though more intelligent, and who also is offered, though as a kind of treasure. Certainly the novel is full of such balancings.

There is even more one can say. There is, for example, the absolute skill with which Ford ties together the castle scene with its digressions. In the dining room scene, Dowell focuses our attention on Leonora's bracelet with the dangling golden key, which we discover twenty pages later she had just shortly before caught in Maisie's hair so deeply that Florence had had to extricate it. In the pictures which the scenes paint, our eyes are constantly directed to the wrists, the hands, the telling glances which communicate more than the relatively sparse dialogue does. And there is the ironic foreshortened view of the scene to come, as Dowell, on the way to the castle, laughs (the only time he does) at seeing one cow throwing another cow into a stream, an action which serves as an oblique hint of the human action to follow.

And so on and on. Gradually, as we sort out impressions, and as the narrative shifts from considering public to private behavior, from moods of calm to those of panic and nightmare, from paralysis to breakdowns to outbursts and back to paralysis again, the design emerges.

Probably even before the end of Part I, we are aware that Ford is intentionally setting Florence and Leonora against Ashburnham and Dowell, that each of the women is from opposite sides of the same cloth and the two men from opposite sides of another cloth. Florence and Leonora, as different as they are, are essentially predatory females. Florence is an amoral materialist for whom emotions and sex are weapons for acquiring a "gentleman of leisure" and "a European establishment" (p. 79). Leonora is an efficient manager of the properties whose ambivalent passions ultimately lead to recklessness and disaster. She is a "sheer individualist" who cannot fathom Ashburnham, for his traditions are "entirely collective," prescribed as they are by "the feudal theory of an overlord doing his best by his dependents, the dependents meanwhile doing their best for the overlord" (p. 146). Ashburnham is finally able to find strength in the simplicities of his feudalism and sentimentalism. But Dowell, who seeks to emulate him, lacks both Ashburnham's moral stamina and inherited sense of honor, is relegated to being a nursemaid and solicitor, and remains at the end a mere shell of the Ashburnham traditions. The four are alike only in their appalling ignorance of sex or of the consequences of released passions. Florence is the one sexual initiate before marriage, a marriage she finds it convenient not to consummate; Leonora comes to her arranged union with Ashburnham "like some patient mediaeval virgin" (p. 140), and until some two years later neither knows how babies are produced (p. 147).

Once Florence is dead, Nancy steps in to make a foursome again. She is central to the novel's structure. The novel is divided into four parts, actually four frameworks, bound by crisis in action or emotion. Each section moves carefully toward its own melodramatic climax. The first two parts center on Dowell's and Ashburnham's relationship with Florence, and the last two on their attachment to Nancy; throughout Leonora paces along the sidelines struggling to possess Ashburnham, while she talks endlessly in private sessions, first with Florence and then with Nancy. Even the time shifts are contained mostly within these two major frameworks. The shiftings, which are so complex within chapters or blocks of action (as in the key castle scene), are found to be relatively few between the two main structural units. In general, most events prior to Florence's suicide and most of the references to them are recounted in the first two books, and the events following her suicide in the last two.[6] Such a structure makes clear that both Florence's promiscuity and Nancy's innocence play central roles in the destruction of "the extraordinarily safe castle" the foursome originally appears to be. But Florence's role, it turns out, is minor so far as Ashburnham's destruction is concerned; her disintegrating influence embraces Dowell and Leonora instead. Ashburnham is not to be ruined until he discovers his true passion for Nancy and is victimized along with her. All of the preliminary crises in the novel lead to the final climactic scene of Nancy's offering herself to Ashburnham, which is then followed by the coda of her departure, her telegram from Brindisi, Ashburnham's suicide, her madness, and her return to England.

The figurative language is carefully contrived to render and evaluate all of the action. The contradictory metaphors of the first chapter, though some are not directly mentioned again, are in effect structural images which help establish the ambiguities of pattern in the novel. Indeed, much of the imagery throughout is structural as it reveals the shifting impressions of Dowell superimposing present attitudes upon recollected ones. Contributory to both the effect of the moment and to the accumulated effect, the figurative language is drawn from the range of Dowell's experience. He searches for illustrations from nature, hunting, invalidism, common and domestic animals, games, with emphasis on "playing the game" (hockey, billiards, and whist in particular), household china and porcelain, opera, and heroic romances. He also evokes imagery of the heart, of fate and fortune, and of destruction and decay. Often exaggerated and contradictory, often either under- or over-keyed, the imagery reflects the imbalance of a man who has been an unseeing witness to the collapse from within of an apparently placid and indestructible way of life.

In a rather conventional way, some metaphors characterize and by repetition intensify our image of each personality. The three women are visualized in metaphors of bright light and whiteness in contrast with the dark inscrutable passions moving them. Shallow, flighty Florence, "a gay tremulous beam (p. 15), "as radiant as the track of sunlight along the sea" (p. 30), seeks to leave the world "a little lighter than she had found it" (p. 40). Rushing into the hotel the night of her suicide, her face is "whiter than paper" against her black dress (p. 102), an image Dowell remembers later when he refers to her "personality of paper" (p. 121). On her deathbed she lies—"Oh, extremely charming and clear-cut–looking with a puzzled expression at the electric-light bulb that hung from the ceiling, or perhaps through it, to the stars above" (p. 120), a picture which may be an oblique, sardonic reference to her having been "positively electric" in the castle scene. Leonora, more substantial than Florence, is "clean-run," "clear in outline" (pp. 205, 227), and in her black dinner dress (both Florence with her copper hair and Leonora with her blonde hair affect black) "seemed to stand out of her corsage as a white marble bust might out of a black Wedgewood vase" (p. 32). Nancy's whiteness is more ghostly and mysterious. Her white complexion against her black hair suggests the life-in-death she is to come to. She is a "spectre" (p. 201) who always wears white and in the moonlight reminds Dowell of "a phosphorescent fish in a cupboard" (p. 109).

Certain of the repeated figurative expressions offer little ironic commentaries on the action or point to larger thematic developments. Rodney Bayham is described as "rather like a rabbit" (p. 239), an image of Leonora's second husband that is perhaps prefigured by her statement: "Edward has been dead only ten days and yet there are rabbits on the lawn" (p. 105). Florence and Dowell on the night of their elopement sit for several hours in the woods "listening to a mocking-bird imitate an old tom-cat" (p. 86), the perfect image, as we come to see later, of Dowell's sexual sterility in relation to Ashburnham's virility. Of more structural significance is Dowell's writing that

Florence's death is a relief to him like "an unbearably heavy knap-sack" falling from his shoulders (p. 120). It is a simile he had used a few pages earlier (p. 115) to describe what happens when a man finds his consummate passion. By recalling an image he had used previously with reference to Ashburnham's passion for Nancy at the time that he realizes he loves her himself, Dowell is giving another hint of his final grotesqueries: "But I guess that I myself, in my fainter way, come into the category of the passionate, of the headstrong, and the too-truthful. For I can't conceal from myself the fact that I loved Edward Ashburnham—and that I love him because he was just myself" (p. 253). That he comes to see himself as even a pale reflection of the excellency Ashburnham represented is his final illusion.

In another development of pattern in the design, Dowell sees Ash-burnham in a series of images which become increasingly more tragic and heroic. In the first, actually a recurrent dream of Dowell's, Ash-burnham is embracing Nancy on the palm of God, while Florence stands alone. The dream is "a vision of judgment" (pp. 70–71), of what, in Dowell's view, should ideally happen if people could get what they wanted. In the second, Dowell seems "to see him stand, naked to the waist, his forearms shielding his eyes, and flesh hanging from him in rags," as "Leonora and Nancy banded themselves to do execution, for the sake of humanity, upon the body of the man who was at their disposal" (p. 239). In the third and final one, he is "naked and reclin-ing amidst darkness, upon cold rocks, like one of the ancient Greek damned, in Tartarus or wherever it was" (p. 252). Ashburnham's plight is elevated to the universal level of classical legend and tragedy, but at the same time, as with the exaggerated commonplace meta-phors applied to him earlier, it is difficult not to believe that Dowell, perhaps unconsciously, belittles Ashburnham by overstating the significance of his suffering and sacrifice. At the very end, recounting Ashburnham's suicide, Dowell is calmer and with studied reserve de-scribes him as "the English gentleman" but also still "a sentimentalist, whose mind was compounded of indifferent poems and novels" (pp. 255–56).

As Dowell writes, a similar reserve seems to take over on at least one other level and leads him to certain insights about social realities. He is constantly seeking out definitions which will illuminate the heart of darkness opened to him. Again the metaphors help to reflect the emerging design. Near the beginning he believes that Ashburnham was destined to be ruined by "tempestuous forces" (p. 52), and tries to enlist our sense of pity by asking, "Is it possible that such a luckless

devil should be so tormented by blind and inscrutable destiny?" (p.
49). Sometime later, when he is summarizing Ashburnham's passionate affairs and has just finished considering the one with the Spanish
dancer La Dolciquita, Dowell interrupts to say that he has not titled
this story "The Ashburnham Tragedy" because

> it is so sad, just because there was no current to draw things along
> to a swift and inevitable end. There is about this story none of the
> elevation that accompanies tragedy; there is about it no nemesis, no
> destiny. Here were two noble people—for I am convinced that both
> Edward and Leonora had noble natures—here then, were two noble
> natures, drifting down life, like fireships afloat on a lagoon and causing
> miseries, heartaches, agony of the mind, and death. And they them-
> selves steadily deteriorated? And why? For what purpose? To point
> what lesson? It is all a darkness. (p. 164)

The denial of "blind and inscrutable destiny" here suggests that Dowell
has come to see human forces at work. But the paradox of "noble
natures" being forces of destruction does seem to suggest "the elevation that accompanies tragedy," except that classical tragedy implies
that the noble ones will be further ennobled by their sacrifice and
death and hence gives us assurance that man can transcend self and
be better than he seems. Dowell leaves us with no such assurance.
When he describes the last weeks before Nancy leaves, he comes to
see that "there was a great deal of imbecility about the closing scenes
of the Ashburnham tragedy" (p. 238). The saddest story has truly
acquired the meaning of "shocking" and "wicked," but only in a
grimly playful sense. Because imbecilities and madness are not ele-
vating, Dowell's contradictory reversion to the term "tragedy" here
forces us to seek a less classical definition. The imbecility is both in
Ashburnham taking the "conventional line," by sending Nancy to
India and her father, and in Leonora and Nancy ignoring it. Dowell
finally realizes that it is not destiny or the forces of elevated tragedy
but "conventions and traditions" that doom to extinction the qualities
of Ashburnham's virtues.

> I dare say it worked out for the greatest good of the body politic.
> Conventions and traditions I suppose work blindly but surely for the
> preservation of the normal type; for the extinction of proud, resolute,
> and unusual individuals.
> Edward was the normal man, but there was too much of the sen-
> timentalist about him and society does not need too many sentimental-

ists. Nancy was a splendid creature but she had about her a touch of madness. Society does not need individuals with touches of madness about them. So Edward and Nancy found themselves steam-rolled out and Leonora survives, the perfectly normal type, married to a man who is rather like a rabbit. (p. 238)

If Dowell comes to see so clearly the social realities, he still is unable to understand human motivations, for they remain unanswerable doubts. "Did the girl love Edward, or didn't she?" he asks (p. 243). Did she love him either before or after Leonora shattered her illusions about Ashburnham? Dowell is "pretty certain" she loved him before, but does not know whether she did afterwards. He cannot even decide if she loved him when she went mad upon hearing about the suicide, or when she sent the telegram. "Because that may just as well have been for the sake of Leonora as for the sake of Edward. Or it may have been for the sake of both of them. I don't know. I know nothing. I am very tired" (p. 245). Leonora wanted to believe she did not, Ashburnham that she did. "I don't know. I leave it to you." He also leaves to us whether or not Edward was a "monster of selfishness" in wishing Nancy would still love him, although five thousand miles away (p. 246). Nancy is clearly the key here to the explication of the darkness and to the dilemmas which beset them all upon the release of passion.

First of all, Nancy in her innocence, corrupted by Leonora's management, is most instrumental in bringing Ashburnham to his pitiful end. In a careful *progression d'effet,* in what might be called the Nancy motif, Ford moves by hint and oblique reference toward the climactic scene. His hand does falter when he reveals private thoughts and actions of Nancy she could not possibly have told Leonora or anyone else. Almost all the revelations of Nancy's consciousness break the narrative illusion, unless we can accept them as Dowell's imaginative reconstructions or sentimental elaborations. Our credulity is threatened, but Ford manages in almost every instance to sustain our suspension of disbelief by the skill with which he engages our attention and renders Nancy's involvement in the final crisis.

The first five of the six casual allusions to Nancy in the first two parts refer to her only as "the girl" or "the poor girl." We do not learn her name until almost the end of Part II. Here Dowell reports her praise of Ashburnham's public virtues, which is followed a few pages later at the beginning of Part III, just after Florence's suicide, with Dowell's unconscious remark about marrying the girl. Not until after this do we learn that on the same night Ashburnham had first realized he loved Nancy. Moving to the center, Nancy involves herself and the others in moral tensions which precipitate the climax. Just before the climactic scene in Ashburnham's bedroom, we have the first direct mention of Nancy's madness (p. 233), a foreshadowing of our final view of her.

In loving Ashburnham, in allying herself with Leonora "with the swift cruelty of youth, and with the swift solidarity that attaches woman to woman" (p. 241), and in being loved by Ashburnham and Dowell, Nancy seems to bridge the gap between male honor and feminine possessiveness. Male honor is the embodiment of the order of the past, female possessiveness of the chaotic morality of the present, an idea Ford had developed earlier, notably in *The New Humpty-Dumpty*, and was to use later in *Parade's End*. When Nancy's idealization of Ashburnham is brought into conflict with Leonora's stories about his lechery, and when Leonora's needling of her and Ashburnham ends in his suicide, she breaks down into madness. Hence, the gap between the order of the past and the chaos of the present cannot be bridged, an interpretation the figurative language bears out.

Ashburnham finds release in death, and Leonora, her passion spent, seeks out the innocuous Rodney Bayham. But Nancy's madness is no release, for she is neither alive nor dead. Ultimately, it seems, she is symbolic of the plight the novel renders. Although Dowell at one point denies the forces of destiny, Nancy is certainly a nemesis for the four characters. She precipitates Florence's suicide, Leonora's moral breakdown (because Leonora cannot bear the thought of Nancy possessing Ashburnham's soul), Ashburnham's suicide, and Dowell's miserable loneliness. As blind and as inscrutable as destiny she brings out the best and the worst there is in all of them.

Except possibly for Ashburnham, Nancy at each reference is presented in sharper paradoxical terms than any of the others are. She is a maze of contradictions, and her sudden shifts between the extremes in her actions and emotions warn us that profound shock will probably immobilize her. Her Catholic training coupled with her sordid childhood had combined to give her personality a combination "of saturnalia and discipline" (p. 125). She has "a tortured mouth, agonized eyes, and a quite extraordinary sense of fun" (p. 123). She is by turns "grotesque" and "beautiful," and both young and "as old as the hills." She can shift suddenly from talk of the saints to "tumbling all over the lawn with the St. Bernard puppy." She can ride furiously or sit quietly for hours nursing Leonora's headaches. "She was, in short, a miracle of patience who could be most miraculously impatient" (p. 124).

Most significantly, she is the epitome of the ambivalent sexual innocence and cruelty which plagues them all. She loves Ashburnham for "the public side of his record—for his good soldiering, for his saving lives at sea, for the excellent landlord that he was and the good sportsman" (p. 244). Once Leonora shatters her illusions about him, Nancy, in her complete sexual innocence and with the instinctive sexual cruelty of the adolescent girl—a part of the "immense and automatically working instinct that attaches . . . [women] to the interest of womanhood" (p. 244)—allows herself to be offered to Ashburnham but without any awareness of what she is doing or saying. When she reads of Ashburnham's suicide, she becomes mad and speechless, except to repeat periodically *Credo in unum Deum Omnipotentum,*" an ominous echo from the past, perhaps to remind us that she still believes in the god that was the gentle man Ashburnham, and in the God whom the world had irrevocably denied.

Finally, on the day before Dowell finishes his memoirs, she says three times "shuttlecocks," drawn from her memory of having been "tossed backwards and forwards between the violent personalities of Edward and his wife" (p. 253). Again the *mot juste* which belittles and illuminates. The word exactly describes how the Ashburnhams have used her; ironically, both Leonora and Ashburnham also had felt the other two had used each of them as a shuttlecock. The paralysis of communication is final and absolute; like every other character in the novel, Nancy is an island unto herself. Even the endless, frenetic talks every night which dominate the last sections of the novel do not lead to any real communication. Instead they precipitate disaster, and, as Dowell complains, no one got what he wanted (p. 237). At the end, Nancy becomes the human embodiment of the unrealized passions underlying society, whose victim she is. Mad, without moral resources, she is perfectly proper, "utterly well behaved as far as her knife and fork go"; she looks beautiful, healthy, and poised, but she signifies nothing, is "a picture without a meaning" (p. 254). She is a personification of both the minuet and the prison, except that now the prison houses nothing but dead passions.

From the first, we have seen some of our way before us but have not discerned the end until we got there. The paradoxes of the first chapter have not been resolved but have been explained and revealed for what they are. The minuet *is* the prison, and the very forms and manners of public behavior which seem to give such stability and insurance against confusions are really a prison to the passions. Once passions are released, hell breaks loose. The whole last part of the book up to Nancy's departure includes an increasing number of references to hell, night, storm, half-lights, cruelty, torture, and agony, recalling the destructive images of the first chapter. Still as Dowell reminds us, the minuet goes on, and outwardly in daytime everyone's behavior seems as calm and as reserved as ever (pp. 201–202).

Ashburnham is the only one who acts as though the minuet still has meaning. The only one to meet a test of moral courage, he refuses to let passion overthrow social order and remains a sentimentalist and a gentleman. The others render him obsolete, and all who remain are wasted by the expense of passion. Leonora breeds but does not love; Nancy is mindless; Dowell himself is merely the chaste eunuch, emotionally and sexually sterile. When his emotions do bubble to the surface, he can find release only in self-pity and lonely fears. He is a sentimentalist, as he says, but one who lacks every emotion of the man of passion and honor he emulates. At every turn, emotional and moral inertia and total meaninglessness—such is Ford's "unbiassed picture of the world we live in."

NOTES

1. *The Good Soldier* (New York: Vintage Books, 1957), p. 183. All page references are to this edition, which is a reprint of the hard-cover edition published by Knopf in 1951.

2. *Henry James: A Critical Study* (New York: Albert and Charles Boni, 1915), p. 155.

3. *Henry James*, p. 168.

4. Mark Schorer, "An Interpretation," which serves as an introduction to the Vintage Book edition, p. vii.

5. *Henry James*, p. 46.

6. The only jumps ahead in the first two parts are references—some of them more than once—to Dowell's return to America, his receiving the cablegrams from Edward and Leonora, his arrival in England, Ashburnham's outburst to him, Ashburnham's death, and Leonora's revelations to him (woven throughout the novel, mostly by summary interspersed with dialogue). Parts III and IV contain references to the courtship and early married life of the Ashburnhams, Leonora boxing Maisie Maidan's ears, the trip to the castle at M—, Maisie's death, the talks between Leonora and Florence, Leonora's attempts at an affair with Bayham, Ashburnham's declaration of love to Nancy at the Casino in Nauheim, and Florence's suicide. There are no more cross references here than one might expect to find in a traditionally plotted novel, but, of course, my listing does not suggest the complex repetitions and dislocations or the varying lengths of these references within the two main frameworks of *The Good Soldier*.

12

FREDERICK C. CREWS

The Longest Journey
and the Perils of Humanism

I

It is a commonly accepted and easily verifiable fact that E. M. Forster is a skeptical humanist both by temperament and by philosophical conviction; as he has remarked himself, his lawgivers are not Moses and St. Paul but Erasmus and Montaigne. His essays and biographies, with their tone of casual disenchantment and their elevation of private human values, are clearly informed with this spirit, and most of the philosophizing in his novels can be traced to the same source. What is less apparent, though scarcely less important, is that the *form* of his novels is also radically affected by his humanism. I do not mean that Forster's "disbelief in belief" is to be blamed for the apparently loose structure of his works; on the contrary, all five of his published novels strike me as being remarkably purposeful and economical in form. Their purposefulness, however, can only be seen in the light of the philosophical issues that stand behind their plots. The plots by themselves, at least in *The Longest Journey, Howards End,* and *A Passage to India,* seem frivolous or over-ingenious if we do not take their implicit metaphysics into account. As soon as we do this, however, things begin to fall into place. My effort here will be to explain how the plot and symbolic framework of *The Longest Journey* are controlled by a

This essay in a slightly different form is reprinted from *English Literary History* (XXVI, 4) with the permission of the Johns Hopkins Press and the author.

philosophical attitude, and to show how the buried argument of this novel reflects upon Forster's entire career as a writer of fiction.

The Longest Journey (1907), which Forster has repeatedly called his favorite of the five novels and the one in which he is most deeply involved, is a product of the years immediately following his graduation from Cambridge. It is not surprising that his semi-autobiographical hero, Rickie Elliot, suffers from the common dilemma of the young man who, B.A. in hand, begins to discover that the world is not what it seemed from within the walls of his college. Rickie's business in the novel is not simply to meet the demands of ordinary existence, to compromise the donnish temperament with the mundane. He has to decide the ponderous question whether an individualistic pursuit of the Good and the Beautiful—the way of life that Forster himself discovered in the Cambridge of Lowes Dickinson and G. E. Moore—has a proper right to existence at all. Will the pages of Shelley and Plato remain legible in the glare of everyday?

Cambridge, of course, does not stand for any fixed position in metaphysics, but for both Rickie and Forster it does signify an openminded zeal for truth. Apart from the ethical problem of whether this attitude is worth perpetuating beyond one's adolescence, *The Longest Journey* burdens its hero with anxiety over his relation to the cosmos at large. Indeed, Rickie cannot review his ethics until he has faced the consequences of his metaphysics. The novel thus becomes centrally entangled in such matters as whether the world is One or Many, and whether a man will do better to place his faith in this life or the next. That a story of some three hundred pages should purport to make meaningful statements on these subjects is evidence enough that its author had not been out of school very long. Yet *The Longest Journey* is surprisingly rewarding when read in philosophical terms. Its drama of opposed views of existence can tell us more about Forster's processes of thought and art than any of his more explicit writings.

To admire a book for what it reveals is not, I grant, to call it a successful work of art; it is hard to disagree with those who have found *The Longest Journey* uneven and sometimes grossly clumsy in execution.[1] This line of criticism, however, has tended to say that the novel is messy because Forster's vision of life is confused. I should say, rather, that Forster presents an extremely dense *clash* of visions, and that this clash is manipulated with conscious intelligence and brought to a carefully prepared resolution. The novel's confusion is aesthetic rather than thematic. Forster has difficulty in maintaining his narrative distance from Rickie Elliot, who is required to bear meaning both as a spokesman for Forster and as a victim of certain errors and weaknesses. Because Rickie's mind provides the controlling point of view behind the narrative, we have to rely on him for most of our knowledge of the other characters. Yet one of Forster's crucial points is that Rickie's mode of vision is a falsifying one. There is, consequently, an uneasy marriage of representation and irony in what Forster permits us to see through Rickie's eyes. Forster's method of compensating for this is to blurt out, every now and then, an exact confession of what he himself wants the story to mean. The total result is a hodgepodge of concealment and revelation that does not make for smooth reading.

Forster's "confessional" passages, nevertheless, prove very handy for the critic. The most significant of these, Chapter XXVIII, can be taken as a philosophical gloss on the total action of the book. It is a chapter unique in all of Forster's work, not only for its brevity but because it makes no mention of the characters or their immediate problems. Here is the entire chapter:

> The soul has her own currency. She mints her spiritual coinage and stamps it with the image of some beloved face. With it she pays her debts, with it she reckons, saying, "This man has worth, this man is worthless." And in time she forgets its origin; it seems to her to be a thing unalterable, divine. But the soul can also have her bankruptcies.
>
> Perhaps she will be the richer in the end. In her agony she learns to reckon clearly. Fair as the coin may have been, it was not accurate; and though she knew it not, there were treasures that it could not buy. The face, however beloved, was mortal, and as liable as the soul herself to err. We do but shift responsibility by making a standard of the dead.
>
> There is, indeed, another coinage that bears on it not man's image but God's. It is incorruptible, and the soul may trust it safely; it will serve her beyond the stars. But it cannot give us friends, or the embrace of a lover, or the touch of children, for with our fellow-mortals it has no concern. It cannot even give the joys we call trivial—fine weather, the pleasures of meat and drink, bathing and the hot sand afterwards, running, dreamless sleep. Have we learnt the true discipline of a bankruptcy if we turn to such coinage as this? Will it really profit us so much if we save our souls and lose the whole world? [2]

Forster's question here is whether we should place our trust in a this-worldly or an other-worldly hope, in the "spiritual coinage" of man's soul or rather in the "incorruptible" coinage of God. Man's soul is liable to "bankruptcies," that is, it may ascribe value wrongly and is bound to be thwarted eventually by the mortality of the objects of its faith. On the other hand, if we place our allegiance in God we may find ourselves deprived of richness in our present experience. The metaphor of coinage was perhaps suggested to Forster by the Biblical phrase, "For where your treasure is, there will your heart be also." Forster, however, would reverse the two terms: where your heart is, he implies, there will your treasure be. And his own decision is still more directly an inversion of Scripture: "Will it really profit us so much if we save our souls and lose the whole world?" Although he makes a token gesture of deference to the belief in personal immortality, Forster clearly believes that our present world is the only one that ought to concern us. Though we seem doomed to failure, there is a "true discipline of bankruptcy" which may somehow make our souls "the richer in the end."

This argument bears upon all the principal characters of *The Longest Journey*, but most conspicuously upon Rickie Elliot. Rickie's entire career may be viewed as an effort to "reckon clearly." He has temperamental leanings toward both the ascetic and the humanistic positions, and he vacillates precariously between renouncing life and committing himself recklessly to it. Neither attitude, according to Forster's gloss, will be ultimately profitable: Rickie must avoid asceticism and yet beware of the "bankruptcy" that follows from overestimating the worth and permanence of the people he loves. The tripartite structure of *The Longest Journey* emphasizes Rickie's problem of arriving at a moderate and discerning humanism, for the names of the book's three sections, "Cambridge," Sawston," and "Wiltshire," are representative of rival outlooks that contend for his loyalty. At Cambridge he commits himself to the detached life of the mind, as epitomized in his friend Steward Ansell. At Sawston he is dominated by his wife and his brother-in-law, Agnes and Herbert Pembroke, whose values are those of the public school they administer: teamwork, self-sacrifice, conformity to rules and duties. And in Wiltshire Rickie learns a kind of natural piety from his half-brother, Stephen Wonham, who is, in E. K. Brown's words, "a pure expression of the novel of ideas." [3]

Rickie's problem is to bring together the "Ansell" and "Stephen" sides of himself, that is, to connect the life of the mind with the life of the body. Both Ansell and Stephen are individualists and humanists: to be loyal to them is, for Rickie, equivalent to being loyal to his own better self. Sawston, which lies between Rickie and his spiritual goal like a Cave of Error or a House of Pride, offers him two spurious rewards for capitulating to "Society": sexual love (from his wife Agnes) and a position of authority (as a schoolmaster). Rickie's discovery that these temptations have ruined his life might be called the "bankruptcy" whose true discipline he tries to learn. And though the

effort is only partially successful for Rickie, it does make Stephen
Wonham "the richer in the end," as we shall find.

If we take the word *asceticism* to mean the suppression of human
values in the interest of a desire for incorruptibility, we may say that
anti-asceticism is the dominant theme of *The Longest Journey*. The
very phrase, "longest journey," which is taken from Shelley's *Epipsychidion*, bears this force in the novel. The relevant lines from Shelley
are these:

> I never was attached to that great sect,
> Whose doctrine is, that each one should select
> Out of the crowd a mistress or a friend,
> And all the rest, though fair and wise, commend
> To cold oblivion, though it is in the code
> Of modern morals, and the beaten road
> Which those poor slaves with weary footsteps tread,
> Who travel to their home among the dead
> By the broad highway of the world, and so
> With one chained friend, perhaps a jealous foe,
> The dreariest and the longest journey go.
>
> (II. 149-159)

Shelley's attitude here toward the "one chained friend" or the
"jealous foe" is reflected in Forster's treatment of Agnes Pembroke,
who marries Rickie and forces him to "commend to cold oblivion"
both Stephen and Ansell (the "fair and wise," respectively). Rickie's
decline from self-loyalty and his eventual resurgence are exactly
parallel to his degree of subservience to Agnes, and Forster reminds us
at several points that we should see this fact in Shelleyan terms. At
Cambridge Rickie comes across the passage from *Epipsychidion* and
marks it "very good" in the margin, but two years later, when he has
become engaged to Agnes, he rereads the lines and finds them "a
little inhuman." (p. 147) When married, he is confident that "Never
again must he feel lonely, or as one who stands out of the broad high-
way of the world and fears, like poor Shelley, to undertake the longest
journey." (p. 192) And when he has finally escaped from Agnes he
announces to Herbert Pembroke: "I never did belong to that great sect
whose doctrine is that each one should select—at least, I'm not going
to belong to it any longer." (p. 283) At this point he finds a new
pleasure in reading the poems of Shelley, "a man," Forster adds help-
fully, "less foolish than you supposed." (p. 298) Such heavy-handed
allusions leave us in no doubt that a simple equation is intended between Rickie's freedom from Agnes and his faithfulness to what

Forster (now misquoting Keats) designates as "the holiness of the heart's imagination." (p. 240)

It is significant that both Stephen and Ansell, despite their profound differences of temperament, are distrustful of Agnes and opposed to the "longest journey" in general. Stephen, whose moral creed is simply "here am I and there are you," has no desire to find a soulmate: "love for one person was never to be the greatest thing he knew." (p. 276) He is convinced, as he puts it, that "all one's thoughts can't belong to any single person." (p. 307) Ansell's view is identical with Stephen's, though phrased more aphoristically: "Man wants to love mankind; woman wants to love one man." (p. 97) [4] Ansell is a prophet of the religion of which Stephen is the living embodiment: the religion of freedom from spiritual constraint. Though he looks up at the dome of the British Museum reading room "as other men look at the sky" (p. 207), what he finds there is substantially what Stephen finds in the countryside of Wiltshire. Ansell (following George Meredith) calls it "the Spirit of Life." "Myself I've found it in books," he explains. "Some people find it out of doors or in each other. Never mind. It's the same spirit, and I trust myself to know it anywhere, and to use it rightly." (p. 209) Ansell does recognize it at his first contact with Stephen, and he does use it rightly: he persuades Rickie to accept Stephen as his brother.

Stephen and Ansell have, to be sure, very different motives for their common attitude toward the longest journey. Stephen fully intends to marry and eventually he does; his only reservation is his belief that "You can't own people." (p. 307) Ansell's misgivings are more deeply seated. Though critics of *The Longest Journey*, with unanimous delicacy, have avoided mentioning the fact, there is more than a hint of homosexuality in Ansell's temperament. His intense disapproval of Rickie's engagement to Agnes stems from simple jealousy as much as from his awareness that Agnes will make a poor wife. For, as he acknowledges to himself late in the novel, his feeling for Rickie has been one of love (see p. 238). In this light an early scene between Rickie and Ansell takes on a special meaning. The two boys have been lying in a meadow outside Cambridge, and Rickie gets up to leave in order to keep an appointment with Agnes. Ansell seizes him by the ankle:

"Don't go," he said idly. "It's much better for you to talk to me."
"Lemme go, Stewart."
"It's amusing that you're so feeble. You—simply—can't—get—away. I wish I wanted to bully you."

Rickie laughed, and suddenly overbalanced into the grass. Ansell, with unusual playfulness, held him prisoner. They lay there for [a] few minutes, talking and ragging aimlessly. (p. 79)

The nature of this "unusual playfulness" is not out of keeping with Ansell's general disaffection with women (see, e.g., pp. 94, 98) nor with his confessed inability to cope with the facts of sex and birth (see p. 210). It is noteworthy that Agnes, who has a highly developed sense of danger to her unique possession of Rickie, is intensely jealous of Ansell (see p. 202).

These suggestions, which are by no means conspicuous in the total pattern of the novel, nevertheless take on a considerable importance when we discover that Rickie, too, is unable to live happily with a woman. The early speculation by one of Rickie's Cambridge friends that he is "a little effeminate" (p. 95) and Ansell's admonition that he is "not a person who ought to marry at all" (p. 97) seem to be at least partially borne out by his total surrender of authority to Agnes. Rickie, who suffers from a hereditary defect of lameness, has never regarded himself as altogether fit to raise a family, and when his one daughter by Agnes is born lame and soon dies of pneumonia, he concludes that he should never again attempt to have a child. He is not, strictly speaking, a homosexual, but his physical handicap and his effeminacy are such that the more genuine strains of homosexuality in Ansell strike a responsive chord in him.[5]

Rickie's vaguely homosexual imagination, indeed, seems largely responsible for his original interest in Agnes. He is attracted to her not for her own sake but because he has idolized the athletic prowess of her dead fiancé, Gerald Dawes; a single glimpse of Gerald embracing Agnes becomes his introduction to the idea of sexual love and his permanent emblem for it (see pp. 51–53). It is not Agnes, but the image of Agnes and Gerald together that enraptures Rickie. When Gerald dies in a football match, Rickie forces Agnes to "mind" her loss because he himself minds it, and he marries her on the perverse assumption that both he and she will remain loyal to Gerald's memory. Thus Rickie interprets his role as a husband altogether vicariously. Having attached a masochistic significance to the fact that Gerald bullied him as a boy (see pp. 49–50), he is more than half willing to be bullied by Agnes, who has shared Gerald's embrace.[6]

This complicated rationale behind Rickie's marriage exposes his most incurable habit of thought and his greatest weakness, an inherent tendency to view his experience symbolically rather than realistically. Gerald and Agnes do not appear to him as human beings but as figures in an emblem of sexual passion, and thus he is unable to perceive the threat that Agnes poses to his spiritual freedom. Ansell, who lives wholly in a world of books, and Stephen, who is wholly "natural," are equally qualified to see Agnes as she is, but Rickie is blinded by his efforts to equate the world of books to the world of nature—to find fixed literary symbols in his everyday experience. This temptation is particularly strong in his dealings with Stephen, who is deeply involved in Rickie's sense of his own identity. Rickie's morbid temperament is governed by the idea of the suffering that his beloved mother endured at the hands of his father, a philanderer and a hereditary weakling who has bequeathed his lameness to Rickie. When Rickie first learns that Stephen is his illegitimate brother he assumes that he and Stephen share the same father, and he willingly defers to Agnes' opinion that Stephen is a self-seeking boor. All is changed, however, when Ansell explains that Stephen is the son of Rickie's mother, not his father. In this revelation Rickie sees an opportunity of fulfilling his ambition to have a brother and, more importantly, to "resurrect" his dead mother. He and Stephen have, he thinks, "got behind right and wrong, to a place where only one thing matters—that the Beloved should rise from the dead." (p. 283)

We know, of course, from the "coinage" chapter that this effort of Rickie's cannot bring him out of his spiritual bankruptcy: "We do but shift responsibility by making a standard of the dead." Nevertheless, Stephen does possess a legitimate symbolic value both for Rickie and in the total scheme of *The Longest Journey*. This value hinges upon the other half of Stephen's parentage. We learn toward the end of the novel that Mrs. Elliot's lover, a man designated only as Robert, was a civilized and imaginative farmer, a "natural man" who yet was a highly articulate spokesman for naturalness. "As he talked, the earth became a living being—or rather a being with a living skin,—and manure no longer dirty stuff, but a symbol of regeneration . . ." (p. 264) This implausible person is himself a symbol of man's secular vigor and potential decency. He rejects the Christian antithesis between sensual and spiritual, admitting only that love, whether illicit or not, is more valuable than the barren "duty" of renunciation: he too is among the characters who win Forster's approval by placing an individual notion of propriety above a social one. He and Mrs. Elliot run off to Stockholm to achieve their liberty, but, significantly, Robert drowns as the two of them "raced for the open sea." (p. 271) First, however, Stephen is conceived, a boy who is destined to have "a cloudless spirit—the spirit of the seventeen days in which he was created." (p. 276) The reader need not be reminded that the actual begetting of

children takes something less than seventeen days, yet Forster means
just what he says: Stephen's spirit is an expression of the whole undertaking of the trip to Stockholm, i.e. of the symbolic rupture with society. When Stephen persuades Rickie to desert Agnes he performs the
identical service that his father did for Mrs. Elliot. He intrudes the wisdom of nature into a custom-ridden marriage, enabling one of the
partners to experience both the perilousness and the desirability of
obeying "the heart's imagination."

II

This brings us to the question of the ultimate philosophy projected
by *The Longest Journey* as a whole. It is evident from the size and
complexity of Forster's plot that he is not constructing a simple
"moral" about the wisdom of the heart. Nor could we say that Platonic
or homosexual friendship is presented as an absolute ideal. The Robert-
Mrs. Elliot episode contradicts this, and Rickie correctly ascribes the
failure of his own marriage to his shortcomings of character (see p.
313). Nor can we entirely reconcile Ansell's disinterested pursuit of
truth with Stephen's anti-intellectualism. Stephen himself, though a
model of independence and masculinity, is by no means a perfect
character; through most of the novel he is something of a drunkard
and a sullen bully. If we are to find a unifying principle in *The Longest Journey* I think we must look beyond the immediate moral issues
to a larger question that is posed by the common situation of the
various characters. Forster's attitude toward this question sets the
tone of the novel and establishes the most important connection between the characters' adventures and Forster's own passages of commentary.

The central difficulty, as the "coinage" chapter suggests, is that of
properly evaluating human life. How large is man when viewed against
the backdrop of his universe? Is it possible, or even worthwhile, to
uphold our private standards of value in a world that is indifferent to
our existence? The issue is raised obliquely on the opening page of the
book, in the form of still another question: what is real? The rather
inept debate in Rickie's Cambridge room over the existence or nonex-
istence of an unperceived cow is, as Lionel Trilling observes, a clue
to the novel's theme.[7] One of Rickie's friends, apparently under the
momentary sway of Bishop Berkeley, argues that the cow ceases to
exist when the perceiver removes his attention. Significantly, it is
Ansell who takes the opposite stand: "Whether I'm in Cambridge or
Iceland or dead, the cow will be there." (p. 11) Though he later denies the existence of Agnes, he does so on grounds that are at least

superficially consonant with his original position. Seeing the gap between Agnes' true character and the Agnes whom Rickie thinks he
knows, Ansell calls her "the subjective product of a diseased imagination." (p. 27) His point here is ethical rather than metaphysical, and
elsewhere he is consistent in his anti-Berkeleyanism. Since he believes
that there is a more or less unchanging world which exists inde-
pendently of any human mind, and that no single person is equipped
to perceive more than an infinitesimal fraction of this whole, he will
not allow himself to be persuaded that his own experience is any less
valid than another's. Unlike Rickie, he does not brood over the seeming
isolation of Cambridge from the "great world," and at one point he
states his philosophy outright:

> There is no great world at all, only a little earth, for ever isolated
> from the rest of the little solar system. The earth is full of tiny so-
> cieties, and Cambridge is one of them. All the societies are narrow,
> but some are good and some are bad . . . The good societies say,
> "I tell you to do this because I am Cambridge." The bad ones say,
> "I tell you to do that because I am the great world" . . . They lie.
> And fools like you [Rickie] listen to them, and believe that they
> are a thing which does not exist and never has existed, and confuse
> "great," which has no meaning whatever, with "good," which means
> salvation. (p. 77)

Ansell's sense of value thus hinges upon what we might call his
cosmology; he feels that since the universe has no distinctive character
after which we can model our lives, we must develop a private idea of
"the Good" and cling to it at all cost. It is not coincidental that Rickie,
who expects his Cambridge ideals to be refuted by the "great world,"
falls an easy victim to the Pembrokes' philosophy that "school is the
world in miniature," nor that it is the unsymbolical, frankly bookish
Ansell who rescues him from error. Ansell's notion of the Good is un-
clouded because he feels no need to seek confirmation for it in the
outside world.[8]

One's notion of the Good need not be derived solely from books,
however; Ansell himself confesses, as we have seen, that "some people
find it out of doors." Robert and his son Stephen exemplify this possibility. This is not to say that they find nature itself an unmixed good
or an Emersonian preceptor of moral truths, but simply that they find
good *within* nature. Both Robert and Stephen are in agreement with
Ansell over the necessity of maintaining a human code of values in
opposition to the blind wastefulness of nature, but at the same time
their own virtues—masculinity, practicality, independence of thought-

seem somehow to have been drawn from the soil. They are strong because their sense of the Good is contiguous with their sense of reality in the countryside.

Rickie, by contrast, is burdened with two incompatible views of nature, one overly poetic and the other quite disillusioned and prosaic. His sense of beauty leads him to believe that "poetry, not prose, lies at the core" (p. 201) of the natural world, but his Christian training and his own deformity, in conjunction with the "natural" cruelty that he witnesses among the pupils at Herbert Pembroke's school, convince him that nature is essentially wanton. He secretly understands that "Nature has no use for us: she has cut her stuff differently." (p. 78; see also p. 97) In the suffering of a schoolboy he "perceived more clearly the cruelty of Nature, to whom our refinement and piety are but as bubbles, hurrying downwards on the turbid waters. They break, and the stream continues." (p. 221) And Stephen, too, presents Rickie temporarily with an instance of nature's fickleness. It seems the height of injustice that Stephen should be allowed to continue the worthless line of Rickie's father while Rickie himself is to die without an heir. Rickie shields himself from such reflections by seeking in his relationship with Agnes a purity altogether exempt from reality and by composing a series of mythological fantasies about communion with nature—stories that are convincing neither to a publisher nor to Stephen, the touchstone of the "natural" in *The Longest Journey*.

Rickie's outlook is significantly altered, however, when he learns that Stephen is his mother's son, for this suggests to him that "natural selection" may preserve the best as well as the worst hereditary strains. To Rickie's emblematic imagination the crucial fact about Stephen is that he represents a survival of their wholly "spiritual" mother; his very existence strikes Rickie as evidence that the spiritual and the natural need not be contradictory. He comes to feel that we can only perpetuate what we love by accepting the earthly side of our lives as a legitimate fact—by living within nature rather than erecting a rival world of impossibly sexless ideals. This is the "clear reckoning" that emerges from his bankruptcy.

Stephen's own views on the natural world are far from irrelevant to Rickie's philosophical problem. Although he has no personal grievances against nature, he wonders "what lucky chance had heated him up, and sent him . . . into a passive world." "He was proud of his good circulation, and in the morning it seemed quite natural. But at night, why should there be this difference between him and the acres of land that cooled all round him until the sun returned?" (p. 274) His reaction to such doubts is in conspicuous contrast to Rickie's. Instead

of clinging to a dualistic theology that gives a subordinate importance
to the realm of nature, Stephen becomes an enthusiastic though inex-
pert freethinker: "He worried infinity as if it were a bone." (p. 106)

This phase is brief, but Stephen never abandons his contempt for
religion, and Forster plainly intends us to see his attitude as at once
more practical and more reasonable than a Christian one. The point is
brought home in an incident that occurs while Rickie and Agnes are
journeying to Cadover to visit Mrs. Failing, Rickie's aunt. Their train,
as Stephen informs them, has struck and killed a small child. Mrs.
Failing, the Christian, taunts Stephen with questions about the fate of
the dead child's soul. Stephen's "natural" conscience is horrified by
such an impersonal way of thinking about death. " 'There wants a
bridge,' he exploded. 'A Bridge instead of all this rotten talk and the
level-crossing. . . . Then the child's soul, as you call it—well, nothing
would have happened to the child at all.' " (pp. 112f.) Not believing,
as Mrs. Failing does, that this present world is merely a way-station
to heaven or hell, Stephen places a high value on the preservation of
life; he agrees with Forster that it will not profit us to save our souls
and lose the world. And in this connection it is worth remembering
that Stephen and Ansell share the same criterion for judging their
acquaintances: "they must be convinced that our life is a state of
some importance, and our earth not a place to beat time on."
(p. 302)

The moral victory of humanism in *The Longest Journey* is costly
but unmistakably plain. Rickie dies, unable to make use of his "clear
reckoning," but in dying he saves Stephen from being crushed by a
train—possibly the same train that killed the child. It is, perhaps, the
train of indifference to human life, or, as James McConkey suggests,
the train of temporality that threatens to sever the human past from the
human future; it must be "bridged" by an intelligent reverence for
life.[9] The bridge is built both in fact and in metaphor: Stephen survives to raise a family and to cherish the memory of Rickie and their
common mother, and the final chapter of the novel projects a hope
that Stephen and his children will hold their own against both "society"
and mutability, the two enemies of humanistic value in *The Longest
Journey*. The waste and decay that have befallen the other characters,
however, make it fitting that even in the final scene of his happiness
Stephen should be troubled by the ultimate metaphysical question of
the novel: "He was alive and had created life. By whose authority?
Though he could not phrase it, he believed that he guided the future
of our race, and that, century after century, his thoughts and his passions would triumph in England. The dead who had evoked him,

the unborn whom he would evoke—he governed the paths between them. By whose authority?" (p. 326)

III

A full treatment of the intricate symbolism of *The Longest Journey* would require another essay of this size; here I can do no better than refer the reader to James McConkey's extremely acute, though unfortunately brief, analysis of the major symbols.[10] McConkey is correct in arguing that the entire symbolic pattern of the novel is build around the characters' pursuit of uniformity and stability in a treacherously changeable world. Just as the pervasive imagery of streams and rivers is employed to suggest the purposeless flux of nature and the difficulty of asserting our human sense of importance (as Rickie thinks, "We fly together, like straws in an eddy, to part in the open stream"; p. 78), so the imagery of chalk and chalk-pits shows us the other face of nature, its continuity and oneness. Ridges of chalk constitute "the fibres of England" (p. 147), uniting Cambridge and Wiltshire and implying a consistent "substratum" of natural impulse beneath the artificial distinctions of society. At one point, for example, Stephen twists Herbert Pembroke around and forces him to see the chalk of Salisbury Plain: "There's one world, Pembroke," he insists, "and you can't tidy men out of it." (pp. 323f.)

The humanistic theme of *The Longest Journey* depends upon our simultaneous awareness of these contradictory symbols, of what McConkey calls "the coexistence of unity with mutability." [11] As in *Howards End*, the central problem of the novel is "Only connect": only connect the past with the future, the mind with the body, the human with the natural. A sense of difficulty and peril is essential to this undertaking, for the human condition is itself perilous; we must recognize and acquiesce in our tenuous position if we are to make use of the few opportunities for true meaning that are afforded us. This attitude is summed up in the posthumous words of Rickie's uncle, Anthony Failing, whose epigrams provide much of the moral gloss to *The Longest Journey:* "Let us love one another. Let our children, physical and spiritual, love one another. It is all that we can do. Perhaps the earth will neglect our love. Perhaps she will confirm it, and suffer some rallying-point, spire, mound, for the new generations to cherish." (p. 311) *The Longest Journey* is full of symbolic rallying-points, many of which fail to meet Forster's austere standard of validity. The Catholic Church at Cambridge, for example, "asserting, however wildly, that here is eternity, stability, and bubbles unbreakable upon a windless sea" (p. 71), is clearly disparaged, for this description comes shortly after Rickie has learned "once for all that we are all of us bubbles on an extremely rough sea." (p. 70) Sawston School is an inadequate symbol for the opposite reason: by selling out to "society" it has failed to assign any importance to private human values. It is in Wiltshire, where man's life is properly related to the earth, that the most convincing monuments stand: Salisbury Cathedral and the burial mound of the Cadbury Rings (the "spire" and "mound" respectively in Anthony Failing's credo). Both are valid symbols by virtue of asserting the persistence of human love amidst the forgetfulness of nature rather than apart from it.[12]

This criterion applies, of course, not only to the literal monuments in the novel but also to the memories and relationships that Rickie attempts to "immortalize," such as the voice of his mother, his brotherhood with Stephen, and the embrace of Gerald and Agnes—all of which he distorts by removing them from their natural context. Furthermore, Rickie's shortcomings as a writer appear to stem from this very inability to distinguish between symbol and prosaic fact. Most of his extravagantly allegorical short stories about communion with nature are products of his "Agnes" period, when "the heart of all things was hidden" from him. (p. 167) The difficulty with his stories is identical with the difficulty in his life: he permits his imagination to isolate a few moments of heightened experience and to forget the chaotic flux from which those moments were abstracted. After he has deserted Agnes and absorbed some of Stephen's matter-of-factness, he finds himself able to write a realistic novel which becomes posthumously successful.

So far I have said little of the autobiographical implications of The Longest Journey, but at this point the connection between Rickie's career and Forster's becomes too overt to be ignored. Rickie's allegory that literally puts Stephen to sleep is identical in plot with Forster's story, "Other Kingdom" (see pp. 86, 140), and Rickie's other stories reflect the allegorical classicism of Forster's early fantasies. When Stephen drops the counterpart of "Other Kingdom" into a rain gutter we can hardly avoid concluding that a slur is intended upon Forster's own tales. And, in a broader sense, the thinness of Rickie's stories makes us ask whether The Longest Journey may not be, among other things, an implicit critique of the symbolic habit of mind and hence a statement of dissatisfaction with Forster's own over-dependence upon symbolism. Though heavily weighted with symbols itself, the novel seems to provide a standard of realism by which most symbols would be judged invalid.

The issue may become clear if we bear in mind a distinction between the intended meaning of symbols and the act of symbolization. The symbols in Rickie's stories are designed to convey the idea of harmony with nature, but the act of distilling nature into mere symbols is "unnatural." The writer's problem is to represent the real world as meaningful without rendering it static—in other words, to find symbols in nature rather than placing them there in order to illustrate a point. It is a legitimate criticism of Forster's mythological stories that they advertise the virtues of the natural, unrestricted life wihout giving the reader the slightest illusion of living that life. Quite a few of the tales about casting off one's inhibitions are told from the point of view of a narrator who is himself inhibited to a comical degree.[13] Furthermore, the desired escape from society in most of Forster's stories is, like Mrs. Elliot's, furtive and only partially successful.[14] Society has the last word in nearly every case; the teacup of experience, as Forster calls it, is dropped but not broken. It is significant that not a single one of the stories is told as a realistic narrative: those that do not deal openly in fantasy are, nonetheless, didactic rather than descriptive. At no point do we see the sustained representation of actual life that Forster does achieve in his novels, and which Rickie, too, apparently masters in his eventual novel "about a man and a woman who meet and are happy." (p. 313)

I do not mean to imply that Forster abandoned his commitment to symbolism; *Howards End* and *A Passage to India* are as richly studded with symbols as any of the earlier works. But it does seem that Forster became concerned over the problem of reconciling his symbolic technique with literal representation of life, and that *The Longest Journey* projects an answer to the problem, a kind of manifesto of future intentions. If we grant that Forster's attitude toward his art is reflected in the dilemmas of his characters, we can see this problem of symbolism taking shape throughout his early career. In the first place, many of the short stories themselves present their central characters with "symbolic moments" that must be seized and cherished.[15] Since "the years are bound either to liquefy a man or to stiffen him," [16] it is the part of wisdom to transfix some moment of youthful endeavor and freedom in which one has been loyal to his finest instincts; the memory of such an "eternal moment" will prove more valuable than any amount of adaptation to the great world of the Pembrokes. The same idea appears prominently in each of the early novels. Caroline Abbott in *Where Angels Fear to Tread* (1905) is "saved" from Sawston values by an unforgettable glimpse of Gino Carella fondling his baby, and another character, Philip Herriton, is likewise saved by his memory of Caroline's passion for Gino. Though Philip's experience is hardly less vicarious than Rickie's, he has discovered "something indestructible—something which she, who had given it, could never take away." [17] Lucy Honeychurch, the heroine of A Room With a View (1908), has three "eternal moments": a murder scene in the Piazza Signoria in Florence; an encounter with her future husband, George Emerson, on a hillside near Fiesole; and an unexpected sight of George in a wood near her home. Each episode produces a significant change in her total frame of mind, though she does not realize this until later. Her struggle to free herself from social inhibition—the perennial struggle of Forster's protagonists— is identical with her effort to "recall" these symbolic occasions. When she has understood that they refute what she has learned from "society," she too will have been saved.

Forster's early fiction, then, provides a realistic justification for symbolic thinking. This justification is spelled out by Rickie in The Longest Journey: "It seems to me that here and there in life we meet with a person or incident that is symbolical. It's nothing in itself, yet for the moment it stands for some eternal principle. We accept it, at whatever costs, and we have accepted life. But if we are frightened and reject it, the moment, so to speak, passes; the symbol is never offered again." (p. 158; see also p. 289) Rickie knows whereof he speaks, for he has had two such moments himself: his confrontation of Gerald and Agnes and his meeting with Stephen just after he has learned that Stephen is his brother. He has, in a sense, "accepted life" by remembering the Gerald-Agnes emblem of sexual passion, but his subsequent tragedy implies that this abstraction, this fixation of Agnes has been destructive. It is no longer sufficient, as it was in Where Angels Fear to Tread, for the hero to experience a symbolic moment in order to be "saved"; he must also return to the prosaic everyday world and make his peace with "nature." The irony of Rickie's fate is that his new-found interest in nature (i.e. in heterosexual love) is precisely what prevents him from behaving naturally; his unrealistic attitude toward Agnes draws him unawares into the heresies of Sawston. As for his second opportunity for symbolism, Agnes has, as she boasts (p. 159), prevented him from seizing it. Rickie's life from that day onward is a continual effort to recapture his true relationship to Stephen; but, since the crucial moment has come and gone already, the effort is doomed to failure. And in a parallel sense, Rickie's allegories are equally doomed by their unnaturalness. Because they imply that communion with nature is merely an ideal, an intellectual concept rather than a possible reality, they fail to support Rickie's meager faith that "poetry, not prose, lies at the core" of nature.

It appears, then, that the significant connection between Rickie's

art and Forster's lies in the fact that both men are hampered by their
latent skepticism about the availability of meaning. Forster is convinced, as Rickie is, that certain moments in life have a legitimate symbolic value, but he is also aware of the obverse of this: most moments
are not symbolic at all. Yet, since the artist must find his symbols within
the natural world rather than impose them from without, he cannot
afford to turn his back on the humdrum experience of life, as Rickie
tries to do. The artist's problem, in short, is essentially the problem of
the humanist as Forster outlined it in his "coinage" chapter: to seek
for meaning only in the real world, yet somehow to forestall the "bankruptcy" of disillusionment.

In this light the humanist and the symbolist are not to be separated;
as Charles Feidelson has said, "Symbolism is humanism, but a critical
humanism." [18] In asserting the transcendent important of certain occurrences, symbolism implies a want of meaning in all other occurrences;
it points not only to a continuous need for order but also to a continuous doubt that order will be found. The symbolist deliberately runs
the risk of incurring the spiritual bankruptcy of the disillusioned humanist, for he repeatedly subjects himself to the uncertain flux of the
natural world in order to seek for meaning. Forster's critique of the
various symbols in his own novel seems to imply a franker acceptance
of this peril than we can find in the other early works; he subjects
Rickie's symbols (and by extension, his own) to a more austere standard of validity, a more skeptical standard than before. *The Longest
Journey*, in short, attempts to come to grips with the aesthetic consequences of Forster's pessimism.

This attempt is, to be sure, only partially successful. In abandoning
the comic framework of *Where Angels Fear to Tread* and *A Room
With a View*,[19] Forster occasionally lapses into passages of bathos and
Meredithian philosophizing—of which the "coinage" chapter is perhaps
the most extreme example. The inconvenience is not permanent, however; in *Howards End* Forster regains his urbanity of tone while man-
aging to treat the same serious theme he broached in *The Longest
Journey*. The "goblins" of panic and emptiness that are met and temporarily exorcised in that novel are representative of the same misgivings that haunt Rickie Elliot, and they seem more conspicuous and
menacing than in the earlier novel. And in *A Passage to India*, Forster's
major achievement as a novelist, his skepticism has in a sense become
the subject of the book. No effort is made to contradict the fear that
certain knowledge of God is unavailable; that our friendships, though
important to us, have no bearing on the rest of the universe; and that
we are doomed by our nature to be victimized by prejudice and delu-

sion. From insisting thinly that we ought to love one another, Forster passes to admitting that whether we do or not, the gods will not take note of it. Rickie Elliot's bankruptcy, which is presented as a result of personal limitations of character and vision, is generalized in *A Passage to India* to encompass the bankruptcy of any and every attempt to find human meaning endorsed by the physical universe.

It may seem perverse to say that *The Longest Journey* is chiefly valuable because it points Forster toward this dead-end. Our interest, however, lies primarily in his art, and it does seem true that his artistic maturity is connected with the way he accommodates his philosophical doubts. Those doubts remain constant from first to last, but Forster's art accepts them with increasing wholeness and poise. The result, imperfectly projected in *The Longest Journey*, is an art that tries to accept the consequences of our subjection to nature, yet which seeks finally to create an order rival to nature's—to become a humanistic monument that stands out the more clearly because the space surrounding it lies in darkness.

NOTES

1. See, e.g., Lionel Trilling, *E. M. Forster* (London, 1944), p. 67, and John Harvey, "Imagination and Moral Theme in E. M. Forster's *The Longest Journey*," *Essays in Criticism*, VI (October, 1956), 418–433.

2. *The Longest Journey* (Norfolk, Connecticut, n.d.), p. 260.

3. E. K. Brown, "The Revival of E. M. Forster," *Yale Review*, XXXIII (1944), 673.

4. Ansell may have borrowed the thought from Byron, *Don Juan*, I. 1545f., but he could also have learned it from Lowes Dickinson. See Forster, *Goldsworthy Lowes Dickinson* (New York, 1934), p. 41.

5. In this connection one is reminded of Rickie's early exchange of letters with Ansell on the subject of Rickie's engagement. When Ansell warns his friend against "the eternal feminine," Rickie answers that "this letter of yours is the most wonderful thing that has ever happened to me yet—more wonderful (I don't exaggerate) than the moment when Agnes promised to marry me." He assures Ansell that Agnes will never come between them, and asks rhetorically: "Can't I love you both?" (p. 98)

6. A similar motive may be involved in Agnes' willingness to marry Rickie. She too is incapable of genuine passion apart from Gerald, but she has heard of Gerald's early treatment of Rickie, and "she had a thrill of joy when she thought of the weak boy in the clutches of the strong one." (p. 63) The same sadist-masochist relationship that held between Gerald and Rickie is resumed between Agnes and Rickie. In a sense, therefore, it is proper to say that Rickie and Agnes are brought together by their memories of Gerald's treatment of *each other* rather than of themselves.

7. *E. M. Forster,* p. 67.

8. We may note in passing that Ansell's argument corresponds roughly to the main point in G. E. Moore's *Principia Ethica.* Ansell, like Moore, remains Platonistic in believing that ethical attributes really exist, but he also shares Moore's rejection of the "naturalistic fallacy" of finding these *a priori* attributes within the perceived "great world." Under Ansell's tutelage Rickie thus suffers an intellectual revolution parallel to the revolution that Moore imposed on Lowes Dickinson and others.

9. See James McConkey, *The Novels of E. M. Forster* (Ithaca, 1957), pp. 115–117.

10. *Ibid.,* pp. 107–117.

11. *Ibid.,* p. 117.

12. It may seem inconsistent that Forster should praise a Christian cathedral in so un-Christian a novel, but this is not in real violation of his anti-asceticism. Salisbury has value because generations of simple villagers "have found in her the reasonable crisis of their lives." (p. 281) The ascetic side of Christianity is epitomized in Cadover Church, whose weak, cracked bell reminds Rickie of his own unsturdiness. Forster's contrast of this bell with the rich, harmonious bell of Salisbury emphasizes the difference between Rickie and Stephen. It possibly also recalls a passage from Nietzsche's *Genealogy of Morals:* "The right of the happy to existence, the right of bells with a full tone over the discordant cracked bells, is verily a thousand times greater: they alone are the *sureties* of the future, they alone are *bound* to man's future." (*The Philosophy of Nietzsche.* New York, 1927, p. 751.) The sentence could stand as an epigraph for the whole of *The Longest Journey.*

13. See, e.g., "The Story of a Panic," "The Other Side of the Hedge," "Other Kingdom," and "The Curate's Friend," in Forster's *Collected Tales.*

14. See *Ibid.,* "The Celestial Omnibus," "The Road from Colonus," "The Machine Stops," "The Point of It," "The Story of the Siren," and "The Eternal Moment."

15. See *Ibid.,* "The Road from Colonus," "The Story of a Panic," "Other Kingdom," "The Curate's Friend," "The Point of It," and "The Eternal Moment."

16. "The Point of It," *Ibid.,* p. 218.

17. *Where Angels Fear to Tread* (New York, 1958), p. 183.

18. Charles N. Feidelson, Jr., *Symbolism and American Literature* (Chicago, 1953), p. 218.

19. Though *A Room With a View* was published a year later than *The Longest Journey,* much of it had been written before the latter was completed. *A Room With a View,* in fact, reads like what we might expect from Rickie Elliot's novel "about a man and a woman who meet and are happy."

13

LIONEL TRILLING

◆──◆

Howards End

BIOGRAPHY intrudes itself into literary judgment and keeps it from being "pure." As we form our opinion of a particular work, certainly the sole object of our thought should be the work itself. But it seldom is—and although we call extraneous the facts that thrust themselves upon us, they inevitably enter into our judgment. We are always conscious of an author, and this consciousness does not rise only from elements in the work; the extraneous personal facts that reach us are never wholly ignored. Literary facts are as intrusive as personal facts, though no doubt they are more "legitimate." The author's whole career presents itself to us not improperly as an architectonic whole of which each particular work is a part; and the shape of that career, the nature and pace of its development, the past failures and successes or those which we know are to come, the very size of the structure, the place of any single unit in the logic of the whole—all bear upon our feelings about any particular work.

In reading Forster there are two literary facts that affect us. One is that, despite an early fecundity which produced four remarkable novels in five years, Forster waited fourteen years to produce his fifth, after which he produced nothing for an even longer period. Perhaps his future biographer will be able to explain his temporary retirement between 1910, the year of *Howards End*, and 1924, the year of *A*

Passage to India, and the second and possibly permanent retirement after the great success of this last novel. But even unexplained, the facts suggest an unusual relation of a man to his craft. In our feeling about Henry James, for instance, it is an element, with a meaning which could no doubt be expressed, that his production is so very large; and we find a similarly implicit significance in the fact that Stendhal waited until he was forty-eight to produce the first of his great novels and until he was fifty-six to produce the second. Just so, it intrudes upon us as an important element in our feeling about Forster that, having mastered his art, he has twice abandoned it. No doubt, with some difficulty, that feeling could be made precise; it fluctuates between disapproval of a dereliction from duty and a sense of relief that a fine artist has not seen art as a grim imperative.

The other literary fact that is likely to influence our feelings about all of Forster's novels is that they are by the author of *Howards End.* This is not to imply a denigration of the other work or to suggest a significant difference in quality. But *Howards End* is undoubtedly Forster's masterpiece; it develops to their full the themes and attitudes of the early books and throws back upon them a new and enhancing light. It justifies these attitudes by connecting them with a more mature sense of responsibility.

For when we have emerged from the immediate seduction of *Where Angels Fear To Tread, The Longest Journey* and *A Room with a View* we can sometimes feel that their assumptions have been right but rather too easy. In one disguise or another, the mythology and fantasy of the early stories have found their way into the novels, and the mythology formulates well but abstractly, the fantasy solves dashingly but sometimes facilely. The formulations and the solutions have been just, but they have not been worked out against sufficient resistance. We have learned that naturalness is to be trusted, that authority and society are stupid and insincere. But we have learned this in a mythological way, as if by parable, and with a great deal of attractive *brio* and *bravura;* we have not seen it put to the test. In the early novels what is bad in life has indeed the look of reality, but what is good has the appearance of myth.

Forster is wonderfully accurate in his perception of the failures in human relationships and he accurately names causes. But although the true relationships he sets up against the false do indeed adequately illuminate badness, they are never in themselves real. Thus Gino can stand as a criticism of English feeling, but he cannot be part of Caro-

line's life. Agnes and Mrs. Failing are entirely alive, but Rickie's
mother, the symbol of life, is dead and a spirit; and although Stephen
marries happily we never see his wife, she is only a voice. It is certainly significant that although we hear much about the transcendent
value of sexual love, we are never shown a happy marriage, and when
we consider the importance of Ansell in *The Longest Journey* we
cannot ignore the weight of his condemnation of marriage.[1] Lucy and
George, we feel, are too impalpable for anything but a merely symbolic union.

Then too, we can become a little weary of Forster's way of dealing
with authority. I. A. Richards speaks of Forster's hatred of doctors,
schoolmasters and clergymen; they are the representatives of authority
and always stupid and insincere. Mr. Richards is mistaken when he
says that Forster's "real audience is youth, caught at that stage when
rebellion against the uncomfortable conventions is easy because the
cost of abandoning them has not been fully counted." Forster's real
audience is maturity, but Mr. Richards has located the element which
might possibly alienate mature people.

The attack on authority is not itself a fault, it may even be a virtue;
but it requires some equally forceful indication of what *right* authority
should be. For example, Mr. Fielding of *A Passage to India* is the
single example of a responsible man who is admirable, but significantly
he is admirable only so long as he rather despises the job he does so
well; when he takes it seriously he is less to be trusted. Again, although
the emotion of parenthood has been so important in the novels, it is
never adequately represented beyond its lyric expression. With the
exception of Mr. Ansell, a shadowy figure who never actually appears
in *The Longest Journey,* and of Mr. Emerson, who is not entirely convincing because he is motherly rather than fatherly in his love for
George, there are no effective fathers in the novels—for Gino's father-
hood is mythological and soon ends, and Mr. Wilcox's relation to
Charles (in *Howards End*) is good but formal; on the other hand,
Caroline Abbott's father is a nag, Rickie's father is cruel, and all the
other fathers, to a remarkable number, are dead.

Of course it is possible that an American cannot judge fairly what
a revolt against the English tradition of authority should be. The
English father is said to be more dominant in the home than the
American father; in England the school authority is stronger than here
and expressed in corporal punishment; the firmness of English class
lines is also significant; and perhaps most important of all is the neces-

sity in a colonial empire of putting a premium on the authoritative type, even in its excess. Yet even taking into account these provocations to rebelliousness, we cannot but feel that through all of Forster's early novels we are being led away from officialism and stuffed-shirtism not toward maturity but toward youth. In none of his novels does Forster give us a mature hero. When George Emerson says that "youth matters intellectually" we want to reply that what matters intellectually is not youth and not age but rightness: we begin to feel that a certain irresponsibility is here at work.

Yet it is never entirely fair to invalidate a negative criticism by saying that it is not sufficiently positive—Forster's criticism of modern life is certainly not the less valid because he fails to exemplify what he means by the good life. What my comments do suggest, however, is that Forster, in the three early novels, has not fully done his job as a novelist: he represents the truth but he does not show the difficulties the truth must meet. And the criterion by which this judgment is made is a work of Forster's own: *Howards End* is a work of full responsibility. Its theme is "Only connect the prose and the passion," and it shows how almost hopelessly difficult it is to make this connection. That the insights of Forster's earlier novels could have come to face this difficulty is their justification.

Howards End is a novel about England's fate. It is a story of the class war. The war is latent but actual—so actual indeed that a sword is literally drawn and a man is really killed. England herself appears in the novel in palpable form, for the story moves by symbols and not only all its characters but also an elm, a marriage, a symphony, and a scholar's library stand for things beyond themselves. The symbol for England is the house whose name gives the title to the book. Like the plots of so many English novels, the plot of *Howards End* is about the rights of property, about a destroyed will-and-testament and rightful and wrongful heirs. It asks the question, "Who shall inherit England?"

The class struggle is not between the classes but within a single class, the middle class. Neither the aristocracy nor the proletariat is represented and the very poor are specifically barred—"We are not concerned with the very poor," the novelist says. "They are unthinkable, and only to be approached by the statistician or the poet. This story deals with gentlefolk, or with those who are obliged to pretend that they are gentlefolk." At the far end of the vast middle class scale is Leonard Bast, the little clerk. He stands "at the extreme verge of gentility," at the very edge of the "abyss" of poverty. At the upper end of the scale is Mr. Wilcox, the business man, rich and rapidly growing richer. Between are the Schlegels, Margaret and Helen, living comfortably on solid, adequate incomes. The Schlegels are intellectuals and constitute the point of consciousness of the novel; upon them the story balances, touching and connecting the wealthy middle class and the depressed middle class.

But the character who dominates the novel belongs to none of these groups. She is Mrs. Wilcox, who, despite her position in the story, soon leaves it. It is perhaps significant that her name is Ruth, for her heart is sad, the home for which she is sick is her chief passion and she stands amid alien corn. She herself is descended from the yeoman class to which Forster gives his strongest sympathies.

It is said of Ruth Wilcox by a "wise" character in the book, that she should have married a soldier, and Margaret Schlegel, who hated armies but liked soldiers, understands what is meant. For although Plato's *Republic* is not mentioned, it is nevertheless pervasive throughout the novel and Margaret, whose father had been a soldier before he became a philosopher, might well have remembered Plato's Watchdogs, the military Guardians from whom the philosophical Guardians were chosen; she might have remembered too that when the Just State is translated into the Just Man, the soldiers represent what Plato called the Spirited Element,—the will, the love of honor and all generous things—which supports the reason.

Certainly the man Ruth Wilcox married had nothing of the Spirited Element in him. Henry Wilcox could give what his second wife in a moment of anger called an "unweeded kindness," but he lived the life of the Platonic Artisans, gainful, mediocre and unaware. The result for Ruth Wilcox was not frustration or unhappiness but tragedy, and her death was marked by cynicism, "not the superficial cynicism that snarls and sneers, but the cynicism that can go with courtesy and tenderness." Her husband had loved her, but his best praise had been for her "steadiness." Nor could her children draw on her for anything good. Her daughter Evie, handsome and tight-lipped, is a breeder of puppies, a dull and cruel girl; her younger son Paul, a vague figure in the novel, is a competent colonial administrator but a weak and foolish man; her elder son Charles is a bully and a righteous blunderer: her family, whom she loves and who adore her, are her alien corn. She is not sorry to die in her early fifties.

Mrs. Wilcox is not a clever woman—a whole scene is devoted to showing how clever people can even find her dull—and she is not, in the usual meaning of the word, a "sensitive" woman. But she has wisdom which is traditional and ancestral.

She seemed to belong not to the young people and their motor, but to the house and the trees that overshadowed it. One knew that she worshipped the past and that the instinctive wisdom the past alone can bestow had descended upon her—that wisdom to which we give the clumsy name of aristocracy. High born she might not be. But assuredly she cared about her ancestors and let them help her.

The house to which she "belongs" is a small though beautiful farmhouse and her ancestors were simple people, yeomen, for Forster in this novel, as in *The Longest Journey*, puts his faith in the men of the English countryside.

Here men had been up since dawn. Their hours were ruled, not by a London office, but by the movements of the crops and sun. That they were men of the finest type only the sentimentalist can declare. But they kept to the life of daylight. They are England's hope. Clumsily they carry forward the torch of the sun, until such time as the nation sees fit to take it up. Half clodhopper, half boardschool prig, they can still throw back to a nobler stock, and breed yeomen.

As a character Ruth Wilcox is remarkably—and perhaps surprisingly —successful. Her "reality" is of a strange kind and consists in her having no reality in the ordinary sense—she does not have, that is, the reality of personality, of idiosyncrasy or even of power. Her strength comes exactly from her lack of force, her distinction from her lack of distinguishing traits. She suggests Shakespeare's "gentle" women, the Countess of *All's Well* or an older Imogen; or she has a touch of Chaucer's Griselda. It is appropriate that we find her kind in the past, for she represents England's past. But for all her lack of contemporary "reality," she is more successful as a real person than as a symbol; she must be seen to be believed and when she dies and becomes the brooding ghost of the story, she becomes a little trying, as perhaps all such symbolic spirits in novels do.

Before Mrs. Wilcox dies she has found the heir for her Howards End. She could not leave it to her family—"to them Howards End was a house: they could not know that to her it had been a spirit for which she sought a spiritual heir." As she lay on her death-bed she had pencilled a note expressing the wish that the house go to Margaret Schlegel. To the Wilcox family nothing could have seemed a greater betrayal. For the Wilcoxes and the Schlegels had had dealings. They had met, joined for a moment when Paul and Helen had thought they were in love, and then had separated in a storm of "telegrams and anger." The Wilcoxes had been aware of how nearly they had been tricked in that affair. Now, with Ruth Wilcox's note before them, they must defend themselves again; they manage to convince themselves that the note should never have been written and is not binding; they destroy it and send Margaret Mrs. Wilcox's vinaigrette.

In the end Howards End comes to Margaret; but it is to pass beyond her to a little classless child, the son of Helen Schlegel and the pitiful Leonard Bast. For each of these intellectual sisters has reached out to the mysterious extremes of the middle class, Margaret upward to the Wilcoxes, Helen downward to the Basts. Such, in this novel, is their function as intellectuals.

Perhaps the intellectual first came into historical notice when Burke, attacking the French Revolution, spoke with contempt of the many small lawyers and small priests in the Assembly. They were, he said, merely men of mind, therefore ill-suited to the management of a state. Burke, we know, had a quarrel of long standing with the rational intellect and with those who used it. With his usual insight, he knew that a great change was coming about in the conduct of human affairs. The French Revolution was the first great occasion when Mind—conscious, verbalized mind—became an important element in national politics. Interest, of course, was also in play, and force too, but mind had the new function of generalizing interest and justifying force. And since Burke's day mind has played an increasing part in politics. Matthew Arnold spoke of the "idea-moved" masses of France and indeed ideas, far more than actual interests, have moved masses, so that even the most repressive and obscurantist systems are systems of ideas.

But the intellectual class does not descend only from the political priests and lawyers Burke attacked. Its origins are also to be found in the religious groups of the 18th century—further back than that, no doubt, in the beginnings of Protestantism: perhaps Erasmus and Milton are its true ancestors, but the 18th century witnessed such a notable breaking up of religious orthodoxies and such a transference of the religious feelings to secular life that it is surely the true seed-time of the intellectual as we now know him. One observes in the social circles of the first generation of English romantic poets the sense of morality, the large feelings and the intellectual energy that had once been given to religion.

This moral and pious aspect of the intellectual's tradition is important. Intellectuals as a class do not live by ideas alone but also by ideals. That is, they must desire the good not only for themselves but for all, and we might say that one of the truly new things in human life in the last two centuries is the politics of conscious altruism. To be sure, the sword and the stiletto have always had to be supplemented by this language, but the 18th century produced and the 19th century multiplied a class of people who sincerely thought or sincerely spoke of politics in terms of the freedom and privilege of groups less advantageously placed than their own; the word "underprivileged" is a key to the nature of the intellectual's political attitude.

Consequently, liberal intellectuals have always moved in an aura of self-congratulation. They sustain themselves by flattering themselves with intentions and they dismiss as "reactionary" whoever questions them. When the liberal intellectual thinks of himself, he thinks chiefly of his own good will and prefers not to know that the good will generates its own problems, that the love of humanity has its own vices and the love of truth its own insensibilities. The choice of the moral course does not settle the quality of morality; there is, as it were, a morality of morality.

And one of the complications of the intellectual's life is his relation to people who are not intellectuals. The very fact of being articulate, of making articulateness a preoccupation, sets up a barrier between the intellectual and the non-intellectual. The intellectual, the "freest" of men, consciously the most liberated from class, is actually the most class-marked and class-bound of all men. With the business man his relation is likely to be unreal; the man who makes money can easily be worried by the intellectual's judgment of him, so pervasive and so coercive (up to a point) is the modern respect for the ideal of disinterestedness. And if we plumb the true feeling of the intellectual (it is not done often enough) we must see his own obscure admiration for the powers of the business man. Then too, because the intellectual, whatever his social origin, always becomes a member of the middle class, he is obscurely aware how dependent is his existence upon the business civilization he is likely to fear and despise.

The relation of the intellectual to the lower classes is no less confused. There is a whole mass of mankind, the enormous majority, indeed, whom he considers it his duty to "protect." To these people he vaguely supposes himself to be in a benevolent superior relation, paternal, pedagogic, even priestlike. He believes it necessary to suppose that they are entirely good; the essential goodness of the masses is for him as much a certainty as the essential badness of the business classes. He is supposed to have nothing but the most benevolent feelings toward them; in *The Longest Journey*, for example, everyone is shocked when Stephen, who is a democrat but not an intellectual, feels the normal angry, aggressive emotions toward humble people. And so the intellectual, in addition to the barrier of his articulateness which cuts him off from the masses as well as from the middle classes, stands behind another barrier, the necessity of regarding the mass of men as objects of his benevolence.

The situation is sad but comic. It is the situation of the Schlegel sisters in *Howards End*. The comedy begins when Helen Schlegel is momentarily seduced by the Wilcox way of life. Visiting at Howards End, she finds her new friends strong; she likes them because they are all "keen on games" and because they put everything to use. Her own life of ideas seems suddenly inadequate.

> She had liked giving in to Mr. Wilcox, or Evie or Charles; she had liked being told that her notions of life were sheltered or academic; that Equality was nonsense, Art and Literature nonsense. One by one the Schlegel fetiches had been overthrown, and, though professing to defend them, she rejoiced. When Mr. Wilcox said that one sound man of business did more good to the world than a dozen of your social reformers, she had swallowed the curious assertion without a gasp, and had leant back luxuriously among the cushions of his motor-car. When Charles said, "Why be polite to servants? they don't understand it," she had not given the Schlegel retort of, "If they don't understand it, I do." No; she vowed to be less polite to servants in the future. "I am swathed in cant," she thought, "and it is good for me to be stripped of it."

Actually, however, it was not a set of ideas that Helen was admiring—it was sex. It was with masculinity that she had fallen in love. It was the idea of men "taking hold," being efficient, having families and supporting them. Perhaps, too, of men owning motor-cars, for in 1910 the automobile is already the totem of the Wilcox males; it pervades the novel, but never attractively, and the Wilcox's chauffeur, Crane, in contrast to Shaw's genial Ennery Striker, is represented as a vaguely malevolent figure. Mr. Wilcox's smoking room, decorated to the masculine taste, is furnished with chairs of maroon leather, "as if a motor-car had spawned."

Howards End is not only a novel of the class war but of the war between men and women. Margaret, like Helen, is to respond to the Wilcox masculinity. Indeed, she marries Henry Wilcox. More perceptive than Helen, she knows this masculinity for what it is—far from adequate—but she accepts it more simply, demanding less of it. Perhaps neither of these young women would have been so urgent toward masculinity had their father lived or had their younger brother Tibby been brought up by a man to be manly. But they feared their own feminine lives and the clever men of their acquaintance offered them no escape. And so Helen, when she is kissed by Paul Wilcox in the garden of Howards End, is quite carried away. The normal life seems suddenly open to her, the life, one guesses, of the body.

> It is so easy for an Englishman to sneer at these chance collisions of human beings. To the insular cynic and the insular moralist they offer an equal opportunity. It is so easy to talk about "passing emotion" and to forget how vivid the emotion was as it passed. Our impulse to sneer, to forget, is at root a good one. We recognize that emotion is not enough, and that men and women are personalities capable of sustained relations, not mere opportunities for an electrical discharge. Yet we rate the impulse too highly. We do not admit that by collisions of this trivial sort the doors of heaven may be shaken open. To Helen, at all events, her life was to bring nothing more intense than the embrace of this boy who played no part in it. . . . In time his slender personality faded, the scene that he evoked endured. In all the variable years that followed she never saw the like of it again.

Helen responded to the masculine principle, but it turned out not to be masculine at all. At breakfast next morning, Paul, who had a career to make in Africa, was frightened and abashed. To Helen the sight is never to be forgotten. " 'When that kind of man looks frightened, it is too awful. It is all right for us to be frightened, or for men of another sort—father, for instance; but for men like that!' " She never does forget, though she thinks she does; the sexual betrayal by the Wilcoxes generates in her a hatred for Wilcoxism that is to make her act desperately, even insanely.

The sexual theme plays through the book, lightly, without much pressure save at one point, but with great seriousness. The great fact about the Wilcoxes is that which D. H. Lawrence saw, the fact of sexual deficiency. Paul with his fear, Charles with his silly wife, Dolly —"She was a rubbishy little creature, and she knew it"—Evie with her heavy love-banter, Mr. Wilcox with his lofty morality and his single, sordid, clandestine love-affair, all exhibit the deficiency.

The sexual lack has its concomitance and perhaps its result in the lack of a developed sense of personality. Helen says:

> "Perhaps the little thing that says 'I' is missing out of the middle of their heads, and then it's a waste of time to blame them. There's a nightmare of a theory that says a special race is being born which

will rule the rest of us in the future just because it lacks the little thing that says 'I.' There are two kinds of people—our kind, who live straight from the middle of their heads, and the other kind who can't because their heads have no middle. They can't say 'I.' They *aren't* in fact. . . . Pierpont Morgan has never said 'I' in his life. No superman can say 'I want' because 'I want' must lead to the question 'Who am I?' and so to Pity and to Justice. He only says 'want'—'Want Europe,' if he's Napoleon; 'want wives' if he's Bluebeard; 'want Botticelli' if he's Pierpont Morgan. Never 'I' and if you could pierce through him, you'd find panic and emptiness in the middle."

She has no doubt been reading H. G. Wells with aversion and perhaps she has been having a bout with the romantic philosophers in her German father's library: certainly she makes an admirably accurate defense of the best of romantic egoism.

The recipient of her little speech is Leonard Bast on the night of the lowest ebb in his sad fortunes. Leonard is an insurance clerk whom the Schlegels had picked up in a concert-hall in a little farce of mistaken umbrellas and forgotten purses. The Schlegels had met the Wilcoxes touring a cathedral; they meet Leonard Bast at a concert: culture comically brings the middle class together and separates it. For Leonard is under the terrible necessity of being cultured.

This is the new obligation that democracy has brought. It will always be one of the mysteries of our civilization. Culture does not help us make our way in a business civilization, yet it has its value and yields its return. In our attitude toward the poet and the professor we are perfectly ambivalent: we know they are useless, yet they make us humble-defiant, and the business man who declares himself a lowbrow is aggrieved if anyone agrees with him.

Leonard is "one of the thousands who have lost the life of the body and failed to reach the life of the spirit, who had given up the glory of the animal for a tail coat and a couple of ideas." His grandparents had been agricultural laborers, a fact of which he is ashamed; reading Ruskin is for him what a revival meeting was for his grandparents—he hopes for a sudden conversion, for the secret of life. When he touches the Schlegel world where art is breathed with the air and where ideas are not the secret of life but its very stuff, he is wholly confused. Margaret, as she observes him, questions all the 19th century's faith in education:

Culture had worked in her own case, but during the last few weeks she doubted whether it humanized the majority, so wide and widening is the gulf that stretches between the natural and the philosophic man, so many the good chaps who are wrecked trying to cross it. She knew the type very well—the aspirations, the mental dishonesty, the familiarity with the outsides of books.

What the Schlegel sisters cherished in Leonard was the solid grain of honesty under the pitiful overlay of culture. He has walked all one night to see the dawn in the country, moved by an impulse which was half native sensibility, half literary sentimentality. " 'But was the dawn wonderful?' " Helen asks him. "With unforgettable sincerity he replied, 'No.' The word . . . flew like a pebble from the sling. Down toppled all that seemed ignoble or literary in his talk, down toppled tiresome R.L.S. and the 'love of the earth' and his silk top-hat." But Leonard cannot understand this of himself; indeed, he is not interested in himself, only in his soul. Just so he cannot be interested in the Schlegel girls except as sounding boards for his culture; in this he is like the Wilcoxes, for, like them, he is not aware of people but only of their status and function: he is obsessed by class. And even the Schlegel girls cannot see Leonard for his class; their very passion for democracy makes them less aware of him than of the abyss that is at his feet, the abyss of wasted lives, of "panic and emptiness" of which Helen especially is so conscious. Listening to the Allegro of Beethoven's Fifth Symphony she hears its terror truthfully stated:

> . . . The music started with a goblin walking quietly over the universe from end to end. Others followed him. They were not aggressive creatures; it was that that made them so horrible to Helen. They merely observed in passing that there was no such thing as splendour or heroism in the world. After the interlude of elephants dancing, they returned and made the observation for the second time. Helen could not contradict them, for, once at all events, she had felt the same, and had seen the reliable walls of youth collapse. Panic and emptiness! Panic and emptiness! The goblins were right.
>
> Her brother raised his finger: it was the transitional passage on the drum.
>
> For, as if things were going too far, Beethoven took hold of the goblins and made them do what he wanted. He appeared in person. He gave them a little push, and they began to walk in major key instead of in a minor, and then—he blew with his mouth and they were scattered! Gusts of splendour, gods and demi-gods contending with vast swords, color and fragrance broadcast on the field of battle, magnificent victory, magnificent death! Oh, it all burst before the girl, and she even stretched out her gloved hands as if it were tangible. Any fate was

titanic; any contest desirable; conqueror and conquered would alike
be applauded by the angels of the utmost stars.

And the goblins—they had not really been there at all? They were
only the phantoms of cowardice and unbelief? One healthy impulse
would dispel them? Men like the Wilcoxes, or President Roosevelt
would say yes. Beethoven knew better. The goblins had really been
there. They might return—and they did. It was as if the splendour of
life might boil over and waste to steam and froth. In its dissolution
one heard the terrible, ominous note, and a goblin with increased
malignity, walked quietly over the universe from end to end. Panic and
emptiness! Panic and emptiness! Even the flaming ramparts of the
world might fall.

Beethoven chose to make all right in the end. He built the ramparts
up. He blew with his mouth for the second time, and again the goblins
were scattered. . . . But the goblins were there. They could return.
He had said so bravely, and that is why one can trust Beethoven when
he says other things.[2]

Panic and emptiness make the dreadful fate that awaits people in
this novel; they are the modern doom. And they threaten the unformed
Leonard Bast as well as the cultivated Helen Schlegel.

Leonard is destroyed. The immediate cause of his destruction is
Mr. Wilcox, who casually remarks to the sisters that Leonard's firm
is unsound and advises that Leonard leave before the crash. The company turns out to be perfectly sound but Leonard has taken and lost
another job and he and his wife Jacky fall quite destitute. Thus Helen
finds them. Paul's betrayal has done its work on her; she hates all
Wilcoxes, the idea of Margaret marrying Henry is inconceivable and
when she fantastically drags the Basts to Henry's country place in
Wales on the night of his daughter's wedding, her action is not so
much humane as vengeful. Here the story takes its operatic turn, for
poor Jacky is discovered to be Henry's former mistress and Margaret
supports Henry in his refusal to help the Basts. That night Helen gives
herself to Leonard, joylessly, out of an hysterical sense of justice.

Margaret's impulse toward Henry Wilcox is precisely the same as
Helen's had been toward Paul, except that hers is more explicit and
less sexually romantic. Henry is one of the race that runs the world,
and he is masculine. She cannot continue to despise the people who
control the ships and trains that carry "us literary people around."
" 'More and more,' " she says, " 'do I refuse to draw my income and
sneer at those who guarantee it.' " To be sure, it disturbs her that the
man she is to marry thinks that both money and sex are unclean. He

cannot talk directly about the one or feel at ease with the other. Yet she loves Henry and she looks for fulfillment in her marriage with him; she looks for reality. Writing to Helen at the time of the affair with Paul, she had said:

> The truth is that there is a great outer life that you and I have never touched—a life in which telegrams and anger count. Personal relations, that we think are supreme, are not supreme there. There love means marriage settlements, death, death duties. So far I'm clear. But here my difficulty. This outer life, though obviously horrid, often seems the real one—there's grit in it. It does breed character. Do personal relationships lead to sloppiness in the end?

The outer life betrays Margaret; it is the inner life which "pays" and which, in the end, takes over the outer life. Howards End has for some time stood empty, a mere storage place for the Schlegels' furniture and their father's library. Miss Avery, the sibylline character who cares for the house, cherishing the memory of Ruth Wilcox and identifying Margaret with her, has arranged the furniture in the rooms and put the books on the shelves: thus, by the agency of women, the best of traditional England is furnished with the stuff of the intellect. And over the bookcase Miss Avery has hung the father's sword: [3] it was she who had said that Ruth Wilcox should have married a soldier. And in Howards End, thus furnished, Margaret and Helen meet after their long separation. For Helen has kept herself hidden from her family and has declared that she is going to live in Germany; Margaret, unable to understand the estrangement, has tempted her to Howards End to choose some souvenir of their old life before her departure. At the meeting she discovers that Helen is pregnant with Leonard's child. The reconciliation of the sisters precipitates what seems the end of Margaret's relation with Henry, for Helen wishes to spend the night among their old possessions and although Henry has no feeling except ownership for Howards End, he refuses to have it desecrated by Helen's presence.

The outer life that fails Margaret now fails itself; but the inner life comes to its rescue. Leonard, torn by remorse over his relation with Helen, comes down to Howards End to confess to Margaret. The dull moral blunderer, Charles Wilcox, is in the library when Bast arrives. Knowing Leonard to be Helen's "lover," he snatches down the old Schlegel sabre to beat him with the flat. Leonard dies, not of the blow but of a weak heart, and as he drops he clutches the bookcase which falls and sends the books tumbling down on him in a shower—the books that in life had promised him so much and given him so little. Charles is jailed for manslaughter and his father, quite broken, relies wholly on Margaret, who establishes him in Howards End together with Helen and Helen's baby.

Not for nothing do Margaret and Helen bear the names of the heroines of the two parts of *Faust*, one the heroine of the practical life, the other of the ideal life; Henry Wilcox bears Faust's Christian name and he and Leonard together, the practical man and the seeker after experience, make up the composite hero. Helen's child is the Euphorion—he is the heir not only of Leonard Bast but of Henry Wilcox, for Howards End is to go to Margaret and from her to Helen's child. And the Eternal Feminine has taken complete control of the England which the masculine outer life has so sadly muddled. It is not entirely a happy picture on which Forster concludes, this rather contrived scene of busyness and contentment in the hayfield; the male is too thoroughly gelded, and of the two women, Helen confesses that she cannot love a man, Margaret that she cannot love a child. And the rust of London, with its grim promise of modern life "melted down, all over the world," creeps toward Howards End. Meanwhile the Euphorion, the classless heir of all the classes in this novel, plays in the hayfield and suggests a hope.[4] He is not only the symbol of the classless society but, as he takes his pleasure among the busy workers in the hay, he is also the symbol of the "Only connect!" which was Margaret's clue to the good life. "Only connect the prose and the passion, and both will be exalted, and human love will be seen at its height."

NOTES

1. On the other hand, Rickie, in his moment of regeneration, asserts that happy marriages are possible. But his statement is not nearly so passionate as Ansell's aphorisms on the deep incompatibility of men and women.

2. This would seem an apt occasion to mention Forster's belief that "music is the deepest of the arts and deep beneath the arts." Forster is himself a devoted amateur of the piano.

3. One cannot help thinking of Schiller's sword which Thackeray bought in Weimar and which he hung in his study over his books.

4. I am indebted to my friend Alan Brown for the suggestion of the significance of the names of Margaret and Helen, but any extravagance in the use of the suggestion is my own. And it should be mentioned that Forster, in his biography of Dickinson, speaking of Dickinson's love of *Faust*, is explicit about his own lack of admiration for the work.

14

REUBEN A. BROWER

The Twilight of the Double Vision:
Symbol and Irony in *A Passage to India*

> *. . . the twilight of the double vision . . .*
> *A Passage to India*

In *A Passage to India,* as in all of E. M. Forster's novels, there are admirable scenes of social comedy that remind us of the sunny repose of Jane Austen. We can enjoy the behavior of Mrs. Turton, the great lady of a British civil station, with the same satisfaction with which we view the absurdities of Mrs. Bennet and Lady Catherine de Bourgh. Here is Mrs. Turton commenting on her Indian guests at the Bridge Party given for Adela Quested and Mrs. Moore soon after their arrival in India:

> "They ought never to have been allowed to drive in; it's so bad for them," said Mrs. Turton, who had at last begun her progress to the summer-house accompanied by Mrs. Moore, Miss Quested, and a terrier. "Why they come at all I don't know. They hate it as much as we do. Talk to Mrs. McBryde. Her husband made her give purdah parties until she struck."
> "This isn't a purdah party," corrected Miss Quested.
> "Oh, really," was the haughty rejoinder.
> "Do kindly tell us who these ladies are," asked Mrs. Moore.
> "You're superior to them, anyway. Don't forget that. You're su-

From *The Fields of Light. An Experiment in Critical Reading,* by Reuben Arthur Brower. Copyright 1951 by Oxford University Press, Inc. Reprinted by permission.

perior to everyone in India except one or two of the Ranis, and they're on an equality."

Advancing, she shook hands with the group and said a few words of welcome in Urdu. She had learnt the lingo, but only to speak to her servants, so she knew none of the politer forms and of the verbs only the imperative mood. As soon as her speech was over, she enquired of her companions, "Is that what you wanted?"

"Please tell these ladies that I wish we could speak their language, but we have only just come to their country."

"Perhaps we speak yours a little," one of the ladies said.

"Why, fancy, she understands!" said Mrs. Turton.

"Eastbourne, Piccadilly, High Park Corner," said another of the ladies.

"Oh yes, they're English-speaking."

"But now we can talk: how delightful!" cried Adela, her face lighting up.

"She knows Paris also," called one of the onlookers.

"They pass Paris on the way, no doubt," said Mrs. Turton, as if she was describing the movements of migratory birds. Her manner had grown more distant since she had discovered that some of the group was Westernized, and might apply her own standards to her.

From a politically liberal, cosmopolitan point of view we may be amused at Mrs. Turton's having "learnt the lingo" or at the charming rudeness of her grammar. But we shall not be able to maintain this comfortable frame of mind for long. Or if we suppose so, like Adela we have been taken in by a surface simplicity and by our own excellent principles. Reading a little further, we realize that our enlightened point of view has itself been undermined:

Miss Quested now had her desired opportunity; friendly Indians were before her, and she tried to make them talk, but she failed, she strove in vain against the echoing walls of their civility. Whatever she said produced a murmur of deprecation, varying into a murmur of concern when she dropped her pocket handkerchief. She tried doing nothing, to see what that produced, and they too did nothing.

The scene leaves us in a most discomforting state of mind. The essence of its irony is expressed in a metaphor, "the echoing walls of their civility": friendly conversational gestures are so perfectly reproduced as to prove that nothing whatever has been communicated. But the phrase sends out tentacles of connection well beyond the immediate context. We are reminded of the more sinister echoes of a Marabar cave or of the image that came to Mrs. Moore after telling her son that the British must love the Indians because it "satisfies God":

Mrs. Moore felt that she had made a mistake in mentioning God . . .
She must needs pronounce his name frequently, as the greatest she
knew, yet she had never found it less efficacious. Outside the arch there
seemed always an arch, beyond the remotest echo a silence.

"The echoing walls" adds a new level of irony to the dialogue of the
Bridge Party and at the same time introduces one of the major symbols of A Passage to India.

It is characteristic of A Passage to India, as it is utterly uncharac-
teristic of Pride and Prejudice, that the irony should be expressed
through metaphor and that the meaning of an ironic expression can
be appreciated only in relation to other expressions that are clearly
symbolic. The central design of Forster's novel is composed of a group
of symbolic metaphors, and his irony is inherent in the meaning of his
symbols. By interpreting them and seeing how they unify the experience of the novel, we can also understand the peculiar character of
Forster's irony, how like and how unlike it is to that of Jane Austen.

The main symbols of A Passage to India are named in the titles to
the three Parts of the novel: Mosque, Caves, and Temple. Each is more
or less closely related to a corresponding variant: Arch, Echo, and
Sky. To anyone familiar with the book the three title words [1] are
immediately and richly expressive. Each conveys a generalized impression of a salient object or event in the narrative, an impression that
stands for and is inseparably connected with various large meanings.
To get a sense of Forster's total design it is necessary to see how the
meanings of these symbols are built up through the dramatic structure.
What follows is an attempt to display the kind of design—symbolic,
ironic, and dramatic—peculiar to A Passage to India. (I shall also indicate where and why the design seems to break down.)

The most general meaning of the Mosque symbol is perhaps best
expressed in the scene between Mrs. Moore and Aziz, the young
Indian doctor whom she meets in a mosque near the civil station. In a
dialogue which is a blend of minor mistakes and underlying sympathy
Mrs. Moore and Aziz reach a surprisingly intimate relationship, Aziz
declaring that the Englishwoman is "an Oriental." Although in a later
scene Mrs. Moore calls him her friend, there is something precarious
about their intimacy. In spite of his affectionate declarations Aziz
quickly forgets that he has promised to take Mrs. Moore and Adela to
visit the Marabar Caves. From the scene in the mosque and from
similar episodes, the Mosque comes to symbolize the possibility of
communication between Britons and Indians, and more generally the
possibility of understanding relationships between any two persons.

And in every instance this larger meaning always implies its opposite or near-oppisite, an ambivalence finely suggested by the first description of the mosque. Aziz is especially pleased by the dualism of "black and white" in the frieze above the arches, and he appreciates the stillness and beauty of the building in contrast with "the complex appeal" of the night. At the end of the scene,

> As he strolled downhill beneath the lovely moon, and again saw the lovely mosque, he seemed to own the land as much as anyone owned it. What did it matter if a few flabby Hindus had preceded him there, and a few chilly English succeeded?

In relation to this and various other points in the narrative, the Mosque represents the ambiguous triumph of Islam, the belief Aziz shares with his Moslem friends "that India was one; Moslem; always had been; an assurance that lasted until they looked out of the door."

The Mosque also expresses Fielding's friendship with Aziz and more generally Fielding's conviction that "The world . . . is a globe of men who are trying to reach one another and can best do so by the help of good will plus culture and intelligence . . ." But this Anglo-Indian relationship is a precarious one, too, its instability being finely expressed in the crisscross of the conversation when Fielding visits Aziz during his illness. After his friend leaves, the Indian goes to sleep, dreaming happily of "good Fielding," in a Moslem paradise with domes "whereunder were inscribed, black against white, the ninety-nine attributes of God." The ironic dualism of color echoes the half-hearted comment on his rapprochement with Fielding: ". . . affection had triumphed for once in a way."

Miss Quested's blundering attempts to "know" Indians and her shifting relationship with her fiancé, Mrs. Moore's son, Ronny, reinforce the negative meanings of the symbol. She naïvely imagines that Mrs. Moore in meeting Aziz at the mosque had seen "the real India," a remark that imparts to the symbol still another ironic connotation. Ronny, who interprets the same episode as a piece of native insolence, reveals as always the reduction of human intercourse to the automatic responses of a governing class.

The opening section of the novel is thus composed as a series of dramatic variations on Mosque themes. While the connection between the narratives and the symbol is always clear, there is hardly ever a point where, as in *The Longest Journey*, we feel the cold hand of allegory. Our attention is always more engaged by what is happening than by any generalized significance. The dialogue is always sufficiently confusing; it mirrors the complex play of interests, amusements, and mistakes that is fairly typical of social intercourse. There is also in the Mosque section complexity of a sort that is more important in the structure of the whole novel. Through the oddly interrupted episodes run lines of symbolic meaning that point to the scene in the Marabar Caves.

By focusing attention on this episode, particularly on Mrs. Moore's curious "vision," we can see how admirably Forster has prepared us for a moment of dramatic change through building up meanings of various major symbols. What does the experience of hearing the echo mean for Mrs. Moore? The sentence that best sums up her situation and its significance is one describing her state of mind as she "surrenders to her vision":

> Then she was terrified over an area larger than usual; the universe, never comprehensible to her intellect, offered no repose to her soul, the mood of the last two months took definite form at last, and she realized that she didn't want to write to her children, didn't want to communicate with anyone, not even with God.

The change in Mrs. Moore's relation to her family and friends is the most obvious effect of her jarring experience. She "loses all interest, even in Aziz," and in her later conversations with Adela and Ronny she exhibits the most snappish and capricious irritability and a complete indifference concerning the "unspeakable attempt" in the cave, an attitude that extends to marriage and love in general:

> "Why all this marriage, marriage? . . . The human race would have become a single person centuries ago if marriage was any use. And all this rubbish about love, love in a church, love in a cave, as if there is the least difference, and I held up from my business over such trifles!"

All distinctions of feeling and of moral value have become confused and meaningless:

> . . . the echo began in some indescribable way to undermine her hold on life. Coming at a moment when she chanced to be fatigued, it had managed to murmur, "Pathos, piety, courage—they exist, but are identical, and so is filth. Everything exists, nothing has value."

The doctrines of Western religious faith become equally empty:

> But suddenly, at the edge of her mind, Religion appeared, poor little talkative Christianity, and she knew that all its divine words from "Let there be Light" to "It is finished" only amounted to "boum."

Finally, the comforting belief in a universe or in some eternal setting for human life is shaken; and at the same time serene acceptance of this world as an end in itself is impossible:

> She had come to that state where the horror of the universe and its smallness are both visible at the same time—the twilight of the double vision in which so many elderly people are involved. If this world is not to our taste, well, at all events there is Heaven, Hell, Annihilation—one or other of those large things, that huge scenic background of stars, fires, blue or black air. All heroic endeavour, and all that is known as art, assumes that there is such a background, just as all practical endeavour, when the world is to our taste, assumes that the world is all. But in the twilight of the double vision, a spiritual muddledom is set up for which no high-sounding words can be found; we can neither act nor refrain from action, we can neither ignore nor respect Infinity.

Mrs. Moore has had a somewhat more than adequate glimpse of complete muddle, an exposure to chaos in personal relations and in the universe.

These are certainly large and varied meanings for a novelist to press from the story of an old woman's visit to some not so "extraordinary" Indian caves. Forster's surprising success in bringing us to accept the strange and wonderful significance of the event depends on his earlier building up of symbolic meanings of Cave, Sky, and Echo. Throughout the preceding narrative, beginning with the opening sentence of the novel, he has imparted to the caves a twofold significance, suggestions of mystery and order that are constantly countered by suggestions of disillusionment and muddle. At the moment of climax the more unpleasant alternatives emerge with the force of truths already experienced and half acknowledged.

The preparation begins in the Mosque symbolism, through which hints of communication between persons and peoples have been accompanied by "clinging forms" of uncertainty. The Cave symbol is not (as I once supposed) simply the antithesis of the Mosque, but in part a parallel symbol repeating the same oppositions. When at Fielding's tea party Aziz first proposes a trip to the Marabar, it seems that the expedition will be a triumph of Anglo-Indian friendship. And during the ecstatic moments of the later tea party outside the caves, this possibility is apparently about to be realized. Once the horrid tour has taken place, the Caves symbolize the failure of all communication, the collapse of human relationships ironically foreshadowed in the less pleasant meaning of the Mosque symbol.

That the Caves should symbolize "mystery" as well as "muddle" depends on preparations that are fairly subtle, particularly in relation to Mrs. Moore. From her first appearance in the novel Mrs. Moore has been presented as ready for "a mystery," for some revelation of unity. Shortly after meeting Aziz in the mosque, she has a minor mystical vision:

> She watched the moon, whose radiance stained with primrose the purple of the surrounding sky. In England the moon had seemed dead and alien; here she was caught in a shawl of night together with earth and all the other stars. A sudden sense of unity, of kinship with the heavenly bodies, passed into the old woman and out, like water through a tank, leaving a strange freshness behind.

This mood is recalled much later, when Mrs. Moore is caught "in the twilight of the double vision" and able neither to "ignore nor respect Infinity":

> Mrs. Moore had always inclined to resignation. As soon as she landed in India it seemed to her good, and when she saw the water flowing through the mosque-tank, or the Ganges, or the moon, caught in the shawl of night with all the other stars, it seemed a beautiful goal and an easy one. To be one with the universe! So dignified and simple. But there was always some little duty to be performed first, some new card to be turned up from the diminishing pack and placed, and while she was pottering about, the Marabar struck its gong.

The Sky (or the "heavenly bodies") as a symbol of the universe and of infinity had also been introduced in other, nondramatic contexts: in the picture of the "overarching sky" at the very beginning of the novel,

> . . . the stars hang like lamps from the immense vault. The distance between the vault and them is as nothing to the distance behind them, and that farther distance, though beyond colour, last freed itself from blue . . .

and in the ironic setting for the Bridge Party:

> Some kites hovered overhead, impartial, over the kites passed the mass of a vulture, and with an impartiality exceeding all. the sky, not deeply coloured but translucent, poured light from its whole circumference. It seemed unlikely that the series stopped here. Beyond the sky must not there be something that overarches all the skies, more impartial even than they? Beyond which again . . .

But in Mrs. Moore's reflections on God and love the infinite series of arches had also been associated with an echo, an association that anticipates the later link between Sky and Caves. God, the traditional Christian order that had sheltered and contained her world, oddly recedes in her thoughts like a fading echo. (The Sky, like the other symbols, has its antithetical and ironic connotations.) Imagery used in various descriptions of the caves also tends to link the two symbols. They are circular, perhaps numberless, and "when a match is struck" and reflected in the "marvellously polished walls . . . two flames approach and strive to unite" in something like an ecstasy of love. The caves take on some of the mysterious qualities of the night sky, and the reader is not altogether surprised that Mrs. Moore finds cosmic significance in making a visit to them. It is quite appropriate that she should have a vision of infinity, though it turns out to be less acceptable than she had imagined.

The preparation for the caves episode as a revelation of "muddle" extends through nearly every phase of the narrative up to the moment of Mrs. Moore's panic. All of the kinds of muddledom that she consequently experiences are anticipated and connected more or less subtly with the Marabar. The conversation in which she first hears that "India's a muddle" is a nice example of this twofold preparation. Miss Quested has been describing a tiny social muddle that began at the Bridge Party in a "shapeless discussion" with two Hindus, Mr. and Mrs. Bhattacharya. The "couple with the unpronounceable name" (a significant comment) change their plans in order to have Mrs. Moore and Adela visit them, and then on the appointed day fail to send their carriage for their guests. Adela wants Fielding to help her clear the matter up:

> "I do so hate mysteries," Adela announced.
> "We English do."
> "I dislike them not because I'm English, but from my own personal point of view," she corrected.
> "I like mysteries but I rather dislike muddles," said Mrs. Moore.
> "A mystery is a muddle."
> "Oh, do you think so, Mr. Fielding?"
> "A mystery is only a high-sounding term for a muddle. No advantage in stirring it up, in either case. Aziz and I know well that India's a muddle."
> "India's— Oh, what an alarming idea!"
> "There'll be no muddle when you come to see me," said Aziz, rather out of his depth. "Mrs. Moore and everyone—I invite you all—oh, please."

The old lady accepted: she still thought the young doctor excessively nice; moreover, a new feeling, half languor, half excitement, bade her turn down any fresh path.

In a few moments Aziz shows that he is as unstable as the Hindus. Having issued his invitation, he thinks with horror of his detestable bungalow and changes the place to the Marabar Caves.

Another symbolic connection is anticipated a little later in a conversation that takes place between Aziz and Professor Godbole, the "Deccani Brahman." The echo, we recall, produced in Mrs. Moore a curious spiritual confusion. What she had known as religion became meaningless, and yet she had had an experience that was somehow religious, a glimpse of evil, of "the undying worm itself." The Caves, it appears, stand for a type of religious experience accessible only to a peculiar type of Oriental intelligence. When Aziz questions Godbole about the Marabar Caves, he gets nowhere. But it is perfectly clear that the Hindu was "concealing something." Adela, who listens without understanding, does "not know that the comparatively simple mind of the Mohammedan was encountering Ancient Night." Just after the caves are mentioned again Godbole sings a Hindu song, the effect of which is described in imagery that suggests the baffling caves and their echoes:

> His thin voice rose, and gave out one sound after another. At times there seemed rhythm, at times there was the illusion of a Western melody. But the ear, baffled repeatedly, soon lost any clue, and wandered in a maze of noises, none harsh or unpleasant, none intelligible. It was the song of an unknown bird.

Somehow—and the "how" cannot be very well defined—we are made to feel that the Marabar may be the scene of a revelation, perhaps confused and murky, but comprehensible to the Hindu mind.

Mrs. Moore's indifference to values and her moral confusion focused in her loss of faith in Christian marriage. The dramatic appropriateness of this is obvious, especially in relation to Adela's discovery on entering the second cave, that she has left out love in deciding to marry Ronny. Mrs. Moore has observed the unsteady course of her "young people's" relations with growing signs of irritation and disillusionment. She hears the word of their engagement with no joy: ". . . though it was all right now she could not speak as enthusiastically of wedlock or of anything as she should have done." The connection between the caves and the unsatisfactoriness of marriage is made at various points in the narrative of Adela's and Ronny's engagement. They quarrel rather bitterly over Aziz's invitation, while Mrs. Moore listens to them with extreme annoyance:

> "I've never heard of these caves, I don't know what or where they are," said Mrs. Moore, "but I really can't have"—she tapped the cushion beside her—"so much quarrelling and tiresomeness!"

Adela, declaring (with unconscious irony) that what she has to say has "nothing to do with the caves," proceeds to tell Ronny that she will not marry him. It is symbolically a little too neat that they get re-engaged during an accident while driving at night on the Marabar Road. The car in which they were riding hits a hyena or a ghost or . . . ?

But the most subtle preparation for Mrs. Moore's disillusioning vision of marriage comes in the superb account of the approach to the caves. Here the main symbols—Mosque, Caves, and Sky—all appear, unobtrusively woven into a narrative that has a predominant tone of dullness and nightmarish confusion. The party itself is made up of an incredible jumble of persons whom Aziz barely succeeds in holding together; in fact Fielding and Godbole arrive only when Adela is rushing away in panic. As the "train half asleep" moves along in a scene of "timeless twilight," Mrs. Moore and Adela apathetically discuss plans for Adela's married life. Mrs. Moore's reflections indicate an approaching crisis in her uncertainty about marriage:

> She felt increasingly (vision or nightmare?) that, though people are important, the relations between them are not, and that in particular too much fuss has been made over marriage; centuries of carnal embracement, yet man is no nearer to understanding man. And to-day she felt this with such force that it seemed itself a relationship, itself a person who was trying to take hold of her hand.

The sky, with appropriate irony, brightens up as if for a "miracle," but there is no sunrise, only a "false dawn." There is ". . . a spiritual silence which invaded more senses than the ear. Life went on as usual, but had no consequences, that is to say, sounds did not echo or thoughts develop." There was, for example, ". . . a confusion about a snake which was never cleared up." (The echoes are later described as serpent-like in their coiling movement.) It is again suggested that the mystery of the Marabar could be understood only by a Hindu:

> . . . he [Aziz] had no notion how to treat this particular aspect of India; he was lost in it without Professor Godbole, like themselves.

For a few minutes before entering the caves, the happy Mosque relationship between Mrs. Moore and Aziz is revived, and understanding
between individuals and even peoples seems possible. But Aziz warns
Adela of the deceptions of "Akbar's universal religion": "Nothing
embraces the whole of India," he tells her, "nothing, nothing, and that
was Akbar's mistake." As the oddly assorted members of the party go
into the first cave, we get a final and tremendous impression of annihilation of human relationships and distinctions:

> The small black hole gaped where their varied forms and colours had
> momentarily functioned. They were sucked in like water down a drain.
> Bland and bald rose the precipices; bland and glutinous the sky that
> connected the precipices; solid and white, a Brahminy kite flapped be-
> tween the rocks with a clumsiness that seemed intentional. Before man,
> with his itch for the seemly, had been born, the planet must have
> looked thus. The kite flapped away . . . Before birds, perhaps . . .
> And then the hole belched and humanity returned.

The pressure felt behind each of the details in this narrative, their
power of evoking at once a sequence of dramatic relationships and a
rich variety of feelings, is due to the kind of far-reaching preparation
we have been tracing. When the echo comes, it seems to the reader
as to Mrs. Moore that this is what he has been waiting for all along.
As the "echoes generate echoes," the layers of meaninglessness unfold
and the whole range of "muddles," in personal relationships, in moral
and religious values, and in concepts of the universe, is revealed. The
symbolic values of Caves, Mosque, and Sky were being built up for
this moment, the perfect aptness of their ironic character now being
clear.

The Echo, though less ambiguous than the other symbols, has a
dual value for the reader. As an image linked with the receding arches
of the sky and with Mrs. Moore's glimpses of infinity it recalls the
possibility of a revelation. But through its monotonous meaningless
"bou-oum" the echo brings to the surface uglier levels of experience
already associated with the Marabar and hinted at in the less sinister
symbols of Mosque and Sky. The vision turns out to be a nightmare.
Forster's success in making it so convincing and so meaningful arises
from his handling of a complex design which is at once dramatic, symbolic, and ironic. As an artist he has earned the right to attribute large
and various meanings to Mrs. Moore's curious experience and to
express a significance that goes well beyond the immediate dramatic
moment. While presenting a seemingly personal crisis Forster has
expressed the vision perhaps most characteristic of the twentieth cen-

tury, the discovery that the universe may not be a unity but chaos, that older philosophic and religious orders with the values they guaranteed have dissolved. The vision of *A Passage to India* has its counterparts in *The Education of Henry Adams* and in "Gerontion" and "The Waste Land." All these visions are—with differing emphases—the result of various kinds of over-exposure, to too many civilizations (which seem to make nonsense of one another), to too many observations of complexity in the mind and in the physical world—

> After such knowledge, what forgiveness?

We are not concerned here with the proper action after such a vision, but with Forster's novel and with how he completes the structure which he began with such art. I think there can be few readers who will say that the concluding Temple section of *A Passage to India* gives them no pause. Is this section of the novel merely a *tour de force*, or does it have an integrity of design comparable to that of the earlier sections? Is its structure complementary to the design we have been tracing? We can answer these questions best by asking and answering a question of the sort we have put to each of the other symbols: what does the Temple symbol mean in dramatic terms?

It signifies most clearly Hinduism, the religion of Godbole, who presides over the ceremony at Mau in which the worshippers "love all men, the whole universe" and in which "the Lord of the Universe" is born. But from a Western point of view, the narrator observes, "this . . . triumph of India was a muddle . . . a frustration of reason and form." Forster's account of the ceremony is shot through with comic, sometimes farcical touches, with the result that of all the symbols the Temple seems the most crudely ironic. Its twofold meaning is expressed very well in the final picture of Fielding's and Aziz's relationship. For a brief time, after being reconciled during the jumble of the Hindu ceremony, they are friends; but their friendship, like the unity of India, is unstable. In the concluding words of the novel we are told that the "temples" as well as "the tank" (i.e. the Mosque), and "the sky" do not want them to be friends. This, we may say, is a finely poised irresolution, the only possible conclusion for a novel of irony. The Temple is a symbol of Hindu unity in love which is no unity.

But if we try to interpret the Temple symbol in terms of the dramatized experiences of Mrs. Moore and of her children, we get into difficulties. We find "muddle" in the relations between symbolic and dramatic designs and at some points a kind of dramatic vacuum. For example, the temple ceremony has an odd meaning in the account of what has happened to Fielding's wife and her brother, Ralph. Fielding tells Aziz that his wife now "believes that the Marabar is wiped out," and after adding that Ralph "rides a little behind her, though with her," he says:

> "From her point of view, Mau has been a success. It calmed her—both of them suffer from restlessness. She found something soothing, some solution of her queer troubles here."

Though there is a notable lack of irony in Fielding's remarks, it is not wholly out of character for him to describe such changes as conceivable, for he has several times shown tolerance for religious experiences that he cannot himself share. For example, he has asked Aziz to sing of "something in religion . . . that the Hindus have perhaps found." But for some reason we are embarrassed by the injection of such vague and solemn mysticism at this point in the novel. We are embarrassed not because the possibility of mystical experience is to be rejected, but because we cannot believe in it here as a part of the fictional experience. Something has gone wrong, or perhaps something is wanting, in the literary structure. The test again is to ask what the metaphors mean in the dramatic context. How has "Mau" (the temple ceremony) "calmed" Fielding's wife, and what is this "wiping out of the Marabar"? If "the Marabar" was "muddle" and panic, the "calming" is apparently an experience of unity and peace, a Hindu vision in which chaos is reduced to order. But once we refer these mystical effects to the narrative of the Mau celebration and recall the glorious muddle of Godbole's "vision," we can no longer solemnly accept "Mau" as a symbol of a soothing revelation of unity.

The "peace of Mau" also seems to be induced through some queer telepathic influence of Mrs. Moore and her children, who have apparently inherited something more marvelous than their mother's "restlessness." In the operatic scene in which Aziz and Ralph hear the chant of "Radhakrishna Radhakrishna," Aziz forgets the wrong done him at Marabar and "focusing his heart on something more distant than the caves, something beautiful," he becomes reconciled with Mrs. Moore's son and discovers that he, like his mother, is "an Oriental." The imagery reminds us of the "distant" sky, of the ultimate unity, but the dramatic preparation for the mystical effect of Mrs. Moore's influence is lacking or unconvincing. More than once after the caves episode we hear that Mrs. Moore "knew something" inaccessible to Fielding and Adela. The queer girl also believes that "only Mrs. Moore could drive" the sound of the echo "back to its source and seal the broken reservoir.

Evil was loose . . ." Mrs. Moore can somehow restore the broken unity and give peace to those who, like her children and Aziz, are in communication with her as Esmiss Moore, a sort of Hindu demigoddess. The impression created before the Marabar visit, that the caves were comprehensible only to a Hindu, prepared us for Mrs. Moore's bafflement but hardly for her "reincarnation." When we recall in contrast with such fragmentary hints what has been so completely and wonderfully presented, the cave nightmare, we can hardly accept this about-face in Mrs. Moore's role and its symbolic value. We cannot at the end of the novel regard Mrs. Moore as in tune with the infinite and conveniently forget the mocking denial of her echo. "To be at one with the universe! So dignified and simple." The exquisite irony of that comment has been too vividly realized in "the muddle" of the Caves.

Put crudely, there is little dramatic evidence that Mrs. Moore or her children ever had any experience of cosmic unity and the peace that passeth understanding. There are some marvelously clever bits of sleight of hand, oblique allusions to being "calmed" and to "knowing something," but not much more. It can be said that Forster, like his characters, was up against the inexpressible: visions of unity are not to be dramatized. Or perhaps they are not easily presented in fiction. They lend themselves better to self-dramatization, as in the poetry of Wordsworth or Vaughan or St. John of the Cross. But it is always unwise to say what cannot be done in literature; in the present instance it is better to say that Forster did not succeed in giving dramatic meaning to the Temple as a symbol of unity. By contrast, the positive meaning of the Mosque—the attainment of closer understanding—is portrayed with sharp particularity as in the scenes between Aziz and Mrs. Moore or between Aziz and Fielding. As Forster's other novels triumphantly prove, he commands this area of experience: he is above all the novelist of personal relations.

It is fortunate that Forster did not succeed in recovering for Temple and Sky single meanings of peace and unity, for the total design of his novel moves toward no such clear resolution. Whenever he emphasizes these simply serious connotations, he is in effect attempting to transcend the limits of his own ironic vision. (Sweet are the uses of ambiguity to the ironist, especially to one who presents experience through richly ambiguous symbols.) In the best of *A Passage to India* Forster enjoys to the full the freedom of giving varied and even opposite meanings to his symbolic metaphors. In the Mosque-Cave sequences the narrative precisely and fully defines the double meanings of the symbols, and there is complete harmony between symbolic and dramatic designs: we saw how beautifully Forster built up the unpleasant implications of Mosque, Caves, and Sky to prepare for the climactic moment when their full force was realized.

The contrast between his ironic-fictional design and Jane Austen's is now clear. Her balancing of possible interpretations, since it depended on well-defined beliefs, led inevitably to a choice and a resolution. Hers was the irony that moves toward the cancellation of irony. Forster's pattern leads to no such resolution. Playing, sometimes capriciously, with every possible meaning of an experience, he cannot reach conclusions. For his basic assumption, best expressed through Fielding, is that anything may be true, that the unreasonable explanation may be as valid as the reasonable one. Only one allegiance remains unshaken throughout the novel, a belief in the possibility and value of communication between individuals, a belief accompanied by the reservation that human relationships are always on the verge of breakdown. The hope of communication is generous, but skeptical, and hints of unity among all men or all nations or all things can hardly be accepted without an ironic smile. The design of Forster's fiction suffers only when he deviates into solemnity.

NOTES

1. It would be hard to find purer examples of symbolic expressions. They are obviously "iconic"; the reader is to think of something (the subject) in terms of the Mosque or the Caves or the Temple (i.e. the generalized impressions). And the "subject" is not otherwise stated. Throughout this chapter expressions of the type, "the Mosque," "the Caves," et cetera, refer to the iconic half of the metaphor. The terms without the article, Mosque, Caves, et cetera, refer to the symbol as a complete metaphor.

15

GRAHAM HOUGH

———◆———

Sons and Lovers

The novels and poems come unwatched out of one's pen. And then the absolute need one has for some sort of satisfactory mental attitude towards oneself and things in general makes one try to abstract some definite conclusions from one's experience.[1]

So Lawrence accounts for the relation between his imaginative and his expository writing. One of the clearest examples of the relation seems to be *Sons and Lovers*. We have the novel, the most complete and integrated of Lawrence's works; and we have his own excellent analysis of it, quite the best that has ever been done, in a letter to Garnett.

A woman of character and refinement goes into the lower class, and has no satisfaction in her own life. She has had a passion for her husband, so the children are born of passion, and have heaps of vitality. But as her sons grow up, she selects them as lovers—first the eldest, then the second. These sons are *urged* into life by their reciprocal love of their mother—urged on and on. But when they come to manhood, they can't love, because their mother is the strongest power in their lives, and holds them. . . . As soon as the young men come into contact with

From *The Dark Sun* by Graham Hough, Macmillan Co., 1956; world rights, Curtis Brown, Ltd.; the quotations from *Sons and Lovers, Fantasia of the Unconscious,* and *Letters* are reprinted by permission of the Viking Press, Inc.

women there is a split. William gives his sex to a fribble, and his
mother holds his soul. But the split kills him, because he doesn't know
where he is. The next son gets a woman who fights for his soul—fights
his mother. The son loves the mother—all the sons hate and are jealous
of the father. The battle goes on between the mother and the girl, with
the son as object. The mother gradually proves the stronger, because
of the tie of blood. The son decides to leave his soul in his mother's
hands, and, like his elder brother, go for passion. Then the split begins
to tell again. But, almost unconsciously, the mother realises what is the
matter and begins to die. The son casts off his mistress, attends to his
mother dying. He is left in the end naked of everything, with the drift
towards death.[2]

The broad psychological outlines emerge more clearly in this exposition, which is evidently the fruit of later reflection, than in the novel
as it stands. But the matter is not quite as simple as that, for both
elements are present in the novel itself. There are several layers of
experience in *Sons and Lovers*, some very close to biographical actuality, some more remote. The element of autobiography constantly
obtrudes itself in Lawrence's fiction. It does not always repay minute
inquiry, and external evidence is often lacking. But *Sons and Lovers*
is a special case, and its relation to reality is a peculiar one. The book
is a catharsis, achieved by re-living an actual experience—re-living it
over and over again; and the achievement is a necessary preliminary
to all the later work. As it happens, we have more detailed information about its genesis, from several sources, than we have for any other
novel of Lawrence; both the means and the incentive to make the biographical connection present themselves. So there is something to be
said for standing for a time outside the completed work to observe
how it arose from its matrix in Lawrence's early life.

The first version was begun some time in 1910, before his mother's
death, in the ambience of the conflict which it describes. Miriam was
created under the direct supervision of her actual prototype; and as
we can see from her memoir, her pressure was constantly exercised
towards presenting things just as they were. Like *The White Peacock*,
Sons and Lovers began with a contrived and conventional plot, and
it was at Jessie Chambers' suggestion that Lawrence re-wrote it as a
far more direct embodiment of the actuality. We first hear of the book
in October 1910, under the name of *Paul Morel*, which it long retained. Lawrence wrote to Sydney Pawling at the time he was nego-
tiating with Heinemann over *The Trespasser* about "my third novel,

Paul Morel, which is plotted out very interestingly (to me), and about one-eighth of which is written. *Paul Morel* will be a novel—not a florid prose-poem, or a decorated idyll running to seed in realism."

The antitheses in the last phrase are of course with *The Trespasser*—the florid prose-poem, and *The White Peacock*—the decorated idyll. It is not quite clear what is meant by saying that *Paul Morel,* by contrast, will be a novel, but probably that it had something like a regular and conventional novelist's plot. The earliest surviving manuscript is described by L. C. Powell, and in it "the father accidentally kills Paul's brother, is jailed, and dies on his release." Even this early version was, it appears, re-worked, for Helen Corke says that Lawrence was re-writing the early chapters about Whitsun 1911. Then in the autumn of that year he showed the manuscript to Jessie Chambers. This was evidently not the same as the manuscript described above, for she says that the brother Ernest does not appear in the story at all. She found the writing strained and tired. "He was telling the story of his mother's married life, but the telling seemed to be at second-hand and lacked the living touch." She herself was presented as Miriam in the story, but placed in a bourgeois setting—in the same family from which the Alvina of *The Lost Girl* was taken. The theme of the mother's hostility to Paul's love for Miriam was explicit from the start; among the sentences she quotes from his early draft are these:

What was it he wanted of her? Did he want her to break his mother down in him? . . . Mrs. Morel saw that if Miriam could win her son's sex sympathy there would be nothing left for her.

But the mother-and-son relationship was presented with a story-book falsity verging on sentimentalism. She said that "what had really happened was much more poignant and interesting than the situations he had invented." Finally she suggested, as she had done about *The White Peacock,* that he should cut out the fiction, and tell the story of his mother, his home life and his adolescence as simply as possible.

Lawrence appealed to her to help him, because of her much clearer recollection of their early days together, and a second re-writing began, under her influence, and with passages for the Paul and Miriam relationship supplied by her. Lawrence worked on this version at Eastwood, in late 1911 and early 1912. It was immediately after the serious illness that followed his mother's death. He had left his teaching job in Croydon, and was writing again on his home ground, again under

Miriam's guidance, but with the being of his mother almost more vivid to him than it had been in her life. He is thus back in the thick of the conflict that *Sons and Lovers* describes.

The passages supplied by Jessie Chambers, or as many of them as survive, are recorded in Appendix D to Moore's *Life and Works of D. H. Lawrence*. Lawrence took them over pretty well wholesale, and the existing evidence goes far to suggest that the whole of the "Lad and Girl Love" chapter and parts of "Strife in Love" and "Defeat of Miriam" may have been written up from notes supplied by her. However, things did not progress as she wished. When she saw the new version, she was greatly impressed by the force and truth of the home life of the Morels but "bewildered and dismayed" at the Paul and Miriam portion. The hero's bondage to his mother, she felt, was "glorified and made absolute." "His mother had to be supreme, and for the sake of that supremacy every disloyalty was permissible." Worse still, she felt he had betrayed the essential nature of their young relationship. Fragments of a commentary by her, also recorded by Moore, show us how. It was by the premature introduction of sexual conflict, the attribution to her of a sexual self-consciousness and a desire for kisses to which Paul was unable to respond. She feels in essence that Lawrence is complicating and distorting a deep, innocent and unselfconscious adolescent tenderness, which in fact was only crossed by his mother's hostility, and that he is doing this in the interests of his mother's point of view. She wrote bitterly to Helen Corke: "The Miriam part of the novel is a slander—a fearful treachery. David has interpreted her every word, action and thought in the light of 'Mrs. Morel's' hatred of her."

It can be argued, and with a good deal of truth, that Jessie obstinately regarded the work as biography not fiction, and every departure from actuality as a falsification. And Lawrence was writing a novel. But this is not the whole story. In the last stages of his relation with Jessie Chambers, Lawrence was endeavouring to convince her, not only of the artistic appropriateness of his version, but of its truth. Inspired by maturer understanding or the need for self-justification, or whatever it might be, he was imposing his own interpretation on events, giving his own interpretation of the failure of their love, and desperately seeking to make it finally convincing to himself by persuading Jessie to accept it, too. The biographical situation is a moving and complicated one, but this is not our concern. Critically speaking, two points of importance become clear. First, the extraordinarily intimate connection between Lawrence's writing and his experience; what he writes as fiction must be retrospectively accepted as fact. And secondly, the co-presence in the Paul and Miriam parts of *Sons and Lovers* of two different kinds of experience—more or less simple recollection, checked and assisted by Jessie Chambers; and a later interpretation of the whole sequence of events. Jessie, as we have seen, believed that this interpretation was a posthumous assertion of his mother's power.

She is unlikely to have been wholly right—but the temptation to biographical speculation must be resisted. The effect of this literary episode on their personal life was a pathetic failure, and it led directly to the ultimate breach between them. The last stage of Lawrence's love for Jessie Chambers was crossed and broken by relations with other women, and then all these were decisively interrupted by the meeting with Frieda. This was the end of his youthful pilgrimage. He left England with Frieda in 1912. For a time they were together in Metz. Then Frieda remained there with her relatives, and Lawrence went off to cousins of his own in Waldbröl. There, unsettled, uprooted but free, utterly severed from all former ties and associations, he took up *Paul Morel* again and worked on a further revision. When he and Frieda were together again at Icking, the work continued with furious intensity. "I lived and suffered that book, and even wrote bits of it," she says, thus fulfilling the rôle that Jessie Chambers had first assumed. On November 11th, 1912, the novel, now called *Sons and Lovers*, was finished, and the manuscript sent to Garnett.

Since the whole situation presents the Freudian Œdipus imbroglio in almost classic completeness, it has naturally raised the question of Freudian influence on the composition of *Sons and Lovers*. The first thing to be said about this is that the situation was there in actuality, and was pretty well recognised for what it was at the time. Jessie herself wrote:

> The day before his mother's funeral we went a walk together. . . .
> At the end of that same walk, as we stood within a stone's throw of the house where his mother lay dead, he said to me:
> "You know, J., I've always loved mother."
> "I know you have," I replied.
> "I don't mean that," he answered. "I've loved her—like a lover—that's why I could never love you."

At this time (1910), the general diffusion of Freudian ideas was of course still far distant, and it is exceedingly unlikely that Lawrence had ever heard Freud's name. Later on Lawrence said that he had not

read Freud in the *Sons and Lovers* period, but had heard of him. He
does not say when or from whom. But there need be no mystery about
this. It was in 1912, and from Frieda. Freud's name occurs on the
first page of her memoir *Not I but the Wind*: "I had met a remarkable
disciple of Freud and was full of undigested theories"; and on the day
of their first meeting she and Lawrence "talked about Œdipus and
understanding leaped through our words." Later she wrote that she
was a great admirer of Freud when she met Lawrence in 1912, and
that he and she had long arguments about Freud together. And of
course the final draft of *Sons and Lovers* was written as strongly under
Frieda's influence as the earlier ones had been under Miriam's. *Sons
and Lovers* is indeed the first Freudian novel in English, but its
Freudianism is mediated not by a text-book but by a person—a person,
moreover, who was at the same time offering an object-lesson in many
of the matters with which Freud deals.

It cannot be supposed that Frieda Lawrence's Freudianism (which
is unlikely to have been very scholastically complete) materially
altered the conception of the story, most of which, in any case, was in
being before she came on the scene. What it could and almost certainly did do is set a theoretical seal on a situation that had been very
thoroughly explored in actuality. Its influence can surely be detected
in the analysis of the novel sent to Garnett. Frieda herself says nothing
about this. But she does say that the bits she wrote or suggested are,
curiously enough, passages presenting the mother's point of view.
Or perhaps it is not curious. By this time she had taken possession of
Lawrence's soul, masterless since his mother's death. She had given
up her own children to do so. She had renounced her maternal rôle in
life, but can play it over again in the book. Lawrence had at last
renounced his mother, but had found someone who could still present
her point of view. So the last fragment needed to make the experience
behind *Sons and Lovers* into an intelligible whole was added. But
Frieda's rôle does not appear directly in the book, and it is right that
it should not. It says more for Lawrence's restraint and sense of form
than we can generally say that he is able to keep out of *Sons and
Lovers* the emancipation, geographical, physical and mental, that
Frieda brought him; that he can see it artistically in its proper place—
as the external standpoint which made the whole vision possible, without the temptation to drag it between the covers.

So much for the genesis of *Sons and Lovers*. To indicate, as we have
just done, different strata of composition in a single work usually leads
to a process of disintegration, to the perception of some failure in unity

and wholeness. With *Sons and Lovers* it is quite otherwise. It is the very presence of these several points of view, differing in time, in degree of maturity and in kind, that gives the book its depth and richness. The solid establishment of character and setting in the early part would be incomplete without its flowering in the Miriam idyll: and the puzzled groping of the later relations with Miriam would be nebulous without its firm, realistic foundation. Lawrence was quite incapable of the sort of conscious æsthetic planning that gives their form to the novels of Henry James. Form for him was the embodiment of an experience, and a form not lived through in experience was impossible to him. This is why even a formal criticism of *Sons and Lovers* must be in part a discussion of the actuality, as far as that can be discovered, or of Lawrence's changing attitudes to it. Certainly the analysis sent to Garnett in November 1912 represents far more than was in Lawrence's mind at the outset.

Even quite late in its composition Lawrence refers to *Sons and Lovers* as "the colliery novel," and it seems quite likely that the original idea was a well-made story of colliery life, to get away from the shapelessness of *The White Peacock* and the factitious emotionalism of *The Trespasser*. Then by Jessie Chambers' advice he abandons the attempt at strength through plot, at any rate plot of the contrived, deliberate kind, and reverts at first to pure naturalism. The whole of Part I up to the death of William is of this kind—strong, straightforward, deeply felt, the best picture of industrial, working-class life in English, probably the only one written completely from the inside. Lawrence describes, as he does again in *Women in Love,* two stages of English industrial development—the small-scale, manageable, quasi-paternalist system, which still allowed some scope for human feelings and genuine human relations; and its supersession by huge mechanistic organisations that inevitably negate the life of the men who are engaged in them. It is the beginning of a lifelong preoccupation with the effects of industrialism, though in *Sons and Lovers* the element of social protest is not strong; there is simply the direct presentation of an intimately known and accepted reality. The very fully developed picture of colliery life is neither an intrusion into the novel nor a mere background; it is integrally connected with the plot. The life of Eastwood offers nothing to a vital, instinctive, unambitious man like Walter Morel, except the pit and the public-house. To Lydia his wife, with her intelligence and her longing for refinement, it offers nothing but the chapel and the hope of getting up into the middle class—through her children if not through her disappointing husband.

Their marriage, therefore, after the first flush of passion has died down, can be nothing but a sterile conflict; on the one hand, brutal toil and the relief from it in brutal drinking; on the other, pinched material struggle and the aspiration after a meagre superiority. This is Paul Morel's heritage, and the neurotic refusal of life engendered in him is the direct result of his parents' failure. And the parents' failure is the direct result of the pressures of an inhuman system. Their strong, disparate personalities make conflict inevitable; it might in another setting have been fruitful conflict: in Eastwood it can only be life-destroying.

With the advent of Miriam, the nature of the novel changes. It is no longer a decisive setting down of experience that has been thoroughly understood. There is no need to apply Jessie Chambers' criticisms, which are essentially of an ethical and personal nature, to the novel as a novel. That Lawrence's treatment of this story was a personal tragedy for her is true and demands our sympathy; but that is another matter. The essential literary point is that here Lawrence begins to do something new and something that is far more peculiar to himself than the admirable first part of *Sons and Lovers*—to use the novel as a deliberate means of exploring an experience that has not been fully understood. "It is the way our sympathy flows and recoils that determines our lives"; and the central Paul and Miriam section of *Sons and Lovers* is a study of the way Paul's sympathies flowed and recoiled. It is not possible that such a study should be true to Miriam's different experience of the same events or to objective fact. Or rather, the only objective fact that is in question is the fluctuation of feeling in Paul-Lawrence's own mind. And leaving aside, as we must, her sense of pain and betrayal, all we can say is that Jessie Chambers was right, and showed acute literary, as well as personal, judgment in feeling the contrast between the first part of the book and the second. For it is here that Lawrence begins to turn the novel to his own purpose, to use it as a means of coming to understand a situation where understanding had not been achieved in ordinary experience.

Any judgment of Lawrence as an artist must depend in some measure on how this process is viewed. "The only way of representing emotion in the form of art," writes Mr. Eliot, "is by finding an 'objective correlative'; in other words, a set of objects, a situation, a chain of events which shall be the formula of that *particular* emotion; such that when the external facts, which must terminate in sensory experience, are given, the emotion is immediately evoked." For those who hold this view much of Lawrence's most characteristic writing must fail. We recall, however, that from this point of view *Hamlet* was also an artistic failure. Of course in what many people consider his best—his descriptive—writing, Lawrence is superbly successful at finding in landscapes, beasts and flowers objective equivalents for emotion. But in writing of human relations he often leaves a residue of the unobjectified. A situation is suggested, it is illuminated in one or two brilliant flashes, and for the rest—a frank confession of the residual mystery.

And gradually the intimacy with the family concentrated for Paul on three persons—the mother, Edgar, and Miriam. To the mother he went for that sympathy and that appeal which seemed to draw him out. Edgar was his very close friend. And to Miriam he more or less condescended, because she seemed so humble.

But the girl gradually sought him out. If he brought up his sketch-book, it was she who pondered longest over the last picture. Then she would look up at him. Suddenly, her dark eyes alight like water that shakes with a stream of gold in the dark, she would ask:

"Why do I like this so?"

Always something in his breast shrank from these close, intimate, dazzled looks of hers.

"Why *do* you?" he asked.

"I don't know. It seems so true."

"It's because—it's because there is scarcely any shadow in it; it's more shimmery, as if I'd painted the shimmering protoplasm in the leaves and everywhere, and not the stiffness of the shape. That seems dead to me. Only this shimmeriness is the real living. The shape is a dead crust. The shimmer is inside really."

And she, with her little finger in her mouth, would ponder these sayings. They gave her a feeling of life again, and vivified things which had meant nothing to her. She managed to find some meaning in his struggling, abstract speeches. And they were the medium through which she came distinctly at her beloved objects.

Another day she sat at sunset whilst he was painting some pine-trees which caught the red glare from the west. He had been quiet.

"There you are!" he said suddenly. "I wanted that. Now, look at them and tell me, are they pine-trunks or are they red coals, standing-up pieces of fire in that darkness? There's God's burning bush for you, that burned not away."

Miriam looked, and was frightened. But the pine-trunks were wonderful to her, and distinct. He packed his box and rose. Suddenly he looked at her.

"Why are you always sad?" he asked her.

"Sad!" she exclaimed, looking up at him with startled, wonderful brown eyes.

"Yes," he replied. "You are always, always sad."

"I am not—oh, not a bit!" she cried.

"But even your joy is like a flame coming off of sadness," he persisted. "You're never jolly or even just all right."

"No," she pondered. "I wonder—why."

"Because you're not; because you're different inside, like a pine-tree, and then you flare up; but you're not just like an ordinary tree, with fidgety leaves and jolly——"

He got tangled up in his own speech; but she brooded on it, and he had a strange, roused sensation, as if his feelings were new. She got so near him. It was a strange stimulant.

Then sometimes he hated her. Her youngest brother was only five. He was a frail lad, with immense brown eyes in his quaint, fragile face—one of Reynolds' "Choir of Angels," with a touch of elf. Often Miriam kneeled to the child and drew him to her.

"Eh, my Hubert!" she sang, in a voice heavy and surcharged with love. "Eh, my Hubert!"

And, folding him in her arms, she swayed slightly from side to side with love, her face half lifted, her eyes half closed, her voice drenched with love.

"Don't!" said the child, uneasy—"don't, Miriam!"

"Yes; you love me, don't you?" she murmured deep in her throat, almost as if she were in a trance, and swaying also as if she were swooned in an ecstasy of love.

"Don't!" repeated the child, a frown on his clear brow.

"You love me, don't you?" she murmured.

"What do you make such a *fuss* for?" cried Paul, all in suffering because of her extreme emotion. "Why can't you be ordinary with him?"

She let the child go, and rose, and said nothing. Her intensity, which would leave no emotion on a normal plane, irritated the youth into a frenzy. And this fearful, naked contact of her on small occasions shocked him. He was used to his mother's reserve. And on such occasions he was thankful in his heart and soul that he had his mother, so sane and wholesome.[3]

This is a typical passage from the central part of *Sons and Lovers*. It defines with extraordinary sensitiveness the nature of the girl, with her deep intelligence and feeling, only just awaking to consciousness, newly aware of the possibilities of sympathy and communication; and the boy, slightly arrogant and cocksure, deeply attracted, but unwilling to submit to the demands of her emotional intensity. Yet a great deal of the effect is gained by the admission of the unrealised, the uncomprehended.

"Always something in his breast shrank from this close, intimate, dazzled look of hers." Miriam *"doesn't know"* why she likes Paul's sketches. She would *"ponder* his sayings"; "She *managed* to find some meaning in his *struggling* abstract speeches". She *wonders why* she always appears to be sad. And Paul for his part "gets *tangled up* in his own speech"; "experiences a *strange* roused sensation. It was a *strange* stimulant". And all this disturbing, ill-understood emotion is placed by contrasting it with his mother's sanity and reserve.

It might be said that a good deal of this is an evasion of real difficulties, a mere token payment, a gesture towards defining a relationship, but an uncompleted gesture. This is true of the word *strange,* which Lawrence constantly overworks and makes into a mere rubber stamp for the undefinable. Otherwise, however, the passage is remarkable for the precision with which it establishes the situation. The actors in the scene are faintly bewildered, unaware of what is happening to them; and the writing refrains from going beyond their actual awareness; yet the material for a fuller understanding is there. It is there in the contrast between her feeling and his, and in the use of the mother as a point of reference. Another writer would have had to make use of the tape-recorder, stream of consciousness technique, or endow the characters with preternatural insight and self-consciousness, or provide a commentary of his own. Lawrence's method gives the actual process of living, with all the groping, the intermittence of vision associated with life as it is lived.

Later in the same chapter comes the episode of the algebra lesson. Miriam hates her status as a household drudge, and is eager for learning. Paul offers to teach her. But she is slow and self-conscious, and too anxious to be able to learn with ease.

> She was poring over the book, seemed absorbed in it, yet trembling lest she could not get at it. It made him cross. She was ruddy and beautiful. Yet her soul seemed to be intensely supplicating. The algebra-book she closed, shrinking, knowing he was angered; and at the same instant he grew gentle, seeing her hurt because she did not understand.
>
> But things came slowly to her. And when she held herself in a grip, seemed so utterly humble before the lesson, it made his blood rouse. He stormed at her, got ashamed, continued the lesson, and grew furious again, abusing her. She listened in silence. Occasionally, very rarely, she defended herself. Her liquid dark eyes blazed at him.

"You don't give me time to learn it," she said.

"All right," he answered, throwing the book on the table and lighting a cigarette. Then, after awhile, he went back to her, repentant. So the lessons went. He was always either in a rage or very gentle.

"What do you tremble your soul before it for?" he cried. "You don't learn algebra with your blessed soul. Can't you look at it with your clear simple wits?" [4]

The scene is repeated again and again; and always Paul is ashamed of his anger. All that appears on the surface is her humility, his arrogance and impatience. Yet what appears between the lines is different. Miriam puts her soul and its complexities into the algebra lesson because to her it stands for learning and the life of the mind, all that has been denied her. It has been granted to Paul: this is his world, and learning is a means of access to him; she is timid and self-conscious because she already loves him, and already with prophetic insight fears that he will go beyond her. Paul is angry with her hesitation, her slowness and her emotional intensity because it already begins to constitute a claim on him. Strongly drawn to Miriam, he cannot and will not give himself to her; he wants to keep their encounter, all her life that touches him, on the level of her "clear simple wits," where he knows he is safe and knows he is her master.

"Then he often avoided her and went with Edgar. Miriam and her brother were naturally antagonistic. Edgar was a rationalist, who was curious and had a sort of scientific interest in life." Here Paul feels secure.

Most of this material is already present in one of the earliest written portions of Sons and Lovers. None of the explanation of Paul's and Miriam's motives suggested above is in the book at any stage. It is doubtful whether Lawrence could have explained them at the time this part of the book was written. He is not writing an interpretation of the Paul-Miriam relation in the light of full psychological knowledge. He is portraying it from the inside, as it seemed at the time. If he is deluded about it, he portrays the delusions. But he puts their grounds and causes into the picture, too. Paul thinks he is a clearheaded, rational creature, irritated by the obscure complexities of Miriam's nature. But in fact he is in a far more complex emotional tangle than she; and the matter for such a reading of the situation is presented quite fully at the same time as his own quite different view. This is not a common achievement—to give the false judgment of a participant in a situation, to give it almost entirely through his eyes, yet to incorporate in it the grounds of a true judgment. It is not a necessary part of the novelist's business to give a final omniscient judgment; but it is his business to give the material on which a final judgment could be based.

The Paul and Miriam chapters are the essential core of *Sons and Lovers*. Adolescent love has been treated in fiction both before and since, tenderly or ironically; but never with such penetration, so little sentimentality or such honest determination to show its nature and the corruptions to which it is subject. Lawrence takes it seriously, and this is rarely done; and he treats it, under the pressure of an urgent personal necessity, from the inside. But quantitatively the Miriam relationship occupies only about a third of the book. The letter to Garnett, after describing the battle between the mother and Miriam for the soul of Paul, continues: "The son decides to leave his soul in his mother's hands, and like his elder brother, go for passion." But this, with other passages in the commentary, is not quite borne out by the text. It is wisdom after the event. At the end of the "Defeat of Miriam" chapter Paul recognises that he cannot love her physically, but he does not know why. He does not clearly recognise the power of the mother-image. It is true that he returns to his mother; the seal is set on his return by their trip to Lincoln together, in which he treats her like "a fellow taking his girl for an outing". But he thinks that he is still faithful to Miriam, that she still holds him in the depths of his soul. Yet her possession of his soul comes to matter less and less, for at the same time another woman is arousing his physical passion.

Clara Dawes represents all that Miriam does not. She is independent, emancipated, experienced and physically uninhibited. She is also separated from her husband, whom she has written off as an insensitive brute. While Miriam trespasses on the sanctities that had been the mother's preserve, Clara Dawes stands freely on unoccupied ground. Miriam wants a completely committed love—with all its concomitants of fidelity, tenderness and understanding. This Paul cannot give; his fidelity and tenderness are already bespoken; and Miriam is condemned to sterile conflict. But Clara's is a frank, physical appeal. The temperamental difference is subtly emphasised. Shortly before his first meeting with Clara, Paul has been reading the Bible to Miriam, and he boggles at a passage about a woman in travail. Anything suggesting the physical relation of man and woman is taboo between them. Not long after, when they are walking with Clara, they meet an elderly spinster lovingly caressing a great horse. They find

her odd, and Clara blurts out flatly, "I suppose she wants a man".
Immediately after as he sees Clara striding ahead, Paul feels a hot
wave of excitement run through him.

The excitement grows. Paul drifts away from Miriam into a Socialist-
Suffragette-Unitarian group around Clara. She comes to work under
Paul in the factory where he is employed, and her husband also works
there. The development of their relation is wholly without the tender
pastoral glow of the farmhouse idyll with Miriam, but also, in spite
of obvious complications, without the hidden obstacles and inhibitions. He does not even realise at first that he desires her sexually.

> Sex had become so complicated in him that he would have denied
> that he ever could want Clara or Miriam or any woman whom he *knew*.
> Sex desire was a sort of detached thing, that did not belong to a woman.
> He loved Miriam with his soul. He grew warm at the thought of Clara,
> he battled with her, he knew the curves of her breast and shoulders as
> if they had been moulded inside him; and yet he did not positively de-
> sire her. He would have denied it for ever.[5]

His mother is not displeased; she thinks he is getting away from
Miriam. And even Miriam is little disturbed by the new situation; she
is sure there is nothing in it.

> Miriam knew how strong was the attraction of Clara for him; but
> still she was certain that the best in him would triumph. His feeling for
> Mrs. Dawes—who, moreover, was a married woman—was shallow and
> temporal, compared with his love for herself. He would come back to
> her, she was sure.[6]

Yet she is afraid to let Paul become her lover, and he can never
bring himself to push things to a crisis. The situation between them
grows steadily more unsatisfactory. Paul's physical desires are becoming more importunate, and it seems on the face of things that it is
Miriam's reluctance which stands in the way. We may read between
the lines that her reluctance is the consequence of his earlier inhibitions; but this is never said. And from this time on the suspicion obtrudes itself that the author is identifying himself too closely with
Paul's point of view. The truth of the presentation is not impaired, as
far as it goes; but less than justice is done to Miriam's side, and Paul's
ex parte explanations have it too much their own way, as they did
not in the earlier chapters of the story. Eventually he breaks with
her, after eight years of friendship and love.

Of course he goes straight to Clara; and easily, naturally, without forethought or complication, he has of her what he has wanted for years. Their first encounter is not even described. Paul has not yet realised that women need to be satisfied as well as men relieved, and at the time of writing Lawrence probably shared his ignorance. At any rate, he is not at the stage when he wishes to analyse and differentiate sexual experience. The mere fact of its occurrence is enough. Paul is immensely elated. He takes Clara to tea with his mother, without embarrassment, and his mother thinks, "What a man he seems." He is growing up, and the mists that clung round the Miriam relationship have cleared. Even on Clara's visits to the Morel household "it was a clear, cool atmosphere, where everyone was himself and in harmony." Paul still sees Miriam, but now his bitter comment on the affair is that it was only talk—"There never *was* a great deal more than talk between us." The sense of tension relieved is vivid enough; but we are obstinately left with the impression that Lawrence does not want to convey—that the relation with Miriam was far the stronger and more meaningful of the two. There is a slightly smug satisfaction about Paul, for having got what he wants without forfeiting his mother's approval, in which the author seems at least partly implicated. It is not the women whom their sons sleep with that possessive mothers hate—it is the women whom they love; and it is not hard to see here the cause for Jessie Chambers' charge of capitulation to the mother's point of view.

Paul has at last succeeded in finding pleasure without the sense of guilt; and his need for this is probably the key to another curious episode, otherwise hard to explain. Baxter Dawes, Clara's husband, has degenerated into a drunken bully. He wants his revenge on Paul, waylays him and beats him up. Paul is severely hurt and becomes ill as a result. Pneumonia follows, and while his mother nurses him, both Clara and Miriam are rejected. Paul has had his pleasure, allowed himself to be punished for it, and now returns safely to his mother's care. But it is too late. Immediately afterwards his mother's illness declares itself; it is a fatal cancer. Paul is prostrated with grief. While visiting his mother in hospital, he learns that Dawes is there, too, and he goes to visit him. Between typhoid and drink, Dawes is brought pretty low, and the two meet on the ground of their common misery. A sort of friendship develops between them, and a little later we have the curious situation of Paul's suggesting to Clara that she has used her husband badly. Clara is even inclined to agree with him. Paul is so broken by his mother's illness that he becomes indifferent to Clara,

and she begins to tire of him. He tells Dawes that she has finished
with him. During the last days of his mother's illness he sees
little of Clara and Miriam, and they mean nothing to him when
he does; but his rôle as Dawes' friend and protector continues to
develop. He visits him in a convalescent home, tries to cheer
him up and give him the courage to start in life again. Paul says that
he feels in a worse mess than Dawes—"in a tangled sort of hole, rather
dark and dreary, and no road anywhere." Paul indeed is withering
away. Clara joins them, and she finds Paul paltry and insignificant,
finds that her husband in his defeat has more manly dignity—even a
certain nobility. Paul is convinced that he is finished, and in a final
act of self-negation he slips away and leaves the two together. And
it does not take Clara long to recognise her real mate.

> "Take me back!" she whispered, ecstatic. "Take me back, take me
> back!" And she put her finger through his fine, thin dark hair, as if she
> were only semi-conscious. He tightened his grasp on her.[7]

So Paul is cleared of his only real sexual relation, and the bond with
the dead mother is unimpaired.

A last effort with Miriam fails. They meet again, with all the old
tension. She suggests marriage, and in a scene of tortured, enigmatic
confusion he rejects it. The situation hardly explains itself—or rather,
two inconsistent explanations are offered. Paul says: "You love me so
much, you want to put me in your pocket. And I should die there,
smothered." But we are also told that he longs for the comfort and
understanding she could give him, and wants her to take possession
of him, as it were by force; she will not take that initiative, and as
long as the decision rests with him he cannot make it. Again we are
placed at the centre of the entanglement, with all the blindness and
lack of comprehension that this implies. It is hard to resist the conviction that there is some impurity of motive here. It is as though
Lawrence himself is forcing the blame on Miriam for refusing to live
Paul's life for him. Paul has been growing weaker and less positive
since his first rejection of Miriam. This is the climax of his nullity,
and invites the final condemnation of his neurotic refusal of responsibility for his own existence.

Lawrence studiously avoids all attempts at such a final judgment.
We are familiar, in the more developed kinds of novel, with the spectator character who stands apart from the action and serves as a
vehicle for the novelist's point of view. There is no such character in

Sons and Lovers. No one is right. No one can claim a superior insight to the others. All the main characters—Paul, Miriam, Mrs. Morel, Clara Dawes—make extremely penetrating remarks on each other. All are blind to much that is going on around them. Even Lawrence the author, whom we must distinguish from his own portrait of himself in Paul, is not in this position. Lawrence's exposition of the novel closes with these words: "He is left in the end naked of everything, with the drift towards death." But never trust the author, trust the tale, as Dr. Leavis puts it. What does the tale actually tell us? It has not often been observed (Anthony West, I believe, is alone in calling attention to it) that at the ghastly climax of his mother's illness Paul, with the connivance of his sister, kills her with an overdose of sleeping tablets to spare her further agony. Realistically considered, it is simply an act of despairing mercy. Symbolically, it has another significance. Here, where the regression of Paul's character has reached its farthest point, there is still something within him which is capable of decisive action—capable even of killing the mother to whom he is bound, to liberate both of them and to end her agony and his. And this prepares us for the actual end of the novel, which is not as Lawrence describes it, but as follows:

"Mother!" he whimpered—"mother!"

She was the only thing that held him up, himself, amid all this. And she was gone, intermingled herself. He wanted her to touch him, have him alongside with her.

But no, he would not give in. Turning sharply, he walked towards the city's gold phosphorescence. His fists were shut, his mouth set fast. He would not take that direction, to the darkness, to follow her. He walked towards the faintly humming, glowing town, quickly.[8]

In fact, he refuses to give in and the final motion is towards life. Paul, whose vacillations and refusals have worn him away till he has reached something like nonentity, proves in the end capable of a regenerating spark. At whatever cost to himself and others he has kept his frail independence alive. And then he puts the whole imbroglio behind him as Lawrence was putting it behind him by writing the book.

"The novels and stories come unwatched out of one's pen." And Lawrence the man is not clearly aware of what has come from the pen of Lawrence the writer. Lawrence the writer, at any rate at this stage, fulfils the conditions demanded by Keats: he is "capable of being in uncertainties, mysteries, doubts, without any irritable reach-

ing after fact and reason." The part of the book which is most contrived, most written to a thesis, is the love-affair with Clara Dawes.
It represents, or is supposed to represent, Paul's attempt at a simple
physical relationship as a relief from the obscure psychic complexities
of the love between himself and Miriam. Yet it is far less powerful,
far less successful, in expressing the essential nature of love than the
unfulfilled and tormented passages with Miriam. Lawrence, in fact, is
at his strongest when he is exploring a state of affairs which is obscure,
which he has not exhausted in life. The writing is a catharsis. When
a situation has been lived through and completed, his best and most
characteristic powers are not called out. Lawrence's limited experience
of mere physiological satisfaction without any stronger bond seems to
have been completed before 1912; it never seems to have interested
him much in life, and it provides no lasting satisfaction and no solution
to the conflict in the novel. Indeed, the emptiness of the affair with
Clara Dawes makes it an inadequate counterpoise to the relation with
Miriam.

Again, like *The White Peacock,* a novel about frustration and failure
and contradictions that are never reconciled. But in *The White Peacock* the human failures are almost absorbed in the quivering joy of
earth, the vibration of the non-human world that surrounds them. In
Sons and Lovers the human conflicts have become more intense and
more pressing, and the necessity for following them to a conclusion
more absolute. The idyllic passages are not a diversion from the plot;
they occur only in the Miriam episodes, and they are strictly subordi-
nated to Miriam herself. They are the necessary setting for her character, and the shared love of Paul and Miriam for flowers, birds'-eggs
and trees is only a pathetic extension of their feeling for each other.
The intense realisation of personal forces burns away all the minor
social falsities that impair the reality of *The White Peacock;* and it
also burns away most of the lyrical tenderness that makes that novel
a springtime story in spite of the frustrations of the plot. So that *Sons
and Lovers* becomes incidentally a full, intimate, sympathetic, but
also a harsh and unrelieved presentation of working-class life—the
oppressively close-knit family system, the narrow play for the individual sensibilities; the strength of individual development when it
manages to survive among the massive forces that press upon it. Lawrence never captures this continuous sense of actuality in a novel
again, though he does in some of the shorter tales. For this reason
Sons and Lovers remains his masterpiece to those who abide by the
central tradition of the novel. Possibly they are right, but those who

hold this view are still not penetrating to what is essential in Lawrence. The naturalistic success of *Sons and Lovers* is only incidental; the growing point of the book is the psychological adventurousness, the resolute beginning of an exploration into the tangled relations between men and women. In his next two novels this is to be Lawrence's only theme.

NOTES

1. *Fantasia of the Unconscious* (1922), xiv.
2. *Letters*, ed. A. Huxley (1932), 78–79.
3. *Sons and Lovers* (Modern Library), 180–182.
4. *Ibid.*, 185–186.
5. *Ibid.*, 323–324.
6. *Ibid.*, 324.
7. *Ibid.*, 478.
8. *Ibid.*, 491.

16

MARVIN MUDRICK

The Originality of *The Rainbow*

MANNERS and morals: they are, critics agree, what novels properly concern themselves with; and the specialist in the English novel can readily demonstrate the English novelist's expert attention to both from *Moll Flanders* to the latest thriller by Graham Greene. Certainly, fiction is of all literary genres the most intractable to description or definition, and we are grateful for any indices to its nature. We are also proud of our language and literature; and the novel in English has an illustrious history, no doubt about it. So the manners and morals, and the fiction we are specially interested in are English and American. It may not, then, seem chauvinistic to us when Caroline Gordon [1] discovers the world history of the novel to be a triumphant progress toward apotheosis in the work of the Anglo-American, Henry James, who was obliging enough to scrutinize, with the tact of an exquisite sensibility, Anglo-Saxon manners and morals—of only a few social groups, to be sure—on *both* sides of the Atlantic. Even Dr. Leavis, who demotes or dismisses Richardson, Fielding, Sterne, Smollett, Dickens, Thackeray, Hardy, and Joyce, expresses much admiration for Hawthorne, and finds a great tradition in Jane Austen, George Eliot, James, Conrad, and Lawrence, in whose work, as it seems to him, manners are so chosen and placed as to reflect on their particular surfaces the image of that sober absolute morality, essentially secular and embattled, which for two centuries has been the strength of England if not of the entire civilized world.

Reprinted from *Spectrum* (III, 1) with the permission of the editors and the author.

It is just here, regarding the rest of the world, that a doubt arises. Compare, for instance, George Eliot and Tolstoy, or Conrad and Dostoievsky—comparisons that Dr. Leavis, at any rate, ought to accept as fair, since one great tradition ought to be able to stand up against another, and since George Eliot and Tolstoy share a preoccupation with the social and ordinary as Conrad and Dostoievsky share a preoccupation with the psychological and extraordinary. Or compare Stendhal and Jane Austen, or Turgenev and James, or almost any nineteenth-century French or Russian novelist and Hawthorne.

Fiction, and a tradition of fiction, may be genuine without being great. Greatness is, after all, relative, and when we compare George Eliot and Tolstoy we˙are aware of such differences in magnitude that to describe the two of them by the same honorific epithet is to do no service to either. Nor is George Eliot a feeble representative of the tradition Dr. Leavis singles out: *Middlemarch,* at least, is a very impressive novel, with a breadth of intelligent sympathy it fixes for all time the manners and morals of its own place and time, it is perhaps the only English novel that sensitively registers something like a whole society. Yet it is, as the author notes, "A Study of Provincial Life." There is, in fact,.no English novel that registers a whole society; and, in the balance with Continental fiction, there is almost no English novel that cannot fairly be described as provincial.

It is not, of course, merely a question of subject: a novelist may be as cosmopolitan as he pleases in treating provincial life—Flaubert or Galdós, for example. The point is that for the English novelist a provincialism of temperament is liable to go along with his provincialism of subject. Mme. Bovary, not to mention Bouvard and Pécuchet, has written some of the better known English novels, and the sturdy pragmatism of the English petty bourgeoisie has penetrated and sustained English fiction since those redoubtable self-made innovators and moral men of practical affairs, Defoe and Richardson. The English novel has chacteristically been partisan, either protective or rebellious; and the standard of conduct—of manners and morals—which˙it lavishly illustrates, and by which it measures itself, is the middle-class standard. *Wuthering Heights* and *Tristram Shandy* are as pertinent to the case as *Pamela,* and together they exemplify the three major modes of English fiction: romance as protest, satire as protest, and sentiment as affirmation. Perhaps Dr. Leavis recoils with such a spasm of distaste from Sterne because *Tristram Shandy* is the most subversive protest in English fiction against the bourgeois imperatives that Dr. Leavis, by implication, finds so congenial to the flowering of a great tradition.

These imperatives are, of course, overwhelmingly materialistic. Tom Jones in the hay (sowing his wild oats) with a pretty chambermaid, Scrooge converted to the obsession of giving rather than withholding smiles and crowns and guineas, Pamela indignantly rejecting pre-marital advances for the sake of wealth and rank later—all of them are enjoying the satisfactions of a morality that ultimately, despite its solemn façade, repays its adherents and sinks human problems in cash and Christmas pudding, a morality of trivial appetites. Whether the English novelist is examining, with intelligence or sentimentality or cynicism, the manners and squeamishness of the cultivated provinces, or the local color of urban and rural low life, or the sinister fascinations of the *haut monde*, or the convulsive freakishness of grand supersexual and asexual passions, or the palpitating idealism of young women who—not having been told what they can importantly do—are looking for something important to do: whatever the English novelist tries, the manners and morals of the earliest and most oppressively successful middle class in history are breathing down his neck and directing his pen into the official view of a life that is in any case considerably less exhilarating than the life visible to the great Continental novelists. Or, for that matter, to Chaucer and Shakespeare.

We must come to it at last, the bourgeois imperative which has defended the materialist order against its gravest threat, and which Anglo-Saxon fiction had perforce to accept for two centuries, the imperative against human normality. You may, the imperative declares, transcend sex by the rhetoric of a grand passion, you may cheapen it as by Fielding's characteristic resort to comic-strip prurience, you may ignore it or jeer at it, you may even in extremity be clinical about it, but you may not regard it as a serious, normal, central preoccupation of mankind, and you may not attempt to understand it.

The first literary effect of such a proscription was to deprive English fiction of normal women. The sphere of decision for women, in Western civilization at least, has always been love and marriage; and if the woman is not permitted to take into account the most serious impulse of her private existence, she may surrender to domesticity or the vapors and become one of Dickens' brave Biddys or dumb Doras, or she may be encouraged to transcend sex before going to the trouble of learning what it is, like George Eliot's Dorothea or Emily Brontë's Cathy or any other Gothic or Romantic heroine. There are even relatively few *interesting* women in English fiction, and most of these are interesting because their authors understand and document the pathology of their reduction: Jane Austen's Emma, Dickens' Estella (his only powerful insight into a woman's sensibility).

And there are a very few whose normality has the protective colora-
tion of intelligence and so passes undetected: Jane Austen's Elizabeth
Bennet and Anne Elliot, for example. Generally speaking, however,
the heroine of English fiction is liable to be a dead loss—think of all
the unrememberable Amelias hung like decorative albatrosses round
the necks of the heroes of Victorian novels. And then think of Tolstoy's Natasha and Anna, Dostoievsky's women supreme in their
passionate abnormality, the whole range of unapologetic women in
Stendhal and Balzac and Flaubert, the gallery of unhurried female
sensuality in Colette: not only a definable *sex* in contrast to the poor
sticks of English heroines, but almost a different species. The English
hero, true, has always been allowed some scope of heroic action in
adventure (often commercial), in working his way up, in "becoming
a success." Still, to eradicate half the human race, and to confine the
energies of the other half mainly within the bounds of materialistic
aspiration—this is not to survey, through morals and manners, the limits
of human possibility. It was this order of things that D. H. Lawrence
confronted when he began writing the novel the first part of which
eventually became *The Rainbow*.

Literary revolutions are as various and frequent as political elec-
tions: some are important, most are not. When what has been called
the Flaubertian tradition (a French import which, though it deeply
influenced two representatives of his own "native" tradition, Dr.
Leavis regards with a somewhat xenophobic distaste) was introduced
into English fiction, and such novelists as James, Conrad, Ford, and
Joyce adopted and developed the techniques available to a conscious
craftsmanship in fiction, one important and irreversible revolution had
occurred—the most important, some critics believe, in the history of
English fiction. Certainly, it produced important and original work,
even though it has inflicted upon us, unavoidably, all the gimmickry
of craft-conscious and myth-mongering and symbolifying criticism,
as well as some of the doleful justification for such criticism in those
pointless manipulations of technique into which the tradition may
tempt the novelist: Conrad, for example, somberly picking his way
through the underbrush of half a dozen intervening points of view, in
that disastrous virtuoso exercise *Chance*, to report on a man's tying a
shoelace.

To this tradition, and to the revolution it achieved, Lawrence does
not belong. Joyce belonged to them, but he participated in another
literary revolution, the revolution against the Anglo-Saxon (and
Irish) censor; and here he and Lawrence may be said to have stood
in a common cause. Joyce's publishing and distributing difficulties

with *Dubliners* and *Ulysses* strikingly resemble Lawrence's with *The Rainbow* and *Lady Chatterley's Lover*. Nevertheless, there is censorship and censorship. When Judge Woolsey issued his celebrated decision admitting *Ulysses* into the United States, he remarked, in denying that it came within the legal definition of obscenity, that its effect on the reader was more likely to be "emetic" than "aphrodisiac." The interesting judicial principle was thus established that, for the Anglo-Saxon commonwealth, to vomit is, if not positively healthier, at least less baneful than to engage in sexual intercourse. The judge rightly inferred that Joyce's sexual imagery and naughty language were no vital threat at all to Anglo-Saxon mores, but only the signs by which a whole culture manifested its nausea and self-disgust. The Joycean Revolution of the Word has brought freedom, it is now obvious, mainly for cynical clinicians and cautious pornographers, the freedom to spit and hiss (and leads directly to such a May-fly oddity of literary entomology as the San Francisco Renaissance). Today, a quarter-century after the canonization of Molly Bloom, the Woolseyan principle has been challenged: *Lady Chatterley's Lover*, which audaciously attempted to rehabilitate sexual imagery and the old Anglo-Saxon words as signs of health and tenderness (and which, by the way, succeeded), has at last been legally published in both the United States and the United Kingdom.

Still, *Lady Chatterley's Lover* is, by the pressures of its subject and of the lateness of its hour, as close to being hortatory as a work of art can afford to be; even without its four famous words (all of them used more frequently, of course, in *Ulysses* and in almost any current popular novel), its radical extra-literary intent is clear. *The Rainbow*—which marked the outbreak of the Lawrencian revolution— is in fact a more dangerous work because it is less open to philistine retaliation, because it bases itself confidently on no exhortation at all, only on the assumption that sex is a serious, normal, central preoccupation of mankind. After its early skirmish with suppression (which showed, not how acutely prescient, but how very silly, English censors could be in 1915), *The Rainbow* has been widely accessible in print, and is even becoming generally accepted—at least the first half of it —as a brilliant record of English manners and morals over three generations, a *really* great English family-chronicle novel, not less respectable and beyond comparison better than anything in this line by Arnold Bennett.

True enough, there is, beside it, no family-chronicle novel in English that deserves mention; and anything that will certify the respectability of *The Rainbow* is to be prized, just as we ought to prize Lawrence's subliterary reputation as a sensational novelist for making more of his fiction accessible in cheap-paperback American reprints than that of any other major English author. *The Rainbow* is not, after all, so respectable as Galsworthy: there are reasons for Lawrence's notoriety, as well as for his boring and disappointing the common reader to whom he is notorious; and the reasons are all in *The Rainbow*. Nothing promises to be more, and proves on inspection to be less, sensational than this family-chronicle novel which assumes not only that generations are generated, but that the relationship between husband and wife is the central fact of human existence, that the living nucleus of this relationship is the act of sexual union, that the act of sexual union is infinitely serious, complex, and difficult, and that an act of such radiant significance must be fairly treated by the honest novelist.

Graham Hough, however, disapproves of Lawrence's candor: "As for physical passion . . . no one should try to present it as . . . [Lawrence] does, and traditional literary good sense has always known it." [2] This appeal to timeless good taste would be plausible, if it were not for the very special conditions against which Lawrence had to contend. Most authors of the past, and of other cultures, who have dealt with physical passion have not, indeed, presented it directly. Chaucer did not, nor did Colette; but the reason is that neither needs to: for Chaucer, the sacramental nature of passion and, for Colette, the various joys of an indulged sensuality are self-evident and unchallenged; medieval Catholic humanism and modern French hedonism meet in their conviction of the power of sexual gratification, which can bring to peace and stillness men and women alike. Lawrence, very much on the other hand, has a unique problem: he must reassert this life-renewing power against two centuries of a culture and literature that have muffled and denied its very existence, and he can reassert it only by presenting its actuality as a reminder to the deaf and blind. Lawrence's terrible candor is necessary only because there has been so mendacious and destructive a silence; and yet, because it is so peremptorily called for, it not only reclaims old truths but rushes on to make discoveries. The long reign of English philistinism—in both life and letters—is Lawrence's provocation and his unexampled opportunity.

Of course Lawrence has the advantage of springing from the country community of English workingmen-farmers, a community not bound or even much influenced by the shopkeeper code, and he comes to maturity at a time when the whole structure of class and community is about to encounter the disintegrating shock of the First World War. In his historic moment, Lawrence has before him the life of the last English community: not the manners of the province (which are in any case the manners of the provincial petty bourgeoisie and minor gentry), but a life rich in productive labor and in continuity with the passing seasons, rooted in the earthly and physical, inarticulate without grossness or stupidity, a life seemingly permament yet fated to pass away in the general breakdown of codes and communities and to be replaced or transcended—if by anything—by individual aspiration. It is this process, over three generations, which is the subject and theme of *The Rainbow;* the process is the most momentous human fact of the past century; and it is a process which, in *The Rainbow,* discloses itself poignantly and most crucially in the sexual histories of individuals. The revolutionary nature of *The Rainbow* is, then, twofold: it is the first English novel to record the normality and significance of physical passion; and it is the only English novel to record, with a prophetic awareness of consequences, the social revolution whereby Western man lost his sense of community and men— more especially, women—learned, if they could, that there is no help any longer except in the individual and in his capacity for a passional life.

As soon as the critic of Lawrence begins to favor such terms as "community" and "passion," he risks being suspected of imagining, obsequiously on cue from his author, a unanimity of social feeling that never was and a potency of personal feeling that never could be, under idyllic and perpetually recurring circumstances in the rural districts of the English Midlands up to, say, the turn of our century. But Lawrence presents no idylls. The community in *The Rainbow,* like every other, is an abstraction from its individuals, who are its only embodiment; and it lives as more than a mere term of discourse only so long as it provides forms and sanctions for the abiding impulses of their separate natures. These impulses are, besides, not all of them communal and sympathetic: Lawrence's individuals are just that, different and distinct from one another except when a strength of sympathy draws them together for moments out of the reciprocal alienations of individuality; and every relationship in *The Rainbow* testifies, not how easy and renewable, but how hard to come by, how precarious, and how irrecoverably unique each instance of passion is, even in a nature as faithful to itself and as sensitively patient as Tom Brangwen's:

Then she said:
     "You will be good to me, won't you?"
She was small and girlish and terrible, with a queer, wide look in her

eyes. His heart leaped in him, in anguish of love and desire, he went blindly to her and took her in his arms.

"I want to," he said as he drew her closer and closer in. She was soothed by the stress of his embrace, and remained quite still, relaxed against him, mingling in to him. And he let himself go from past and future, was reduced to the moment with her. In which he took her and was with her and there was nothing beyond, they were together in an elemental embrace beyond their superficial foreignness. But in the morning he was uneasy again. She was still foreign and unknown to him. Only, within the fear was pride, belief in himself as mate for her. And she, everything forgotten in her new hour of coming to life, radiated vigour and joy, so that he quivered to touch her.

It made a great difference to him, marriage. Things became remote and of so little significance, as he knew the powerful source of his life, eyes opened on a new universe, and he wondered in thinking of his triviality before. A new, calm relationship showed to him in the things he saw, in the cattle he used, the young wheat as it eddied in a wind.

And each time he returned home, he went steadily, expectantly, like a man who goes to a profound, unknown satisfaction. At dinnertime, he appeared in the doorway, hanging back a moment from entering, to see if she was there. He saw her setting the plates on the white-scrubbed table. Her arms were slim, she had a slim body and full skirts, she had a dark, shapely head with close-banded hair. Somehow it was her head, so shapely and poignant, that revealed her his woman to him. As she moved about clothed closely, full-skirted and wearing her little silk apron, her dark hair smoothly parted, her head revealed itself to him in all its subtle, intrinsic beauty, and he knew she was his woman, he knew her essence, that it was his to possess. And he seemed to live thus in contact with her, in contact with the unknown, the unaccountable and incalculable.

They did not take much notice of each other, consciously.

"I'm betimes," he said.

"Yes," she answered.

He turned to the dogs, or to the child if she were there. The little Anna played about the farm, flitting constantly in to call something to her mother, to fling her arms round her mother's skirts, to be noticed, perhaps caressed, then, forgetting, to slip out again.

Then Brangwen, talking to the child, or to the dog between his knees, would be aware of his wife, as, in her tight, dark bodice and her lace fichu, she was reaching up to the corner cupboard. He realized that he lived by her. Did he own her? Was she here for ever? Or might she go away? She was not really his, it was not a real marriage, this marriage between them. She might go away. He did not feel like a master, husband, father of her children. She belonged elsewhere. Any moment, she might be gone. And he was ever drawn to her, drawn after her, with ever-raging, ever-unsatisfied desire. He must always turn home, wherever his steps were taking him, always to her, and he could never quite reach her, he could never quite be satisfied, never be at peace, because she might go away.

At evening, he was glad. Then, when he had finished in the yard, and come in and washed himself, when the child was put to bed, he could sit on the other side of the fire with his beer on the hob and his long white pipe in his fingers, conscious of her there opposite him, as she worked at her embroidery, or as she talked to him, and he was safe with her now, till morning. She was curiously self-sufficient and did not say very much. Occasionally she lifted her head, her grey eyes shining with a strange light, that had nothing to do with him or with this place, and would tell him about herself. She seemed to be back again in the past, chiefly in her childhood or her girlhood, with her father. She very rarely talked of her first husband. But sometimes, all shining-eyed, she was back at her own home, telling him about the riotous times, the trip to Paris with her father, tales of the mad acts of the peasants when a burst of religious, self-hurting fervour had passed over the country.

Tom Brangwen's apprehensions are not, after all, merely the customary timeless ones of husbands, but unprecedented seismic shocks: *The Rainbow* is recording a community in its last flare of vitality and gradual dying away, and all relationships and feelings are shaken by the great change. The foreignness of Tom's wife represents, disturbingly enough, the essential distance between all men and especially between the sexes; but it is already a terrifying difference beyond natural difference. Tom is no simple farmer: his aspiration toward the irreducibly alien woman is an inarticulate but not unconscious aspiration toward the experience of a life beyond the receding satisfactions of a community in process of dissolution. Till he meets Lydia he refuses, in drink and solitude, the only life his community offers him. Now, his dissatisfactions are new, and the brave chances he takes are new.

It was the coming of the colliery, years before, bringing canal and railway through the Brangwen land, which cut across the past and offered a promise of the future:

As they drove home from town, the farmers of the land met the blackened colliers trooping from the pit-mouth. As they gathered the harvest, the west wind brought a faint, sulphurous smell of pit-refuse burning. As they pulled the turnips in November, the sharp clink-clink-clink-clink-clink of empty trucks shunting on the line, vibrated in their hearts with the fact of other activity going on beyond them.

Tom, the young farmer awakened to a troubled sense of the restrictions of the Brangwen life, comes eventually into his own vision of a life beyond, once he has had his encounter with the complaisant pretty girl and his little talk with her Frenchman escort, the "ageless" and "monkey-like," gracious and imperial gentleman from elsewhere. When Tom sees the foreign lady walking toward him on the road, he knows that she is the awful chance he must take, and the best he can do. Yet the impulse outward moves, necessarily, more rapidly than the possibility of comprehending and fulfilling it: the breakup of the community is too sudden and unanticipated as railways and canals cut across the enclosed spaces of the mind, and the individual is freed from traditional unquestioned preoccupations in order to think and do—what? Tom Brangwen seeks out and lives with strangeness; but his satisfaction and his anguish remain equally resistant to statement or analysis, shy of words, still therefore plausibly connected with the old inarticulate traditional world. His steadiness, halfway between two worlds, is constantly in danger from the incompleteness of its commitment to either; it can be shaken, as by his step-daughter, Anna, whom he desperately loves but who has come too far from the past to rest in mute suspensions of judgment:

> She tried to discuss people, she wanted to know what was meant. But her father became uneasy. He did not want to have things dragged into consciousness. Only out of consideration for her he listened. And there was a kind of bristling rousedness in the room. The cat got up and stretching itself, went uneasily to the door. Mrs. Brangwen was silent, she seemed ominous. Anna could not go on with her fault-finding, her criticism, her expression of dissatisfactions. She felt even her father against her.

Individual aspiration, once it is released, has no certain or obvious goal; and how can it be held in check somewhere, how can one keep it from making all action or repose seem premature and insufficient, how can the skeptical analytic mind be quieted? In fact, even for Tom these question have force, the speechless remoteness of his marriage—for all of its passion—is finally not enough, his pathetic paternal jealousy of his stepdaughter's choice of a husband poisons even as it recalls to him his sense of his own life:

> What was missing in his life, that, in his ravening soul, he was not satisfied? He had had that friend at school, his mother, his wife, and Anna? What had he done? He had failed with his friend, he had been a poor son; but he had known satisfaction with his wife, let it be enough; he loathed himself for the state he was in over Anna. Yet he was *not* satisfied. It was agony to know it.
> Was his life nothing? Had he nothing to show, no work? He did not

count his work, anybody could have done it. What had he known, but
the long, marital embrace with his wife! Curious, that this was what his
life amounted to! At any rate, it was something, it was eternal. He
would say so to anybody, and be proud of it. He lay with his wife in his
arms, and she was still his fulfillment, just the same as ever. And that
was the be-all and the end-all. Yes, and he was proud of it.

But the bitterness, underneath, that there still remained an unsatis-
fied Tom Brangwen, who suffered agony because a girl cared nothing
for him. He loved his sons—he had them also. But it was the further, the
creative life with the girl, he wanted as well. Oh, and he was ashamed.
He trampled himself to extinguish himself.

So Tom Brangwen dies, drunk as Noah to forget the wearying puzzles
of his middle age, drowned in the flood of rain, and his women
mourn him:

They cleared and washed the body, and laid it on the bed.

There, it looked still and grand. He was perfectly calm in death, and,
now he was laid in line, inviolable, unapproachable. To Anna, he was
the majesty of the inaccessible male, the majesty of death. It made her
still and awe-stricken, almost glad.

Lydia Brangwen, the mother, also came and saw the impressive, inviolable body of the dead man. She went pale, seeing death. He was
beyond change or knowledge, absolute, laid in line with the infinite.
What had she to do with him? He was a majestic Abstraction, made
visible now for a moment, inviolate, absolute. And who could lay claim
to him, who could speak of him, of the him who was revealed in the
stripped moment of transit from life into death? Neither the living nor
the dead could claim him, he was both the one and the other, inviolable,
inaccessibly himself.

"I shared life with you, I belong in my own way to eternity," said
Lydia Brangwen, her heart cold, knowing her own singleness.

"I did not know you in life. You are beyond me, supreme now in
death," said Anna Brangwen, awe-stricken, almost glad.

This is Everyman, not at all the conventional individualist hero
of English fiction; and Lawrence, anticipating perplexity, provided
his critics with a long peg on which to hang their theories about *The
Rainbow* and *Women in Love*. "You mustn't look," he wrote to Edward Garnett, who had been disappointed to find no trace of *Sons
and Lovers* in the new work, ". . . for the old stable *ego* of the
character. There is another ego, according to whose action the individual is unrecognizable, and passes through, as it were, allotropic
states which it needs a deeper sense than any other we've been used
to exercise, to discover are states of the same single radically un-

changed element." And he goes on to make obligingly explicit the analogy of diamond-carbon to the mode of characterization he has just begun to feel at home in Now this tip from the essentially kindly Lawrence to his bewildered English friend is a useful one; for the elucidation of *Women in Love* especially, as Mark Schorer has pointed out.[3] It is nevertheless not so simple, or perhaps even so accurate, as it looks; and it does not indicate anything nearly so unprecedented— if one takes into account Continental fiction—as Lawrence appears to think.

The trouble is that, in this formulation, Lawrence does not yet seem to have made clear to himself why the old mode of characterization is being discarded and how the new mode functions, and what sort of novel employs one or the other. *Sons and Lovers* is—like *A Portrait of the Artist as a Young Man*—a wilful and confused post-Victorian novel of youthful longing and self-discovery, written by a young man whose *parti pris* rejects or ignores the values of the community which has helped to make him; *The Rainbow*, on the other hand, is an elegiac novel about the dissolution of a community whose values, even as these pass away, the author neither rejects nor ignores but seeks to understand and somehow, for his characters' sake, to transcend. The characters (Mr. Morel excepted) in *Sons and Lovers* are post-Victorian individualists colliding with an angry young individualist of a hero; the characters in *The Rainbow* breathe and move, as long as they can, in the large atmosphere of a community. Not that Tom Brangwen is less *individual* than, say Paul Morel; quite the contrary, he is more honestly and totally imagined, and therefore more human and more of a man. If the novelist creates his characters as more or less aggressive bundles of recognizable traits, as egos stabilized by manners and morals, and his novel as a sequence of collisions between such bundles, he will produce the kind of novel that Lawrence is now giving up, the novel preoccupied—whether in affirmation or in protest—with manners and morals, the class novel, the standard English novel. If, however, the novelist creates his characters in a life-size medium, fictional and communal, which nurtures, provokes, and makes room for the strength of impulse, he will produce a novel like *The Rainbow*—or *Anna Karenina*, or *The Idiot*, or *The Red and the Black*. Characters in novels like these are not caricatures or even conventional heroes, mere victims or arbiters of manners and morals, they are passions and first principles; and they are all the more human and individual for being so. Nor, of course, is Lawrence's new mode of characterization unprecedented or revolutionary, it is only not very English.

What *is* revolutionary in *The Rainbow*—what makes Lawrence, in perhaps the most important sense, the only modern novelist—is not the mode of characterization, but the new awareness which finds this mode necessary: the awareness that with the dying away, in the age of technology, of genuine communal relations between men, with the inevitable thwarting of what Lawrence was later to call "the societal impulse," the only hope for man lies in those remaining potentialities of human relationships which depend for their realization on the fullest (not necessarily the most various or complicated) possible realization of the sexual impulse. Lawrence, being English, had in this respect no choice but to be revolutionary. English novelists, as spokesmen for the most advanced middle class in the world, had since Defoe been advocating the simplest escape from the intolerable human problems posed by industrialism—the escape into materialist success, the pursuit of what Dickens' Wemmick poignantly euphemizes under the phrase "portable property"; but with the end of the expansive romantic phase of English industrialism, no serious English writer could any longer believe in this escape and pursuit, as Dickens and others before and after could believe in it once it had been sweetened by contrition, materialist benevolence, and marital union with another form of portable property. (We cannot imagine a French or an Italian or a Russian Lawrence, just as we cannot imagine an English Dostoievsky, though the awareness of which Lawrence is both creator and instrument has, finally, as much to say to the Continent as Dostoievsky has to say to the English.) For Lawrence, then, the hope, in fact the last resort, of modern man is—the unhappy word stares at us as it did at Lawrence's censors—sex: not as cold appetite, not as self-imposed exile from the teeming world, not as the exploiting of sensation or the temporary allaying of an itch, but as the bond of tranquillity and faith between man and woman, those polar opponents, and the last removable proof of human community.

The Rainbow is midpassage and arrival. Tom Brangwen still has roots, connections, the virtue of quietness in solitude; of these vestiges of community Anna and Will still keep something by, as it were, barely remembering them, Anna in her slovenly cheerful maternity, Will in his mute satisfaction with manual labor or minor artisanship. Only Ursula—modern woman and therefore, in her unforeseen and disastrously unprepared-for homelessness, true representative of modern mankind—has nothing at all of what, outside themselves, sustained the two generations before her. And for all three generations the unmapped territory to be explored, with increasing desperation and hope, is sex.

Tom Brangwen has a real marriage, notwithstanding its ultimate vulnerability to the stress of uncomprehended change; his apparently unwarrantable youthful waiting for a strangeness beyond his ordinary experience is rewarded and vindicated, and his life is transfigured by the reality of passion. If his marriage fails to give him everything, it nevertheless gives him much, even enough to make him at length unhappily sensitive to the unknown vibrations of what he must do without.

For Anna and Will, on the other hand, marriage seems at first sunnier and more simple. They have moved very far out of the shadow of the old Brangwen world; Anna, at least, is impatient with established sanctities; and both of them rejoice on their prolonged honeymoon in an uninhibited mutual exploration of sexuality, day after day of vital time-dissolving ease:

> As they lay close together, complete and beyond the touch of time or change, it was as if they were at the very centre of all the slow wheeling of space and the rapid agitation of life, deep, deep inside them all, at the centre where there is utter radiance, and eternal being, and the silence absorbed in praise: the steady core of all movements, the unawakened sleep of all wakefulness. They found themselves there, and they lay still, in each other's arms; for their moment they were at the heart of eternity, whilst time roared far off, forever far off, towards the rim.
>
> Then gradually they were passed away from the supreme centre, down the circles of praise and joy and gladness, further and further out, towards the noise and the friction. But their hearts had burned and were tempered by the inner reality, they were unalterably glad.
>
> Gradually they began to wake up, the noises outside became more real. They understood and answered the call outside. They counted the strokes of the bell. And when they counted midday, they understood that it was midday, in the world, and for themselves also.
>
> It dawned upon her that she was hungry. She had been getting hungrier for a lifetime. But even yet it was not sufficiently real to rouse her. A long way off she could hear the words, "I am dying of hunger." Yet she lay still, separate, at peace, and the words were unuttered. There was still another lapse.
>
> And then, quite calmly, even a little surprised, she was in the present, and was saying:
>
> "I am dying with hunger."
>
> "So am I," he said calmly, as if it were of not the slightest significance. And they relapsed into the warm, golden stillness. And the minutes flowed unheeded past the window outside.
>
> Then suddenly she stirred against him.
>
> "My dear, I am dying of hunger," she said.

It was a slight pain to him to be brought to.

"We'll get up," he said, unmoving.

And she sank her head on to him again, and they lay still, lapsing. Half consciously, he heard the clock chime the hour. She did not hear.

"Do get up," she murmured at length, "and give me something to eat."

"Yes," he said, and he put his arms round her, and she lay with her face on him. They were faintly astonished that they did not move. The minutes rustled louder at the window.

"Let me go then," he said.

She lifted her head from him, relinquishingly. With a little breaking away, he moved out of bed, and was taking his clothes. She stretched out her hand to him.

"You are so nice," she said, and he went back for a moment or two.

Then actually he did slip into some clothes, and, looking round quickly at her, was gone out of the room. She lay translated again into a pale, clearer peace. As if she were a spirit, she listened to the noise of him downstairs, as if she were no longer of the material world.

In such moments as Lawrence here presents, there can be no "characters" in the conventional fictional sense: the mode of characterization is dictated by the focus of attention, which here is on a core of impulse anterior to personality. It is, of course, easy to misunderstand such a passage in the context of English fiction, especially that sort of woman's fiction of which *Jane Eyre* is a quasi-serious instance: the emotion of romantic love reduces heroine (or hero) to a fluttering impotency—especially in anticipation—that may resemble a reduction to impulse. But the conjugal satisfactions of Tom Brangwen, or Anna, or Will, are not reductive at all, they liberate universal human powers, far from making romantic victims they make those relations between people without which there are only egos in collision and no persons. Nobody, it is true, can live indefinitely at such a depth of impulse; and the comic ascension of Anna and Will to the level of a more mundane appetite testifies not only to the existence of a daylight world in which we are all, more or less, scrupulously differentiated fictional characters, but also to that respect for full human truth which disciplines even the most rhapsodic utterances in this novel. The careful reader never forgets that *The Rainbow* is, in one large and traditional aspect, a great realistic novel: Tom Brangwen's life outside marriage, for example, is registered with an immediacy and resonance that would establish him as one of the great figures in English fiction even if he were nothing more; and one thinks of such superb set-pieces as Tom's efforts at comforting the child Anna while Lydia is bearing his first child, Tom's drunkenly inspired eulogy of marriage, his death in the flood—a luminous pertinence of detail, a fidelity to locale, a sternness of pathos not readily matched in any other fiction. Nevertheless, as the rhythm of the style—always near, when not actually, the rhythm of rhapsodic utterance—persists in implying, life is renewable only and perpetually at the springs of impulse, in celebration and praise, where we are less unique than human; and only to the degree to which we have renewed ourselves there, can we breathe and move as individuals in the daylight world.

Renewal, the gift and aim of life, becomes in modern marriage less and less the gift of repose, more and more pressingly the aim of conscious and personal exploration: woman is less passive and man more anxious, approaching an uneasy identity of rôles. Lydia is still withdrawn and enigmatic, a woman of the old dispensation, unharried, immured in domesticity and unamenable to self-questioning; so Tom is the explorer—joyous or baffled—in this first marriage, moving doubtfully at the rim of awareness. Anna, on the other hand, has come awake, because the invasion of all things by mechanism and the conscious mind has made Lydia the last possible woman of her kind: having lost what her mother unquestionably had, Anna must make up for it by becoming explorative in her own right, the free companion of her husband. But, after the shared bliss of the honeymoon, the difficulties of the new dispensation become gradually manifest. When the communal sanction for marriage is dissipated and only free and equal individuals remain, the burden on accidents of personality grows suddenly enormous. The temperamental differences between Lydia and Tom were unbridgeable, and of no significance to Lydia. Yet Will's soft inarticulateness drives the skeptical articulate Anna wild, and Anna's attacks on her husband's temperament drive him into retaliatory fury:

> She . . . clung to the worship of human knowledge. Man must die in the body but in his knowledge he was immortal. Such, somewhere, was her belief, quite obscure and unformulated. She believed in the omnipotence of the human mind.
>
> He, on the other hand, blind as a subterranean thing, just ignored the human mind and ran after his own dark-souled desires, following his own tunnelling nose. She felt often she must suffocate. And she fought him off.
>
> Then he, knowing he was blind, fought madly back again, frantic in sensual fear. He did foolish things. He asserted himself on his rights, he arrogated the old position of master of the house.
>
> "You've a right to do as I want," he cried.
>
> "Fool!" she answered. "Fool!"

"I'll let you know who's master," he cried.

"Fool!" she answered. "Fool! I've known my own father, who could put a dozen of you in his pipe and push them down with his finger-end. Don't I know what a fool you are!"

In the perilous colloidal tension of modern marriage, too much depends on merely personal qualities. And—at least for persons living in the delusive afterglow of the old world, still unalert to the swarming problems of consciousness—too much depends on the increasingly elaborate and conscious satisfactions of sexuality: the man, having lost his inherited mastery, comes to depend on these as on a drug, and the woman comes to resent what she will eventually regard as his infantile male weakness. Variety, the avoidance of monotony, becomes more and more a brutal conjugal compulsion. At length, reciprocally excited by Will's brush with infidelity, Anna and Will give themselves to the pleasures of a sort of democratic sexual cannibalism, to the fetishistic daylight fevers of sensuality, the manipulation of bodies as instruments for pleasure; and if Lawrence's imagery in this passage plainly obliges us to find the experience analogous to the Fall, it obliges us also to see the new experiences as a necessary expansion of man's knowledge in the time of another forced departure from the garden. Still, Anna and Will never reclaim their honeymoon fulfillment of passion or seem capable of the reconciliation between passion and sensuality; and their lives dwindle away in subtle disorganization, in the minor consummations and complaints of Anna's rôle as the fecund housewife and Will's as a woodwork teacher for the town, "very happy and keen in his new public spirit." Since their imperfect truce is the first modern marriage, it is appropriate that they bring into being the first complete modern woman, totally dispossessed and therefore totally explorative.

The child Ursula still has her father's environing and sometimes overpowering love; and she has, also in conversation with her grandmother, a window on the certainties of the past even as the thought of growing up without such certainties begins to trouble her:

. . . Ursula asked her deepest childish questions of her grandmother. "Will somebody love me, grandmother?"

"Many people love you, child. We all love you."

"But when I am grown up, will somebody love me?"

"Yes, some man will love you, child, because it's your nature. And I hope it will be somebody who will love you for what you are, and not for what he wants of you. But we have a right to want what we want."

Ursula was frightened, hearing these things. Her heart sank, she felt she had no ground under her feet. She clung to her grandmother. Here was peace and security. Here, from her grandmother's peaceful room, the door opened on to the greater space, the past, which was so big, that all it contained seemed tiny; loves and births and deaths, tiny units and features within a vast horizon. That was great relief, to know the tiny importance of the individual, within the great past.

Lydia's wisdom in old age is wasted on her granddaughter, and reverberates outward into the large implications of the novel. One of the dangers of marriage in the time of a breaking of bonds is, as Lydia suggests, that a man may be driven to seek in a mate not a distinct and different person as generous and needy as himself, but only what will compensate him, somehow, for his sense of loss—though, tragically, he must have both in order to have either. The marriage of Anna and Will is, at last, a deadlock because neither wife nor husband has the generosity and wisdom to acknowledge and accept the unbreakable differentness of the other; and Tom's response to Lydia's strangeness—at the beginning so compelling an attraction for him—is, at last, to drift back into confusion and the oblivion of drink. Moreover, the grandmother's words to the child Ursula are a prophecy; for Skrebensky will desperately seek in Ursula (as Will sought in Anna) only what might make up for his unmanning sense of loss, and Ursula herself will not understand, not at least till very late, that her promiscuity with Skrebensky is no generous gift of love but only a confession of mutual weakness, no passionate resolution but an increasingly unsatisfactory escape into sex from the unprecedented problems of the modern consciousness.

In the new world there are no landmarks or guideposts, the great past is no longer even a memory, everyone is free and dispossessed; so Ursula's life becomes, necessarily enough, a kind of adventure in limbo. Yet it is this concluding section—in bulk, more than half—of the novel that has been most vexatious and unrewarding for readers; and any effort to assess *The Rainbow* bumps hard against it. No doubt, the section is less satisfying than most of what has come before: it is unduly repetitive, it is occasionally content to make points by assertion rather than by incident, it sometimes mistakes mere detailed documentation for thematic illustration and development, its tone sometimes verges on stridency. There are, after all, too many and too similar descriptions of Ursula and Skrebensky making hopeless love; the career of Ursula as a teacher, however interesting it may be in its own right, is recorded at too much length and with too little relevance to the theme of the novel; and when Lawrence, in his haste to dismiss dry book-learning, tries to palm off on us so trivially literary a truism about college life as this—

> College was barren, cheap, a temple converted to the most vulgar, petty commerce. Had she not gone to hear the echo of learning pulsing back to the source of the mystery?—The source of mystery! And barrenly, the professors in their gowns offered commercial commodity that could be turned to good account in the examination-room; ready-made stuff too, and not really worth the money it was intended to fetch; which they all knew.

—when Lawrence settles for this sort of thing, we are persuaded that he is no longer, for the time being at any rate, attending to the seriousness of his theme. It is perhaps more to the point to agree with Dr. Leavis that Lawrence, his mind already on the very different second novel which had detached itself from this original conception of a single novel on marriage, was trying to finish *The Rainbow* with less sympathy than conscientiousness: in this view, the frustrating account of Ursula's long and strenuous career of frustration may be taken as the result of Lawrence's prudent desire to save her consummation for *Women in Love.*

Still, *The Rainbow* is, finally, not about consummation but about promise. The rainbow that Ursula sees at the very end of the novel need not be dismissed as a despairing symbolic stroke to allow a nominal conclusion and to release Lawrence for *Women in Love;* though the two novels are obviously related in ways more important than the continuance of several characters through the second, it may be that those readers who find the end of *The Rainbow* wanting have turned their minds prematurely to the next book, and are expecting what it is not in the theme of the earlier novel to give. No doubt Lawrence's original intention was to write a single novel which would encompass and illustrate in the lives of a family the great social and psychological change of our century, and which would conclude with a treatment of such individual problems and individual solutions as, indeed, are treated in *Women in Love.* But it must have become eventually clear to him that the breakdown of community was a subject in itself, and that it culminated appropriately in the coming to consciousness of emancipated, modern woman. If Lawrence had ended the novel with modern woman numbed in her grimace of freedom, he would have been merely cynical; if he had ended with Ursula still unsure of her feelings for Skrebensky, the novel would trail off in a puzzle. The novel does, in fact, end as Ursula, having freed herself of her struggle with Skrebensky, is for the first time genuinely free not only of the unrevivable past but of those false ties she has tentatively accepted in place of it. To require any more—at least schematically—is to require an unequivocal happy ending, and even in *Women in Love* or *Lady Chatterley's Lover* Lawrence is not so obliging as that.

The fault is, then, not of scheme but of execution: much of the last half of *The Rainbow* seems to have been written with a slackening of Lawrence's attention to proportion and detail. Yet much is finely done. Something as difficult, for instance, as the relationship between Ursula and Miss Inger comes off without damage to our sympathy for Ursula, and with strong pertinence to the theme. In a time when the injunctions of community and family have been broken, when the individual is responsible only to himself and to his own impulses, why should not Ursula first admire and then fiercely love the handsome, independent woman who so resembles what she herself wishes to be? And why should the warmth and physical responsiveness of her feelings be curbed? No mere prohibition will do, for sanctions and prohibitions alike have gone under. It is only by living through the experience that Ursula can judge its sinister misleadingness for her: to be free like Winifred Inger is to take pleasure only in the thrill of physiological or mechanical process, to handle and reject, to give nothing, to hate one's humanness and to deny the possibility of relationship—as Ursula discovers during the visits to her uncle's colliery:

> His real mistress was the machine, and the real mistress of Winifred was the machine. She too, Winifred, worshipped the impure abstraction, the mechanisms of matter. There, there, in the machine, in service of the machine, was she free from the clog and degradation of human feeling. There, in the monstrous mechanism that held all matter, living or dead, in its service, did she achieve her consummation and her perfect unison, her immortality.

The narcissistic delights of homosexuality are not enough, even for Winifred Inger; even she must make a commitment to something outside herself, and she finds her consummation and her unison, her immortality, in the machine. But Ursula continues to seek hers in the flesh. Perhaps the repetitive savageries of Ursula's sexual encounters with Skrebensky are partly justifiable on the ground that with Skrebensky Ursula's attempt is so much more plausible and at the same time so much more exacerbating: at least Skrebensky is a man and no narcissistic projection of herself, though she can master and break him; at least Skrebensky is not positively evil, though he is weak and inchoate. If we do not lose sympathy with Ursula for her annihilating cruelty toward Skrebensky, it is because we are convinced that she suffers in the grip of an impulse which is, if it can ever be fulfilled, the sanest and most healing impulse accessible to her; if she appears at moments in the guise of a female spider devouring her sexually spent and useless mate, she is in any case obeying a brute instinct more vital than Skrebensky's attachment to political abstractions or Miss Inger's attachment to mechanism. Ursula's quest is desperate, so therefore are her feelings often; but the discoveries she must make cannot be arrived at by theorem, and she has no immediately recognizable allies. To contain and to be blocked from fulfilling so mastering an impulse is, finally, punishment and promise enough, as Lawrence indicates in the marvelous passage in which Ursula has her heart-stopping encounter with the stampeding horses, hallucination or reality:

> She knew they had not gone, she knew they awaited her still. But she went on over the log bridge that their hoofs had churned and drummed, she went on, knowing things about them. She was aware of their breasts gripped, clenched narrow in a hold that never relaxed, she was aware of their red nostrils flaming with long endurance, and of their haunches, so rounded, so massive, pressing, pressing, pressing to burst the grip upon their breasts, pressing forever till they went mad, running against the walls of time, and never bursting free. Their great haunches were smoothed and darkened with rain. But the darkness and wetness of rain could not put out the hard, urgent, massive fire that was locked within these flanks, never, never.

The new woman is too strong, and the new man is too weak, the woman suddenly conscious of long-sleeping powers and the man suddenly confronted with a rival. It is as if, for the new broken reed of a man like Skrebensky, all the long history of patriarchal Western civilization—its dream of wholeness and community, its exaltation of the family and of romantic love—has been man's dogged postponement of woman's inevitable supremacy. It all leads to Skrebensky, totally dependent, beaten child and rejected lover, hearing his doom on the final morning-after:

> He tapped at her bedroom door at the last minute. She stood with her umbrella in her hand. He closed the door. He did not know what to say.
> "Have you done with me?" he asked her at length, lifting his head.
> "It isn't me," she said. "You have done with me—we have done with each other."
> He looked at her, at the closed face, which he thought so cruel. And he knew he could never touch her again. His will was broken, he was seared, but he clung to the life of his body.

"Well, what have I done?" he asked, in a rather querulous voice.

"I don't know," she said, in the same dull, feelingless voice. "It is finished. It has been a failure."

In this contest—though Skrebensky thinks otherwise—there is no kindness and cruelty, only life and death, all and nothing; the issue is beyond the condescensions of charity, and the time is very late. There must be, somewhere, men to face up to the new dispensation: men like Tom Brangwen, who did much and might have done more had he known better what had overtaken him. Anna, in paralyzing contempt of Will when he tried to assert an authority he had already yielded by his unmanly surrender to her flesh, cried out that her stepfather "could put a dozen of you in his pipe and push them down with his finger-end." The new woman is strong in her power to wound and even to kill man's spirit if she has no male counterforce to match her. Yet life somehow continuously renews itself: in a time of human degradation, the unique powers of woman have at last asserted themselves; and such powers, coming so unexpectedly out of the very sources of life, cannot be without a commensurate object and response. What remains, in the compulsive ugliness of modern industrialism, as all values except those preservable by the conscious individual are swept away, is promise:

> In everything she saw she grasped and groped to find the creation of the living God, instead of the old, hard barren form of bygone living. Sometimes great terror possessed her. Sometimes she lost touch, she lost her feeling, she could only know the old horror of the husk which bound in her and all mankind. They were all in prison, they were all going mad.
>
> She saw the stiffened bodies of the colliers, which seemed already enclosed in a coffin, she saw their unchanging eyes, the eyes of those who are buried alive: she saw the hard, cutting edges of the new houses, which seemed to spread over the hillside in their insentient triumph, the triumphs of horrible, amorphous angles and straight lines, the expression of corruption triumphant and unopposed, corruption so pure that it is hard and brittle: she saw the dun atmosphere over the blackened hills opposite, the dark blotches of houses, slate roofed and amorphous, the old church-tower standing up in hideous obsoleteness above raw new houses on the crest of the hill, the amorphous, brittle, hard edged new houses advancing from Beldover to meet the corrupt new houses from Lethley, the houses of Lethley advancing to mix with the houses of Hainor, a dry, brittle, terrible corruption spreading over the face of the land, and she was sick with a nausea so deep that she perished as she sat. And then, in the blowing clouds, she saw a band of faint irridescence colouring in faint colours a portion of the hill. And for-

getting, startled, she looked for the hovering colour and saw a rainbow forming itself. In one place it gleamed fiercely, and, her heart anguished with hope, she sought the shadow of iris where the bow should be. Steadily the colour gathered, mysteriously, from nowhere, it took presence upon itself, there was a faint, vast rainbow. The arc bended and strengthened itself till it arched indomitable, making great architecture of light and colour and the space of heaven, its pedestals luminous in the corruption of new houses on the low hill, its arch the top of heaven.

And the rainbow stood on the earth. She knew that the sordid people who crept hard-scaled and separate on the face of the world's corruption were living still, that the rainbow was arched in their blood and would quiver to life in their spirit, that they would cast off their horny covering of disintegration, that new, clean, naked bodies would issue to a new germination, to a new growth, rising to the light and the wind and the clean rain of heaven. She saw in the rainbow the earth's new architecture, the old, brittle corruption of houses and factories swept away, the world built up in a living fabric of Truth, fitting to the overarching heaven.

The pledge of the future is Ursula's knowledge of what is terrible about the present, and her knowledge derives from a power of passion which must at length be consummated because it would otherwise have had no cause to spring into being. Dostoievsky called the Russians the "god-bearing" people, those who carry the secret of life within them and preserve it for that remote apocalypse when all the world will be fit to receive it. At the conclusion of *The Rainbow* Ursula is the single god-bearing person left in the world. It is a tribute to the prodigious optimism and persuasiveness of Lawrence's vision that the secret she holds seems worth the keeping till the world is fit to receive it.

NOTES

1. In *How to Read a Novel*, Viking, 1957.
2. In *The Dark Sun*, Duckworth (London), 1956, p. 63.
3. "*Women in Love*," in *The Achievement of D. H. Lawrence*, ed. Frederick J. Hoffman and Harry T. Moore, 1953, pp. 163–177.

17

ANGELO P. BERTOCCI

———◆———

Symbolism in *Women in Love*

It is not until chapter xxviii, "In the Pompadour," that Birkin abstracts completely into the language of theory the compulsive vision irradiating the whole of *Women in Love*. It is the vision of modern man and modern society with little time left to choose between death-in-life and, indeed, the imminent destruction of civilization, and the radical renewal and reintegration of a whole mode of being that is salvation. The moment is well chosen. The action of the novel has reached a great divide: the two couples, Ursula and Birkin, Gudrun and Gerald, have been united in their contrasting ways and in the final chapters, "Continental" and "Snowed In," will be put to the trial by ice. Birkin's message itself is dramatized; it is in the form of a letter to Halliday and the "Crème de Menthe" crowd. The young man, himself an effeminate figure of decay, declaims Birkin's analysis of the present crisis amid the jeering comments of the coterie. Among them is Pussum, that modern embodiment of the West African wooden figurine which itself had objectified the very state of being denounced in the letter. To add to the tension, the letter is read in the presence of Gerald, Birkin's friend. But it is Gudrun who acts, in a state no doubt partly of jealousy of Pussum, who had for a night been Gerald's mistress and has just flaunted that fact, partly out of loyalty to her sister Ursula who is now Birkin's wife, but chiefly with that ambiva-

From *A D. H. Lawrence Miscellany* ed. Harry T. Moore; © 1959, by Southern Illinois University Press. Reprinted by permission of Southern Illinois University Press.

lence of attitude that has characterized her throughout. She hardly knows whether to be angry at what she considers Birkin's promiscuous sermonizing or afraid of the portent for herself in that letter. At any rate, she snatches it away and walks off with it amid the jeers of the crowd and then holds on to it in that *amor fati* that is to grow upon her among the snow-clad mountains.

The message, pronounced against an opposition making for "irony," is briefly that modern society is dominated by the desire for destruction which in the individual is "ultimately a desire for destruction in the self." This means a return to the original rudimentary conditions of being along the Flux of Corruption. It promises, "beyond knowledge, the phosphorescent ecstasy of acute sensation," which is a kind of *fleur du mal*, a "flower of mud," born of sex used as a reductive agent. It invites us "to *lose* ourselves in some ultimate black sensation, mindless and infinite."

The message turns out to be a program for Gerald and Gudrun under the influence of snow and of that artist in corruption, Loerke, the "wizard rat that swims ahead" "in the river of corruption just where it falls over into the bottomless pit." When the trial by ice is over and Birkin looks half in disgust and half in despair upon the frozen stallion that is Gerald, his prophetic words to Gerald come to the reader's mind: "I suppose you want the same . . . only you want to take a quick jump downwards, in a sort of ecstasy—and he [Loerke] ebbs with . . . the sewer stream." Gerald is always the diver and for the last time he has let himself fall into the *cul de sac* of snow where, only a little way farther up, opens the imperial road to Italy. And Birkin takes recourse in the final bitter consolation of the religious when they see man forsaking God. It is the thought that God does not need man and that the "creative mystery" will, as ever, bring to birth "new species . . . more lovely . . . always surpassing wonder." Even in Lawrence the vision of betrayal, for (in spite of the jeers of his enemies and of his own self-criticism) Birkin always remains the *Salvator Mundi*, the vision of death is capped by a Resurrection, or, better, a recurring Re-creation.

To seem to make "the head of the corner" the "stone" that Dr. F. R. Leavis, that master builder in things Lawrencean (and not the least in his study of *Women in Love*) [1] has "rejected" might seem an unnecessary challenge to critical wisdom. Nevertheless, I think it will not do to call Birkin's letter "Lawrencean self-parody." The hoots are those of Birkin's former friends and associates to be sure, but their jeers are to be taken at a discount, for these individuals have already been shown as marked for death. Gudrun's snatching the letter from Halliday's hands has more organic relation to the novel than would the mere survival in Lawrence's memory of the scene when Katherine Mansfield impounded a Lawrence book at the Café Royal.

Dr. Leavis' interpretations at this point suggest too much preoccupation with Middleton Murry's assertion that Lawrence is no artist (even if that constitutes, at the present stage of civilization, his unique greatness) or T. S. Eliot's belief that Lawrence is not sufficiently the artist. Strategy for Lawrenceans no longer requires a defensive-offensive against Murry and Eliot. Birkin's letter and its presentation is quite sufficiently dramatized. But it is no mere parody, or if there is parody, it is parody of tone and not of substance. The proof of this is the way the novel turns out. Further proof is the lifting of the outcome for Gerald, who is Birkin's chief concern as well as the bearer of the social-industrial theme, to the level of religious despair and religious affirmation at the end of the novel. Or is Birkin, at this moment, once more exhibiting his unlovely *Salvator Mundi* propensities? If so, the central situation in the novel would descend, at the very last moment, into bathos.

It is easy to understand how defenders of Lawrence should center their attention on what can be related to the actualities of our personal and social existence, or to what in his vision can be verified in the objectives of our common life. They want to save him from the connotations, for some people, of the word "prophet." Yet it seems to be a fact that any drastic vision of social death and renewal is a religious vision, as Rousseau's was a religious vision. Nor was Lawrence's desire to save mankind any more intense nor explicit in his conscience as a man than Dante's. One need not feel uneasy, therefore, because the novelist, at the proper moment, makes explicit what had been more largely implicit in the texture and structure of the novel. It is one of the ways of binding an esthetic structure, and Dante uses it. If Birkin occasionally gives the impression that heaven and earth have important stakes in the outcome of the action, Dante goes even further when he declares that heaven, too, has set a hand to his work.

The important question is always, esthetically, whether what seem like propositions can be seen as part of a texture. The answer in *Women in Love* I think is very largely "yes," and the novelistic structure deserves all Dr. Leavis' praise. This is especially true if more attention is paid to Lawrence's symbolism, and from this Dr. Leavis shies away. To define "symbol" as what merely "stands for," and to suggest that in Lawrence we have far more complex significances than symbol can handle, is to ignore a distinction between symbol and allegory made by Goethe and Coleridge. Indeed, what Dr. Leavis uses as an example of symbol—the passage where Gerald, sitting in the canoe with Gudrun, feels his distance from her ("Water-Party") —would, from this point of view, be considered an example of "symbol" which, failing to be realized, falls into mere "allegory."

It is my belief, then, that *Women in Love* is best seen as taking its origin in religious vision, as any drastic proposal for destruction and re-creation, be it Rousseau's or Marx's, is the translation of religious vision into action. I do not speak specifically of the vision of the Hebrew prophets, or the Christian vision, for I am not persuaded by efforts to make of Lawrence almost a Christian. It seems more likely that, as Birkin says of Ursula's relation with her father, that his is a "love of opposition." But like the Hebrew-Christian, Lawrence has the religion of the "one thing needful." Happiness on earth, even existence itself whatever it may be, true productivity and creation, depend upon the faith with which men and women consent to meet in a Third, a principle of being which is neither of the participants. And the way for man is woman, and for woman man.

Thus the religious quality of Lawrence's vision makes for expression, and sometimes a straining toward expression, which carries characters and situations beyond the "universality," let us say, of a Homer at one end or of a good modern realist at the other. To realize this means a clearer understanding of problems of characterization and action in Lawrence's novels. For these problems will go with an art of symbol more radical than Dr. Leavis, or even Graham Hough perhaps, are ready to admit.

What this means is that Lawrence uses not merely the symbols at hand which seem natural to all expression and which have been developed in social experience, but that he strives to create new fusions of meaning and even to *enforce* new meanings based upon created premises. I hope that all this will be clearer after illustration. I will therefore proceed, without seeking otherwise to define symbol, to show how symbol functions in *Women in Love*. Does the novel, or any important portion of it, *behave* like a symbolic work?

Where there is a symbol, a kind of magnetic field of incident, image, and rhythm is set up, drawing to itself clusters of interrelated suggestion. Of course the bond of the logical relation of ideas is not completely missing; on the other hand the images and rhythms are not to be thought of as wild vines intertwining about a supporting line of logic, embellishing it with their foliage and giving it the factitious air of a living thing. Rather does image call to image, scene to scene, rhythm to rhythm, as color calls to color, the same or the opposite, in a painting. There is "logic" here, but the logic is not merely discursive. What seem necessities are set up for reasons that are more than the logically necessary reasons. The effect of discursive relations is linear, of symbolic relations the effect is circular. It suggests a to-and-fro in all directions at once. What is "evermore about to be" but is not yet, calls its parts organically into being.

Again, where a structure is truly symbolic, any vigorous cutting should seem to live by the life of the whole because it is constituted by the meeting of the forces of the whole on their way to other and busier intersections. I propose to examine "Water-Party" (Chapter xiv) because of the very challenge of its contrast to the snow and ice images of the final extended carnival at the ski lodge. This chapter is also the culmination of that first rhythm of action bringing commitment of the women, now "in love," to their men. I shall work backward and forward from this center, enough to show that it is indeed a "center." Of course, any intersection in a symbolic structure—and this is a way of defining symbol—seems "the center."

II

The world of the colliery has been invited to the annual ritual of the "Water-Party" at Shortlands. The affair is an appeasement of conscience for the elder Crich, his way of sharing with his miners the products of what, in spite of himself—for Crich is not the man to look too closely at what his "love" destroys, be it his wife or his colliers—he knows is their enslavement. But the man responsible for the water, and anxious to avoid any accident, is Gerald, he who has carried organization of industry to the point of death for the spirit in exchange for the certainty of *panem et circenses*. And Gerald has already been presented in some sort as a master of the watery element. In "Diver" (iv) though the "morning was full of a new creation," he had been present as a "white" figure, launched in a "white" arc through the air, moving in the "translucency of the grey, uncreated water," that "whole otherworld" which he dominated "just himself of the watery world," "immune and perfect," "like a Nibelung," and loving the "violent impulse of the very cold water against his limbs, buoying him up." This Nibelung, master of water and cold, had exacted a cry of admiration from Gudrun, envying him "this momentary possession of pure isolation and fluidity." He has "go," the sisters agree, though Ursula adds that "it goes in applying the latest appliances." And then, she adds, as though it were relevant, a dark "non sequitur": "You know he shot his brother?"

At the water-party the two girls have succeeded in obtaining a release from this redoubtable master of waters with his right hand bandaged, for it had been "trapped . . . in machinery." They had rowed off in rejection of the collier crowd for a little idyll of happiness around the bend. Ursula had sat "unconsciously crooning her song, strong and unquestioned at the center of her own universe," but Gudrun, as ever suffering from "the sense of her own negation," and demanding "the other to be aware of her," dances as though possessed before Highland cattle which usually frighten her. A little later Gerald's sister Diana, that other "negated" being, as Birkin says, will dance perilously on the top of the boat, tumble into the water, and drown carrying her rescuer down with her.

For Gerald and Gudrun things have not as yet gone so far. There is a quarrel as he takes the part of the cattle being driven "mad." Gudrun strikes him a first blow and prophesies a last. He does not contradict her statement. As he had involved her somehow in the submission to which he had reduced the red Arab mare (ix), so now her aggression strikes the spark of a declaration of love from him. Gerald, a "terrible swooning burden on his mind," grasps her hand "as if his hand were iron." Thus begins the long imprisonment that Gerald's love will bring Gudrun, in a novel rich with suggestions of imprisonment due to profane love.[2] Gudrun's "blood ran cold," but she acquiesces softly.

Gerald walks on beside her, "a mindless body." Then the author comments: "He suffered badly. He had killed his brother when a boy, and was set apart, like Cain." As often happens when Lawrence is building up his texture of meanings, this second seeming irrelevance, coming after the first, Ursula's reference to that fatal shooting, now drops into its place. He is a threat to Gudrun as well as a man somehow consigned to death. Even though she will indeed strike the last blow later in the snow after he has almost strangled her, yet Gerald will be his own murderer up in that *cul de sac* of snow. For Birkin has already detected the death-wish in Gerald.

As they lower a canoe into the water soon afterward, Gudrun refers again to the wounded hand. She continues to have power over them both. As they paddle, he who "was set apart, like Cain," and who in "Diver" had felt perfect and immune in the water, now feels the distance between himself and Gudrun. She assures him of her nearness, "Yet we cannot very well change, while we are in the water." And now Gerald, "who always kept such a keen attentiveness, concentrating and unyielding in himself," melts "into oneness with the whole" (always in this novel a bad sign) as in "pure, perfect sleep . . . and perfect lapsing out." [3] Gudrun cannot avoid a certain wistfulness even now. Later, on the night that Gerald comes from his father's grave with clay-clogged feet to take her, he certainly does not give sleep to his beloved. He "destroys" her into consciousness. Her awakened consciousness apropos of Gerald will, at the end of the novel, be translated into the awful vision of the clock-face of existence.

But even this relative contentedness now in the canoe is broken by Gudrun's uneasy feeling that someone is in need of Gerald and calling for him. "Then as if the night smashed, suddenly there was a great confusion of shouting, warring on the water." "Wasn't this *bound* to happen?" says Gudrun, her heart grown "cold, because of his sharp, impersonal face. It was as if he belonged naturally to dread and catastrophe, as if he were himself again."

Thus the momentary promise of a true polarity between Gerald and Gudrun in their canoe is dissipated. Just before this, in that magically "illusive" scene with the lanterns, Gerald and Gudrun had stood together "in one luminous union, close together and ringed round with light" in the primrose yellow with butterflies hovering about them. (Generally it is Ursula who is associated with yellow and primrose and gold and who "drifts off like a butterfly.") But a second lantern had shown a cuttlefish with a "face that stared straight from the heart of the light, very fixed and coldly intent." And Gudrun had insisted on exchanging the lantern for one of Ursula's which, Birkin remarked, suggested "the heavens above, and the waters under the earth." It was the cuttlefish that in "Moony" (xix) Ursula was to see in the bright moon under stoning, "shooting out arms of fire like a cuttle-fish, like a luminous polyp." Tonight, for Gudrun, everything speaks of the death for which she has affinity.

A far different fate, however, awaits Birkin and Ursula. As deep calleth unto deep so one image in the reader's mind, coming later, gives meaning to an earlier image. In "An Island" (xi), Birkin and Ursula had set out on Willey Water, in a leaky punt. "It will float us all right," he had said. He wanted no *Paul et Virginie,* no Watteau picnics. Indeed Ursula had shrunk from the "little jungle of rank plants before her, evil-smelling fig-wort and hemlock." But Birkin, determined as ever to encompass all experience, had "explored" it. They quarreled bitterly about love; never had Ursula found him so insufferable. Yet, at one point, when he is dropping daisies on the pond which float away, face up, like "points of exaltation" here and there, she felt "some sort of control was being put on her." And when they were once more on the "free land" Ursula saw that the boat of purple chocolate paper which she had made and dropped carelessly into the water was escorting the daisies and that they had become a convoy of rafts. Surely these two people seem marked for salvation. We feel the full force of this incident only when the Gudrun-Gerald-in-the-canoe episode provides its pendant and contrast.

To return to the scene of the accident, Gerald and Gudrun hear the voice of Winnie, imploring help for her drowning sister, "Get her out." It is the same Winnie whom Gudrun is later to tutor to please the dying elder Crich and to yield to her seemingly ineluctable urge to imprisonment. It is that same charming child who makes evilly satirical caricatures of her pets, who mocks as a Gudrun mocks, as a Loerke mocks, and yet who loves her rabbit Bismarck, so "mysterious" and individual and untamed, even though she cannot resist the temptation to "do" him too, as she had "done" her Pekinese Looloo.

But images of prison and oppression, of death and fate, accumulate. The "beauty and subjection of his loins," as Gerald climbs hopelessly with his bandaged hand into the boat from which he has dived, becomes a sign for Gudrun of the "terrible hopelessness of fate," the end of a "great phase of life," indeed the "final approximation" of life for her. And though it is now she who yearns for "connection with him, across the invisible space of water," she feels an unbearable isolation as she hears the "decisive, instrumental voice." Death has made Gerald revert to mechanism and mechanism in that water means isolation and death.

Now when Gerald climbs back to the boat, it is "slowly, heavily, with the blind climbing nature of an amphibious beast, clumsy, his head blunt and blind like a seal's." He has discovered "a whole universe under there; and as cold as hell." Again he insists on the "cold" of the water. "It is so cold, actually, and so endless, so different really from what it is on top, so endless—you wonder how it is so many are alive, why we're up here." "I'm afraid it's my fault. But it can't be helped . . . I could go on diving, of course—not much, though—and not much use—." The situation is the reverse of that in "Diver." The watery realm of immunity and perfection in isolation is the realm of death and cold as hell. But he lingers on, doing what he can. And Birkin must pull him away, this "instrumental" Cain of modern life, who has killed his brother and feels responsible for his sister, scolding him, "You waste yourself . . . to put a mill stone of beastly memories round your neck."

Thus the "water-party" has ended in death by water. There have been some happier results too. Ursula finds herself "deeply and passionately in love" with Birkin. But Gudrun, though shocked and frightened, has been left with a commitment to Gerald and only one problem: "the real thrill: how she should act her part."

In this same chapter, Gerald and Gudrun had come upon Birkin discoursing to Ursula on Aphrodite born of the "first spasm of universal dissolution"—then the snakes and swans and lotus—marsh flowers—and Gudrun and Gerald, all issuing from "the process of destructive creation," when the "stream of synthetic creation lapses." He had smelled the little marsh, for him a kind of Stygian swamp, where seethed the "river of darkness . . . putting forth lilies and snakes, and the *ignis fatuus*" with the "*fleurs du mal*" that is the best modern civilization can do. Where are the roses "warm and flamy" with which Ursula identifies her happiness? Ursula objects to this obsession with death; Gerald coming up, chimes in his support of Ursula. "I only want to know what we are," Birkin had insisted, the Hamlet of this unreal and death-dealing carnival on the water.

III

Thus an examination of "Water-Party" has confirmed suspicion. It is a living cross section of an organic unity. All the major motifs of the novel are here, in full sight or by implication. Moreover Birkin's marsh with its "alarming" odor, its unhealthy flowers and reptiles, is watered by the "black river of corruption which has unfathomed depths of death by perfect cold."

But let us try the water again, this time in an earlier chapter, at "Breadalby" (VIII). The pond into which Hermione has marshaled her more docile guests is turned into an alarming aquarium where "great lizards" like Sir Joshua "crawled about," belonging to a primeval world. A Miss Bradley, "plump and big and wet, looked as if she might roll and slither in the water almost like one of the slithering lions in the Zoo." As for the little Contessa, who can compare with her for evocative but unflattering animal names except those other denizens of the underworld, the young man who is being forced to marry in "A Chair" (XXVI), that silky "dark-eyed, silent rat," and, of course, that reptilian nonpareil of a Loerke who bears the full brunt of Lawrencean intemperance in epithet? The Contessa is at her most charming when "small and like a cat, her white legs twinkling as she went, ducking slightly her head," she stands "like a tiny figurine of ivory and bronze, at the water's edge," watching, of course, those lovely shapes of dissolution, "the swans which came up in surprise." [4] In her refusal to give herself though taking amusement from everything, she is, like Loerke, a "weasel," and in the water she "sits like a rat." Lawrence is prone to "see" and "feel" his characters not only in their psychological individuality but also, and sometimes more emphatically, in relation to the central problems of existence. Not that he creates mouthpieces for preconceived ideas, but his vision of character seems to originate in an intense vision of particular qualities of existence, to which the author reacts in attraction and repulsion. Hence a certain patterning of characters and epithets, visible in the instances of the Contessa, the young man of "A Chair," Loerke, and one might add Pussum, to mention only minor figures. Hence, too, a certain narrowing of focus, a loss at times in three-dimensional quality of character in return for a gain in intensity. Lawrence, like Dostoevsky, often "dis-realizes" his characters and for the same reason: their source is not in a "philosophy" but in a religious vision of good and evil. It is not that they "stand" for such and such ideas but they do "stand" in relation to intensely felt reaction to ultimate qualities of existence. To be sure, they are usually endowed with enough psychological characteristics to make them viable in the ordinary sense. But all characters are created characters and Lawrence's quite properly bear the stigmas of his vision. Thus even Lawrence's humor is bound by his fundamental feeling. It is amusing to see Sir Joshua Malleson with his "eighteenth-century appearance," the center of "talk going on, ceaselessly, Joshua's voice dominating," reduced to a great lizard of the primeval world even before he discourses on the "*social* equality of man." These "saurians" in their rites of immersion have something amusing about them, and yet are presented also, in Gudrun's words, as "terrifying." Among them is Gerald who has made a "scarlet silk handkerchief around his loins" do very well for a bathing suit. Looking "white but natural in his nakedness," he flaunts himself in the sun, dives, and dominates the scene from the wall at the end of the pond, as the "shoal of seals" breaks to gather around him. To the silent Ursula with his "really yellow hair, his figure so full and laughing" he seems Dionysius. (It is the Dionysius in Gerald that Birkin cannot save, he who loathes the Dionysian ecstasies and prefers a "dry soul.") Near Gerald-Dionysius leans Hermione, earlier called "Cassandra," she who with her insane and obscene will has insisted on this water-party over the refusal of Birkin and the Brangwen sisters. In her sinister "grace" she was "frightening, as if she were not responsible for what she might do," but Gerald laughed all the more, in his *amor fati* at her "convulsive madness."

Hermione belongs to death. In her the analytic and discursive reason is keen enough to desire the spontaneity it lacks, but having no true source of life in itself, it tries to create through will power. Hence her awful weariness and fatigue of utterance, and her chanting intonations as though of a priestess more than a little mad. As she sits "erect and silent and somewhat bemused, and yet so potent, so powerful," Birkin sees her and those about her as figures "in the hall of kings in some Egyptian tomb, where the dead all sat immemorial and tremendous." [5]

Through Hermione, too, another land of death comes into view, to be added to West Africa, with the "beetle-like face" of the totem and Egypt, with its "ball-rolling scarab." In an earlier skirmish with her, as Birkin was copying a picture of a goose given to Hermione by the Chinese ambassador, he had filled her with despair as he had described too recognizably the centers the Chinese live from, "the hot, stinging centrality of a goose in the flux of cold water and mud . . . fire of the cold-burning mud—the lotus mystery." So truly does a novel become for Lawrence a scheme of colors and animals, flowers, and sensations transformed, as in the lines just quoted, into a landscape of the soul that it becomes almost inevitable that, if Hermione is to make an attempt on Birkin's life, it will be with a Chinese ball of lapis-lazuli. And if Birkin, refusing to be murdered, is to find healing in nature, it will be on the "wet hillside," where fine soft wet grass will be more delicate than the touch of any woman, but where nevertheless he will seek its opposite, the "sting on the thigh" of the firs and the "light whip of the hazel" on the shoulders.

It was Birkin who had seen the social game as played at Breadalby in all its mechanical perversity: "The game is known, its going on is like a madness, it is so exhausted." Yet the social ritual at Breadalby, too, barely escapes a termination, like "Water-Party," in death.

IV

To continue to follow the traceries of relationships would be tedious. Yet I must at least point to some images found in "Water-Party" and "Breadalby" in order to insist on the richness of symbolic context.

The "whiteness" of Gerald everywhere emphasized (together with his "softness" and the "softness" of Gudrun) might seem a puerile analogy to the snow-death near Innsbruck. But connect it with his Nibelung and Nordic quality, "the strange white wonderful demons from the North," relate it to the "vast abstraction of ice and snow" and the "mystery of ice-destructive knowledge," and a major pattern is seen developing.[6]

Even in other contexts "whiteness" exploits the same suggestion. Thus in "Moony" it is the "white and deathly smile of the moon," the Syria Dea, the "white body of fire" in the water that "leaping up white," in fragments like "white birds," refuses to be violated. When its white petals take the rose shape, then especially must this whiteness be destroyed, for the rose is life-giving and Ursula sees herself as a rose of paradisal bliss. Is it the peace of death that the moon recovers as its rose recomposes itself? At any rate, Birkin has fought well against the "moon-brilliant hardness," mocking the "magic peace" of the woods. The alternative was the "lovely golden light of spring," transfused through Ursula's eyes, "though this was a paradisal bird that could never be netted, it must fly by itself to the heart." [7]

But "whiteness," because it belongs to death, can even be related to the flowers of mud, and—of all seemingly antithetical things—to mechanism. Thus in "Sketch-Book" (x) the image of lotus and other *fleurs du mal* is taken up and woven further into the pattern. This time Gudrun is "seated like a Buddhist" as she stares fixedly at the water-plants that rise from the "festering chill": "She *knew* how they rose out of the mud." Then a "man in white" appears rowing on the water, to her "keen frisson of anticipation." Gerald, she recognized, "was her escape from the heavy *slough* of the pale, underworld, *automatic* colliers" (italics mine). He started out of the mud. He was "master." As he bent forward rowing, there was a "whiteness he seemed to enclose." Yet he "seemed to stoop to something"; and soon he will be made to stoop for Gudrun's "Sketch-Book" in the water while his "white loins" were "exposed" behind him.

The images in this context reach out toward Birkin's letter calling for "positive creation, relations in ultimate faith, when all this process of active corruption, with all its flowers of mud, is transcended." Again, Pussum is a "flower of mud," also a "red lotus in dreadful flowering nakedness." Another "mud-child" is Loerke, though he will also be, in his way, a master of the snow.

In Gudrun's knowledge of the mud, much as she may seek to escape the vision of the Thames mud in "Water-Party" and the crowd that evokes it, lies her destiny. Hence the strange attraction, after all, to the "automatic colliers," the cinema where with the engineer Palmer she may sit half-fascinated and half-repelled. Gerald's kiss under the bridge will be a collier's kiss; he will take her with the mud from his father's grave on his boots; and in the dawn, as he puts on trousers and braces, what saves him from her ridicule is his resemblance to a collier.

This knowledge, deep in her bones, of how things grow out of mud will attract her to a new master Loerke, the genius of the mud and the sewer. And just as in Gerald she sought to be saved from the mud by the master of mechanisms who started out of the mud, so in Loerke she sought that transcendence of man's abjectness through the art of mockery or the mockery that is art. She will reject marriage with Gerald; she sees the futility of creation in mechanism. "Let them become instruments, pure machines, pure wills that work like clockwork, in perpetual repetition," with a "slumber of constant repetition." Yet her own face is like a "twelve-hour clock-dial," she is "unsheathed in sleep, unrelieved, unsaved." But the "female, subterranean recklessness and mockery" revealed in "Breadalby" by her dance as Ruth in her desperate but subtly malevolent clinging to Ursula as Naomi, finds its affinity in Loerke, "absolute in himself," promising nothing but the wakefulness of exacerbated sensation. And he is even more the slave of mechanism than Gerald; his art is the *fleur du mal* of mechanism in its tendency to exploit and abandon its models in the very flush of youth and in its effort to transmute subjection to mechanism into some kind of a victory by the alchemy of an inhuman art.

For Gudrun this abandonment to Loerke and to the ultimate "reduction in sensation" is the other side of her transport before the snow peaks and ridges which "glowed with living rose, incandescendent like immortal flowers against a brown-purple sky." To Gerald she seems to be seeking to "gratify herself among the rosy snow-tips" leaving him utterly alone and with a mad desire to destroy the scene and Gudrun with her "strange religion." But this is more *amor fati* coupled, with the ambivalence that especially characterizes Gudrun, with the last despairing hope of salvation. Even the "rosy pistils" of the snow peaks will reject her, for she has not learned Ursula's lesson of the "catkins." She is more envious than indignant at Gerald's stallion-like promiscuousness; with her incapacity for marriage, she has chosen the *Glücksritter,* and she will re-enact the ride of the little girlish figure on the huge horse.

Nevertheless, in one of the finer pages of the novel, where Lawrence succeeds completely in becoming a "changer" like Birkin, capable of giving everything its due thanks to the centered strength of vision, a foretaste of Gudrun's union with Loerke at its best is pre-

sented in a vividly imagined scene. The section seems to balance both
Gudrun and Gerald's moment of unity and Birkin's and Ursula's earlier
consummation scene at the end of "Excurse."

In the snow Gerald has been "happy by himself" as he had been
in the water in "Diver," "isolated as if there were a vacuum around
his heart, or a sheath of pure ice." With Gerald, the instrumentalist,
the toboggan had been a means of dangerous exploration of earth and
air and sky and "carried the souls of human beings into an inhuman
abstraction of velocity and weight and eternal, frozen snow." Gudrun
and Gerald had been "brought into perfect static unity" but "unseeing
and unwitting." And Gudrun had had the "complete moment" of her
life; she had "fused like one molten, dancing globule." The scene had
looked "like a garden, with the peaks for pure flowers and her heart
gathering them." Yet she had had "no separate consciousness for
Gerald," and even her joy had been "like a fine blade in his heart."

Gudrun's toboggan scene with Loerke effects a sharp contrast. For
Loerke, "pert as a pixie," the toboggan went "wildly and gaily, like a
flying leaf." When they pitched over, he made ironical remarks, the
kind he would make "as he wandered in hell." And this gave them
amusement, careless and timeless, and seemed to lift them above the
"dreariness of actuality." The "comble de joie" was a large thermos
flask, a packet of Keks, and a Schnapps, heidel-beer, "from the bilber-
ries under the snow." "How very perfect it was, this silvery isolation
and interplay," Gudrun had thought.

But this momentary release through fancy, using snow and even
the products from under the snow, could not in fact deal with the
facts of life, "the monotony of contingencies." Gerald appears, Loerke
is beaten to the ground, Gudrun strikes her last blow, and is almost
strangled to death, and Gerald climbs under the "unremitting" light
of a "small bright moon" forbidding sleep until he lets himself fall,
within the reach of the road outward, in the final cradle of snow, the
cul de sac, where "something broke in his soul, and immediately he
went to sleep."

v

It is time to pull away from the compulsive magnetism of the field
of forces that is Women in Love to essay some conclusions valid at
least for this novel. The theme of death-in-life with its counter-theme
of the life-still-possible for the saving remnant seems to have been, in
Lawrence's consciousness, a core of intuitive force, an intensely radiant
focus reaching out to assimilate and fuse idea, image, character, epi-

sode, and scene. In the number of chapters which we have explored, attracted especially by water-situations, we have seen water, boating, diving woven together with the denizens of river and pond, earth and sky, with the cold fires of the marsh, with the lily and the lotus and other *fleurs du mal*, with whole landscapes of static corruption, West Africa, Egypt, China, and the religions of Buddha, the Magna Mater, and the Mater Dolorosa. We have been taught to see in terms of water and mud and flower and whiteness and soft blondness and snow. As the reader advances he carries with him not merely a line of action or a "tenor" of ideas but also a sensuous vocabulary of images with its own syntax and reaching out toward a perfection of its own "logic." He has the experience of an ever-expanding *globe* of apprehension where the whole that, in one sense, is to be paradoxically integrates into itself the part that is. I submit that this is the experience of the symbol.

But what is the mode of this symbolism? It is less the symbolism of the Metaphysicals, with their "image of thought," than that of the Romantics, of Shelley, Keats, Coleridge, and Wordsworth with their "image of impression." [8] Like Baudelaire in "L'Albatros," Lawrence will work with the illustrative image which presents the sensuous equivalent of an idea easily expressible in itself in order to insure a certain support for it in sensation, emotion, and prestige. In "Mino" (XIII) didactic illustration becomes excessive and perhaps humorless: Birkin is to be to Ursula as Mino to the fluffy female with her incipient promiscuity. On the other hand in "Class-room" the catkins are at once plausible action, illustration, and the base for the meaning of the "pistils" of the mountain peaks late in the novel.

The best Baudelaire is in such a poem as "La Chevelure," where the hair of the beloved becomes the means by which we conceive an exotic seascape and an oasis which is the paradise of memory. It points toward that order "anywhere out of this world," of *"luxe, calme et volupté,"* toward which the poet is ever *en voyage.* Lawrence's symbols, as I have shown, often behave in this way.

For the novelist that is Lawrence the symbols must of course advance the action. Symbolic episodes such as that of the red Arab mare and the rabbit, among other functions, serve to carry forward the reader's perception of Gudrun's most secret processes of development. From a half-frightened and subjected admiration, she evolves to a connivance with Gerald in tyranny over the quick and the individual and to a cynical self-recognition in a universe of cruelty and death. Furthermore, since Lawrence's expression is always straining toward the symbol, it is only in the light of such more fully developed episodes that the reader can find his way into scenes as that of the conflict, immediately after the *Schuhplatteln*, between "Gudrun's ordinary consciousness and his [Gerald's] uncanny, black art consciousness."

To illustrate briefly from a minor instance. Pussum at the Pompadour is described as "leaning forward, her dark, soft hair falling and swinging against her face. There was something curiously indecent, obscene about her small, longish dark skull, particularly when the ears showed." The reader is not made to *see* what makes Pussum look "indecent, obscene," and even less why such a quality is connected with the ears showing. It is thanks to other contexts where the image is more fully fleshed, indeed it is because of the magnetism of the whole system of symbols, that we grant our poetic faith to such moments instead of accusing Lawrence of exploiting illegitimately his vague "somethings." The *created* meanings have provided the faith for the *enforced* meaning.

Our samplings, I submit, like Harry T. Moore's in the study of *The Rainbow*, reveal Lawrence as one of the workers in *symbolisme*.[9] One may argue that Lawrence moves toward even that form of *symbolisme* that seems his antipodes. Mallarmé with his apparently sterile love of a very suggestion of the suggestive, for the rose that is "absent" from all bouquets, relies increasingly on what I should call *enforced* meanings written in some ultimate abstraction of shorthand. He tends to forget that his "enforced" meanings, to be poetic meanings at all, must, though the shadow of a shadow, live by the antecedent fleshed and created meanings. The petal or the fragrance of the rose evokes the rose only for one who has seen the rose. Lawrence, though like any symbolist working toward some more efficient language of poetic abstraction, stops far short of the falling-off place because of his very distrust of abstraction. Even his flame must be a living flame. He will never seek life in that perfect cold whose "*azur*" haunts Mallarmé's imagination. Nevertheless, like any symbolist, he runs Mallarmé's risks. Lawrence fails when he seeks to enforce meanings which he has not created or when he yields to a didactic passion for the explication, forgetting meanings he has already created dramatically.

Fundamentally, Lawrence, like the major writers of his time, belongs to *symbolisme* in that common effort on the part of poetry, as Valéry said, to take back its own from music. Perhaps, in the end, amid the confusions of the *symbolistes* themselves as well as of theorists of the symbol, "*reprendre à la musique leur bien*" is the clue to the true meaning of this way of seeing and working. *Symbolisme* seems to have been a conscious and determined effort, based essentially upon Romantic theory and Romantic experimentation, to elaborate all those possibilities of language, its syntax, and its structures that will distinguish poetry from prose even when it is well written. It has sought to attain in varying degree to the "condition of music," that is, not merely vowel and consonant music, not merely melodic line, but a structure suggestive of fugue and sonata and other musical forms, in the hope that poetry may "mean" and "be" as music means and is. The new ideal spread from poem to novel. *Women in Love,* in Mark Schorer's words, bears "perhaps, a more immediate relationship to the traditional art of dance than to the traditional art of fiction . . . in the shifting allegiances between the members, and the configuration of characters." [10] A full study of *Women in Love* I think would show something of the dance in the shifting allegiances and the configuration of images.

For Lawrence understood the theory of language as paradox and gesture, though also holding to expression as simple, sensuous, and passionate. Birkin, seeking analogies between love, sleep, and death, realizes that "there was always confusion in speech. Yet it must be spoken . . . [though] to give utterance was to break a way through the walls of the prison as the infant in labor strives through the walls of the womb." And Ursula, listening, knows that "words themselves do not convey meaning, that they are but the dumb gesture we make, a dumb show like any other."

The reason for this sense of the inadequacy of vocabulary and syntax, as I have suggested, is that, though Lawrence is ardent in his desire to help shape the affairs of men in this world, his commission, as it were, lies in the religious vision. The search for an appropriate language is a characteristic result of the religious impulse, an attempt to make a gesture toward some newly sensed relation between the seen and the unseen, the social and the overriding reality upon which both a man's integrity and the good society are based. But for Lawrence even the new language is the language of men and not of angels.

NOTES

1. *D. H. Lawrence: Novelist* (New York: Alfred Knopf, 1956). All references will be to the chapter on *Women in Love* (IV).

2. One thinks of the elder Crich who had tamed the "hawk" that was his wife. The earliest image of imprisonment is that of Laura Crich.

3. Sleep is for Birkin, too, related to love and death, little as he may understand the relationship. But for him sleep is more than a "lapsing out" as for Gerald; it is a death into birth and new life, a vulnerability like a babe's to experience and not a drug. Elsewhere, the paradisal state between lovers is described as without thought or desire or will, "to be perfectly still and together, in a peace that was not sleep, but content in bliss . . . this was heaven: to be together in happy stillness." The scene on the water is to be contrasted as an ideal opposite to Birkin's and Ursula's state of love.

4. Hermoine earlier in this chapter, speaking of the swans, had told with vengeful glee how the "ousted lover had sat with his head buried beneath his wing," after being defeated in combat for the sole female. She herself loves to exert power over the stag; she fondles and dominates her kitten Micio. In this control over the "young, animal-like spontaneity and detachment" which Birkin loves, and which he exhibits at his work, she belongs with the mechanists and the dealers in death. Lawrence uses animals in a dual role: they are valued for their spontaneity and they are used, as in this context, to suggest "reduction in sensation."

5. In the much discussed passage in "Excurse" (XXIII), the "Egyptian" quality in Birkin is presented in a favorable light. But the Egyptian quality of "pure concentration in darkness" is positive when counterbalanced in Birkin by a "Greek" quality of "lambent intelligence."

6. Gerald's "whiteness" of body develops into the "magic, hideous white fire," the "white-cruel-recognition" in "Rabbit" and becomes even a "white aura, as if he were a visitor from the unseen" when Gerald first kisses Gudrun.

7. Lawrence insists in many passages on the "strange golden light" radiating from Ursula. Like Novalis' "beloved object," who also can be reached only through an "accord" (*Stimmung*), she seems to be the "center of a paradise." But at times this same quality of luminousness can ring her round in "supreme repudiation" and "perfect hostility."

8. There is an excellent discussion of the difference in R. A. Foakes, *The Romantic Assertion* (New Haven: Yale University Press, 1958), pp. 32–34.

9. Frederick J. Hoffman and Harry T. Moore, *The Achievement of D. H. Lawrence* (Norman: University of Oklahoma Press, 1953).

10. *Ibid.*, p. 169.

18

MARK SCHORER

On *Lady Chatterley's Lover*

I

Lady Chatterley's Lover came into being under the umbrella pines
of an Italian wood where Lawrence liked to sit writing beside a spring
of San Eusebio, before the cave where the saint had lived. The air was
golden, wild flowers embroidered the ground, nightingales sang to
him. He wrote: "Civilized society is insane." He had put himself at
last as far as possible "outside the made world" in order to deliver this
last judgment upon it, and yet, writing his condemnation of industrial
society in the peace of this Tuscan *pinèta,* he was also closing a circle.

As is known to all who read, D. H. Lawrence was born, the son of
a coal miner and a schoolteacher, in the village of Eastwood in the
English midlands of Nottinghamshire where they edge on Derbyshire.
What the life of that countryside was like at the end of the last and
the beginning of the present century, and what Lawrence's youth,
lived in that countryside, was like, is best told in his novel *Sons and
Lovers.* The background of that novel, as of his first, *The White Peacock,* is a slow cultural convulsion about to reach its end, a convulsion
in which the ancient pastoralism of the yeoman way of life yields to
the new mechanization of the industrial way of life, and in which, incidentally, a lovely landscape yields itself to an iron horror. What was
lovely and peaceful in that older life and landscape was Lawrence's

Reprinted from *Evergreen Review* (I, 1) and Grove Press edition of *Lady
Chatterley's Lover* by D. H. Lawrence (1957) with the permission of the
publishers.

peculiar treasure; what was ugly and new, his special anathema. Just before his death (and very shortly after he had published *Lady Chatterley's Lover*), as with a gasp of nearly desperate nostalgia, he wrote to a boyhood friend, J. D. Chambers, the younger brother of that girl "Miriam" who is at the center of the conflict in *Sons and Lovers*.

> Dear David,—
>
> I hardly recognized you as J. D.—and you must be a man now, instead of a thin little lad with very fair hair. Ugh, what a gap in time! it makes me feel scared.
>
> Whatever I forget, I shall never forget the Haggs—I loved it so. I loved to come to you all, it really was a new life began in me there. The water-pippin by the door—those maiden-blush roses that Flower would lean over and eat and Trip floundering round.—And stewed figs for tea in winter, and in August green stewed apples. Do you still have them? Tell your mother I never forget, no matter where life carries us.— And does she still blush if somebody comes and finds her in a dirty white apron? Or doesn't she wear work-aprons any more? Oh, I'd love to be nineteen again, and coming up through the Warren and catching the first glimpse of the buildings. Then I'd sit on the sofa under the window, and we'd crowd round the little table to tea, in that tiny little kitchen I was so at home in.
>
> *Son' tempi passati, cari miei! quanto cari, non saprete mai!*—I could never tell you in English how much it all meant to me, how I still feel about it.
>
> If there is anything I can ever do for you, do tell me.—Because whatever else I am, I am somewhere still the same Bert who rushed with such joy to the Haggs.

This recollection is in sharp contrast to a fresher one that appears in the second version of *Lady Chatterley*. There, late in the novel, Lawrence has his lovers go to the Eastwood country; they meet in the church at Hucknall where "the pinch of dust that was Byron's heart" (Byron, "that fat lad"!) is enshrined, and they survey the old Lawrence landscape—Haggs Farm now deserted, Felley Mill still and abandoned, everything "dead as Nineveh," all life sacrificed to "coal and iron." This bitterly personal scene disappears from the final version of the novel, but here we have a comparable episode in the long motor trip that Constance Chatterley makes through Derbyshire:

> The car ploughed uphill through the long squalid straggle of Tevershall, the blackened brick dwellings, the black slate roofs glistening their sharp edges, the mud black with coal-dust, the pavements wet and black. It was as if dismalness had soaked through and through everything. The utter negation of natural beauty, the utter negation of the

gladness of life, the utter absence of the instinct for shapely beauty which every bird and beast has, the utter death of the human intuitive faculty was appalling. The stacks of soap in the grocers' shops, the rhubarb and lemons in the greengrocers'! the awful hats in the milliners'! all went by ugly, ugly, ugly, followed by the plaster-and-gilt horror of the cinema with its wet picture announcements, "A Woman's Love!" . . . Tevershall! That was Tevershall! Merrie England! Shakespeare's England! No, but the England of to-day, as Connie had realized since she had come to live in it. It was producing a new race of mankind, over-conscious in the money and social and political side, on the spontaneous, intuitive side dead,—but dead! Half-corpses, all of them: but with a terrible insistent consciousness in the other half. There was something uncanny and underground about it all. It was an underworld. . . . This is history. One England blots out another.

Constance Chatterley's drive, we may assume, duplicates in fact and feeling a drive through the same countryside that Lawrence made in 1925. "Been motoring all over my well-known Derbyshire," he wrote mildly enough to Martin Secker. "But I can't look at the body of my past, the spirit seems to have flown." The Lawrences had been living above Taos and in Oaxaca; now they had paused in England on their way to Italy again. For a few months they settled at Spotorno (where Angelo Ravagli, the "Tenente" of Lawrence's letters, was their landlord). Lawrence was weary and felt no incentive to write a long book, but he did, during this period, write in its rough form the novelette, *The Virgin and the Gypsy*, which returns him to the English setting and is in some ways a thematic anticipation of *Lady Chatterley* as well. Then they moved south to Florence and the Villa Mirenda. In the summer of 1926 they made one more visit to England, and late in that year, after the composition of *Lady Chatterley* was well under way, Lawrence wrote to Rolf Gardiner about this visit. In this letter he tells Gardiner in explicit detail of the familiar landmarks in Eastwood and its environs—the houses in which he lived as a boy, Haggs Farm and Felley Mill and other places that had figured prominently in the first half dozen novels and in so many of his stories. "That's the country of my heart," he writes; but painfully, for he concludes as follows:

> I was at my sister's in September, and we drove round—I saw the miners—and pickets—and policemen—it was like a spear through one's heart. I tell you, we'd better buck up and do something for the England to come, for they've pushed the spear through the side of *my* England.

What he could do for "the England to come" was to write *Lady*

Chatterley, and we are reminded of a letter from as far back as 1913:

> Pray to your gods for me that *Sons and Lovers* shall succeed. People should begin to take me seriously now. And I do so break my heart over England when I read the *New Machiavelli*. And I am so sure that only through a readjustment between men and women, and a making free and healthy of this sex, will she get out of her present atrophy. Oh, Lord, and if I don't "subdue my art to a metaphysic," as somebody very beautifully said of Hardy, I do write because I want folk—English folk— to alter, and have more sense.

Fourteen years after his death, his widow said of Lawrence and *Lady Chatterley* and the English people, "he spoke out of them and for them, there in Tuscany, where the different culture of another race gave the impetus to his work."

Between the cottage on Walker Street in Eastwood, or Haggs Farm outside it, and the Villa Mirenda outside Florence, lay a long history. In that history, three items loom large: Lawrence's marriage to Frieda von Richthofen, the first World War, and travels all over the globe. His marriage is one of the most exploited subjects in our memoir literature, and all one need say of it here is that, whatever stresses it may have undergone, it had more of blessedness, and that without that blessed- ness, the lyrical portions of *Lady Chatterley*, which comprise a great hymn to true marriage, could not have been written. Lawrence's per- sonal experiences in the war are the subject of the chapter called "The Nightmare" in the novel, *Kangaroo*, and the atmosphere of the war and of a war-made world hangs over all his works from 1916 on but is most prominent in the quality of that social world that threatens the lyrical world of *Lady Chatterley*, for Lawrence felt as early as 1916 what we all feel today, "the violence of the nightmare released now into the general air." The travels (southern and central Europe, the Far East, Australia, the United States and Mexico, Europe again) not only provided him with a series of settings through which his novels make their march and so lead him to their end at the Villa Mirenda, but also provided him with images of utopia (always smashed) that would give him the community relationship that he sometimes desper- ately felt he needed. It was only when he gave up that hope, and the programs that his novels sometimes developed out of that hope, that he could have come to rest in *Lady Chatterley*, where there is no pro- gram at all, only the inspired plea that the human being become what he already is, that is, human. The journey from the humanity and the inhumanity of his youth, to his discovery at the end of the essentially human as it could be defined in drama against that background—this is another circle that his last novel closes.

There were times in Lawrence's career when the whole beautiful line of it, as it was finally drawn, threatened to blow up completely. After the purely autobiographical novel, *Sons and Lovers,* Lawrence wrote his two most complex works, *The Rainbow* and *Women in Love.* These were novels that attempted to seize directly on the psychic realities. They end with regenerate heroes who have experienced visions of human felicity for which they can find no place either in this world or in the realistic convention of the novel. Then begins a period for which bitter, surely, is a mild word—bitter, galled, the withers wrung. And yet, in this period, where Lawrence tries to bring his characters into vital social relationships, we are at the center of the most fascinating and alarming elements in Lawrence, the artist.

Aaron's Rod (the novel that, in its first paragraph, announces the end of war, the violence released now into the general air) was published in 1922, the year of Mussolini's *coup d'état; Kangaroo,* in 1923; *The Plumed Serpent,* in January 1926. Unable to see any but negative virtues (that is, vices) in democracy, which seemed to Lawrence a means of freeing the individual to mediocrity and a numbed anxiety only, he was still fairly desperate to find some means of satisfying what he himself called his "societal impulse" and of making his novels end positively in this world. So he turned to undemocratic ideas, a part of the violence released now; and in these three novels, in three different ways, tried them out to see if they would work either for the novel or for life. They did not. This is the imaginative test of theoretical abstraction, and Lawrence's greatness of mind shows in the necessity he felt to reject the abstraction when it would not work for the imagination. The first two of these novels are fragmentary, implosive structures because the author, while he cannot prove the abstraction right, is unwilling to let his story prove it wrong and so lets the story jar to a stop in negation. The third is a unified work because the lives of the characters, in the actualities of the plot, prove that the abstraction is merely abstract, that is, wrong, and the novel ends in its rejection.

Aaron's Rod presents Lawrence in the character of Lilly, who assures Aaron Sisson that he will not find himself until he finds a greater man to whom he can submit his partial individuality; but in the end, Lilly can produce no such leader, not even himself. In *Kangaroo,* Lawrence puts himself in Aaron's position, as the man who seeks the leader; but, confronted by the alternative of the socialist, Struthers, and the fascist, Kangaroo, the Lawrentian hero departs for America, where he hopes to find a more plausible choice. Then, in *The Plumed Serpent*, Lawrence tries still another device: he transforms his seeker into a woman, a jaded European who has severed her connections with her own social past and seeks fulfillment in Mexico through the leadership of two men who are trying to institutionalize a primitive religion which is not in the least unlike Lawrence's own religion of "the dark gods"; but it will not work. As the two leaders fail her, so she fails them, and discovers, with Lawrence, that there are two kinds of power: the power to dominate others, and the power to fulfill oneself. "The leader-cum-follower relationship is a bore," Lawrence wrote then, in a letter. "And the new relationship will be some sort of tenderness, sensitive, between men and men, and between men and women." *Lady Chatterley's Lover*, his last novel, was first to be called *Tenderness*.

This is the final Lawrence, the Lawrence who kicked out, although with a dragging reluctance, the hypothetical fragments that he had tried to shore against the world's ruin and his own, and who was determined to attempt still to be free in the actualities of human relationship. He was an artist who had gone through a purgatorial period that sought escapes from freedom, and then settled with small content and no complacency into the paradise that knows what freedom is, or at least where it begins. This is the paradise that is allowed to human life when human beings can recognize that after all the sweat for something else, for something either more or less, the value of life exists in the act of living; that living means full living, or the life of the full and not the partial self, the self that realizes its powers rather than the self that seeks power or submits to it. And this is, after all, the beginning of the true democracy, as it is of the true marriage, because it is total integration, and therefore makes possible the only creative spontaneity, even though that be in isolation, in an Italian wood.

At the Villa Mirenda—a great square block of whitish-gray stone that stands, like the typical farm villa of Tuscany, alone on its hill, its clusters of cypresses thrusting up blackly green against the blue, its fields and vineyards falling away from it in all directions, and the matchstick dwellings of the *contadini* scattered here and there among the fields—here, the Lawrences saw few people. Chiefly they had the peasants and themselves. One reason that they took the place was because this was "a region of *no* foreigners." Lawrence knew quite well what he was facing ("Have you built your ship of death, oh, have you?") and he was trying to face it. ". . . people don't mean much to me, especially casuals; them I'd rather be without," he wrote;

and, "the Florence society is no menace." He did not want what he could have, and he could not have what he felt that he needed. He took his isolation, then, with small content and no complacency. In July of 1926 he wrote to Rolf Gardiner as follows:

> I believe we are mutually a bit scared. I of weird movements, and you of me. I don't know why. But if you are in London even for a couple of days after the 30th, do come and see us, and we can talk a little, nervously. No, I shall ask you questions like a doctor of a patient he knows nothing about.
>
> But I should like to come to Yorkshire, I should like even to try to dance a sword-dance with iron-stone miners above Whitby. I should love to be connected with something, with some few people, in something. As far as anything *matters*, I have always been very much alone, and regretted it. But I can't belong to clubs, or societies, or Freemasons, or any other damn thing. So if there is, with you, an activity I *can* belong to, I shall thank my stars. But, of course, I shall be wary beyond words, of committing myself.
>
> Everything needs a beginning, though—and I shall be very glad to abandon my rather meaningless isolation, and join in with some few other men, if I can. If only, in the dirty solution of this world, some new little crystal will begin to form.

And even after he had finished the second version of *Lady Chatterley* (and among the truths that this novel most forcibly urges is the meaning and the necessity of isolation), he could still write as follows to Dr. Trigant Burrow:

> I suffer badly from being so cut off. But what is one to do? One can't link up with the social unconscious. At times, one is *forced* to be essentially a hermit. I don't want to be. But anything else is either a personal tussle, or a money tussle; sickening: except, of course, just for ordinary acquaintance, which remains acquaintance. One has no real human relations—that is so devastating.

Better to have no social relationships at all than to have them and pretend that they are real! So he wrote disgustedly to Huxley of Beethoven, whose letters he was reading, "always in love with somebody when he wasn't really, and wanting contacts when he didn't really—part of the crucifixion into isolated individuality—*poveri noi*." Every future holds only one final fact, and what Lawrence loved about Villa Mirenda was that it served to school him in that ultimate isolation.

I never know what people mean when they complain of loneliness.

To be alone is one of life's greatest delights, thinking one's own thoughts,
doing one's own little jobs, seeing the world beyond
and feeling oneself uninterrupted in the rooted connection
with the centre of all things.

In those barely furnished rooms, in that quiet country landscape, the
rooted connection might yet be found.

There is nothing to save, now all is lost,
but a tiny core of stillness in the heart
like the eye of a violet.

Violets grew there in profusion, and Lawrence was dying among
them. He was ill much of the time at the Mirenda, and his was an
illness that could be alleviated, not cured. If illness and the image of
a black ship lay under his isolation, they affected in a curious way
Lawrence's attitude toward his work. During the months at Spotorno,
after the English visit of 1925, he wrote only a few stories, his longest
effort being that piece about an English girl called *The Virgin and the
Gypsy*, which is preparatory to *Lady Chatterley*. At Villa Mirenda, the
lethargic indifference, a weary kind of rest after all the high-strung
battles, grew in him. He wrote his British publisher:

> In the real summer, I always lose interest in literature and publica-
> tions. The *cicadas* rattle away all day in the trees, the girls sing, cutting
> the corn with sickles, the sheaves of wheat lie all afternoon like people
> dead asleep in the heat. *E più non si frega.* I don't work, except at an
> occasional scrap of an article. I don't feel much like doing a book, of any
> sort. Why do any more books? There are so many, and such a small
> demand for what there are. So why add to the burden, and waste one's
> vitality over it.

But news of the General Strike in England renewed the images of iron
and of an "underground humanity" in his mind.

> I feel bad about that strike. Italian papers say: "The government will
> maintain an iron resistance." Since the war, I've no belief in iron re-
> sistances. Flesh and blood and a bit of wisdom can do quite enough
> resisting and a bit of adjusting into the bargain—and with iron one only
> hurts oneself and everybody. Damn iron!

Then, once more, with the visit to England in the summer of 1926,
mere images of iron became the monstrous realities of the senses, and
soon after his return to Italy, he writes, "I've nearly done my novel."

II

The story of *Lady Chatterley's Lover* is among the simplest that Lawrence devised: Constance Chatterley, the frustrated wife of an aristocratic mine owner who has been wounded in the war and left paralyzed and impotent, is drawn to his gamekeeper, the misanthropic son of a miner, becomes pregnant by him, and hopes at the end of the book to be able to divorce her husband and leave her class for a life with the other man. Through all his career Lawrence had been concerned with the general theme of this book—the violation or the fulfillment of individuality in relationship—and many times he had handled the theme in the concrete terms here presented where fulfillment involves the crossing either of class or cultural lines, and often of both, where violation results from resisting this necessity. The familiar construction, then, is of a woman in a relatively superior social situation who is drawn to an "outsider" (a man of lower social rank or a foreigner) and either resists her impulse or yields to it. The two possibilities are embodied, of course, and respectively, in the situation into which Lawrence was born and in the situation into which he married. Inevitably, it became a favorite situation of his fiction.

Among the short stories, one might mention five as clear illustrations: one of his juvenile works, *A Fragment of Stained Glass*, deals with a medieval serf who flees his bondage with a miller's daughter; in *The Daughters of the Vicar*, one daughter chooses to defy her family in order to marry a miner; in *The Shades of Spring*, a Miriam-like girl reveals to her old, poetic lover that a gamekeeper has taken his place; in *Mother and Daughter*, the daughter chooses to upset her mother's values and her own by committing the absurdity of going off with an Armenian known to the mother as "the Turkish Delight"; in *None of That*, an enormously wealthy daughter of the jazz age invites an involvement (to her destruction) with a Mexican bullfighter.

Among the novelettes, one might again mention five. In *The Fox*, a constrictive relationship between two girls is shattered by the intrusion of a farmer-soldier and his passion for one of them; in *The Ladybird*, an aristocratic Englishwoman yields to a mysterious central European, Dionys Psanek; in *St. Mawr*, Mrs. Witt and her daughter Lou are attracted by a Welsh groom and a half-breed Navajo; in *The Princess*, a New England virgin wishes to yield to a Mexican guide and discovers only too late that she cannot truly yield; in *The Virgin and the Gypsy*, an English virgin yields to a gypsy.

From the ten novels, we can once more choose five, although the situation is omnipresent. There is *Lady Chatterley's Lover* itself. In *Sons and Lovers*, the parental situation is not only an obvious example but the archetype. In *The Lost Girl*, a middle-class English girl leaves the comforts (and depredations) of home for a rigorous life with an Italian peasant. In *The Plumed Serpent*, Kate Forrester, a refined European, yields (temporarily) to the intellectual leadership of one Mexican and the physical leadership of another. And in the very first novel, *The White Peacock*, the situation not only presents itself in the Lettie-George relationship, but a gamekeeper, Annable, appears briefly but volubly as the earliest version of Parkin-Mellors, the gamekeeper of the last novel.

Such a catalogue as this takes two risks: it suggests a limited imaginative range, and it seems to denigrate the subject by a tone of frivolity. Neither risk is serious, for the theme itself, however badly one may state the situations that embody it, is pushed into every area that concerns us most seriously in this century. *Lady Chatterley's Lover*, like everything that Lawrence wrote, is an affirmation of life values as against the mechanization of human nature. This, his general subject matter, may be broken down into two major themes; the relation of men and women, and the relation of men and machines. In the works as they are written, the two are one, and his most subtle and penetrating perception, the knowledge that social and psychological conflicts are identical, is so firmly integrated in the structure of his books that it is almost foolhardy to speak of his having two themes when in fact he had one vision. But a vision has both a background and a foreground, and one may say, perhaps without distortion, that the men and machines relationship is the background, the man and woman relationship, the foreground. This division does not mean that the first determines the second, for it would be just as true to say that the second determines the first. They are, in fact, inextricable. We might say that one provides the scene, and the other, the drama enacted on that scene.

Who *was* Annable? One must remind oneself of the British novel as it was in the year 1911 to recognize what an extraordinary figure he is, standing there so clearly from the beginning, in that first novel, written when Lawrence was a very young man. Whether he had some prototype in actuality we will probably never know, and it is of no importance that we should know; certainly he had none in fiction. What is important is simply to observe that he was uniquely *there*—there from the beginning in Lawrence's imagination as the figure who asserts that modern civilized society is insane, and who without compromise rejects it. Nothing that one might say of ideas of primitivism and of the natu-

ral man as these had been used in the writing of the two preceding
centuries would in any way reduce his uniqueness.

> He was a man of one idea:—that all civilisation was the painted fungus
> of rottenness. He hated any sign of culture. I won his respect one after-
> noon when he found me trespassing in the woods because I was watching
> some maggots at work in a dead rabbit. That led us to a discussion of
> life. He was a thorough materialist—he scorned religion and all mysti-
> cism. He spent his days sleeping, making intricate traps for weasels and
> men, putting together a gun, or doing some amateur forestry, cutting
> down timber, splitting it in logs for use in the hall, and planting young
> trees. When he thought, he reflected on the decay of mankind—the
> decline of the human race into folly and weakness and rottenness. "Be
> a good animal, true to your animal instinct," was his motto. With all
> this, he was fundamentally very unhappy—and he made me also
> wretched.

Annable's difficulty is that he is not only an animal (as his name is not
quite that word), but also a human being with a civilized experience
behind him. The son of a prosperous father, he had been enrolled at
Cambridge, had taken orders and served as curate to a fashionable
rector, and had married (unhappily, in the end) a lady; yet now he
lives in brutish squalor, amid a swarm of soiled children and a slat-
ternly, illiterate woman, and strives not to lift his mind above these
chosen circumstances. He does not manage to survive his choice. Yet
he serves his function in providing a kind of choral emphasis in a novel
that is concerned with the thinning out of human relationship amid a
general deterioration of life. He serves no less to emphasize Lawrence's
success in developing the character and situation of his last gamekeeper. His success with this figure is Lawrence's vindication of his
crude attempt with Annable, just as it is the payment of his longstand-
ing debt to the humanity of his own father. This is not so much a matter of psychological as it is of aesthetic maturity; Lawrence had found
precisely the way that he wished to speak. For if *Lady Chatterley's
Lover* concludes a long thematic history, it concludes no less a history
of forms.

Lawrence was, of course, three things: he was a man in search of
a life; he was a prophet in search of a revelation; and he was an artist
in search of a convention. The first formed the second, and the second
created the problems of the third, but it is only the third, finally—or
the third as containing the others—that we can with much profit consider in the name either of criticism or of thought.

In a recent enthusiastic book on Lawrence by an Anglican priest who writes under the name of Father Tiverton, we are shown that the spirit of Lawrence's work was not at all inimical to much that is central in Christian thought, and also that this spirit makes him the kind of artist that he is. And how simply Father Tiverton puts it! "He reached the point in imaginative being at which the preacher and the poet coincide, since the poem is the sermon." The *whole* poem, of course, or the *whole* story, or the *whole* novel, not any set of extractable words or scenes that exist only as a portion of those wholes. This primary axiom of all reading and all criticism applies nowhere more drastically than to *Lady Chatterley's Lover.*

To reach the point where the preacher and the poet coincide *formally* was not a simple matter. We have already observed something of Lawrence's intellectual progress, how in novel after novel, the imaginative test qualifies the theoretical conviction. Thus Lawrence's mind constantly moved as each novel shrugged off its predecessor, at the same time that his techniques moved through a wide range of fascinating experimentation (still almost entirely unexamined by criticism) in his attempt to accommodate what was theoretically dear to him to the dearer forms of fiction. In both the broadest and the most special sense, Lawrence is first of all the artist; he gives primacy to the "living tissue" of imaginative experience and his craft is constantly moving always on a dynamic base.

All this is to say nothing at all about those sporadic bursts of "genius" ("A great genius, but no artist," runs the cliché) that even the unfriendliest critics grant, those "fitful and profound insights" that even Mr. Eliot, for example, finds it possible to allow; it is only to say that in the one imporant way that a man is an artist, Lawrence was an artist: that he knew where his real life was lived. Once this obvious matter can be established (and Father Tiverton went far in doing just that), we can begin to analyze the spurts of genius and their place in the whole art, or even, conceivably, to decribe the constant artist.

Lawrence, the constant artist, made constant demands on the forms of fiction that had not been made in the past. "It is the way our sympathy flows and recoils that really determines our lives," he wrote in the famous ninth chapter of *Lady Chatterley's Lover.*

> And here lies the vast importance of the novel, properly handled. It can inform and lead into new places the flow of our sympathetic consciousness, and it can lead our sympathy away in recoil from things gone dead. Therefore, the novel, properly handled, can reveal the most secret places of life; for it is in the *passional* secret places of life above all, that the tide of sensitive awareness needs to ebb and flow, cleansing and freshening.

Among the "things gone dead" (and it is only one) is the conventional-
ized, the calcified ethic of Christianity, and it was Lawrence's belief
that the human consciousness was capable of regeneration if only it
could be led away from the rubble into "new places." ". . . for wide
masses of people," John Lehmann wrote in 1947, in a plea for a renewal of "the world of love,"

> the Christian symbols as they have known them have ceased to be sig-
> nificant, and their desperate need is to find new symbols—even if those
> symbols should lead us back to a rediscovery of the central meaning of
> Christianity, restored through the discarding of outworn and corrupted
> images, and irrelevant accretions of fact.

Although Mr. Lehmann himself found the mass of Lawrence's symbols
inadequate to this end, one can argue—and so Father Tiverton argued
—that this attempt was precisely Lawrence's. His wish was to take the
sacraments out of their merely institutional bindings and to reassert the
sacramental nature of life itself.

> The old Church knew best the enduring needs of man, beyond the
> spasmodic needs of today and yesterday. . . . For centuries the mass of
> people lived in the rhythm, under the Church. And it is down in the
> mass that the roots of religion are eternal. When the mass of a people
> loses the religious rhythm, that people is dead, without hope. But
> Protestantism came and gave a great blow to the religious and ritualistic
> rhythm of the year, in human life. Non-conformity *almost* finished the
> deed. Now you have a poor, blind, disconnected people with nothing but
> politics and bank-holidays to satisfy the eternal human need of living
> in ritual adjustment to the cosmos in its revolutions. . . . Mankind has
> got to get back to the rhythm of the cosmos, and the permanence of
> marriage.

"I am a profoundly religious man," Lawrence once said of himself, and
when Father Tiverton comes to the concluding point in his discussion,
where he wishes to state the central fact about Lawrence's view and
his art, he writes: "I should claim that one of the great virtues of Lawrence was his sense of the ISness rather than the OUGHTness of religion . . . he believed in his dark gods not because they 'worked,' but
because they were true."

But how, in the realistic tradition of the British novel, was the artist
to communicate the "ISness of religion"? Of the first three novels,
where the content is suited to the realistic convention, *Sons and Lovers*
is successful even though it is in that work that Lawrence discovers
that what he wants his work to communicate is a more essential reality

than "that hard, violent style full of sensation and presentation" (as Lawrence himself described it) was capable. *The Rainbow* and *Women in Love* are his extended attempt at a form that will accomplish this end. The first begins as a traditional family chronicle and ends in a Blakean vision; the second consolidates the visionary and the hallucinatory effects of the first, and they dominate the whole. Neither is a novel in any traditional sense, not even a "psychological novel." They are psychic dramas in which primary human impulses rather than human personalities struggle and embrace, and they end with heroes who have made a journey of the soul and whose regeneration puts them beyond the conditions of that social world out of which the novel as we have known it has always come and in which it has always been rooted. In *Aaron's Rod* and *Kangaroo* the strenuous formal attempt is relinquished; these are rather rough chronicles of real journeys in which the soul's journey is *discussed* but in which no attempt is made to embody its destination in the drama. In *The Plumed Serpent,* an extremely ambitious work, the myth of the soul's journey coalesces happily with the primitive Mexican myth that the heroes are attempting to revitalize in Mexican political life and that makes up the bulk of the story; it ends with the European heroine's conclusion that the Mexican myth may be good for the Mexicans but that it is of small use to her, and she lapses back into the condition of her social world, saying, *"But I can fool them so they shan't find out."* She will take from them what is of use to her, for as long as may be.

In many of his short stories and in his short novels, Lawrence managed to maintain a realistic framework within which rich symbolic modulations that far transcend realism could be beautifully contained. In the shorter fiction, too, he could break into pure symbolic forms, as in *The Woman Who Rode Away,* or into splendid fable, as in *The Man Who Died.* But even as he managed more and more successfully to handle action that in itself was ritualistic and prose that was liturgical, the convention of the realistic novel could not be made wholly to yield. The progress from the first through the third version of *Lady Chatterley* is the history of an effort to make the events at once maximally plausible in realistic terms and maximally meaningful in psychic terms. The result in the third version is a novel in a solid and sustained social context, with a clear and happily developed plot, in which the characters function fully and the author allows them to speak for themselves; at the same time it is a novel in which everything is symbolic, in which "every bush burns," and which in itself finally forms one great symbol, so that one can easily remember it as one remembers a picture. In the background of this picture black machinery looms cruelly against a darkening sky; in the foreground, hemmed in and yet separate, stands a green wood; in the wood, two naked human beings dance.

III

The first *Lady Chatterley* is a relatively short, dark, and above all rough sketch written under the pall of recently experienced English gloom; the second, written after the Etruscan adventure, is much longer and leaps out of the dreariness of the first, with a strong infusion of lyric feeling and natural vitality that must derive from Lawrence's experience of the brilliantly sensuous tomb paintings at Tarquinia and elsewhere; the third, written after a hard and alarming illness, is about the same length as the second, but there is a sharpening of intellectual issues and a deepening of pathos. These are the large general changes, and if we add to them the fact that in each version as it succeeds an earlier, the treatment of the sexual act becomes more and more explicit, a development as necessary to the achievement of the four qualities just listed as it was to the full dramatization of Lawrence's theme, we have encompassed the major changes in tone and feeling. At the other end of the scale of revision are thousands of alterations in technical detail, and a systematic analysis of these changes would tell us a great deal about Lawrence the writer, but the place and time for such an analysis is a scholarly monograph that could best be published when all three texts of the novel are available to interested readers. Between these two extremes of revisionary method are a variety of changes in dramatic structure, many of which have been observed by E. W. Tedlock, Jr., in an appendix to his *The Frieda Lawrence Collection of D. H. Lawrence Manuscripts* (1948). It is in the interest of the present account to observe a few of these.

Lawrence's first problem in revision seems to have been to tell his story in such a way as to achieve maximum plausibility within the terms of his own aspiration: he had to make the love of the lady and the gamekeeper convincing, and he had also to give their love a chance for survival in the world as he saw it. If we follow the alterations in the character of the keeper, in the character of Constance, and finally, in the nature of the resolutions, we will be able to see how he achieved his end.

In all three versions, the gamekeeper (called Parkin in the first two, Mellors in the third) is a man of about forty, a miner's son who has misanthropically withdrawn from the industrial world into work in the wood. In the first and second versions, he is of medium height, with reddish-brown eyes and a shaggy mustache; in the third, he is taller, with blue eyes. In the first version he is physically strong; in the second, not so strong; in the third, sometimes rather frail. The Parkin of the first version speaks only in the vernacular; the second uses the Derbyshire dialect in scenes of affection and the king's English when he wishes; Mellors speaks more or less like the second Parkin but is capable of much more conceptual language. The Parkin of the first version has least motivation for his misanthropy but is the most violent in asserting it. He delights in trapping poachers and getting summonses for them; to Mellors, this is an unpleasant part of his work. Where Parkin is positively churlish with Constance, Mellors is ironical and mildly derisive. The first Parkin's motivation lies in a smashed marriage with a brutish woman; the second Parkin's motivation lies in the same marriage, but with a background of an awkward sexual trauma that unfits him for any other woman and yet does not fit her for him. In Mellors, the sexual background is amplified but the traumatic experience disappears: he has had love affairs with young women drawn exactly on the models of the Helena and Miriam of Lawrence's second and third novels—romantic, "spiritual" women who offended his manhood, and from these he had turned to the "common" girl, Bertha, whom he married, but who revealed at once a ferocious sexual will under the force of which the marriage passed swiftly into brutish deterioration. From this marriage, Mellors escaped into the world, and the world of gentlemen: he had become an officer's aide in India. Now, in his cottage, he has books that he can read and talk about, and he is Constance's equal in all but birth. The original Parkin is something of a clown as well as a boor: "The skirts of his big coat flapped, his brown dog ran at his heels. He was once more going to take the world by the nose. . . . He strode with a grand sort of stride, baggy coattails flapping. The son of man goes forth to war! She smiled to herself grimly." The second Parkin still has "a rather sticking-out brown mustache," but "His bearing had a military archness and resistance that was natural to him." Mellors has not only the military background itself, but, along with "a certain look of frailty," natural gentility, and when Constance sees him in town, "tall and slender, and so different, in a formal suit of thin dark cloth," she reflects that "he could go anywhere. He had a native breeding which was really much nicer than the cut-to-pattern class thing."

In Constance Chatterley, the changes are perhaps less drastic, but they are no less important to her motivation. In the first version, she has had a certain continental experience but it has hardly made her worldly; in the second version, she has had a continental education; in the third version, she has not only had a continental education but also a series of casual, "intellectual" love affairs before her marriage. She is still "a ruddy, country-looking girl with soft brown hair and a sturdy body, and slow movements, full of unused energy," but she is also a woman whose experience has equipped her to take the full measure of her world. Her marriage ruined by Clifford's physical incapacity, she has, in her third figuration, a casual postmarital affair (and is encouraged in this conduct by her friends, her father, even her husband). In the third version, Lawrence introduces the character of Michaelis, a successful, trivial playwright, to put Constance at the very center of the full emptiness of this social-intellectual world. This motivation is of first importance, for it places Mellors and Constance in precisely the same situation: an experienced man and woman, both disillusioned with their experience, both capable of a better experience. With the minimization of the class barrier between Connie and Mellors and the amplification of their similar sexual defeat, Lawrence achieves the psychological realism of the final version.

If they are ready for one another, they still face the problem of finding a world that is ready for them. As only a glance at the variation in the three endings will show, Lawrence had solved this problem only in part by the alterations that we have already observed. In the first version, where class barriers are strongest, and where Lawrence is still hoping for some social role for his characters, Parkin ends as a worker in a Sheffield steel mill and as the secretary of the local branch of the Communist party. Just before the end, after Constance is shown in an impossible scene in a worker's home, she and Parkin quarrel, and the likelihood of their finding any way out is small. In the final scene, she hopes to become his wife, simply his wife, living on his terms, sharing his interests, politics included; but our hope for her is small. In the second version, Parkin is no longer a political man and the Sheffield mills are an abomination to him; he plans to leave them for farm work. He is perhaps a little less unwilling to spend more of Connie's money in order to find a life for themselves, if she is so determined. The novel ends with his promising to "come to Italy" in her wake, when she needs him. But here Lawrence has tried to write out the class barrier by fiat. While Constance is visiting on the Continent, she has this revelation:

Class is an anachronism. It finished in 1914. Nothing remains but a vast proletariat, including kings, aristocrats, squires, millionaires and working-people, men and women alike. And then a few individuals who have not yet been proletarianised. . . .

It was a great relief to her that the vague, yet very profound class-mistrust which had laid like a negating serpent at the bottom of her soul, was now gone. Vitally, organically, in the old organic sense of society, there were no more classes. That organic system had collapsed. So she need not have any class-mistrust of Parkin, and he need have none of her.

This discovery presumably frees them to live in the world as it is, on their terms. The end of the second version is very explicitly uninterested in any retreat to the colonies. It is the world or nothing, this time. "To Connie, the wood where she had known Parkin in the spring had become the image of another world," but the implication is that she can make *that* world bloom in this one, probably in Italy. On this subject, Lawrence had taken his personal stand, and interested readers should examine his *Autobiographical Sketch*, written at this time and published posthumously in *Assorted Articles*. There he writes:

> Class makes a gulf, across which all the best human flow is lost. It is not exactly the triumph of the middle classes that has made the deadness, but the triumph of the middle-class *thing*. . . . the middle class is broad and shallow and passionless. Quite passionless. At the best they substitute affection, which is the great middle-class positive emotion. . . . Yet I find, here in Italy, for example, that I live in a certain silent contact with the peasants who work the land of this villa. I am not intimate with them . . . and they are not working for me; I am not their *padrone*. Yet it is they, really, who form my *ambiente*. . . . I don't expect them to make any millenium here on earth, neither now nor in the future. But I want to live near them, because their life still flows.

But Connie and Mellors are not Frieda and D. H. Lawrence, and Lawrence has the dramatic tact to recognize as much in the third version. While the entire implication (underlined by the *rapport* that develops between Mellors and Connie's father) is that class is an anachronism, and that the moment we can make better assumptions about what we are in the potential human facts, this will be the first of many anachronisms to vanish from the actual social facts, Lawrence wisely allows the matter to remain in the realm of implication rather than forcing it to solve his dramatic problem. Again, with the question of marriage as it is *versus* marriage as it should be, the second version is as explicit as this:

> So it must be: a voyage apart, in the same direction. Grapple the two vessels together, lash them side by side, and the first storm will smash them to pieces. This is marriage, in the bad weather of modern civilisation. But leave the two vessels apart, to make their voyage to the same

port, each according to its own skill and power, and an unseen life connects them, a magnetism which cannot be forced. And that is marriage as it will be, when this is broken down.

In the third version, the dramatic presentation of a true marriage is permitted to speak for itself, and the fact that this true marriage must exist in a wasteland leaves the end of the third version in some uncertainty, which is supremely right. The whole seems to slow down into a *decrescendo* as it begins to breathe out an uneasiness that is aesthetically fine, among Lawrence's really great effects. Political affirmations (and some impossible scenes) vanish, both the earliest assertions of class war and the middle assertions of the absence of class, and the novel ends with a long letter from Mellors to Constance, written from a farm where he is working, as both characters await their divorces and Connie awaits her child. Mellors hopes to find a farm of his own, perhaps in Canada, where they can make their life; but he does not hope for more, and he is hardly bold in the hope he has.

> . . . what I live for now is for you and me to live together. I'm frightened, really. I feel the devil in the air, and he'll try to get us. Or not the devil, Mammon: which I think, after all, is only the mass-will of people, wanting money and hating life. Anyhow I feel great grasping white hands in the air, wanting to get hold of the throat of anybody who tries to live, live beyond money, and squeeze the life out. There's a bad time coming! If things go on as they are, there's nothing lies in the future but death and destruction, for these industrial masses. I feel my inside turn to water sometimes, and there you are, going to have a child by me. But never mind. All the bad times that ever have been, haven't been able to blow the crocus out: not even the love of women. So they won't be able to blow out my wanting you, nor the little glow there is between you and me. We'll be together next year. And though I'm frightened, I believe in your being with me. A man has to fend and fettle for the best, and then trust in something beyond himself. You can't insure against the future, except by really believing in the best bit of you, and the power beyond it. So I believe in the little flame between us. For me now, it's the only thing in the world. I've got no friends, not inward friends. Only you.

Earlier in the novel, we encounter this exchange between the lovers:

> "I would like to have all the rest of the world disappear," she said, "and live with you here."
> "It won't disappear," he said.
> They went almost in silence through the lovely wood. But they were together in a world of their own.

In the end, Lawrence permits them to meet the world as it is with the only armor that they have: the courage of their own tenderness. But the reader remembers, perhaps, for his comfort and theirs, the echoing promise of Clifford himself, meant with such an ironic difference and delivered in the cadences of the later T. S. Eliot, that "every parting means a meeting elsewhere. And every meeting is a new bondage."

If Lawrence's first problem in revision was to achieve maximum plausibility within the terms of his aspiration, his second problem was to achieve maximum meaning through the amplification of his symbols. If the first problem involved him primarily in the solid realities of a class situation, the second involved him in the modulations of psychic reality. The basic contrast between life-affirming and life-denying values, between "tenderness" and the "insentient iron world" is the sole subject of Lawrence's symbolic amplifications, and nearly any line of revision, no matter how minor, that he chose to follow through the three versions of his novel would demonstrate the swelling connotative richness with which this contrast is presented.

Perhaps the most obvious development over the three texts is Lawrence's increase in descriptions of both the mechanical world and the wood on the Chatterley estate, for this juxtaposition in the setting of the novel is the first symbolic form of the basic thematic contrast of the novel. It is developed until the new consciousness of the lovers is itself like a wood in flower, and the shrinking consciousness of Clifford is itself like a machine in gear.

> She was like a forest, like the dark interlacing of the oak wood, humming inaudibly with myriad unfolding buds. Meanwhile the birds of desire were asleep in the vast interlaced intricacy of her body.
> But Clifford's voice went on, clapping and gurgling with unusual sounds.

Hardly less obvious is Lawrence's development of two kinds of scene —the intimate sexual scenes between the lovers in the wood and the intellectual and abstract discussions (including discussions of sex) inside Wragby Hall. This development is important not only in that it dramatizes the two ways of life but more especially in that it presents symbolically two ways of conceiving life. Incidentally, one might observe that in his amplification of the Wragby scenes, Lawrence also benefits the dramatic force of his novel, for insofar as the character of Clifford undergoes changes through these revisions, the physical barrier between him and his wife, which was the only real barrier in the first version, takes on relative unimportance as the temperamental and intellectual barrier between them becomes much more important. Again, in this whole growth, one might observe that changes in characterization are likewise in symbolic support of the basic thematic contrast of the book, for as Constance, in the third version, grows into the mature woman with a consciousness like a flowering wood, so Clifford, at the very height of his industrial efficiency, sags into a horrible infantilism, and the whole relationship of Clifford and Mrs. Bolton becomes an enormously subtle trope of class relations. Finally, one might view the alterations in Lawrence's language, from text to text, as integral to his symbolic intentions, and the contrast in language between the two kinds of scene as absolutely primary to the whole aesthetic purpose of the work. In the Hall, language is over-intellectualized, abstract, polite, and cynical; in the wood, it is intuitive, concrete, coarse, and earthy. "We have no language for the feelings," Lawrence wrote in his essay, *The Novel and the Feelings,* "because our feelings do not even exist for us." In a novel which attempts to direct the consciousness to its source in the feelings, Lawrence necessarily employed the only language that English convention provides.

Whatever one may feel as to Lawrence's success, one cannot for a moment question the purity of his intention. Lawrence, who is perhaps the only important puritan in his generation, is eloquent and complete in his remarks on this novel in *A Propos of Lady Chatterley's Lover.* To those remarks one might add only a few observations that he made in other places. His purpose, he always asserted, was "to make the sex relation valid and precious, not shameful," and sex, he said, "means the whole of the relationship between man and woman." Given his intention, he could quite rightly say that "anybody who calls my novel a dirty sexual novel is a liar," and, "It'll infuriate mean people; but it will surely soothe decent ones."

With one friend, Lady Ottoline Morrell, who was apparently disturbed by the novel, he debated in calm protest:

> About *Lady C.*—you mustn't think I advocate perpetual sex. Far from it. Nothing nauseates me more than perpetual sex in and out of season. But I want, with *Lady C.*, to make an *adjustment in consciousness* to the basic physical realities. . . . God forbid that I should be taken as urging loose sex activity. There is a brief time for sex, and a long time when sex is out of place. But when it is out of place as an activity there still should be the large and quiet space in the consciousness where it lives quiescent. Old people can have a lovely quiescent sort of sex, like apples, leaving the young quite free for *their* sort.

The basic physical realities have, as any thoughtful reading of this novel will reveal, enormous reverberations throughout the whole of life. The urgency for the modern world no less than the precise descriptive relevance of Lawrence's vision is constantly brought home to us by psychologists. Erich Fromm, for example, in that notable book, *Escape from Freedom*, writes:

> The word "power" has a twofold meaning. One is the possession of power over somebody, the ability to dominate him; the other meaning is the possession of power to do something, to be able, to be potent. The latter meaning has nothing to do with domination; it expresses mastery in a sense of ability. If we speak of powerlessness we have this meaning in mind; we do not think of a person who is not able to dominate others, but of a person who is not able to do what he wants. Thus power can mean one of two things, *domination* or *potency*. Far from being identical, these two qualities are mutually exclusive. Impotence, using the term not only with regard to the sexual sphere but to all spheres of human potentialities, results in the sadistic striving for domination; to the extent to which an individual is potent, that is, able to realize his potentialities on the basis of freedom and integrity of his self, he does not need to dominate and is lacking the lust for power. Power, in the sense of domination, is the perversion of potency, just as sexual sadism is the perversion of sexual love.

In the second version of *Lady Chatterley*, Lawrence, in the poetic terms of his novel, made the same distinction when he spoke of the two "energies"—"the frictional, seething, resistant, explosive, blind sort" and "the other, forest energy, that was still and softly powerful, with tender, frail bud-tips and finger-ends full of awareness."

The pathos of Lawrence's novel arises from the tragedy of modern society. What is tragic is that we cannot feel our tragedy. We have slowly grown into a confusion of these terms, the two forms of power, and, in confusing them, we have left almost no room for the free creative functions of the man or woman who, lucky soul, possesses "integrity of self." The force of his novel probably lies in the degree of intensity with which his indictment of the world and the consequent solitude of his lovers suggest such larger meanings. Certainly it is these meanings that make these characters, in Edmund Wilson's word, "heroic," and that give them the epic quality that was felt by no less a poet than Yeats. "These two lovers," he wrote to his friend, Mrs. Shakespear—

These two lovers the gamekeeper and his employer's wife each separated from their class by their love and by fate are poignant in their loneliness; the coarse language of the one accepted by both becomes a forlorn poetry, uniting their solitudes, something ancient humble and terrible.

Ancient, humble, and terrible. *Lady Chatterley's Lover* is all of those; but it is also this: triumphant. Lawrence sings in his novel, like Stephen Spender in a short poem of twenty years later, our first and final hymn.

> Through man's love and woman's love
> Moons and tides move
> Which fuse those islands, lying face to face.
> Mixing in naked passion,
> Those who naked new life fashion
> Are themselves reborn in naked grace.

Acknowledgment is made to these publishers for their kind permission to quote from the works of D. H. Lawrence: to Alfred A Knopf, Inc., for quotation from "Autobiographical Sketch," in *The Later D. H. Lawrence;* to Twayne Publishers for quotation from *A Propos of Lady Chatterley's Lover,* in *Sex, Literature and Censorship;* and to The Viking Press, Inc., for excerpts from *The Letters of D. H. Lawrence* and *Last Poems.*

1961. It is to be regretted that I could not obtain permission to reprint from Encounter *(February, 1960) Katherine Anne Porter's essay, "A Wreath for the Gamekeeper," which takes sharply feminine issue with the point of view of my essay. Miss Porter quite understandably wishes to reprint this work for the first time in a collection of her essays.*

M. S.

19

DAVID DAICHES

Dubliners

JAMES JOYCE left his native Dublin at the age of twenty-two, and lived ever after in self-imposed exile on the Continent. Yet all his work is concerned with Dublin; his characters are Dubliners, his background is Dublin, his atmosphere is Dublin, and all the tremendous resources of his symbolic realism were employed in creating in language the essence and reality of the Dublin he turned his back on as a young man. This fact is in itself symbolic. Joyce's literary career was a progressive attempt to insulate himself against the life which is his subject as an artist until he reached the point at which what one may call ideal comedy became possible There are many definitions of comedy, but the definition that is most relevant to a consideration of such a work as *Ulysses* as comedy is that which identifies the comic spirit with the author's renunciation of any share in the world he portrays. Tragedy and comedy, insofar as they arise from differences in attitude, differ essentially on this point. Comedy is written by one who, temporarily or permanently, has renounced his share in human destiny; tragedy is the work of one who is all too conscious of his share. Indeed, the same story may be comic or tragic according to whether the arrangement and emphasis of the events result in stressing or in minimizing the author's (and so, for the critic, the reader's) sense of community with the life he creates. The failure of Hamlet to cope with the circumstances in the midst of which he finds himself is tragic be-

From *The Novel and the Modern World*, by David Daiches, University of Chicago Press, rev. ed., 1960.

cause those circumstances are presented as part of the author's world, of our world:[1] it would be comic if the details of style and organization were handled so as to insulate author and reader from any such community and the theme became an intellectual one of frustration—the theme of most comedies. The theme of *Ulysses*—if we can differentiate the theme from the treatment—is in itself neither comic nor tragic; but it is presented with the supreme aloofness that makes supreme comedy. Joyce leaves Ireland in order to write about Ireland; he shuns the life which is his subject in order to be able to embody that life in his art as an artist only and not as a fellow country-many or even as a fellow mortal. So the main fact about Joyce's biography has a direct connection with the main fact about his art—the fact that *Ulysses* (and, though with obvious differences, *Finnegans Wake*) constitute comedy at its ultimate point.

Joyce's work, however, is not so homogeneous that such an explanation can fit all of it. It fits *Dubliners* only to a limited extent (and *Dubliners* was written while Joyce was still in Dublin) and it does not fit *A Portrait of the Artist as a Young Man* at all. The road to the renunciation that produced *Ulysses* and *Finnegans Wake* was not a straight one. In *Dubliners* Joyce is simply the clear-eyed observer, and he is observing what is around him, so that these stories have none of the symbolizing qualities that memory lends. *A Portrait of the Artist* is a work of exorcism. Joyce seems to have decided that until he had come to terms with the life which had molded him he would not be free to embody that life in his art. He grapples directly with himself considered as a product of his environment; in doing so he attains complete self-consciousness about the process he is describing; and so henceforth he can defy determinism—he has faced the problem squarely and won the right to dismiss it. He has shaped his own connection with Ireland into a work of art and has exorcised the evil spirit of self-consciousness—that spirit which has such an inhibiting influence on the production of comedy. Exorcism or catharsis, *A Portrait of the Artist* certainly enabled Joyce to get certain inhibiting forces out of his system, and by doing so made *Ulysses* possible.

There are thus four periods in Joyce's life as a writer. First, the period of *Dubliners* where he gives us thumbnail sketches of characteristic situations of the life of which he is still a part, in spite of the studied objectivity of his approach. Joyce is a part of the Ireland of *Dubliners* in the same dim way that Chekhov is a part of the Russia he presents in his plays and stories. The second period, producing the autobiographical *Portrait,* is one of candid study of his relation to the forces that have made him, with the gradual realization of the impossibility of his remaining longer in such an environment if he was to achieve that kind of artistic integrity which he had already set for himself as his aim. The third period, to which the conclusion of the *Portrait* had so directly pointed, follows; the period when he is free to re-create in language, on both the realistic and the symbolic levels, the life he had renounced, making that renunciation as the price he deemed necessary for artistic integrity and the objectivity of true comedy, but conscious of the risk involved in thus severing his ties with that microcosm of civilization which had produced him and which for him stood for humanity. Stephen tells Cranly toward the end of *A Portrait*:

". . . I do not fear to be alone or to be spurned for another or to leave whatever I have to leave. And I am not afraid to make a mistake, even a great mistake, and perhaps as long as eternity too."

Cranly, now grave again, slowed his pace and said:

"Alone, quite alone. You have no fear of that. And you know what that word means? Not only to be separate from all others but to have not even one friend."

"I will take the risk," said Stephen.

Ulysses was produced as the result of Joyce's having taken that risk. The fourth period produced *Finnegans Wake*. Here Joyce created in a purely symbolic manner an epitome of the life he renounced, rejecting the realistic narrative basis on which *Ulysses* was organized and enlarging the symbolic element to include both theme and technique, and further to the point where it involves interfering with the very English language itself. From one point of view at least, it marks the completion of Joyce's journey from realism to symbolism.

Let us now turn back to *Dubliners* and consider in more detail the nature of Joyce's achievement here. The short stories that make up this book have certain common features in aim and technique; they are realistic in a certain sense, and they have a quite extraordinary evenness of tone and texture, the style being that neutral medium which, without in itself showing any signs of emotion or excitement, conveys with quiet adequacy the given story in its proper atmosphere and with its proper implications. Only the last story in the collection, "The Dead," stands apart from the others; here Joyce has done something different—he has presented a story in a way that implies comment, and he has deliberately allowed his style to surrender, as it were, to that comment, so that the level objectivity of the other stories is replaced by a more lyrical quality.

The first three stories are told in the first person, the principle of
selection, which determines the choice, organization, and emphasis of
the incidents, being provided by the recollected impressions of the narrator. Thus, in "The Sisters" Joyce gives the constituent parts of what,
to a sensitive boy, made up (whether actually or not is irrelevant) a
single and memorable experience; and these parts are arranged and
patterned in such a way as to give a sense of the unity of the experience to the reader. And although it is irrelevant to the critic whether
events actually occurred or not, it is very relevant that the pattern of
events should be one which produces a recognizable experience with
its attendant atmosphere. A purely "formal" analysis of any of these
stories would be useful—in fact, indispensable—in an endeavor to assess their value as literature, but such an analysis is only the first step
in a process; it is not in itself able to tell us why that particular arrangement of incident and description constitutes a totality which has more
value than a mere symmetrical pattern or intriguing design. The arrangement of events in "The Sisters" or "Araby" produces a good short
story because the result is not merely a pattern *qua* pattern (such has
no *necessary* value in literature), but a pattern which corresponds to
something in experience. For those who, owing to the circumstances
of their life or the limitations of their sensibility, are unable to recognize that correspondence, the story loses most of its worth: there is
always this limitation to the universality of great literature, this stum-
bling-block to the purely formal critical approach. A study of *Dubliners*
can tell us a great deal about the function of pattern in fiction and
about the relation between realism as a technique and as an end. No
English short-story writer has built up his design, has related the parts
to the preconceived whole, more carefully than Joyce has done in
stories such as "The Sisters," "Two Gallants," or "Ivy Day in the Committee Room." Observation is the tool of imagination, and imagination
is that which can see potential significance in the most casual seeming
events. It is the more specifically and consciously artistic faculty that
organizes, arranges, balances emphases, and sets going undercurrents
of symbolic comment, until that potential significance has become
actual.

In the second of these stories, "An Encounter," the organizing and
selecting principle is again the boy's impressionable mind and memory
as recalled or conceived by Joyce. It is worth noting how Joyce sets the
pattern going in this and other stories. Descriptive comment concerning the chief characters constitutes the opening paragraph—comment
that wanders to and fro in its tenses, not starting with a clear edge of

incident but with a jagged line, as though memory were gradually searching out those events which really were the beginning of the design which is a totality in the retrospective mind. Similarly, in "The Sisters," the opening paragraph consists of an almost regular alternation of imperfect and pluperfect tenses:

> Night after night I had passed the house . . . and studied the lighted square of window. . . . If he was dead, I thought, I would see the reflection of candles on the darkened blind.
> . . . He had often said to me: "I am not long for this world," and I thought his words idle. Now I knew they were true. . . .

These deliberately wavering beginnings serve a double function. First, they give the author an opportunity of presenting to the reader any preliminary information that is necessary to his understanding of the story; they enable him, too, to let out those pieces of information in the order which will give them most significance and throw the necessary amount of emphasis onto what the author wishes to be emphasized. Second, on a simple, naturalistic level they give us the pattern of an experience as it actually is to memory or observation. The beginning is vague (the reader should study the evidence of witnesses in reports of court trials to understand how wavering the beginning of a unified experience is to both observer and sufferer), but once under way the jagged line becomes straight, until the end, which is precise and definite. Our own memories of experiences which have been significant for us will provide sufficient comment on this technique. In those stories which are told in the first person, as memories, the jagged-line openings are more conspicious than in the stories narrated in the third person: Joyce has not done this accidentally.

Very different are the conclusions of the stories. A series of events is recognized as having constituted a totality, a "significant experience," in virtue of its close, not of its opening. The conclusions of these stories are level and precise, the last lines denoting a genuine climax of realization (if told in the first person) or in the pattern of the objective situation (if told in the third). And the pause is genuine. If the reader were taken on five minutes farther he might find the addition unnecessary or silly, but it would not cancel out the effect of the whole story, as the prolongation of the trick conclusions of so many modern short-story writers would. In many of O. Henry's short stories, for example, where the final point is contained in a fraction of a moment sustained in print simply by the author's refusing to go farther, the conclusion is not a genuine one, no real end to a pattern, but simply a piece of wit on the author's part. The stories they tell are not real patterns or wholes but are made to appear so only by the epigrammatic form of the conclusion, and the point would be lost if the author told his readers the succeeding event. Joyce is not in this tradition—he has more respect for his art. His final pauses are as genuine as the final bars of a Beethoven symphony, though not nearly so obvious. The degeneration of the short story—and the short stage play, too—into the extended epigram was a feature of the 1920's and 1930's. Perhaps it is due to some extent to the influence of the curtain stage, where the author is absolved from the necessity of creating a genuine conclusion by the rapid descent of the curtain, cutting off the audience from the stage at a single stroke. The platform stage of the Elizabethans encouraged healthier tendencies: there the end of the pattern had to be real, the pause a real pause, for there was no slick curtain to relieve the writer of his responsibility. Genuine pause does not imply a long-drawn-out conclusion or an uneconomical art: Joyce's endings are subtle and rapid:

"What do you think of that, Crofton," cried Mr. Henchy. "Isn't that fine? What?"

Mr. Crofton said that it was a very fine piece of writing.

Or:

Gazing up into the darkness I saw myself as a creature driven and derided by vanity; and my eyes burned with anguish and anger.

And there is the immensely subtle and effective ending of "Grace," concluding in the middle of Father Purdon's sermon. The platform-stage ending does not require verbosity or obviousness; it requires only that the last line shall really conclude the pattern; that the reader's pause shall be real and not forced on him by a trick of the author in refusing to say more when there is more to be said.

"Two Gallants," a gray, unexciting incident whose predominant mood is illustrated by the setting—late Sunday evening in a deserted street of Dublin—is one of Joyce's minor triumphs. It is a perfect example of the organization of the casual until, simply by the order and relation of the parts, it becomes significant, not only a sordid incident that happened at a given moment but a symbol of a type of civilization. The arrangement of detail so as to give the utmost density to the narrative is a striking quality here, as it is in "Ivy Day in the Committee Room." Joyce will pause to elaborate the description of a character at a certain point of the story, and it is only by a careful, critical analysis

that we appreciate the full effect of having that pause in that place
and in no other. Always the location of particularizing detail is such
that it suggests the maximum amount of implication. In "Ivy Day in the
Committee Room" two features of Joyce's technique are dominant:
first, every action is symbolic of the atmosphere he wishes to create,
and, second, the pauses for description are carefully arranged and
balanced so as to emphasize the symbolic nature of the action. The
introduction of candles to light up the bareness of the room at the
particular point in the story when Joyce wishes to draw the reader's
attention to its bareness is one of many examples:

> A denuded room came into view and the fire lost all its cheerful
> colour. The walls of the room were bare except for a copy of an election
> address. In the middle of the room was a small table on which papers
> were heaped.

A simple enough piece of description, but it has been held back till
now and allowed to emerge naturally as a result of the candle incident
at a point where the emphasis on bareness, on the loss of the fire's
cheerful color, and on the dreary untidiness of the room, gains its maximum effect as regards both structure and atmosphere. Similarly, the
manipulation of the Parnell motif in this story shows great skill. It is
suggested in the title, but does not break through to the surface of the
story until, at a point carefully chosen by Joyce, Mr. Hynes takes off his
coat, "displaying, as he did so, an ivy leaf in the lapel." And henceforth this motif winds in and out until its culmination in Mr. Hynes's
recitation. And no more effective symbol of the relation between two
of the main interests of Dubliners in the beginning of this century has
ever been created than in this simple, realistic piece of dialogue and
description:

> "This is Parnell's anniversary," said Mr. O'Connor, "and don't let us
> stir up any bad blood. We all respect him now that he's dead and gone—
> even the Conservatives," he added, turning to Mr. Crofton.
> Pok! The tardy cork flew out of Mr. Crofton's bottle. Mr. Crofton got
> up from his box and went to the fire. As he returned with his capture
> he said in a deep voice:
> "Our side of the house respects him because he was a gentleman."

The claims of liquor impinge naturally on those of politics, as anyone
who has seen a certain section of the Scottish Nationalists at work in
Edinburgh today can well understand. A similar point is made in Mr.
Kernan's remark in "Grace."

" 'Course he is," said Mr. Kernan, "and a damned decent Orangeman, too. We went into Butler's in Moore Street—faith I was genuinely moved, tell you the God's truth—and I remember well his very words. *Kernan*, he said, *we worship at different altars*, he said, *but our belief is the same*. Struck me as very well put."

This time it is religion and liquor that mingle so effortlessly. The slipping-in of the name of the bar right beside Mr. Kernan's expression of his genuine religious emotion is realistic and convincing in itself and is also symbolic in that it makes, thus economically, a point about the Irish character.

Joyce's realism in *Dubliners* is not therefore the casual observation of the stray photographer, nor is it the piling-up of unrelated details. All the stories are deliberately and carefully patterned, all have a density, a fulness of implication, which the even tone of the narrative by disguising only renders more effective. The almost terrifying calm of "An Encounter," the aloof recording of "Eveline," the hard clarity of carefully ordered detail in "After the Race," the carefully balanced interiors in "A Little Cloud," the penetrating climax of "Counterparts," the quiet effectiness of "Clay"—to select only some of the more obvious points—are the work of an artist whose gift of observation, tremendous as it is, is never allowed to thwart his literary craftsmanship—his ability to construct, arrange, organize. The two most impressive stories in the collection are "Ivy Day in the Committee Room" and the concluding story, "The Dead." The former has in a high degree all the qualities we have noted; it is as careful a piece of patterned realism as any writer has given us. But "The Dead" differs both in theme and technique from all the other stories in *Dubliners* and deserves some discussion to itself.

In "The Dead" Joyce uses a much more expansive technique than he does elsewhere in *Dubliners*. He is not here merely concerned with shaping a series of events into a unity; he has a specific point to make —a preconceived theme in terms of which the events in "The Dead" are selected and arranged. In the other stories there is no point other than the pattern that emerges from his telling of the story; no argument can be isolated and discussed as the "theme" of the story, for the story is the theme and the theme is the story. The insight of the artist organizes the data provided by observation into a totality, but no external principle determines that organization; the principle of organization is determined simply by further contemplation of the data themselves. But "The Dead" is the working-out, in terms of realistic narrative, of a preconceived theme, and that theme is a man's withdrawal into the circle of his own egotism, a number of external factors trying progressively to break down the walls of that circle, and those walls being finally broken down by the culminating assault on his egotism coming simultaneously from without, as an incident affecting him, and from within, as an increase of understanding. Only when we have appreciated this theme does the organization of the story become intelligible to us. On the surface it is the story of Gabriel returning from a jolly time at a party given by his aunts in a mood of desire for his wife and the frustration of that desire on his learning that a song sung by one of the guests at the party had reminded his wife of a youth who had been in love with her many years ago and who had died of pneumonia caught through standing outside her window in the cold and the rain; so that his wife is thinking of that past, in which Gabriel had no share, when he was expecting her to be giving herself to him, the final result being that Gabriel loses his mood of desire and falls asleep in a mood of almost impersonal understanding. But about three-quarters of the story is taken up with a vivid and detailed account of the party, and on first reading the story we are puzzled to know why Joyce devotes so much care and space to the party if the ending is to be simply Gabriel's change of mood on learning how his wife is really feeling. As a piece of simple patterning the story seems lopsided; we have to discover the central theme before we realize how perfectly proportioned the story is.

The theme of the story is the assault on the walled circle of Gabriel's egotism. The first character we see is Lily, the caretaker's daughter, rushed almost off her feet in the performance of her various duties. Then comes a pause, and Joyce turns to describe the Misses Morkan, who are giving the party, and the nature of the function. Then, when this retrospect had been brought up to the time of the opening of the story, Gabriel and his wife enter—late for the party, everyone expecting them. The external environment is drawn first before Gabriel enters and makes it merely an environment for himself. Lily is an independent personality, quie outside Gabriel's environment; she is introduced before Gabriel in order that when Gabriel arrives the reader should be able to feel the contrast between the environment as Gabriel feels it to be (a purely personal one), and as it is to a quite objective observer—the caretaker's daughter to whom the party is just an increase of work. Gabriel is greeted as he enters with a great deal of fuss; he enters naturally into the environment his aunts are preparing for him, but immediately after the greeting he has an illuminating encounter with Lily. He patronizes her, as he had known her since she was a child. He remarks gaily that one of these days he will be going to her wedding. Lily resents the remark and replies bitterly that "the men that is now is only all palaver and what they can get out of you."

What part does this little incident play in the story? It is the first attempt to break down the circle of Gabriel's egotism. He has questioned Lily, not with any sincere desire to learn about her, but in order to indulge his own expansive mood. He does not recognize that Lily and her world exist in their own right; to him they are merely themes for his genial conversation. Gabriel colors at Lily's reply; his egotism is hurt ever so slightly, but the fortress is still very far from taken. How slight the breach was is illustrated by his subsequent action—he thrusts a coin into the girl's hand, warming himself in the glow of his own generosity and not concerned with finding a method of giving that will obviate any embarrassment on Lily's part. On thinking over his encounter with Lily he sees it simply as a failure on his part to take up the right tone, and this failure of his own hurts his pride a little and makes him wonder whether he ought not to change the speech he has prepared for after dinner—perhaps that is the wrong tone too. He sees the whole incident from a purely egotistical point of view; Lily exists only as an excuse for his gesturing, and he is worried lest his gestures are not those which will get most appreciation from his audience.

Then we have Gabriel again in his relation with his aunts. He was always their favorite nephew, we are told. We see his possessive attitude to Gretta, his wife. We see him patting his tie reassuringly when his wife shows a tendency to laugh at him. When that tendency is manifested by Aunt Julia as well he shows signs of anger, and tactful Aunt Kate changes the conversation. The picture of Gabriel as withdrawn behind the walls of his own egotism is carefully built up.

The second assault on Gabriel's egotism is made by Miss Ivors, the Irish Nationalist, who attacks his individualism and asks what he is doing for his people and his country. She succeeds in making Gabriel very uncomfortable, and when she leaves him he tries to banish all thought of the conversation from his memory with the reflection that "of course the girl, or woman, or whatever she was, was an enthusiast but there was a time for all things." He goes on to reflect that "she had tried to make him ridiculous before people, heckling him and staring at him with her rabbit's eyes." And so fails the second attempt to break down the circle of Gabriel's egotism.

Then we see Gabriel in a more congenial atmosphere, where his egotism is safe. He is asked to carve the goose—as usual. But Gabriel has been upset, and his cold refusal of a request by Gretta shows his egotism on the defensive. He runs over the heads of his speech in his mind. It must be changed—changed in such a way as to squash these assaults that are being made on his ego. And so he thinks up a nice, cozy talk about hospitality and humor and humanity and the virtues of the older generation (with which, as against the generation represented by Miss Ivors, he temporarily identifies himself). Eventually the meal begins, and Gabriel takes his seat at the head of the table, thoroughly at ease at last.

Mr. Bartell D'Arcy is Gabriel's counterpart—a figure merely sketched, to serve the part of a symbol in the story. There is deliberate irony on Joyce's part in making Gretta refer to him as conceited in an early conversation with Gabriel. When at dinner a group of guests are discussing with their hostesses the singers of Ireland, their complacency is such as to dismiss Caruso almost with contempt: they had hardly heard of him. Only D'Arcy suggests that Caruso might be better than any of the singers mentioned, and his suggestion is met with skepticism. D'Arcy alone of the guests refuses to drink either port or sherry until persuaded by nudges and whispers. And it is D'Arcy who sings the song that removes Gretta to another world.

Gabriel's speech takes place as planned, and for some time he revels happily in the little world of which he is the center. The party ends and the guests stand with coats on in the hall, about to take their leave. Gabriel is waiting for Gretta to get ready, and as he and others are waiting the sound of someone playing the piano comes down to the hall:

> "Who's playing up there?" asked Gabriel.
> "Nobody. They're all gone."
> "Oh no, Aunt Kate," said Mary Jane. "Bartell D'Arcy and Miss O'Callaghan aren't gone yet."
> "Someone is fooling at the piano anyhow," said Gabriel.

D'Arcy is first "nobody"; then—and it is significant for the structure of the story that it is Gabriel who says this—he is "fooling at the piano." While Gabriel, a little disturbed again, is making a final effort to reestablish his full sense of his own importance by telling a humorous story to the circle in the hall and thus becoming again the center of attraction, the sound of someone singing comes downstairs, and Gabriel sees his wife listening, standing near the top of the first flight "as if she were a symbol of something." D'Arcy stops abruptly on being discovered (again the contrast with Gabriel) and finally Gabriel and

Gretta set out for the hotel where they are to spend the night, as it is too far to go home at such an hour.

Then comes the climax, when the fortified circle of Gabriel's egotism is battered down by a series of sharp blows. Just at the moment of his greatest self-confidence and desire for her, Gretta tells him that she is thinking about the song D'Arcy had sung. He questions her, first genially, and then, as he begins to realize the implications of the song for Gretta, more and more coldly:

> "I am thinking about a person long ago who used to sing that song."
> "And who was the person long ago?" asked Gabriel, smiling.
> "It was a person I used to know in Galway when I was living with my grandmother," she said.
> The smile passed away from Gabriel's face. . . .

Miss Ivor had talked about Galway; it was one of the symbols of that world of otherness against which Gabriel had been shutting himself in all evening. This is the beginning of the final assault. Then Gabriel learns that the "person" was a young boy that Gretta used to know, long before she knew him. He had been in love with her, and they used to go out walking together. With cold irony Gabriel asks whether that was the reason that Gretta had earlier in the evening expressed a desire to go to Galway for the summer holidays. When she tells him that the young man is dead—dying long since, when he was only seventeen—this line of defense is taken away from Gabriel and he falls back onto his final line:

> "What was he?" asked Gabriel, still ironically.
> "He was in the gasworks," she said.
> Gabriel felt humiliated by the failure of his irony and by the evocation of this figure from the dead, a boy in the gasworks.

Gabriel has no further defenses left. He burns with shame, seeing himself

> as a ludicrous figure, acting as a pennyboy for his aunts, a nervous, well-meaning sentimentalist, orating to vulgarians and idealising his own clownish lusts, the pitiable fatuous figure he had caught a glimpse of in the mirror. Instinctively he turned his back more to the light lest she might see the shame that burned upon his forehead.

The full realization that his wife had all along been dwelling in another world, a world he had never entered and of which he knew nothing, and the utter failure of his irony to bring his wife back to the world of which he, Gabriel, was the center, finally broke the walled circle of his egotism. A dead youth, a mere memory, was the center of the world in which Gretta had all this while been living. As a result of this knowledge, and the way it has been conveyed, Gabriel escapes from himself, as it were, and the rest of the story shows us his expanding consciousness until the point where, dozing off into unconsciousness, he feels a sense of absolute unity, of identity even, with all those elements which before had been hostile to his ego:

> Generous tears filled Gabriel's eyes. . . . The tears gathered more thickly in his eyes and in the partial darkness he imagined he saw the form of a young man standing under a dripping tree. . . . His own identity was fading out into a grey impalpable world: the solid world itself, which these dead had one time reared and lived in, was dissolving and dwindling.
> A few light taps upon the pane made him turn to the window. It had begun to snow again. He watched sleepily the flakes, silver and dark, falling obliquely against the lamplight. The time had come for him to set out on his journey westward. Yes, the newspapers were right: snow was general all over Ireland. It was falling on every part of the dark central plain, on the treeless hills, falling softly upon the bog of Allen and, further westward, softly falling into the dark mutinous Shannon waves. It was falling, too, upon every part of the lonely churchyard where Michael Furey lay buried. It lay thickly drifted on the crooked crosses and headstones, on the spears of the little gate, on the barren thorns. His soul swooned slowly as he heard the snow falling faintly through the universe and faintly falling, like the descent of their last end, upon all the living and the dead.

The snow, which falls indifferently upon all things, covering them with a neutral whiteness and erasing all their differentiating details, is the symbol of Gabriel's new sense of identity with the world, of the breakdown of the circle of his egotism to allow him to become for the moment not a man different from all other men living in a world of which he alone is the center but a willing part of the general flux of things. The assault, which progressed through so many stages until its final successful stage, had this result, and the contrast with the normal Gabriel is complete.

It is only as a result of some such analysis that the organization and structure of "The Dead" can be seen to be not only effective but inevitable. It is a story which, in the elaborateness of its technique and variations of its prose style (the cadenced inversions of the final passage form a deliberate contrast with the style of the earlier descriptions, adding their share to the presentation of the main theme), stands apart from the others in *Dubliners*. Joyce's versatility is already apparent. "Ivy Day in the Committee Room" has the texture of a Katherine Mansfield story but with a firmness of outline and presentation that Katherine Mansfield lacked in all but two or three of her works. "The Dead" is in a more traditional style, but done with a subtlety and a virtuosity that makes it one of the most remarkable short stories of the present century.

"The Dead" was not part of the original draft of *Dubliners*. It was added later, at a time when Joyce was becoming increasingly preoccupied with the problem of aesthetics. The story is, indeed, a symbolic statement of the aethetic attitude that he came to accept. Gabriel moves from an egocentric to an impersonal point of view just as the artist (according to Joyce's explanation in *A Portrait of the Artist as a Young Man*) moves from the personal lyrical method to the impersonal dramatic approach. The indifferent acceptance of life as something revolving not round the artist's ego but on its independent axis is for Joyce the ideal aesthetic attitude. Thus "The Dead" is, in some sense, a fable illustrating Joyce's view of the nature of the artist's attitude. It reflects his preoccupation with the problem of defining the aesthetic point of view at this period.

NOTE

1. Not, of course, on the physical level.

20

HARRY LEVIN

———◆———

The Artist

THE HISTORY of the realistic novel shows that fiction tends toward auto-biography. The increasing demands for social and psychological detail that are made upon the novelist can only be satisfied out of his own experience. The forces which make him an outsider focus his observation upon himself. He becomes his own hero, and begins to crowd his other characters into the background. The background takes on a new importance for its influence on his own character. The theme of his novel is the formation of character; its habitual pattern is that of apprenticeship or education; and it falls into the category which has been distinguished, by German criticism at least, as the *Bildungsroman*. The novel of development, when it confines itself to the professional sphere of the novelist, becomes a novel of the artist, a *Künstlerroman*. Goethe's *Wilhelm Meister*, Stendhal's *Vie d'Henri Brulard*, and Butler's *Way of All Flesh* amply suggest the potentialities of the form.

The *Künstlerroman* offered a tentative solution to the dilemma of Joyce's generation, by enabling writers to apply the methods of realism to the subject of art. It enabled Marcel Proust to communicate experience more fully and subtly than had been done before, because it was

---

From *James Joyce: A Critical Introduction*, by Harry Levin; copyright 1941 by New Directions; reprinted by permission of New Directions.

his own experience that he was communicating, and because he was an artist to his finger-tips. *A la recherche du temps perdu* has been described as a novel that was written to explain why it was written. But, having come to be written, it offers other novelists little stimulus toward self-portraiture. It is singularly fitting that *Ulysses* should have appeared in the year of Proust's death. The perverse logic of André Gide can still present, in his *Journal des faux-monnayeurs*, the diary of a novelist who is writing a novel about a novelist who is keeping a diary about the novel he is writing. Of course, the *Künstlerroman* has no logical limit; but, like the label on the box of Quaker Oats, it has a vanishing-point. Already it is beginning to look as old-fashioned as Murger's *Vie de Bohême*.

The *Künstlerroman*, though it reverses the more normal procedure of applying the methods of art to the subject of reality, is the only conception of the novel that is specialized enough to include *A Portrait of the Artist as a Young Man*. In 1913, the year before Joyce finished his book, D. H. Lawrence had published his own portrait of the artist, *Sons and Lovers*. Both books convey the claustral sense of a young intelligence swaddled in convention and constricted by poverty, and the intensity of its first responses to esthetic experience and life at large. The extent to which Lawrence warms to his theme is the measure of Joyce's reserve. Characteristically, they may be reacting from the very different institutions behind them—evangelical English protestantism and Irish Catholic orthodoxy—when Lawrence dwells on the attractions of life, and Joyce on its repulsions. The respective mothers of the two artists play a similar role, yet May Dedalus is a wraith beside the full-bodied realization of Mrs. Morel. The characters in *Sons and Lovers* seem to enjoy an independent existence; in the *Portrait of the Artist* they figure mainly in the hero's reveries and resentments. Joyce's treatment of childhood is unrelieved in its sadness: endless generations of choirs of children sounded, for Stephen Dedalus, the same note of pain and weariness that Newman had heard in Vergil. "All seemed weary of life even before entering upon it."

The attitude of the novelist toward his subject is one of the critical questions considered by Joyce's subject. Stephen expounds his own esthetic theory, which he designates as "applied Aquinas," during a walk in the rain with his irreverent friend, Lynch. *Solvitur ambulando*. It should be noted that the principal action of the *Portrait of the Artist*, whether in conversation or revery, is walking. The lingering images of *Dubliners* are those of people—often children—in the streets. And it was reserved for Joyce to turn the wanderings of Ulysses into a peripatetic pilgrimage through Dublin. He was, in that respect, a good Aristotelian. But he added a personal touch to the critical theory of Aristotle and Aquinas, when he based the distinction between the various literary forms on the relation of the artist to his material. In the lyric, it is immediate; in the epic, the artist presents his material "in mediate relation to himself and others"; in drama, it is presented in immediate relation to others.

The lyrical form is in fact the simplest verbal vesture of an instant of emotion, a rhythmical cry such as ages ago cheered on the man who pulled at the oar or dragged stones up a slope. He who utters it is more conscious of the instant of emotion than of himself as feeling emotion. The simplest epical form is seen emerging out of lyrical literature when the artist prolongs and broods upon himself as the centre of an epical event and this form progresses till the centre of emotional gravity is equidistant from the artist himself and from others. The narrative is no longer purely personal. The personality of the artist passes into the narration itself, flowing round and round the persons and the action like a vital sea. This progress you will see easily in that old English ballad *Turpin Hero,* which begins in the first person and ends in the third person. The dramatic form is reached when the vitality which has flowed and eddied round each person fills every person with such vital force that he or she assumes a proper and intangible esthetic life. The personality of the artist, at first a cry or a cadence or a mood and then a fluid and lambent narrative, finally refines itself out of existence, impersonalizes itself, so to speak. The esthetic image in the dramatic form is life purified in and reprojected from the human imagination. The mystery of esthetic like that of material creation is accomplished. The artist, like the God of the creation, remains within or behind or beyond or above his handiwork, invisible, refined out of existence, indifferent, paring his fingernails.

This progress you will see easily in the succession of Joyce's works. The cry becomes a cadence in *Chamber Music;* the mood becomes a *nuance* in *Dubliners.* If *Exiles* is unsuccessful, it is because the epiphany is not manifest to others; the artist has failed to objectify the relations of his characters with each other or with the audience. The narrative of the *Portrait of the Artist* has scarcely emerged from the lyrical stage. Whereas *Dubliners* began in the first person and ended in the third, the *Portrait of the Artist* takes us back from an impersonal opening to the notes of the author at the end. The personality of the artist, prolonging and brooding upon itself, has not yet passed into the narration. The shift from the personal to the epic will come with *Ulysses,* and the

center of emotional gravity will be equidistant from the artist himself
and from others. And with *Finnegans Wake,* the artist will have retired
within or behind, above or beyond his handiwork, refined out of existence.

Except for the thin incognito of its characters, the *Portrait of the
Artist* is based on a literal transcript of the first twenty years of Joyce's
life. If anything, it is more candid than other autobiographies. It is distinguished from them by its emphasis on the emotional and intellectual
adventures of its protagonist. If we can trust the dates at the end of
the book, Joyce started to write in Dublin during 1904, and continued
to rewrite until 1914 in Trieste. There is reason to believe that he had
accumulated almost a thousand pages—and brought Stephen to the
point of departure for Paris—when the idea of *Ulysses* struck him, and
he decided to reserve those further adventures for the sequel. His
provisional title, *Stephen Hero,* with its echo of the ballad of Dick
Turpin, marks the book as an early point in his stages of artistic imper-
sonality. As the hero of a pedagogical novel, Stephen is significantly
baptized. Saint Stephen Protomartyr was patron of the green on which
University College was located, and therefore of the magazine with
which Joyce had had his earliest literary misadventures.

Stephen is ever susceptible to the magic of names—particularly of
his own last name. Names and words, copybook phrases and schoolboy slang, echoes and jingles, speeches and sermons float through his
mind and enrich the restricted realism of the context. His own name
is the wedge by which symbolism enters the book. One day he pene-
trates its secret. Brooding on the prefect of studies, who made him
repeat the unfamiliar syllables of "Dedalus," he tells himself that it is
a better name than Dolan. He hears it shouted across the surf by some
friends in swimming, and the strangeness of the sound is for him a
prophecy: "Now, at the name of the fabulous artificer, he seemed to
hear the noise of dim waves and to see a winged form flying above
the waves and slowly climbing the air. What did it mean? Was it a
quaint device opening a page of some medieval book of prophecies
and symbols, a hawklike man flying sunward above the sea, a prophecy
of the end he had been born to serve and had been following through
the mists of childhood and boyhood, a symbol of the artist forging
anew in his workshop out of the sluggish matter of the earth a new
soaring impalpable imperishable being?"

The *Portrait of the Artist,* as we have it, is the result of an extended
process of revision and refinement. The original version—if an *Ur-
Portrait* can be remotely discerned—must have been securely founded

upon the bedrock of naturalistic narrative. It must have been a human document, virtually a diary, to which Joyce confided his notions and reactions not very long after they occurred. In turning from a reproductive to a selective method, he has foreshortened his work. A fragmentary manuscript, now in the Harvard College Library, touches only the period covered by the last chapter of the printed book, and yet it is nearly as long as the book itself. What is obliquely implied in the final version is explicitly stated in this early draft. The economic situation, for example, as the Dedalus household declines from the genteel to the shabby, is attested by a series of moving vans. In the book there is just one such episode, when Stephen arrives home to hear from his brothers and sisters that the family is looking for another house. Even then the news is not put in plain English, but in evasive pig-Latin. And the book leaves us with only the vaguest impression of the brothers and sisters; Stephen himself is not sure how many there are.

With revision, the other characters seem to have retreated into the background. Stephen's mother, because of the tension between her love and his disbelief, should be the most poignant figure in the book, just as her memory is the most unforgettable thing in *Ulysses*. But the actual conflict is not dramatized; it is coldly analyzed by Stephen in the course of one of his interminable walks and talks—this time with the serious-minded Cranly. In the manuscript it gives rise to a powerful scene, on the death of Stephen's sister, when his mother's orthodox piety is humbled before the mysteries of the body. The heroine of the book has been refined out of existence; she survives only in veiled allusions and the initials E—— C——. Emma Clery, in the manuscript, is an enthusiastic young lady with whom Stephen attends a Gaelic class. Their prolonged and pallid romance comes to an unexpected climax when he sees her mackintosh flashing across the green, and abruptly leaves his lesson to confront her with the proposal that they spend the night together and say farewell in the morning. Her reaction explains the interview so cryptically reported in the book, when Stephen turns on the "spiritual-heroic refrigerating apparatus, invented and patented in all countries by Dante Alighieri."

The esthetic theory plays a more active part in the earlier version. Instead of being dogmatically expounded to Lynch, it is sounded in the debating society, where it occasions a bitter argument. As Joyce rewrote his book he seems to have transferred the scene of action from the social to the psychological sphere. As he recollected his "conflicts with orthodoxy" in the comparative tranquility of exile, he came to the conclusion that the actual struggles had taken place within the mind of Stephen. Discussions gave way to meditations, and scenes were replaced by *tableaux*. Evasion and indirection were ingrained in Joyce's narrative technique. The final effect is that which Shakespearean actors achieve by cutting out all the scenes in Hamlet where the hero does not appear. The continuity of dynastic feuds and international issues is obscured by the morbid atmosphere of introspection. Drama has retired before soliloquy.

The Stephen we finally meet is more sharply differentiated from his environment than the figure Joyce set out to describe. How can he be a poet—the other boys have asked him—and not wear long hair? The richness of his inner experience is continually played off against the grim reality of his external surroundings. He is trying "to build a breakwater of order and elegance against the sordid tide of life without him." He is marked by the aureole of the romantic hero, like Thomas Mann's outsiders, pressing their noses against the window panes of a bourgeois society from which they feel excluded. "To merge his life in the common tide of other lives was harder for him than any fasting or prayer, and it was his constant failure to do this to his own satisfaction which caused in his soul at last a sensation of spiritual dryness together with a growth of doubts and scruples." At school he takes an equivocal position, "a free boy, a leader afraid of his own authority, proud and sensitive and suspicious, battling against the squalor of his life and against the riot of his mind. At home he feels "his own futile isolation." He feels that he is securely of the same blood as his mother and brother and sister, but stands to them "rather in the mystical kinship of fosterage, foster child and foster brother."

Joyce's prose is the register of this intellectual and emotional cleavage. It preserves the contrast between his rather lush verse and his rather dry criticism, between the pathetic children and the ironic politicians of *Dubliners*. All his sensibility is reserved for himself; his attitude toward others is consistently caustic. The claims to objectivity of a subjective novel, however, must be based on its rendering of intimate experience. If Joyce's treatment of Stephen is true to himself, we have no right to interpose any other criteria. Mr. Eliot has made the plausible suggestion that Joyce's two masters in prose were Newman and Pater. Their alternating influence would account for the oscillations of style in the *Portrait of the Artist*. The sustaining tone, which it adopts toward the outside world, is that of precise and mordant description. Interpolated, at strategic points in Stephen's development, are a number of purple passages that have faded considerably.

Joyce's own contribution to English prose is to provide a more fluid medium for refracting sensations and impressions through the author's mind—to facilitate the transition from photographic realism to esthetic impressionism. In the introductory pages of the *Portrait of the Artist*, the reader is faced with nothing less than the primary impact of life itself, a presentational continuum of the tastes and smells and sights and sounds of earliest infancy. Emotion is integrated, from first to last, by words. Feelings, as they filter through Stephen's sensory apparatus, become associated with phrases. His conditioned reflexes are literary. In one of the later dialogues of the book, he is comparing his theory to a trimmed lamp. The dean of studies, taking up the metaphor, mentions the lamp of Epictetus, and Stephen's reply is a further allusion to the stoic doctrine that the soul is like a bucketful of water. In his mind this far-fetched chain of literary associations becomes attached to the sense impressions of the moment: "A smell of molten tallow came up from the dean's candle butts and fused itself in Stephen's consciousness with the jingle of the words, bucket and lamp and lamp and bucket."

This is the state of mind that confers upon language a magical potency. It exalts the habit of verbal association into a principle for the arrangement of experience. You gain power over a thing by naming it; you become master of a situation by putting it into words. It is psychological need, and not hyperfastidious taste, that goads the writer on to search for the *mot juste*, to loot the thesaurus. Stephen, in the more explicit manuscript, finds a treasure-house in Skeat's *Etymological Dictionary*. The crucial moment of the book, which leads to the revelation of his name and calling, is a moment he tries to make his own by drawing forth a phrase of his treasure:

—A day of dappled seaborne clouds.—
    The phrase and the day and the scene harmonised in a chord. Words. Was it their colours? He allowed them to glow and fade, hue after hue: sunrise gold, the russet and green of apple orchards, azure of waves, the greyfringed fleece of clouds. No, it was not their colours: it was the poise and balance of the period itself. Did he then love the rhythmic rise and fall of words better than their associations of legend and colour? Or was it that, being as weak of sight as he was shy of mind, he drew less pleasure from the reflection of the glowing sensible world through the prism of a language manycoloured and richly storied than from the contemplation of an inner world of individual emotions mirrored perfectly in a lucid supple periodic prose.

The strength and weakness of his style, by Joyce's own diagnosis, are those of his mind and body. A few pages later he offers a cogent illustration, when Stephen dips self-consciously into his word-hoard for suitable epithets to describe a girl who is wading along the beach. We are given a paragraph of word-painting which is not easy to visualize. "Her bosom was as a bird's, soft and slight, slight and soft as the breast of some dark-plumaged dove," it concludes. "But her long fair hair was girlish: and girlish, and touched with the wonder of mortal beauty, her face." This is incantation, and not description. Joyce is thinking in rhythms rather than metaphors. Specification of the bird appeals to the sense of touch rather than to the sense of sight. What is said about the hair and face is intended to produce an effect without presenting a picture. The most striking effects in Joyce's imagery are those of coldness, whiteness, and dampness, like the bodies of the bathers who shout Stephen's name.

The most vital element in Joyce's writing, in the *Portrait of the Artist* as in *Dubliners*, is his use of conversation. As a reporter of Irish life, for all his reservations, Joyce is a faithful and appreciative listener. It is a tribute to Stephen's ear that, in spite of the antagonism between father and son, Simon Dedalus is such a ripe and congenial character. Like Sean O'Casey's *Paycock*, with all his amiable failings, he is Ireland itself. Though he takes pride in showing Cork to Stephen, and in showing off his son to his own native city, he is really the embodiment of Dublin: "A medical student, an oarsman, a tenor, an amateur actor, a shouting politician, a small landlord, a small investor, a drinker, a good fellow, a storyteller, somebody's secretary, something in a distillery, a tax-gatherer, a bankrupt and at present a praiser of his own past." The improvident worldliness of John Stanislaus Joyce had made him, in the unforgiving eyes of his son, a foster-parent. So young Charles Dickens, hastening from the blacking-factory to the Marshalsea, came to look upon his father as a horrible example of good-fellowship, a Mr. Micawber.

This disorder, "the misrule and confusion of his father's house," comes to stand in Stephen's mind for the plight of Ireland. Like Synge's *Playboy*, he must go through the motions of parricide to make good his revolt. Religion and politics, to his adult perception, are among the intimations of early childhood: harsh words and bitter arguments that spoil the taste of the Christmas turkey. Again, as in "Ivy Day in the Committee Room," or in Lennox Robinson's *Lost Leader* on the stage, it is the ghost of Parnell that turns conversation into

drama. "Dante," the devout Mrs. Riordan, is true to the Catholic
Church in denouncing the disgraced nationalist leader. Mr. Casey,
the guest of honor, is of the anti-clerical faction. Mr. Dedalus is by
no means a neutral, and some of his mellowist profanity is enlisted in
the cause of his dead hero. Mrs. Dedalus softly rebukes him:

—Really, Simon, you should not speak that way before Stephen. It's
not right.
—O, he'll remember all this when he grows up, said Dante hotly—the
language he heard against God and religion and priests in his own home.
—Let him remember too, cried Mr Casey to her from across the table,
the language with which the priests and the priests' pawns broke Parnell's heart and hounded him into his grave. Let him remember that too
when he grows up.

The *Portrait of the Artist,* as Joyce's remembrance finally shaped
it, is a volume of three hundred pages, symmetrically constructed
around three undramatic climaxes, intimate crises of Stephen's youth.
The first hundred pages, in two chapters, trace the awakening of religious doubts and sexual instincts, leading up to Stephen's carnal sin
at the age of sixteen. The central portion, in two more chapters, continues the cycle of sin and repentance to the moment of Stephen's
private apocalypse. The external setting for the education of the artist
is, in the first chapter, Clongowes Wood College; in the second, third,
and fourth, Belvedere College, Dublin. The fifth and final chapter,
which is twice as long as the others, develops the theories and projects
of Stephen's student days in University College, and brings him to the
verge of exile. As the book advances, it becomes less sensitive to outside impressions, and more intent upon speculations of its own. Friends
figure mainly as interlocutors to draw Stephen out upon various
themes. Each epiphany—awakening of the body, literary vocation,
farewell to Ireland—leaves him lonelier than the last.

A trivial episode at Clongowes Wood seems fraught for Joyce with
a profoundly personal meaning. Young Stephen has been unable to get
his lessons, because his glasses were broken on the playing-field.
Father Dolan, the prefect of studies, is unwilling to accept this excuse,
and disciplines Stephen with the boys who have shirked their books.
Smarting with pain and a sense of palpable injustice, Stephen finally
carries his case to the rector, who shows a humane understanding of
the situation. Many years later Father Conmee, the rector, takes a
walk through a chapter of *Ulysses;* and Father Dolan—who was actually a Father Daly—pops up with his "pandybat" in Stephen's night-

mare. This schoolboy incident lays down a pattern for Joyce's later behavior. When he cabled Lloyd George, who had other things on his mind during the first World War, *re* a pair of trousers and *The Importance of Being Earnest*, he was behaving like an aggrieved schoolboy unjustly pandied.

The physical handicap, the public humiliation, the brooding sensibility, the sense of grievance, the contempt for convention, the desire for self-justification, and the appeal to higher authority—these are all elements of Joyce's attitude toward society and toward himself. He had begun his education by questioning the Jesuit discipline; he would finish by repudiating the Catholic faith. Having responded to the urgent prompting of his senses, he would be treated as a sinner; he would refer the ensuing conflict, over the head of religious authority, to the new light of his scientific and naturalistic studies; he would seek, in the end, to create his own authority by the light of his senses. In turning away from Ireland toward the world at large, he would appeal from the parochial Daly to the enlightened Conmee. That miserable day at Clongowes Wood, like that long evening at Combray when M. Swann's visit kept Marcel's mother downstairs, had unforeseen consequences.

Adolescence complicates the second chapter. Stephen is beginning to appreciate beauty, but as something illicit and mysterious, something apart from the common walks of life. Literature has begun to color his experience, and to stimulate his mind and his senses. His untimely enthusiasm for Lord Byron—"a heretic and immoral too"— provokes a beating at the hands of his classmates. Now in jest and again in earnest, he is forced to repeat the *confiteor*. One of his essays had been rewarded with the taunt of heresy from his English master, and he takes rueful consolation in the self-conscious part of the Byronic hero. He will not agree that Lord Tennyson is a poet, though he gives tacit consent to the assertion that Newman has the best prose style. But it is his other master, Pater, whose influence is felt at the climax of the chapter. Stephen's sexual initiation is presented in empurpled prose, as an esthetic ritual for which his literary heresies have been preparing him. In trying to find a cadence for his cry, he harks back to the lyricism of *Chamber Music* and the anguish of the small boy in *Dubliners*:

> He stretched out his arms in the street to hold fast the frail swooning form that eluded him and incited him: and the cry that he had strangled for so long in his throat issued from his lips. It broke from him like a wail of despair from a hell of sufferers and died in a wail of furious

entreaty, a cry for an iniquitous abandonment, a cry which was but the echo of an obscene scrawl which he had read on the oozing wall of a urinal.

The unromantic reader is prone to feel that a scrawl would have been more adequate to the occasion. The incidence of the word "swoon" is a humorless symptom of the Pateresque influence on Joyce's early writing. There is many "A swoon of shame" in *Chamber Music*, and "a slowly swooning soul" in the last paragraph of *Dubliners*. "His soul was swooning" at the end of the fourth chapter of the *Portrait of the Artist*, having been darkened by "the swoon of sin" at the end of the second chapter. Though the scene is clouded with decadent incense, it is clear that Stephen is still a child, and that the woman plays the part of a mother. Joyce's heroes are sons and lovers at the same time; his heroines are always maternal. It is like him to lavish his romantic sensibility on an encounter with a prostitute and to reserve his acrid satire for the domain of the church. In Stephen's mind a symbolic association between art and sex is established, and that precocious revelation helps him to decide his later conflict between art and religion.

Meanwhile, the third chapter is devoted to his remorse. It embodies at formidable length a sermon on hell, suffered by Stephen and his classmates during a retreat. The eloquent Jesuit preacher takes as his object-lesson the sin of Lucifer, pride of the intellect, his great refusal and his terrible fall. Stephen's repentant imagination is harrowed by the torments of the damned. This powerful discourse provides an ethical core for the book, as Father Mapple's sermon on Jonah does for *Moby-Dick*, or Ivan's legend of the Grand Inquisitor for *The Brothers Karamazov*. Joyce is orthodox enough to go on believing in hell, and—as Professor Curtius recognized—to set up his own *Inferno* in *Ulysses*. Like another tormented apostate, Christopher Marlowe, he lives in a world where there is still suffering, but no longer the prospect of salvation. Like Blake's Milton, he is a true poet, and of the devil's party. Stephen's ultimate text is the defiance of the fallen archangel: *"Non serviam!"*

Temporarily, there is confession and absolution. When Stephen sees the eggs and sausages laid out for the communion breakfast, life seems simple and beautiful after all. For a time his restlessness seems to be tranquilized by church and satisfied by school. Seeking to order his existence, he contemplates the possibilities of the Jesuit order itself: the Reverend Stephen Dedalus, S. J. After a conference with a member of that order, he is fascinated and terrified by the awful assumption of powers which ordination involves. In the fourth chapter the call comes unexpectedly—the call to another kind of priesthood. Stephen dedicates himself to art, and enters upon his peculiar novitiate. The church would have meant order, but it would also have meant a denial of the life of the senses. A walk along the strand brings him his real vocation —an outburst of profane joy at the bird-like beauty of a girl, a realization of the fabulous artificer whose name he bears, a consciousness of the power of words to confer an order and life of their own. Like the birds that circle between the sea and the sky, his soul soars in "an ecstasy of flight," in a metaphor of sexual fulfilment and artistic creation. "To live, to err, to fall, to triumph, to recreate life out of life!"

The fifth chapter is the discursive chronicle of Stephen's rebellion. He moves among his fellow-students, an aloof and pharasaic figure, unwilling to share their indignation at the first performance of the *Countess Cathleen,* or their confidence in a petition to ensure world peace. His own struggle comes when his mother requests him to make his Easter duty and his diabolic pride of intellect asserts itself. Cranly, with the sharpest instruments of casuistry, tries to probe his stubborn refusal. It is less a question of faith than of observance. Stephen will not, to please his mother, do false homage to the symbols of authority, yet he is not quite unbeliever enough to take part in a sacrilegious communion. If he cannot accept the eucharist, he must be anathema; he respects the forms by refusing to observe them. "I will not serve that in which I no longer believe, whether it call itself my home, my fatherland or my church: and I will try to express myself in some mode of life or art as freely as I can and as wholly as I can, using for my defence the only arms I allow myself to use, silence, exile and cunning."

With this peremptory gesture, emancipating himself from his petty-bourgeois family, and from Ireland and Catholicism at the same time, Stephen stands ready to take his solitary way wherever the creative life engages him. In a previous argument with other friends, he abandoned the possibility of fighting these issues out at home. "Ireland is the old sow that eats her farrow." Davin, the nationalist, is willing to admit that Stephen's position is thoroughly Irish, all too typical of their gifted countrymen. "In your heart you are an Irishman but your pride is too powerful." Stephen is unwilling to compromise: "When the soul of a man is born in this country there are nets flung at it to hold it back from flight. You talk to me of nationality, language, religion. I shall try to fly by those nets." In exile, silence, and cunning he trusts to find substitutes for those three forms of subjection.

On his way to and from Belvedere College, his soul was "disquieted and cast down by the dull phenomenon of Dublin." With his realization of the end he was soon to serve, a new vista of "the slowflowing Liffey" became visible "across the timeless air." Nomadic clouds, dappled and seaborne, voyaging westward from Europe, suggested strange tongues and marshalled races. "He heard a confused music within him as of memories and names . . ." At University College, the time-worn texts of Ovid and Horace have filled him with awe for the past and contempt of the present: ". . . it wounded him to think that he would never be but a shy guest at the feast of the world's culture and that the monkish learning, in terms of which he was striving to forge out an esthetic philosophy, was held no higher by the age he lived in than the subtle and curious jargons of heraldry and falconry."

English is as strange a tongue as Latin. "His language, so familiar and so foreign, will always be for me an acquired speech," Stephen reflects, while conversing with the dean of studies, an English convert to Catholicism. "I have not made or accepted its word. My voice holds them at bay. My soul frets in the shadow of his language." The last pages are fragments from Stephen's notebook, duly recording his final interviews with teachers and friends, with his family and "her." Spring finds him setting down "vague words for a vague emotion," his farewell to Dublin, and to sounds of the city which will never stop echoing in his ears:

> *April 10.* Faintly, under the heavy night, through the silence of the city which has turned from dreams to dreamless sleep as a weary lover whom no caresses move, the sound of hoofs upon the road.

Toward the end, his purpose stiffens into a flourish of blank verse:

> *April 26.* Mother is putting my new secondhand clothes in order. She prays now, she says, that I may learn in my own life and away from home and friends what the heart is and what it feels. Amen. So be it. Welcome, O life! I go to encounter for the millionth time the reality of experience and to forge in the smithy of my soul the uncreated conscience of my race.

On the eve of departure he makes his final entry:

> *April 27.* Old father, old artificer, stand me now and ever in good stead.

The mythical and priestly figure of Dædalus is known for more than one work of genius—for a pair of wings, as well as a labyrinth. Stephen invokes his namesake under both aspects, the hawklike man and the fabulous artificer. Sometimes it is the cunning of the craftsman, the smithy of the artist, that is symbolized. At other times, soaring, falling, flying by the nets of Ireland, it is life itself. Yet these images of aspiration can also be associated with Icarus, the son of Dædalus. That ill-fated and rebellious spirit, who borrowed his father's wings and flew too near the sun, is an equally prophetic symbol: in a classical drama, *Icaro*, the young anti-fascist poet, Lauro de Bosis, adumbrated the heroism of his own death. The epigraph of Joyce's book is a quotation from Ovid—or rather a misquotation (the correct reference is to the *Metamorphoses*, VIII, 188). Here we are told that Dædalus abandoned his mind to obscure arts, *et ignotas animum dimittit in artes."* But Joyce does not tell us Ovid's reason:

> *. . . longumque perosus*
> *exsilium, tractusque soli natalis amore . . .*

The artificer was weary of his long exile and lured by the love of his natal soil, the Roman poet and exile goes on to say, and the rest of his myth rehearses the filial tragedy. The father cries out for the son; Joyce's confused recollection, in *Ulysses*, makes the son cry out for the father: *"Pater, ait."* On the brink of expatriation, poised for his trial flight, Stephen, in the *Portrait of the Artist*, is more nearly akin to the son. His natural father, Simon Dedalus, is left standing in the mystical kinship of fosterage. The Jesuit fathers, who supervised his education, no longer call him son. He has appealed from Father Dolan to Father Conmee; now he appeals from the church to another paternity. His wings take him from the fatherland. The labyrinth leads toward a father.

21

PHILIP TOYNBEE

◆━◆

A Study of *Ulysses*

THE EARLY pages of *Ulysses* read like an immediate sequel to *A Portrait of the Artist*. Not only is the life of Stephen Dedalus resumed, after a short interval in Paris, at the point where it was left off in the earlier book, but there is an absolute continuity of manner, mood, and method. The color is still a melancholic silver-gray. The high and uncertain note of expectation struck at the very end of *A Portrait of the Artist* ("Welcome, O Life! I go to encounter for the millionth time the reality of experience and to forge in the smithy of my soul the uncreated conscience of my race") has been muted by the death of Stephen's mother. It was a note struck only to be muted. The vocabulary has not changed, and there is no new complexity of method. The interval has filled Stephen's mind with new knowledge, has changed him from a provincial Irish boy into an educated European; but it has also, by the circumstances of his mother's death, given him a heavier burden of guilt than could all the adolescent vices of the earlier book. This is a guilt which has come to stay, not only throughout this book but, by strong implication, throughout the whole of Stephen's future life.

Early (page 3) the first note of remorse is struck. When Mulligan mocks Stephen for refusing his mother's last request, to kneel down and pray for her, an image of death is evoked. "Silently, in a dream she had come to him after her death, her wasted body within its loose

Reprinted from *James Joyce: Two Decades of Criticism*, ed. by Seon Givens, Vanguard Press, Inc. 1948, by permission of the author.

brown graveclothes giving off an odour of wax and rosewood, her breath, that had bent upon him mute, reproachful, a faint odour of wetted ashes." Five pages later this sentence is repeated with a slight variation. Seventeen pages later again, when Stephen is reflecting that even the deplorable, the scraggy and bespectacled boy had once a mother who loved him, another faint echo of the image returns. "She was no more: the trembling skeleton of a twig burnt in the fire, an odour of rosewood and wetted ashes." In the third section of the book the echo dies away: "Wombed in sin-darkness I was, too, made not begotten. By them, the man with my voice and my eyes and a ghost-woman with ashes on her breath." But the image has not simply appeared and reappeared, to be forgotten. It is not Joyce's way to give even so delicate an emphasis as this without a profound purpose. Not only does the theme of Stephen's guilt broaden into one of the main currents which run through the book, but a smaller stream flows from this particular image to all the images of death evoked in Bloom by the funeral of Paddy Dignam. "Much better to seal up all the orifices. Yes, also. With wax. The sphincter loose. Seal up all." The odor of wax has been particularized by Bloom, whose keen, earthy, reflective mind is forever particularizing concepts which in Stephen's mind remain vague, general, and poetic. Finally, a more leisurely study than this can be would discover in Stephen's original image the first use in the book of the word "mute" and would follow all the subtly changing tones of that important word in later passages.

On page 16, Mulligan, still mocking Stephen, tells Haines that "He proves by algebra that Hamlet's grandson is Shakespeare's grand-father and that he himself is the ghost of his own father." This, too, is re-echoed in the schoolroom when Stephen is solving an algebraic problem for the same backward and unprepossessing boy. "Sitting at his side Stephen solved out the problem. He proves by algebra that Shakespeare's ghost is Hamlet's grandfather." Fifty pages later Bloom's first soliloquy turns to "Mrs. Bandmann Palmer. Like to see her in that again. Hamlet she played last night. Male impersonator. Perhaps he was a woman. Why Ophelia committed suicide? Poor Papa!" and this leads on to Bloom's first reflection on his father's suicide. Fifty pages later again the lines

> Hamlet, I am thy father's spirit
> Doomed for a certain time to walk this earth

insinuate themselves again into the mind of Bloom. From that point onward the Hamlet theme echoes and re-echoes throughout the book, now violent, now subdued, now implicit, and now explicit. Indeed, but for the fact that Molly Bloom escapes the pattern, it would be possible to make a complete exegesis of the book in these terms. Hamlet is the secondary mythological framework of the book, supplying those complex father-mother-son relations which are lacking in the *Odyssey* but which are demanded by the roles of Bloom and Stephen.

By these two sets of theme and variation, the first a verbal image with more than verbal implications, the second a beam running the whole length of the building, much of Joyce's strength and originality is illustrated. He was both an architect and a musician. The image of Mrs. Dedalus' corpse is like some quiet subsidiary subject in the first movement of a symphony, reappearing later in remote keys, never forgotten but never insistent. The Hamlet theme is architectural rather than musical, for its reappearances are not so much evocative as constructional. Throughout *Ulysses* Joyce is engaged on these two more or less distinct artistic functions—the building of a house out of certain traditional blocks of granite, and the orchestral accompaniment within the rising walls. In this article I am concerned only with the early pages of this book, with the foundations of the walls, the exposition of the musical themes, but I would insist that this isolation of certain sections from the rest is an artificial necessity of criticism. Confronted with this book the critic can adopt one of two methods. Either he can select certain elements and pursue them from the beginning to the end—in which case he must neglect all the artistic coherence of the current's actual flow, neglect, that is to say, the flowing water itself for a cartographical description of the banks. Or else he must choose different points on the bank and immerse himself from each, thereby paying only an occasional and preoccupied attention to the river's destination. I have chosen the second method, fully conscious, I hope, of its alarming inadequacies, only because the first has been used far more often.

Ulysses is divided into three movements, of very different lengths, and each movement into a number of sections. Here I shall try to confine myself to the first movement and the first three sections of the second. I shall hope to consider the third section of the second movement in some detail.

The three sections of the first movement might be entitled "Stephen on the Shore Accompanied," "Stephen in School," and "Stephen on the Shore Alone." Setting aside the esoteric detail of symbol and Homeric analogy (since it would be impossible to discover anything here which has escaped the eagle and instructed eye of Mr. Stuart Gilbert), we find that the first section neatly provides the reader with nearly all the essentials of Stephen's general and particular predicament, the second lays a brief emphasis on the humiliation of his material conditions, and the third gives the first continuous insight into the poetic workings of his conscious mind. The third section also reviews and transforms much of the material provided by the first and second. In musical terms one might say that the first section provides the principal themes, the second develops several of the themes, and the third recapitulates them all in a new key. It is really astonishing how much information is provided by the twenty short pages of the first section, without the author once stepping intrusively forward to provide it in his own person. It reads like a complete and independent unit, an innocent description of the relations of three young men living in a Martello tower on the Dublin coast. In fact, it is a masterpiece of introductory skill, and the apparent "innocence" is a tour de force. Joyce's problem, as I see it, was to begin quietly and with apparent simplicity, to begin also with an air of freedom and discursiveness, yet to pack into those twenty pages not only all the essential information about Stephen's present condition but also all the leitmotivs of his future saga. He achieves this with almost incredible skill. There is nothing indigestible about this first section; it reads smoothly and easily, yet at the end of it the trick has been done, the information delicately purveyed, the main themes memorably played.

By the time that we reach page 20 of *Ulysses* we know that Stephen is living in the tower with Haines and Mulligan, that he has literary ambitions, that he is poor and obliged to earn his living by teaching, that his mother has recently died, that he is a lapsed but not an emancipated member of the Roman Catholic Church, that he is possessed of a sparse but bitter humor. We also know that he is obsessed by guilt caused by his refusal to obey his mother's last request, that he is humiliated by his companions (consciously by the ribald and blasphemous Mulligan, quite unconsciously by the obtuse and pedantic Englishman); we know that he is half aware of his need of a father (Hamlet and the heresy of Sabellius). Finally, and with the most delicate subtlety, we are provided, through the words and the bearing of Haines, with a vivid picture of Ireland's political condition. Something more must be said about this. *Ulysses* satisfies all the principal requirements of the naturalists. It is a book set firmly in the context of a particular time and place, as socially and politically conscious as the most intransigent Marxist could wish. But the environment is not an armor-casing in which puppet characters are tightly constricted; it is not even a hard framework, but a theme running through the minds and actions of the characters from one end to the other, from Haines through Privates Carr and Compton to the young English naval officer whose virginity Molly stole at Gibraltar. The subjection of Ireland lies as deep in Stephen's mind, echoing and reinforcing his personal subjection, as the humiliation of the Jews lies in the mind of Bloom.

The thirteen pages of the second section show us Stephen suffering the two-faced humiliation imposed by his employment, first at the hands of the boys and then at the hands of the headmaster. In the weary questions which he puts to the boys on Pyrrhus and then Lycidas, in their inane or dishonest answers, it is not only Stephen who is mocked in his own person but history and poetry themselves, Stephen's most sacred shrines. Then comes humiliation at the hands of Mr. Deasy, at first a repetition of the financial humiliation he had already suffered at the hands of Mulligan, and then the outrage of being obliged to listen sycophantically to his Protestant and Unionist views (echoes of Haines) and to his preposterous letter to the Press on foot-and-mouth disease. In this letter, which Mr. Deasy forces Stephen to urge on the editors of his acquaintance, there appears the first passage of that rich parody which is later to swell into such monstrous and perhaps excessive proportions.

"May I trespass on your valuable space. That doctrine of *laissez-faire* which is so often in our history. Our cattle trade. European conflagration. Pardoned a classical allusion. Cassandra. By a woman who was no better than she should be. To come to the point at issue. 'I don't mince my words, do I?' Mr. Deasy asked as Stephen read on." Finally Mr. Deasy issues, by his conventional but spirited anti-Semitism, a sort of fortuitous warning against the particular manifestation of the father which Stephen will seek during the course of the day.

> Mr. Deasy halted, breathing hard and swallowing his breath. "I just wanted to say," he said. "Ireland, they say, has the honour of being the only country which never persecuted the Jews. Do you know that? No. And do you know why?"
>
> He frowned sternly on the bright sun.
>
> "Why, sir?" Stephen asked, beginning to smile.
>
> "Because she never let them in," Mr. Deasy said solemnly.
>
> A coughball of laughter leaped from his throat, dragging after it a rattling chain of phlegm. He turned back quickly, coughing, laughing, his lifted arms waving to the air.

"She never let them in," he cried again through his laughter as he stamped on gaitered feet over the gravel of the path. "That's why." On his wise shoulders through the chequerwork of leaves the sun flung spangles, dancing coins.

I have quoted these last lines of the second section less to illustrate the headmaster's anti-Semitism, which has been expressed much more forcibly before, than to give an example of Joyce's prose style in the early part of the book. How lively it is, how vivid and clear; above all, how flexible! Even if he had confined himself to this instrument alone, *Ulysses* would have been remarkable for the quality of its writing.

Yet with what freshness, with how sharp and profound a change in mood and key, does the opening of the third section follow on the passage I have quoted! "Ineluctible modality of the visible: at least that if no more, thought through my eyes. Signature of all things I am here to read, seaspawn and seawrack, the nearing tide, that rusty boot. Snot-green, blue-silver, rust: coloured signs. Limits of the diaphane." How magnificently Joyce rings the changes between the simplicity of his Anglo-Saxon words and the deliberate pomposity of the Latin phrases! "On his wise shoulders through the chequerwork of leaves the sun flung spangles, dancing coins. . . . Ineluctible modality of the visible." [1]

This last section of the first movement marks the first qualitative change in his method. The first two sections are narrative interspersed with interior comment. This section is a continuous interior monologue, interspersed with short passages of description. The first paragraph is entirely within the mind of Stephen: the second begins, "Stephen closed his eyes to hear his boots crush crackling wrack and shells." And then immediately continues: "You are walking through it howsomever. I am, a stride at a time. A very short space of time through very short times of space. . . ." A page and a half later comes another brief rise to the surface. Stephen has sunk a deep shaft into his own mind by this point and is preoccupied with the death of Arius. "Illstarred heresiarch. In a Greek water-closet he breathed his last: euthanasia. With beaded mitre and with crozier, stalled upon his throne, widower of a widowed see, with upstiffed omophorion, with clotted hinderparts. *Airs romped around him, nipping and eager airs.* They are coming, waves. The whitemaned seahorses, clamping, brightwind-bridled, the steeds of Mananaan." Joyce is not yet ready to plunge into unrelieved interior monologue. His own words enter from time to time, unobtrusive but informative, a guide to the changing external circumstances which are continually altering the direction of Stephen's thoughts. But henceforth the information which he will feel himself obliged to supply thus directly will dwindle away into nothing. It is simply not true to say that Joyce shows no consideration for his reader. That he probably shows too little I suggested in my first article, but at least his method advances with some caution, providing information at the beginning and utilizing the information later.

The fourteen pages of this third section are as tightly packed as the twenty pages of the first. Paris, the condition of Ireland, the sea, the Fathers of the Church, his mother and the demoralization of his family, poetry, history, and the mere mundane details of his day, these are some of the many themes which are subtly and beautifully woven together in Stephen's mind. The quiet voice of the narrator with its sea-shore descriptions does not intrude awkwardly on Stephen's reflections but rather paints a continuous and delicate background to their progression. By the end of the section not only has a great deal of new information been provided about Stephen, filling out the barer facts of the first two sections, but a new tone has been introduced, a mass of new and brighter colors have been laid on the canvas.

With the opening of the second movement and the first appearance of Bloom, Joyce is obliged to beat a stylistic retreat. Once again he must provide, as succinctly as he can, a great deal of new information —even more, indeed, than at the beginning of the book, for the reader is assumed to know something of Stephen from *A Portrait of the Artist:* he can know nothing whatever about Bloom. A minor but informative theme is played in the first paragraph: "Mr. Leopold Bloom ate with relish the inner organs of beasts and fowls. He liked thick giblet soup, nutty gizzards, a stuffed roast heart, liver slices fried with crust-crumbs, fried hencod's roes. Most of all he liked grilled mutton kidneys which gave to his palate a faint tang of faintly scented urine." Throughout the fifteen pages of the first section (Bloom at Home) and the sixteen pages of the second (Bloom in the Streets), the kidney makes its symbolic reappearances, but the whole first paragraph is really an analogy of the character of Bloom. Bloom is an imaginative man, but an earthy one who takes a sly, half shamefaced pleasure in seamy sides (faintly scented urine).

It is noteworthy that the narrator has stepped forward again, and at the beginning of the section he is prominent. Yet he does not do much more than introduce us to Bloom in the setting of his home at breakfast time. Almost at once the interior monologue begins, and it is Bloom himself who gives us all the important information about his general situation. But Bloom's interior monologue is a very different thing from Stephen's—not different only in degree, not different only because their two characters are different, but different in kind, different in purpose. Approximately one might say that Stephen reflects in poetry and Bloom in prose; that Stephen's monologue is meant to be something more than a mere literal account of his stream of consciousness, while Bloom's is severely realistic. Stephen's mind works in symbols which have a strict relevance to the whole purpose of the book; the early Bloom is a photographic collage on a largely symbolic canvas. Bloom's monologue is discursive, and many of the thoughts which pass through his mind are purely ephemeral; they have no relevance beyond the immediate and photographic. Of course, there are symbolic themes in Bloom's monologue—his romantic feeling for the East, the death of his son, the humiliation of his race, and many, many more. But these are set in a background of photographic irrelevancies.

"He walked southward along Westland Row. But the recipe is in the other trousers. O, and I forgot that latchkey, too. Bore this funeral affair. O well, poor fellow, it's not his fault. When was it I got it made up last? Wait. I changed a sovereign, I remember. First of the month it must have been or the second. O he can look it up in the prescriptions book." This very typical passage is worth analyzing. First, the narrator gives his flat necessary morsel of information. The second sentence is pure realism, having no significance beyond its present context. The third sentence is symbolic, echoing the theme of the key to the Martello tower in the first movement, anticipating the advertisement of The House of Keys which is to preoccupy Bloom at the newspaper office. The fourth sentence is informative, telling us for the first time that Bloom must attend a funeral that morning. The fifth sentence is also informative, telling us something about Bloom's reactions and character. The rest of the quotation is again discursive, photographic, and relevant only to its present context.

The problem is clear enough. Joyce has to provide information; he has to introduce new themes and echo old ones in a new key; he has to present the inner nature of Bloom and distinguish absolutely the reality behind Bloom from the reality behind Stephen. I think he succeeds magnificently in all these aims, but at a certain unavoidable cost. The trouble is that although the necessity of the realistic setting may be obvious, the setting itself is extremely unstimulating. Fortunately, it is fairly unobtrusive in this early part of the second movement, because these sections are packed with necessary information and memorable themes. Also one feels a certain relief in this descent to earth after the high poetic flights of Stephen. But I shall try to show . . . that the problem becomes acute at a much later stage in the book.

Yet Bloom is by no means incapable of poetry, even at this early stage, though it is a poetry which does not yet rise above the level of realistic speculation. "A dead sea in a dead land, grey and old. Old now. It bore the oldest, the first race. A bent hag crossed from Cassidy's clutching a naggin bottle by the neck. The oldest people. Wandered far away over all the earth, captivity to captivity, multiplying, dying, being born everywhere. It lay there now. Now it could bear no more. Dead: an old woman's: the grey sunken cunt of the world." It is at least arguable that this kind of language provides a sufficient contrast to the language of Stephen and gives a more concise, a more intense revelation of Bloom than the prosaic details of his anxiety about the chemist's prescription. At any rate much of Bloom's later language is as rich in symbol, as far from realism as Stephen's. He is not essentially the creature of prose, and I am inclined to think it a failure that he is confined to this medium for so much of the book.

But this is an anticipatory criticism, for Bloom's first two sections are wonderfully successful. The mingling of prose and poetry becomes more and more subtle until the opening of that astonishing funeral section, perhaps the most faultless piece of writing in the whole book. "Nathan's voice! His son's voice! I hear the voice of Nathan who left his father to die of grief and misery in my arms, who left the house of his father and left the God of his father.

"Every word is so deep, Leopold.

"Poor Papa! Poor man! I'm glad I didn't go into the room to look at his face. That day! O dear! O dear! Ffoo! Well, perhaps it was the best for him."

This passage is typical of Bloom's early soliloquy at its best. The Old Testament quotation serves a triple purpose at least. It reminds us of Bloom's orthodox Jewish background; it emphasizes his guilt toward his dead father and his abandoned faith, and it echoes in a more robust key the guilt of Stephen. The contrast of the everyday language which follows is extremely moving, a broken, personal application of Abraham's words, comparable to the parallelism of Biblical verse.

By the end of the second section of this movement Bloom, both man and symbol (for it is possible to distinguish them), has emerged with extreme clarity. As in the first movement, we have seen and studied the hero both at home and in private soliloquy. The elegiac third section shows him in the presence of death and of his fellows.

> Martin Cunningham, first, poked his silk-hatted head into the carriage and, entering deftly, seated himself. Mr. Power stepped in after him, curving his height with care.
> "Come on, Simon."
> "After you," Bloom said.
> Mr. Dedalus covered himself quickly and got in, saying:
> "Yes, yes."
> "Are we all here now?" Martin Cunningham asked. "Come along, Bloom."

These opening lines immediately present Bloom in his role of Outsider. Not only is he the last to enter the carriage, not only is he patronized by Martin Cunningham, but, in sharp distinction to Simon Dedalus, he is addressed by his surname. This is to be his relationship with his companions throughout the funeral, a relationship which is to be emphasized and fortified by the fact that he is a Jew among Gentiles. On the second page, "Mr. Bloom at gaze saw a lithe young man, clad in mourning, a wide hat. 'There's a friend of yours gone by, Dedalus,' he said. 'Who is that?' 'Your son and heir.' " This is the first time in the book that the paths of Stephen and Bloom cross. It receives no further emphasis, except in the snarling attack on Stephen launched by Mr. Dedalus, and in the fact that Bloom's thoughts are sent violently after the death of his own son, little Rudi. Death enters here and gradually takes full possession of Bloom's mind. One by one all the *trappings* of death appear to him, a prosaic but increasingly alarming spectacle, while a sort of bass accompaniment is played by his memories of Rudi and of his father's suicide.

The musical analogy is not inapt. Bloom's surface mind is like the eager quarrying nose of a terrier, eagerly sniffing out the paraphernalia of death down to the seamiest details of corruption and necrophily. But on a deeper level of his mind the same sad themes are being played, "My son died in childhood. My father killed himself." There is an extraordinarily clear differentiation, yet an extraordinarily subtle blending of Bloom, the terrier, the prosaic and inquisitive individual, and Bloom the symbol, Bloom the sonless father and the fatherless son.

The terrier begins cautiously, sniffing at the faded language of obituary notices. "Thanks to the Little Flower. Sadly missed. To the inexpressible grief of his. Aged 88 after a long and tedious illness." A galloping hearse with a tiny coffin on it turns his mind to Rudi. "A dwarf's face, mauve and wrinkled like little Rudi's was. Dwarf's body, weak as putty in a white-lined deal box." But immediately after this Mr. Power's tactless attack on suicides (mitigated by the patronizing kindness of Martin Cunningham) sends Bloom in pursuit of his father. "The coroner's ears, big and hairy. Boots giving evidence. Thought he was asleep at first. Then saw little yellow streaks on his face. Had slipped down to the foot of the bed. Verdict: overdose. Death by misadventure. The letter. For my son Leopold.

No more pain. Wake no more. Nobody owns."

But soon Bloom, the terrier, is sniffing at the odors of decomposition, and the passage follows which I have already quoted. "Then the insides decompose quickly. Much better to close up all the orifices. Yes, also. The sphincter loose. Seal up all." Murder preoccupies him next: "Her clothing consisted of. How she met her death. Recent outrage. The weapon used. Murderer is still at large. Clues. A shoelace. The body to be exhumed. Murder will out." A little later his thoughts lead Bloom to a sort of angry and eloquent despair: "Seat of the affections. Broken heart. A pump, after all, pumping thousands of gallons of blood every day. One fine day it gets bunged up and there you are. Lots of them lying around here: lungs, hearts, livers. Old rusty pumps: damn the thing else. The resurrection and the life. Once you are dead you are dead." But two pages after this his nose has routed out the richer and more satisfying odors of necrophily: "Still they'd kiss all right if properly keyed up. Whores in Turkish graveyards. Learn anything if taken young. You might pick up a young widow there." But at the end it is Bloom's father who provides the last death image of the section, an image which faintly echoes Stephen's Hamlet theme and anticipates the Hamlet quotation which will occur to Bloom's mind thirty pages later. "Last time I was here was Mrs. Sinico's funeral. Poor papa, too . . . I will appear to you after death. My ghost will haunt you after death. You will see my ghost after death."

Although the principal themes of this section are death in general and the particular deaths of Bloom's son and father, the other general themes of the book are running through it. No more than any other section of the book is it a separable anthology passage, and if I isolate it here that is only by the artificial necessities of criticism. I have already shown that the loneliness of Bloom, both as an individual and as a Jew, is an important element in the section, and it is not the only one. Yet the whole passage can also be described as a dirge, for death usurps more and more of Bloom's mind as the climax approaches. It would therefore be reasonable to ask what it is that Joyce has to say about death. Unfortunately, the more austere, the more "pure," a creative writer is, the harder is it to answer this kind of question. In a very real sense what Joyce has to say about death is said in this section and cannot be said in any other way. If he had some theory or message to convey we should be able to paraphrase it. But in fact there is not one of Bloom's discursive reflections which announces the faith of the writer himself. "Once you are dead, you are dead" is Bloom's statement, not Joyce's, and it is not even the final or uncontradicted opinion of Bloom. A few pages later, for example, he is so possessed by the present reality of his father that he cannot reject the possibility of ghosts. In fact, the very nearest one can come to any general statement of Joyce's attitude is that birth, sex, and death are so intermingled in Bloom's mind that we become strongly conscious of the common element in all three. But this is both vague and feeble. The final fact is that Joyce's statement is made *there* and cannot be made *here*. Since it is an almost intolerably powerful statement we can deduce that in this passage Joyce shows himself to be a pure artist whose purity is altogether free from the anemia which the word not unjustly suggests in some other contexts.

By the end of the funeral scene Joyce's exposition is over. We are now in possession of all the preliminary information that we need, and armed with it we are expected to embark on the long development which ends only with the beginning of Molly's soliloquy. It is at this point that Joyce's stylistic problem became really formidable.

No writer in the world has ever achieved even two distinct styles of equal excellence. It is not a possible achievement. Inevitably it must seem to a writer that certain kinds of words are better than other kinds, certain phrases more vivid than other phrases, certain rhythms more pleasing and evocative than others. He can, of course, ring the changes on words, phrases, and rhythms to suit the changing situations. His sentences can become more abrupt or languorous, his vocabulary more colloquial or more grandiloquent, but the passages which a critic selects as his best will all be in the same language at any given stage of the writer's development. We think of the crystal simplicity of Turgenev, the opulence of Pater, the gymnastic complexities of Henry James's style. Whatever prose writer we admire, when we consider him we think of one distinctive style. Many writers had other ways of writing which they used with dexterity at appropriate moments, but one predominant style stands out as their best. Consider that very conscious stylist Virginia Woolf. There are passages in her novels of extreme severity, of irony and bitterness, but it is not of these that we think when her name is mentioned. The secondary styles are not only rarer than the dominant ones; they are less successful.

In the early passages of *Ulysses* we have seen that there are already two distinct styles; there is the "high" language of Stephen, rich, supple, and poetical, and there is the "low" language of Bloom, earthy, colloquial, and disjointed. Now, admirable though the language of Bloom may be, it is admirable rather as a contrast than in its own right. Taking the styles out of their contexts (and of course it is just this which writers, and Joyce above all writers, reproach the critic for doing, yet which critics feel themselves obliged sometimes to do), out of their contexts there is no doubt that Stephen's style is superior. By this I do not simply mean that the language is more beautiful; I mean that it moves us at a greater variety of levels. Both the matter and the manner are Joyce extended to his utmost, using all the resources of his spirit. In Bloom's soliloquies, on the other hand, we are conscious of a brilliant tour de force; we are inevitably conscious of something almost patronizing in the author's choice of a suitable medium for an *inferior* being. Joyce has done everything in his power to avoid giving this impression, and he has come nearer to succeeding than any writer of any time could have done. But he could not quite succeed.

His recognition of this is shown by the tactic which he adopted in the main body of the book. He resolutely rejected the conception of a writer's function which demands that he be always aiming at his own highest possibility. He moved back from the page before him and aimed at a *total* impression in a way which no novelist had done before. Each page was to be, not a thing of individual excellence, but the most potent contribution to the whole. It goes without saying that this did not involve a careless or indifferent attitude to the single page; in some ways it demanded an even more ferocious concentration on the immediate detail. The older novelists, who had made a plan indeed, but compared to Joyce's a plan of great flexibility, could always digress by at least a hair's breadth. They could, without obvious disloyalty to their plan, embark suddenly on some little exquisite poem in prose, merely because they felt that a contrast was demanded to a long piece of cerebration. But Joyce's pages were to fit into one another and into the whole book like files into a cabinet. In many, many cases their excellence was to depend strictly on their context, and on nothing else. It was a magnificent decision, and by taking it Joyce raised the possible ambition of the novelist to new heights. In his hands the novel become as integrated, as *unarbitrary* as a poem. Valéry's old gibe would no longer apply. If the countess accepted a cup of tea in a novel by Joyce, it would not be merely to fill an empty moment; it would be for some very good and very explicit intellectual purpose.

Having achieved this distant view of his whole purpose, his task became almost painterly. He would apply to the different areas of his canvas a wide variety of preselected colors, none of which need have meaning in itself, but each of which would contribute to the total color pattern. The analogy demonstrates the extreme difficulty of the task. Percy Lubbock has admirably shown that the great disadvantage of the novel is the simple sad fact that time must elapse in reading it. A total and instantaneous impression cannot be made; pages are turned, the book is put down for a day or a month. By the time that the end is reached, even by the model reader who has read the whole at a single sitting, the beginning and middle are only a vague memory. To circumvent this difficulty (it cannot be overcome) the older novelists had tried to make each single moment as palatable as possible, to make each brief passage a self-sufficient artistic whole. In this way a total impression was hoped for, but, should it fail through the failing memories of the readers, at least a succession of impressions would have been made. With great pride and integrity Joyce rejected this palliative. When, for example, it is necessary to be dull, he deliberately bores us and at great length. If we are too bored to read what he has written for us to read, then it is so much the worse for us. We shall miss the total impression even more widely than if we had read but forgotten. In any case Joyce will not sugar our pill. It is not true, of course, that none of the independent passages in the middle and later pages of *Ulysses* have any independent merit. It would be a lamentable plan which jealously forbade any value to its components, and many of these later passages are masterpieces in their own right. But they remain subordinate masterpieces.

The stylistic problem was solved in this way. Different styles were apportioned to different passages, strictly on their relevance and not at all on their abstract merit. *No* style was bad unless it was unsuitable. No style which was unsuitable was good. Now it was not possible to invent a whole series of new styles; that task was beyond even Joyce's ingenuity. Nor did it seem necessary to do so. There already existed a limitless variety of English prose styles, each rich with poignant, repulsive, or affectionate associations. By making a selection from these it was possible for Joyce to do all that he wanted to do, and in making that selection he became the greatest parodist there has ever been.

Though credit is given to the parodies of the hospital scene, it is not generally recognized that half of the whole of *Ulysses* is written in a parodied language. Where Flaubert and Henry James tried to rid themselves of a narrator's personality, opinions, and sympathies, Joyce denied himself even the distinctive language of a single narrator. For this reason the critical method which I elected to follow in these articles becomes exceedingly difficult. How can I examine in detail a single sample from this variegated material without depriving it, by isolation, of all its meaning? And if I were to select one of those rare passages in which Joyce allows his own high poetic tone to be heard then I could, it is true, examine it on its isolated merits, but this would be to avoid confronting his most important stylistic innovaton.

My own conservative and perhaps cowardly feeling is that Joyce's whole theory was wrong. It was a brilliant theory, bravely executed, but he carried it to doctrinaire extremes which often made its practice intolerable. It is a depressing fact that no activity demands such constant and such humiliating compromise as the writer's. It is not enough to write for the *lecteur idéal*, that will-o'-the-wisp of all original writers which is seen, when approached, to be only the reflected image of the writer himself. Whatever high claims may be made for the ideal of clarity it is essentially a base and utilitarian quality of communication. Stylists have always claimed that it is important first to be clear to oneself, and this is so obviously true that it hardly needed to be said. But clarity to oneself is so far from being the same as clarity to others that the process of writing is often one of deliberately surrendering an attained precision simply for the sake of rendering oneself intelligible. From a pure and private height of clarity the writer must *debase* his words and method into intelligibility. This is the ugly professional secret.

So, although there is one sort of courage in Joyce's refusal to compromise, there is also cowardice in his fear of sullying his hands with the dirty work. For the pill *must* be sweetened; the individual passage must have a merit of its own which is not dependent merely on its context in the whole. Even in pictures, after all, the greatest painters achieved colors and details which had a virtue of their own. We cannot achieve the distant view which Joyce demands of us when we are plunged into the thick of his absorbing detail. The whole and the parts, the retrospective and the immediate view, remain distinct, and Joyce has not been able to cure us of the distinction. Fortunately, as I have said, his theory did not demand that each individual section should be without individual merit; it merely allowed that it might be. I discover that even my retrospective view of the book rejects those passages to which too free a permission was given to have merit only as components. In fact, not only do they fail as we read them, for which Joyce was prepared, but, having failed then, they fail also to make their contribution to the whole.

Discretion? Compromise? These words have an ugly ring in any criticism of the arts. But in his method every great writer has been influenced by them, just as no great writer has allowed his matter to be touched by either. When Joyce's fitting of style to matter is discreetly done, we can see how admirable and interesting an innovation his extreme form of this age-old ambition can be. The Nausicaa passage (pages 329 to 365) is a short one, divided into two parts by the narrations of Gerty MacDowell and Bloom. It opens in the appropriate language of Gerty: "The summer evening had begun to fold the world in its mysterious embrace. Far away in the west the sun was setting and the last glow of all too fleeting day lingered lovingly on sea and strand. . . ." And, leaving the initial high tone of the novelette it continues in novelette colloquialism: "Madcap Ciss with her golliwog curls. You had to laugh at her sometimes. For instance when she asked you would you have some more Chinese tea and jaspberry ram and when she drew the jugs too and men's faces on her nails with red ink make you split your sides or when she wanted to go where you know she said she wanted to run to the Miss White. That was just like Cissycums." One reads on with growing nausea and growing fascination. The effect is made with a force which no other method could have given. And the voice stops at the point of repletion. Had it continued for the whole of the section, the nausea and fascination would have turned sour, and the effect would have been destroyed. Instead of this we are returned, to our overwhelming relief, to the familiar racy language of Bloom. "Tight boots? No. She's Lame! O!

"Mr. Bloom watched her as she limped away. Poor girl, That's why she's left on the shelf and the others did a sprint. Thought something was wrong by the cut of her jib. Jilted beauty. A defect is ten times worse in a woman. But makes them polite. Glad I didn't know it when she was on show. Hot little devil all the same. Wouldn't mind. . . ." Nor does this familiar voice weary us by continuing too long. The section ends with the sound of the cuckoo clock from the priest's house, marking the moment when Bloom is being cuckolded by Blazes

Boylan. No device could have recalled us more vividly to the chronological architecture of the book. The whole section seems to fall suddenly into its proper place in the total scheme. The individual impression made by the skill and vividness of the writing is fortified, is given
another dimension, by the skill and vividness with which the part is
related to the whole.

This section has always seemed to me to be the most perfect justification for the later method of *Ulysses*. It proves that the method can
be used and, when used discreetly, can be more effective than the
method of any earlier novelist.

In the hospital scene which follows we are *conscious* of the mechanism in quite a different way. It is as unnatural as the Nausicaa section
is bewilderingly natural. For one thing, Joyce has now rid himself of
any single narrator, of any narrator at all unless it be the embodied
spirits of Malory, Addison, Carlyle, and the other dead prose-writers
whom he parodies. Everything has become deliberately artificial, deliberately literary, and, in spite of the fact that there is not one word in
the authentic voice either of Joyce himself or of any *Ulysses* character,
we are conscious of the writer's personality as in no other section of
the book. I cannot believe that this was Joyce's intention. On the contrary, it is clear that he hoped, by his self-effacing use of the language
of others, to conceal himself entirely. He fails to do this for the most
obvious of reasons. We are never for a moment lulled into believing
that we are really reading the words or Malory or Carlyle, word-perfect
though each one of the parodies is. We gasp at the skill with which it
is done, and we are never unaware of the brilliant man who is doing
it. When we discover the *reason* for the use of parody here (and I did
not do so myself until I read Mr. Gilbert's book), we are still less surprised that the section failed to make the impression which Joyce
intended. The embryo would appear to be the symbol of the scene,
and we are therefore presented with the development of the English
written language from embryo to maturity. It is nearly incredible that
the writer who painted Bloom and Gerty on the shore with such marvelous assurance should have tumbled so quickly into such a bathetic
pit of false analogy and doctrinaire blindness. Nothing could be
cleverer; nothing could be more unsuitable or more wrongheaded. It
is precisely as if a painter, working hitherto by the authority of his
eye, were suddenly to destroy his growing picture by the application
of a color which he had selected purely by some a priori theory of
chromatics. The logical, almost scholastic, mind of Joyce seems to

have been suddenly left to fend for itself, abandoned by the controlling intuition of the artist, by that controlling artistic *discretion* whose vital function it is to forbid excess to any element of the work.

The remaining three hundred and thirty pages of *Ulysses* are divided into four long sections, to none of which excess has been effectively forbidden. Edmund Wilson has made a sharp distinction between the nighttown section and Molly's soliloquy on the one hand, the coffee-stall and question-and-answer sections on the other. The first two he finds "among the best things in the book," while he condemns the others as "artistically absolutely indefensible." Of Molly's soliloquy he even writes that it seems to him to be "among the supreme expressions in literature of the creative powers of humanity." Yet my own strong feeling is that the only logical distinction which can be made is between the nighttown scene and the other three sections. In other words, I find it hard to find any logical justification for praising Molly's soliloquy and condemning the two sections which precede it. Of the nighttown section, that strange ballet which marks the climax of the book, the coming together of Bloom and Stephen, the recognition of their roles in the crammed and multicolored world of their common unconscious mind, I shall write very little. I find it by far the most difficult part of the book, and the meaning of many of the apparitions is still altogether obscure to me. The central episodes, Bloom's catharsis at the hands of Bella, Stephen's at the hands of Privates Carr and Compton, are difficult neither to understand nor to appreciate. They are the necessary purgations which each must suffer in order to understand and fulfill his role. It is equally easy to see that in this section Joyce is restating all the principal, and, indeed, all the minor, themes of the book in the language of a new dimension. The day's memories of Bloom and Stephen begin to overlap, so that Haynes and Mother Grogan, for example, appear without any incongruity in the mind of Bloom, although they belong only to the past of Stephen. But, spurred to condemn perhaps only through failure to understand, I cannot help feeling that the section is far too tightly packed. Joyce seems to have lost his capacity to leave well alone. One imagines him inserting and reinserting new episodes and apparitions at each revision. Does it, for example, really add to our understanding or to the strength of our impression when Stephen's mother makes her exceedingly melodramatic appearance? ("Stephen's mother, emaciated, rises stark through the floor in leper grey with a wreath of faded orange blossoms and a torn bridal veil, her face worn and noseless, green with grave mould.

Her hair is scant and lank. She fixes her blue-circled hollow eyesockets on Stephen and opens her toothless mouth uttering a silent word. . . .") In the context—a succession of apparitions, each more vivid than the last—this ghastly image fails to impress us. Though clearly more important than most of the other apparitions, she does not stand out from them. She is simply another horror, appearing at a point where we have grown accustomed to horrors. In fact, everything in this section is lit by the same garish and distorting light; no distinction of tone or color is made between the different events, and they therefore fail to make the impression which each might have made in a more moderate setting.

I think that little distinction can be made among the three last sections, because in all of them Joyce is putting the same theory into practice with equal ferocity. My own feeling is that the greatest tour de force (and it is largely in these terms that we are now forced to criticize) are the fifty anticlimactic pages devoted to the coffee-stall. "His (Stephen's) mind was not exactly what you would call wandering but a bit unsteady and on his expressed desire for some beverage to drink Mr. Bloom in view of the hour it was and there being no pumps of Vartry water available for their ablutions, let alone drinking purposes, hit upon an expedient by suggesting, off the reel, the propriety of the cabman's shelter, as it was called, hardly a stone's throw away near Butt Bridge. . . ." This language of the provincial gossip column is unflaggingly maintained throughout the whole section. It shows all the ingenuity and endurance which have been exhibited to more stimulating purpose in many earlier passages of *Ulysses*. Does it succeed? It succeeds in providing a flat and savorless contrast to the brilliance of the nighttown section. It succeeds in giving us a strong sense of exhausted minds and spirits. It succeeds also in providing the kind of relief which is clearly demanded now that the search is over, now that Stephen and Bloom are at last united. But at what a high, at what an uneconomic, price, this success is achieved! At this point in the book Joyce seems to have fallen into a chronological error of astonishing simplicity. He seems to have retreated into the strictest unity of time. We are to spend exactly that period of time in the reading which is supposed to elapse in the period of which we read. There was no attempt to impose this burden on us in the earlier parts of the book, and it is most unwelcome here. Had he described the moments spent at the cabman's shelter with the economy and compression of the opening in the Martello tower I am convinced that he could have achieved all his effects in fifteen pages instead of fifty. The theory demanded a rambling long-windedness, but a subtler practice could have achieved enough even of that in less than a third of the pages Joyce has imposed on us. The oldest and least impeachable of critical axioms demands that if the same impression can be made in more or in fewer words it is better to make it in fewer. Even long-windedness need not be long-winded, and this will seem paradoxical only to those who have never understood the nature of artistic transmutation.

I shall say nothing of the seventy-page question-and-answer section which follows, because it has become, and not unjustly, the *point de mire* of all hostile critics. It is more dispiriting to have to admit to a very qualified admiration for the soliloquy with which the book ends. For not only has this section been held to mark the highest culmination of Joyce's method in *Ulysses;* clearly it foreshadows the further development of his method in *Finnegans Wake.*

Molly Bloom's soliloquy can be judged in at least three different ways. It can be considered simply as the closing section of Joyce's symphony, as the final chords which have meaning only in relation to what has gone before. It can be considered as a literary unit on its own; and it can be considered as a photographic attempt to reproduce a particular stream of consciousness. Finally, of course, it must be considered in the common light of all these three judgments. The first judgment is by far the easiest to make. Up to this point in the book I believe that Joyce's *architectural* sense has been impeccable. Whatever faults one may find with his detailed execution, the scheme is still magnificent. Never was a novel constructed with so visionary a quality of shape, of development, of balance and counterbalance. Nor do I believe that this sense deserted him at the end. The idea of closing this epic of male peregrination and search in the deep female current of Molly's mind is surely an idea of genius. After the angularity of Stephen and Bloom, their talk, their labored actions, their cogitations, whether earthy or ethereal, we are to sink here into the contrast which was always implicit, whether we had known it or not. Within the limits of the judgment we are making we need not decide whether this *is* the female mind or not; it is, in any case, the *anima,* the female image in the mind of the male, sensual, intuitive, submarine. And as a purely technical device it is equally happy. Woven into Molly's memories and anticipations, all the complex strands of the book are smoothed out; they do not cease abruptly on the last page as in nearly all other novels, but seem to flow onward, to be literally interminable.

Is it possible, after paying such high praise to the purpose, to make strong reservations about the execution? In this book I believe that it is, for it is unique in the distinction it seems to make between the two. Here one cannot say simply that the passage is too long, for I am surprised to find that it extends only to forty pages. Yet I find that much of it is very dull, and that it is the dullness of superfluity. Edmund Wilson writes of the "long, unbroken rhythm of brogue, like the swell of some profound sea," and by these words admirably demonstrates what the language of this passage should have been. But not, I think, what it is. In the first place Molly's language is not brogue, if, as Mr. Wilson suggests, brogue is taken to mean a vocabulary as well as a tone of voice. The daughter of Major Tweedy reflects in the rather weary language of the English lower middle class. Then the impressive word "unbroken" merely means unpunctuated, and the impressive word "rhythm" can have only the most recherché application. "They're all so different Boylan talking about the shape of my foot he noticed at once even before he was introduced when I was in the DBC with Poldy laughing and trying to listen I was waggling my foot we both ordered 2 teas and plain bread and butter I saw him looking with his two old maids of sisters when I stood up and asked the girl where it was what do I care with it dropping out of me and that black closed breeches he made me buy takes you half an hour to let them down wetting all myself always with some brand new fad every other week. . . ." I have taken the quotation at random, for wherever one may dip into this stream one finds exactly the same rather muddy liquid.

It is hard to exaggerate the difficulty of Joyce's task. Edmund Wilson's words may suggest that he might have written this passage in the rich, poetical language of Synge, but it needs very little reflection to see how disastrous that would have been. Yet I cannot help feeling that he made his task more difficult still by offering himself an additional and a superfluous problem. At a much earlier stage in the book he seemed to have rid himself of the ambition, both pedestrian and unattainable, to give a photographic representation of the mind's arbitrary peregrinations. In this last section he seems to have returned with renewed zest to that once abandoned will-o'-the-wisp. It was a foolish naïveté in so clever a man, for no words can ever convey the half-wordless wanderings of the mind. And even if words could be found to do so, what would be achieved by finding them? Raw material for the psychologist, but nothing for the artist. Indeed, the attempts to make this literal representation thwarts the artist in his own difficult and delicate task, for art *always* involves stylization, selection, concentration; art can never be diffuse as life is diffuse. Joyce appears to have been so afraid of the worst extreme, that of falsifying the image of Molly Bloom by making her language "beautiful," that he rushed into the other extreme of attempting no transmutation of his material. God alone knows how it should have been done, but the critic may say not like this.

How could it all have been better done? That remains a question which I, at any rate, would never dare to answer. It may even be that some of the problems which Joyce set himself were by their nature insoluble. There was never a more ambitious book than this, or a braver one. And in the main, in that final perspective which was never out of the writer's mind, *Ulysses* remains a very great novel. The total, the architectural impression is overwhelming. Indeed, this book is almost unique in the retrospective satisfaction which it gives in spite of the frequent irritation and weariness which one has felt while reading it. The superfluities seem to fall away, and the vivid unforgettable passages (which constantly recur in the most unpromising surroundings) come together in a supreme pattern. Had every part been worthy of the tremendous whole, this would have been the greatest prose work ever written.

NOTE

1. A more pointed example of this device appears a few pages later: "Morose delectation Aquinas tunbelly calls this, frate porcospino. Unfallen Adam rode and not rutted. Call away let him: they quarrons dainty is. Language no whit worse than his. Monk-words, marybeads jabber on their girdles: roguewords, tough nuggets patter in their pockets." Here the Anglo-Saxon words make deliberate assault on the initial Latin phrase.

22

EDMUND   WILSON

The Dream of H. C. Earwicker

JAMES Joyce's *Ulysses* was an attempt to present directly the thoughts
and feelings of a group of Dubliners through the whole course of a
summer day. *Finnegans Wake* is a complementary attempt to render
the dream fantasies and the half-unconscious sensations experienced
by a single person in the course of a night's sleep.

This presents a more difficult problem to the reader as well as to
the writer. In *Ulysses*, the reader was allowed to perceive the real
objective world in which the Blooms and Dedalus lived, and their
situation and relationships in that world, so that its distortions or
liquefactions under the stress of special psychological states still usually remained intelligible. But in *Finnegans Wake* we are not supplied
with any objective data until the next to the last chapter, when the
hero—and then only rather dimly—wakes up for a short time toward
morning; and we are dealing with states of consciousness which,
though they sometimes have something in common with the drunken
imaginations of the Night Town scene in *Ulysses* or the free associations of Mrs. Bloom's insomniac reveries, are even more confused and
fluid than these; so that it becomes on a first reading the reader's
prime preoccupation to puzzle out who the dreamer is and what has
been happening to him. And since Joyce has spent seventeen years
elaborating and complicating this puzzle, it is hardly to be expected
that one reading will suffice to unravel it completely.

Reprinted from *The Wound and the Bow,* copyright 1940 by Edmund Wilson, Oxford University Press, 1947, by permission of the author.

Let me try to establish, however, some of the most important facts which provide the realistic foundation for this immense poem of sleep. The hero of *Finnegans Wake* is a man of Scandinavian blood, with what is apparently an adapted Scandinavian name: Humphrey Chimpden Earwicker, who keeps a pub called The Bristol in Dublin. He is somewhere between fifty and sixty, blond and ruddy, with a walrus mustache, very strong but of late years pretty fat. When embarrassed, he has a tendency to stutter. He has tried his hand at a number of occupations; has run for office and has gone through a bankruptcy. He is married to a woman named Ann, a former salesgirl, who is more or less illiterate and whose maiden name seems to have begun with Mac. They are both Protestants in a community of Catholics, he an Episcopalian and she a Presbyterian; and by reason both of his religion and of his queer-sounding foreign name, he feels himself, like Bloom in *Ulysses*, something of an alien among his neighbors. The Earwickers have three children—a girl named Isobel, who has evidently passed adolescence, and two younger boys, twins: Kevin and Jerry. There are also a maid-of-all-work called Kate and a man about the place called Tom.

It is a Saturday night in summer, after a disorderly evening in the pub. Somebody—probably Earwicker himself—has been prevailed upon to sing a song; later, when it was closing time, he had to put a man outside, who abused him and threw stones at the window. There has also been a thunderstorm. Earwicker has been drinking off and on all day and has perhaps gone to bed a little drunk. At any rate, his night is troubled. At first he dreams about the day before, with a bad conscience and a sense of humiliation: then, as the night darkens and he sinks more deeply into sleep, he has to labor through a nightmare oppression.

He and his wife are sleeping together; but he has no longer any interest in her as a woman. He is preoccupied now with his children. His wife is apparently much younger than he, was only a girl when he married her; so that it is easy for him to confuse his first feelings for her with something like an erotic emotion which is now being aroused by his daughter. And his affection for his favorite son is even acquiring homosexual associations. Little Kevin is relatively sedate: named after the ascetic St. Kevin, he may be destined for the Catholic priesthood. Jerry (Shem) is more volatile and has given evidences of taste for writing; and it is Jerry rather than Kevin (Shaun) with whom the father has tended to identify himself.

To tell the story in this way, however, is to present it the wrong way around. It depends for its dramatic effect on our not finding out till almost the end—pages 555–590, in which Earwicker partially wakes up—that the flights of erotic fantasy and the horrors of guilt of his dream have been inspired by his feelings for his children. The pub is on the edge of the Phoenix Park, between it and the River Liffey and not far from the suburb of Chapelizod, which is said to have been the birthplace of Iseult. At the very beginning of the dream, we find Earwicker figuring as Tristram; and through the whole night he is wooing Iseult; he carries her off, he marries her. The Freudian censor has intervened to change *Isobel* into *Iseult la Belle*—as well as to turn the ana (upper)-Liffey, which figures in the dream as a woman, into *Anna Livia Plurabelle*. The idea of incest between father and daughter is developed on page 115; the transition from Isobel to Iseult is indicated in the "Icy-la-Belle" of page 246; and the sister of the twins is designated by her family nickname "Izzy" on page 431. But, though the boys have been given their real names and planted pretty clearly—on pages 26–27—it is not until almost the end—on page 556—that a definite identification of Earwicker's daughter with Iseult is made. In the same way, it is not until the passage on pages 564–565 that we are led to connect with Earwicker's son the homosexual motif which has first broken into his dream with the ominous incident of the father's accosting a soldier in the park and subsequently being razzed by the police, and which works free toward morning—page 474—to the idea, not related to actuality, of "some chubby boy-bold love of an angel."

In the meantime, the incest taboo and the homosexuality taboo have together—as in the development of Greek tragedy out of the old myths of cannibalism and incest—given rise, during Earwicker's effortful night, to a whole mythology, a whole morality. He is Tristram stealing Iseult, yes; but—at the suggestion of an Adam's mantelpiece in the bedroom where he is sleeping—he is also Adam, who has forfeited by his sin the Paradise of the Phoenix Park; at the suggestion of a copy of Raphael's picture of Michael subduing Satan which hangs on the bedroom wall, he is an archangel wrestling with the Devil. And he has fallen not merely as Adam but also as Humpty Dumpty (he is fat and his first name is Humphrey); as the hero of the ballad of *Finnegans Wake*, who fell off a scaffold while building a house (but came to life again at the sound of the word "Whisky"); and as Napoleon (an obelisk dedicated to Wellington is a feature of the Phoenix Park, though there is apparently no Wellington Museum). Since the landmarks of the life of Swift still keep their prestige in Dublin, he is Swift, who loved Stella and Vanessa with the obstructed love of a father and whose mind was finally blotted by madness: Swift's cryptic name for Stella, "Ppt," punctuates the whole book.

And Earwicker is also making up in sleep for an habitual feeling of helplessness due to his belonging to a racial and religious minority. He is sometimes the first Danish conqueror of Ireland, who sailed up that very Liffey; sometimes Oliver Cromwell, that other hated heathen invader.

But it is Joyce's further aim to create, through Earwicker's mythopoeic dream, a set of symbols even more general and basic. He has had the idea of making Earwicker, resolved into his elemental components, include the whole of humanity. The river, with its feminine personality, Anna Livia Plurabelle, comes to represent the feminine principle itself. At one time or another all the women who figure in Earwicker's fantasy are merged into this stream of life which, always renewed, never pausing, flows through the world built by men. The daughter, still a little girl, is early identified with a cloud, which will come down to earth as rain and turn into the rapid young river; the Anna Livia Plurabelle chapter describes a lively woman's coming-of-age; in the end, the mature river, broader and slower now, will move toward her father, the sea. The corresponding masculine principle is symbolized by the Hill of Howth, which rises at the mouth of the Liffey; and the idea of the hill as a citadel and the idea of the city as a male construction associate themselves with this: the man is a hill that stands firm while the river runs away at his feet; he is a fortress, he is Dublin, he is all the cities of the world.

And if Earwicker is animated in sleep by the principles of both the sexes, he has also a double existence in the roles of both Youth and Old Age. Canalizing his youthful impulses in a vision of himself as his favorite son, he dreams himself endowed with a resilience to go out and try life again; exalted by a purity of idealism which has not yet been tainted by experience, and yet bubbling with roguish drolleries, blithely beloved by the girls. On the other hand, foreshadowing his own decline, he sees the vision of a chorus of old men, who, drivelingly reminiscent, at the same time gloat and scold at the thought of the vigorous young Tristram kissing Iseult on the other side of the bushes, and exclaim in admiration—an expansion of Earwicker's feelings at the sight of his own sleeping son—over the form of the sleeping Earwicker (Shaun—Jerry). The old men are named Matthew Gregory, Marcus Lyons, Luke Tarpey, and Johnny MacDougall; and they are identified variously with the four apostles, the Four Masters (early sages of Irish legend), the Four Waves of Irish mythology, the four courts of Dublin, and the four provinces of Ireland (Johnny MacDougall is evidently Ulster: he always follows at some distance behind the others). These fathers are always associated with a gray ass and sycamore trees, and have perhaps been suggested to Earwicker by four sycamore trees on the Liffey, among which a neighbor's donkey has been grazing. All of these major motifs are woven in and out from beginning to end of the book, and each at a given point receives a complete development: the woman-river in pages 196–216—the well-known Anna Livia Plurabelle chapter; the male city-fortress-hill in pages 532–554 (already published separately as *Haveth Childers Everywhere*); the Young Man in the chapters about Shaun, pages 403–473; and the Old Men, providing a contrast, just before, in pages 383–399.

There are also a stone and an elm on opposite sides of the Liffey, which represent the death principle and the life principle (Ygdrasil). The tree has several graciously rustling solos (a notable one at the end, beginning on page 619), and in the Anna Livia Plurabelle chapter she has a long conversation with the stone, which blends with the gossip of two old washerwomen drying clothes on the riverbank. This dialogue is only one of many dialogues which are really always the same disputation, and in which one of the parties, like the stone, is always hard-boiled, immobile, and prosaic, while the other is sensitive, alive, rather light-mindedly chattering or chirping. The tougher of the two parties in these interchanges is always browbeating or bullying the other. Sometimes they are Satan and Saint Michael; sometimes they are transmogrified antitheses derived from Aesop's fables: the Mookse and the Gripes (the Fox and the Grapes), the Ondt and the Gracehoper (the Ant and the Grasshopper); but all these dualisms are evidently connected with the diverse temperaments of Earwicker's twins (who sometimes appear as Cain and Abel) and represent the diverse elements in the character of Earwicker himself, as these struggle within his own consciousness, the aggressive side sometimes reflecting certain powers in the external world—the force of hostile opinion or the police —which he now fears, now feels he can stand up to. The various pairs, however, shift their balance and melt into one another so readily that it is impossible to give any account of them which will cover all the cases in the book.

Besides all this, just as Joyce in *Ulysses* laid the *Odyssey* under requisition to help provide a structure for his material—material which, once it had begun to gush from the rock of Joyce's sealed personality at the blow of the Aaron's rod of free association, threatened to rise and submerge the artist like the flood which the sorcerer's apprentice let loose by his bedeviled broom; so, in the face of an even more formidable danger, he has here brought in the historical theory of the eighteenth-century philosopher, Giambattista Vico, to help him to organize *Finnegans Wake*. It was Vico's idea that civilizations always pass through three definite phases: a phase when people imagine gods, a phase when they make up myths about heroes, and a phase when they see things in terms of real men. It will be noted that the figures mentioned above divide themselves among these three categories of beings. Vico further believed that history moved in cycles and that it was always repeating itself, which—to the frequent exasperation of the reader —*Finnegans Wake* is also made to do. And there is also a good deal more out of Vico, which you can find out about in *Our Exagmination* [1] but which seems even more idle and forced than the most forced and idle aspects of the Odysseyan parallel in *Ulysses*. The fact that there is a Vico Road in the Dublin suburb Dalkey—"The Vico Road goes round and round to meet where terms begin"—gives Joyce a peg in actuality on which to hang all this theory.

There is one important respect in which Joyce may seem to depart from Vico. Vico, so far as is known, did not believe in progress: his cycles did not spiral toward an earthly goal; his hope for salvation was in heaven. But the cycles of *Finnegans Wake* do result in a definite progression. As Earwicker lives through from darkness to light, he does slough off his feeling of guilt. By morning the Devil has been vanquished by Michael; Youth has bounded free of Age; the Phoenix of Vico and the Phoenix Park has risen from its ashes to new flight; Tristram has built a castle (Howth Castle) for his bride; and Iseult, once the object of an outlawed love, now married and growing older, turns naturally and comfortably at last into the lawful wife in the bed beside him, whom Earwicker is making an effort not to jab with his knees; the tumult and turbidity of Saturday night run clear in the peace of Sunday morning; the soul, which has been buried in sleep, is resurrected, refreshed, to life.

Yet if one looks at the book as a whole, one finds that the larger cycle does return upon itself. This will be seen when I discuss the last pages. In the meantime, let me merely point out that we do not find in *Finnegans Wake* any climax of exaltation comparable either to the scene where Stephen Dedalus realizes his artist's vocation or to Molly Bloom's great affirmative. The later book represents an aging phase in the constant human subject with which the series of Joyce's books has dealt. This subject—which must never be lost sight of, though in this case it is easy to do so—is the nexus of intimate relationships involved in a family situation. We find it first in the *Portrait of an Artist* in the attitude of Dedalus toward his family, and in the delicate but vital displacement in the relations of the young married couple who figure in the short story called "The Dead." In *Exiles*, another young married couple come back from abroad with a son, and a more serious displacement takes place when the wife meets an old lover. In *Ulysses*, the relations of man and wife, by this time almost middle-aged, have been affected by more serious readjustments, and they are related in a complex way to the relations of the Blooms to their children, of Dedalus to his parents, and of both the Blooms to Dedalus. Now, in *Finnegans Wake*, the husband and wife have reached an age at which, from the emotional point of view, they seem hardly important to one another, and at which the chief source of interest is the attitude of the father toward the children—"the child we all love to place our hope in," as Earwicker thinks in the last moments before the rising sun wakes him up. (We have already had intimations of this relationship in the adoptively paternal instincts of Bloom toward the spiritually parentless Dedalus; in Joyce's little lyric poems, poignant to the point of anguish, that deal with his own children; and in the poem called "Ecce Puer," in which the family cycle appears.)

Here this family situation has been explored more profoundly by Joyce than in any of his previous books. In sleep, the conventions and institutions with which we discipline and give shape to our lives are allowed partly to dissolve and evaporate, so as partly to set free the impulses of the common human plasm out of which human creatures are made; and then the sexual instincts of the man and the woman, the child's instinct and the parent's instinct, the masculine and feminine principles themselves, come into play in confusing ways, shadow forth disturbing relationships, which yet spring from the prime processes of life. *Finnegans Wake* carries even farther the kind of insight into such human relations which was already carried far in *Ulysses;* and it advances with an astounding stride the attempt to find the universally human in ordinary specialized experience which was implied in the earlier book by the Odysseyan parallel. Joyce will now try to build up inductively the whole of human history and myth from the impulses, conscious and dormant, the unrealized potentialities, of a single human being, who is to be a man even more obscure and even less well endowed, even less civilized and aspiring, than was Leopold Bloom in *Ulysses*.

Finnegans Wake, in conception as well as in execution, is one of the boldest books ever written.

II

In order to get anything out of *Finnegans Wake,* you must grasp a queer literary convention. It has been said by T. S. Eliot that Joyce is the greatest master of language in English since Milton. Eliot has also pointed out that Milton is mainly a writer for the *ear.* Now Joyce through a large part of his adult life has been almost as blind as Milton; and he has ended, just as Milton did, by dealing principally in auditory sensations. There is as little visualization in *Finnegans Wake* as in *Samson Agonistes.* Our first criticism, therefore, is likely to be that nothing is *seen* in Earwicker's dream. It is, after all, not uncommon in dreams to have the illusion of seeing people and places as clearly as when we are awake; and in the dream literature with which we are already familiar—*Alice in Wonderland, The Temptation of Saint Anthony*—the dreamers are visited by plain apparitions, not merely by invisible voices. But we must assume with *Finnegans Wake* that Earwicker's imagination, like Joyce's, is almost entirely auditory and verbal. We have been partly prepared by *Ulysses,* in which we listen to the thoughts of the characters but do not see them very distinctly.

But there is another and more serious difficulty to be got over. We are continually being distracted from identifying and following Earwicker, the humble proprietor of a public house, who is to encompass the whole microcosm of the dream, by the intrusion of all sorts of elements—foreign languages, literary allusions, historical information—which could not possibly have been in Earwicker's mind. The principle on which Joyce is operating may evidently be stated as follows. If the artist is to render directly all the feelings and fancies of a sleeper, primitive, inarticulate, infinitely imprecise as they are, he must create a literary medium of unexampled richness and freedom. Now it is also Joyce's purpose in *Finnegans Wake* to bring out in Earwicker's consciousness the processes of universal history: the languages, the cycles of society, the typical relationships of legend, are, he is trying to show us, all implicit in every human being. He has, as I have indicated, been careful to hook up his hero realistically with the main themes of his universal fantasia: the Bible stories, the Battle of Waterloo, Tristram and Iseult, and so forth. But since Earwicker's implications *are* shown to be universal, the author has the right to summon all the resources of his superior knowledge in order to supply a vehicle which will carry this experience of sleep. He has the same sort of justification for mak-

ing the beings in Earwicker's dream speak Russian in fighting the siege
of Sebastopol (which has got in by way of a picture hanging in Earwicker's house) as Thomas Hardy has, for example, to describe in his
own literary vocabulary a landscape seen by an ignorant person. If
it is objected that in *Finnegans Wake* the author is supposed to be not
describing, but presenting the hero's consciousness directly, Joyce
might reply that his procedure had precedent not only in poetry, but
also in pre-naturalistic fiction: even the characters of Dickens were
allowed to make speeches in blank verse, even the characters of Meredith were allowed to converse in apothegms. Why shouldn't H. C.
Earwicker be allowed to dream in a language which draws flexibility
and variety from the author's enormous reservoir of colloquial and literary speech, of technical jargons and foreign tongues?

Yet here is where the reader's trouble begins, because here, in spite
of the defense just suggested, a convention that seems indispensable
has been disconcertingly violated. What Joyce is trying to do is to
break out of the Flaubertian naturalism into something that moves
more at ease and that commands a wider horizon, something that is
not narrowly tied down to the data about a certain man living in a
certain year on a certain street of a certain city; and the reaction is
of course quite natural: it was inevitable that the symbol and the
myth, the traditional material of poetry, should have asserted themselves again against the formulas of scientific precision which had begun to prove so cramping. But here the act of escaping from them
shocks, just as it sometimes did in Proust. Proust argues in an impressive
way, in the final section of his novel, the case against nineteenth-
century naturalism; yet who has not been made uncomfortable at finding that Proust's personal manias have been allowed to affect the structure of his book: that a story which has been presented as happening
to real people should not maintain a consistent chronology, that it
should never be clear whether the narrator of the story is the same
person as the author of the book, and that the author, who ought to
know everything, should in some cases leave us in doubt as to the facts
about his hero? One had felt, in reading *Ulysses*, a touch of the same
uneasiness when the phantasmagoria imagined by Bloom in the drunken
Night Town scene was enriched by learned fancies which would seem
to be more appropriate to Dedalus. And now in *Finnegans Wake* the
balloon of this new kind of poetry pulls harder at its naturalistic anchor.
We are in the first place asked to believe that a man like H. C. Earwicker would seize every possible pretext provided by his house and
its location to include in a single night's dream a large number of his-

torical and legendary characters. And is it not pretty far-fetched to assume that Earwicker's awareness of the life of Swift or the Crimean War is really to be accurately conveyed in terms of the awareness of Joyce, who has acquired a special knowledge of these subjects? Also, what about the references to the literary life in Paris and to the book itself as Work in Progress, which take us right out of the mind of Earwicker and into the mind of Joyce?

There are not, to be sure, very many such winks and nudges as this, though the shadow of Joyce at his thankless task seems sometimes to fall between Earwicker and us. Joyce has evidently set himself limits as to how far he can go in this direction; and he may urge that, since Earwicker is universal man, he must contain the implications of Joyce's destiny as he does those of Swift's and Napoleon's, though he has never heard of him as he has of them, and that to give these implications a personal accent is only to sign his canvas. Yet, even granting all this and recognizing the difficulty of the task and accepting without reservation the method Joyce has chosen for his purpose, the result still seems unsatisfactory, the thing has not quite come out right. Instead of the myths' growing out of Earwicker, Earwicker seems swamped in the myths. His personality is certainly created: we get to know him and feel sympathy for him. But he is not so convincing as Bloom was: there has been too much literature poured into him. He has exfoliated into too many arabesques, become hypertrophied by too many elements. And not merely has he to carry this load of myths: he has also been all wound round by what seems Joyce's growing self-indulgence in an impulse to pure verbal play.

Here another kind of difficulty confronts us. There is actually a special kind of language which people speak in dreams and in which they sometimes even compose poetry. This language consists of words and sentences which, though they seem to be gibberish or nonsense from the rational point of view, betray by their telescopings of words, their combinations of incongruous ideas, the involuntary preoccupations of the sleeper. Lewis Carroll exploited this dream language in "Jabberwocky," and it has been studied by Freud and his followers, from whom Joyce seems to have got the idea of its literary possibilities. At any rate, *Finnegans Wake* is almost entirely written in it.

The idea was brilliant in itself, and Joyce has in many cases carried it out brilliantly. He has created a whole new poetry, a whole new humor and pathos, of sentences and words that go wrong. The special kind of equivocal and prismatic effects aimed at by the symbolist poets have here been achieved by a new method and on psychological principles which give them a new basis in humanity. But the trouble is, it seems to me, that Joyce has somewhat overdone it. His method of giving words multiple meanings allows him to go on indefinitely introducing new ideas; and he has spent no less than seventeen years embroidering *Finnegans Wake* in this way.

What has happened may be shown by the following examples. First, a relatively simple one from a passage about the Tree: "Amengst menlike trees walking or trees like angels weeping nobirdy aviar soar anywing to eagle it!" It is quite clear in the last seven words how an ornithological turn has been given to "nobody ever saw anything to equal it." Here is a more complex one: Earwicker, picturing himself in the chapter in which he partially wakes up, is made to designate his hair with the phrase "beer wig." This has as its basis *bar wig*, which has rushed into the breach as *beer wig* under the pressure of Earwicker's profession as a dispenser of drinks in his pub, of the fact that his hair is yellow, and of his tendency to imagine that his queer last name is being caricatured by his neighbors as "Earwigger"—a tendency which has led to his dream being impishly haunted by earwigs. There are thus four different ideas compressed in these two words. But let us examine —with the aid of the hints provided by the *Exagmination*—an even more complicated passage. Here is Earwicker-Joyce's depiction of the madness and eclipse of Swift: "Unslow, malswift, pro mean, proh noblesse, Atrahore, melancolores, nears; whose glauque eyes glitt bedimmed to imm; whose fingrings creep o'er skull: till quench., asterr mist calls estarr and graw, honath Jon raves homes glowcoma." This passage, besides the more or less obvious ones, contains apparently the following ideas: Laracor, Swift's living in Ireland, combined with the *atra cura, black care*, that rides behind the horsemen in the first poem of Book Three of Horace's *Odes;* the Horatian idea that death comes to the mean and the noble alike; *proh*, the Latin interjection of regret, and *pro*, perhaps referring to Swift's championship of the impoverished Irish; *melancolores, melancholy* plus *black-colored; glauque*, French, *gray-blue*, plus Greek *glaux, owl*—gray evening plus Swift's blue eyes, which also had an owlish appearance; in *glitt bedimmed to imm*, the doubled consonants evidently represent a deadening of the sense; *creep o'er skull*, French *crépuscule, twilight; asterr*, Greek *aster, star*, Swift's Stella, whose real name was Esther; Vanessa's real name was Hester—so Stella calls Hester a (q)wench; perhaps German *mist, dung, trash*, plays some part here, too—as well as German *starr, rigid;*

graw evidently contains German *grau, gray; honath Jon* is *honest John* and *Jonathan; glowcoma* is *glaucoma,* a kind of blindness, plus the idea of a pale glow of life persisting in a coma. This passage has some beauty and power; but isn't it overingenious? Would anyone naturally think of Horace when he was confronted with "Atrahore"? And, even admitting that it may be appropriate to associate Latin with Swift, how does the German get in? Swift did not know German nor had he any German associations.[2]

In some cases, this overlaying of meanings has had the result of rendering quite opaque passages which at an earlier stage—as we can see by comparing the finished text with some of the sections as they first appeared—were no less convincingly dreamlike for being more easily comprehensible. You will find three versions of a passage in *Anna Livia Plurabelle* on page 164 of the *Exagmination;* and on page 213 of the book you will see that Joyce has worked up still a fourth. My feeling is that he ought to have stopped somewhere between the second and the third. Here is Version 1 of 1925: "Look, look, the dusk is growing. What time is it? It must be late. It's ages now since I or anyone last saw Waterhouse's clock. They took it asunder, I heard them say. When will they reassemble it?" And here is Version 4 of 1939: "Look, look, the dusk is growing. My branches lofty are taking root. And my cold cher's gone ashley. Fieluhr? Filou! What age is at? It saon is late. 'Tis endless now senne eye or erewone last saw Waterhouse's clough. They took it asunder, I hurd thum sigh. When will they reassemble it?" There is a gain in poetry, certainly; but in the meantime the question and the answer have almost disappeared. Has it really made Anna Livia any more riverlike to introduce the names of several hundred rivers (*saon* is *Saône* doing duty as *soon,* and *cher* is the *Cher* for French *chair*)—as he also introduces in other sections the names of cities, insects, trees? And why drag in *Erewhon?* In the same way, the talk of the Old Men, which, when it first came out in *Navire d' Argent,* seemed almost equal in beauty to the Anna Livia Plurabelle chapter, has now been so crammed with other things that the voices of the actual speakers have in places been nearly obliterated.

Joyce has always been rather deficient in dramatic and narrative sense. *Ulysses* already dragged; one got lost in it. The moments of critical importance were so run in with the rest that one was likely to miss them on first reading. One had to think about the book, read chapters of it over, in order to see the pattern and to realize how deep the insight went. And *Finnegans Wake* is much worse in this respect The main outlines of the book are discernible, once we have been tipped off as to what it is all about. It is a help that, in forming our hypothesis, the principle of Occam's razor applies; for it is Joyce's whole design and point that the immense foaming-up of symbols should be reducible to a few simple facts. And it must also be conceded by a foreigner that a good deal which may appear to him mysterious would be plain enough to anyone who knew Dublin and something about Irish history, and that what Joyce has done here is as legitimate as it would be for an American writer to lay the scene of a similar fantasy somewhere on Riverside Drive in New York and to assume that his readers would be able to recognize Grant's Tomb, green buses, Columbia University and the figure of Hendrik Hudson. A foreign reader of *Finnegans Wake* should consult a map of Dublin and look up the articles on Dublin and Ireland in the *Encyclopedia Britannica*.

Yet it seems to me a serious defect that we do not really understand what is happening till we have almost finished the book. *Then* we can look back and understand the significance of Earwicker's stuttering over the word *father* on page 45; we can see that "Peder the Greste, altipaltar" on page 344 combines, along with Peter the Great and *agreste*, *pederast* and *pater*; we can conclude that the allusion on page 373 about "begetting a wife which begame his niece by pouring her youngthings into skintighs" refers back to the little story on pages 21–23, and that this whole theme is a device of the "dream-work" to get over the incest barrier by disguising Earwicker's own children as the children of a niece.

But in the meantime we have had to make our way through five hundred and fifty-four pages; and there is much that is evidently important that we still do not understand. How, for example, is the story of the "prankquean" just mentioned related to the motif of the letter scratched up by the chicken from the dump heap; and what is the point about this letter? The theme is developed at prodigious length in the chapter beginning on page 104; and it flickers all through the book. It turns up near the end—pages 623–624—with new emotional connotations. The idea of letters and postmen plays a prominent part all through. Little Kevin is represented as giving the postman's knock; and Earwicker—though he here seems to be identifying himself with the other son, Jerry—is caught up into a long flight of fantasy in which he imagines himself a postman. The letter comes from Boston, Massachusetts, and seems to have been written by some female relation, perhaps the niece mentioned above. One feels that there is a third woman in the story, and that something important depends on this. Yet a considerable amount of rereading has failed, in the case of the present writer, to clear the matter up.

Finnegans Wake, in the actual reading, seems to me for two thirds of its length not really to bring off what it attempts. Nor do I think it possible to defend the procedure of Joyce on the basis of an analogy with music. It is true that there is a good deal of the musician in Joyce: his phonograph record of *Anna Livia* is as beautiful as a fine tenor solo. But nobody would listen for half an hour to a composer of operas or symphonic poems who went on and on in one mood as monotonously as Joyce has done in parts of *Finnegans Wake*, who scrambled so many motifs in one passage, or who returned to pick up a theme a couple of hours after it had first been stated, when the listeners would inevitably have forgotten it.[3]

I believe that the miscarriage of *Finnegans Wake*, in so far as it does miscarry, is due primarily to two tendencies of Joyce's which were already in evidence in *Ulysses*: the impulse, in the absence of dramatic power, to work up an epic impressiveness by multiplying and complicating detail, by filling in abstract diagrams and laying on intellectual conceits, till the organic effort at which he aims has been spoiled by too much that is synthetic; and a curious shrinking solicitude to conceal from the reader his real subjects. These subjects are always awkward and distressing: they have to do with the kind of feelings which people themselves conceal and which it takes courage in the artist to handle. And the more daring Joyce's subjects become, the more he tends to swathe them about with the fancywork of his literary virtuosity. It is as if it were not merely Earwicker who was frightened by the state of his emotions but as if Joyce were embarrassed, too.

Yet, with all this, *Finnegans Wake* has achieved certain amazing successes. Joyce has caught the psychology of sleep as no one else has ever caught it, laying hold on states of mind which it is difficult for the waking intellect to recreate, and distinguishing with marvelous delicacy between the different levels of dormant consciousness. There are the relative vividness of events reflected from the day before; the nightmare viscidity and stammering of the heavy slumbers of midnight; the buoyance and self-assertive vitality which gradually emerge from this; the half-waking of the early morning, which lapses back into the rigmaroles of dreams; the awareness, later, of the light outside, with its effect as of the curtain of the eyelids standing between the mind and the day. Through all this, the falling of twilight, the striking of the hours by the clock, the morning fog and its clearing, the bell for early mass, and the rising sun at the window, make themselves felt by the sleeper. With what brilliance they are rendered by Joyce! And the voices that echo in Earwicker's dream—the beings that seize upon him and speak through him: the Tree and the River, the eloquence of Shaun, the mumbling and running-on of the Old Men; the fluttery girl sweetheart, the resigned elderly wife, the nagging and jeering gibberish—close to madness and recalling the apparition of Virag in the Walpurgisnacht scene of *Ulysses*, but here identified with the Devil—which comes like an incubus with the darkness and through which the thickened voices of the Earwicker household occasionally announce themselves startlingly: "Mawmaw, luk, your beeftay's fizzin' over" or "Now a muss wash the little face." Joyce has only to strike the rhythm and the timber, and we know which of the spirits is with us.

Some of the episodes seem to me wholly successful: the Anna Livia chapter, for example, and the end of *Haveth Childers Everywhere*, which has a splendor and a high-spirited movement of a kind not matched elsewhere in Joyce. The passage in a minor key which precedes this major crescendo and describes Earwicker's real habitations—"most respectable . . . thoroughly respectable . . . partly respectable," and so forth—is a masterpiece of humorous sordidity (especially "copious holes emitting mice"); and so is the inventory—on pages 183–184—of all the useless and rubbishy objects in the house where Shem the Penman lives. The *Ballad of Persse O'Reilly* (*perce-oreille*, earwig) —which blazons the shame of Earwicker—is real dream literature and terribly funny; as is also the revelation—pages 572–573—of the guilty and intricate sex relationships supposed to prevail in the Earwicker family, under the guise of one of those unintelligible summaries of a saint's legend or a Latin play. The waking-up chapter is charming in the passage—page 565—in which the mother comforts the restless boy and in the summing-up—page 579—of the married life of the Earwickers; and it is touchingly and thrillingly effective in throwing back on all that has gone before the shy impoverished family pathos which it is Joyce's special destiny to express.

Where he is least happy, I think, is in such episodes as the voyage, 311 ff., the football game, 373 ff., and the siege of Sebastopol, 338 ff. (all in the dense nightmarish part of the book, which to me is, in general, the dullest). Joyce is best when he is idyllic, nostalgic, or going insane in an introspective way; he is not good at energetic action. There is never any direct aggressive clash between the pairs of opponents in Joyce, and there is consequently no real violence (except Dedalus' smashing the chandelier in self-defense against the reproach of his dead mother). All that Joyce is able to do when he wants to represent a battle is to concoct an uncouth gush of language. In general one feels, also, in *Finnegans Wake* the narrow limitations of Joyce's interests. He has tried to make it universal by having Earwicker take part in his dream in as many human activities as possible: but Joyce himself has not the key either to politics, to sport, or to fighting. The departments of activity that come out best are such quiet ones as teaching and preaching.

The finest thing in the book, and one of the finest things Joyce has done, is the passage at the end where Ann, the wife, is for the first time allowed to speak with her full and mature voice. I have noted that Joyce's fiction usually deals with the tacit readjustment in the relationships between members of a family, the almost imperceptible moment which marks the beginning of a phase. In *Finnegans Wake*, the turning point fixed is the moment when the husband and wife know definitely—they will wake up knowing it—that their own creative sexual partnership is over. That current no longer holds them polarized—as man and woman—toward one another; a new polarization takes place: the father is pulled back toward the children. "Illas! I wisht I had better glances," he thinks he hears Ann-Anna saying (page 626) "to peer to you through this baylight's growing. But you're changing, acoolsha, you're changing from me, I can feel. Or is it me is? I'm getting mixed. Brightening up and tightening down. Yes, you're changing, sonhusband, and you're turning, I can feel you, for a daughterwife from the hills again. Imlamaya. And she is coming. Swimming in my hindmoist. Diveltaking on me tail. Just a whisk brisk sly spry spink spank sprint of a thing theresomere, saultering. Saltarella come to her own. I pity your oldself I was used to. Now a younger's there." It is the "young thin pale soft shy slim slip of a thing then, sauntering, by silvamoonlake" (page 202 in the Anna Livia Plurabelle section) that she herself used to be, who now seems to her awkward and pert, and the wife herself is now the lower river running into the sea. The water is wider here; the pace of the stream is calmer: the broad day of experience has opened. "I thought you were all glittering with the noblest of carriage. You're only a bumpkin. I thought you the great in all things, in guilt and in glory. You're but a puny. Home!" She sees him clearly now: he is neither Sir Tristram nor Lucifer; and he is done with her and she with him. "I'm loothing them that's here and all I lothe. Loonely in me loneness. For all their faults. I am passing out. O bitter ending! I'll slip away before they're up. They'll never see me. Nor know. Nor miss me. And it's old and old it's sad and old it's sad and weary I go back to you, my cold father, my cold mad father, my cold mad feary father."

. . . The helpless and heartbreaking voices of the Earwicker children recur: "Carry me along, taddy, like you done through the toy fair"— for now she is herself the child entrusting herself to the sea, flowing out into the daylight that is to be her annihilation . . . "a way a lone a last a loved a long the" . . .

The Viconian cycle of existence has come full circle again. The unfinished sentence which ends the book is to find its continuation in the sentence without a beginning with which it opens. The river which runs into the sea must commence as a cloud again; the woman must give up life to the child. The Earwickers will wake to another day, but the night has made them older: the very release of the daylight brings a weariness that looks back to life's source.

In these wonderful closing pages, Joyce has put over all he means with poetry of an originality, a purity, and an emotional power, such as to raise *Finnegans Wake*, for all its excesses, to the rank of a great work of literature.

1961. This was written when Finnegans Wake *first came out and I had not yet grasped its simple and solid structure. I had not even identified Shem and Shaun, Earwicker's twin sons, who dominate, respectively, the two halves of the book and whose antithetical personalities are reflected in all the other pairs of opposites: the Mookse and the Gripes, the Ondt and the Gracehoper, the two washerwomen, etc. It appears from one of Joyce's published letters that I was not correct in assuming that old Johnny MacDougall represented Ulster. E. W.*

NOTES

1. *Our Exagmination Round His Factification for Incamination of Work in Progress*, published by New Directions at Norfolk, Connecticut. This is a collection of papers from *Transition*, the Paris magazine in which *Finnegans Wake* first appeared. The writers have taken their cues from Joyce himself, and he seems to have chosen this way of providing the public with a key. It is, in fact, rather doubtful whether without the work done by *Transition* it would be possible to get the hang of the book at all. See also Mr. Max Eastman's account of an interview with Joyce on the subject in Part III, Chapter III, of *The Literary Mind*.

2. I chose this passage because a partial exposition of it, which I take to be more or less authoritative, had appeared in the *Exagmination* (in the paper by Mr. Robert McAlmon). I did not remember to have read it in its place in *Finnegans Wake*, and was unable to find it when I looked for it. Since then I have been told by another reader who has been over and over the book that this sentence about Swift is not included. This is interesting

because it indicates the operation of a principle of selection. Joyce suffered himself from glaucoma, and it may be that he eliminated the reference because he felt that it was too specifically personal.

3. This essay was written in the summer of 1939, just after *Finnegans Wake* came out, and I have reprinted it substantially as it first appeared. Since then an article by Mr. John Peale Bishop in *The Southern Review* of Summer, 1939, and studies by Mr. Harry Levin in *The Kenyon Review* of Autumn, 1939, and in *New Directions* of 1939, have thrown further light on the subject; and I have also had the advantage of discussions with Mr. Thornton Wilder, who has explored the book more thoroughly than anyone else I have heard of. It is to be hoped that Mr. Wilder will some day publish something about *Finnegans Wake;* and in the meantime those interested in the book should consult the essays mentioned, upon which I have sometimes drawn in revising the present study.

One suggestion of Mr. Bishop's should certainly be noted here. He believes that the riddle of the letter is the riddle of life itself. This letter has been scratched up from a dung-heap and yet it has come from another world; it includes in its very brief length marriage, children and death, and things to eat and drink—all the primary features of life, beyond which the ideas of the illiterate writer evidently do not extend; and Earwicker can never really read it, though the text seems exceedingly simple and though he confronts it again and again.

I ought to amend what is said in this essay on the basis of a first reading by adding that *Finnegans Wake,* like *Ulysses,* gets better the more you go back to it. I do not know of any other books of which it is true as it is of Joyce's that, though parts of them may leave us blank or repel us when we try them the first time, they gradually build themselves up for us as we return to them and think about them. That this should be true is due probably to some special defect of *rapport* between Joyce and the audience he is addressing, to some disease of his architectural faculty; but he compensates us partly for this by giving us more in the long run than we had realized at first was there, and he eventually produces the illusion that his fiction has a reality like life's, because, behind all the antics, the pedantry, the artificial patterns, something organic and independent of these is always revealing itself; and we end by recomposing a world in our mind as we do from the phenomena of experience. Mr. Max Eastman reports that Joyce once said to him, during a conversation on *Finnegans Wake,* when Mr. Eastman had suggested to Joyce that the demands made on the reader were too heavy and that he perhaps ought to provide a key: "The demand that I make of my reader is that he should devote his whole life to reading my works." It is in any case probably true that they will last you a whole lifetime.

23

E. M. FORSTER

———◆❖◆———

Virginia Woolf

WHEN I was appointed to this lectureship the work of Virginia Woolf was much in my mind, and I asked to be allowed to speak on it. To speak on it, rather than to sum it up. There are two obstacles to a summing up. The first is the work's richness and complexity. As soon as we dismiss the legend of the Invalid Lady of Bloomsbury, so guilelessly accepted by Arnold Bennett, we find ourselves in a bewildering world where there are few headlines. We think of *The Waves* and say "Yes—that is Virginia Woolf"; then we think of *The Common Reader*, where she is different, of *A Room of One's Own* or of the preface to *Life As We Have Known It:* different again. She is like a plant which is supposed to grow in a well-prepared garden bed—the bed of esoteric literature—and then pushes up suckers all over the place, through the gravel of the front drive, and even through the flagstones of the kitchen yard. She was full of interests, and their number increased as she grew older, she was curious about life, and she was tough, sensitive but tough. How can her achievement be summed up in an hour? A headline sometimes serves a lecturer as a life-line on these occasions, and brings him safely into the haven where he would be. Shall I find one today?

The second obstacle is that the present year is not a good date on which to sum up anything. Our judgements, to put it mildly, are not at their prime. We are all of us upon the Leaning Tower, as she called it, even those of us who date from the nineteenth century, when the earth was still horizontal and the buildings perpendicular. We cannot judge the landscape properly as we look down, for everything is tilted. Isolated objects are not so puzzling; a tree, a wave, a hat, a jewel, an old gentleman's bald head look much as they always did. But the relation between objects—that we cannot estimate, and that is why the verdict must be left to another generation. I have not the least faith that anything which we now value will survive historically (something which we should have valued may evolve, but that is a different proposition); and may be another generation will dismiss Virginia Woolf as worthless and tiresome. However this is not my opinion, nor I think yours; we still have the word, and when you conferred the Rede Lectureship on me—the greatest honour I have ever received—I wondered whether I could not transmit some honour to her from the university she so admired, and from the central building of that university. She would receive the homage a little mockingly, for she was somewhat astringent over the academic position of women. "What? I in the Senate House?" she might say; "are you sure that is quite proper? And why, if you want to discuss my books, need you first disguise yourselves in caps and gowns?" But I think she would be pleased. She loved Cambridge. Indeed, I cherish a private fancy that she once took her degree here. She, who could disguise herself as a member of the suite of the Sultan of Zanzibar, or black her face to go aboard a Dreadnought as an Ethiopian[1]—she could surely have hoaxed our innocent praelectors, and, kneeling in this very spot, have presented to the Vice-Chancellor the exquisite but dubious head of Orlando.

There is after all one little life-line to catch hold of: she liked writing.

These words, which usually mean so little, must be applied to her with all possible intensity. She liked receiving sensations—sights, sounds, tastes—passing them through her mind, where they encountered theories and memories, and then bringing them out again, through a pen, on to a bit of paper. Now began the higher delights of authorship. For these pen-marks on paper were only the prelude to writing, little more than marks on a wall. They had to be combined, arranged, emphasised here, eliminated there, new relationships had to be generated, new pen-marks born, until out of the interactions, something, one thing, one, arose. This one thing, whether it was a novel or an essay or a short story or a biography or a private paper to be read to her friends, was, if it was successful, itself analogous to a sensation. Although it was so complex and intellectual, although it might be large and heavy with facts, it was akin to the very simple things which had started it off, to the sights, sounds, tastes. It could be best described as we describe them. For it was not about something. It was something. This is obvious in "esthetic" works, like *Kew Gardens* and *Mrs. Dalloway;* it is less obvious in a work of learning, like the *Roger Fry,* yet here too the analogy holds. We know, from an article by Mr. R. C. Trevelyan,[2] that she had, when writing it, a notion corresponding to the notion of a musical composition. In the first chapter she stated the themes, in the subsequent chapters she developed them separately, and she tried to bring them all in again at the end. The biography is duly about Fry. But it is something else too; it is one thing, one.

She liked writing with an intensity which few writers have attained, or even desired. Most of them write with half an eye on their royalties, half an eye on their critics, and a third half eye on improving the world, which leaves them with only half an eye for the task on which she concentrated her entire vision. She would not look elsewhere, and her circumstances combined with her temperament to focus her. Money she had not to consider, because she possessed a private income, and though financial independence is not always a safeguard against commercialism, it was in her case. Critics she never considered while she was writing, although she could be attentive to them and even humble afterwards. Improving the world she would not consider, on the ground that the world is man-made, and that she, a woman, had no responsibility for the mess. This last opinion is a curious one, and I shall be returning to it; still, she held it, it completed the circle of her defences, and neither the desire for money nor the desire for reputation nor philanthropy could influence her. She had a singleness of purpose which will not recur in this country for many years, and writers who have liked writing as she liked it have not indeed been common in any age.

Now the pitfall for such an author is obvious. It is the Palace of Art, it is that bottomless chasm of dulness which pretends to be a palace, all glorious with corridors and domes, but which is really a dreadful hole into which the unwary aesthete may tumble, to be seen no more. She has all the aesthete's characteristics: selects and manipulates her impressions; is not a great creator of character; enforces patterns on her books; has no great cause at heart. So how did she avoid her appropriate pitfall and remain up in the fresh air, where we can hear the sound of the stable boy's boots, or boats bumping, or Big Ben; where we can taste really new bread, and touch real dahlias?

She had a sense of humour, no doubt, but our answer must go a little deeper than that hoary nostrum. She escaped, I think, because she liked writing for fun. Her pen amused her, and in the midst of writing seriously this other delight would spurt through. A little essay, called *On Being Ill,* exemplifies this. It starts with the thesis that illness in literature is seldom handled properly (de Quincey and Proust were exceptional), that the body is treated by novelists as if it were a sheet of glass through which the soul gazes, and that this is contrary to experience. There are possibilities in the thesis, but she soon wearies of exploring them. Off she goes amusing herself, and after half a dozen pages she is writing entirely for fun, caricaturing the type of people who visit sick-rooms, insisting that Augustus Hare's *Two Noble Lives* is the book an invalid most demands, and so on. She could describe illness if she chose—for instance, in *The Voyage Out*—but she gaily forgets it in *On Being Ill.* The essay is slight, and was not offered for public sale, still it does neatly illustrate the habit of her mind. Literature was her merry-go-round as well as her study. This makes her amusing to read, and it also saves her from the Palace of Art. For you cannot enter the Palace of Art, therein to dwell, if you are tempted from time to time to play the fool. Lord Tennyson did not consider that. His remedy, you remember, was that the Palace would be purified when it was inhabited by all mankind, all behaving seriously at once. Virginia Woolf found a simpler and a sounder solution.

No doubt there is a danger here—there is danger everywhere. She might have become a glorified diseuse, who frittered away her broader effects by mischievousness, and she did give that impression to some who met her in the flesh; there were moments when she could scarcely see the busts for the moustaches she pencilled on them, and when the bust was a modern one, whether of a gentleman in a top hat or of a youth on a pylon, it had no chance of remaining sublime. But in her writing, even in her light writing, central control entered. She was master of her complicated equipment, and though most of us like to write sometimes seriously and sometimes in fun, few of us can so manage the two impulses that they speed each other up, as hers did.

The above remarks are more or less introductory. It seems convenient now to recall what she did write, and to say a little about her development. She began back in 1915 with *The Voyage Out*—a strange tragic inspired novel about English tourists in an impossible South American hotel; her passion for truth is here already, mainly in the form of atheism, and her passion for wisdom is herein the form of music. The book made a deep impression upon the few people who read it. Its successor, *Night and Day,* disappointed them. This is an exercise in classical realism, and contains all that has characterised English fiction, for good and evil, during the last two hundred years: faith in personal relations, recourse to humorous side-shows, geographical exactitude, insistence on petty social differences: indeed most of the devices she so gaily derides in *Mr. Bennett and Mrs. Brown.* The style has been normalised and dulled. But at the same time she published two short stories, *Kew Gardens* and *The Mark on the Wall.* These are neither dull nor normal; lovely little things; her style trails after her as she walks and talks, catching up dust and grass in its folds, and instead of the precision of the earlier writing we have something more elusive than had yet been achieved in English. Lovely little things, but they seemed to lead nowhere, they were all tiny dots and coloured blobs, they were an inspired breathlessness, they were a beautiful droning or gasping which trusted to luck. They were perfect as far as they went, but that was not far, and none of us guessed that out of the pollen of those flowers would come the trees of the future. Consequently when *Jacob's Room* appeared in 1922 we were tremendously surprised. The style and sensitiveness of *Kew Gardens* remained, but they were applied to human relationships, and to the structure of society. The blobs of colour continue to drift past, but in their midst, interrupting their course like a closely sealed jar, stands the solid figure of a young man. The improbable has occurred; a method essentially poetic and apparently trifling has been applied to fiction. She was still uncertain of the possibilities of the new technique, and *Jacob's Room* is an uneven little book, but it represents her great departure, and her abandonment of the false start of *Night and Day.* It leads on to her genius in its fulness; to *Mrs. Dalloway* (1925), *To the Lighthouse* (1927), and *The Waves* (1931). These successful works are all suffused with poetry and enclosed in it. *Mrs. Dalloway* has the framework of a London summer's day, down which go spiralling two fates: the fate of the sensitive worldly hostess, and the fate of the sensitive obscure maniac; though they never touch they are closely connected, and at the same moment we lose sight of them both. It is a civilised book, and it was written from personal experience. In her work, as in her private problems, she was always civilised and sane on the subject of madness. She pared the edges off this particular malady, she tied it down to being a malady, and robbed it of the evil magic it has acquired through timid or careless thinking; here is one of the gifts we have to thank her for. *To the Lighthouse* is, however, a much greater achievement, partly because the chief characters in it, Mr. and Mrs. Ramsay, are so interesting. They hold us, we think of them away from their surroundings, and yet they are in accord with those surroundings, with the poetic scheme. *To the Lighthouse* is in three movements. It has been called a novel in sonata form, and certainly the slow central section, conveying the passing of time, does demand a musical analogy. We have, when reading it, the rare pleasure of inhabiting two worlds at once, a pleasure only art can give: the world where a little boy wants to go to a lighthouse but never manages it until, with changed emotions, he goes there as a young man; and the world where there is pattern, and this world is emphasised by passing much of the observation through the mind of Lily Briscoe, who is a painter. Then comes *The Waves*. Pattern here is supreme—indeed it is italicised. And between the motions of the sun and the waters, which preface each section, stretch, without interruption, conversation, words in inverted commas. It is a strange conversation, for the six characters, Bernard, Neville, Louis, Susan, Jinny, Rhoda, seldom address one another, and it is even possible to regard them (like Mrs. Dalloway and Septimus) as different facets of one single person. Yet they do not conduct internal monologues, they are in touch amongst themselves, and they all touch the character who never speaks, Percival. At the end, most perfectly balancing their scheme, Bernard, the would-be novelist, sums up, and the pattern fades out. *The Waves* is an extraordinary achievement, an immense extension of the possibilities of *Kew Gardens* and *Jacob's Room*. It is trembling on the edge. A little less—and it would lose its poetry. A little more—and it would be over into the abyss, and be dull and arty. It is her greatest book, though *To the Lighthouse* is my favourite.

It was followed by *The Years*. This is another experiment in the realistic tradition. It chronicles the fortunes of a family through a documented period. As in *Night and Day*, she deserts poetry, and again she fails. But in her posthumous novel *Between the Acts* (1941) she returns to the method she understood. Its theme is a village pageant, which presents the entire history of England, and into which, at the close, the audience is itself drawn, to continue that history; "The curtain rose" is its concluding phrase. The conception is poetic, and the text of the pageant is mostly written in verse. She loved her country—her country that is "the country," and emerges from the unfathomable past. She takes us back in this exquisite final tribute, and she points us on, and she shows us through her poetic vagueness

something more solid than patriotic history, and something better
worth dying for.

Amongst all this fiction, nourishing it and nourished by it, grow
other works. Two volumes of *The Common Reader* show the breadth
of her knowledge and the depth of her literary sympathy; let anyone
who thinks her an exquisite recluse read what she says on Jack Mytton
the foxhunter, for instance. As a critic she could enter into anything—
anything lodged in the past, that is to say; with her contemporaries
she sometimes had difficulties. Then there are the biographies, fanci-
ful and actual. *Orlando* is, I need hardly say, an original book, and the
first part of it is splendidly written: the description of the Great Frost
is already received as a "passage" in English literature, whatever a
passage may be. After the transformation of sex things do not go so
well; the authoress seems unconvinced by her own magic and somewhat fatigued by it, and the biography finishes competently rather
than brilliantly; it has been a fancy on too large a scale, and we can
see her getting bored. But *Flush* is a complete success, and exactly
what it sets out to be; the material, the method, the length, accord
perfectly, it is doggie without being silly, and it does give us, from
the altitude of the carpet or the sofa-foot, a peep at high poetic personages, and a new angle on their ways. The biography of Roger Fry
—one should not proceed direct from a spaniel to a Slade Professor,
but Fry would not have minded and spaniels mind nothing—reveals
a new aspect of her powers, the power to suppress herself. She in-
dulges in a pattern, but she never intrudes her personality or over-
handles her English; respect for her subject dominates her, and only
occasionally—as in her description of the divinely ordered chaos of
Fry's studio with its still-life of apples and eggs labelled "please do
not touch"—does she allow her fancy to play. Biographies are too
often described as "labours of love," but the *Roger Fry* really is in
this class; one artist is writing with affection of another, so that he
may be remembered and may be justified.

Finally, there are the feminist books—*A Room of One's Own* and
Three Guineas—and several short essays, etc., some of them significant.
It is as a novelist that she will be judged. But the rest of her work
must be remembered, partly on its merits, partly because (as Mr.
William Plomer has pointed out [3]) she is sometimes more of a novelist
in it than in her novels.

After this survey, we can state her problem. Like most novelists
worth reading, she strays from the fictional norm. She dreams, designs,

jokes, invokes, observes details, but she does not tell a story or weave
a plot, and—can she create character? That is her problem's centre.
That is the point where she felt herself open to criticism—to the criticisms, for instance, of her friend Hugh Walpole. Plot and story could
be set aside in favour of some other unity, but if one is writing about
human beings, one does want them to seem alive. Did she get her
people to live?

Now there seem to be two sorts of life in fiction, life on the page
and life eternal. Life on the page she could give; her characters never
seem unreal, however slight or fantastic their lineaments, and they
can be trusted to behave appropriately. Life eternal she could seldom
give; she could seldom so portray a character that it was remembered
afterwards on its own account, as Emma is remembered, for instance,
or Dorothea Casaubon, or Sophia and Constance in *The Old Wives'
Tale*. What wraiths, apart from their context, are the wind-sextet from
The Waves, or Jacob away from *Jacob's Room*! They speak no more
to us or to one another as soon as the page is turned. And this is her
great difficulty. Holding on with one hand to poetry, she stretches
and stretches to grasp things which are best gained by letting go of
poetry. She would not let go, and I think she was quite right, though
critics who like a novel to be a novel will disagree. She was quite
right to cling to her specific gift, even if this entailed sacrificing
something else vital to her art. And she did not always have to sacrifice; Mr. and Mrs. Ramsay do remain with the reader afterwards, and
so perhaps do Rachel from *The Voyage Out,* and Clarissa Dalloway.
For the rest—it is impossible to maintain that here is an immortal portrait gallery. Socially she is limited to the upper-middle professional
classes, and she does not even employ many types. There is the bleakly
honest intellectual (St. John Hirst, Charles Tansley, Louis, William
Dodge), the monumental majestic hero (Jacob, Percival), the pompous amorous pillar of society (Richard Dalloway as he appears in *The
Voyage Out,* Hugh Whitbread), the scholar who cares only for young
men (Bonamy, Neville), the pernickety independent (Mr. Pepper,
Mr. Bankes); even the Ramsays are tried out first as the Ambroses. As
soon as we understand the nature of her equipment, we shall see
that as regards human beings she did as well as she could. Belonging
to the world of poetry, but fascinated by another world, she is always
stretching out from her enchanted tree and snatching bits from the
flux of daily life as they float past, and out of these bits she builds
novels. She would not plunge. And she should not have plunged. She

might have stayed folded up in her tree singing little songs like *Blue-Green* in the *Monday or Tuesday* volume, but fortunately for English literature she did not do this either.

So that is her problem. She is a poet, who wants to write something as near to a novel as possible.

I must pass on to say a little—it ought to be much—about her interests. I have emphasised her fondness for writing both seriously and in fun, and have tried to indicate how she wrote: how she gathered up her material and digested it without damaging its freshness, how she rearranged it to form unities, how she was a poet who wanted to write novels, how these novels bear upon them the marks of their strange gestation—some might say the scars. What concerns me now is the material itself, her interests, her opinions. And not to be too vague, I will begin with food.

It is always helpful, when reading her, to look out for the passages which describe eating. They are invariably good. They are a sharp reminder that here is a woman who is alert sensuously. She had an enlightened greediness which gentlemen themselves might envy, and which few masculine writers have expressed. There is a little too much lamp oil in George Meredith's wine, a little too much paper crackling on Charles Lamb's pork, and no savour whatever in any dish of Henry James', but when Virginia Woolf mentions nice things they get right into our mouths, so far as the edibility of print permits. We taste their deliciousness. And when they are not nice, we taste them equally, our mouths awry now with laughter. I will not torture this great university of Oxbridge by reminding it of the exquisite lunch which she ate in a don's room here in the year 1920; such memories are now too painful. Nor will I insult the noble college of women in this same university—Fernham is its name—by reminding it of the deplorable dinner which she ate that same evening in its Hall—a dinner so lowering that she had to go to a cupboard afterwards and drink something out of a bottle; such memories may still be all too true to fact. But I may without offence refer to the great dish of Bœuf en Daube which forms the centre of the dinner of union in *To the Lighthouse*, the dinner round which all that section of the book coheres, the dinner which exhales affection and poetry and loveliness, so that all the characters see the best in one another at last and for a moment, and one of them, Lily Briscoe, carries away a recollection of reality. Such a dinner cannot be built on a statement beneath a dish-cover which the novelist is too indifferent or incompetent to remove. Real food is necessary, and this, in fiction as in her home, she knew how to provide. The Bœuf en Daube, which had taken the cook three days to make and had worried Mrs. Ramsay as she did her hair, stands before us "with its confusion of savoury brown and yellow meats and its bay leaves and its wine"; we peer down the shiny walls of the great casserole and get one of the best bits, and like William Bankes, generally so hard to please, we are satisfied. Food with her was not a literary device, put in to make the book seem real. She put it in because she tasted it, because she saw pictures, because she smelt flowers, because she heard Bach, because her senses were both exquisite and catholic, and were always bringing her first-hand news of the outside world. Our debt to her is in part this: she reminds us of the importance of sensation in an age which practises brutality and recommends ideals. I could have illustrated sensation more reputably by quoting the charming passage about the florists' shop in *Mrs. Dalloway*, or the passage where Rachel plays upon the cabin piano. Flowers and music are conventional literary adjuncts. A good feed isn't, and that is why I preferred it and chose it to represent her reactions. Let me add that she smokes, and now let the Bœuf en Daube be carried away. It will never come back in our lifetime. It is not for us. But the power to appreciate it remains, and the power to appreciate all distinction.

After the senses, the intellect. She respected knowledge, she believed in wisdom. Though she could not be called an optimist, she had, very profoundly, the conviction that mind is in action against matter, and is winning new footholds in the void. That anything would be accomplished by her or in her generation, she did not suppose, but the noble blood from which she sprang encouraged her to hope. Mr. Ramsay, standing by the geraniums and trying to think, is not a figure of fun. Nor is this university, despite its customs and costumes: "So that if at night, far out at sea over the tumbling waves, one saw a haze on the waters, a city illuminated, a whiteness in the sky, such as that now over the hall of Trinity where they're still dining or washing up plates: that would be the light shining there—the light of Cambridge."

No light shines now from Cambridge visibly, and this prompts the comment that her books were conditioned by her period. She could not assimilate this latest threat to our civilisation. The submarine perhaps. But not the flying fortress or the land mine. The idea that all stone is like grass, and like all flesh may vanish in a twinkling, did not enter into her consciousness, and indeed it will be some time before it can be assimilated by literature.[4] She belonged to an age which distinguished sharply between the impermanency of man and the durability of his monuments, and for whom the dome of the British Museum Reading Room was almost eternal. Decay she admitted: the delicate grey churches in the Strand would not stand for ever; but she supposed, as we all did, that decay would be gradual. The younger generation—the Auden-Isherwood generation as it is convenient to call it—saw more clearly here than could she, and she did not quite do justice to its vision, any more than she did justice to its experiments in technique—she who had been in her time such an experimenter. Still, to belong to one's period is a common failing, and she made the most of hers. She respected and acquired knowledge, she believed in wisdom. Intellectually, no one can do more; and since she was a poet, not a philosopher or a historian or a prophetess, she had not to consider whether wisdom will prevail and whether the square upon the oblong, which Rhoda built out of the music of Mozart, will ever stand firm upon this distracted earth. The square upon the oblong. Order. Justice. Truth. She cared for these abstractions, and tried to express them through symbols, as an artist must, though she realised the inadequacy of symbols.

> They come with their violins, said Rhoda; they wait; count; nod; down come their bows. And there is ripples and laughter like the dance of olive trees. . . .
> "Like" and "like" and "like"—but what is the thing that lies beneath the semblance of the thing? Now that lightning has gashed the tree and the flowering branch has fallen . . . let me see the thing. There is a square. There is an oblong. The players take the square and place it upon the oblong. They place it very acurately; they make a perfect dwelling-place. Very little is left outside. The structure is now visible; what is inchoate is here stated; we are not so various or so mean; we have made oblongs and stood them upon squares. This is our triumph; this is our consolation.

The consolation, that is to say, of catching sight of abstractions. They have to be symbolised, and "the square upon the oblong" is as much a symbol as the dancing olive trees, but because of its starkness it comes nearer to conveying what she seeks. Seeking it, "we are not so various or so mean"; we have added to the human heritage and re-affirmed wisdom.

The next of her interests which has to be considered is society. She was not confined to sensations and intellectualism. She was a social creature, with an outlook both warm and shrewd. But it was a peculiar outlook, and we can best get at it by looking at a very peculiar side of her: her Feminism.

Feminism inspired one of the most brilliant of her books—the charming and persuasive *A Room of One's Own*; it contains the Oxbridge lunch and the Fernham dinner, also the immortal encounter with the beadle when she tried to walk on the college grass, and the touching reconstruction of Shakespeare's sister—Shakespeare's equal in genius, but she perished because she had no position or money, and that has been the fate of women through the ages. But Feminism is also responsible for the worst of her books—the cantankerous *Three Guineas*— and for the less successful streaks in *Orlando*. There are spots of it all over her work, and it was constantly in her mind. She was convinced that society is man-made, that the chief occupations of men are the shedding of blood, the making of money, the giving of orders, and the wearing of uniforms, and that none of these occupations is admirable. Women dress up for fun or prettiness, men for pomposity, and she had no mercy on the judge in his wig, the general in his bits and bobs of ribbon, the bishop in his robes, or even on the harmless don in his gown. She felt that all these mummers were putting something across over which women had never been consulted, and which she at any rate disliked. She declined to co-operate, in theory, and sometimes in fact. She refused to sit on committees or to sign appeals, on the ground that women must not condone this tragic male-made mess, or accept the crumbs of power which men throw them occasionally from their hideous feast. Like Lysistrata, she withdrew.

In my judgement there is something old-fashioned about this extreme Feminism; it dates back to her suffragette youth of the 1910's, when men kissed girls to distract them from wanting the vote, and very properly provoked her wrath. By the 1930's she had much less to complain of, and seems to keep on grumbling from habit. She complained, and rightly, that though women today have won admission into the professions and trades they usually encounter a male conspiracy when they try to get to the top. But she did not appreciate that the conspiracy is weakening yearly, and that before long women will be quite as powerful for good or evil as men. She was sensible about the past; about the present she was sometimes unreasonable. However, I speak as a man here, and as an elderly one. The best judges of her Feminism are neither elderly men nor even elderly women, but young women. If they, if the students of Fernham, think that it expresses an existent grievance, they are right.

She felt herself to be not only a woman but a lady, and this gives a further twist to her social outlook. She made no bones about it. She was a lady, by birth and upbringing, and it was no use being cowardly about it, and pretending that her mother had turned a mangle, or that Sir Leslie had been a plasterer's mate. Working-class writers often mentioned their origins, and were respected for doing so. Very well; she would mention hers. And her snobbery—for she was a snob—has more courage in it than arrogance. It is connected with her insatiable honesty, and is not, like the snobbery of Clarissa Dalloway, bland and frilled and unconsciously sinking into the best armchair. It is more like the snobbery of Kitty when she goes to tea with the Robsons; it stands up like a target for anyone to aim at who wants to. In her introduction to *Life As We Have Known It* (a collection of biographies of working-class women edited by Margaret Llewellyn Davies) she faces the fire. "One could not be Mrs. Giles of Durham, because one's body had never stood at the wash-tub; one's hands had never wrung and scrubbed and chopped up whatever the meat is that makes a miner's supper." This is not disarming, and it is not intended to disarm. And if one said to her that she could after all find out what meat a miner does have for his supper if she took a little trouble, she would retort that this wouldn't help her to chop it up, and that it is not by knowing things but by doing things that one enters into the lives of people who do things. And she was not going to chop up meat. She would chop it badly, and waste her time. She was not going to wring and scrub when what she liked doing and could do was write. To murmurs of "Lucky lady you!" she replied, "I am a lady," and went on writing. "There aren't going to be no more ladies. 'Ear that?" She heard. Without rancour or surprise or alarm, she heard, and drove her pen the faster. For if, as seems probable, these particular creatures are to be extinguished, how important that the last of them should get down her impressions of the world and unify them into a book! If she didn't, no one else would. Mrs. Giles of Durham wouldn't. Mrs. Giles would write differently, and might write better, but she could not produce *The Waves*, or a life of Roger Fry.

There is an admirable hardness here, so far as hardness can be admirable. There is not much sympathy, and I do not think she was sympathetic. She could be charming to individuals, working-class and otherwise, but it was her curiosity and her honesty that motivated her. And we must remember that sympathy, for her, entailed a tremendous and exhausting process, not lightly to be entered on. It was not a half-crown or a kind word or a good deed or a philanthropic sermon or a godlike gesture; it was adding the sorrows of another to one's own. Half fancifully, but wholly seriously, she writes:

> But sympathy we cannot have. Wisest Fate says no. If her children, weighted as they already are with sorrow, were to take on them that burden too, adding in imagination other pains to their own, buildings would cease to rise; roads would peter out into grassy tracks: there would be an end of music and of painting; one great sigh alone would rise to Heaven, and the only attitudes for men and women would be those of horror and despair.

Here perhaps is the reason why she cannot be warmer and more human about Mrs. Giles of Durham.

This detachment from the working-classes and Labour reinforces the detachment caused by her Feminism, and her attitude to society was in consequence aloof and angular. She was fascinated, she was unafraid, but she detested mateyness, and she would make no concessions to popular journalism, and the "let's all be friendly together" stunt. To the crowd—so far as such an entity exists—she was very jolly, but she handed out no bouquets to the middlemen who have arrogated to themselves the right of interpreting the crowd, and get paid for doing so in the daily press and on the wireless. These middlemen form after all a very small clique—larger than the Bloomsbury they so tirelessly denounce, but a mere drop in the ocean of humanity. And since it was a drop whose distinction was proportionate to its size, she saw no reason to conciliate it.

"And now to sum up," says Bernard in the last section of *The Waves*. That I cannot do, for reasons already given; the material is so rich and contradictory, and ours is not a good vintage year for judgements. I have gone from point to point as best I could, from her method of writing to her books, from her problems as a poet-novelist to her problems as a woman and as a lady. And I have tried to speak of her with the directness which she would wish, and which could alone honour her. But how are all the points to be combined? What is the pattern resultant? The best I can do is to quote Bernard again. "The illusion is upon me," he says, "that something adheres for a moment, has roundness, weight, depth, is completed. This, for the moment, seems to be her life." Bernard puts it well. But, as Rhoda indicated in that earlier quotation, these words are only similes, comparisons with physical substances, and what one wants is the thing that lies beneath the semblance of the thing; that alone satisfies, that alone makes the full statement.

Whatever the final pattern, I am sure it will not be a depressing one. Like all her friends, I miss her greatly—I knew her ever since she started writing. But this is a personal matter, and I am sure that there is no case for lamentation here, or for the obituary note. Virginia Woolf got through an immense amount of work, she gave acute pleasure in new ways, she pushed the light of the English language a little further against darkness. Those are facts. The epitaph of such an artist cannot be written by the vulgar-minded or by the lugubrious. They will try, indeed they have already tried, but their words make no sense. It is wiser, it is safer, to regard her career as a triumphant one. She triumphed over what are primly called "difficulties," and she also triumphed in the positive sense: she brought in the spoils. And sometimes it is as a row of little silver cups that I see her work gleaming. "These trophies," the inscription runs, "were won by the mind from matter, its enemy and its friend."

NOTES

1. See Adrian Stephen, *The Dreadnought Hoax*. See, still more, an unpublished paper which she herself once wrote for a Women's Institute, leaving it helpless with laughter.
2. *The Abinger Chronicle*, April 1941.
3. *Horizon*, May 1941.
4. Elizabeth Bowen is, so far as I know, the only novelist who has assimilated the bombed areas of London into her art; descriptions of them are of course frequent.

24

ERICH AUERBACH

—◆—

The Brown Stocking

"And even if it isn't fine to-morrow," said Mrs. Ramsay, raising her eyes to glance at William Bankes and Lily Briscoe as they passed, "it will be another day. And now," she said, thinking that Lily's charm was her Chinese eyes, aslant in her white, puckered little face, but it would take a clever man to see it, "and now stand up, and let me measure your leg," for they might go to the Lighthouse after all, and she must see if the stocking did not need to be an inch or two longer in the leg.

Smiling, for an admirable idea had flashed upon her this very second— William and Lily should marry—she took the heather mixture stocking, with its criss-cross of steel needles at the mouth of it, and measured it against James's leg.

"My dear, stand still," she said, for in his jealousy, not liking to serve as measuring-block for the Lighthouse keeper's little boy, James fidgeted purposely; and if he did that, how could she see, was it too long, was it too short? she asked.

She looked up—what demon possessed him, her youngest, her cherished?—and saw the room, saw the chairs, thought them fearfully shabby. Their entrails, as Andrew said the other day, were all over the floor; but then what was the point, she asked herself, of buying good chairs to let them spoil up here all through the winter when the house, with only one old woman to see to it, positively dripped with wet? Never mind: the rent was precisely twopence halfpenny; the children loved it; it did her husband good to be three thousand, or if she must be accurate, three hundred miles from his library and his lectures and his disciples; and there was room for visitors. Mats, camp beds, crazy ghosts of chairs and tables whose London life of service was done—they did well enough here; and a photograph or two, and books. Books, she thought, grew of themselves. She never had time to read them. Alas! even the books that had been given her, and inscribed by the hand of the poet himself: "For her whose wishes must be obeyed . . ." "The happier Helen of our days . . ." disgraceful to say, she had never read them. And Croom on the Mind and Bates on the Savage Customs of Polynesia ("My dear, stand still," she said)—neither of those could one send to the Lighthouse. At a certain moment, she supposed, the house would become so shabby that something must be done. If they could be taught to wipe their feet and not bring the beach in with them—that would be something. Crabs, she had to allow, if Andrew really wished to dissect them, or if Jasper believed that one could make soup from seaweed, one could not prevent it; or Rose's objects—shells, reeds, stones; for they were gifted, her children, but all in quite different ways. And the result of it was, she sighed, taking in the whole room from floor to ceiling, as she held the stocking against James's leg, that things got shabbier and got shabbier summer after summer. The mat was fading; the wall-paper was flapping. You couldn't tell any more that those were roses on it. Still, if every door in a house is left perpetually open, and no lockmaker in the whole of Scotland can mend a bolt, things must spoil. What was the use of flinging a green Cashmere shawl over the edge of a picture frame? In two weeks it would be the colour of pea soup. But it was the doors that annoyed her; every door was left open. She listened. The drawing-room door was open; the hall door was open; it sounded as if the bed-room doors were open; and certainly the window on the landing was open, for that she had opened herself. That windows should be open, and doors shut—simple as it was, could none of them remember it? She would go into the maids' bedrooms at night and find them sealed like ovens, except for Marie's, the Swiss girl, who would rather go without a bath than without fresh air, but then at home, she had said, "the mountains are so beautiful." She had said that last night looking out of the window with tears in her eyes. "The mountains are so beautiful." Her father was dying there, Mrs. Ramsay knew. He was leaving them fatherless. Scolding and demonstrating (how to make a bed, how to open a window, with hands that shut and spread like a French-woman's) all had folded itself quietly about her, when the girl spoke, as, after a flight through the sunshine the wings of a bird fold them-selves quietly and the blue of its plumage changes from bright steel to soft purple. She had stood there silent for there was nothing to be said. He had cancer of the throat. At the recollection—how she had stood there, how the girl had said "At home the mountains are so beautiful," and there was no hope, no hope whatever, she had a spasm of irritation, and speaking sharply, said to James:

"Stand still. Don't be tiresome," so that he knew instantly that her severity was real, and straightened his leg and she measured it.

The stocking was too short by half an inch at least, making allowance for the fact that Sorley's little boy would be less well grown than James.

"It's too short," she said, "ever so much too short."

Never did anybody look so sad. Bitter and black, half-way down, in the darkness, in the shaft which ran from the sunlight to the depths, perhaps a tear formed; a tear fell; the waters swayed this way and that, received it, and were at rest. Never did anybody look so sad.

But was it nothing but looks? people said. What was there behind it— her beauty, her splendour? Had he blown his brains out, they asked, had he died the week before they were married—some other, earlier lover, of whom rumours reached one? Or was there nothing? nothing but an incomparable beauty which she lived behind, and could do nothing to disturb? For easily though she might have said at some moment of intimacy when stories of great passion, of love foiled, of ambition thwarted came her way how she too had known or felt or been through it herself, she never spoke. She was silent always. She knew them—she knew without having learnt. Her simplicity fathomed what clever people falsified. Her singleness of mind made her drop plumb like a stone, alight exact as a bird, gave her, naturally, this swoop and fall of the spirit upon truth which delighted, eased, sustained—falsely perhaps.

("Nature has but little clay,' 'said Mr. Bankes once, hearing her voice on the telephone, and much moved by it though she was only telling him a fact about a train, "like that of which she moulded you." He saw her at the end of the line, Greek, blue-eyed, straight-nosed. How incongruous it seemed to be telephoning to a woman like that. The Graces assembling seemed to have joined hands in meadows of asphodel to compose that face. Yes, he would catch the 10:30 at Euston.

"But she's no more aware of her beauty than a child," said Mr. Bankes, replacing the receiver and crossing the room to see what progress the workmen were making with an hotel which they were building at the back of his house. And he thought of Mrs. Ramsey as he looked at that stir among the unfinished walls. For always, he thought, there was something incongruous to be worked into the harmony of her face. She clapped a deerstalker's hat on her head; she ran across the lawn in goloshes to snatch a child from mischief. So that if it was her beauty merely that one thought of, one must remember the quivering thing, the living thing (they were carrying bricks up a little plank as he watched them), and work it into the picture; or if one thought of her simply as a woman, one must endow her with some freak of idiosyncrasy; or suppose some latent desire to doff her royalty of form as if her beauty bored her and all that men say of beauty, and she wanted only to be like other people, insignificant. He did not know. He did not know. He must go to his work.)

Knitting her reddish-brown hairy stocking, with her head outlined

absurdly by the gilt frame, the green shawl which she had tossed over
the edge of the frame, and the authenticated masterpiece by Michael
Angelo, Mrs. Ramsay smoothed out what had been harsh in her manner
a moment before, raised his head, and kissed her little boy on the forehead. "Let's find another picture to cut out," she said.

This piece of narrative prose is the fifth section of part 1 in Virginia
Woolf's novel, *To the Lighthouse,* which was first published in 1927.
The situation in which the characters find themselves can be almost
completely deduced from the text itself. Nowhere in the novel is it set
forth systematically, by way of introduction or exposition, or in any
other way than as it is here. I shall, however, briefly summarize what
the situation is at the beginning of our passage. This will make it easier
for the reader to understand the following analysis; it will also serve
to bring out more clearly a number of important motifs from earlier
sections which are here only alluded to.

Mrs. Ramsay is the wife of an eminent London professor of philosophy; she is very beautiful but definitely no longer young. With her
youngest son James—he is six years old—she is sitting by the window
in a good-sized summer house on one of the Hebrides islands. The
professor has rented it for many years. In addition to the Ramsays,
their eight children, and the servants, there are a number of guests in
the house, friends on longer or shorter visits. Among them is a well-
known botanist, William Bankes, an elderly widower, and Lily Briscoe,
who is a painter. These two are just passing by the window. James is
sitting on the floor busily cutting pictures from an illustrated catalogue.
Shortly before, his mother had told him that, if the weather should be
fine, they would sail to the lighthouse the next day. This is an expedition James has been looking forward to for a long time. The people at
the lighthouse are to receive various presents; among these are stock-
ings for the lighthouse-keeper's boy. The violent joy which James had
felt when the trip was announced had been as violently cut short by
his father's acid observation that the weather would not be fine the
next day. One of the guests, with malicious emphasis, has added some
corroborative meteorological details. After all the others have left the
room, Mrs. Ramsay, to console James, speaks the words with which
our passage opens.

The continuity of the section is established through an exterior occurrence involving Mrs. Ramsay and James: the measuring of the
stocking. Immediately after her consoling words (if it isn't fine tomorrow, we'll go some other day), Mrs. Ramsay makes James stand up
so that she can measure the stocking for the lighthouse-keeper's son

against his leg. A little further on she rather absent-mindedly tells him to stand still—the boy is fidgeting because his jealousy makes him a little stubborn and perhaps also because he is still under the impression of the disappointment of a few moments ago. Many lines later, the warning to stand still is repeated more sharply. James obeys, the measuring takes place, and it is found that the stocking is still considerably too short. After another long interval the scene concludes with Mrs. Ramsay kissing the boy on the forehead (she thus makes up for the sharp tone of her second order to him to stand still) and her proposing to help him look for another picture to cut out. Here the section ends.

This entirely insignificant occurrence is constantly interspersed with other elements which, although they do not·interrupt its progress, take up far more time in the narration than the whole scene can possibly have lasted. Most of these elements are inner processes, that is, movements within the consciousness of individual personages, and not necessarily of personages involved in the exterior occurrence but also of others who are not even present at the time: "people," or "Mr. Bankes." In addition other exterior occurrences which might be called secondary and which pertain to quite different times and places (the telephone conversation, the construction of the building, for example) are worked in and made to serve as the frame for what goes on in the consciousness of third persons. Let us examine this in detail.

Mrs. Ramsay's very first remark is twice interrupted: first by the visual impression she receives of William Bankes and Lily Briscoe passing by together, and then, after a few intervening words serving the progress of the exterior occurrence, by the impression which the two persons passing by have left in her: the charm of Lily's Chinese eyes, which it is not for every man to see—whereupon she finishes her sentence and also allows her consciousness to dwell for a moment on the measuring of the stocking: we may yet go to the lighthouse, and so I must make sure the stocking is long enough. At this point there flashes into her mind the idea which has been prepared by her reflection on Lily's Chinese eyes (William and Lily ought to marry)—an admirable idea, she loves making matches. Smiling, she begins measuring the stocking. But the boy, in his stubborn and jealous love of her, refuses to stand still. How can she see whether the stocking is the right length if the boy keeps fidgeting about? What is the matter with James, her youngest, her darling? She looks up. Her eye falls on the room—and a long parenthesis begins. From the shabby chairs of which Andrew, her eldest son, said the other day that their entrails were all over the floor, her thoughts wander on, probing the objects and the people of her environment. The shabby furniture . . . but still good enough for up here; the advantages of the summer place; so cheap, so good for the children, for her husband; easily fitted up with a few old pieces of furniture, some pictures and books. Books—it is ages since she has had time to read books, even the books which have been dedicated to her (here the lighthouse flashes in for a second, as a place where one can't send such erudite volumes as some of those lying about the room). Then the house again: if the family would only be a little more careful. But of course, Andrew brings in crabs he wants to dissect; the other children gather seaweed, shells, stones; and she has to let them. All the children are gifted, each in a different way. But naturally, the house gets shabbier as a result (here the parenthesis is interrupted for a moment; she holds the stocking against James's leg); everything goes to ruin. If only the doors weren't always left open. See, everything is getting spoiled, even that Cashmere shawl on the picture frame. The doors are always left open; they are open again now. She listens: Yes, they are all open. The window on the landing is open too; she opened it herself. Windows must be open, doors closed. Why is it that no one can get that into his head? If you go to the maids' rooms at night, you will find all the windows closed. Only the Swiss maid always keeps her window open. She needs fresh air. Yesterday she looked out of the window with tears in her eyes and said: At home the mountains are so beautiful. Mrs. Ramsay knew that "at home" the girl's father was dying. Mrs. Ramsay had just been trying to teach her how to make beds, how to open windows. She had been talking away and had scolded the girl too. But then she had stopped talking (comparison with a bird folding its wings after flying in sunlight). She had stopped talking, for there was nothing one could say; he has cancer of the throat. At this point, remembering how she had stood there, how the girl had said at home the mountains were so beautiful—and there was no hope left—a sudden tense exasperation arises in her (exasperation with the cruel meaninglessness of a life whose continuance she is nevertheless striving with all her powers to abet, support, and secure). Her exasperation flows out into the exterior action. The parenthesis suddenly closes (it cannot have taken up more than a few seconds; just now she was still smiling over the thought of a marriage between Mr. Bankes and Lily Briscoe), and she says sharply to James: Stand still. Don't be so tiresome.

This is the first major parenthesis. The second starts a little later, after the stocking has been measured and found to be still much too short. It starts with the paragraph which begins and ends with the motif, "never did anybody look so sad."

Who is speaking in this paragraph? Who is looking at Mrs. Ramsay here, who concludes that never did anybody look so sad? Who is expressing these doubtful, obscure suppositions?—about the tear which —perhaps—forms and falls in the dark, about the water swaying this way and that, receiving it, and then returning to rest? There is no one near the window in the room but Mrs. Ramsay and James. It cannot be either of them, nor the "people" who begin to speak in the next paragraph. Perhaps it is the author. However, if that be so, the author certainly does not speak like one who has a knowledge of his characters—in this case, of Mrs. Ramsay—and who, out of his knowledge, can describe their personality and momentary state of mind objectively and with certainty. Virginia Woolf wrote this paragraph. She did not identify it through grammatical and typographical devices as the speech or thought of a third person. One is obliged to assume that it contains direct statements of her own. But she does not seem to bear in mind that she is the author and hence ought to know how matters stand with her characters. The person speaking here, whoever it is, acts the part of one who has only an impression of Mrs. Ramsay, who looks at her face and renders the impression received, but is doubtful of its proper interpretation. "Never did anybody look so sad" is not an objective statement. In rendering the shock received by one looking at Mrs. Ramsay's face, it verges upon a realm beyond reality. And in the ensuing passage the speakers no longer seem to be human beings at all but spirits between heaven and earth, nameless spirits capable of penetrating the depths of the human soul, capable too of knowing something about it, but not of attaining clarity as to what is in process there, with the result that what they report has a doubtful ring, comparable in a way to those "certain airs, detached from the body of the wind," which in a later passage (2, 2) move about the house at night, "questioning and wondering." However that may be, here too we are not dealing with objective utterances on the part of the author in respect to one of the characters. No one is certain of anything here: it is all mere supposition, glances cast by one person upon another whose enigma he cannot solve.

This continues in the following paragraph. Suppositions as to the meaning of Mrs. Ramsay's expression are made and discussed. But the level of tone descends slightly, from the poetic and non-real to the practical and earthly; and now a speaker is introduced: "People said." People wonder whether some recollection of an unhappy occurrence in her earlier life is hidden behind her radiant beauty. There have been rumors to that effect. But perhaps the rumors are wrong: nothing of this is to be learned directly from her; she is silent when such things come up in conversation. But supposing she has never experienced anything of the sort herself, she yet knows everything even without experience. The simplicity and genuineness of her being unfailingly light upon the truth of things, and, falsely perhaps, delight, ease, sustain.

Is it still "people" who are speaking here? We might almost be tempted to doubt it, for the last words sound almost too personal and thoughtful for the gossip of "people." And immediately afterward, suddenly and unexpectedly, an entirely new speaker, a new scene, and a new time are introduced. We find Mr. Bankes at the telephone talking to Mrs. Ramsay, who has called him to tell him about a train connection, evidently with reference to a journey they are planning to make together. The paragraph about the tear had already taken us out of the room where Mrs. Ramsay and James are sitting by the window; it had transported us to an undefinable scene beyond the realm of reality. The paragraph in which the rumors are discussed has a concretely earthly but not clearly identified scene. Now we find ourselves in a precisely determined place, but far away from the summer house—in London, in Mr. Bankes's house. The time is not stated ("once"), but apparently the telephone conversation took place long (perhaps as much as several years) before this particular sojourn in the house on the island. But what Mr. Bankes says over the telephone is in perfect continuity with the preceding paragraph. Again not objectively but in the form of the impression received by a specific person at a specific moment, it as it were sums up all that precedes—the scene with the Swiss maid, the hidden sadness in Mrs. Ramsay's beautiful face, what people think about her, and the impression she makes: Nature has but little clay like that of which she molded her. Did Mr. Bankes really say that to her over the telephone? Or did he only want to say it when he heard her voice, which moved him deeply, and it came into his mind how strange it was to be talking over the telephone with this wonderful woman, so like a Greek goddess? The sentence is enclosed in quotation marks, so one would suppose that he really spoke it. But this is not certain, for the first words of his soliloquy, which follows, are likewise enclosed in quotation marks. In any case, he quickly gets hold of himself, for he answers in a matter-of-fact way that he will catch the 10:30 at Euston.

But his emotion does not die away so quickly. As he puts down the receiver and walks across the room to the window in order to watch the work on a new building across the way—apparently his usual and characteristic procedure when he wants to relax and let his thoughts wander freely—he continues to be preoccupied with Mrs. Ramsay. There is always something strange about her, something that does not quite go with her beauty (as for instance telephoning); she has no awareness of her beauty, or at most only a childish awareness; her dress and her actions show that at times. She is constantly getting involved in everyday realities which are hard to reconcile with the harmony of her face. In his methodical way he tries to explain her incongruities to himself. He puts forward some conjectures but cannot make up his mind. Meanwhile his momentary impressions of the work on the new building keep crowding in. Finally he gives it up. With the somewhat impatient, determined matter-of-factness of a methodical and scientific worker (which he is) he shakes off the insoluble problem "Mrs. Ramsay." He knows no solution (the repetition of "he did not know" symbolizes his impatient shaking it off). He has to get back to his work.

Here the second long interruption comes to an end and we are taken back to the room where Mrs. Ramsay and James are. The exterior occurrence is brought to a close with the kiss on James's forehead and the resumption of the cutting out of pictures. But here too we have only an exterior change. A scene previously abandoned reappears, suddenly and with as little transition as if it had never been left, as though the long interruption were only a glance which someone (who?) has cast from it into the depths of time. But the theme (Mrs. Ramsay, her beauty, the enigma of her character, her absoluteness, which nevertheless always exercises itself in the relativity and ambiguity of life, in what does not become her beauty) carries over directly from the last phase of the interruption (that is, Mr. Bankes's fruitless reflections) into the situation in which we now find Mrs. Ramsay: "with her head outlined absurdly by the gilt frame" etc.—for once again what is around her is not suited to her, is "something incongruous." And the kiss she gives her little boy, the words she speaks to him, although they are a genuine gift of life, which James accepts as the most natural and simple truth, are yet heavy with unsolved mystery.

Our analysis of the passage yields a number of distinguishing stylistic characteristics, which we shall now attempt to formulate.

The writer as narrator of objective facts has almost completely vanished; almost everything stated appears by way of reflection in the consciousness of the dramatis personae. When it is a question of the house, for example, or of the Swiss maid, we are not given the objective information which Virginia Woolf possesses regarding these objects of her creative imagination but what Mrs. Ramsay thinks or feels about them at a particular moment. Similarly we are not taken into Virginia Woolf's confidence and allowed to share her knowledge of Mrs. Ramsay's character; we are given her character as it is reflected in and as it affects various figures in the novel: the nameless spirits which assume certain things about a tear, the people who wonder about her, and Mr. Bankes. In our passage this goes so far that there actually seems to be no viewpoint at all outside the novel from which the people and events within it are observed, any more than there seems to be an objective reality apart from what is in the consciousness of the characters. Remnants of such a reality survive at best in brief references to the exterior frame of the action, such as "said Mrs. Ramsay, raising her eyes . . ." or "said Mr. Bankes once, hearing her voice." The last paragraph ("Knitting her reddish-brown hairy stocking . . .") might perhaps also be mentioned in this connection. But this is already somewhat doubtful. The occurrence is described objectively, but as for its interpretation, the tone indicates that the author looks at Mrs. Ramsay not with knowing but with doubting and questioning eyes—even as some character in the novel would see her in the situation in which she is described, would hear her speak the words given.

The devices employed in this instance (and by a number of contemporary writers as well) to express the contents of the consciousness of the dramatis personae have been analyzed and described syntactically. Some of them have been named (*erlebte Rede*, stream of consciousness, *monologue intérieur* are examples). Yet these stylistic forms, especially the *erlebte Rede*, were used in literature much earlier too, but not for the same aesthetic purpose. And in addition to them there are other possibilities—hardly definable in terms of syntax—of obscuring and even obliterating the impression of an objective reality completely known to the author; possibilities, that is, dependent not on form but on intonation and context. A case in point is the passage under discussion, where the author at times achieves the intended effect by representing herself to be someone who doubts, wonders, hesitates, as though the truth about her characters were not better known to her than it is to them or to the reader. It is all, then, a matter of the author's attitude toward the reality of the world he represents. And this attitude differs entirely from that of authors who interpret the actions, situations, and characters of their personages with objective assurance, as was the general practice in earlier times. Goethe or Keller, Dickens or Meredith, Balzac or Zola told us out of their certain knowledge what their characters did, what they felt and thought while doing it, and how their actions and thoughts were to be interpreted. They knew everything about their characters. To be sure, in past periods too we were frequently told about the subjective reactions of the characters in a novel or story; at times even in the form of *erlebte Rede,* although more frequently as a monologue, and of course in most instances with an introductory phrase something like "it seemed to him that . . ." or "at this moment he felt that . . ." or the like. Yet in such cases there was hardly ever any attempt to render the flow and the play of consciousness adrift in the current of changing impressions (as is done in our text both for Mrs. Ramsay and for Mr. Bankes); instead, the content of the individual's consciousness was rationally limited to things connected with the particular incident being related or the particular situation being described . . . And what is still more important: the author, with his knowledge of an objective truth, never abdicated his position as the final and governing authority. Again, earlier writers, especially from the end of the nineteenth century on, had produced narrative works which on the whole undertook to give us an extremely subjective, individualistic, and often eccentrically aberrant impression of reality, and which neither sought nor were able to ascertain anything objective or generally valid in regard to it. Sometimes such works took the form of first-person novels; sometimes they did not. As an example of the latter case I mention Huysmans's novel *A rebours.* But all that too is basically different from the modern procedure here described on the basis of Virginia Woolf's text, although the latter, it is true, evolved from the former. The essential characteristic of the technique represented by Virginia Woolf is that we are given not merely one person whose consciousness (that is, the impressions it receives) is rendered, but many persons, with frequent shifts from one to the other—in our text, Mrs. Ramsay, "people," Mr. Bankes, in brief interludes James, the Swiss maid in a flash-back, and the nameless ones who speculate over a tear. The multiplicity of persons suggests that we are here after all confronted with an endeavor to investigate an objective reality, that is, specifically, the "real" Mrs. Ramsay. She is, to be sure, an enigma and such she basically remains, but she is as it were encircled by the content of all the various consciousnesses directed upon her (including her own); there is an attempt to approach her from many sides as closely as human possibilities of perception and expression can succeed in doing. The design of a close approach to objective reality by means of numerous subjective impressions received by various individuals (and at various times) is important in the modern technique which we are here examining. It basically differentiates it from the unipersonal subjectivism which allows only a single and generally a very unusual person to make himself heard and admits only that one person's way of looking at reality. In terms of literary history, to be sure, there are close connections between the two methods of representing consciousness—the unipersonal subjective method and the multipersonal method with synthesis as its aim. The latter developed from the former, and there are works in which the two overlap, so that we can watch the development. This is especially the case in Marcel Proust's great novel. We shall return to it later.

Another stylistic peculiarity to be observed in our text—though one that is closely and necessarily connected with the "multipersonal representation of consciousness" just discussed—has to do with the treatment of time. That there is something peculiar about the treatment of time in modern narrative literature is nothing new; several studies have been published on the subject. These were primarily attempts to establish a connection between the pertinent phenomena and contemporary philosophical doctrines or trends—undoubtedly a justifiable undertaking and useful for an appreciation of the community of interests and inner purposes shown in the activity of many of our contemporaries. We shall begin by describing the procedure with reference to our present example. We remarked earlier that the act of measuring the length of the stocking and the speaking of the words related to it must have taken much less time than an attentive reader who tries not to miss anything will require to read the passage—even if we assume that a brief pause intervened between the measuring and the kiss of reconciliation on James's forehead. However, the time the narration takes is not devoted to the occurrence itself (which is rendered rather tersely) but to interludes. Two long excursuses are inserted, whose relations in time to the occurrence which frames them seem to be entirely different. The first excursus, a representation of what goes on in Mrs. Ramsay's mind while she measures the stocking (more precisely, between the first absent-minded and the second sharp order to James to hold his leg still) belongs in time to the framing occurrence, and it is only the representation of it which takes a greater number of seconds and even minutes than the measuring—the reason being that the road taken by consciousness is sometimes traversed far more quickly than language is able to render it, if we want to make ourselves intelligible to a third person, and that is the intention here. What goes on in Mrs. Ramsay's mind in itself contains nothing enigmatic; these are ideas which arise from her daily life and may well be

called normal—her secret lies deeper, and it is only when the switch
from the open windows to the Swiss maid's words comes, that something happens which lifts the veil a little. On the whole, however, the
mirroring of Mrs. Ramsay's consciousness is much more easily comprehensible than the sort of thing we get in such cases from other
authors (James Joyce, for example). But simple and trivial as are the
ideas which arise one after the other in Mrs. Ramsay's consciousness,
they are at the same time essential and significant. They amount to a
synthesis of the intricacies of life in which her incomparable beauty
has been caught, in which it at once manifests and conceals itself. Of
course, writers of earlier periods too occasionally devoted some time
and a few sentences to telling the reader what at a specific moment
passed through their characters' minds—but for such a purpose they
would hardly have chosen so accidental an occasion as Mrs. Ramsay's
looking up, so that, quite involuntarily, her eyes fall on the furniture.
Nor would it have occurred to them to render the continuous rumination of consciousness in its natural and purposeless freedom. And
finally they would not have inserted the entire process between two
exterior occurrences so close together in time as the two warnings to
James to keep still (both of which, after all, take place while she is on
the point of holding the unfinished stocking to his leg); so that, in a
surprising fashion unknown to earlier periods, a sharp contrast results
between the brief span of time occupied by the exterior event and the
dreamlike wealth of a process of consciousness which traverses a whole
subjective universe. These are the characteristic and distinctively new
features of the technique: a chance occasion releasing processes of
consciousness; a natural and even, if you will, a naturalistic rendering
of those processes in their peculiar freedom, which is neither restrained
by a purpose nor directed by a specific subject of thought; elaboration
of the contrast between "exterior" and "interior" time. The three have
in common what they reveal of the author's attitude: he submits,
much more than was done in earlier realistic works, to the random
contingency of real phenomena; and even though he winnows and
stylizes the material of the real world—as of course he cannot help
doing—he does not proceed rationalistically, nor with a view to bringing a continuity of exterior events to a planned conclusion. In Virginia
Woolf's case the exterior events have actually lost their hegemony,
they serve to release and interpret inner events, whereas before her
time (and still today in many instances) inner movements preponder-
antly function to prepare and motivate significant exterior happenings.
This too is apparent in the randomness and contingency of the exterior

occasion (looking up because James does not keep his foot still), which releases the much more significant inner process.

The temporal relation between the second excursus and the framing occurrence is of a different sort: its content (the passage on the tear, the things people think about Mrs. Ramsay, the telephone conversation with Mr. Bankes and his reflections while watching the building of the new hotel) is not a part of the framing occurrence either in terms of time or of place. Other times and places are in question; it is an excursus of the same type as the story of the origin of Odysseus' scar, which was discussed in the first chapter of this book. Even from that, however, it is different in structure. In the Homer passage the excursus was linked to the scar which Euryclea touches with her hands, and although the moment at which the touching of the scar occurs is one of high and dramatic tension, the scene nevertheless immediately shifts to another clear and luminous present, and this present seems actually designed to cut off the dramatic tension and cause the entire footwashing scene to be temporarily forgotten. In Virginia Woolf's passage, there is no question of any tension. Nothing of importance in a dramatic sense takes place; the problem is the length of the stocking. The point of departure for the excursus is Mrs. Ramsay's facial expression: "never did anybody look so sad." In fact several excursuses start from here; three, to be exact. And all three differ in time and place, differ too in definiteness of time and place, the first being situated quite vaguely, the second somewhat more definitely, and the third with comparative precision. Yet none of them is so exactly situated in time as the successive episodes of the story of Odysseus' youth, for even in the case of the telephone scene we have only an inexact indication of when it occurred. As a result it becomes possible to accomplish the shifting of the scene away from the window-nook much more unnoticeably and smoothly than the changing of scene and time in the episode of the scar. In the passage on the tear the reader may still be in doubt as to whether there has been any shift at all. The nameless speakers may have entered the room and be looking at Mrs. Ramsay. In the second paragraph this interpretation is no longer possible, but the "people" whose gossip is reproduced are still looking at Mrs. Ramsay's face—not here and now, at the summer-house window, but it is still the same face and has the same expression. And even in the third part, where the face is no longer physically seen (for Mr. Bankes is talking to Mrs. Ramsay over the telephone), it is nonetheless present to his inner vision; so that not for an instant does the theme (the solution of the enigma Mrs. Ramsay), and even the moment when the problem is formulated (the expression of her face while she measures the length of the stocking), vanish from the reader's memory. In terms of the exterior event the three parts of the excursus have nothing to do with one another. They have no common and externally coherent development, as have the episodes of Odysseus' youth which are related with reference to the origin of the scar; they are connected only by the one thing they have in common—looking at Mrs. Ramsay, and more specifically at the Mrs. Ramsay who, with an unfathomable expression of sadness behind her radiant beauty, concludes that the stocking is still much too short. It is only this common focus which connects the otherwise totally different parts of the excursus; but the connection is strong enough to deprive them of the independent "present" which the episode of the scar possesses. They are nothing but attempts to interpret "never did anybody look so sad"; they carry on this theme, which itself carries on after they conclude: there has been no change of theme at all. In contrast, the scene in which Euryclea recognizes Odysseus is interrupted and divided into two parts by the excursus on the origin of the scar. In our passage, there is no such clear distinction between two exterior occurrences and between two presents. However insignficant as an exterior event the framing occurrence (the measuring of the stocking) may be, the picture of Mrs. Ramsay's face which arises from it remains present throughout the excursus; the excursus itself is nothing but a background for that picture, which seems as it were to open into the depths of time—just as the first excursus, released by Mrs. Ramsay's unintentional glance at the furniture, was an opening of the picture into the depths of consciousness.

The two excursuses, then, are not as different as they at first appeared. It is not so very important that the first, so far as time is concerned (and place too), runs its course within the framing occurrence, while the second conjures up other times and places. The times and places of the second are not independent; they serve only the polyphonic treatment of the image which releases it; as a matter of fact, they impress us (as does the interior time of the first excursus) like an occurrence in the consciousness of some observer (to be sure, he is not identified) who might see Mrs. Ramsay at the described moment and whose meditation upon the unsolved enigma of her personality might contain memories of what others (people, Mr. Bankes) say and think about her. In both excursuses we are dealing with attempts to fathom a more genuine, a deeper, and indeed a more real reality; in both cases the incident which releases the excursus appears accidental and is poor in content; in both cases it makes little difference whether the excursuses employ only the consciousness-content, and hence only interior time, or whether they also employ exterior shifts of time. After all, the process of consciousness in the first excursus likewise includes shifts of time and scene, especially the episode with the Swiss maid. The important point is that an insignificant exterior occurrence releases ideas and chains of ideas which cut loose from the present of the exterior occurrence and range freely through the depths of time. It is as though an apparently simple text revealed its proper content only in the commentary on it, a simple musical theme only in the development-section. This enables us also to understand the close relation between the treatment of time and the "multipersonal representation of consciousness" discussed earlier. The ideas arising in consciousness are not tied to the present of the exterior occurrence which releases them. Virginia Woolf's peculiar technique, as exemplified in our text, consists in the fact that the exterior objective reality of the momentary present which the author directly reports and which appears as established fact—in our instance the measuring of the stocking—is nothing but an occasion (although perhaps not an entirely accidental one). The stress is placed entirely on what the occasion releases, things which are not seen directly but by reflection, which are not tied to the present of the framing occurrence which releases them.

Here it is only natural that we should recall Proust's work. He was the first to carry this sort of thing through consistently; and his entire technique is bound up with a recovery of lost realities in remembrance, a recovery released by some externally insignificant and apparently accidental occurrence. Proust describes the procedure more than once. We have to wait until volume 2 of *Le Temps retrouvé* for a full description embracing the corresponding theory of art; but the first description, which occurs as early as section 1 of *Du Côté de chez Swann*, is impressive enough. Here, one unpleasant winter evening, the taste of a cake (*petite Madeleine*) dipped in tea arouses in the narrator an overwhelming though at first indefinite delight. By intense and repeated effort he attempts to fathom its nature and cause, and it develops that the delight is based on a recovery: the recovery of the taste of the *petite Madeleine* dipped in tea which his aunt would give him on Sundays when, still a little boy, he went into her room to wish her good morning, in the house in the old provincial town of Combray where she lived, hardly ever leaving her bed, and where he used to spend the summer months with his parents. And from this recovered remembrance, the world of his childhood emerges into light, becomes depictable, as more genuine and more real than any experienced present—and he begins to narrate. Now with Proust a narrating "I" is preserved throughout. It is not, to be sure, an author observing from without but a person involved in the action and pervading it with the distinctive flavor of his being, so that one might feel tempted to class Proust's novel among the products of the unipersonal subjectivism which we discussed earlier. So to class it would not be wrong but it would be inadequate. It would fail to account completely for the structure of Proust's novel. After all, it does not display the same strictly unipersonal approach to reality as Huysmans's *A Rebours* or Knut Hamsun's *Pan* (to mention two basically different examples which are yet comparable in this respect). Proust aims at objectivity, he wants to bring out the essence of events: he strives to attain this goal by accepting the guidance of his own consciousness—not, however, of his consciousness as it happens to be at any particular moment but as it remembers things. A consciousness in which remembrance causes past realities to arise, which has long since left behind the states in which it found itself when those realities occurred as a present, sees and arranges that content in a way very different from the purely individual and subjective. Freed from its various earlier involvements, consciousness views its own past layers and their content in perspective; it keeps confronting them with one another, emancipating them from their exterior temporal continuity as well as from the narrow meanings they seemed to have when they were bound to a particular present. There is to be noted in this a fusion of the modern concept of interior time with the neo-Platonic idea that the true prototype of a given subject is to be found in the soul of the artist; in this case, of an artist who, present in the subject itself, has detached himself from it as observer and thus comes face to face with his own past.

I shall here give a brief passage from Proust in order to illustrate this point. It deals with a moment in the narrator's childhood and occurs in volume 1, toward the end of the first section. It is, I must admit, too good and too clear an example of the layered structure of a consciousness engaged in recollection. That structure is not always as evident as it is in this instance; elsewhere it could be made clearly apparent only through an analysis of the way the subject matter is arranged, of the introduction, disappearance, and reappearance of the characters, and of the overlapping of the various presents and consciousness-contents. But every reader of Proust will admit that the whole work is written in accordance with the technique which our passage makes apparent without comment or analysis. The situation is this: One evening during his childhood the narrator could not go to sleep without the usual ceremony of being kissed good night by his mother. When he went to bed his mother could not come to his room because there was a guest for supper. In a state of nervous hypertension he decides to stay awake and catch his mother at the door when, after the guest's departure, she herself retires. This is a serious offense, because his parents are trying to correct his excessive sensitivity by sternly suppressing such cravings. He has to reckon with severe punishment; perhaps he will be banished from home and sent to a boarding school. Yet his need for momentary satisfaction is stronger than his fear of the consequences. Quite unexpectedly it happens that his father, who is usually far stricter and more authoritarian but at the same time less consistent than his mother, comes upstairs directly behind her. Seeing the boy, he is touched by the desperate expression in his face and advises his wife to spend the night in the child's room to calm him down. Proust continues:

> On ne pouvait pas remercier mon père; on l'eût agacé par ce qu'il appelait des sensibleries. Je restai sans oser faire un mouvement; il était encore devant nous, grand, dans sa robe de nuit blanche sous le cachemire de l'Inde violet et rose qu'il nouait autour de sa tête depuis qu'il avait des névralgies, avec le geste d'Abraham dans la gravure d'après Benozzo Gozzoli que m'avait donné M. Swann, disant à Hagar, qu'elle a à se départir du côté d'Isaac. Il y a bien des années de cela. La muraille de l'escalier, où je vis monter le reflet de sa bougie n'existe plus depuis longtemps. En moi aussi bien des choses ont été détruites que je croyais devoir durer toujours et de nouvelles se sont édifiées donnant naissance à des peines et à des joies nouvelles que je n'aurais pu prévoir alors, de même que les anciennes me sont devenues difficiles à comprendre. Il y a bien longtemps aussi que mon père a cessé de pouvoir dire à maman: "Va avec le petit." La possibilité de telles heures ne renaîtra jamais pour moi. Mais depuis peu de temps, je recommence à très bien percevoir si je prête l'oreille, les sanglots que j'eus la force de contenir devant mon père et qui n'éclatèrent que quand je me retrouvai seul avec maman. En réalité ils n'ont jamais cessé; et c'est seulement parce que la vie se tait maintenant davantage autour de moi que je les entends de nouveau, comme ces cloches de couvents que couvrent si bien les bruits de la ville pendant le jour qu'on les croirait arrêtées mais qui se remettent à sonner dans le silence du soir.

> (It was impossible for me to thank my father; what he called my sentimentality would have exasperated him. I stood there, not daring to move; he was still confronting us, an immense figure in his white nightshirt, crowned with the pink and violet scarf of Indian cashmere in

which, since he had begun to suffer from neuralgia, he used to tie up his head, standing like Abraham in the engraving after Benozzo Gozzoli which M. Swann had given me, telling Hagar that she must tear herself away from Isaac. Many years have passed since that night. The wall of the staircase, up which I had watched the light of his candle gradually climb, was long ago demolished. And in myself, too, many things have perished which, I imagined, would last for ever, and new structures have arisen, giving birth to new sorrows and new joys which in those days I could not have foreseen, just as now the old are difficult of comprehension. It is a long time, too, since my father has been able to tell Mamma to "Go with the child." Never again will such hours be possible for me. But of late I have been increasingly able to catch, if I listen attentively, the sound of the sobs which I had the strength to control in my father's presence, and which broke out only when I found myself alone with Mamma. Actually, their echo has never ceased: it is only because life is now growing more and more quiet round about me that I hear them afresh, like those convent bells which are so effectively drowned during the day by the noises of the streets that one would suppose them to have been stopped for ever, until they sound out again through the silent evening air.) *Remembrance of Things Past*, by Marcel Proust. Translated by C. K. Scott Moncrieff. Random House. 1934.

Through the temporal perspective we sense here an element of the symbolic omnitemporality of an event fixed in a remembering consciousness. Still clearer and more systematic (and also, to be sure, much more enigmatic) are the symbolic references in James Joyce's *Ulysses*, in which the technique of a multiple reflection of consciousness and of multiple time strata would seem to be employed more radically than anywhere else. The book unmistakably aims at a symbolic synthesis of the theme "Everyman." All the great motifs of the cultural history of Europe are contained in it, although its point of departure is very specific individuals and a clearly established present (Dublin, June 16, 1904). On sensitive readers it can produce a very strong immediate impression. Really to understand it, however, is not an easy matter, for it makes severe demands on the reader's patience and learning by its dizzying whirl of motifs, wealth of words and concepts, perpetual playing upon their countless associations, and the ever rearoused but never satisfied doubt as to what order is ultimately hidden behind so much apparent arbitrariness.

Few writers have made so consistent a use of reflected consciousness and time strata as those we have so far discussed. But the influence of the procedure and traces of it can be found almost everywhere—lately even in writers of the sort whom discriminating readers are not in the habit of regarding as fully competent. Many writers have invented their own methods—or at least have experimented in the direction—of making the reality which they adopt as their subject appear in changing lights and changing strata, or of abandoning the specific angle of observation of either a seemingly objective or purely subjective representation in favor of a more varied perspective. Among these writers we find older masters whose aesthetic individualities had long since been fully established but who were drawn into the movement in their years of maturity before and after the first World War, each in his own way turning to a disintegration and dissolution of external realities for a richer and more essential interpretation of them. Thomas Mann is an example, who, ever since his *Magic Mountain,* without in any way abandoning his level of tone (in which the narrating, commenting, objectivizing author addressing the reader is always present) has been more and more concerned with time perspectives and the symbolic omnitemporality of events. Another very different instance is André Gide, in whose *Faux-Monnayeurs* there is a constant shifting of the viewpoint from which the events (themselves multilayered) are surveyed, and who carries this procedure to such an extreme that the novel and the account of the genesis of the novel are interwoven in the ironic vein of the romanticists. Very different again, and much simpler, is the case of Knut Hamsun who, for example in his *Growth of the Soil,* employs a level of tone which blurs the dividing line between the direct or indirect discourse of the characters in the novel and the author's own utterances; as a result one is never quite certain that what one hears is being said by the author as he stands outside his novel; the statements sound as though they came from one of the persons involved in the action, or at least from a passer-by who observes the incident. Finally, we have still to mention certain further peculiarities of the kind of writing we are considering—those which concern the type of subject matter treated. In modern novels we frequently observe that it is not one person or a limited number of persons whose experiences are pursued as a continuum; indeed, often there is no strict continuum of events. Sometimes many individuals, or many fragments of events, are loosely joined so that the reader has no definite thread of action which he can always follow. There are novels which attempt to reconstruct a milieu from mere splinters of events, with constantly changing though occasionally reappearing characters. In this latter case one might feel inclined to assume that it was the writer's purpose to exploit the structural possibilities of the film in the interest of the novel. If so, it is a wrong direction: a concentration of space and time such as can be achieved by the film (for example the representation, within a few seconds and by means of a few pictures, of the situation of a widely dispersed group of people, of a great city, an army, a war, an entire country) can never be within the reach of the spoken or written word. To be sure, the novel possesses great freedom in its command of space and time—much more than the drama of pre-film days, even if we disregard the strict classical rules of unity. The novel in recent decades has made use of this freedom in a way for which earlier literary periods afford no models, with the possible exception of a few tentative efforts by the romanticists, especially in Germany, although they did not restrict themselves to the material of reality. At the same time, however, by virtue of the film's existence, the novel has come to be more clearly aware than ever before of the limitations in space and time imposed upon it by its instrument, language. As a result the situation has been reversed: the dramatic technique of the film now has far greater possibilities in the direction of condensing time and space than has the novel itself.

The distinctive characteristics of the realistic novel of the era between the two great wars, as they have appeared in the present chapter—multipersonal representation of consciousness, time strata, disintegration of the continuity of exterior events, shifting of the narrative viewpoint (all of which are interrelated and difficult to separate)—seem to us indicative of a striving for certain objectives, of certain tendencies and needs on the part of both authors and public. These objectives, tendencies, and needs are numerous; they seem in part to be mutually contradictory; yet they form so much one whole that when we undertake to describe them analytically, we are in constant danger of unwittingly passing from one to another.

Let us begin with a tendency which is particularly striking in our text from Virginia Woolf. She holds to minor, unimpressive, random events: measuring the stocking, a fragment of a conversation with the maid, a telephone call. Great changes, exterior turning points, let alone catastrophes, do not occur; and though elsewhere in *To the Lighthouse* such things are mentioned, it is hastily, without preparation or context, incidentally, and as it were only for the sake of information. The same tendency is to be observed in other and very different writers, such as Proust or Hamsun. In Thomas Mann's *Buddenbrooks* we still have a novel structure consisting of the chronological sequence of important exterior events which affect the Buddenbrook family; and if Flaubert —in many respects a precursor—lingers as a matter of principle over insignificant events and everyday circumstances which hardly advance the action, there is nevertheless to be sensed throughout *Madame Bovary* (though we may wonder how this would have worked out in *Bouvard et Pécuchet*) a constant slow-moving chronological approach first to partial crises and finally to the concluding catastrophe, and it is this approach which dominates the plan of the work as a whole. But a shift in emphasis followed; and now many writers present minor happenings, which are insignificant as exterior factors in a person's destiny, for their own sake or rather as points of departure for the development of motifs, for a penetration which opens up new perspectives into a milieu or a consciousness or the given historical setting. They have discarded presenting the story of their characters with any claim to exterior completeness, in chronological order, and with the emphasis on important exterior turning points of destiny. James Joyce's tremendous novel—an encyclopedic work, a mirror of Dublin, of Ireland, a mirror too of Europe and its millennia—has for its frame the externally insignificant course of a day in the lives of a schoolteacher and an advertising broker. It takes up less than twenty-four hours in their lives—just as *To the Lighthouse* describes portions of two days widely separated in time. (There is here also, as we must not fail to observe, a similarity to Dante's Comedy.) Proust presents individual days and hours from different periods, but the exterior events which are the determining factors in the destinies of the novel's characters during the intervening lapses of time are mentioned only incidentally, in retrospect or anticipation. The ends the narrator has in mind are not to be seen in them; often the reader has to supplement them. The way in which the father's death is brought up in the passage cited above—incidentally, allusively, and in anticipation—offers a good example. This shift of emphasis expresses something that we might call a transfer of confidence: the great exterior turning points and blows of fate are granted less importance; they are credited with less power of yielding decisive information concerning the subject; on the other hand there is confidence that in any random fragment plucked from the course of a life at any time the totality of its fate is contained and can be portrayed. There is greater confidence in syntheses gained through full exploitation of an everyday occurrence than in a chronologically well-ordered total treatment which accompanies the subject from beginning to end, attempts not to omit anything externally important, and emphasizes the great turning points of destiny. It is possible to compare this technique of modern writers with that of certain modern philologists who hold that the interpretation of a few passages from *Hamlet, Phèdre,* or *Faust* can be made to yield more, and more decisive, information about Shakespeare, Racine, or Goethe and their times than would a systematic and chronological treatment of their lives and works. Indeed, the present book may be cited as an illustration. I could never have written anything in the nature of a history of European realism; the material would have swamped me; I should have had to enter into hopeless discussions concerning the delimitation of the various periods and the allocation of the various writers to them, and above all concerning the definition of the concept realism. Furthermore, for the sake of completeness, I should have had to deal with some things of which I am but casually informed, and hence to become acquainted with them *ad hoc* by reading up on them (which, in my opinion, is a poor way of acquiring and using knowledge); and the motifs which direct my investigation, and for the sake of which it is written, would have been completely buried under a mass of factual information which has long been known and can easily be looked up in reference books. As opposed to this I see the possibility of success and profit in a method which consists in letting myself be guided by a few motifs which I have worked out gradually and without a specific purpose, and in trying them out on a series of texts which have become familiar and vital to me in the course of my philological activity; for I am convinced that these basic motifs in the history of the representation of reality—provided I have seen them correctly— must be demonstrable in any random realistic text. But to return to those modern writers who prefer the exploitation of random everyday events, contained within a few hours and days, to the complete and chronological representation of a total exterior continuum—they too (more or less consciously) are guided by the consideration that it is a hopeless venture to try to be really complete within the total exterior continuum and yet to make what is essential stand out. Then too they hesitate to impose upon life, which is their subject, an order which it does not possess in itself. He who represents the course of a human life, or a sequence of events extending over a prolonged period of time, and represents it from beginning to end, must prune and isolate arbitrarily. Life has always long since begun, and it is always still going on. And the people whose story the author is telling experience much more than he can ever hope to tell. But the things that happen to a few individuals in the course of a few minutes, hours, or possibly even days—these one can hope to report with reasonable completeness. And here, furthermore, one comes upon the order and the interpretation of life which arise from life itself: that is, those which grow up in the individuals themselves, which are to be discerned in their thoughts, their consciousness, and in a more concealed form in their words and actions. For there is always going on within us a process of formulation and interpretation whose subject matter is our own self. We are constantly endeavoring to give meaning and order to our lives in the past, the present, and the future, to our surroundings, the world in which we live; with the result that our lives appear in our own conception as total entities—which to be sure are always changing, more or less radically, more or less rapidly, depending on the extent to which we are obliged, inclined, and able to assimilate the onrush of new experience. These are the forms of order and interpretation which the modern writers here under discussion attempt to grasp in the random moment—not one order and one interpretation, but many, which may either be those of different persons or of the same person at different times; so that overlapping, complementing, and contradiction yield something that we might call a synthesized cosmic view or at least a challenge to the reader's will to interpretive synthesis.

Here we have returned once again to the reflection of multiple consciousnesses. It is easy to understand that such a technique had to develop gradually and that it did so precisely during the decades of the first World War period and after. The widening of man's horizon, and the increase of his experiences, knowledge, ideas, and possible forms of existence, which began in the sixteenth century, continued through the nineteenth at an ever faster tempo—with such a tremendous acceleration since the beginning of the twentieth that synthetic and objective attempts at interpretation are produced and demolished every instant. The tremendous tempo of the changes proved the more confusing because they could not be surveyed as a whole. They occurred simultaneously in many separate departments of science, technology, and economics, with the result that no one—not even those who were leaders in the separate departments—could foresee or evaluate the resulting overall situations. Furthermore, the changes did not produce the same effects in all places, so that the differences of attainment between the various social strata of one and the same people and between different peoples came to be—if not greater—at least more noticeable. The spread of publicity and the crowding of mankind on a shrinking globe sharpened awareness of the differences in ways of life and attitudes, and mobilized the interests and forms of existence which the new changes either furthered or threatened. In all parts of the world crises of adjustment arose; they increased in number and coalesced. They led to the upheavals which we have not weathered yet. In Eu-

rope this violent clash of the most heterogeneous ways of life and kinds
of endeavor undermined not only those religious, philosophical, ethical, and economic principles which were part of the traditional heritage and which, despite many earlier shocks, had maintained their
position of authority through slow adaptation and transformation; nor
yet only the ideas of the Enlightenment, the ideas of democracy and
liberalism which had been revolutionary in the eighteenth century and
were still so during the first half of the nineteenth; it undermined even
the new revolutionary forces of socialism, whose origins did not go
back beyond the heyday of the capitalist system. These forces threatened to split up and disintegrate. They lost their unity and clear definition through the formation of numerous mutually hostile groups,
through strange alliances which some of these groups effected with
non-socialist ideologies, through the capitulation of most of them during the first World War, and finally through the propensity on the
part of many of their most radical advocates for changing over into
the camp of their most extreme enemies. Otherwise too there was an
increasingly strong factionalism—at times crystallizing around important poets, philosophers, and scholars, but in the majority of cases
pseudo-scientific, syncretistic, and primitive. The temptation to entrust
oneself to a sect which solved all problems with a single formula,
whose power of suggestion imposed solidarity, and which ostracized
everything which would not fit in and submit—this temptation was so
great that, with many people, fascism hardly had to employ force
when the time came for it to spread through the countries of old European culture, absorbing the smaller sects.

As recently as the nineteenth century, and even at the beginning of
the twentieth, so much clearly formulable and recognized community
of thought and feeling remained in those countries that a writer engaged in representing reality had reliable criteria at hand by which to
organize it. At least, within the range of contemporary movements, he
could discern certain specific trends; he could delimit opposing attitudes and ways of life with a certain degree of clarity. To be sure,
this had long since begun to grow increasingly difficult. Flaubert (to
confine ourselves to realistic writers) already suffered from the lack of
valid foundations for his work; and the subsequent increasing predilec-
tion for ruthlessly subjectivistic perspectives is another symptom. At
the time of the first World War and after—in a Europe unsure of
itself, overflowing with unsettled ideologies and ways of life, and
pregnant with disaster—certain writers distinguished by instinct and
insight find a method which dissolves reality into multiple and multi-

valent reflections of consciousness. That this method should have been developed at this time is not hard to understand.

But the method is not only a symptom of the confusion and help-lessness, not only a mirror of the decline of our world. There is, to be sure, a good deal to be said for such a view. There is in all these works a certain atmosphere of universal doom: especially in *Ulysses,* with its mocking *odi-et-amo* hodgepodge of the European tradition, with its blatant and painful cynicism, and its uninterpretable symbolism—for even the most painstaking analysis can hardly emerge with anything more than an appreciation of the multiple enmeshment of the motifs but with nothing of the purpose and meaning of the work itself. And most of the other novels which employ multiple reflection of con-sciousness also leave the reader with an impression of hopelessness. There is often something confusing, something hazy about them, something hostile to the reality which they represent. We not infre-quently find a turning away from the practical will to live, or delight in portraying it under its most brutal forms. There is hatred of culture and civilization, brought out by means of the subtlest stylistic devices which culture and civilization have developed, and often a radical and fanatical urge to destroy. Common to almost all of these novels is haziness, vague indefinability of meaning: precisely the kind of unin-terpretable symbolism which is also to be encountered in other forms of art of the same period.

But something entirely different takes place here too. Let us turn again to the text which was our starting-point. It breathes an air of vague and hopeless sadness. We never come to learn what Mrs. Ram-say's situation really is. Only the sadness, the vanity of her beauty and vital force emerge from the depths of secrecy. Even when we have read the whole novel, the meaning of the relationship between the planned trip to the lighthouse and the actual trip many years later remains unexpressed, enigmatic, only dimly to be conjectured, as does the content of Lily Briscoe's concluding vision which enables her to finish her painting with one stroke of the brush. It is one of the few books of this type which are filled with good and genuine love but also, in its feminine way, with irony, amorphous sadness, and doubt of life. Yet what realistic depth is achieved in every individual occurrence, for example the measuring of the stocking! Aspects of the occurrence come to the fore, and links to other occurrences, which, before this time, had hardly been sensed, which had never been clearly seen and attended to, and yet they are determining factors in our real lives. What takes place here in Virginia Woolf's novel is precisely what was attempted everywhere in works of this kind (although not everywhere with the same insight and mastery)—that is, to put the emphasis on the random occurrence, to exploit it not in the service of a planned continuity of action but in itself. And in the process something new and elemental appeared: nothing less than the wealth of reality and depth of life in every moment to which we surrender ourselves without prejudice. To be sure, what happens in that moment—be it outer or inner processes—concerns in a very personal way the individuals who live in it, but it also (and for that very reason) concerns the elementary things which men in general have in common. It is precisely the random moment which is comparatively independent of the controversial and unstable orders over which men fight and despair; it passes unaffected by them, as daily life. The more it is exploited, the more the elementary things which our lives have in common come to light. The more numerous, varied, and simple the people are who appear as subjects of such random moments, the more effectively must what they have in common shine forth. In this unprejudiced and exploratory type of representation we cannot but see to what an extent—below the surface conflicts—the differences between men's ways of life and forms of thought have already lessened. The strata of societies and their different ways of life have become inextricably mingled. There are no longer even exotic peoples. A century ago (in Mérimée for example), Corsicans or Spaniards were still exotic; today the term would be quite unsuitable for Pearl Buck's Chinese peasants. Beneath the conflicts, and also through them, an economic and cultural leveling process is taking place. It is still a long way to a common life of mankind on earth, but the goal begins to be visible. And it is most concretely visible now in the unprejudiced, precise, interior and exterior representation of the random moment in the lives of different people. So the complicated process of dissolution which led to fragmentation of the exterior action, to reflection of consciousness, and to stratification of time seems to be tending toward a very simple solution. Perhaps it will be too simple to please those who, despite all its dangers and catastrophes, admire and love our epoch for the sake of its abundance of life and the incomparable historical vantage point which it affords. But they are few in number, and probably they will not live to see much more than the first forewarnings of the approaching unification and simplification.

25

JOAN BENNETT

---◆---

The Form of the Novels

VIRGINIA Woolf, in her essay on *Mr. Bennett and Mrs. Brown* in 1924, affirmed that the Edwardian novelists had

> made tools and established conventions which do their business; and
> that business is not our business. For us those conventions are ruin, those
> tools death.

Her own continual experiments with the form of the novel were the consequence of that belief. What then did she feel to be her "business" as a novelist? To say that it was to communicate human experience is not enough; for the same might be said of most novelists. What she most clearly knew that she wanted to do was to record what life felt like to living beings. This was also what Dorothy Richardson had discovered in 1913 that she wished to do, and she shows us, with fine perception, through a long and leisurely progress, what life felt like to Miriam. But Virginia Woolf was not content with the record of a single mind. She wanted also to communicate the impression made by one individual upon others and to reveal human personality partly through its own self-consciousness and partly through the picture projected by it upon other minds. This was the starting point which impelled her to break away from the tradition, in *Jacob's Room*. There she makes her first attempt to remove the narrator from the scene, so that the reader may seem to see the subject solely through the eyes of

From *Virginia Woolf: Her Art as a Novelist,* Cambridge University Press ©
1945; reprinted by permission of Cambridge University Press.

the people in the book. But elimination is not yet completely effected. There are passages of description, events are recorded, comments are made not by the characters themselves but by their author:

> Elizabeth Flanders, of whom this and much more than this had been said and would be said, was, of course, a widow in her prime. She was half-way between forty and fifty.
>
> [*Jacob's Room*]

Later such necessary facts will be given through the reflection of some other mind in the book, not from without; Mrs. Dalloway's age and appearance for instance:

> A charming woman, Scrope Purvis thought her (knowing her as one does know people who live next door to one in Westminster); a touch of the bird about her, of the jay, blue-green, light, vivacious, though she was over fifty, and grown very white since her illness. There she perched, never seeing him, waiting to cross, very upright.
>
> [*Mrs. Dalloway*]

Nor is it only description and the record of event that brings the narrator forward in *Jacob's Room*—she is still, like her forerunners, though less continuously, present as commentator:

> Anyhow, whether undergraduate or shop boy, man or woman, it must come as a shock about the age of twenty—the world of the elderly— thrown up in such black outline upon what we are; upon the reality; the moors and Byron, the sea and the lighthouse; the sheep's jaw with the yellow teeth in it; upon the obstinate irrepressible conviction which makes youth so intolerably disagreeable—"I am what I am, and intend to be it," for which there will be no form in the world unless Jacob makes one for himself.
>
> [*Jacob's Room*]

But the direction, in which already she is moving, is towards complete objectivity, not the objectivity of drama, which is limited to the enacted scene and the spoken word, but an objectivity in which the feelings, the meditations, the memories of the protagonists are projected, without intervention upon the mind of the reader. When James in *To the Lighthouse* emerges into manhood, we receive his impressions of "the world of the elderly," linked as Jacob's are with past memories and with projects for the future, through the medium of his own reflections:

> He had always kept this old symbol of taking a knife and striking his father to the heart. Only now, as he grew older, and sat staring at his

father in an impotent rage, it was not him, that old man reading, whom he wanted to kill, but it was the thing that descended on him—without his knowing it perhaps: that fierce sudden black-winged harpy, with its talons and its beak all cold and hard, that struck and struck at you (he could feel the beak on his bare legs, where it had struck him when a child) and then made off, and there he was again, an old man, very sad, reading his book. That he would kill, that he would strike to the heart. Whatever he did—(and he might do anything, he felt, looking at the Lighthouse and the distant shore) whether he was in business, in a bank, a barrister, a man at the head of some enterprise, that he would fight, that he would track down and stamp out—tyranny, despotism, he called it—making people do what they did not want to do, cutting off their right to speak.

[*To the Lighthouse*]

And just as the passage about Jacob throws the reader's mind back to an earlier scene in which the sheep's jaw figured as the token of his childish self-assertion, so here, but with a richer complexity, James's meditations and the images in which he frames them, recall an earlier scene in which the demanding, uncomprehending figure of his father strode between the little boy and his mother:

At the window he bent quizzically and whimsically to tickle James's bare calf with a sprig of something, she twitted him for having despatched "that poor young man," Charles Tansley. Tansley had had to go in and write his dissertation, he said.

"James will have to write *his* dissertation one of these days," he added ironically, flicking his sprig.

Hating his father, James brushed away the tickling spray with which in a manner peculiar to him, compound of severity and humour, he teased his youngest son's bare leg.

[*To the Lighthouse*]

The will to discover and record life as it feels to those who live it was the originating cause of Virginia Woolf's rejection of existing conventions. It was this primarily that impelled her to eliminate narration and comment. In *Jacob's Room*, however, certain needs arising out of her vision of the subject prevented her from achieving that purpose. She had yet to learn how to communicate all the facts that need to be known, how to mark the passage of time, how to indicate the point of view, without speaking in her own person. In this first experiment she is avowedly conscious of her difficulties and has not learnt the art to conceal her art. Thus she will recount Jacob's words, thoughts, acts and then—much as Fielding used to do—she will insert an essay upon the art of fiction:

But though all this may very well be true—so Jacob thought and spoke—so he crossed his legs—filled his pipe—sipped his whisky, and once looked at his pocket-book, rumpling his hair as he did so, there remains over something which can never be conveyed to a second person save by Jacob himself. Moreover, part of this is not Jacob but Richard Bonamy—the room; the market carts; the hour; the very moment of history. Then consider the effect of sex—how between man and woman it hangs wavy, tremulous, so that here's a valley, there's a peak, when in truth, perhaps, all's as flat as my hand. Even the exact words get the wrong accent on them. But something is always impelling one to hum vibrating, like the hawk moth, at the mouth of the cavern of mystery, endowing Jacob Flanders with all sorts of qualities he had not at all— for though, certainly, he sat talking to Bonamy, half of what he said was too dull to repeat; much unintelligible (about unknown people and Parliament); what remains is mostly a matter of guesswork. Yet over him we hang vibrating.

[*Jacob's Room*]

The essay interrupts the illusion; but it is an invaluable document, for it enumerates the difficulties which, later, her craftsmanship was to overcome. Presently she would devise a form whereby she could communicate directly that "something which remains over" and can only be conveyed by Jacob himself, a form whereby, also, she could indicate the degree in which, at any given moment, a personality is not itself merely, but an instrument played upon by another and affected by the room, the street, the hour and "the very moment of history." She learnt to impart directly "the effect of sex," and to communicate the mysterious complexity of living experience.

Jacob's Room, because no adequate substitute has been devised to replace the old conventions, falls apart. The reader is left with the impression of a series of episodes, each of them conveyed with depth and subtlety, so that at each successive moment he is vividly aware of how life felt to Jacob, or of how Jacob affected some other. But the successive moments build up no whole that can be held in the mind. In the traditional novel the episodes are interwoven to compose a story. In that story one character is central and stands in some significant relation to the other characters and their stories. So, for instance, the story of Emma is interwoven with the story of Jane Fairfax and with the story of Harriet Smith; every other character in the book plays some part in those stories and the combined effect of all is to illuminate the central character. When the reader closes the book he has a complete pattern in his mind, the pattern by which Emma's emerging self-knowledge has been communicated. To that emergence each of the other characters was contributory and Jane Austen selected the episodes so that they might effect it. The episodes of which *Jacob's Room* is composed are chosen to reveal the impact of Jacob's developing personality upon the people with whom he comes into contact and, to a lesser degree, the impact of the external world and of other people upon Jacob. It must be of set purpose that we are given more of Jacob's reflection in other minds than of his own experience. But the result is that Jacob remains a nebulous young man, indeed almost any young man, and the reader does not fully participate in the powerful effect he makes upon others. Moreover, in so far as the writer has succeeded in effacing herself, the people she creates have to take her place. Their consciousness of the world and the people in it must be made adequate to communicate all that the writer requires the reader to know and to feel. Consequently a number of persons become momentarily very prominent. The effect is much as it would be if most of the characters in *Hamlet* were given monologues as soul-searching as the prince's own. From moment to moment, while they hold the stage, the reader is fascinated and deeply attentive. But ultimately his attention is dissipated and diffused. Too many disassociated, or only tenuously related, demands have been made upon it. A similar effect is produced by a later, and, in many ways, greater book than *Jacob's Room, The Years*. By the time Virginia Woolf wrote this, she had developed her own method of presentation very fully, although the scale upon which the book is planned, spanning nearly sixty years and tracing the life-course of two generations, necessitates an element of narration. It is, however, reduced to a minimum, and the reader is continually aware of such facts as the season, the weather, the place as reflected in some human consciousness.

> But in April such weather was to be expected. Thousands of shop assistants made that remark as they handed neat parcels to ladies in flounced dresses standing on the other side of the counter of Whiteley's and the Army and Navy Stores. Interminable processions of shoppers in the West End, of business men in the East, paraded the pavements, like caravans perpetually marching,—so it seemed to those who had any reason to pause, say, to post a letter, or at a club window in Piccadilly.
>
> [*The Years*]

More subtle and complex reflections are given through a particular consciousness, and it is the number of people whom we are invited to know with this degree of intimacy that obscures the pattern of the whole. When a novelist uses the older convention of narrative and characterization a large number of characters living through a long stretch of time can be more easily united. The stories and the groups

of characters in, for instance, *Middlemarch* are all related in a number
of ways to the story of Dorothea. The pattern of each story can be
recalled in isolation and can readily be re-incorporated into the pattern
of the whole. Minor characters are kept, by the novelist, in due sub-
ordination to major characters; neither the events of their lives nor
their experience of living are given prominence. The new method
deepens the reader's intimacy with the persons in the book at the risk,
if there are many of them, of impeding his width of view. He cannot
see the wood for the trees. The trees are magnificent, and one returns
to them again and again with renewed pleasure, Eleanor, Kitty, Edward, Maggie and Sara (especially Sara), Rose, Martin, Morris and
then the younger generation, Peggy and North, each name calls to
mind vivid moments of experience and luminously distinct personalities. But what remains in the mind is a series of episodes rather than
parts of a whole. The episodes illustrate the passage of time and the
diversity of the human scene, and they evoke reflection upon the
changing climate of opinion in sixty years, and upon the impress of
historical happenings in an individual consciousness. All this *The
Years* can give while preserving the illusion that it is all received by
the reader directly, without the intervention of the author. But the
reader feels, as Miss La Trobe in *Between the Acts* fears her audience
will do when she allows the unselected impressions of the present
moment to take the place of her invented pageant:

> something was going wrong with the experiment. "Reality too strong,"
> she muttered.
>
> [*Between the Acts*]

The total effect of *The Years* is too much like life itself; consummate
though the art is with which the parts are constructed, too little has
been done to construct the whole; the book shares in the uncoordinated
character of normal experience.

This does not mean that Virginia Woolf's art is incapable of communicating experience that is wide as well as deep. But to do so she
had to invent conventions as rigid or more rigid than the old ones
that she discards. This she does in her four most satisfying novels,
Mrs. Dalloway, To the Lighthouse, The Waves and *Between the Acts*.
There are certain resemblances between them in structure and in
style. In each case a small group of people is selected, and through
their closely interrelated experience the reader receives his total impression. In each case also certain images, phrases and symbols bind
the whole together. Apart from these general resemblances each of

these novels is a fresh attempt to solve the problems raised by the departure from traditional conventions. Her first problem is to preserve the illusion of direct contact with human beings in the process of immediate and random experience, while in fact so selecting that experience that it will form an ordered whole. Moreover, the totality aimed at, a whole that reflects human consciousness, must include not only the impressions made by physical surroundings and by other human beings but also the threefold effect of time; the passing moments or hours; the voyage from youth to age; and the historic time, or time in relation to nation-wide and world-wide event.

Three years after *Jacob's Room,* in 1925, *Mrs. Dalloway* was published. The subject is similar in so far as the principal theme is one personality, affecting and affected by the others who come into contact with it. But in the later book the composition of the whole is superbly successful. The impression made upon the reader by the central personality is clear and full, whilst a far deeper and wider understanding of the surrounding lives is given than was achieved in *Jacob's Room.* The incidents or episodes are themselves even more vivid, but they cohere firmly together and finally leave an impression of unity. In *Mrs. Dalloway* a convention or art form has been evolved which is more than adequate to take the place of the older convention of narrative and characterization. The necessary circumscription is imposed by the narrow framework of time; the whole of the action takes place within one day. It moves between Mrs. Dalloway's preparation for her party in the morning and her presiding over it in the evening of the same day. Within this narrow frame, by means of the contacts she makes and the memories they evoke in her and in others, her life story from girlhood to her present age of fifty is gradually unfolded. The story of Septimus Warren Smith, who impinges upon her consciousness early in the day and whose death throws a shadow over her party in the evening, is the means of introducing another group of characters, a darker side of life, and a more profound sense of the historic background against which the whole is set. The major characters are no more than five and they stand out from the rest with a distinctive prominence, for it is they alone who reveal their thoughts to the reader in prolonged and repeated soliloquy as well as in conversation. These five major characters move round each other, as it were, in two concentric circles, Clarissa, Peter Walsh and (rather more faintly drawn), Richard Dalloway in the one, Septimus and Rezia Warren Smith in the other. Around each of these two inner circles there is a ring of minor characters such as Sally Seton, Lady Bruton, Hugh Whitbread, Elizabeth Dalloway and, that important foil to

Clarissa, Doris Kilman; round the Warren Smith orbit move Dr. Holmes and Sir William Bradshaw through whose appearance at the party the two themes are ultimately interlocked. Further in the background are a number of figures, unimportant in themselves, but helping to compose the total scene and each one of them supplying an essential part of the pattern.

But there is another point of view from which the subject of the book no longer appears to be the life story of Clarissa Dalloway, nor of Septimus Warren Smith, but human life itself, its tension between misery and happiness and its inevitable consummation in death. From this point of view the fabric of the book is spun between the lines

> Fear no more the heat o' the sun
> Nor the furious winter's rages;

and

> If it were now to die
> 'Twere now to be most happy;

lines from Shakespeare which are woven into Clarissa's reflections or those of Septimus unobtrusively, but which evoke their own poetic context and associations. For within the book there is a poetic pattern, probing to that deeper level at which the mind apprehends timeless values, as well as the prose pattern wherein the reader is given a picture of the modern world with its destructive forces of class-struggle, economic insecurity and war. On the prose plane there are the satiric portraits of the self-made, successful, impermeable nerve specialist (the most cruel and brilliant satiric portrait Virginia Woolf ever drew) and, hardly less harsh, the picture of the neurotic, self-tormenting, embittered governess. On this plane too is one aspect of Septimus, the sympathetic yet slightly mocking account of his intellectual aspirations and romantic notions before war shattered him and, at the same time, lifted him on to the plane of tragedy. On that poetic plane there are only love and death and the evanescent beauty of the world.

From now on Virginia Woolf planned all her books, with the exception of *The Years*, within a narrow framework. She achieved this either by confining the action to a brief period of time, or by limiting the foreground characters to a small number, or by employing both these devices. Despite the narrow area of time within which the story usually moves, she yet contrives to give the reader an intimate knowledge of much that has preceded the action. In this her art is comparable with Ibsen's who, while keeping his drama within the unities of time and place can so draw upon his characters' memories as to unfold for the audience all that is relevant in their past histories. In *To the Lighthouse* the outward structure is simple. It consists of three movements of unequal length and of two different kinds, as it were two acts linked by a chorus. The first and longest act covers less than one day and is framed between Mrs. Ramsay's opening words: "Yes, of course, if it's fine tomorrow,"—that is, if it's fine we shall go to the lighthouse —and, the last words spoken by her in the book, "Yes, you were right, it's going to be wet tomorrow." After this there follows, as it were, a choral ode which marks the passage of ten years. It is framed between the close of the day recorded in the first movement and Lily Briscoe's awakening ten years later, back once more in the Ramsays' house after Mrs. Ramsay's death. The third act again covers less than a day and is enclosed between Lily's morning reflections: "What does it mean, what can it all mean?" and her evening reflections, as she finishes that picture which she began ten years ago and says: "I have had my vision." Only ten characters make any prominent appearance and of those ten only seven, Mr. and Mrs. Ramsay, Lily, Mr. Bankes, Mr. Tansley, James and Cam reveal themselves fully in speech and in soliloquy.

As in *Mrs. Dalloway*, the form is the vehicle for two kinds of experience—one on the plane of prose and the other on the plane of poetry. The double effect is analogous to that of the greatest poetic drama, and to some kinds of lyric poetry, in which the surface statement has, as it were, folded within it, the poetic meaning. The surface statement can be summarized or defined while the other can only be suggested, since it depends upon the thoughts and feelings evoked by imagery and rhythm and these will be different for different readers and at different times. Similarly, Virginia Woolf's novels convey two different kinds of meaning to each of which the form is beautifully adapted.

On the prose plane *To the Lighthouse* tells about the Ramsay family, their relations to one another and to a small representative group of their friends. The visit to the lighthouse, projected and then frustrated by the weather in the first movement, and effected in the last, is an instrument to reveal certain aspects of character such as Mrs. Ramsay's sympathetic understanding of other people's feelings, in particular those of her son James, Mr. Ramsay's insensibility and his ruthless employment of logic and a sense of fact, Mr. Tansley's aggressive self-assertiveness. The expedition provides an instance in relation to which the reader discerns Mr. Ramsay's habitual insensitiveness to other people's feelings, it is remembered in the last movement, when, with

Cam and James, he actually goes to the lighthouse, as the type of event in the past out of which the character of the boy has been formed. On this plane the reader's interest is centred in human character. The group of people assembled at the Ramsays' house, the Ramsays' children and friends, are all revealed in the light of their relation to Mrs. Ramsay and to one another, both before and after her death. Mr. Bankes's disinterested devotion to her physical and moral beauty, like his disinterested scientific curiosity, is a foil to Mr. Ramsay's more self-regarding love and learning. Mr. Tansley's sense of inferiority and consequent aggressiveness are brought out by his introduction, as Mr. Ramsay's disciple, into a house-party to which he feels himself socially inferior and intellectually superior. Looked at from this point of view Lily Briscoe's endeavour to paint a picture of Mrs. Ramsay, sitting on the steps of the house, and her subsequent completion of the picture is the expression of her sense of Mrs. Ramsay's power to create order and harmony out of human relations. The manner in which the characters are presented, partly through their actions and conversation and partly through their own reflections, effects a happy combination of amused appraisal with sympathetic understanding.

On the other plane the lighthouse is a poetic symbol with an uncircumscribed power of suggestion. For the reader, as for Mrs. Ramsay, the alternating light and shadow of the lighthouse beam symbolizes the rhythm of joy and sorrow in human life and the alternating radiance and darkness of even the most intimate human relationships:

> She looked at the steady light, the pitiless, the remorseless, which was so much her, yet so little her, which had her at its beck and call (she woke in the night and saw it bent across her bed, stroking the floor), but for all that, she thought, watching it with fascination, hypnotised, as if it were stroking with its silver fingers some sealed vessel in her brain whose bursting would flood her with delight, she had known happiness, exquisite happiness, intense happiness, and it silvered the rough waves a little more brightly, as daylight faded, and the blue went out of the sea and it rolled in waves of pure lemon which curved and swelled and broke upon the beach and the ecstasy burst in her eyes and waves of pure delight raced over the floor of her mind and she felt, It is enough! It is enough!
>
> [*To the Lighthouse*]

The structure of the book itself reproduces the effect of the lighthouse beam, the long flash represented by the first movement (The Window), the interval of darkness represented by the second movement

(Time Passes) and the second and shorter flash by the last movement (The Lighthouse). When this aspect of the book is thought of the subject is no longer a particular group of human beings; it is life and death, joy and pain—more specifically two themes stand out, the isolation of the individual human spirit and the contrast between the disordered and fragmentary experience of living and the ideal truth or beauty to which the human mind aspires. Mr. Ramsay's habit of murmuring, "Someone had blundered" and "We perished each alone," which on the prose plane is a mere donnish eccentricity, in keeping with his character, on this other plane evokes the sense of chaos and of loneliness. Mr. Carmichael, the remote, inscrutable old poet, addicted to drugs and unfortunate in his domestic life, is used, at the prose level, to illustrate a typical difference between Mr. Ramsay, whose despotic intolerance cannot forgive his behaviour at dinner (he asks for a second helping of soup), and Mrs. Ramsay's larger understanding. But Mr. Carmichael has also another function. Already, in the first movement, his disinterested self-sufficiency causes Mrs. Ramsay to suspect her own motives. In the last movement, while he still remains the remote, inscrutable old man (the reader never comes into direct contact with his reflections), he is also the poet who, Lily feels, shares her quest for beauty and significance.

The second movement in the book, Time Passes, has also a double function. From one point of view it is a method of recording events that mark the passage of ten years. Mrs. Ramsay dies; Prue is married; Prue dies in childbed; Andrew is killed in France; Mr. Carmichael publishes poems; the marriage between Paul and Minta is flawed and patched up; at intervals Mrs. McNab, alone or with Mrs. Bast, airs and cleans the house. Thus the years are marked and scarred, a particular ten years in which such was the history of the Ramsay family, linked with the history of England and the first European war. But, from the other point of view, it is not merely a particular ten years that is represented, but time in relation to eternity, the short span of mortal lives, contrasted with the recurring seasons and the enduring world. The pageant of the seasons is interwoven with the record of human events in such a way as to evoke the illusion of nature's sympathy, or point to the irony of nature's indifference. But in this section, brilliant though it often is, the burden is sometimes too heavy and strain reveals itself in an over-elaborate style.

A similar over-charging of the prose is felt in the decriptive interludes in *The Waves*. Their purpose is to symbolize the progress from youth to age by showing it reflected in the progress from dawn to sunset. Consequently these brief essays are not merely word-paintings of a seascape under the changing light of the sun, but also prose-poems evoking the changing mood and temper of mankind through the seven ages of man. Birds, insects, the objects in the house, the quality of light and sound are made to reflect the altering perceptions of man as he passes from youth to maturity and from maturity to old age. For instance, in the essay introducing that section of the book in which the characters are in the last stage of adolescence (the young men are about to enter the university, or to start their business career), the complex changes in their personality are symbolized by the behaviour of the birds at mid-morning:

> In the garden the birds that had sung erratically and spasmodically in the dawn on that tree, on that bush, now sang together in chorus, shrill and sharp; now together, as if conscious of companionship, now alone as if to the pale blue sky. They swerved, all in one flight, when the black cat moved among the bushes, when the cook threw cinders on the ash heap and startled them. Fear was in their song, and apprehension of pain, and joy to be snatched quickly now at this instant. Also they sang emulously in the clear morning air, swerving high over the elm tree, singing together as they chased each other, escaping, pursuing, pecking each other as they turned high in the air. And then tiring of pursuit and flight, lovelily they came descending, delicately declining, dropped down and sat silent on the tree, on the wall, with their bright eyes glancing, and their heads turned this way, that way; aware, awake; intensely conscious of one thing, one object in particular.
>
> [*The Waves*]

Skilfully the flight and song of the birds has been made to echo the habits of young human beings, uniting in companies, rejoicing in solitude, driven together by fear of a hostile world, competitive yet co-operative, alert yet narrow in vision. But the parallel is over-ingenious; the reader inclines to attend neither to the impressions of the morning scene, nor to the mind of youth, but to the skill of the writer. The ingenuity calls attention to itself, as in some over-elaborate metaphysical conceit, or in a dream passage from De Quincey's *Opium Eater*. For Virginia Woolf's highly wrought style combines the wit of the first "yoking together things apparently unlike" with the evocative rhythms of the second:

> Now it was that upon the rocking waters of the ocean the human face began to reveal itself; the sea appeared paved with innumerable faces, upturned to the heavens; faces imploring, wrathful, despairing; faces

that surged upwards by thousands, by myriads, by generations: infinite was my agitation; my mind tossed, as it seemed, upon the billowy ocean, and weltered upon the weltering waves.

The wind rose. The waves drummed on the shore, like turbaned warriors, like turbaned men with poisoned assegais who, whirling their arms on high, advance upon the feeding flocks, the white sheep.

The first paragraph is by De Quincey, deliberately reproducing the effect of an opium dream, the second is by Virginia Woolf.

There is another reason why the interludes in *The Waves* and the central movement in *To the Lighthouse* are not wholly satisfactory. Inevitably they interrupt the mood of the narrative, they force the reader to abandon one point of view and adopt another and consequently they disturb his "willing suspension of disbelief." When the magic of a fiction works for the reader, he lives in the world the writer creates, "the mariner has his will." Any change of approach which reminds him of the art of the story-teller breaks the illusion. The structure of *To the Lighthouse* is so planned that the time interlude is unavoidable. By some means the passage of ten years must be felt—the consequent re-adjustment of the reader's point of view, his removal to a further distance from the scene of action, so that he observes the characters as tiny, featureless beings whirled about by the winds of chance, is accepted as an inconvenience necessary to the total effect. The necessity of the prose poems in *The Waves* is more doubtful. A simpler device would have been adequate to mark the passage of the years which is in any case implicit in the body of the book.

In *Mrs. Dalloway* and *To the Lighthouse* the concentration necessary for the full effect of Virginia Woolf's mode of presentation is achieved by limiting the time covered by the action, as well as by restricting the number of foreground characters. In *The Waves* the span of time covered by the action is from youth to age in one generation. The reader shares the experience of that generation by direct and intimate observation of the thoughts and feelings of three women and three men. The degree of intimacy achieved, the depths to which human consciousness is explored and the wide relevance to universal human experience necessitates and compensates for this narrowing of attention. Some part of Virginia Woolf's vision of life is sacrificed and will be found again in her two subsequent books. There is less comedy in *The Waves* than in any other of her books and less of the surface of human behaviour. The form of the book allows less variation in pitch then elsewhere, there is no relaxation, and, unless the reader's attention is continually on the stretch, he may fail to notice some such event as a birth, a marriage, a love alliance, or a death which is referred to in meditation and, although submerged beneath the continual flow of life's current, is yet essential to the gradual forming and fixing of personality as well as to the impression of life created by the whole composition. Furthermore unless he gives continually that heightened attention which poetry, but not fiction, normally demands he will not respond adequately to the recurrent images and symbols upon which that impression largely depends. The reward for such vigilant reading is the depth, truth and compassion with which human consciousness is presented. It is true that the six through whom that consciousness is conveyed are in some ways alike and are in some ways exceptional. Each of them is capable of full self-development and, therefore, of that rare integrity which can attain self-knowledge. Each is capable of a sensitive and finely distinguishing response to the experience of living. In this sense they are above the average man or woman in a way comparable to that in which the tragic hero is above the normal stature. Moreover, the six are modern men and women of the upper middle class, so that their peculiar endowment with the powers of perception and of self-realization demands "a willing suspension of disbelief" such as is unquestioningly given when an audience accepts the extraordinary command of poetic language possessed by any Shakesperian character. The language in which the six express themselves even in early youth is a convention without which the writer could not communicate her vision. For instance, the children are doing their lessons and each feels the moment in accordance with his or her own temperament; no child's language could convey what they feel, but the language in the book conveys the feelings of the children, each with that singularity of attitude which will govern their whole life:

"Those are yellow words, those are fiery words," said Jinny. "I should like a fiery dress, a yellow dress, a fulvous dress to wear in the evening."

"Each tense," said Neville, "means differently. There is an order in this world; there are distinctions, there are differences in this world, upon whose verge I step. For this is only a beginning."

"Now Miss Hudson," said Rhoda, "has shut the book. Now the terror is beginning. Now taking her lump of chalk she draws figures, six, seven, eight, and then a cross and then a line on the blackboard. What is the answer? The others look; they look with understanding. Louis writes; Susan writes; Neville writes; Jinny writes; even Bernard has now begun to write. But I cannot write. I see only figures. The others are handing in their answers, one by one. Now it is my turn. But I have no answer.

The others are allowed to go. They slam the door. Miss Hudson goes.
I am left alone to find an answer. The figures mean nothing now. Meaning has gone. The clock ticks. The two hands are convoys marching
through a desert. The black bars on the clock faces are green oases. The
long hand has marched ahead to find water. The other painfully stumbles
among hot stones in the desert. It will die in the desert. The kitchen
door slams. Wild dogs bark far away. Look, the loop of the figure is
beginning to fill with time; it holds the world in it. I begin to draw a
figure and the world is looped in it, and I myself am outside the loop;
which I now join—so—and seal up, and make entire. The world is entire,
and I am outside of it, crying, 'Oh save me, from being blown for ever
outside the loop of time!' "

[*The Waves*]

In the first movement of the book, where the six are children, the
characteristic music of each is first sounded. In a sense the form is
simple while in another it is complex and elaborate. The interrelated
themes, the subtle record of sense perceptions, emotions and thoughts,
move within a simple formal design. The six are assembled together
at their first school; then the group divides in two, the girls at one
boarding school, the boys at another, later we see them singly or in
pair, and twice all six are brought together again. Percival, that shadowy, symbolic figure, the athletic boy and man of action, provides a
centre to which the six converge. They meet for his farewell party before he goes to India, then again, years after his death, and all are
conscious of the loss. As the years accumulate the characteristic music
of each becomes fuller and clearer. Each separates from the others
and lives an individual life. The design resembles some classical ballet
in which from time to time the dancers come forward singly or in pairs
and at times all combine in a concerted movement, while the spectator
remains conscious of the characteristic steps of each. The analogy of
the dance may serve to indicate the outer structure of the book; for its
inner form a better analogy would be a sequence of odes, for the se-
quent monologues are far richer and more complex in their effect than
any dance steps. They convey a developing vision of life seen through
six pairs of eyes and together achieving a balanced picture. The six
temperaments complement one another: Jinny's love of life is the complement of Rhoda's loathing and dread of it; Jinny's impulse to enjoy
variety, to taste all the sweets of life and bind herself to none, is the
counterpart of Susan's need to strike roots and to possess. Bernard's
roving intelligence and unconfined imaginative sympathy is the complement of Neville's desire for an ordered completeness, his passion

for a limited perfection, while Neville's pursuit of the intellectual life complements Louis's need to effect something in the world of affairs: "to lace the world together with our ships," Neville's selection of the finest classical fruits of our cultural heritage complements Louis's sense that he inherits the whole history of the world:

> the long, long history that began in Egypt, in the time of the Pharoahs, when women carried red pitchers to the Nile.

Similarly, each of the six experiences the sexual impulse in a different way, expressing the nostalgia of their individual temperaments, which together compose a complete human being.

In *The Waves* one aspect of Virginia Woolf's vision of life is more completely given than in any other of her books. By narrowing the reader's attention and concentrating it upon the inner monologue of six persons, she is able to reveal, with profound insight, the experience of living. What is presented is the solitary consciousness, the reception of experience rather than its issue in action. The six combine to reveal the basic structure of human personality with its capacity for joy and pain; its earth-rootedness and its fear of life; its bondage to self and its outreaching to others, its fragmentary perceptions and its nostalgia for perfect beauty and truth.

But, while *The Waves* brings to light one aspect of truth as the writer saw it, other aspects are thrown into the shadow. The experience of the passing of the years in a single life is fully felt, but their passing in the history of a nation is more faintly perceived. Particular scenes, school, college, a farm, a room, a London street are vividly seen reflected in the human mind. But the wider sense of place as the background for divers human activities is not felt. Six people are intimately presented, but the crowded world in which they live is almost effaced. It was perhaps the severe formality of the structure of *The Waves* and its focus narrowed on to the individual life that suggested the relaxed form and wider scope of the next book, *The Years*. In it the reader is aware of time and place in relation to the nation's life; he is aware of a social structure; he is aware of economic conditions. If *The Waves* is the nearest of all the novels to poetic drama, *The Years* is the nearest to social comedy. In the last book *Between the Acts* the two effects are beautifully combined.

26

D. H. LAWRENCE

◆━━◆

Surgery for the Novel—or a Bomb

You talk about the future of the baby, little cherub, when he's in the cradle cooing; and it's a romantic, glamorous subject. You also talk, with the parson, about the future of the wicked old grandfather who is at last lying on his death-bed. And there again you have a subject for much vague emotion, chiefly of fear this time.

How do we feel about the novel? Do we bounce with joy thinking of the wonderful novelistic days ahead? Or do we grimly shake our heads and hope the wicked creature will be spared a little longer? Is the novel on his death-bed, old sinner? Or is he just toddling round his cradle, sweet little thing? Let us have another look at him before we decide this rather serious case.

There he is, the monster with many faces, many branches to him, like a tree: the modern novel. And he is almost dual, like Siamese twins. On the one hand, the pale-faced, high-browed, earnest novel, which you have to take seriously; on the other, that smirking, rather plausible hussy, the popular novel.

Let us just for the moment feel the pulses of *Ulysses* and of Miss Dorothy Richardson and M. Marcel Proust, on the earnest side of

Briareus; on the other, the throb of *The Sheik* and Mr. Zane Grey, and, if you will, Mr. Robert Chambers and the rest. Is *Ulysses* in his cradle? Oh, dear! What a grey face! And *Pointed Roofs*, are they a gay little toy for nice little girls? And M. Proust? Alas! You can hear the death-rattle in their throats. They can hear it themselves. They are listening to it with acute interest, trying to discover whether the intervals are minor thirds or major fourths. Which is rather infantile, really.

So there you have the "serious" novel, dying in a very long-drawn-out fourteen-volume death-agony, and absorbedly, childishly interested in the phenomenon. "Did I feel a twinge in my little toe, or didn't I?" asks every character of Mr. Joyce or of Miss Richardson or M. Proust. Is my aura a blend of frankincense and orange pekoe and boot-blacking, or is it myrrh and bacon-fat and Shetland tweed? The audience round the death-bed gapes for the answer. And when, in a sepulchral tone, the answer comes at length, after hundreds of pages: "It is none of these, it is abysmal chloro-coryambasis," the audience quivers all over, and murmurs: "That's just how I feel myself."

Which is the dismal, long-drawn-out comedy of the death-bed of the serious novel. It is self-consciousness picked into such fine bits that the bits are most of them invisible, and you have to go by smell. Through thousands and thousands of pages Mr. Joyce and Miss Richardson tear themselves to pieces, strip their smallest emotions to the finest threads, till you feel you are sewed inside a wool mattress that is being slowly shaken up, and you are turning to wool along with the rest of the woolliness.

It's awful. And it's childish. It really is childish, after a certain age, to be absorbedly self-conscious. One has to be self-conscious at seventeen: still a little self-conscious at twenty-seven; but if we are going it strong at thirty-seven, then it is a sign of arrested development, nothing else. And if it is still continuing at forty-seven, it is obvious senile precocity.

And there's the serious novel: senile-precocious. Absorbedly, childishly concerned with *what I am.* "I am this, I am that, I am the other. My reactions are such, and such, and such. And, oh, Lord, if I liked to watch myself closely enough, if I liked to analyse my feelings minutely, as I unbutton my gloves, instead of saying crudely I unbuttoned them, then I could go on to a million pages instead of a thousand. In fact, the more I come to think of it, it is gross, it is uncivilised bluntly to say: I unbuttoned my gloves. After all, the absorbing adventure of it! Which button did I begin with?" etc.

The people in the serious novels are so absorbedly concerned with themselves and what they feel and don't feel, and how they react to every mortal button; and their audience as frenziedly absorbed in the application of the author's discoveries to their own reactions: "That's me! That's exactly it! I'm just finding myself in this book!" Why, this is more than death-bed, it is almost post-mortem behaviour.

Some convulsion or cataclysm will have to get this serious novel out of its self-consciousness. The last great war made it worse. What's to be done? Because, poor thing, it's really young yet. The novel has never become fully adult. It has never quite grown to years of discretion. It has always youthfully hoped for the best, and felt rather sorry for itself on the last page. Which is just childish. The childishness has become very long-drawn-out. So very many adolescents who drag their adolescence on into their forties and their fifties and their sixties! There needs some sort of surgical operation, somewhere.

Then the popular novels—the *Sheiks* and *Babbitts* and Zane Grey novels. They are just as self-conscious, only they do have more illusions about themselves. The heroines do think they are lovelier, and more fascinating, and purer. The heroes do see themselves more heroic, braver, more chivalrous, more fetching. The mass of the populace "find themselves" in the popular novels. But nowadays it's a funny sort of self they find. A sheik with a whip up his sleeve, and a heroine with weals on her back, but adored in the end, adored, the whip out of sight, but the weals still faintly visible.

It's a funny sort of self they discover in the popular novels. And the essential moral of *If Winter Comes*, for example, is so shaky. "The gooder you are, the worse it is for you, poor you, oh, poor you. Don't you be so blimey good, it's not good enough." Or *Babbitt*: "Go on, you make your pile, and then pretend you're too good for it. Put it over the rest of the grabbers that way. They're only pleased with themselves when they've made their pile. You go one better."

Always the same sort of baking-powder gas to make you rise: the soda counteracting the cream of tartar, and the tartar counteracted by the soda. Sheik heroines, duly whipped, wildly adored. Babbitts with solid fortunes, weeping from self-pity. Winter-Comes heroes as good as pie, hauled off to jail. *Moral:* Don't be too good, because you'll go to jail for it. *Moral:* Don't feel sorry for yourself till you've made your pile and don't need to feel sorry for yourself. *Moral:* Don't let him adore you till he's whipped you into it. Then you'll be partners in mild crime as well as in holy matrimony.

Which again is childish. Adolescence which *can't* grow up. Got into the self-conscious rut and going crazy, quite crazy in it. Carrying on their adolescence into middle age and old age, like the looney Cleopatra in *Dombey and Son,* murmuring "Rose-coloured curtains" with her dying breath.

The future of the novel? Poor old novel, it's in a rather dirty, messy tight corner. And it's either got to get over the wall or knock a hole through it. In other words, it's got to grow up. Put away childish things like: "Do I love the girl, or don't I?"—"Am I pure and sweet, or am I not?"—"Do I unbutton my right glove first, or my left?"—"Did my mother ruin my life by refusing to drink the cocoa which my bride had boiled for her?" These questions and their answers don't really interest me any more, though the world still goes sawing them over. I simply don't care for any of these things now, though I used to. The purely emotional and self-analytical stunts are played out in me. I'm finished. I'm deaf to the whole band. But I'm neither *blasé* nor cynical, for all that. I'm just interested in something else.

Supposing a bomb were put under the whole scheme of things, what would we be after? What feelings do we want to carry through into the next epoch? What feelings will carry us through? What is the underlying impulse in us that will provide the motive power for a new state of things, when this democratic-industrial-lovey-dovey-darling-take-me-to-mamma state of things is bust?

What next? That's what interests me. "What now?" is no fun any more.

If you wish to look into the past for what-next books, you can go back to the Greek philosophers. Plato's Dialogues are queer little novels. It seems to me it was the greatest pity in the world, when philosophy and fiction got split. They used to be one, right from the days of myth. Then they went and parted, like a nagging married couple, with Aristotle and Thomas Aquinas and that beastly Kant. So the novel went sloppy, and philosophy went abstract-dry. The two should come together again—in the novel.

You've got to find a new impulse for new things in mankind, and it's really fatal to find it through abstraction. No, no; philosophy and religion, they've both gone too far on the algebraical tack: Let X stand for sheep and Y for goats: then X minus Y equals Heaven, and X plus Y equals Earth, and Y minus X equals Hell. Thank you! But what coloured shirt does X have on?

The novel has a future. It's got to have the courage to tackle new propositions without using abstractions; it's got to present us with new, really new feelings, a whole line of new emotion, which will get us out of the emotional rut. Instead of snivelling about what is and has been, or inventing new sensations in the old line, it's got to break a way through, like a hole in the wall. And the public will scream and say it is sacrilege: because, of course, when you've been jammed for a long time in a tight corner, and you get really used to its stuffiness and its tightness, till you find it suffocatingly cosy; then, of course, you're horrified when you see a new glaring hole in what was your cosy wall. You're horrified. You back away from the cold stream of fresh air as if it were killing you. But gradually, first one and then another of the sheep filters through the gap and finds a new world outside.

[1923]